C000258081

THE SILENT-FOOTED BUTLER

Life is bottled sunshine and Death the silent-footed butler who draws out the cork.

The Martyrdom of Man – Winwood Reade

THE SILENT-FOOTED BUTLER

CATHY GILES

T-GEM BOOKS

First published in Great Britain in 2011 by
T-GEM BOOKS
11 Queens Road
London E11 1BA

ISBN 978-0-9568321-0-8

Cathy Giles: cathy@t-gembooks.com
T-GEM Books, 11 Queens Road, London E11 1BA
www.t-gembooks.com

Designed, prepared and typeset by Cathy Giles with the assistance of
Toby Hart, BSc (Hons), Dip.Arch, MA RIBA III: toby@artefactestudio.com
Cover design by Cathy Giles
Family trees created and set by Cathy Giles
Illustrations and photographs prepared by Cathy Giles and Toby Hart

Printed in Great Britain by Darwin Press
77a Blackheath Road, Greenwich, London, SE10 8PD
Bound in Great Britain by J. Muir Bookbinders Ltd.
64-68 Blackheath Road, Greenwich, London SE10 8DA

The text pages of this book are printed on CyclusOffset paper, which is produced using 100% recycled fibres and PCF (Process Chlorine Free) according to the RAL UZ-14: Blue Angel, EU Ecolabel no. DK/011/1
The photo pages of this book are printed on G-Print, which contains material sourced from responsibly managed forests, certified in accordance with the FSC (Forest Stewardship Council)
Materials used for the cover and dust jacket are also certified in accordance with the FSC www.fsc.org

For my sister, Izzy,
my children, Toby, George, Emily and Martha
and my nephew, Rory.

In memory of Chris

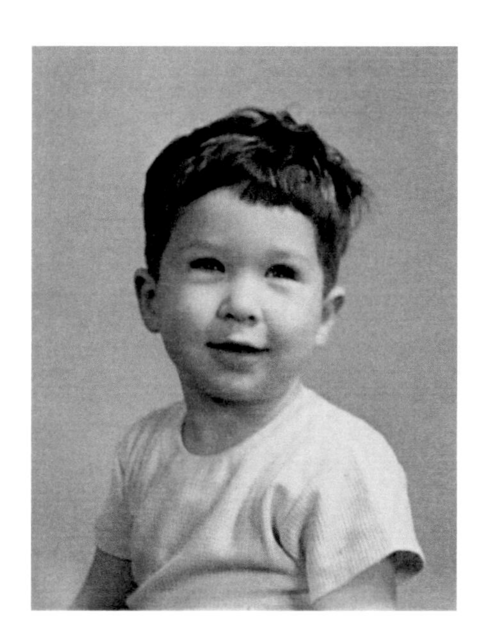

All the illustrations in this book, apart from those that appear in *Dad's Story*, are by Christopher Giles, most of them produced between the ages of seven and twelve. The cartoons in Part Three were drawn between the ages of fifteen and seventeen. The drawings in *Dad's Story* are by Derek Giles, which he drew whilst still at school.

CONTENTS

PART TWO

PART THREE

EPILOGUE

A NOTE ABOUT THE TYPE: ITC Berkeley Old Style

In 1937, the distinguished and prolific American typographer, Frederic W. Goudy (1865-1947), was asked to draw a new typeface for the exclusive use of the University of California Press. It was known as University of California Old Style, but remained the property of the university press and saw little use elsewhere. In 1956, nearly ten years after Goudy's death, Lanston Monotype reissued the typeface under the name Californian, and it became a successful and widely used font for book typography. Then, in the early 1980s, ITC decided to revive University of California Old Style. Tony Stan (1917-1988), a world-class typographer, carefully redrew the fonts for ITC using Goudy's original designs as a foundation. The combined artistry of Goudy and Stan created ITC Berkeley Old Style; a beautiful typeface that is light, crisp, elegant and highly legible.

In the pages that follow, I have taken the liberty of reconstructing some of the past through dialogue. I do not claim that the words were actually spoken, but nevertheless, as I was writing they seemed to flow as if from the characters' mouths. Conversations that I have recounted between myself and others are as I remember them: some I believe to be accurate word for word. Diary and journal entries have been edited, and passages from some letters have been cut, but the original words and meanings have not been altered. I have changed the names of the family described in Chapter 24, *Dad's Mates,* to protect their identities.

PROLOGUE

You will preserve all my Letters and I will secure yours – and thus in the course of time we shall each of us have a good Bundle – which, hereafter, when things have strangely altered and god knows what happened, we may read over together and look with pleasure on times past.

Letter from John Keats to his sister, Fanny, September 10th 1817

I began writing this book in May 2004. Since then, through periods of motivation and progress as well as times of dormancy and doubt, it has expanded and evolved into what it is today. However, not a word would have been written were it not for an unplanned moment that happened six months earlier at a time when I was lacking direction, fed up with myself and drinking too much. As was so often the case, I awoke that morning with a hangover, feeling gloomy and restless. Sitting at the kitchen table slumped over a mug of tea, I knew that unless I made myself do something, it wouldn't be long before I slipped into despondency and opened a bottle of wine. I went through a mental list of suggestions, rejecting one after the other, until, quite unexpectedly, I said to myself: you could find the letters from Chris. I sat up straight; my hand went to my mouth. Through my fingers I whispered, *I could find the letters from Chris*. All at once it seemed a matter of urgency. I fetched the stepladder, carried it upstairs and climbed into the loft. I found what I was looking for – some boxes that had been transported and preserved, unopened, through three house moves, clearly marked 'Letters'. I brought them downstairs and placed them on the kitchen table. The lids lifted easily as the sticky tape that had sealed them was now browned and brittle. Inside was an astonishing number of letters of varying shapes, sizes, and colours. I removed a handful, surprised momentarily to see my old addresses printed on the envelopes. As I began to identify the senders and sort the letters into piles, I couldn't resist reading some of them. The youthful vocabulary of the day made me smile, as did the price of the postage stamps. Before long, I was immersed, swept back to my teenage years. Faces and places, intimacies and friendships coalesced as in a clearly remembered dream. I was infused with warmth and amusement along with the melancholy of time lived and gone.

Then I found one of Chris's letters. It was as unnerving as a sudden scream, the shock of seeing his handwriting. The world seemed to fall away. I felt immobilised, as though I had stumbled upon a secret I was not meant to discover. My heart raced. His handwriting! I couldn't believe the impact it had – to see again the words he had written. As I held the letter, I was aware that his hands had also held it, had once lifted it to his mouth to lick the flap. I visualised him going to find a stamp from our mother's office, leaving the house, crossing the road and posting this very letter in the pillar-box on the corner of Cleveland Road. I laid it in the middle of the table, deciding not to read it until I had found them all. My earlier reverie had gone. I renewed my search with purpose, prepared for the next jolt. By the evening, every kitchen surface was covered and the boxes were empty. In front of me lay five letters from Chris. I assembled them in chronological order, breathed deeply, and eased the first one out of its envelope. His untidy writing pierced me with sadness and pleasure; memories tumbled into my mind; I heard his animated voice, felt his sparkly-eyed smile and pictured his expressive gestures. Overcome by a strange joy, I read every word, spilling tears of long-lived, never-finished grief. Chris, my only brother, died just six weeks after his seventeenth birthday.

The next day my twin sister, Izzy, phoned me. She said, "Do you know what I did yesterday? I've not been able to face it before, but I dug out all the letters Chris wrote to me when I was at university and read them for the first time since he died." We had reached the same point on the same day. It had taken both of us more than twenty-eight years to read his letters again.

My children have often asked me what Chris was like. He is indelibly stored in my memory, he appears in my dreams, yet whenever I have tried to describe the multi-faceted, inspirational person that he was, my words have fallen far short of the sum of him, have failed to illuminate the influence and impression he had on everyone who knew him. It has always bothered me that he is but a shadow to the people who came into my life after his death. I knew I would have to write about him if I wanted to bring his life out of obscurity, but this was a daunting prospect. Although I had kept diaries, composed a few essays and written as a form of therapy, to write a book seemed impossible. I had tried many times to begin and failed just as often to get beyond the first page. If ever I did manage to write something that seemed to have some potential, it was soon torn up or deleted; harsh self-criticism made sure of that. I was further hindered by a notion that I could only write with alcohol flowing through my veins, believing that it lubricated my mind, freed the imagination and opened the windows of creativity. There is some truth in this, yet ultimately, alcohol dims the senses, confuses the thoughts and burns out all attempts at prolonged endeavour. Lacking discipline, incentive, and staying power, I was unable to enter that place of solitary confinement that writing really is.

Then various elements conspired to force my hand. A relationship came to an unhappy end; I was again struggling to deal with loss, negativity and depression. As usual I took up the pen and the bottle, but through the alcoholic haze I became aware that the words spilling onto the paper were more meaningful for me than the relationship had been and that my own neglect of my creativity was the main source of my loneliness.

More distressingly, our mother was diagnosed with Alzheimer's disease. She had been losing her short-term memory for some years, but it had become obvious that her increasingly strange behaviour was far more than occasional forgetfulness. She fought it every step of the way, relying valiantly upon the remnants of her exceptional organisational ability to disguise the fact that her life was slipping out of control. Izzy and I guessed it was Alzheimer's long before we managed to persuade her to see a consultant. By the time tests had eliminated all other possibilities, the words

'Alzheimer's Disease' were as meaningless to her as thousands of others she no longer understood. Her decline was awful to witness: as tangles and plaques destroyed her brain cells, she was stripped of her independence, intellect, grace and dignity. She was almost unable to function in the present, yet she still retained clear memories of the past; memories that became fixed so vividly in her mind that she needed to tell them, always as if for the first time, over and over again. Rather than closing my ears to the repetitions of her identically phrased stories, I decided to write them down, question her further and nudge her to remember more. I am glad I did, for it was the last chance that she or I had to access her memory. My mother's infirmity brought into direct focus the incalculable value of health and the brevity and randomness of life. If I meant to do anything with mine, I must start right now.

I decided to stop pouring poison down my throat, wantonly destroying my brain cells, and made the same decision the next day and the next. In a similar way, I decided to write. I progressed past the first page and wrote another and then another, until the words began to grow into something of substance. What a revelation to learn that I did not need alcohol to write: how reassuring to find inspiration in plentiful supply with just the application of dedication and constructive work. There were no more excuses: I had the motivation; I was sober; I would try to write a book about Chris and this time I would not give up.

Of course I could not write about him in isolation. The book would also be about Izzy and myself – 'the girls', as he used to call us. Remembering the life we shared with Chris would be an undertaking for both of us. As I started on the canvas of our childhood, I realised that I needed to colour in some background about Mum, Dad and Granny, the three adults with whom we lived. Their experiences of life before we were born had established their attitudes, influenced their beliefs, and were brought to bear upon our upbringing. Their history is also ours. I have presented my research of their lives and our ancestry in three separate biographical sections: *Granny's Story, Dad's Story* and *Mum's Story*.

Granny's and Mum's Scottish roots were fairly accessible. I contacted the relatives I knew, none of whom I had spoken to for many years, and began to ask questions. They lent me photographs and recounted tales from the past. With the additional help of Internet access to genealogical websites, my voyage back through the generations and along the lines of siblings and cousins began. As I discovered the many babies and children who had died, the illnesses that had cut adult lives short, the young men killed in wars, the hardship and poverty, even abuse, depravity, crime and intrigue, I had to become an investigator, detective, historian, psychologist and interpreter in order to assemble data, follow leads, track people down, and understand who they were, what they were like and how they survived. I found no dukes or duchesses, knights or dames – our forebears were ordinary folk, most of them living hand-to-mouth in cramped, basic dwellings and labouring in the factories, shipyards, mills, mines and iron foundries. The exploration was, and still is, fascinating, but the material that has accumulated is far too extensive for this book. Consequently, apart from a few stories that almost pleaded to be told, I have given only brief sketches to set the scene for Granny's early life. *Mum's Story* follows on from there and is depicted mainly through the diary she kept during the 1940s.

When it came to writing about my father's history, I barely knew where to begin. He died in 1999. I knew none of his relatives. His mother died before we were born and he had cut himself off from her side of the family. Fortunately, I knew his mother's name. Persistent searches connected me with a second cousin I didn't know I had. With his help and encouragement, I contacted and met other family members, which has been both heart-warming and curative. What has emerged, though, is a labyrinth of mysteries, leading to a dead-end with a Machiavellian great-grandfather, whose identity has been artfully concealed through three generations. As far as Dad's father is concerned, I haven't investigated deeply. We knew him, as we paid weekly visits to Grandad throughout our childhood. Although I found out where he was born, now know the names of his siblings and parents, and have stretched his family tree to previous generations, the picture I have drawn of him is derived from my own recollections and Dad's memoirs.

As I began to write about Chris, a wealth of material came to light. Finding those letters from him was only the beginning. The doors to the past had been opened and people from long ago reappeared. A friend with whom I hadn't had any contact for thirty years wrote to me just as I was writing about his friendship with Chris; somebody who had been occupying my thoughts emailed me after a twenty-five-year silence; I bumped into old acquaintances in unlikely places; names I hadn't heard in ages cropped up in conversation; almost forgotten events, scenarios and images resurfaced. The more absorbed I became in the process of remembering, the more of the past I reclaimed. I contacted as many people who had known Chris as I could; some I hadn't spoken to since he died, others I had never spoken to before. They were incredibly generous in giving me their time, sharing their memories and answering my questions. I am indebted to those who loaned me significant correspondence and photographs and to others who allowed me to use letters that they themselves penned more than thirty-five years ago.

The most invaluable help I have received has been from my sister. Apart from permitting me to use her diaries and letters, she has been my soundboard – answered, discussed and considered every question I have asked, contributed her own thoughts and recollections, read every draft and supported me throughout not just the writing of this book, but every moment of my life. Our memories serve us in differing ways. Izzy has an astonishing memory for dates, places, chronology, names and faces – she can look at a photo of our infant class and name every child. I tend to remember atmosphere, conversations, gestures, expressions, texture, colour and smell. I see the past in cameos, the scenes replaying with the lucidity of a movie, but above all, I remember vividly how I felt.

I intended this book to be about Chris. It is, in as far as I have included as much detail about his life as I have been able to gather, but at the same time it has expanded to include the lives of others, whilst also becoming much more autobiographical than I had anticipated. Nevertheless, Chris has a connection with all I have written. He has been my inspiration, and in that sense he is present on every page.

PART ONE

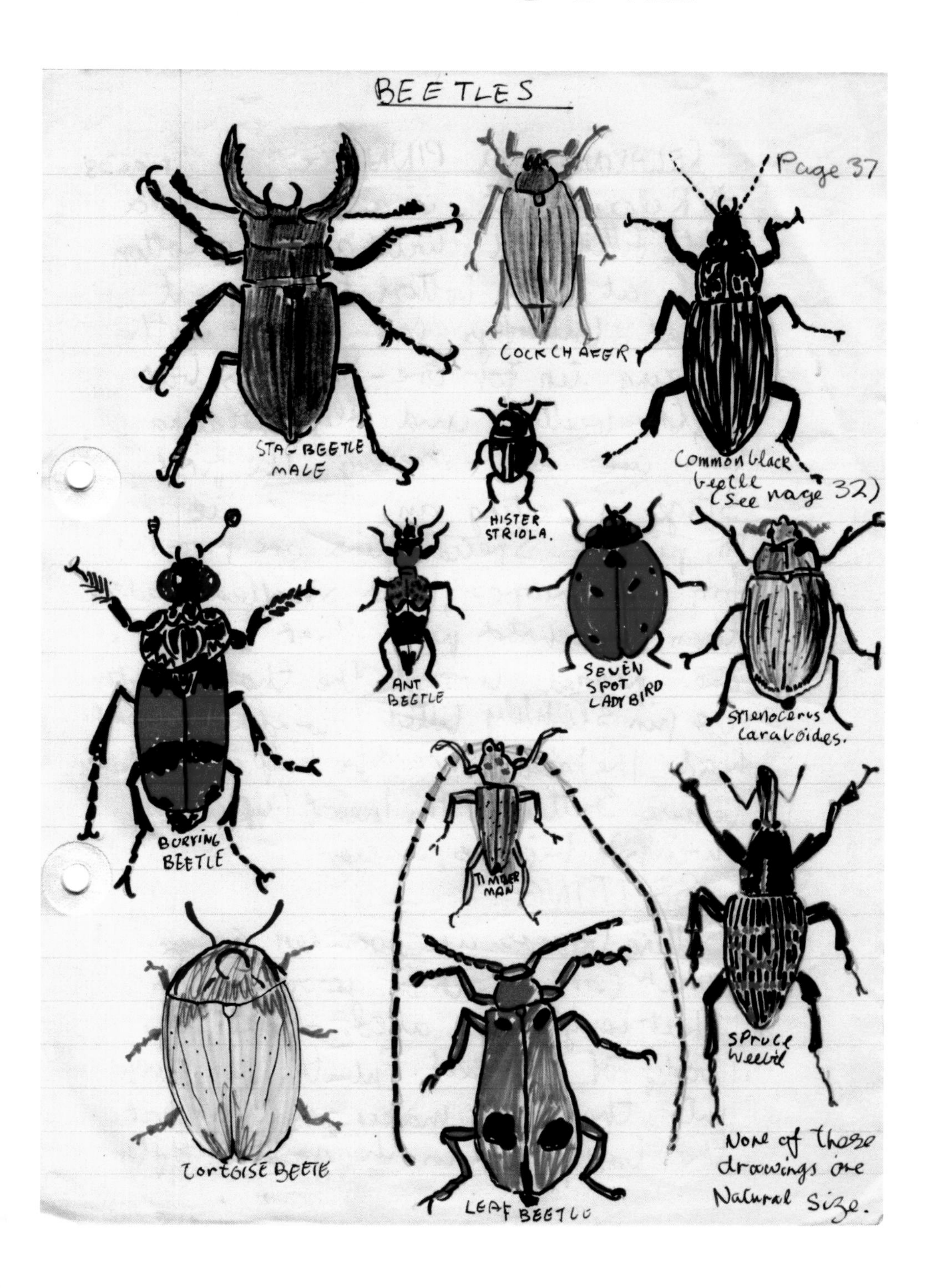

BEETLES
Page 37
COCKCHAFER
STAG-BEETLE MALE
Common black beetle (See page 32)
HISTER STRIOLA.
ANT BEETLE
SEVEN SPOT LADYBIRD
Stenocerus caraboides.
BURYING BEETLE
TIMBER MAN
Spruce Weevil
Tortoise Beetle
LEAF BEETLE
None of these drawings are Natural Size.

Izzy and I adored our baby brother, Chris.

1
32, CLEVELAND ROAD

Born green we were
to this flawed garden

Firesong – Sylvia Plath

I was fourteen when I discovered that the past was not quite as I had supposed. Mum was driving me to a cello lesson, a long journey across London that we had made regularly since I was nine. Our conversation had lapsed into silence. I was content to lose myself in my thoughts, which at the time often focused on members of the opposite sex. I fretted and anguished, replaying conversations in my mind, mortified afresh by the inane things I had said. What had possessed me to talk about my *guinea pigs*? He must have thought me so childish. I burned hours of thought-watts analysing the meaning of simple phrases – "see you next week" – what did it *mean*? Was he looking forward to seeing me again, or had his intonation been slightly dismissive? There were several boys I adored to distraction at the time, all of them distressingly out of reach, it seemed, but they weren't beyond my wildest dreams. I fantasised about them and imagined all sorts of blissful scenarios, alternating the leading man to suit the situation. I wondered whether any of my dreams would come true. Could it be that "see you next week" might by some extraordinary transmutation evolve into "I love you"? Had I perhaps, without knowing it, already met the man I was going to marry? Maybe in years to come, I would be saying to my children, "I remember the first time I set eyes on your father. I was twelve. I used to watch him across the orchestra; sneak secret glances during bars' rests, averting my eyes swiftly if he happened to look in my direction. I swear I fell in love with him then and there, even though it was three more years before he actually spoke to me." Maybe he would admit that he had noticed me too, but had been too overawed to make an approach. We would smile at each other with fond remembrance…

As I daydreamed along these lines, a question I hadn't intended to ask out loud breezed from my mouth. "Mum? How did you and Dad meet?"

There was a hiatus. Her hands tightened on the steering wheel.

"It was probably at a committee meeting," she answered. I could sense her tension, but she made her voice sound vague and indifferent.

"What committee?"

"It would have been something to do with the Communist Party."

"When would that have been?"

"Oh, it's too long ago to remember."

"Where then?" I persisted.

"It must have been at Wanstead House."

I was hoping to hear her describe a romantic first encounter, some affectionate memories perhaps, but she said no more. I drifted back into contemplation, but could not retrieve the boy-thoughts that had been pleasantly occupying me. Mum cleared her throat, shifted in her seat, straightened her back with a purposeful movement and appeared to come to a decision. With a sharp intake of breath, she all at once launched forth.

"I suppose I may as well tell you that Dad and I married only a few weeks before you two were born. I haven't told you before, but I used to be married to someone else. I had to wait for the divorce to come through before I could marry again."

"Oh," I said.

"He was a horror, my first husband," she continued. "He used to hit me, the so-and-so. I was flabbergasted the first time it happened. I'd never been hit before."

"What did you do?" I asked, turning my head to look at her, alarmed to think that Mum had been a battered wife.

"I hit him back. He wasn't much taller than me and I have strong arms and hands from playing the piano. I wasn't just going to take it, but oh, it was so degrading." Her sturdy hands clutched the steering wheel. I studied her wide wrists, her broad, blunt-ended fingers: strong, capable, useful musician's hands, as she described them so unflinchingly, that reached a tenth comfortably on the piano keyboard – an eleventh at a stretch – and only man-sized gloves would fit. There was nothing dainty about Mum. It bothered me when she told me (and she often did) that I was just like her. I had a wide span, but were my hands as big as hers? Surely my fingers were more elegant? No, I thought, I was doomed; they would become like Mum's and I would have to live with them forever.

"Afterwards," she went on, "when things had calmed down, he'd apologise and beg forgiveness, promising it wouldn't happen again. Like a fool, I believed him, but let me tell you, if a man strikes you once, it won't be the last time. I hope it never happens to you, but if it does, you get out immediately." I stared unseeingly at the road ahead, rather taken aback by the bitter tone of her voice, stunned by her revelations. This was a new type of conversation. I felt suddenly older.

"When the fights were over, I'd try to talk to him. We're adults, Bill, I'd say. Grown up people don't behave like this! It's senseless and humiliating to fight. To which he replied: all men beat their wives. Can you believe it? He'd seen his father beat his mother and thought it was the norm! Of course, he was jealous of my involvement with music – resented the time I spent practising; expected me to stop the moment he came in and slammed the piano lid down if I didn't. I put up with him for years, but eventually enough was enough."

We had arrived at our destination. Mum parked on the driveway, I slid my cello out of the back seat, and there was Florence Hooton, my teacher, waiting at her door to welcome us inside.

"Hello Cathy," greeted Miss Hooton energetically. Whilst I was unpacking, she announced that she would like to hear a complete run-through, from memory, of the Lalo concerto. "Think of it as a practice performance for the concert next week," she said, turning to Mum, "OK Elizabeth?"

"Yes, of course," Mum replied, sitting down at the piano to accompany me.

As I played the well-practised notes, my mind revolved with questions. Why had

Mum kept us in the dark? What else had she hidden from us? Had she had children with this man? Bill who? Were we connected to him in some way? Could it be that Dad was not our father?

Substantial passages of the Lalo passed by on automatic pilot. I was quite surprised to find myself in the middle of the second movement. Nevertheless, I reached the end without a memory slip. Miss Hooton, although pleased with my reliability, spent the rest of the lesson trying to draw more drama and ebullience from my playing.

"That's better," she declared. "We need more *pings*, more *vibrato*, more *excitement*."

On the way home, I endeavoured to extract more information. Bill Stewart was his name: no, she had not had any children with him.

"How did it end?"

"Mammy – your Granny – picked up signals that I was unhappy. She has the Highlanders' sixth sense, you know." This I had heard before. Granny, we were told, sometimes had uncanny premonitions, knew of tragedies before the news arrived, and was able to communicate telepathically with her sisters. I was highly sceptical of these claims, having seen no evidence of it myself – quite the reverse, in fact. The Granny I knew appeared to be insensitive and unimaginative. Maybe her sixth sense had departed before we were born.

"She was living in Edinburgh at the time," Mum continued, "running a boarding house in Portobello. I didn't tell her about Bill's violence – it wasn't the sort of thing one discussed – but she knew the marriage was on the rocks. She was concerned about me, so she sold up and moved down to London to be nearby if I needed her. That was when she bought 32, Cleveland Road."

"What happened then?"

"I moved in with her."

"And that was when you met Dad?"

"Some time after that, yes."

We were back where we had started. Before we reached home, however, Mum spilled one last bean: "Of course, I didn't intend to get pregnant. You were accidents. Nice ones, though," she added.

There were still unanswered questions that I would have to consider later, when I had shared Mum's startling disclosures with my sister and brother. She would not volunteer the information to them; it would be up to me to do so.

"Izzy?"

"Yes?" she responded, not lifting her eyes from her book.

"Come up to my room. I've got something to tell you."

"In a minute."

I went upstairs, going through Chris's bedroom to reach mine. Anyone entering his room for the first time would have been astounded. For me, though, the shelves of skulls, skeletons, fossils, insects, butterflies and moths were as familiar as the wallpaper. As I entered, he picked up a sheet of paper and handed it to me. "Do you think you could type this out for me, Cath?"

"Yes, sure."

"It's a list of all the cats of the world – thirty-seven species altogether, including *Felis catus,* the common domestic cat."

I looked at the paper. Arranged in their correct Genus groups he had listed the scientific names of every cat. Beside each one he had written its ordinary name, how rare or common it was and its geographical distribution. For example:

Felis planiceps, Flat-headed cat: Very rare: Malay Peninsula, Borneo, Sumatra.
Panthera uncia, Snow Leopard: Rare: Mountains of Central Asia.

"I'd no idea there were so many different types of cat," I said, impressed. "This is really interesting. Wow, I didn't know the cheetah was rare."

"It is. A lot of these cats are endangered species."

"I like this one – '*Felis rubiginosa*, the Rusty Spotted cat.'" The name caught my eye, as we had a cat called Rusty.

"It's the smallest cat in the world," Chris told me. "Fully grown, it only weighs about two pounds."

Izzy walked in. "What's the big secret?"

We sat on the floor.

"Well, I've just found out that Mum used to be married to somebody else."

"Oh," they said.

"Don't you think it's odd she hasn't told us before?" They shrugged. I was expecting the news to have more impact.

"He used to beat her up," I told them.

"How revolting," said Izzy.

"That's probably why she didn't say anything," Chris suggested.

"She had to wait ages for the divorce to come through and wasn't able to marry Dad until just before Izzy and I were born. That makes us almost illegitimate."

I paused for effect, scanning their faces. They both looked at me, waiting expectantly. "Maybe there was some big scandal we don't know about," I embellished, hoping to make it sound more tantalising.

"Is there?" asked Chris.

I gave up. "No. I don't think so. Mum didn't plan to have us, though, Izzy. We were mistakes."

"Huh, well that explains why she married him. That was the mistake, if you ask me. I mean, they just don't get on, do they?" she said.

"No – but they must have been in love with each other once – surely?"

Dad was staring blankly out of the living room window when I asked him how he and Mum had met.

"What did you say?"

"You and Mum," I repeated tentatively – "about when you first met?"

He grimaced. I wished I hadn't asked my question, but it was too late now.

"Huh," he said bitterly, not turning to face me, "Your mother!" With his gaze still fixed beyond the windowpane, he spoke as if to himself: "You don't know the half of it. I could show you letters she wrote to me back then, promising undying love, wanting me more than anyone else in the world. All lies. She didn't mean a word of it." He gave a scornful laugh, "Yes; *they'd* tell you a different story." Pausing, he narrowed his eyes; "She hoodwinked me alright – changed completely after she married me." His voice dropped to a whisper. "Then I found out what she was really like – cold, unfeeling, frigid..."

I backed out of the room, not wanting to hear any more. I hadn't heard the word frigid before, but his intonation had implications I didn't wish to understand. I shouldn't have asked. I knew they weren't happy together. I had just hoped to see his face light up as he remembered the first time he saw her, to hear that once upon a time it had been different: but neither Mum nor Dad ever wanted to recall the time when they had, presumably, been in love. "Love!" Mum used to say in her later life, "it was sexual attraction, that's all; how ridiculous to take that as a basis for choosing a partner for life." They both felt they had been tricked.

After the Second World War – described then as 'the war to end all wars' – there was a great surge in socialism. The Peace Movement was gathering momentum, although it would be a few more years before various organisations came together to set up the Campaign for Nuclear Disarmament. In the 1950s, some of the shocked post-war population believed that the ideals of communism offered the way forward to create a peaceful 'brave new world' and a better future. Mum and Dad were two of them. Dad was already a member of the Wanstead and Woodford branch of the Communist Party when Mum joined. Mum had just escaped from an abusive marriage, but she was young and optimistic: her bad experience had not dented her hopes of finding a man with whom she could enjoy a happy relationship.

Derek Giles seemed to be all that she was looking for. He was in his mid-thirties, attractive, intelligent, cultured and philosophical – everything that her husband, Bill Stewart, was not. She did not see that Derek was also insecure, needy and depressive. He had never been in a long-term relationship with a woman and still lived with his father and stepmother in a small terraced house in Woodford Bridge. He was not happy where he lived, nor did he like his job. It was with his comrades in the Communist Party where he felt at home, where he could listen to and join in political debate, where he was welcomed and valued. Mum met him on his home ground, joining a group in which he was an established member. She saw him at his best. They fell in love – and how can we judge retrospectively whether it was genuine or not? It always feels like the real thing at the time. If she had any doubts about his stability, or concerns about his tendency to be miserable, I imagine she ignored them. It is, after all, human nature to think that love will overcome all obstacles. For a while anyway, they must have enjoyed being together. When Mum found that she was pregnant, it was a surprise, but not a disaster. Divorce proceedings had begun: she and Dad could marry when the decree absolute was granted. They were intending to marry anyway – their family was just coming along sooner than planned.

Mum was living with her mother in a comfortable house in which she had a music room and was building up her teaching practice. Now that she was pregnant, it seemed obvious that Dad should move in with them. When the baby was born, Granny would be on hand to look after it while Mum taught and Dad was out at work. So it was that Dad moved into Cleveland Road.

Granny and Dad took an instant disliking to each other. Granny was a strong-minded, forthright woman who had lived an independent life for twenty years. She and Mum enjoyed an uncomplicated, companionable relationship. Basically, Dad did not fit in. His personality was the antithesis to Granny's and, as became increasingly clear, to Mum's. If Mum had not conceived at that time, would her relationship with Dad have continued? Was it only the accidental pregnancy that bound them together? When the sexual passion fizzled out, could they have parted and gone their own ways? There are no answers, but what I do know is that their relationship soon began to flounder.

Mum was invited to take part in an international piano competition in Prague. Dad objected strongly to her going, the conflict becoming so extreme that they went to see a marriage-guidance counsellor, even though they were not actually married at that point. The counsellor, a woman, listened to Mum's views with barely-disguised condescension. She smiled sympathetically at Dad.

"Mrs. Giles," she spoke indulgently, "a wife's place is with her husband. How can you think of leaving him for three weeks? You're recently married and in the early stages of pregnancy. The idea is preposterous. Women are apt to get silly notions when they're pregnant; I'm sure that's all this is."

Dad nodded with self-righteous satisfaction. Mum was outraged. "Tell me," she demanded, "if my husband needed to be away on business for three weeks, would you tell *him* that his place was at home with his wife?" Mum went to Prague and Dad seethed ineffectively.

When Mum had her seven-month antenatal check-up, the doctor said he could feel rather too many arms and legs for one baby. With two babies to look after, Mum would definitely need her mother's help. There was no turning back. Granny doubled her hours of knitting. Dad's resentment grew. The dislike they felt for each other deepened into loathing. It was into this triangle of discontent that we made our entrance.

ABOVE: Mum and Dad in about 1950 before they met.
Mum: dressed glamorously for a publicity photo. Dad: a good-looking man apart from the teeth.

BELOW: The only photos I've found of Mum and Dad together before we were born.
Perhaps I am imagining it, but they seem ill-suited even then.

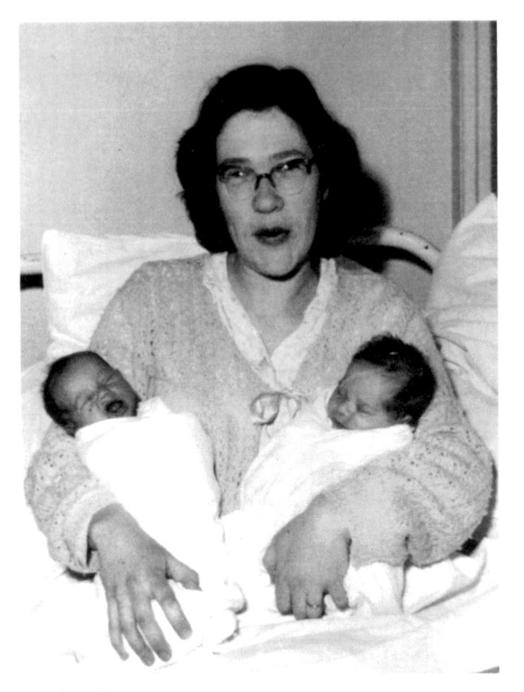

ABOVE:
Mum with her new babies, Catherine (left) and Isabel (right) in Wanstead Hospital.

ABOVE:
With Dad, swaddled in Granny's hand-knitted Shetland shawls. (Izzy on left, Cathy on right)

BELOW:
Out to air in the back garden. Izzy seems to be sleeping peacefully whilst I am frowning.

BELOW:
In our twin pram at the duck pond sporting more of Granny's knitwear.
(Cathy on left, Izzy on right)

Mum and Dad married on February 1st 1956 and we were born on the twenty-sixth. Unusually, we were full-term twins with a combined weight of nearly a stone. Mum must have looked splendid at the Register Office, but the occasion was not photographed.

I was born fifty-five minutes before my twin. Mum called me Catherine and my sister, Isabel. Almost at once, she realised that she had named us the wrong way round. She imagined a Catherine to be gentle, placid and quiet; an Isabel, vigorous, assertive and boisterous. She could have swapped our names around, but having declared her first baby to be Catherine, she felt it wouldn't be right to change her mind. According to Mum, I was the loudest crier in Wanstead hospital. Izzy found feeding almost too much effort and was content to sleep, while I yelled for more. Izzy lost weight and I, although smaller at birth, put it on. We were twins, but not identical; different, yet significantly connected; always together, limbs entwined in our mother's womb, hearts next to each other from the moment they started to beat.

Soon after we were born, Mum produced so much milk that her breasts became engorged and inflamed. She was given a drug that dried up the milk, which resulted in there being only enough for one baby until her breasts recovered. An officious nurse informed her that one of us would have the breast, the other the bottle. Mum refused to comply, insisting that we take turns at the breast. She meant to treat us fairly.

Back from hospital, a four-hourly feeding regime was established. Mum told me that with twins, the routine was essential, but it was also accepted baby-rearing practice in those days. We were fed separately, alternating which baby sucked first. I had imagined that we had taken a breast each, but this was not the case.

"Och no," said Granny, "ye cannae feed two babies at the same time."

"Granny cuddled one of you while I fed the other," Mum explained. "I couldn't have managed without her. Of course that's the advantage of living in an extended family."

After we had been changed and fed, we were trussed in blankets, laid in the twin pram and wheeled out to the garden to air. When the last feed in the evening was over we would be put in our cots and there we would stay until six o'clock in the morning.

"What if we cried in the night?" I asked.

"We left you to cry. You were the demanding one, screaming blue murder for hours! We had a right old battle with you, night after night of it, but you gave up in the end when you realised it wasn't getting you anywhere," remembered Mum with amusement.

"Aye, if you pick a baby up, you're making a rod for your own back," added Granny sagely. "Ye cannae let a baby rule your life. They have to learn who's boss. Your belly was full; we knew there was nothing wrong with you – sheer wilfulness, that's all. Babies need a routine; it gives them security. Now, wee Isabel, we didn't hear a peep out of her; she slept contentedly through your howling." They laughed fondly.

"It was always such a nuisance when the clocks changed – do you remember, Mammy?"

"Aye, puts everyone out of routine. It's a daft idea altogether if ye ask me. Why we don't just keep to British Summertime and be done with it, I don't know. It's the Politicians who mess about with time, if ye want my opinion."

Passers-by stopped to admire us, for in those less fearful days, prams were left in front gardens and outside shops. "You were the talk of the town," Mum boasted. "Everybody knew the twins. How nice, they used to say, a boy and a girl!" She said that I was the one who looked like the boy.

"We used to take you up to the library in the twin pram and leave you outside. You sat at opposite ends and you'd pull each other's booties, hats and mittens off and toss them overboard. Sooner or later, someone would come along and re-dress you. Of course, when they'd gone, you'd undress each other and throw your clothes out of the pram again. It was a great game."

Mum told me that I had four teeth before Izzy had any and walked months before she did. I pulled myself to standing position and tottered round and round our playpen, stepping onto or over Izzy when I came to her sitting in a corner. When we could both walk and were out of the playpen, we toddled around together, and once almost burned the house down when we pushed the couch against the gas fire.

After we had outgrown the pram, the wheels were taken off and it became a seesaw boat. I remember rocking back and forth in it with Izzy, both of us receiving violent jolts as our vessel lurched across the grass.

Chris was born on Midsummer's Day, June 24th 1958. He weighed nine pounds four ounces and was named Christopher Colin Giles. Mum chose to give birth to him at home. As labour progressed, Dad was summoned to get the girls dressed and keep them out of the way. Mum and Dad had recently acquired a car and my recollection is that this was our first ride in it.

"When we get back," said Dad, "there will be a surprise for you." But what could be more thrilling than a car ride? Our car wasn't as smart as the man's next door. His had a wide running board and a secret dickie-seat that popped up out of the boot. He let us sit in it sometimes and laughed when we called it the dickybird. Our car did not have a dickybird and the running board was too narrow to stand on easily, but we climbed excitedly into the back and knelt on the leather upholstery to see out of the windows. The car coughed and spluttered and then we were chugging away.

I have no memory of seeing Chris for the first time, but I know that Izzy and I, nearly two-and-a-half, were smitten with our baby brother. He smiled so readily and laughed when we played with him. We rocked his pram, held out our fingers to feel the clutch of his little fist, stroked and kissed him. Once, when Chris must have been very small, we lifted him out of his carrycot and squashed him into our doll's pram, which teetered on its wheels, overbalanced sideways and our real baby rolled onto the grass. We sucked in our breath. Oh no! What had we done? I picked him up and lay him back in his carrycot while Izzy tucked his blankets around him, hoping nobody had noticed. To our relief he gurgled happily and reached for our fingers, none the worse for his tumble.

ABOVE: Ten months old (Izzy on left, Cathy on right).

BELOW: In the back garden, one year old (Cathy on left, Izzy on right).

Our old twin pram became a see-saw boat (Izzy on left, Cathy on right). Granny knitted all our cardigans and jumpers, many of them in traditional Fair Isle patterns like the ones we are wearing here.

ABOVE: Izzy aged two on the back steps.

RIGHT: Cathy aged two in the front garden.

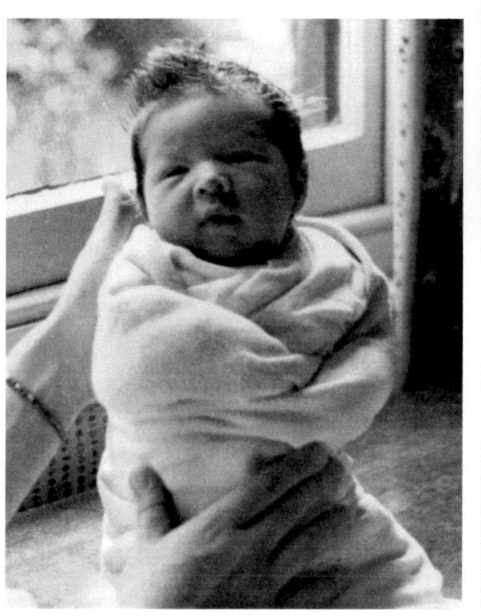

Christopher Giles was born on Midsummer's Day, June 24th 1958.

ABOVE: Three weeks old.

LEFT: From the start Chris made people laugh with his comical smile.

BELOW: Our first car, parked outside 32, Cleveland Road.

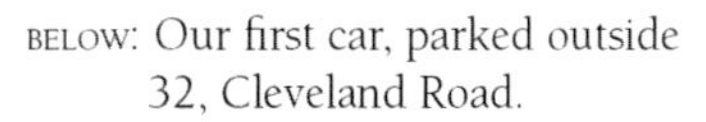

ABOVE: With Mum on Woodford Green, March 1959 (Cathy on right).

BELOW LEFT: With Dad at Cleveland Road; a not-so-happy family (Cathy on left).

BELOW RIGHT: With Granny in Valentine's Park, April 1959 (Cathy on right).

Chris was a cheerful, contented baby. Everybody loved him. If Izzy and I had not been twins, we might perhaps have been jealous of the attention he received, but that was never the case. Granny doted on him. "Oh my bonny boy," she would say as she settled him onto her lap and sang nursery rhymes and Scottish folk songs to him. The song she sang the most was *Loch Lomond*: it was his favourite.

> By yon bonnie banks and by yon bonnie braes,
> Where the sun shines bright on Loch Lomond,
> Where me and my true love were ever wont to gae,
> On the bonnie, bonnie banks of Loch Lomond.
>
> Ye'll take the high road, and I'll take the low road,
> And I'll be in Scotland afore ye;
> But me and my true love will never meet again
> On the bonnie, bonnie banks of Loch Lomond.

Chris could sing a recognisable tune long before he could talk. When he did speak, his chatter was continuous. We had a black and white cat called Sally, who was rather fat and stupid, but good-natured. Chris was very fond of her, and of Whisky, the cat next door. If he ran out of things to talk about, he would say, "Sally's a nice cat, isn't she?" followed by, "Whisky's a nice cat, isn't she?"

We children slept in the smallest bedroom at the back of the house above the kitchen. Chris slept in a cot and Izzy and I shared bunk beds. Mum told me that when the beds had been assembled, I announced that I was going to sleep on the top. Izzy, not to be outdone, stated just as vehemently that she was going to sleep on the bottom. After we had been tucked in and the door was closed, Chris would pipe up, "Is the paraffin fire on?"

"Yes, it is." Mum reassured from the next room. Spoken more quickly, it became "isapaffinfyon?" and sometimes the answer was, "No, you don't need it tonight." But he would ask the same routine question nevertheless.

On Christmas Eve we left Dad's socks at the end of our beds to find them stuffed full in the morning with mostly predictable items: an orange at the bottom, a sugar mouse, a bag of chocolate pennies, a balloon, a comic and, quite usefully, a small torch. The idea was that we would read our comics before waking Mum and Dad. It wasn't until I started filling stockings for my children that Mum told me the secret of replacing the empty sock with its pre-stuffed partner. I had never worked it out. One year, Izzy told us that she heard the bells on Father Christmas's sleigh during the night as he travelled over the rooftops. She was absolutely sure of it, which somehow set her apart: Chris and I had slept through a magical moment that only Izzy had experienced.

Mum and Dad slept in the room next to ours, where Chris had been born. The rest of the upstairs was a landing higher up, a separate area that was let to tenants and comprised a kitchen, two large rooms and a bathroom. Money was tight, so renting part of the house made some necessary extra income. The tenants, Mrs. Blockley and her son, Kit, had a television. We thought they must be very rich.

Occasionally, Mrs. Blockley invited us upstairs to watch *Popeye* or *The Flintstones*, but we didn't feel comfortable in their hot, stuffy room. When the cartoon was over, we sat in awkward silence while they cleared their throats and trawled their minds for something to say to us. Our cue to leave was when Mrs. Blockley rummaged in the bottom of her shopping bag and produced three slightly fluffy, sticky humbugs.

"Here you are dearies. Eat up your spinach!" Puzzled, we said thank you.

"Like Popeye! You know!" she explained, winking. We ran downstairs, pleased to escape. The brown-striped sweets were thrown away immediately, as we knew from past experience how utterly revolting they were.

By the age of three, Chris knew the name and make of every car and could recognise lorries by the sound of their engines. "What kind of lorry is that?" Mum once asked. "It hears like a Bedford," he replied. He was ecstatic if he spotted a transporter or fire engine. Mum and Dad bought him a second-hand pedal car made of red metal with white rubber wheels and the word 'THUNDERBOLT' painted on its sides. He hurtled along Cleveland Road, his little feet pedalling as fast as they would go. Izzy and I followed him with our shared red metal doll's pram, the frayed and faded cloth hood tearing from its rusted frame – but we had to have it up for the pleasure of pressing the side hinges down and feeling the satisfying clonk as they snapped into straightness. One of us pushed our two swaddled dollies along in the pram while the other clutched an old handbag of Mum's and we discussed the cost of living.

I remember childhood winters being deeply cold. During the nights, rivulets of condensation iced solidly to the inside of the bedroom windows. Our breath puffed white plumes into the frozen air and our hot water bottles flopped like cold blubber at the bottom of the beds. We struggled out of our pyjamas and into our clothes under the blankets in an attempt to preserve heat, and emerged with our garments inside out or back-to-front. Downstairs, heating was sparse and spared. An Ideal coal boiler heated the water, giving out some warmth, while various electric fires were switched on if absolutely necessary. I suffered miserably with chilblains: my feet became so cold that they felt as if they were clamped in ice blocks. As they warmed up, a deep ache brought tears to my eyes, followed by painful irritation as the chilblains began to throb and itch. I longed to be warm. It was sometimes all I could think about. But during the summer, winter was forgotten. We complained about going to bed when the sun was still shining and found it impossible to sleep in our stifling west-facing room. Mum or Dad used to hose our bedroom wall from the garden in the belief that the cold dousing would cool the baking bricks. We listened to the water slapping on the wall and sometimes peeked around the curtains to watch, until Mum gestured to us to get back into bed.

Granny and Mum were the anchors in our young lives. Dad was a rather remote character who was mostly absent during the day, but when he was there, the ambience of our environment changed. We sensed the tension and prickliness that existed between him and Mum and Granny even when we were very young. There were many occasions when I felt perplexed by what I witnessed. Here are two examples that I remember clearly from the age of about four.

One happened just before Christmas. Mum tried to create a bit of magic for us. She gave us paper and helped us to write down our Christmas wishes. Grouped around the boiler in our pyjamas, she lifted the lid and told us to drop our lists into the fire. She explained that as the paper burned, the words would float up the chimney and fly straight to Father Christmas, who would read them and know what we wanted. We listened with cautious wonder and decided it must be true, because Mum did not make up stories.

"That's right isn't it dear?" she called to Dad, cajoling him to join in. "Isn't this what you used to do as a boy?"

Dad stood some distance away warming his back by the convector heater, his arms stretched out behind him, palms open, watching us with detachment.

"If you say so," he replied.

Mum looked crestfallen.

"Can we go outside and look at the smoke from the chimney?" I asked, mustering an excitement I no longer felt.

"*May* we go outside," corrected Dad tersely.

"No, dear. It's dark and cold," said Mum wearily. "Time for bed."

The other occurred during a holiday with Mum and Dad in Norfolk. We had gone to the seaside town of Sheringham and were walking along the promenade in the hot sun. For some reason, Chris was miserable and weepy. Mum held his hand, trying to distract him by pointing out the boats, kites, sandcastles and sea. Izzy and I skipped cheerfully beside him in our sand shoes and sundresses, hoping he would cheer up. Dad, who had been ominously silent for most of the day, suddenly exploded. He grabbed Chris by the arm and shook him hard.

"Will you *shut up*. I've had enough of your snivelling. Stop it *now*."

Chris opened his mouth and wailed at full volume, real tears pouring from his eyes. Mum hunkered down and wrapped her arms around him. "Derek! Leave him be. You're making matters worse," she warned.

"I'm fed up with his behaviour. He's been whingeing all day," said Dad angrily. "He needs a good smack. That'll teach him."

"Oh Derek, don't say such things – he's only a wee boy," said Mum. "There, there, sweetie pie, it's all right, shhh," she said soothingly to Chris. Izzy and I stood by helplessly, silent witnesses.

"And you two!" said Dad, lashing out at us, "What are you gawping at? You're just as bad." Passers-by turned to stare at him, casting sympathetic looks down at Mum.

"Derek, please, you're making a scene." She stood up with Chris sobbing in her arms and steadied herself. "Come on girls," she said encouragingly, giving us a brave smile. We each clung to a handful of her cotton-print skirt and walked on.

Dad worked in the City as a clerk for the Guardian Royal Exchange Assurance Company[1] in the overseas accounts department. I am not sure what exactly his job

1. Initially, Dad worked for the Guardian Assurance Company. It merged with Royal Exchange Assurance in 1968 to form the Guardian Royal Exchange Assurance Company.

entailed, but I know it gave him no satisfaction. He left the house at eight o'clock in the morning and commuted on the crowded Central line to Bank station and back five days a week. His office was on one of the upper floors of the Royal Exchange building; the view from his window was the only thing he enjoyed about his job. He was discontented at work and equally discontented at home.

Mum taught the piano and cello to private students and gained such a fine reputation that she was never short of pupils. She also ran an enterprise called 'The James Ching Professional Service', which she took over in 1961 when James Ching died, at the request of his family. Having been one of James Ching's advanced piano students and already made recordings for his Professional Service, she was the only person who could have taken it on. She managed the entire service single-handedly from her office at home. The business's main function was to supply piano teachers with recordings of the Associated Board piano examination pieces. Every year, Mum recorded the entire syllabus of set pieces, from grade I to VIII. Piano teachers from all over the world bought her recordings, along with her annotations and performance advice, to assist their pupils entering for exams. The other role of The James Ching Professional Service was to provide historical notes and annotations of the set works for O and A level music exams. These were much in demand by overworked school music teachers. Mum was always busy. When we returned home from school, she was already teaching her pupils. It was Granny who kept an eye on us and cooked the evening meal. Running the household was Granny's job; what's more it was her house, and therein lay the kernel of discontent, to put it mildly, between Dad and Granny. Mum was caught in the crossfire, but however unbiased she meant to be, her allegiance was ultimately with her mother. Dad's fury turned on Mum. She tried to placate him. They battled silently, each one wanting what the other could not or would not give.

Granny had been running households from the age of fourteen when she was taken out of school to keep house for her father. She had to learn quickly how manage the shopping, cooking, washing and finances on a low budget. A wholesome hot meal every day was an achievement – proof of her efficiency and prudence. When she married and had her own children, she was proud of the fact that through her hard work, economical measures and good sense, her family was well cared for; and it was in this way that she demonstrated her love towards us. She cuddled us when we were very small, but as soon as the unsteady toddling stage was over and we could walk securely on two feet, the days of hands-on tenderness were over. I wonder if this was because she had been deprived of maternal love as a child, as she was only four years old when her mother died.

Like Granny, Mum cuddled us when we were babies, but as we grew into small people, physical affection seeped away. By the time we were at school there were no more hugs; nothing that passed as affectionate contact. Both Mum and Granny disapproved of parents who were overprotective of their children. Life is tough: children must be taught to be independent, to think for themselves, to learn to survive. It was considered that we were perfectly capable of walking to school by ourselves at four-and-a-half. By six we knew our way to the swing park, the forest, the River Roding and our friends' houses. We had the freedom to go where we pleased. If Mum and Granny worried about our safety, they didn't show it. "Och, they'll be back when their bellies start to rumble," declared Granny. Nor did they seem at all interested in where we had been. "Oh, so there you are," was the usual greeting when we materialised after hours of outdoor adventure.

Our relationship with Dad is much more difficult to describe. Mum and Granny were solid, definable people. We felt comfortable with them; the boundaries were clear; we knew how far we could go before we got a ticking off. Subliminally, we understood that despite the absence of hugs, we were loved. There was no such security with Dad. The signals we picked up from him were inconsistent and confusing. We often had the impression that we were somehow at fault, but were not sure why. Sometimes he flew off the handle at us for no comprehensible reason; at other times he seemed not to notice us at all. Unable to interpret his messages towards us, our perception of him was never clear. His reaction to accidents, illness or injury was to go to pieces and panic, as if he were the sick or wounded party. Discomfited by his agitation, Izzy, Chris and I played down our fevers, cuts and bruises, reassuring him that we were fine. Mum and Granny offered us kindness and sympathy when we were unwell, and I was the one who was often ill, but by then the lack of physical contact between us had rendered embraces awkward and embarrassing. Absence of endearment in our family was etched so heavily that Izzy and I are still unable to hug one another spontaneously. It is unlikely that this one place of discomfort between us will ever ease. Thankfully, we have no difficulties in giving or receiving heartfelt cuddles with our children or embracing our friends.

Izzy and I started to have ballet lessons when we were five. Dad took us to our classes, as Mum taught on Saturday mornings. We carried our second-hand vanity cases with pride. They were grey, lined with red satin and contained our ballet shoes, leotards and skirts. Dad rang the bell and we entered a forbidding, dark house. We were shown into a small area at the end of the hall, which was full of other little girls changing into or out of ballet costumes. Not quite sure what we should be doing, we put our cases down and struggled out of our clothes. There was so little light, we couldn't see what we were doing. The girls left the room, telling us we had better hurry up. Somewhat dishevelled, we followed them into a large studio with French windows at one end, a polished wooden floor, mirrors and rails along two walls and an ancient upright piano against the other. A woman was sitting at the instrument with her back to us. To the side of her was someone I saw at once as the Witch from *Hansel and Gretel*. Old and wrinkled, her grey hair knotted into a tight bun on top of her head, she was dressed from head to foot in black. In her right hand, she held a walking stick.

"Come along, come along," she ordered, as we all huddled into one corner of the room.

"Music!" she barked. A vaguely recognisable melody erupted from the twangy, out-of-tune piano. The girl in front of us skipped diagonally across the room to the other side.

"Point your toes, back straight. Next!" The second pupil launched herself across the floor. We eyed the Witch nervously. I knew that Izzy was as scared as I was. We were the only two left.

"Come on," she shouted impatiently.

I galumphed into action with the grace of a seal out of water.

"Lift your feet! Don't wave your arms! Head up!"

Izzy skipped daintily after me.

"You two," she said, pointing her cane ominously at us, "come here."

We walked towards her with trepidation.

"Closer!" she said, and prodded her stick into my belly.

"Where are your belts? And why is there no elastic across your slippers? As for your hair... what is it girls?"

"A disgrace," intoned our classmates, en masse.

We hung our heads in shame. She waved her stick dismissively.

"Get in line. Tell your mother I want to see her."

We then 'danced' back across the room one after the other. As far as I can recall, that is all we did. In the changing room it was pandemonium. The girls for the next class were battling for space and our clothes had been strewn all over the floor, trampled underfoot. The following week we fared no better.

"You! Come here!" I assumed my position in front of her.

"What is the meaning of this? I will *not* have grey socks in class. White ankle socks and nothing else." She struck the floor angrily with her stick. As if on cue, Izzy's hair cascaded out of its bun, pins and Kirby grips skittering in all directions. Our enthusiasm for ballet was severely dampened.

Mum found us another ballet school. We were again aware that we didn't look quite right. Granny had knitted us pink wraparound cardigans, but the pink was the wrong shade and the four-ply wool too bulky. We longed for the elegant shop-bought ones the other girls wore. Our tap shoes were old-fashioned, our skirts too long, and even our cherished vanity cases looked drab compared to the rest. We stuck with it for a while and Mum came up trumps when we had to have costumes made for our first show. Our class (the youngest) were to perform the Flower Dance. We were divided into groups of daisies, tulips, daffodils and forget-me-nots. Izzy and I were to be forget-me-nots. Mum asked Mrs. Blunden, a large, homely woman, too big for her tiny house in Cowslip Road, to make us tutus. They were truly lovely – green satin bodices with delicate straps and flounce after flounce of pale blue net that stuck out just as it should. We couldn't have been more pleased with ourselves.

On the day of the performance, Mum took us to the Sir James Hawkey Hall in Woodford Green with our hair pinned tightly into buns and our special tutus in plastic bags. Backstage was mayhem, but Mum helped us to dress before leaving to find her seat. Our excitement was complete when a helper came over to us, painted lipstick on our mouths and powdered our noses. We were on first and danced as well as we could, but it was over in minutes. We then had to wait until the very end of the interminably drawn out show to take a final bow. Long before that, the flowers had wilted.

Young Chris Giles. Note the oversized duffle coat he is wearing in the picture on the right above. Our clothes were always bought to grow into.

ABOVE: Cathy aged three
TOP AND MIDDLE: Cathy aged four
BELOW: Izzy aged four
Clearly we are not identical twins, yet people often told us how alike we were.

2
WASTE NOT, WANT NOT

A penny saved is a penny gained.

Scottish proverb

Mum and Granny shopped together, compared prices in the local grocery stores and bought the least expensive. Small luxuries such as hand cream, bubble bath or pleasant smelling soap were thought unnecessary extravagances. Glycerine mixed with water was the emollient for all skin conditions, and if that failed, lanolin was the back up. Stomach upsets were treated with bicarbonate of soda, all other ailments with Aspirin. We used the cheapest soap, which looked and smelled like lard and made about as much lather. Boots, the chemists, sold low-cost shampoo, which was bought in the largest economy size then diluted. Washing-up liquid and scouring pads were unnecessary when soap powder and Ajax would do. As for tissues: a disgraceful waste of paper when we could blow our noses on rags. Nor did new-fangled machines seduce them:

Hair-dryers: "Why on earth people waste money on those things is a mystery. Hair will dry perfectly well if you just leave it."

Electric toasters: "What a con: much better to put bread under the grill where you can see it."

Electric kettles: "So extravagant! You end up heating far more water than you need, besides which, gas heats the water more quickly."

Electric blankets: "Well, they're just plain dangerous."

They had an odd aversion to electricity. We had a gas fridge as well as a gas cooker. Gadgets to make the daily chores easier were also rejected out of hand. The long-handled mop was ridiculed: "There's only one way to get a floor clean – get down on your hands and knees and scrub."

Spray polish was ineffective and used by the lazy. To bring a true shine to wood, Mansion polish out of a tin must be spread thinly over the surfaces then rigorous elbow grease applied. Even the modest vegetable peeler was scorned: "A good sharp paring knife is all you need."

However, there were some things that were not economised. Cheap white sliced bread, instant coffee and poor quality meat were not allowed across the threshold. Granny selected her meat from the family butcher on the High Road; bread came warm from the bakery; Dad bought coffee beans and tea from a specialist shop in the City – one of his few contributions to the household that was appreciated. Margarine was a dirty word: the cheapest salted butter was bought for baking, but extra pennies were spent on fresh butter for spreading on bread and scones. 'Fresh' is the Scottish term for 'unsalted' – as in salt-water/fresh-water – but I didn't understand this when I was little, thinking that the cooking butter was somehow off. When I realised that the delicious butter I tasted at other peoples' houses was salted and asked if I could have that kind instead, Granny was angry that I preferred it to fresh butter. I need hardly mention that all South African produce was boycotted.[1]

Although Granny, Mum and Dad protested against racism and inequality, they were themselves prejudiced. They could not abide American, South African, Canadian, Australian or New Zealand accents. As a race, all Americans were brash and stupid. Granny and Mum moaned about the inferiority of the English education and legal system, complained about the inhospitable nature of Londoners and the lack of generosity of Southerners in general. To Granny and Mum, all things Scottish were best. Dad was intolerant of people who did not speak perfect English or who exposed a lack of education, calling them 'ignorant fools' or 'blithering idiots'. Young men were without exception 'long-haired louts', 'spotty good-for-nothings' or 'lazy yobbos'. Yet he slipped into Cockney slang when he was with his 'common' friends. Despite the statement he was fond of repeating – "a person who uses profanities lacks intelligence and shows ignorance" – he used swear words himself when he lost his temper. The three of them agreed that pop music was vulgar trash; transistor radios should be banned along with ITV and all advertising; churchgoers were fools or religious nutcases. Yet hand in hand with prejudice went hypocrisy. Izzy was berated for reading Catherine Cookson novels – cheap rubbish, they called it. When Granny was old and her eyesight failing, Mum borrowed 'Talking Books' from the library for her and Granny thought them 'awful good'.

"But these ones are by Catherine Cookson," said Izzy indignantly, "you used to tell me they were rubbish." Mum and Granny denied ever having said such a thing.

Granny made jam, jelly and marmalade. It would have been unthinkable to buy it. We went strawberry and raspberry picking to pick-your-own farms in Essex. Once I ate so many strawberries during our hour in the field that Mum had to stop the car umpteen times on the way home for me to pee by the side of the road.

"For heaven's sake, Catherine, how many strawberries did you eat?" They were irresistible – bright red fruits lying lusciously beneath the leaves, slightly warm on the outside from the hot sun, cool and succulent within, the juice bursting into the mouth. I had lost count of the number I'd eaten: hundreds, probably.

We collected crab apples and went brambling in Epping Forest, coming home with purple mouths, tongues and hands, and scratched arms. Mum and Granny bought boxes of apricots, plums, greengages, blackcurrants and crates of Seville oranges when the fruits were in season and low-priced. Out came the huge copper pot and the kitchen would be turned over to jam making. For bramble, crab apple or blackcurrant jelly, an old chair with the seat taken out was brought in from the hut. The corners of a large square of muslin were tied to the four legs and the cooked fruit

1. Apartheid, a system of legal racial segregation, was introduced by South Africa's National Party in 1948. In 1958, the ANC (African National Congress) and its allies called for an international boycott of all South African goods. In Britain, the TUC, Labour, Liberal and Communist parties backed the campaign and twenty-two local authorities banned South African fruit from their schools and canteens. On March 9th 1960, Labour Party leader Hugh Gaitskell went on television to ask viewers not to buy South African products. Granny, Mum and Dad were vehemently Anti-Apartheid, boycotting all South African goods. Granny and Mum were even known to take local grocers to task for selling it. For thirty-five years hundreds of thousands of people in Britain joined Anti-Apartheid Movement campaigns until in April 1994 South Africa held its first one-person, one-vote general election.

mulch poured in. The juice dripped into a bowl beneath for hours. Granny squeezed the bag to catch the last drop, then the liquid was boiled up with sugar until she was satisfied it had reached the point where it would set. When the jam jars had been filled, circles of greaseproof paper were laid on the jam's surface, cellophane stretched across the rims and secured with thin elastic bands. The jars were labelled, dated and stacked in the jam cupboard.

The mincer was set up for marmalade making – a heavy iron contraption that clamped to the side of the table. First the pips had to be removed from the oranges and soaked in a bowl overnight to jellify. The fruit was fed through the mincer and boiled up with sugar in the copper pan. After hours of cooking, it was removed from the heat and the pip jelly added to help the marmalade solidify.

Granny made sure that no leftover food was chucked away. The remains of a joint of beef or lamb would be turned into stovies or shepherd's pie the next day. Vegetable and fruit peelings were tipped onto the compost heap, the teapot emptied onto the earth around the bushes, and any food scraps the birds might eat were thrown onto the grass. We were severely rebuked if we discarded a bruised apple, brown banana or piece of festering cheese. The squishy, mouldy bits would be cut out and the rest given back to us to eat. It was also a mortal sin to leave the tiniest scrap of food on our plate. "If you didn't want it you shouldn't have asked for it," we were told. After a struggle, when we could not eat the last potato or piece of fatty meat, Granny or Mum would scrape it onto their plate and polish it off. Waste was a crime. Sheets, when they wore thin, were cut in half lengthways and the outer edges sewn together – many of the sheets we slept on had an uncomfortable ridge down the middle. Cardboard, brown paper and string were saved from parcels; clothes were patched and darned, but never thrown away. At the end of their wearable life they would be used for dusters and floor cloths.

Mum and Granny would not have dreamt of buying cakes or puddings. Granny made delicious scones, pancakes (drop scones), sponges, pastry, jam tarts, fruit crumble, bread and butter pudding, lemon meringue, apple dumplings and chocolate cake. Mum's speciality was 'tablet' (a Scottish version of fudge), which was scrumptious. Breakfast cereals were banned. We had porridge and that was that. We were told that cornflakes tasted of cardboard and there was more nourishment in the packaging. I remember going to friends' houses after school and being offered food as soon as we stepped through the door. It struck us as strange that these mums gave their children sandwiches, buns, biscuits and drinks at four o'clock. At home, we were not allowed to eat until dinnertime, as snacking between meals would ruin our appetite. Feeling terribly naughty, we would eat the plates of food – sliced white bread and margarine with shop-bought Robertson's jam – yummy; iced buns, jam doughnuts, penguin biscuits and chocolate fingers. Sometimes we dared to ask whether we could have a bowl of cereal. What bliss – cornflakes, or better still – Rice Krispies.

Granny wore an apron in the house. She had several of the same design with deep pockets that extended across the whole width, and bibs with straps that crossed over the back to tie at the waist. Worn and washed over and over, the floral prints were faded and the binding frayed. She often sneezed in the mornings, as did I, and always kept a handkerchief tucked under the cuff of her cardigan. I also stuffed my hankies up my sleeve, but it was not pleasant to feel them against the wrist when they became soaked and snotty.

She knitted our clothes, which, I am sorry to say, we did not always appreciate. She was an expert at Fair Isle knitting and made us jumpers, cardigans and gloves in traditional Fair Isle patterns. For Mum she knitted twin sets, skirts and short-sleeved lacy tops. Even Dad wore Fair Isle waistcoats and plain cardigans with pockets that she knitted for him, which in retrospect seems uncharacteristic of them both – she *make* something for him? He *wear* it?

She showed us how to make pom-poms for woolly hats by cutting out two circles of cardboard, making a hole in the middle and winding a ball of wool through the hole and over the edges, round and round and round. When the card was thick with wool, we pushed scissors between the two pieces of card, snipped the wool around the circumference and tied the strands tightly together. It was a satisfying moment when the card was pulled away to reveal a perfect woolly ball. She also taught me how to knit and crochet. Izzy was not interested, but I was.

Yarn was ordered from a wholesaler in Scotland, which arrived in skeins. Granny would call for my assistance: "Cath-er-reen! Come and help me wind the wool." (She pronounced my name with three clear syllables, the emphasis on the last, which made it sound as if she were permanently cross with me.) She would place the looped skein around my extended arms and roll the wool into balls, while my arms went up and down like a wooden doll as I helped the yarn around my wrists. Sometimes the roles were reversed and she held the skein while I did the rolling. "Not too tight, mind. Keep it loose. There's a knack to winding wool."

The rhythmical sound of busy needles was a familiar background noise. When a garment was finished, Granny tied and trimmed the loose ends and threw the snippets into the garden for the birds. Sure enough, they swooped down and carried off beakfuls of coloured scraps to line their nests. They also picked up hair clippings after Mum had given Chris or Dad a haircut in the garden. Chris looked but never found a woolly-lined or hair-quilted nest.

Our clothes were purchased to last, not to flatter or fit. They were invariably bought several sizes too big and far removed from any style that appealed to us. Fabric was examined for durability. Synthetic fibres were rejected in favour of linen, cotton or wool, although our grey pleated skirts were made of Terylene. Footwear was a matter of great importance. When the sales were on, we were taken to a shoe shop where our feet were properly measured. Shoes were bought to allow the recommended room for growth and were made by Clarks' or Start-Rite. We longed for more stylish models, but a raised heel or pointed toe was out of the question.

The front door of our house was always on the latch – we just pushed the door and in we went, as did all visitors and pupils. Granny and Mum pooh-poohed warnings of intruders: everyone left their doors open in the tenements, they said. The neighbours were in and out of one another's homes and there was never any trouble. The car was not locked either, until the day the cat's dinner disappeared.

Sally was fed on whiting, a cheap fish from the fishmonger. Granny and Mum had bought the cat's food first. They left it in the car while they made other purchases and then drove home. The bag of whiting had gone. They could not understand what had happened to it. Mum searched under the car seats, but it was nowhere to be found. Eventually they concluded that it must have been stolen. Shocked that there were people who would steal from a car, Mum began reluctantly to lock the car doors. It did not seem to occur to her that there must also be people who would gladly enter and take from an unlocked house. The front door remained on the latch.

The time came when Sally had to be put down. She was old, ill and in pain. Mum explained that putting Sally to sleep, as she called it, was the kindest thing to do, but we were very upset, particularly Chris. To cheer us up, Mum got another cat straight away; an affectionate, intelligent ginger called Rusty. He had a loud, rumbling purr, which he turned on full for anyone willing to make a fuss over him.

To our dismay, just a few weeks after his arrival, he went missing. We made posters to stick on trees and lampposts and went round the streets knocking on doors. A week later we found him several streets away settled in comfortably with another family who were most reluctant to part with him. It transpired that Rusty had made friends with the milkman and followed him on his round. When the milk float departed, Rusty couldn't find his way home and simply moved into another house. Such is the infidelity of cats. Still, we were glad to get him back and he didn't disappear again. We were not glad, however, when Rusty's antics put an end to us having Christmas trees. He couldn't resist pawing at the glass baubles, swiping them so hard that one after the other fell off and smashed. Mum made a barrier to try and stop him, but he managed to jump over it and leapt right into the tree, which toppled and crashed to the ground. The lights fused and earth was strewn all over the newly washed floor. Rusty fled from the room and Granny said enough was enough. The decorations that were still intact were removed and the tree put out in the garden. We begged to have a tree the next year, but were refused. Granny disliked Christmas trees anyway – unnecessary, messy things and an utter waste of money. Christmas itself was superfluous, created needless work and put her routine out of kilter.

Some years later, we acquired a tabby kitten whom we named Tinker. She was completely neurotic, afraid to go outside and all too frequently found peeing in corners. She did improve a bit, but could never be trusted. Rusty tolerated Tinker, but the two were never great friends – at least, that is how it appeared to me.

Granny listened to the weather forecast without fail every morning. It was almost a religious ritual, which demanded her full concentration and our compliance, as the broadcast coincided with our breakfast time. She came through from the kitchen to stand, hands on hips, in the middle of the living room. The wireless was in the corner, its speaker mounted above the table.

"Wheesht now, I want to hear the weather," ordered Granny, her voice rising above our chatter. "Will ye turn it up a wee bit?" One of us reached for the brown Bakelite knob, second from the right, and raised the volume. Breakfast was suspended. If we didn't pipe down and keep our cutlery still she shouted, "Och, *wheesht* the lot of ye, I cannae hear the man speak." Chris, if his back was to her, pulled faces at Izzy and me, while I nudged his legs, receiving kicks in return. The table jogged, rattling cups and plates. "Stop your fidgeting, Christopher," Granny chided.

Dad, sitting beside us, said not a thing. He flinched at every word Granny uttered while he chewed his toast grimly and took measured sips of tea. Granny, head cocked to one side, feet planted apart, absorbed the weather forecast dourly before returning to the kitchen to relay her own interpretation to Mum. Dad followed her retreating figure with lancing looks of hatred. He left the table, pulled on his jacket, picked up his briefcase and announced that he was going to work. Mum hurried through, fixed a smile on her face and placed a kiss on his cheek – a charade that was performed every morning. Dad left the house while Granny continued with her diagnosis of the weather. The forecast was gospel: from the long-range outlook she determined the best week for the tomato plants to go in the ground, when to sow the carrot seeds, chit the potatoes or prune the hydrangeas – such ugly bushes, I thought, but Granny admired them and turned the flowers blue by sprinkling aluminium sulphate around the roots. I always wondered why – pink seemed fine to me.

When breakfast was over, Mum chivvied us to get ready for school, the forecast dictating what we should wear. "Och, they won't be needing their cardigans," Granny might say to Mum, "it's going to be in the seventies today." I cannot count the number of mornings I walked shivering to school, wearing just a flimsy summer dress with only sandals on my bare feet. Standing in the playground with goose-pimpled limbs waiting for the doors to open, I longed for my cardigan. On other occasions, she would declare, "They'll be needing their raincoats today." Often we did not, but Granny would not have it that the forecast was ever wrong.

Mum and Granny did not have breakfast with the rest of us. They were up early and brewed the first large pot of tea – a blend of two parts ordinary Indian to one part Lapsang Souchong. Surprisingly, all three adults drank from the same pot. They were of the opinion that this particular combination of teas was the best, the pine-smoked, coarse black leaves from China adding a refreshing, piquant flavour to the Indian. It was one thing they agreed about. When we had gone to school, Mum and Granny shopped. At eleven o'clock, a pot of freshly ground coffee was percolated, which they drank with their mid-morning brunch. Three o'clock was afternoon tea – another Indian/Lapsang Souchong brew, and six o'clock was dinnertime. This, their weekday routine, was set in stone. On Saturdays and Sundays, dinner[2] was at one o'clock after Mum had finished her morning teaching.

Our bath was in the kitchen. It was a hipbath, covered during the day with a wooden lid, which could be used as a work surface. The downstairs lavatory was also accessed from the kitchen, a situation that would probably not gain planning permission today. The fun of the hipbath was that we could submerge ourselves up to the neck in the deep end. There were a few quarrels about whose turn it was to have the last bath. Last was the best position as we could carry on with whatever we were doing for longer. We decided to settle the arguments by drawing up a rota, and the first list was pinned to the wall.

2. In our household, the main meal of the day was called dinner, whether eaten in the middle of the day or in the evening.

The kitchen floor was Marley[3] tiled, cold and slippery for wet feet. When we had finished our bath, Dad lifted us out, wrapped us in towels that had been warming in the hot cupboard, and swung us into the living room where we dried by the boiler. When I was about six, the routine ended for me. I was in the privileged position of last. Izzy and Chris were already dried and in their pyjamas. I called to Dad that I'd finished. "Oh you're much too heavy to lift out of the bath any more," he said. I was taller and broader than Izzy – the difference in our size was often commented upon – not just at home, but by outsiders: "Well, how strange that they're twins and she's bigger." It seemed to me that the comparison was unflattering. Izzy was little and cute; I was big and ungainly. Happiness drained down the plughole with the bath water. I was too heavy now. I hauled myself out, ashamed of my hugeness, self-conscious of my body. Izzy and Chris continued to enjoy their flights across the kitchen tiles, but I had to walk barefoot over the cold floor.

The next list we drew up was the custard skin list. Granny made custard, poured it into a bowl and left it to stand, so that by the time it came to be served, a skin had formed. This would be pinched in the middle and pulled up whole, like a blanket. We all wanted the skin, so the rota distributed the treat fairly. There was also the washing-up, drying-up and putting-away list, each day crossed off meticulously.

After dinner, Granny lumbered through to her room to knit, Mum went to the music room to teach, the three of us washed up, dried up and put away, and Dad descended to the cellar, his private domain, where he kept the things he picked up at jumble sales, Oxfam shops and white-elephant stalls, and where he restored paintings, mended clocks and French-polished chairs. Mum had to remember to tell him when the coal was due to be delivered so that he could hang dustsheets across the partitioned coal store to protect his treasures.

The coalmen looked like enormous alien beetles. They wore oily black leather hoods that extended over their shoulders and down their backs. Around their middles they had wide double-buckled belts. Sweating and straining they heaved the bulging coal sacks onto their leathered backs and clumped through the shed. The shed, as we called it, was actually a covered side entranceway to the back garden. Just past the shed was the coalhole. They lifted the heavy iron cover and with mighty grunts tipped the coal into the chute. The black rocks rumbled in an avalanche down into the cellar. Then Mum counted money into one of their huge blackened hands and they were gone.

We were expected to help with household chores, and did. We polished the shoes, laid the table, ran errands for Granny, went to the Post Office to weigh parcels for Mum and helped to fold sheets. We didn't have a washing machine. Granny used a service called 'The Bag-Wash' for cotton and linen whites. All articles were crammed into sacks, which were collected from the door once a week, boiled in the bag and returned damp. The contents were hung out on the washing line, draped around the boiler, or folded and left to dry in the hot tank cupboard. Everything else

3. Marley Homelay floor tiles were manufactured in the 1950s and 60s. Made of a synthetic material, harder and tougher than Vinyl, they were about 8 inches (20cm) square, about ⅛ inch (3mm) thick and laid onto a solid floor. They were produced in various colours, speckled with distinctive, contrasting flecks.

was washed by hand.

Dad collected handkerchiefs – other people's that had dropped on the ground. When he came home, he pulled the puddle-soaked mucky hankies out of his pockets and described his finds proudly – for example, "a good haul today – look, a couple of lacy ones and three gents'." Granny took them without comment and stuffed them into the bag-wash. They came back clean enough. Dad ironed and folded each one lovingly before placing them with the others in the hanky drawer. The embroidered initials set me wondering about the names of those who had lost them. Dad did most of the ironing, but this was not without danger.

"What are you ironing it like *that* for?" demanded Granny. Dad lifted the iron, looking set to hurl it at her. She flinched and we all tensed as Dad crashed the iron onto the ironing board and shouted, "Mind your own business. I'll iron as I damn well please."

The atmosphere at home affected us deeply on levels beyond our understanding. We knew that Dad and Granny did not like each other; that much was obvious. We sensed that there was something not quite right between Mum and Dad, but that was intangible. On a subconscious level, it bothered us, but when we were involved with our games and adventures, we forgot all about it. Together we created a happier world, trusting and relying upon one another, plaited together like a harvest loaf.

Before I go any further with the story of our childhood, I would like to fill in some historical background, which must begin with the matriarch of the family – Granny. For her, down to earth practicality, hard work and economy were the valuable essentials of life. The imagination was brushed aside along with physical affection and 'all that nonsense'. There were reasons why this attitude prevailed. Granny, and generations before hers, had lived in times of poverty and hardship, when infant mortality was commonplace. Grief was an indulgence, an expensive emotion that wouldn't pay the rent. As Granny said, "If your babies died, you had to get on with life. There were other mouths to be fed. You weren't the only one who'd lost a child or a husband or wife."

I am sure that feelings were no less profound than they are today, or have ever been. To talk about them, though, was rare. As far as Granny was concerned, there was no time to let the heart linger or the mind wander. Dreaming and blathering wouldn't put bread on the table. But for all the stoicism, folks still mourned, wondered and loved – even Granny. I shall take you back now to the early nineteenth century, to before she was born, in order to set the scene. As I will be moving swiftly through the branches of the family, and names are repeated in successive generations, it might be helpful to refer to the 'Greig, Glass and Mouat' and the 'Fraser' family trees printed at the end of the book.

CLEVELAND ROAD

ABOVE: Cleveland Road. Photo: *Woodford Times* 1966

BELOW: Mum and the three of us, and me with the red-hooded doll's pram, 1960.

ABOVE: Chris aged two, twins aged four-and-a-half sitting on the kitchen step. Izzy is in the middle.

RIGHT AND BELOW RIGHT: Cathy in the middle.

BELOW: Summer holiday 1960. Izzy in the middle.

GRANNY'S STORY: GATHERING THE CLANS

All the world's a stage,
And all the men and women merely players;
They have their exits and their entrances;
And one man in his time plays many parts.

As You Like It – William Shakespeare

3
GRANNY'S FATHER'S PARENTS

Granny's father's father, William Greig (pronounced and originally spelled 'Gregg'), was born in 1839 in County Antrim, Northern Ireland, into a Protestant family. From accounts that have passed down through the generations, the Greigs were tenant farmers of a smallholding in Ballymena. They probably employed a few farm hands and a couple of women or girls to help in the house, but they worked alongside their employees, undertook the same jobs and sat down together at one large table to eat. Although they made no distinction between themselves and their employees, the Greigs were nevertheless better placed than many of their country-folk.

William played the fiddle and was able to rattle off tunes by ear, which suggests that despite the demands of running a smallholding, there was time found for entertainment. It would also seem that they were compassionate people from this story I was told: one day, during the potato famine of 1845-1850, a destitute and starving family came past the farm looking for food and shelter. William's mother was so overcome with pity that she took them all in, and not just for the night – they remained for several months until they had regained their health and strength.

In the early 1860s, William met Martha Long, a woman six years his senior. Martha was from Randalstown, about ten miles south of Ballymena. Her father, Alexander Long, was a weaver. She and her siblings had a more puritanical upbringing than William, as her family were devout Presbyterians – a doctrine that Martha maintained all her life.

Although the north of Ireland was not affected so severely as the south by the Great Hunger, there was still a shortage of food, homelessness, unemployment and extreme poverty in the 1860s. Perhaps circumstances had changed for the worse for the Greigs by this time, as Martha Long, a strong-willed, resolute woman, decided that Ireland was no place to bring up a family. As soon as she and William were married they crossed the waters to Scotland, sailing up the Firth of Clyde to Glasgow where they hoped a better future awaited them.

Initially, the couple settled south of Glasgow in Busby, Renfrewshire, where William found work and accommodation as an outdoor labourer. Their first three children were born there: Henry in 1864, William (Granny's father) in December 1866, and Robert in 1868. At this point, the Greigs moved to Calton, a central district of Glasgow, where two more children were born – their only daughter, Lizzie, followed by the last son, John. William Greig worked long hours as a labourer at the Print Works, and later the Iron Foundry, while Martha brought up their five children. The family lived on the bread line, but were scrupulously respectable. Martha made sure that they were well turned out on a Sunday, hands and faces scrubbed, shoes and buttons shining. To church they went without fail, Martha wearing her black bonnet, William his top hat. By all accounts, Martha was very strict with her children. When her third son, Robert, was nine, he was messing about with fireworks when one exploded in his face. The pain of his injuries was more bearable than the contemplation of his mother's wrath, for he spent hours walking the streets before returning home to face the consequences. He lost an eye as a result and had to live with a glass one for the rest of his life. The children's father was less severe and lightened the atmosphere when he fetched his fiddle and played the ballads, jigs and reels of Ireland. His second son, William, showed particular interest in music, and after some instruction became a proficient folk fiddler himself. He would dance around the room while he played, until his mother had had enough of such time-wasting frivolity and made him stop.

Economic hardship in Glasgow meant that many parents sent their children to work in the cotton mills. Some were only ten when they entered the factories as part-time workers. By the age of thirteen, they were labouring twelve-hour days, often in appalling conditions. Martha Greig was adamant that none of her children were going to work in the mills. Her sheer determination ensured that all of them were given apprenticeships or jobs. She dressed herself and her eldest sons, Henry and William, in their best Sunday clothes and marched them to the Post Office, where her powers of persuasion gained them both jobs as telegraph messengers. She then established her younger sons, Robert and John, as apprentices in the boot and shoe trade. Lizzie was apprenticed into the dressmaking trade.

Of the five children, Robert was the first to marry. A son was born, but the birth was complicated, infection set in, and a month later Robert's young wife died from septicaemia. Robert moved back to his parents' house where his sister, Lizzie, took on the role of mother to the baby boy. Let us hope that Martha had mellowed a little and was not as stern with her grandson as she had been with her children. Yet despite her harshness, Martha Greig was fiercely protective of her family. Her eldest son, Henry, was considered to be 'not quite right in the head', but she took care of him and ensured that he had work and a roof over his head. He lived with her for his entire life until he died in his forties of heart failure caused by asthma.

Soon after Robert had returned home with his baby son, his brother, William, departed to marry Annie Glass. William Greig (junior) and Annie Glass were to be our Granny's parents.

4
GRANNY'S MOTHER'S PARENTS

Granny's mother's mother, Ann Mouat (also spelt Mowat), was born in Dunrossness, the southernmost tip of the Shetland Islands, in 1837. The Islands are way out in the North Atlantic, a good hundred miles north of the Scottish mainland. Exposed to the sea, wind and harsh weather, living on rough terrain and infertile land, the Shetlanders had to be tough to survive. Sheep and Shetland ponies populated the common grazing land, both species managing to live on the coarse grass found amid the heather on the moorlands. Sheep were essential to the Shetlanders for milk, meat, and particularly wool, the animals' fine quality fleece giving the Shetland Wool Industry world renown. Crofters used the ponies to carry cut peat from the hills to fuel their fires. In springtime, the ponies' thick manes and tails were cropped to provide raw material for fishing nets and lines. The animals were also put to work in the copper and talc mines, and bred, sold and exported south to work as pit ponies. Their small stature made them valuable, as they could travel into the narrowest shafts. It is only relatively recently that they have been used as mounts for young children.

Whaling also provided Shetland sailors with a living. Although it wasn't until the 1900s that major whaling stations were established on the Shetland Islands, fleets sailing into the North Atlantic from the large whaling ports on the east coast of Scotland often stopped to pick up crews from Shetland. It was big business, British whaling vessels in fierce competition with Norwegian and Dutch companies, as well as the Icelandic hunters. Whales were slaughtered indiscriminately and horribly. The huge creatures generated enormous revenue – a sperm whale yielded around seventy-five barrels of oil (over 2,300 gallons). The whale population and the lives of the men who hunted them were of little or no consequence to the whaling companies, whose sole motivation was profit. There were numerous whaling disasters. Granny related one tragic story of three Shetland brothers who drowned together. The boys, along with countless other young men, died in the Atlantic waters. Life was cheap.

Ann Mouat grew up in a large family of two boys and five girls. There were no schools in Shetland at this time and she and her siblings were illiterate, as were most of the Shetland population. The children would have been taught to knit, mend sails, make fishing nets and cut peat. Their father was a crofter, so they would have been used to tending sheep and helping with the necessary tasks from an early age. The sea that surrounded them, that giver and taker of life, pounded out the rhythm of their existence incessantly, sending its winds to howl at their doors and slice through their bones.

When they were children, the story goes that Ann and her sisters, Catherine and Barbara, were very ill with diphtheria. They had lost their hair, which is one of the distressing side effects of the disease, and wore cotton head-caps to cover their baldness. One summer morning they went for an early walk. The mist still hung in the air, the sun shone, and as there was nobody to see them, they removed their caps to feel the warmth and wind on their scalps. The girls noticed tiny droplets of dew settling on one another's heads. They realised that it was a downy growth of new hair that was catching the beads of moisture. Overjoyed, they held hands and danced in the morning sunshine, celebrating their survival and recovery.

When Ann was seventeen, her mother developed tuberculosis and died six months later. Ann became her father's housekeeper until he remarried eight years later. Ann and her stepmother did not see eye to eye. I have been told that the new wife was cruel to Ann and wanted her out of the house. Whatever the truth, it was then that Ann decided to leave Shetland, to get away from the remote, comfortless islands. She was twenty-five and single with an independent spirit and the courage to take her chance. She left behind her entire family and the only community and way of life she knew. She must have been aware that she would probably not see her kin or the islands again, but something stronger pulled at her – a yearning for more. To the mainland she sailed, where she hoped to find live-in work as a domestic servant. It is thought that she was employed in Glasgow initially, but at some point she lived and worked in Ayr. It was in one of those places that she met Andrew Glass.

Andrew Glass was born in Girvan, Ayrshire, in 1820. His Irish-born parents, John Glass and Margaret Lang, earned their living as handloom weavers. As soon as their children were able, they helped too, the whole family working at the looms from their rented dwelling. However, the invention of the power loom, along with other developments in textile machinery, would fundamentally change the lives of handloom weavers. The first steam-powered textile factory had been built in Nottingham in 1790. From around 1810, handloom weaving in the home was progressively replaced by power-loom weaving in the factories. This was accompanied by a massive reduction in handloom weavers' earnings. Struggling to survive, weavers worked regularly from six in the morning until ten or eleven at night, using all available daylight, often working ninety-hour weeks.

Although the Glass family laboured intensively at the looms, it appears that the children did get some schooling, as there is no doubt that Andrew was taught to read and write. When he was in his early twenties, his father died and the cottage industry died with him. The family dispersed, Andrew's brothers marrying and his sisters becoming servants, two of them later emigrating to Australia. His mother moved to Kilmarnock and became a grocer and spirit dealer. Andrew remained in Girvan, continuing to earn a meagre living as a handloom weaver in other households.

In 1846 he married Agnes Smith. What became of her, I do not know. It is probable that she died, as in 1851 he married Elizabeth Connelly. After the birth of their second child, Andrew moved his family to Glasgow where he found employment as a cotton weaver in a factory. A third child was born, but died three days later. Their last child, a daughter, was born in 1862. Information on her birth registration indicates that at this time Andrew was still a cotton weaver. However, his life was about to move in a different direction. He was made redundant. Instead of looking for another job as a weaver, he decided, astonishingly, to become a journalist. Unlike so many of his contemporaries, he was literate, he had somehow managed to pick up a degree of education, and there was nothing he liked better than to write.

Moving his occupation from the loom to the desk was not the only change in Andrew's life. During his travels as a journalist, he met and fell in love with Ann Mouat, a Shetland-born woman seventeen years younger than himself. He abandoned his wife and children and set up home with Ann in Glasgow. Elizabeth and the children moved back to Ayrshire. Whether Andrew ever saw them again is not known.

Ann Mouat was never legally Andrew's wife, but they did not advertise their unmarried state. Despite their differing backgrounds and disparity in age, I believe they shared a kindred spirit. Ann had departed from Shetland in search of broader horizons, while Andrew, discontented with a life of manual labour, had taken his chance as a writer, weaving words rather than cotton. Although Ann was illiterate, it seems reasonable to assume that she was intelligent. I think it likely that Andrew taught her the basics of reading and writing. I imagine, too sentimentally no doubt, that he read his pieces to her and was keen to hear her response. Ann would almost certainly have knitted him Fair Isle garments – perhaps he liked to hear the click of her needles as he wrote.

Andrew had just turned forty-nine when Ann gave birth to her first child, a daughter, born on May 22nd 1869, who was named Annie Glass – my great grandmother. Ann, maybe for the first time, wrote her name rather than a cross on the birth certificate in large, childish letters. Eighteen months later she bore her first son, Andrew, followed by Maggie in 1873 and Magnus in 1875. Magnus's birth registration describes Ann as a Smallware Hawker and Andrew a Book Canvasser. With four young children to support, it appears they were struggling financially. Ann must have been traipsing around the neighbourhood knocking on doors with baskets of household goods trying to make some extra money. Two more children were born: Hannah in 1877 and James in 1880, by which time Andrew was sixty and Ann, forty-two. All six children were registered illegitimate. Ann managed, clumsily, to sign every birth certificate.

Andrew spent the rest of his working life earning an unsteady living as a freelance writer. He published several collections of stories and poetry, which consist largely of his narratives of Scottish tales and legends, written in a typically Victorian style with much of the dialogue in Scots. As a prefatory note to *Tales and Traditions of Ayrshire and Galloway*, he writes:

> Let not the reader suppose that I wish to impress him with the idea that there is something strikingly original in this little book. By no means. I know its shortcomings as well as paterfamilias is supposed to know the faults and failings of his children. I may briefly say, however, by way of enlisting the reader's sympathy, that the tales were written under all the disadvantages incidental to a wandering life, whilst representing the press in the west and south of Scotland.

It is dated 8th May 1873, two months after the birth of Ann's third child, Maggie. In another preface, dated 1878, he writes: "Hotels are not conducive to *sober thought*." [*The italics are his.*] Both extracts bear out accounts that Andrew was not a supportive partner, often away from home and not often sober. It would appear that Ann had little help from Andrew in raising her children. My romantic picture of their relationship seems sadly inaccurate. It was, however, a poignant experience to read the words that Andrew Glass, my great-great-grandfather, wrote some hundred and thirty years ago. I liked what I read, and felt that he was something of a romantic himself – certainly imaginative, poetic and perceptive. I quote here from his introduction to another volume:

> The author's chief difficulty has been in deciding what to select, from the extraordinary rich field of legendary lore with which Scotland abounds. Every strath and glen, every feudal ruin and hoary abbey, every village, however humble and obscure, nay, even every stream and mountain have tales to record of love, war, hatred, envy and revenge; all furnishing a boundless variety of historical and social incidents that ought to be of the highest interest to Scotchmen at large.
>
> The extraordinary changes brought about in recent times by the introduction of the locomotive engine, the steamboat, and the electric telegraph have far exceeded the wildest dreams of the most imaginative, and have in most respects tended to lessen the interest in local historical incidents. The whole physical aspect of the country is being changed to such an extent that the rising generation can scarcely comprehend the simple, primitive life of former times, when each locality, with its local associations, well-nigh comprised a world in itself to its inhabitants. Now all this is being changed, and surely it is a good thing to gather up and preserve all interesting legends ere they pass into oblivion, and to hand them down to successive generations, not orally, as in former times, but by means of the all powerful press.

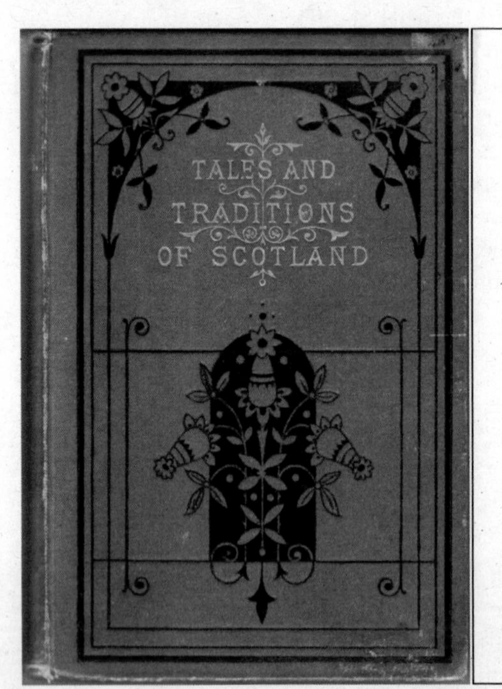

TALES AND TRADITIONS

OF

SCOTLAND.

BY ANDREW GLASS,

AUTHOR OF "POEMS AND SONGS," ETC.

SECOND AND ENLARGED EDITION.

GLASGOW:
PRINTED BY HAY NISBET, 219 GEORGE STREET.
1878.

ABOVE: Granny's father's parents, Martha Long and William Greig from Northern Ireland.

BELOW: Granny's mother's parents, Ann Mouat from Shetland and Andrew Glass from Ayrshire. Andrew, a journalist, chose to pose at a writing desk for this photograph.

ABOVE: William Greig (1866-1952), Granny's father

ABOVE: Henry Greig (1864-1913)

BELOW: John Greig (1873-1953), born on his brother Henry's ninth birthday.

BELOW LEFT: Lizzie Greig (1870-1939), foster mother to her brother Robert's son and her brother William's daughter, Bessie.

BELOW RIGHT: Robert Greig (1868-1945), foster father to William's daughter, Bessie. He lost an eye in a fireworks accident. The glass eye he wore gives the impression of a squint.

ABOVE: Annie Glass (1869-1896), Granny's mother, who died of tuberculosis aged twenty-seven.

ABOVE: Sisters Annie and Maggie Glass (1873-1955)

BELOW: Hannah Glass (1877-1955) with her husband, Jim Davidson. I have no photographs of Andrew or James Glass.

BELOW: Magnus Glass (1875-1897), who died from the same illness as his sister.

ABOVE: The formidable Grandmother Greig (Martha Long), holding her great-grandson.

ABOVE: Grandma Glass (Ann Mouat) with her daughter, Hannah. Ann is pictured wearing one of her hand-made Shetland shawls.

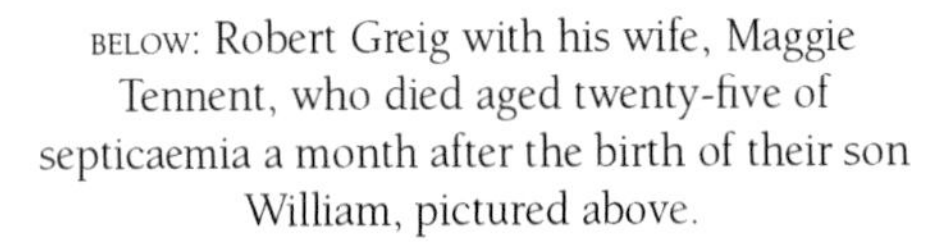

BELOW: Robert Greig with his wife, Maggie Tennent, who died aged twenty-five of septicaemia a month after the birth of their son William, pictured above.

BELOW: Hannah with her husband, Jim Davidson, and their two daughters, Ann and Mary.

5
GRANNY'S CHILDHOOD

I have now reached the point in family history where I have been able to glean information from living relatives – in particular, Mum's first cousins, Ailsa Land and Marie Smith, and my first cousin, David Fraser. I also have the stories that Granny and Mum passed on to me stored in my memory. Other accounts from Mum are those I wrote down before her long-term memory faded.

Ann Mouat and Andrew Glass's eldest daughter, Annie Glass, was employed as a carpet sewer in a factory when she met William Greig. According to Granny, Annie Glass was an open-minded, intelligent young woman. She had gentle blue eyes and rich, chestnut-coloured hair, which she twisted and fastened into a thick coil at the nape of her neck. William Greig was a questioning, thoughtful man with a steady job and income, having worked for the Post Office since he left school. Granny told me they were a well-matched couple.

In 1891, William and Annie married. He was twenty-four, she twenty-two. They moved into a rented tenement flat in Hutchesontown, Glasgow. Nine months later almost to the day, their first daughter, our Granny, was born. As was customary in Scotland, she was named after her mother's mother, and was called Annie Mouat Greig. From all accounts, William was thrilled to be a father and delighted when his wife told him she was expecting again. Baby Annie was a sixteen-month-old toddler when another girl was born. She was given the names of her father's mother – Martha Long Greig.

By now, Andrew Glass was an old man suffering from senile dementia. In October 1895 he died aged seventy-five. His death certificate states, incorrectly, that he was single. Ann, his devoted partner and mother of six of his children, is described as his 'Inmate'. Maybe it was too much of a struggle to write her name without Andrew there to encourage her, so the document of her partner's death bears her mark – 'X'. Perhaps she was saying goodbye to him with a kiss.

William and Annie Greig moved to a larger tenement flat at 29, Parnie Street, around the corner from Glasgow Cross, where their third daughter, Bessie, was born. However, William's elation at the arrival of another bonny girl was soon crushed, for not long after the birth, his wife contracted pulmonary tuberculosis. On October 6th 1896, aged twenty-seven, she died. After a brief five years of marriage, William Greig was a widower with three small daughters – Annie, aged four, Martha, not yet three and eight-month-old Bessie.

Baby Bessie was sent to live with her Uncle Robert and Aunt Lizzie, her father's brother and sister, who became her foster parents. She was raised with Uncle Robert's motherless boy, Willie, who was then five years old. The children's formidable grandmother, Martha Greig, as tough as ever and with twenty-eight years of life left in her yet, also brought her influence to bear.

Ann Mouat, or Grandma Glass, as her grandchildren knew her, had helped nurse her daughter and taken care of the little girls, but she could not continue indefinitely. Another tragedy struck: her son Magnus became gravely ill and died from pulmonary tuberculosis just a year after his sister Annie had succumbed to the same disease. Ann placed another 'X' on his death certificate and bade a second child farewell. In October 1895 she had lost her partner, October 1896 her daughter, and October 1897 her son.

William had to find someone who would move into Parnie Street to help him. At his mother's suggestion, her older maiden sister, Eliza Long, agreed to become housekeeper. Whether she came over from Northern Ireland to take on the task of caring for her nephew and his daughters, or was already settled in Glasgow, I don't know, but it would seem that she arrived on a metaphorical broomstick. Great Aunt Eliza was a humourless, dour woman whose staunch Presbyterianism did nothing to soften her nature. She wore stiff, sombre clothes, an expression of disapproval and was as rigidly set in her ways as the corsets that bound her.

William, used to his mother's similar temperament, got along with her well enough, but she did not treat his daughters, Annie and Martha, with love or affection. Grandma Glass visited when she could and found the time to teach young Annie to knit in the traditional Shetland way, but overall the girls were deprived of motherly care. Martha was a nervous, insecure child. Annie tried to protect her little sister, whom she talked of as "poor wee Martha". At school, Annie looked out for Martha, who was afraid of the teachers and sometimes wet herself.

Their father, unlike his parents, was not too bothered about religion. He paid lip service to it by sending the girls to Sunday school and taking them to church occasionally, but he did not bring them up wielding the fearful stick of a punishing God over their heads. God was an occasional visitor but not an oppressive presence. It was Great Aunt Eliza who made them say their prayers every night. Although William knew the Bible backwards, he saw it more as an interesting text rather than a book from which to be preached. He enjoyed his drink and his pipe too much to be puritanical, and although he never remarried, there's no reason to suppose that he did not take pleasure in the company of women. He had a quick brain, played chess masterfully and was a wizard card player, reportedly winning every whist drive he attended. He was an excellent dancer and a natural musician. His daughters loved it when he took the fiddle in his hands and started up a tune. I like to think of his two lassies dancing to the jigs and reels he had learnt from his Irish father.

Annie had a good singing voice and a musical ear. She picked up the basics of the fiddle and became competent enough to rattle off a few reels herself. (I was amazed to hear this tale – not once did she demonstrate her skill to us, nor did she give any hint that she had ever touched a musical instrument.) In 1901, Queen Victoria died. The images of street processions, mourning clothes, sombre faces and black armbands made a lasting impression on eight-year-old Annie as the Victorian era came to an end.

Meanwhile, Annie and Martha's younger sister, Bessie, was growing up in a different environment. She regarded Aunt Lizzie and Uncle Robert as her parents and was effectively separated from her sisters and father. Although they saw one another from time to time, their upbringings were not the same. Uncle Robert had done well for himself and was now Managing Director of the Shieldhall boot and shoe factory, one of the Co-operative Society's businesses. It was a secure, well-paid job that enabled him to rise socially. Bessie benefited from better quality food and clothing – Robert made her shoes and Lizzie her clothes – than her big sisters.

In 1902, aged sixty-two, Grandfather William Greig from Ireland died. The whole household gathered around his bed to watch his last breaths: his wife, Martha; their children, Henry, Robert, Lizzie and John, and the grandchildren – ten-year-old Willie and five-year-old Bessie. The witnessing of her grandfather's death had a deep effect on young Bessie. It was a scene she would often remember. William's widow, Martha Greig, wore black for the rest of her life.

Just before she turned fourteen, Annie's childhood came to an abrupt end. She was taken out of school and Great Aunt Eliza upped and left. She told William that his eldest daughter was old enough to keep house and should have been doing so long before this. Annie had to learn fast. Her father handed over the housekeeping money and left her to get on with it. Naturally efficient, she organised her chores, worked out a routine, and taught herself how to cook, to shop and to handle the finances. She carted the dirty laundry in an old pram to the 'steamies', where she did the washing along with dozens of other women. Annie had inherited her mother's thick chestnut-coloured hair, which led to the women at the steamies describing her as "the lass wi' the heer" – something that Granny never forgot.

Annie was up early every morning to make her father porridge before he left for work. After Martha had gone to school, Annie spent her days managing the house and preparing meals. William often went out in the evenings, sometimes returning home a little the worse for drink, but on Saturday nights he would invariably get drunk. Annie waited up listening for her father's return. She could tell by the sound of his steps on the stairs leading up to the flat how bad a state he was in. He was never violent towards her, but she often had to help him undress and get him into bed. There were occasions when he was so inebriated that he fell to the floor in a stupor. Unable to lift him, even with Martha's help, she would haul his mattress off the bed, roll his body onto it, put a pillow under his head and leave him to sober up. Great Aunt Eliza descended on Parnie Street from time to time, but only visited to criticise Annie's housekeeping.

When Annie was seventeen, she took a job at the Post Office as a telegraphist. Martha left school at fourteen and went to work in a department store in Glasgow, where she had to stand at the door to greet customers. With her diffident and reserved nature, the situation didn't suit her. She felt intimidated by rude, haughty patrons and hated the work. She left to go into apprenticeship as a tailoress, but learned nothing about dressmaking. Her duties were no more than those of a char and dogsbody. Later, she found a job in a factory as a machinist, sitting with other girls in rows sewing garments on a production line. When she turned sixteen, she was sacked, not for poor work or behaviour, but because employers had to pay higher wages to girls over sixteen. There was no law to prevent this practice and it was a ruse that most employers adopted. Martha's next job was in the linen room of a hotel, pressing sheets, pillowcases, napkins and tablecloths.

Both girls were working and their father was still employed as a postman. Although their wages were low, there were nevertheless three pay packets coming into the house every week. Financially, the family were better off than they had ever been before, but such were the hardships they had endured, they knew the value of money and were not about to squander their hard-earned wages. Prudently, Annie and Martha started paying weekly sums into individual Insurance Bonds, well aware that by saving some money now, they would be investing in a more secure future.

When Bessie left school she also joined the Post Office as a telegraphist. It was there that she properly established her relationship with her eldest sister, Annie. Although they had been separated during childhood, they discovered that they could communicate telepathically. "If you need to speak to me," Annie told Bessie, "you have only to stand outside your door for a few moments and I'll come to you as soon as I have the opportunity." Annie worked in a different part of the building and was not able to see Bessie waiting for her. Yet she would know that Bessie was there and would go to meet her. Or so we were told.

Our Martha, as we have heard, was a rather vulnerable, reticent girl. Annie, aware of her younger sister's lack of confidence, always tried to reassure and protect her, but Annie's job entailed her working shifts: on the late shift, she did not get home until ten o'clock at night. When their father was also out, it was perhaps on these evenings that an uncle began to take advantage of Martha. His identity is not known – the term 'uncle' might be misleading – but from all accounts the man was a member of the family. Martha was in her early twenties at the time.

One evening, I imagine, there is a knock on the door and Martha, seeing the familiar face of a relative, invites him in, unwittingly allowing her captor across the threshold.

"If you're wanting to speak to Daddy, he's out."

"Is he now? And Annie?"

"She's on the late shift."

"Then it's just you and me, which gives us the opportunity to get to know each other a little better."

His presence makes her feel uncomfortable, but how can she ask him to leave? It wouldn't be right to cause offence or appear rude to a member of the family.

"How about a pot of tea for your uncle, lass?"

Martha makes the tea, brings it on a tray into the room and places it on the table. She pours it out and hands him a cup. He invites her to come and sit beside him. She perches nervously on the edge of the chair. He studies her appraisingly.

"You're turning into a fine girl, Martha. Quite the young lady now. Tell me, are you stepping out with a young beau?" She shakes her head. "No? I cannae believe that. A pretty lass like you must have plenty of gentlemen admirers." He lays his hand on her knee and winks at her.

Alarmed, she rises and picks up the tea tray. She feels flustered by the insinuation that she is keeping secrets. Annoyingly, a blush heats her face and her uncle chuckles knowingly. She stumbles slightly. He leaps up.

"Here now, let me help you with that."

"It's fine, I can manage."

He follows her through to the scullery, takes the tray from her and leaves it by the sink. He does not allow her to start on the washing up. Instead, he puts his hands on her shoulders, turns her around and leads her back to the living room. His arm circles her waist fleetingly as he guides her to the couch, settles her down and sits beside her. Martha feels uneasy in her uncle's company. She chides herself for her shyness. After all, he is just being friendly, chatting kindly to her, drawing her into conversation.

After a while, he says, "Well now, I'd best be going before your Daddy and Annie get back. We don't want their tongues a-wagging do we!"

Worried now that she has somehow done something wrong, she sees him out.

"How about a wee kiss for your uncle before I leave?"

He pats his hand against his cheek. She places a hasty kiss where indicated.

"There now, that didn't hurt, did it? You're a bonny lass, sure enough." He drops a rather lingering kiss on her forehead and leaves with a conspiratorial wave. She washes and dries the teapot, cups and saucers and puts them away. She is not sure why, but she is anxious to conceal any evidence that someone has called round. When her Daddy and sister return, she doesn't mention the uncle's visit. He has succeeded in covertly administering the first milligram of poison – the transference of collusion and blame and the intravenous drip of guilt.

Disturbingly, he calls again a couple of days later, and again the following week and the week after. The word for it now is grooming. She doesn't know it, but she has walked into his trap. Slowly, carefully and with the utmost subtlety, he begins to draw in the net. At last, she is so hemmed in that there is no way out. Unprotected, unable to defend herself and without hope of rescue, she is coerced into succumbing to sexual abuse; a shameful secret that Martha cannot speak of to anyone.

How exactly it happened (the above is a fictional realisation) or for how long it continued is unknown. Marie, Martha's daughter, suspects that it went on for some time before Martha realised that she was pregnant. In those days, indeed until as late as the 1950s, young unmarried women who became pregnant were all too often sectioned by their own families and sent to mental institutions, so great was the social stigma. Immediately after the birth, the babies were removed for adoption. In some appalling cases the young women remained incarcerated in lunatic asylums for the rest of their lives. Such a ruinous course of action would not have occurred to Martha's father or sister, but nevertheless, Martha kept the terrible knowledge to herself. She was the victim, steeped in victims' guilt, carrying the blame and the child of rape. There was nothing she could do but run away.

Her father and sister were beside themselves. They must have guessed that Martha was pregnant, for why else would she have disappeared? William was frantic. Every day he walked the streets looking for her. He knocked on doors, asked questions and followed leads, desperate to find her. Annie worried and waited, hoping her sister would come home; but she didn't. Months went by while William continued his frenzied search.

He found her just a few days before she was due and took her to a safe place – maybe a hospital, but more likely a nursing home, where she gave birth to a baby boy who was given away for adoption. He then arranged for her to recuperate for a couple of weeks, after which he brought his daughter home.

She had managed to survive by scrubbing doorsteps. Clean flights of steps up to front doors were an obsession at the time. Owners of handsome houses employed charladies to keep the entranceways of their properties pristine – a twice-daily chore, as the streets were filthy with soot and horse-dung. It would have been difficult for an unmarried, pregnant woman to be given lodging, but there must have been somebody somewhere who was kind to her. There is no doubt that her father was, and she did at last confide in him, although the identity of her abuser went no further than his ears. We do not know what became of Martha's son, but he has not been forgotten. It is unlikely that he is still alive, as he would be in his nineties now, but he holds an absent place in the family.

6
MAGGIE

Every battered woman learns early on not to expect help. Eventually she's fractured inside by the continuing degradation and her emotional world is a landscape of desperation. Of course she smiles in public and is a good wife. He insists – and so do we.

Life and Death – Andrea Dworkin

My research uncovered some fascinating stories. Many have been excluded from this narrative, as the individuals to whom they relate are far removed from the main characters in my story. However, I feel that this one needs to be told. It is an account of one woman's suffering, victimisation, and heartbreak. Through my investigation of census, birth, marriage and death records I have assembled some facts, not necessarily completely accurate, but documented information nevertheless. I also have stories and details passed on to me by living descendants. Put together, a picture begins to form. Add to that one's contemplation and reflection and a sense of the life one is trying to fathom begins to surface. Whilst not all of the following can be read as fact, neither is it purely fictitious. That said, I shall write it as my instincts feel it was and trust that the above is a sufficient disclaimer.

Maggie Glass, the second daughter of Andrew Glass and Ann Mouat, was born in Glasgow in March 1873. It must have been her father's book publishing connections that led to her taking a job as a bookseller's packer at the age of about sixteen. There she met David Anderson, the bookseller's assistant. He was five years older than her and maybe appeared worldly to the young, impressionable girl. It did not take long for him to seduce her – Maggie was only seventeen when she became David Anderson's wife in 1889. There is no evidence to suggest that they married because she was pregnant, but if it were so, she must have miscarried. David Anderson registered himself a 'Bookseller' on the marriage certificate, omitting the 'Assistant' part of his job title – a small deceit, but a foretaste of his nature. The couple lived first in a tenement block on Gallowgate Street, Bridgeton; an address with ominous connotations.

Maggie was soon to find out that her husband was not the man she had thought him to be. She had married a cruel, sadistic bully: her life was to become a living hell. The abuse she suffered might have been infrequent at first; restrained perhaps, but Maggie was mistreated from the start.

As soon as she was married, she had to give up her job; a common occurrence in those days. Without her own income, she was now financially dependent on her husband. However, David Anderson's job was not secure. He may have thought he held a senior position in the bookstore, but it was an illusion. Two years after the marriage, he was made redundant. Perhaps this was when his brutality towards his wife escalated; for at some point he began to bring men home with him and forced Maggie to have sex with them.

Maggie's first baby, James, was born in January 1893 at the home of her parents. On James's birth certificate, David Anderson describes himself as a 'Grocer', implying proprietorship, when in fact he was just a butter packer. After her confinement, Maggie moved to Dennistoun where her husband had rented cheaper accommodation. A daughter, Margaret, was born there in December 1894. Maggie again went home to her mother's to give birth to her third child – a boy, David, born in June 1896. By this time Maggie's father, Andrew Glass, was dead; her sister Annie was dying from pulmonary tuberculosis; only her younger sister Hannah and brothers, Magnus and James, still lived at home. It must have been a short respite to be back with her mother and siblings, but if Maggie entertained any thoughts of escaping her marriage, they could have been no more than hopeless wishes. She had nowhere to go, no place to hide. It is still difficult for any battered woman to speak about what has been done to her and by whom. Terror, shame, intimidation, subjugation and isolation effectively silence the victim, removing any likelihood of the abuser being exposed. David Anderson's horrific treatment of his wife went on behind closed doors, unseen and unimpeded.

Maggie's enforced prostitution continued whilst her husband lost one job after the other, the family moving to poorer and poorer areas of Glasgow. A fourth child, Annie Mowat, was born in January 1899 and the fifth, Catherine, in February 1901, by which time the family were living in what can only be described as a slum. The 1901 census has them registered at 59, Barloch Street, Maryhill, Glasgow. It does not state how many rooms they are renting, but just one has a window. They are listed as David Anderson, Head (33), Maggie Anderson, Wife (28), James (8), Margaret (6), David (4), Annie (2) and Catherine (2 months). It is of course possible, indeed likely, that her husband did not in fact father all of Maggie's children.

Later that year, Maggie made what must have been the bravest and most harrowing decision of her life. She took her five little children to the home of her husband's parents, left them there and walked out of her marriage. What was it that gave her the courage she must have needed to abandon her children and flee at this point? I am as certain as I can be that Maggie did not forsake them to save her own skin. I believe that she acted as she did in order to protect them. As they grew older they would have been increasingly exposed to the attacks on their mother. They were witnessing violence and terror on a daily basis. It is also not beyond speculation that they too were being sexually assaulted. The only way she knew she could save them was to run away. Her husband would not be able to look after five children on his own. For the time being she hoped they would be out of harm's way with his parents. I also conjecture that she did not take her children to her own mother (although that would have surely been her preference), as she knew that they would soon have been removed and taken to her husband's parents anyway.

David Anderson immediately charged his wife with Desertion. Maggie had to appear in Court where she was required to prove that she could not stay in the marriage and could not support her children. She must have clutched at one last straw – that custody of the children would be awarded to her by pleading her husband's cruelty. She was forced to disclose in public the appalling acts of sexual exploitation to which she had been subjected – yet another humiliating, offensive ordeal she had to endure. Her sister Hannah stood in court with her as her witness, but as Hannah had not been an eyewitness to the rapes, and as Maggie had no witnesses willing to corroborate her defence, her case collapsed. David Anderson denied all his wife's allegations and was given custody of her five children. His parents brought them up: Maggie never saw them again.

She now needed work and somewhere to live that might give her some protection. Leaving her husband did not achieve freedom or safety. An abuser does not let his victim go. It is likely that he continued to persecute and harass, keeping tabs on her whereabouts, turning up out of nowhere to menace and threaten. She succeeded in finding employment at 59, Queen Street in Govan, where she lived in as a charwoman. According to Post Office directories, Jean Fulton, a widow, and her son John were living at that address, so I have to assume that the Fultons were her employers.

I try to imagine how Maggie felt – living in fear of her husband, cruelly deprived of her children, desolate, destroyed, broken. It is hardly surprising that she succumbed to another man and fell pregnant. To date I have not been able to identify the father, but John Fulton is a possibility. Whoever he was, he promised to stand by her, but when it came to it, reneged. Maggie's son, her sixth baby, was born in June 1905. She named him William Glass. His birth registration contains the following statement: 'Name of Mother: Maggie Glass, Charwoman, Wife of David Anderson, Gun Maker, who she declares is not the father of the child'. No name is given for the father.

Maggie was determined to keep her baby, but she faced several predicaments. She had to find work and accommodation. It was out of the question to think she could find either as a single woman with a baby. She turned to her mother, Ann Mouat, and sister, Hannah, for help. It was decided that Billy (as baby William was called) would live with them. Maggie felt that it was imperative to conceal her son's illegitimacy. Together, the three women agreed to bring him up to believe that his parents had died in an influenza epidemic and that Maggie and Hannah were his aunts.

Once again Maggie had to make a brave decision. Determined to protect Billy, and aching constantly for a futile sight of her lost children, she concluded that the best course of action was to move away from Glasgow altogether. Maggie kissed her baby goodbye. In another world she would never have left him, but for his sake, nobody must guess she was his mother. Apart from an occasional visit, Maggie was absent from most of her precious son's early childhood. Knowing he would be loved and well cared for, she boarded the train for London, where she had been offered the position of Nanny, caring for another woman's infants. Perhaps she drew some comfort from living with children; I do not know. How Maggie might have felt has passed beyond my imagination.

Hannah Glass married Jim Davidson in 1907. Ann Mouat and two-year-old Billy moved in with them. Jim was not enlightened about Billy's pedigree, the secret kept even from him. Hannah and Jim had two daughters: Ann, born in 1908, and Mary, in 1910. To them, Billy was like a big brother. In about 1912, the Davidsons, Ann and Billy moved to Oban, a coastal town some seventy miles northwest of Glasgow. It put them at a safer distance from David Anderson, and Maggie felt she could risk returning to Scotland to be reunited with her son and family.

Grandma Ann Mouat died in Oban in 1916, aged seventy-nine, a Shetland-born woman whose devotion to her family never wavered. After her death, Jim Davidson, Hannah and Maggie took the decision to emigrate with their children to Canada. Jim was offered land in Lynn Valley in trade for his military service. It seemed a good opportunity for them all to make a new life. Billy Glass was now fourteen. In May 1920 the family boarded the ship *Cassandra* run by the Steamship line 'Anchor Donaldson' as third class passengers, embarking upon the long passage to Quebec. From Quebec they journeyed by train across the continent, arriving in North Vancouver five days later.

When Billy turned fifteen, he joined a ship as an engineer and went to sea. His Aunts Maggie and Hannah stood at the harbour to wave him goodbye, but it was Maggie whom Billy held in his sight until she disappeared from view, for of the two aunts, he felt a greater closeness with Maggie – almost as if she were his own mother.

After a number of years at sea, Billy returned to Vancouver and rejoined his family. He dropped the 'y' from his name and became known as Bill in his adult life. In a quiet moment, Maggie told him that he was her son. It was surely something that he had been longing to hear and which his heart had known instinctively, but she asked him to keep the secret. Nobody else must know the truth. The story that Bill was an orphan raised by his aunts was maintained. But there were other secrets that Bill never knew. His mother breathed not a word to him of his five half brothers and sisters. Bill lived his whole life in ignorance of their existence, just as they lived theirs knowing nothing of Bill or their mother.

I wanted to find out what happened to Maggie's first five children, but Anderson is a common name and therefore difficult to research. However, I did find this: Margaret, Maggie's second child, married John Horne in Glasgow in 1913 when she was eighteen. Annie, Maggie's fourth child, married William Fitzgerald in 1927, also in Glasgow. Both marriage registrations enter the bride's mother as 'Margaret Anderson m.s. Glass (deceased)'. This struck me as painfully sad. It is also persuasive evidence that Maggie's five children were brought up believing that their mother was dead. In fact, she lived until 1955, aged eighty-two, dying in the same year as her sister Hannah. Before Hannah died, she felt that she must tell her daughters about their Aunt Maggie's tragic life. It was then that Ann and Mary were enlightened. Mary later shared the information with her own children, thus some of Maggie's history was preserved. Hannah's husband, Jim Davidson, lived to the age of ninety-three. When Chris, my brother, was born in 1958, Jim visited England and called on his niece (Granny) and great niece (Mum) at 32, Cleveland Road, leaving a gift of a silver sixpence to mark the birth of his great-great nephew.

Maggie's son, Bill Glass, married Winnifred Marr in 1933. Bill worked up and down the coast of British Columbia as a shipyard engineer for the same company until he retired. He and Winnifred had one son, Barry. In 2005, I made contact with Barry's daughter, Brenda Glass Alexander, and with Ann Goddard, Hannah's granddaughter. The information and memories they shared with me have helped enormously in fitting some pieces of the jigsaw puzzle of this branch of the family together.

LEFT:
Maggie Glass aged about eighteen soon after her disastrous marriage to David Anderson.

ABOVE AND BELOW LEFT:
Maggie, looking sad and weary during the time she worked as a Nanny in London.

BELOW:
Maggie's illegitimate son, William Glass, marrying Winnifred Marr in 1933. William was brought up believing that Maggie was his aunt.

LEFT TO RIGHT: Sisters Bessie, Martha and Annie Greig (Granny).
Bessie was brought up by her Uncle Robert and Aunt Lizzie together with her cousin Willie, Uncle Robert's motherless son. Robert was more affluent than his brother William. In this photograph it is evident that Bessie is better dressed than her sisters.

7
HUSBANDS

Having travelled swiftly through time in the telling of Maggie's story, I will now go back and pick up from the end of the previous chapter, before Maggie, Hannah and Jim emigrated. Martha had just given birth to a son who had been given away for adoption.

Following her dreadful ordeal, Martha wanted to get away from Glasgow. She went to Oban to live with her Aunt Hannah and Uncle Jim Davidson. There she found work in O'Hare's, a tailoring establishment with premises on the front looking out to sea. She had no experience of tailoring and knew little more than how to operate a sewing machine. However, she was observant and dextrous, and with help and instruction from a fellow employee, she picked up the methods quickly. Although she became an expert at the job, she always disliked sewing. She did it when she had to, but it gave her little pleasure.

Before long, she met Archibald McKillop, a postman. He was born in Cork in 1889, but was now living in Oban with his parents and a number of younger siblings. Oddly, when men were drafted for the War in 1914, he was declared unfit, yet he was a postman walking twenty miles a day. Whatever his lack of fitness, it spared him from the trenches and no doubt protected his life. Quiet and undemanding, he kept his own counsel and asked no questions. Martha did not tell him about the baby boy she had borne: it was something he never knew about. The couple married in Oban in June 1919 when Martha was twenty-five and Archibald, thirty. Martha's sister, Annie, was her witness and Hannah and Jim's daughters, Ann and Mary, were her bridesmaids. Nine months later their first child, William, was born – yet another William to add to the family tree – and he too was known as Billy.

When Hannah, Jim, Maggie and family emigrated to Vancouver, Martha and Archibald moved to Edinburgh where they had two more children: Archie, born in 1924 and their daughter, Marie, in 1930.

At the time they were renting a ground floor, purpose-built council flat in Northfield Broadway. Archibald was earning £3 a week and the rent was £1 a week. Martha took in dressmaking to make extra money, which she used to pay for her sons to go to the Royal High School. However, she began to contemplate the possibilities of buying their own place. If they could find somewhere large enough, they could let out a room or two, which would cover the cost of a mortgage. I write 'they', but it was actually Martha who thought out the scheme. She saw an ideal property for sale in South Trinity Road. It had the benefit of two large front rooms, which could be rented out, still leaving plenty of space for the family.

The price was £600. She found a building society willing to lend £540 at a repayment cost of £1 per week, the same as the rent they were currently paying – but what about the £60 down payment? Fortunately, those Insurance Bonds that Annie and Martha had set up all those years ago had just matured and were each worth £30. Annie lent her £30 to Martha, enabling the purchase to be made. Two rooms were let at ten shillings a week each. The mortgage was therefore covered. With Martha continuing to take in dressmaking, she was able to provide extras for her children. Marie, for example, took dancing lessons. Martha was a canny woman, as were her sisters.

In 1917, Bessie, Granny's youngest sister, joined the Women's Voluntary Army. After some basic training in Aldershot, she was posted to Rouen in France where she met her future husband, Harold (Hal) Dicken, a trainee pilot in the RAF Army Air Corps. Hal was discharged at the end of the war after the signing of the 1918 Armistice, but Bessie stayed on in Rouen, as there was still much work to be done telegraphing casualty lists. The war had been over for more than a year before she was demobbed. She and Hal married in Glasgow in August 1920 and immediately left Scotland to live in West Bromwich in the Midlands. Bessie was once again separated from her sisters. Their daughter, Ailsa, was born in June 1927, seven years into the marriage. She was to be their only child.

Annie, our Granny, and the eldest of the Greig sisters, was the last to marry. David Fraser was the man she fell in love with. David Turnbull Fraser was born in Dundee, a coastal city in the east of Scotland situated to the north of the Firth of Tay. It was a busy port; whaling, shipbuilding and cloth manufacture its major industries. Quite by chance, Dundee also became famous for marmalade when a ship carrying a cargo of oranges was forced to put into Dundee harbour during a severe storm. A local grocer bought the oranges, his wife turned them into marmalade and another trade was born. Dundee was dirty and unsanitary, as were all overpopulated nineteenth-century towns. Piped water was introduced in 1845, but as it cost to be connected, poor areas did without. Sewers were not laid until the 1870s. Filth and contaminated water were breeding grounds for disease. Inevitably, cholera and typhus epidemics struck with fatal frequency. In 1859, John and Janet Turnbull, one pair of my sixteen pairs of great-great-great-grandparents, and several of their children all died from cholera in the same week. John Turnbull signed every death certificate before dying himself.

For generations, both sides of David Fraser's family had lived in Dundee. David's father, Robert Fraser, was working as a stonemason and his mother, Jessie Sturrock, as a powerloom weaver at the time of their marriage in 1876. Their first child, George, was born in 1877. A year later, Jessie gave birth to twins. The first was a boy, the second a girl, the gap between them fifty-five minutes, precisely the same as between my sister and me. They were named Andrew and Betsey after their mother's parents. Sadly, Betsey did not live for long, dying from hydrocephalus when she was four months old. A year and a half later, her twin brother, Andrew, died of croup, an infection of the trachea and larynx that was a killer in the days before antibiotics.

About six weeks before little Andrew died, Dundee suffered an appalling disaster. On 28th December 1879, the bridge over the Firth of Tay collapsed during a violent storm, taking with it a train, six carriages and some seventy-five people to their death. The bridge, opened only nineteen months before, had already taken the lives of twenty men during its six-year construction. It cost over £300,000 to build, and at nearly two miles long was at the time the longest bridge in the world. The collapse of the Tay Bridge remains the worst structural engineering disaster in the British Isles and shocked the Victorian engineering profession and the public alike. More than 125 years after the catastrophe, it still holds a peculiar fascination, in part because there remains speculation as to the cause of the collapse and also because the police recorded the names of only sixty passengers. From the number of ticket stubs counted, seventy-five people had boarded the train.

The Tay Bridge disaster must have affected Jessie and Robert and only added to the grief they were feeling over the deaths of their twins. However, they still had their three-year-old son George, who seemed robust, and Jessie was pregnant again. Perhaps there was a better future ahead.

In 1880, Jessie bore another son, Robert, but less than a year later, a double tragedy was to strike. George, now a lively four-year-old, came down with croup. Within five days he was dead. The infection was passed to baby Robert, who died three days later. Infant mortality was commonplace, but it cannot have made loss any easier to bear. To have four children and lose them all in just over four years is more than I can contemplate. George, Andrew, Betsey and Robert Fraser were dead – all long-forgotten children whose missing shapes have, at last, been fitted into the mosaic of our family. I am glad to have found and acknowledged them.

On March 13th 1883, eighteen months after the deaths of George and Robert, Jessie gave birth again to a boy, David Turnbull Fraser, who lived to survive childhood illnesses. Their last child was a girl, Jean. According to Granny, Robert and Jessie were rather parochial, superstitious people. Davie (as he was called) was not of the same mould. He had an inquisitive mind and from a young age was drawn to music. He asked his parents if he could learn to play the violin, but they refused saying that it was 'the instrument of the devil'. That Davie was not allowed to learn the violin or take music lessons did not quash his interest. He borrowed textbooks from the library and searched the second-hand bookshops on the look out for publications that explained the theory of music and its notation. He taught himself the basics, learned how to read music and entered himself for an Associated Board Rudiments of Music examination, which he passed [*a copy of his certificate can be seen on the next page*]. By the time he was eighteen, he was established as a sorting clerk and telegraphist for the GPO. His sister Jean, at fourteen years of age, was working as an apprentice jute weaver.

I look at the photograph [*on page 65*] taken in a Dundee studio of Robert and Jessie Fraser with their children, Davie and Jean, who appear to be in their twenties, and contemplate the image of Jessie seated beside her husband. She is in her fifties, her face looking surprisingly unlined and youthful. Death has been a frequent visitor throughout her life, yet still she manages a smile for the camera. One can almost see a twinkle of amusement in her eyes. Robert, sporting a splendid moustache, appears relaxed, his deep-set eyes holding a warm expression. Davie stands with excellent posture next to his sister, the photograph suggesting a close, contented family. Pictures tell many stories: the images, motionlessly framed, become projections of one's imagination. The dead, it seems, convey their thoughts to the living.

Soon after this photograph was taken, the Frasers left Dundee and moved to

Glasgow. Why they departed from their hometown, I don't know, but it wasn't long after this that Robert Fraser died, aged fifty-five, of heart failure caused by anaemia. Davie, excluded from the Armed Forces for health reasons, continued to work as a postal sorting clerk and telegraphist for the GPO, which is where he later met his future wife, Annie Greig. They married in Scotstoun, Glasgow, in June 1922, when she was twenty-nine and he thirty-nine.

The newlyweds moved to 37, Albert Road, a rented tenement flat in the building next door to Davie's mother, Jessie, and sister, Jean. William Greig, Annie's father, moved into lodgings around the corner. However, he was such a frequent visitor to his daughter and son-in-law's home that paying for full-board accommodation in the next street seemed a waste of money. It was agreed that he might just as well move in with them, which was perhaps what he had been angling for all along.

After a very long and difficult labour, Annie gave birth to their first baby on March 23rd 1923, a boy who was named Robert. Twenty-one months later, on December 30th 1924, their daughter was born; our mother, Elizabeth Greig Fraser. Throughout her childhood she was known as Betty.

R.A.M. R.C.M.

GLORIA IN EXCELSIS DEO

ET IN TERRA PAX

DIEU ET MON DROIT

ARS

SCIENTIA

The Associated Board of the Royal Academy of Music and The Royal College of Music.

Patron—HIS MAJESTY THE KING.

President—H.R.H. THE PRINCE OF WALES, K.G.

LOCAL CENTRE EXAMINATION.

PASS CERTIFICATE.

This is to Certify that at the Local Centre Examination held at Glasgow in 1909, David T. Fraser was Examined in Rudiments of Music and satisfied the requirements of the Board.

William L. Bygge, Chairman of the Board

A. C. Mackenzie, Principal of R.A.M.

C. Hubert H. Parry, Director of R.C.M.

These Certificates do not entitle the holders to append any letters to their names nor are the holders thereof certified as Teachers.

R.A.M. R.C.M.

ABOVE: Annie (Granny) and Martha Greig.

BELOW: Bessie Greig with her husband, Hal Dicken.

Robert and Jessie Fraser (née Sturrock) with their children, David Fraser (my grandfather) and Jean. Their first four children had all died before David was born. I gasped when I first saw this picture, so strong is the resemblance between young Davie (as he was called) and Chris at the same age.

Sheila Jelley very kindly gave me the original photograph from her family album when I met her for the first time in 2008. Her father, David Bradford, was David Fraser's first cousin.

The Fraser family c1910
SEATED: Jessie and Robert Fraser
STANDING: their son, David, and daughter, Jean

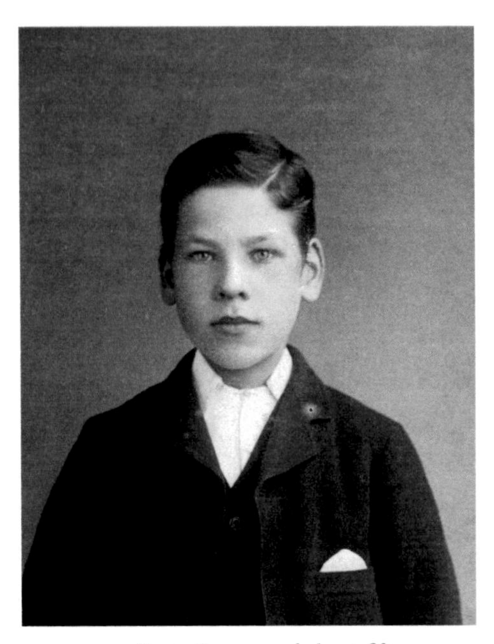

ABOVE: Davie Fraser aged about fifteen.

BELOW: Davie aged about thirty-eight soon after he and Annie met. He died in 1935 aged fifty-two.

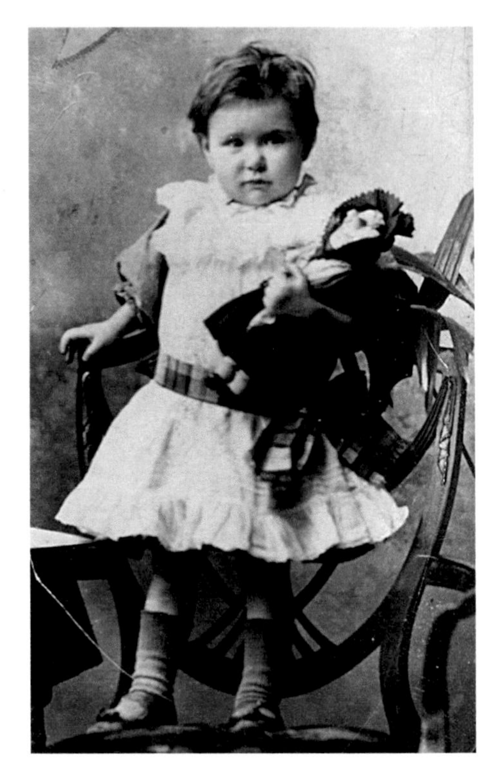

ABOVE: Annie Greig (Granny) aged about three.

BELOW: Annie in her twenties, before she met her future husband.

Granny's wedding, Glasgow, June 1922

ABOVE LEFT TO RIGHT: Sister Martha, Annie, William Greig and sister Bessie.

BELOW LEFT: Aunt Lizzie, William, Grandmother Greig, Uncle Robert.

RIGHT: The bride and groom, Annie and Davie Fraser.

ABOVE: Betsey Turnbull Sturrock (1835-1901) and Andrew Smith Sturrock (c1834-1915), David Fraser's maternal grandparents from Dundee (one pair of my eight pairs of great-great grandparents).

BELOW: Dundee c1930: Back row right is Annie Fraser. Middle row centre are George Bradford and his wife Mary Bradford (née Sturrock). The children are, left to right: Robert Fraser, twins Audrey and David Bradford, (George and Mary's grandchildren) and Betty Fraser (Mum). I met Audrey for the first and, sadly, the only time in 2006.

8
ANNIE AND DAVIE

A word now about tenement housing: the addresses that have so far been mentioned refer to whole blocks of tenements, not individual houses or flats. 37, Albert Road, for example, was a four-storey building, the entrance to which was called the 'close'. Within the close was a central staircase with dwellings on either side of every floor. The tenements of Albert Road were structurally substantial with thick walls, solid doors and well-fitting windows. (Mum told me she didn't know what a draught was until she came to London.) Davie, Annie and their family lived on the second floor. Cooking was done on the iron range in the kitchen, which had to be blacked to keep it polished – a filthy job. To one side of the range was a bed recess, which could be used for visitors or when one of the family was unwell. There was a lavatory but no bath. The children were sat on the side of the sink to be washed, and a tin bath brought through once a week for the adults to bathe. There were three bedrooms; one for Annie and Davie, one for Annie's father (who was known as Gran) and one for the children. Lastly, there was 'The Room', which was kept as clean and tidy as possible and was not a place in which children were allowed to play noisy games.

At the Post Office, Davie made friends with some amateur musicians. He asked them where he might purchase a violin and was sent to Mr. Smiley's music shop on the Great Western Road. At long last he held in his hands the instrument he had always wanted to play, and he was determined to learn how to play it properly. With a combination of good teaching, dedicated practice and natural aptitude, Davie became a competent fiddle player. After work, he got together with his colleagues to play chamber music. The talent that had lain dormant and suppressed for all those years now grew and blossomed. It was in The Room that Davie held his musical evenings and where visitors were entertained.

The rear windows of the tenements looked down on the Cathcart railway line, the clatter and rumble of trains providing a noisy background accompaniment. There was terrible poverty after the First World War. Soldiers, many crippled with war wounds, congregated on the back green by the railway begging for money and food. Those who hadn't died in the trenches had come back home to nothing. They caught ha'pennies and farthings thrown down to them from the tenement windows.

Davie Fraser got on well with Gran, his father-in-law, and became Gran's chess partner and golf companion. In Scotland, golf was not an exclusive pastime for the well-to-do. Ordinary working-class people enjoyed the game too – Annie was a good golfer herself. Gran had also discovered crosswords, which became a new passion in his life. Crosswords were first published in 1923 in the American newspapers, the craze soon reaching Britain. For Gran, with a refined chess and card-player's mind coupled with the knowledge he had amassed from reading, crosswords were made for him. With the Bible and the complete works of Shakespeare for reference, he filled in the puzzles, priding himself on finishing the *Times* and the *Herald* crosswords nearly every day. He often won crossword and chess competitions and was cock-a-hoop when one week, instead of just printing his name as the winner, the newspaper caption read, "W. Greig does it again!"

Football was a key element in Gran's life too. He had no allegiance to Rangers, whose fans were traditionally Loyalist/Protestant, but was a fanatical supporter of Queen's Park, who were famously non-aligned. He took his grandson, Robert, to all the home matches at Hampden Park. Gran, stocky and dogged, thrust out his elbows and pushed his way through the crowd with Robert hanging onto his coattails. He always succeeded in gaining prime viewing position at the front of the terrace.

Davie knew that his daughter, Betty, was musical when, at the age of four, she started to pick out hymn tunes on the old piano. He bought her a book of beginner piano music – *Scenes at a Farm* by Walter Carroll – showed her how the notes on the page corresponded with the keys on the piano, instructed her to learn the right-hand part first, then the left-hand part and to call him when she had worked it out. Obediently, she did as she was told, "then Daddy said I could play the hands together." She whizzed through the book, learnt the pieces by herself and then, for fun, worked them out in different keys. Davie observed Betty's application and progress: it was obvious that she was gifted. He resolved to find her a teacher and get a better piano. He had just been given a rise at work, so was able to purchase a piano by using the little extra to pay for the instrument in monthly instalments. It was a good Newton upright and survives to this day – Izzy now has it.

Betty's brother, Robert, also showed an interest in music and asked to play the violin. Davie was fortunate to find excellent teachers for his son and daughter. They were Julia and Elsa Ommer, sisters, both unmarried, who lived nearby and ran their house like a small music academy. Julia taught the piano and cello and Elsa taught the violin. For the first few years, Betty just learnt the piano. She progressed at an astonishing speed, loved her lessons and loved to practise. At the age of eleven she took up the cello as well. Although it was always her second instrument, she became a competent player.

Robert had a natural talent for the violin, but was more interested in plants, which became a consuming passion that was to absorb him for the rest of his life. His botanical enthusiasm got him into trouble on one occasion some years later. When he was about fifteen, he decided to climb Ben Ledi to look at the flora. He set off by bus northwards to Callander, a town to the east of Loch Lomond, where he could begin his trek. Unknown to his mother, he was wearing his new boots, a purchase that had made quite a dent in the housekeeping purse. He came back home with one sole flapping off which did not go down at all well.

Mum remembered the excitement when her Daddy bought a wireless. She and Robert would rush back from school to listen to music. She told me: "We'd never heard Beethoven, Haydn, Mozart or Brahms symphonies before. It was absolutely wonderful. Sometimes we'd recognise tunes and realise we'd heard Daddy play them on his violin." She went on to say: "Daddy was a fine person. He didn't raise his voice or hand to us. He was a thinking man; well read, philosophical and considerate. And he was a good husband – Mammy was a happily married woman; but there was a reserve between him and us children. He grew up in a very conformist family and assumed the conventional role of Father. We saw him as a figure of authority and kept a respectful distance. I remember him sitting me on his knees and putting his arms around me, but I wouldn't have climbed onto his lap without invitation."

All children were sent to Sunday school, not necessarily for religious reasons. For parents, it was a God-sent opportunity to enjoy some uninterrupted time in bed. For Betty, it instilled a life-long aversion to the sound of the church organ. She and Robert attended the local Battlefield Primary School on Cathkin Road, which was about a mile away. Robert liked to run to school and time how long it took him. He was chuffed to find that he regularly managed to get there in five minutes.

Scottish primary schools placed music as a standard subject on the curriculum. Curwen's Tonic Sol-fa modulator[1] hung over the blackboard, where it had hung in Scottish classrooms for decades. With a baton, the teacher pointed to the symbols on the modulator (beginning at elementary level with the major scale – Doh-Ray-Me-Fa-Soh-La-Te-Doh'), whilst encouraging his/her pupils to sing the right note. In tandem with time names – 'ta, fa, te, fe, ti, fi', Sol-fa gave every child a starting point for reading pitch and rhythm. Like other teaching methods of the time, such as learning 'times tables' or memorising poems, it was very effective: interval leaps, modulation (changing key) and sight-singing from the modulator became second nature to Scottish children. Betty heard and automatically analysed music in Sol-fa for the rest of her life – and was forever grateful for the invaluable aural training she received courtesy of the Scottish Education System.

In the summer, Annie organised family holidays. She and her sister Martha, with their children and Gran, would head off to St. Andrews or the Isle of Arran for a month or more, their husbands joining them when they were able. Martha's sons, Billy and Archie, were close in age to Robert and Betty. The children had wonderful days playing on the beach, swimming in the sea and picnicking. After Martha's daughter, Marie, was born, the cousins were often told to take "the wee girl" with them in her pushchair, which rather restricted the extent of their adventures. "Why do we have to take *her*?" they moaned, when they were out of earshot. When little Marie was not in their charge, Billy led his brother and cousins on wild adventures, his high spirits infectious. Mum remembered how he was always climbing trees and persuading them across fast flowing streams – "he had longer legs than the rest of us and leapt easily from stone to stone, while we'd end up with wet feet" – and leading them further afield than they should go. Billy and Robert raced ahead, leaving Betty to catch up. Archie slowed his pace to keep her company. He and Betty, the nearest

1. English Congregationalist minister, John Curwen (1816-1880) developed Sarah Glover's (1785-1867) original 'Norwich Sol-fa' into what became known as 'Tonic Sol-fa', a 'moveable doh' system which uses different syllables to indicate each note of the scale and a separate set of syllables to describe lengths and patterns of rhythm. Curwen's Sol-fa was a simple way of teaching how to sing by note, making music easily accessible to all classes and ages of people. Many hymnals were produced in Sol-fa versions. However, Tonic Sol-fa training fell out of use in English schools in the early 1900s. Scottish schools continued to teach it until the 1960s, when, unfortunately, it began to disappear from the timetable. For a detailed treatise on the Sol-fa method, see *The Teacher's Handbook of the Tonic Sol-fa System* by Alexander T. Cringan, Canada Publishing Co. Ltd. 1889, available to download or read online.

in age, were particularly close friends.

Although Billy had an exuberant side, he was also a very sensitive person, occasionally touchy and a bit of a loner, sometimes preferring to go off on his own. It was maybe on those occasions that he took his sketchbook and watercolours and painted. It was obvious when Billy was a small boy that he could draw. From the age of about twelve, he was lucky to have a wonderful art teacher at school, Mr. Gemmell, who recognised his talent and took a keen interest in helping to develop his skills.

One summer Bessie travelled up from the Midlands with her daughter, Ailsa, to join her sisters and father on the Isle of Arran. It was the only holiday when all three sisters and six cousins were together. Mum often talked of that holiday, saying that they all had "a whale of a time". Marie remembered Mum being very kind to her, making sure the "baby" was included in the games, while Ailsa remembered "collecting brambles and watching a vast quantity of bramble jelly being prepared."

Annie and Davie enjoyed a contented relationship. Although money was tight, Annie was scrupulously careful with it. Davie didn't waste it on drink or tobacco and they managed to save enough for music lessons. But Annie's happy marriage was short-lived. Davie contracted Addison's disease, an illness that attacks the kidneys, which in those days was incurable. He kept working for as long as he could until he was bedridden. Twice he went into hospital for a few weeks to give Annie some respite from nursing and to enable her to take the children on holiday. Davie was too sick to go with them again. Unable to work, he no longer had an income, receiving only a small pension from the Post Office. Gran, still in employment, helped out, but there was not enough money to pay for music lessons. Annie, caring for her terminally ill husband, was not able to go back to work herself. She called on Julia and Elsa Ommer to explain. The sisters would not hear of Robert or Betty giving up their music lessons and continued to teach them for nothing.

For seven years Davie clung on to life while the disease gradually destroyed him. Knowing that he was dying, he bought a notebook in which he planned to write a series of letters to his son. It started quite promisingly, but there are just three entries, the first two in August 1928, soon after his condition had been diagnosed, and the last a year before he died. Here are some extracts:

> My Dear Son,
>
> I've thought frequently that I'd like to write you a few letters, not with any definite object in view but only because after my Father had died, I felt a little disappointed that he had left no communication to anyone. I have a little notebook of his yet, but nothing that could be thought interesting appears in it.
>
> Perhaps you will find these lines when I am no more your cheery Daddy and it is my desire that you may find something interesting, amusing, or perhaps even valuable in them. You have not yet gone to school but some day you should be able to read this crabbed script. How these letters, if I manage to continue them, will turn out, I haven't the faintest idea but I felt that I want to tell you such a lot about many things that I shouldn't want for subject matter. What form they will take I do not know. This certainly isn't a diary as I am not to note events as they occur (altho' this may happen also). Rather

it is to be a series of reminiscences or as I think I have seen it named, a "Commonplace Book". I'm afraid it will be commonplace enough.

This is August 1928, ten years after the finish of the Great War. You happily have no experience of it but it shadows all people's thoughts and behaviour yet. Everything seems to revert to it and as long as maimed and disabled men are to be seen and the many lost remembered, the Great War will be remembered and cursed. Perhaps it came as a punishment to a world that was going wrong, who knows. Certainly the world benefited and for a time such was the horror of the battlefield, a better epoch seemed to appear. This has not so far been realised and today there seems to be more ill feeling amongst people and individuals and even crime has become increasingly rife. There is salt in the earth yet, however, and although the outlook isn't bright, I can see a better future.

Conventions, which were almost religious rites, have been swept away and the rising generation, of which you my lad are a member, is looking at things with a clearer vision, seeing things in their proper perspective and I hope following a truer light with saner judgement. Broadmindedness and consideration for others is on the increase.

We are all searchers after truth, but it is so much greater than we, that we cannot grasp it. It behoves us, then, to respect the views of other searchers who perhaps are no further advanced than we are, only they are on a different road and see views that are not ours. The differing aspects will be reconciled one day.

August 1928

You are in Edinburgh with your Mammy and Betty just now and having a rare time, I've no doubt, wi' your cousins Billy and Archie. You are always having good times and I wonder if you will remember them when you grow up. The picnics to Eaglesham and Milngavie – how delighted Betty and you always were to get on to a bus. Your Mammy and Daddy enjoyed these picnics too. They were good and we'll have more of them too, I hope many a one before you scan this. Then there have been the two holidays at St. Andrews last year and this year and what a time you had on the sands and in Mrs. Docherty's house and garden wi' Teddy and Johnny.

I would wish you always to be happy but happiness is lost for a time and regained only after a struggle. Each individual is made up of the physical, mental and spiritual and the greatest of these is the spirit. It is indefinable but in your days of tribulation you will find it. You will realise that a Power, a Great, Tremendous and Kindly, Kingly Power has you in the hollow of a hand. You will want to lie down and rest in it and you know it won't crush you although you are a mite, and you will fear no more.

August 1934

Look at the lapse of time! You are at Whiting Bay[2] this month along with Mammy, Betty, Auntie Martha, Billy, Archie and Marie and all having a whole month's holidays and great times. I find you are a rather anxious customer. Don't worry and don't be afraid. Think things out for yourself, face things squarely and keep your eyes and mind open. There's nothing in either the physical or mental aspects of life that can affect you. You'll find that your physique can be utterly destroyed and you would still be you. There's the Divine spark in all of us. Tend it well and keep its temple in good repair.

Your loving Daddy.

2. Whiting Bay is on the south east coast of the Isle of Arran.

I suppose it was merely a residue of the ingrained hierarchy within the Victorian family structure, but it does seem sad that Davie made no effort to write to his daughter. I asked Mum about this and it was not without a certain resentment that she said, "Och well, that's how it was in those days. The boy was always more important. I'm sure it didn't cross my father's mind to write to me – I was just the girl." She also told me that had her father lived he would not have allowed her to go to London to study at the Academy when she was seventeen: and had she not gone to London, her future would have been entirely different. She would probably have had children, but they would not have been Izzy, Chris and me.

Davie died on July 16th 1935, aged fifty-two. Annie was forty-two, Robert, twelve and Betty, ten. I will return to Mum's life later, but now I am going to skip forward to the 1960s and continue with the story of our childhood.

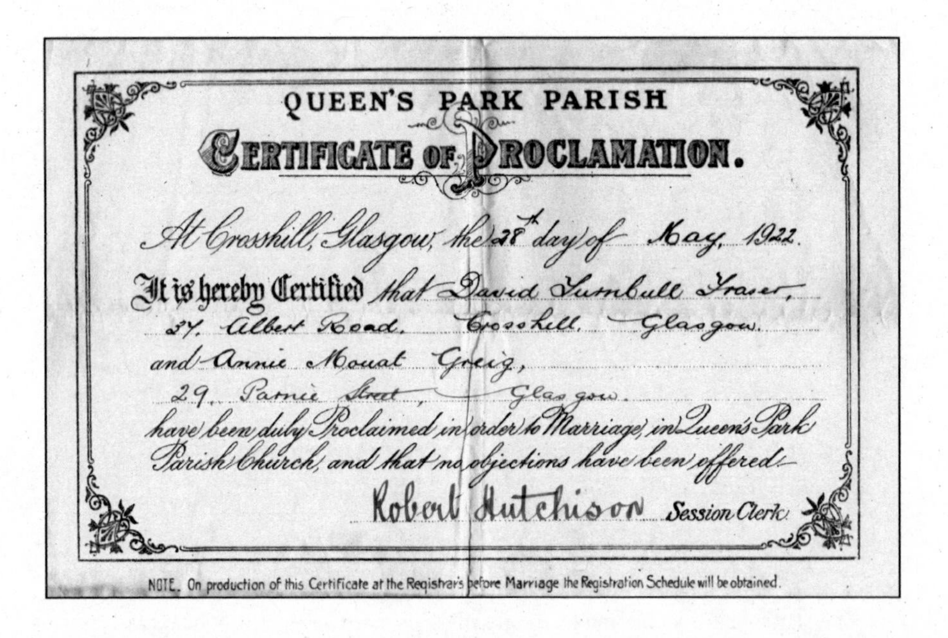
QUEEN'S PARK PARISH

CERTIFICATE OF PROCLAMATION.

At Crosshill, Glasgow, the 28th day of May, 1922.

It is hereby Certified that David Turnbull Fraser,
27. Albert Road, Crosshill, Glasgow.
and Annie Mouat Greig,
29. Parnie Street, Glasgow.
have been duly Proclaimed in order to Marriage in Queen's Park Parish Church, and that no objections have been offered.

Robert Hutchison Session Clerk.

NOTE. On production of this Certificate at the Registrar's before Marriage the Registration Schedule will be obtained.

Mum's childhood was a happy one, with parents who enjoyed a harmonious marriage. She and her brother, Robert, were the best of friends, having a very close bond for their whole lives. Chris's impish little face was clearly inherited from Mum: some of their expressions are almost identical.

37, Albert Road, Glasgow, as it is today (2008), where Davie and Annie Fraser (Granny) lived their married life and where their children, Robert and Elizabeth (Mum) were born. The woman in the picture is standing in the 'close' entrance. When Mum was a girl, the entrance did not have a door. The Fraser family lived in the second floor flat on the left.

Photo by Izzy Giles

BELOW LEFT: Betty and Robert with their Daddy.

BELOW: Betty (Mum)

ABOVE: Billy and Archie McKillop

Billy was a member of the Scouts and proud to be made leader of his pack.

BELOW: Betty, Archie, Marie, Billy and Robert on holiday on the Isle of Arran.

BELOW: Marie McKillop

ABOVE: Holiday on the Isle of Arran, summer of 1934

Rather a poor picture, but the only one of all three sisters with all their children.
STANDING: Billy, Bessie, Archie, Annie, Robert. SEATED: Marie, Martha, Betty, Ailsa.

BELOW: Gran playing cards, and doing the crossword with Archie and Martha.

9
INFANT SCHOOL

Orange makes me think of sand,
Soft, dry and crunchy,
Also it makes me think of fudge,
Sweet, delicious and munchy.

Orange makes me think of oranges,
Fat, juicy and round
Also it makes me think of bees
Who make a buzzy sound.

Orange – Christopher Giles (aged eight)

At the age of twenty-seven, Margaret Sprakes was appointed headmistress of the newly built Oakdale Infant School in South Woodford. She moved from Yorkshire down to London to take up her position and rented a basement flat in Cleveland Road, which meant that she passed number thirty-two frequently. On the gate she noticed a plaque, which read:

Elizabeth Fraser L.R.A.M., A.R.C.M., G.R.S.M.
Teacher of Pianoforte and Violoncello

Margaret played the piano and sang (she was one of the altos in the Philharmonia Chorus), but she had always wanted to play the cello. She bought herself an instrument for ten pounds, mustered her courage and rang the doorbell of number thirty-two. She was concerned that she might be thought too old to begin, but Mum was not bothered by Margaret's age, having no wish to discourage a person with such a strong desire to learn the cello. Mum claims that Margaret was her best pupil. By the end of her first lesson she could already produce a good sound, play a scale of C major and a piece using all four fingers. She whizzed through to Grade VIII in a few years, by which time she had started to teach the cello herself to a few of her Infant pupils. She and Mum became friends and it followed that Izzy and I went to Oakdale Infant School, aged four-and-a-half.

Our first day at school was not the traumatic experience of so many children, as we had each other and Oakdale was already familiar to us. We were deposited in the playground with the new batch of infants, some of them already wailing, and led into Mrs. Wright's reception class. Miss Sprakes was in the classroom and stayed there all day, taking howling children onto her lap, comforting them and encouraging us all to have fun. It surprised me why anyone should cry when there was a sand pit, a dressing-up box, paints and easels, books, crayons, building blocks and a Wendy House. I was wondering who Wendy was when I saw that Izzy was crying and went to ask her what was wrong. She said she wasn't unhappy – it was just that so many others were crying, it made her cry too. I tried to squeeze out a few tears, but my eyes remained dry.

Mum taught Izzy and me to read long before we started school. Izzy was a fluent reader by the time she was four. Mrs. Wright observed her sitting in the reading corner with a book, turning the pages, putting the book back, finding another and flicking through quickly.

"What are you doing?" she asked.

"Reading," Izzy replied.

"You're only looking at the pictures. I can't hear you saying any of the words."

"I read in my head," Izzy explained.

"Do you indeed?" said the amused teacher, "then perhaps you can tell me what the story was about in the book you've just put back?" Izzy recounted it almost word for word. Books were borrowed from the Junior School for her, while most of the class ploughed through *Janet and John*, speaking the words out loud in an expressionless monotone. She had a reading age of thirteen when she was five.

Izzy, petite and adorable, was a favourite with the older girls in the school. Although just six or seven themselves, they mothered and cosseted her as if she were their own baby doll. When I looked for her in the playground, I would often spot her in the arms of a big girl, being carried around like a trophy. I was bigger, heavier, not so cute; not made of the right material for babying. There were times, though, when I would have welcomed a little attention myself. The school seemed enormous; huge classrooms, long corridors, a great hall, a vast playground, whole roomfuls of toilets, and places that we knew must never be entered – the staff room, the caretaker's cupboard and the sheds in the playground. Oakdale shrank to its actual size as we grew older.

The shock for me was the discovery that not everyone liked me. A boy pushed me; another snatched the toy I was playing with; a girl refused to give me a turn with the doll's pram. When I asked if I could join in a game, I was told to go away. It bothered me the way these children behaved, but it also distressed me to be left out. I wanted to be one of the gang. Sometimes I thought it was only because Izzy was so popular that I was included at all. She was my social agent; made sure I was asked to join in and stood up for me in her quiet way.

I was an organiser even then. This sometimes worked to my advantage, for I was good at inventing games. Everyone listened to me as I explained the principles of a new game. They allowed me to divide them into teams, select individuals for roles (Captain, Chief, Wizard, Monster, Hero and so on) and direct groups to parts of the playground that were to be caves, grottoes, castles or dungeons. All was well until the characters started to step outside of their roles.

"STOP! The Dragon's not supposed to *eat* the Princess – he's a friendly Dragon!" I shouted. "And Keith, you're the Knight. You should be galloping over to rescue her right now. And you soldiers – prisoners should be thrown in the dungeon, not the cave."

"We thought this was the dungeon."

"No, no. The dungeon's over *there*."

"Oh, it doesn't matter."

"It does! They're the rules!"

The game disintegrated. Nobody wanted me telling them what to do, yet I couldn't bear to see the story take a wrong turn and run out of control. The children dispersed, going off to make their own entertainment and leaving me out. I wandered away alone, miserable and cross with myself. Izzy came to find me. "It was a really good game. Paul shouldn't have eaten Jennifer. I didn't think she was a good princess anyway. Come and play skipping. We need someone to hold the rope."

Soon after starting school, I caught a cold, which went to my chest and turned into bronchitis. It became a chronic condition and I was often absent from school. At five, I was referred to the London Chest Hospital. At six I had my first asthma attack. We had gone to visit some friends of Mum's who had four children of similar ages to us. I was running around in their large garden, full of boisterous excitement, when I started to cough and splutter and had to stop running. I went to find Mum, but she was already rushing towards me. I was too out of breath to speak, gasping, wheezing and choking. Mum realised at once it was asthma. She told me that her heart sank at that moment: her brother's wife, Lily, suffered terribly, so she knew how debilitating and life-compromising asthma was.

Illness, fevers and coughing became part of my life. Mum used to sit on my bed and talk to me in soothing tones, her cool hands testing the temperature of my brow. I would watch as she ground Aspirin into powder between two spoons and mixed it with jam for me to swallow. She brushed my hair, helped me to bath, and dressed me in clean, open-air-fresh pyjamas. At night I lay beside her at the edge of the bed, but never between her and Dad. I used to say it was because I got too hot. I knew that was not the real reason, but could not explain what it was.

Izzy and I walked to Oakdale unaccompanied, and it wasn't just around the corner. One way to get there was down Clarendon Road, left into Marlborough Road, over the railway line via the footbridge, into Pultney Road, across George Lane and along Cowslip Road. That was probably the quickest route, but we varied it, sometimes using the tunnel by South Woodford station to get to the other side of George Lane. I ran down shrieking, listening for the echo of my voice. Izzy never shouted, but if there was nobody around, she might stamp her feet. Then we cut through a lane called Pigs Alley, sometimes stopping out of necessity to use the public conveniences situated there. Occasionally in winter, smog would descend – thick, mustardy-yellow fog that almost obscured one's vision. We were wrapped up in coats and gloves with woollen scarves tied around our mouths and noses in an attempt to filter the air. Through the murk we navigated, quite excited that we could only see a yard ahead. It wasn't much good for my bronchitis, though.

At Christmas time a big tree went up in the school hall. A small present for every child was laid beneath it and decorations and balloons festooned the room. In assembly, Miss Sprakes spoke to us in a serious voice: "Now, I know that *nobody* here would *dream* of taking a present before Father Christmas gives them out, and not one of you would even *think* of bursting a balloon, would you?"

"No, Miss Sprakes," we agreed solemnly – and nobody did.

It was Dad who dressed up as Father Christmas and gave the presents out at the school party. Izzy and I looked at him suspiciously, but didn't dare ask if he were really our Dad. We sang *We Wish You a Merry Christmas* with great emphasis on 'wish'. The bit I liked best was: 'We all like figgy pudding.'

Every child's birthday was celebrated in assembly. The birthday girl or boy brought in a selection of cards and a present 'to show'. Miss Sprakes read out the cards, holding up the pictures for us to 'aah' over cute animals or laugh at funny cartoons. The present was admired then the whole school sang *Happy Birthday*, some of the naughty boys surreptitiously singing rude words.

We had milk every day, which came in miniature bottles that held a third of a pint. One term I was milk monitor. I had to hand a straw to each child as they picked their bottle out of the crate and make sure that they put the foil tops into a bowl to be washed and added to the aluminium collection for guide dogs. I wasn't keen on school milk, as it was lukewarm with coagulated cream at the top. How I envied the few special children who had a third of a pint of orange juice instead. Why couldn't I be an orange juice child?

Chris joined the Infant School during our last year there. He tore around the playground wearing out his shoes in a matter of weeks. His knees and elbows were usually grazed, grubby and scabby, and his clothing dishevelled from rolling on the ground and tripping over. Learning to read was far less exciting, but his teachers were fond of him even though he didn't pay attention. Every child's name was written out in large letters and pinned to the wall. Although Chris couldn't read, he recognised the word 'Christopher'. He looked at the wall and copied 'Christopher Walker' into his exercise book. He wrote his name correctly, however, in a composition titled 'About Myself'. It reads: "My name is Christopher Colin Giles. I am five years old. I have two sisters." That was it.

One day on the way home, we saw a young girl following her mother out of the sweet shop opposite Cowslip Road. The child stopped to pull the top off a tube of Smarties, wrenched too hard and the tube fell out of her hand. She cried out as the Smarties dropped like hail stones to the pavement. The three of us came to a halt, following the bouncing, rolling, coloured sweets with our eyes. The mother flicked round, spoke sharply and dragged her daughter away by the arm. "Don't you dare pick them up; they're dirty. No you are not having another packet." Our reaction was spontaneous and unanimous. We held hands ready to cross the road, waited until the child had been tugged squealing round the corner, and then ran towards our windfall. We retrieved every last runaway Smartie and ate them then and there, squatting by the gutter.

Religion reared its head for the first time. At some point during the daily assembly, when the whole school sat cross-legged in rows on the hall floor, Miss Sprakes announced, "Hands together, eyes closed." There was a shuffle as the children adjusted their positions, pressed their hands together under their chins and shut their eyes. We copied the gestures: then, within the darkness of our heads, we listened to rhymes thanking God for flowers, trees, homes, friends – even mummies and daddies, brothers and sisters. We also heard that we had to ask God to make us good, kind and loving, and if we were accidentally bad, He would forgive us. It was all very mysterious. Who on earth was this person? We learnt he doesn't live on earth; he has his own special place in the sky called Heaven.

Dinnertime was stranger still. Izzy and I queued for our food, found a place at a table, put our plates down and tucked straight in. "You can't eat yet!" hissed a girl sitting next to us, "We haven't said Grace." Hastily, we placed our cutlery back on the table. A teacher said, "Hands together, eyes closed," and continued with the words, "For what we are about to receive, may the Lord make us truly grateful." On cue, the whole school mumbled, "Ah, Men." Now there was a Lord as well as a God – and a girl called Grace.

At home, we asked, "Who's God? Where's Heaven? Are we Christians?" Mum and Dad rolled their eyes at each other.

"Well, it was bound to happen at some point," said Mum resignedly to Dad.

"Yes, I suppose so," sighed Dad. They explained that God is like a character in a fairy story; he's not real; there's no such thing as God and no such place as Heaven, but some people think there is, like the teachers and children at school. Most of them call themselves Christians because they believe in a religion, a story, called Christianity, but there are lots of other religions in the world based on different made-up stories. No, they said, we are not Christians; we are atheists; we have no religious beliefs at all and do not believe in God; but, they warned us, we should not go around saying that at school. When we asked why not, they replied, "It's just best not to." So we carried a secret.

In 1960, it was compulsory to teach Christianity in State schools. Every day we sang hymns, recited the Lord's Prayer, thanked Grace for dinner, wrote out prayers in our exercise books or made them up. At least we could join in, unlike the girl in Mrs. Vincent's class who sat in the reading corner on her own outside the hall and wasn't allowed Christmas or Birthdays. I felt very sorry for her, but she said she didn't mind because she was Joe's witness. At Easter time, we were taught about the crucifixion of Jesus. Izzy was horror-struck when she heard that nails were hammered through Jesus's hands and feet, that he was whipped, stabbed and tortured. She screamed out in class and had to be taken away crying to be comforted by Miss Sprakes.

As well as atheism, the word communism should be avoided, our parents told us. At this time, to be a member of the Communist party was illegal in the USA. During the 1950s, Senator Joseph McCarthy was leading his fanatical anti-communist crusade, which has been likened to the barbaric witch-hunts of the seventeenth and eighteenth centuries. Thousands were arrested, unfairly tried, fined and imprisoned, whether they were communists, people suspected of having communist connections, or simply those categorized as undesirables. Two were even executed.[1] Although it

1. On June 19th 1953, Ethel and Julius Rosenberg were executed at Sing Sing prison. They were convicted of espionage on March 29th 1951, accused of stealing the secret of the atomic bomb and delivering it to the USSR. The McCarthyite witch-hunters who led the prosecution did not present any evidence that proved the couple were spies, but they did show that the United States was willing to go to any length to destroy communists and their supporters. The Rosenberg's defenders said there was never a chance of a fair trial in the anti-communist 'Red Scare' climate of the time. While the couple's commitment to the communist cause was well-documented, they denied the spying charges even as they faced the electric chair. Ethel was 37 and Julius 35. Their two sons, Michael and Robert, were 10 and 6.

was not illegal to be a member of the Communist Party in Britain, Mum and Dad felt it best for us not to broadcast their political allegiance.

The first anti-nuclear demonstration took place at Easter 1958. Fifteen thousand people marched from London to Aldermaston, where nuclear weapons were (and still are) manufactured. The peaceful protest was planned by the newly formed Campaign for Nuclear Disarmament and the now familiar CND logo made its first appearance. Mum, Dad, Granny and the two of us in borrowed pushchairs marched part of the way, but as Mum was seven-months pregnant, they didn't go too far. Subsequent marches, which became known as May Day Marches, set off from Aldermaston. Many more supporters joined the march along the route, swelling to rally in Hyde Park, where speakers addressed the crowd. Our family participated in the May Day March every year. I remember them being good fun. There were brass bands, hooters and songs, we held banners, wore badges, shouted out slogans with the rest and ate our picnic in the park. We didn't have much idea what it was all about, but everyone seemed to be friends and the atmosphere of good will and optimism was infectious. Even Mum and Dad were happy together on those days.

Our school News Books, of course, gave our secrets away. Quite what our teachers made of our reports, we can only guess.

> **Izzy (aged six):** On Sunday we went on the May-day march and we met Freda and robin and their little girl Cathey. And we all marched together into a park.

Above these words is a crayoned picture showing people marching with prams and holding a huge banner that says STOP ALL TORIES and a smaller one that reads, *ban the bom*.

> **My News (same age):** On Sunday we went on a may day march and we bought a badge and on it said A Happy May day. We marched from Oxford station to the park. Lots of people were there.

My picture shows a horse at the front (one of the mounted police) and lots of multi-coloured people carrying banners saying 'BTB'.

> **Chris (aged five):** We went to a communist march. I made a home made Ban the bomb. And we went to the pigons.

He was referring to the pigeons of Trafalgar Square. His picture is similar to ours except for the excessive number of pigeons.

Another kind of May Day took place every year in Miss Sprakes's school – the crowning of the May Queen. All pupils participated. We carried posies; the girls wore party dresses; the boys, pressed grey shorts and white shirts. Seasonal songs were learnt by heart and sung with gusto to an out-of-tune piano, which was wheeled by the ever-willing caretaker and a few strong lads into the playground. Pupils from the oldest class of six- and seven-year-olds voted for the girl they wanted to be the May Queen. The one who came second in the poll acted as Crown Bearer. Her role was to lead the Queen's procession bearing a coronet of flowers on a satin cushion. The next eight girls with the highest votes had the honour of holding the Queen's train. Following them were the garland bearers – six pairs of boys and girls chosen from younger classes who carried ropes entwined with flowers. When the Queen had been positioned on her decorated throne, she was ceremoniously crowned by a local dignitary, after which every class performed their well-practised dances around the maypole.

When Izzy and I reached the top class, I hoped Izzy would be voted the May Queen. But I was afraid that I wouldn't get enough votes to carry the Queen's train – which meant that I would not have a beautiful white party dress that only the Queen's escorts were entitled to wear. This would be the closest I would ever get to dress like a bridesmaid: to be deprived of the opportunity was unbearable. Overwhelmed, I burst into tears and ran sobbing to Miss Sprakes. I explained the sorry situation to her, which no doubt she had already considered. I was added to the back of the Queen's train, pleased to be wearing a white dress, but rather sad the way it had all worked out. I'd had to negotiate my position, and worse, the class chose tall Vivien Crown to be May Queen on the grounds that Izzy was too small for the role. So it was that Izzy headed the procession as Crown Bearer and I brought up the rear.

Before we had a television, radio programmes like *Children's Hour* and *Listen with Mother* kept us fully absorbed. We listened to *Toy Town* – home of Larry the Lamb, Dennis the Dachshund, the Mayor and other characters. I loved the *Listen with Mother* theme tune – *Berceuse* from Fauré's *Dolly Suite* – and the familiar words: "Are you sitting comfortably?" (Pause) "Then I'll begin."

Granny resisted getting a television until long after most of our friends had one, but when Izzy and I were seven and Chris was five, she decided to rent one. It was installed in her room, which meant that she policed what we watched and called the curfew. There were just two TV channels then – ITV and BBC. We were not allowed to watch ITV because it was thought our susceptible minds would be corrupted by the commercials, so the only option was BBC, until BBC2 was launched in 1964.

Our favourite programmes were *Blue Peter*, *Animal Magic* with Johnny Morris, the series of *The Railway Children*, *Belle and Sebastian*, *The Adventures of Robinson Crusoe*, and *Crackerjack*: "It's Friday, it's five to five, it's *Crackerjack*," announced Leslie Crowther every week, after which he and Peter Glaze propelled the programme along at a fast pace, doling out cabbages and *Crackerjack* pencils to contestants. Then of course there was *Doctor Who*. We were hooked from the very first enthralling episode, which was broadcast at the end of 1963. The weird electronic theme music alone created an aura of suspense. *Doctor Who* was shown on Saturday afternoons at a time that sometimes clashed with other activities. We pleaded to be taken home in time to watch it, a request that caused both Mum and Dad to get annoyed with us. Chris, along with every other boy in the country, did Dalek impersonations, swivelling around with outstretched arms and chanting in manic tones, "I am a Dalek. Exterminate. Exterminate." I was so frightened by the Cybermen that I had to sleep with the landing light on and the door open.

During school holidays, or when we were ill, there was little to watch during the day apart from the programmes intended for the under-fives. Nevertheless, we enjoyed *Playschool*. I loved hearing the harp glissandi that preceded the voyages through the round, square or arched windows. There was also *Watch with Mother*, which showed a variety of programmes. We liked *Tales of the Riverbank* and *The Woodentops*. Just about bearable was *Bill and Ben, the Flowerpot Men*, but we despised *Andy Pandy*. For the rest of the time, all there was to see was the test card – a girl wearing a hair-band playing noughts and crosses with a clown in the middle of what seemed to be a complex board-game. I used to wonder about that girl. What kind of glamorous world did she come from to have been chosen to appear on the test card? Had she been selected from hundreds of hopeful candidates? What must her life be like, being recognised wherever she went? She must live in a huge house and be taught by a governess, I decided. When I asked Mum, she said the child was probably the daughter of someone who worked at the BBC. (She was almost right – the girl was the daughter of George Hersee, the head designer of the card.)

Soon after the television arrived, although not because of it, Mrs. Blockley and Kit, the tenants, moved out. We spread into the whole house. Our bunk beds were moved into the adjacent room – where Mum and Dad had slept – and Chris had our old room to himself. The first-floor bathroom was now free to use, but we usually opted to have our baths in the kitchen. This was partly because it was warmer downstairs, but it was also for safety's sake. On the wall above the tap-end of the bath upstairs was an ancient Ascot gas water heater that self-ignited a few moments after the hot tap was turned on. At least that was what it was supposed to do, but sometimes it hissed gas into the room and refused to light. If you waited, there was a chance it might still ignite, but you couldn't hang about for too long for fear of being gassed. Just as you felt you could wait no longer and lunged to turn off the tap, the Ascot often burst into life with a mighty whoosh, almost leaping from the wall as it sucked back the escaped gas in an implosion of fire.

10
MUSIC LESSONS BEGIN

I think I should have no other mortal wants, if I could always have plenty of music. It seems to infuse strength into my limbs, and ideas into my brain. Life seems to go on without effort, when I am filled with music.

The Mill on the Floss – George Eliot

The sound of the piano was familiar to us even before we were born. We knew a wide range of piano music by heart from hearing Mum's lessons through the walls. But best of all was listening to Mum play herself. She practised for hours. After we had gone to bed, I would sometimes hear her playing a beautiful piece and risk leaving the bedroom to sit at the top of the stairs to hear it more clearly. On some evenings, a cellist and a violinist came over to play piano trios. I simply couldn't stay in bed when I heard the opening of Beethoven's 'Archduke' Trio. I remember getting quite frustrated when they kept stopping to rehearse. Why didn't they just play it? How could they bear to stop in the middle of the tune? Then I would hear a door open, or see Granny or Dad coming into the hall and scamper back to bed.

Mum started us on the piano when we were about five, but decided that she should not continue to teach us herself, so sent us to Dorothy Carter, one of her ex-pupils. We travelled by train on our own to Woodford station and walked from there to the top of Monkhams Avenue to Mrs. Carter's house. We waited on the platform of South Woodford station for a train to arrive and always sat in the first carriage. One Saturday morning, the train driver came out of his door marked 'do not obstruct' and invited us into his cabin to drive the train with him. Izzy writes about this in her school News Book, November 1962:

> On Saturday when me and my sister went to our Music leson we got on the train and a man opend a door and let us come in his cabin to see all what was going on in front of the train then we got out of the train and walked up the Road to our Music lesson and then we went home.

I write:

> When I went to my piano lesson on the train we got on it and the driver came out of his cabin and said wood you like to come in and see all the things in frunt.

I did not like my lessons with Mrs. Carter. A few years later, to my relief, Mum suggested I give them up. I continued to learn and play the music that appealed to me, but I don't think any amount of practice would have turned me into a pianist. I have been asked how old I was when I decided I wanted to play the cello, or whether that decision was made for me. All I can say is that I can't remember a time when I didn't want to play the cello. I loved its rich, vibrant sound, its shape and size. I pestered Mum to let me have a go on her cello, but she told me I would have to wait until I was bigger before I could begin to learn. I was sure I had grown enough when I started school, so was terribly disappointed to find that I hadn't. Eventually, Miss Sprakes started teaching me when I was six-and-a-half on a half-sized instrument, which was still too big. I remember my first lesson. Miss Sprakes came into my classroom and called me over.

"Come on," she said, taking my hand, "I've got a surprise for you." We walked to the room that she used for singing and music classes. It had a piano and lots of percussion instruments – chime bars, glockenspiels, triangles, drums and wood blocks. She opened the door and there was a chair and a little cello lying on its side. I hardly dared to believe that it might be for me. Miss Sprakes sat me down, and then the caretaker came into the room with a footrest he had made.

"Oh you are kind," said Miss Sprakes, "that looks exactly the right size. Let's try it, Catherine."

I couldn't wait to get my hands on the cello, but first Miss Sprakes had to make sure that my feet could go flat down on the footrest – a simple wooden plank raised on blocks to about four inches off the ground that was placed in front of the infant-sized chair. Yes – my feet reached. Now I could play – but then I had to wait again while Miss Sprakes tuned the cello.

"Go and play me an A would you dear?"

I found an A on the piano.

"Play it again will you? No, not the D or G – I only need to hear the A."

A, D, G, C rang out deliciously on the cello.

"There, it's in tune now," she said, satisfied.

I sat down again like a dog waiting for a bone. She handed me the cello. I pulled it towards me, grinning from ear to ear.

"Let's adjust the spike and get you sitting comfortably. Well, it's still a bit too big for you," she said, shortening the spike further.

"Oh, I don't think so," I said positively, "it feels just right to me."

Miss Sprakes laughed. "I'm sure we'll be able to manage. Now, do you know the names of the strings?"

"Yes," I said, plucking the strings, calling out their names with confidence.

"Very good. Now, here's the bow. Give me your hand and I'll show you how to hold it." She wrapped my fingers around the big end and told me, "This part of the bow's called the frog." I giggled rather wildly. She held my hand over the bow and together we drew it across the D string and back again. Oh, what a wonderful sound! I could feel it vibrating in my body.

"Can I do it by myself?"

"Go on then. Imagine your cello's a big fluffy cat and you're going to stroke it and make it purr."

It purred contentedly, sending tingles up my arm and through my tummy. It was the moment I had been waiting for and I couldn't stop smiling. Miss Sprakes reported back to Mum that I had taken to it like a duck to water. I had short lessons almost every day in school and took my cello home to practise.

Mum and Granny went to Ambrose's auction sale in Loughton on the last Thursday of every month. Granny had a good eye for antiques and for bargains. Most of our furniture, crockery, cutlery, linen and bedding came from sales. One of their successful bids was a large Axminster carpet, which fitted perfectly into the music room. When I was practising I followed the patterns in the rug – there were trees, flowers, wreaths and ribbons, and animals that looked like tigers, wolves, mice, humming birds, peacocks and deer. In the centre were two pairs of white swans and two pairs of black swans swimming in a pond. It seemed to me that the whole purpose of the carpet was to provide an exotic setting for the eight graceful swans.

Izzy began learning the violin at the same time as I started the cello. We played in our first concert in December 1962, a couple of months before we were seven. The event was Mum's annual pupils' concert, which was held in Oakdale Infant School hall. Apparently, I played one little piece and was so elated that I asked to play another. I didn't know what nerves were then, unlike Miss Sprakes, who, being one of Mum's pupils, also performed in the concert. She could hardly play for shaking. Afterwards, she decided that she would not put herself through such an ordeal again. Izzy kept to her one modest piece, and then we played a piano duet together. Chris sat attentively in the audience for about ten minutes then tore up and down the corridor for the rest of the concert.

The following April, Izzy and I both gained distinctions in our Grade I. The exams were held in our own house, as Mum had enough examinees for her music room to become an examination centre. Apparently, I was so delighted to be playing my pieces again that I sat on the stairs the evening before singing, "Tomorrow's my exam day." Later that year, we were invited to perform in a local *Soirée Musicale*. I don't remember this event, but it was, I am told, the first time I met and played on the same platform as Paul Hart. I was seven; he was nine.

Chris also started on the piano, but Mum wanted each of us to play a non-keyboard instrument as well. To my disappointment, he opted for the violin rather than the cello. It meant that he and Izzy went to their violin lessons together, which caused Izzy some embarrassment, as Chris could not be persuaded to walk sensibly down the street. He galloped ahead, dragging his violin case along railings, or lagged behind to inspect anthills and stroke cats. He leaped on and off the kerbstones, stamped in puddles and told jokes in an attempt to make Izzy laugh. Invariably, Izzy crossed to the other side of the road and pretended she had nothing to do with him. At the bottom of George Lane, she waited while he shrieked his way down the underpass, and followed at a discreet distance. One week, some Irish workmen were digging up the road. "Give us a tune," they called. Unabashed, Chris opened his violin case on the pavement, drew out his fiddle and played 'God Save the Queen'. They laughed their heads off and threw him a couple of pennies. Izzy was mortified. "Come on. Hurry up, we're going to be late," she chided.

The violin was not his instrument; it was his opponent. He attacked it with his bow like a swordfighter, and although he played in tune and in time, the sound he produced was frightful. We all suffered Chris's violin playing, Chris included, for several years.

Mum had taught Margaret Sprakes all she could. It was time for Margaret to find a teacher who could coach her at a more advanced level. As it happened, a cellist was coming to play to the children in Oakdale Junior School. Her name was Florence Hooton. She performed to the youngsters and Margaret was impressed; so was I – not just by her cello playing, but also by her glamorous sky-blue concert dress. The two women established an enduring friendship and worked closely together, Margaret taking her good pupils to play to Florence, many of whom went on to study full-time with her at the Royal Academy of Music. When I was nine, Miss Sprakes drove me to Miss Hooton's house in Stag Lane, Edgware, to play to her. It was a special occasion. I wore my prettiest dress and Miss Sprakes said I could pick a bunch of flowers from her garden to take with us. Miss Hooton saw us arrive and came out to greet us.

"Maggie," she boomed expansively, "how *marvellous* to see you. And you must be Cathy!" It was the first time anyone had called me Cathy. I handed her the flowers shyly. "Oh, what a *beautiful* posy. Are they from Maggie's garden?" I nodded. "*Thank* you. I do love flowers. I am so looking forward to hearing you play. Maggie's told me *all* about you."

I performed my pieces. She listened and watched intently. When I had finished, she was hearty with her congratulations. Then she began to work with me, talking to Miss Sprakes as she made subtle changes to my bow hold, slightly altered the position of my left hand, suggested I raise my left elbow a little. She was gentle and precise. Everything she said worked and made sense to me. I admired her astuteness and unerring ability to analyse from the start. I was also conscious of her diplomacy – she praised Miss Sprakes's teaching whilst also instructing her how my technique could be improved. Then she taught me exercises, showing me a technical practice routine that I was to go through every day – a regime that served me well from then on. She said I could go and play in the garden while she had a chat to Maggie. I skipped outside, delighted to find a tiny thatched house at the end of the lawn. I peered through the dirty windows. Inside everything was child-sized – a table, chairs, a dresser displaying a half-size tea set. I tried the front door, but it was too stiff to open. I ran back excitedly to ask if I could go into the little house.

"Ah, the Wendy house," said Miss Hooton, "we had it built for our daughters when they were small. I'll see if David can get the door open and you can have a look inside next time you come. Well, Cathy; a big bravo. Thank you for coming to play to me."

I began to have regular lessons with Miss Hooton, whilst Miss Sprakes continued to teach me at school. Month after month I went to Miss Hooton's hoping that David would have unlocked the Wendy house (I still didn't know who Wendy was). I caught glimpses of it through the windows, but I wasn't given the opportunity to go into the garden again.

ABOVE: Oakdale Infant School, May Day 1960

ABOVE: 1962. I am sitting next to Jonathan Turner, whose family became an important part of our lives.

BELOW: May Day 1963. Izzy, the Crown Bearer, is leading the procession. The headmistress, Margaret Sprakes, is walking beside the retiring May Queen and I am bringing up the rear.

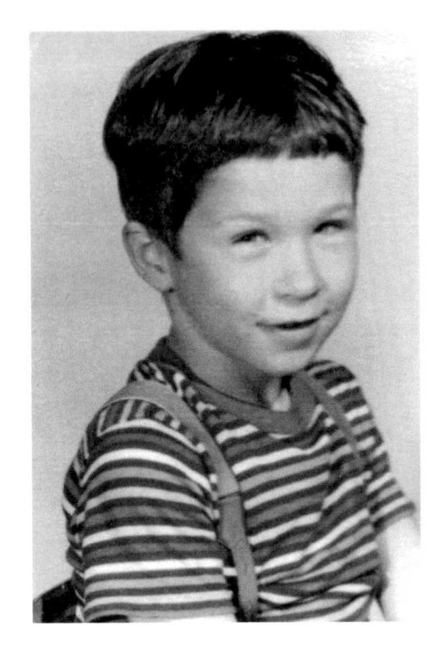

ABOVE LEFT: Chris aged five

ABOVE RIGHT: Izzy trying to show Chris how to hold a cat.

BELOW: Beginners on the violin and cello, aged seven. Chris is listening in the background. The carpet's intricate pattern of plants and animals often drew my attention away from practising.

11
TALL TALES

At seven when I go to bed,
I find such pictures in my head:
Castles with dragons prowling round,
Gardens where magic fruits are found.

A Child's Thought – Robert Louis Stevenson

In our games we invented an imaginary family. Izzy was the mummy figure called Mrs. Kourshy (a name cribbed from an acquaintance of Mum's), I was 'Auntie' and Chris was the baby – a little girl called Sheelee. Izzy and I clomped around in Mum's old high-heeled pointy shoes with scarves tied around our heads and made towel nappies and makeshift rattles for Sheelee. Chris was very convincing with his crawling, babbling, gooing and howling.

Our most secret place was the cupboard on the landing. Half of it was taken up with a copper water tank and on the other side hung old coats. We crawled in on all fours, squished ourselves inside, pulled the door shut and arranged a space within the mangy furs and moth-eaten tweeds. Bodies pressed together, chins on our knees, we ate Co-op chocolate digestive biscuits and had confidential whispered conversations in the dark. If we heard footsteps coming up the stairs, we were as quiet as mice, convinced that nobody knew we were there.

At weekends after we'd had our baths, we all climbed into the same bed, I in the middle with my arms around Izzy and Chris. Snuggled together we escaped to fairyland. I made up stories, the inspiration being in the titles. For example: 'The Wizard Who Couldn't Make Spells', 'The Apple Tree Princess', 'The Ice Castle and the Unhappy Dragon', 'The Dwarf and the Magic Carpet'. It was up to Izzy and Chris to choose the one that most appealed. If they chose the first, it would perhaps be about a wizard who was utterly miserable because he had forgotten how to make spells, had mislaid his spell book, and was in serious trouble because the mighty king of all wizards would soon be paying him a visit. The king expected to be entertained by the latest magic and our poor wizard couldn't even turn a prince into a frog – one of the most basic spells of all. What was he to do? I carried on in that sort of way, making it up as I went along, with no idea as to what would happen next, knowing only that in the end all would be well. Sometimes I deliberately left the tale on a cliff-hanger.

"Oh, don't stop there!" cried Izzy and Chris in unison.

"You'll have to wait till tomorrow," I said meanly.

"Oh, *please*, Kate," (as I was then known), "tell us some more."

Our raised voices alerted Granny.

"Go and tell Cath-er-reen to stop her nonsense and get those children into bed," she told Mum, "it's way past their bedtime."

"Aw, Mummy," we wailed, "just a bit longer."

"Well, be very quiet and you can have another five minutes while I make your hot-water-bottles."

"Goody!"

"Shh: just a few minutes." The story resumed until Mum came back and we had to get into our own beds. Then she tucked us up and said goodnight.

"Isapaffinfyon?" called Chris.

"Yes, it's on. Now go to sleep."

Mum and Dad wanted to record me telling a story (I don't know why, except that they both liked to document our lives. They took huge numbers of photographs of our childhood, of which the ones in this book are just a small selection). The tape recorder was set up. They, Izzy and Chris waited expectantly. For once, I couldn't think of any good titles. The atmosphere was wrong. It wasn't just the three of us cuddled up in our pyjamas at bedtime. Perhaps when I began it would be fine. "Once upon a time…"

"No, not yet," said Dad, "I haven't pressed the record button."

So my first idea flew straight out of the window.

"The tape is running now. You may begin," said Dad. I started again, but floundered. The mediocre story lost direction and I had no idea how to sort out the muddled plot. It became more and more rambling until finally I had to bring it to a feeble end.

"Me now, me now," Chris clamoured. "It's not the same as the last one," he added promptly. He had listened attentively to every word and repeated his own cut-down version. Then it was Izzy's turn. She wasn't a storyteller – she was very good at writing them down, but inventing off the cuff wasn't her forte. Her story was short, but on this occasion a lot better than mine. Chris chipped in with his potted version and the recording session ended.

Mum played us that tape some ten years later and I remembered the rising panic I had felt during the telling of my story – the moment when I knew all was lost. Hearing our high-pitched childish voices was surprising, though. We were so well spoken – every word enunciated clearly with not a vowel out of place. Professor Henry Higgins would have been proud of us. No wonder we were called 'posh' when we went to school. Yet how did this come to be with Mum from the tenements of Glasgow and Dad from Brixton? Both Mum and Dad had cultivated their voices. Mum determined to lose her Glaswegian accent when she arrived in London, as she could not stand being teased about it. Although she came from a working-class background, her parents spoke well and she'd had a good education in Scotland. Dad had a musical ear and found the vernacular ugly. He had also read extensively – in particular the English classics. We became sick of hearing his quotations.

"Who said that?" he would ask, and then supply the answer: "Why, it was Mr. Pickwick" (or Mr. Micawber or Uriah Heap or Hamlet or King Lear). Dickens and Shakespeare were the most common, so we sometimes made lucky guesses, but he liked to catch us out: "Why, no. That is from the novel *Vanity Fair*, penned by William

Makepeace Thackeray." He spoke as if he himself were a character in a Victorian novel.

It took us no time at all to learn playground English. We were of necessity bilingual. It wasn't so easy, though, when friends came round, and there was nothing worse than being corrected in front of them. To Mum, and especially Dad, all three of us were Eliza Dolittles. For example:

"Can I listen to the radio?"

"I'm sure you're perfectly *capable* of listening to the radio. If you're asking whether you *may* listen to it; that is a different question."

He got at us about the unnecessary use of "got": "One doesn't need to say, I've got something – the verb is *to have*. I have something is all that is required."

The difference between the verbs 'to lay' and 'to lie' was explained over and over again. "It is *not* I am going to lay down; it is I am going to *lie* down. A hen *lays* an egg; the table is *laid*. One *lies* down. I *lay* on the bed is correct, however, when 'lay' is used as the past tense of the verb 'to lie'."

The intrusive *r* was a pet hate. "Drawing *not* draw*r*ing; vanilla essence *not* vanilla*r*essence; Law and Order *not* Law *r*and Order; Hosanna in Excelsis *not* Hosanna *r*in Excelsis."

He objected to the way in which the word 'like' is used, stating that it should only be used as a verb. For example: "He cried like a baby" would be bad English. "He cried in the same way as a baby" would be more acceptable. "He looked at me like I was stupid" – oh, dear me, no! – "He looked at me as if I were stupid."

Then there was the *h*: "Are you referring to Wales, the country, or W*h*ales of the sea? Witch way? Do you not mean w*h*ich way?" My children rag me about the way I pronounce w*h*y, w*h*en, w*h*ere, w*h*ite, and w*h*at, but it was dinned into me. 'What' was another bone of contention: "Would you please repeat that?" or "I'm sorry, I didn't hear you", *not* "What?" or "Come again" or, sin of sins, "Wot?" with a silent *t*.

Other serious grammatical misdemeanours were: "I shouldn't of done that." "I got off of the bus." As for "It ain't arf funny" – well, it was not funny at all. We were constantly corrected. It was even worse when it came to pronunciation. Just like (oops, in the same manner as) Professor Higgins, we were made to repeat the offending word until a flawless intonation was achieved: no *f*s were heard in place of a *th*; every word ending in *t* finished with an audible click, and *ing* words were rounded off with a ringing (not ringin') g.

"Plygran? What kind of a word is that? Do you mean playground? Say it correctly."

"Playground, playground, playground, brown, brown, brown, found, found, found, day, day, day, plate, plate, plate, height, height, height, three, three, three, again, again, again, again, again."

Although there are some things I am glad to have been taught, it was intensely irritating; and perhaps we would have learnt anyway without the punishing training.

Dad made up stories for us. 'The Green Men' was an ongoing series about two elves who lived with a man named Wallace. They had pointy ears and long white beards; their hats, jackets, breeches and pantomime-style boots were entirely green; they drank from acorn cups, ate from walnut shells and slept in the pockets of Wallace's favourite jacket – the old tweed one with leather patches on the elbows, which hung on the back of his bedroom door at night. It was during the hours of darkness that the Green Men got up to mischief. I remember enjoying Dad's Green Men tales when we were very young (Izzy, however, never liked them), but as we got older we started to resent Dad calling us for story-time. It became something we had to do to please him. He settled into his armchair expectantly. We had to arrange ourselves around him just so; Chris on his lap, Izzy and I between or beside his knees. None of us liked to be touched by him. His gentle strokes felt creepy, not soothing. I remember once telling him to stop fiddling with my hair because it would make tangles, but it wasn't the real reason. He withdrew his hand as if I had burnt it and my body tensed for an undelivered slap.

He also read to us from a huge hard-backed book that he'd had as a child – *The Brothers Grimm Fairy Tales* with illustrations by Arthur Rackham. Amongst the leaves were a dozen or so full-page colour plates with protective sheets of tracing paper in front of them. The tales are not children's fare; they are quite gruesome in places. Izzy managed to listen to the stories, but she was supremely frightened of the pictures. The one that terrified her above all appeared in *Little Red Riding Hood* (or *Little Red-Cap* in the Grimm version). It depicts the Wolf grinning toothily, lying on a four-poster bed in the cottage. He has just eaten Grandmother and is dressed in his victim's nightclothes, salivating, waiting for Little Red-Cap to arrive. She can be seen through the window, innocently picking flowers in the forest, unaware of the fate awaiting her. Izzy covered her eyes when the page was getting close. "Have you looked yet?" she asked anxiously.

"Yes, yes," Dad assured her, "I've turned the page. You can open your eyes now." Then he would 'accidentally' let the wolf page fall open and Izzy would scream.

Occasionally, my stories became confused with real life. After our fifth birthday party, a mother of one of our friends asked me if her daughter had left her gloves behind. "They were pink and white, a present from her granny," she said.

I had never seen the gloves, but the woman looked so concerned, I was anxious to help. "Pink woolly ones with a pretty white pattern?" I guessed.

"Yes! That's right," said the relieved mother, "you've found them, then?"

"I think so," I said, hoping it might be true. "Yes – in fact, I remember! They went up the Hoover, but Mummy rescued them and I expect she's washed them by now. Don't worry."

The mother called round to pick them up, repeating my far-fetched tale. Mum had to apologise. "It was just one of Catherine's stories, I'm afraid. We don't have your daughter's gloves."

In those days, most children's birthday parties followed the same formula. Dressed in party clothes, we arrived at our friend's house, handed him or her a small gift and played games such as musical chairs (or cushions, bumps or statues), blind man's bluff, stick the tail on the donkey, pass the parcel, squeak piggy squeak, until it was time to eat. One of our favourites was the memory game. Twenty small objects were laid out on a tray and shown to us. We had two minutes to memorise them. The tray was taken away and we had to write down all the things we could remember. Izzy was especially good at this. Once, an inspired mother tried a 'guess the smell' game. Blindfolded, we were taken into the kitchen one by one and asked to identify various aromas that were wafted under our noses – onion, banana, pear, mint, lavender, geranium, boot polish and so on. Sometimes one of the dads would try out a few unconvincing magic tricks that made us laugh rather than gasp in wonder, but there were no hired entertainers – the breed had not yet evolved. Tea consisted of crustless sandwiches cut into dainty triangles with paper flags on cocktail sticks advertising their fillings. There were Twiglets, crisps, chocolate fingers, marshmallows, iced gem biscuits, and always jelly, ice-cream and blancmange, which was usually pink and often in the shape of a rabbit. When we had eaten our fill, the curtains were drawn, the lights switched off and the birthday cake, with an appropriate number of blazing candles, borne in and placed in front of the birthday child. We sang *Happy Birthday*, which settled into an uncomfortable key after the second bar, Izzy and I usually the only ones to reach the octave leap in the third phrase. The song finished with an enthusiastic round of applause, and then there was an expectant hush. We all took a deep breath and held it while the child whose birthday it was attempted to blow out every candle in one go. This was important, or his or her wish might not come true. Then, with eyes squeezed shut, the birthday child made a secret wish. As we wondered what our friend was wishing for, we quietly exhaled and made up our own wishes in our minds.

Our birthday parties were a little different. First of all, Mum typed the invitations: she wasn't going to spend good money buying printed ones. She encouraged parents not to bring us presents as there were two of us – they mustn't go wasting money. Mum played the piano for the musical games – bits of Mozart, Burgmüller, *The Golliwog's Cakewalk*, Chopin – we ought to have appreciated it, but it was not the norm. Our friends' parents played pop songs or tunes from children's shows on a gramophone. Our pass the parcel was wrapped in newspaper without a proper present at the end – sometimes only a ha'penny pink and yellow fruit-salad chew. We did not play stick the tail on the donkey or any of the good games, it seemed. Our sandwiches came in squares with crusts on and our birthday cake was one of Granny's homemade chocolate ones. There were no shop-bought biscuits – just scones, pancakes and jam tarts. Mum kept a watchful eye on our guests as they helped themselves to sandwiches and cocktail sausages.

"That's enough, Raymond. Eat what you have on your plate first. Jennifer! Your sandwich is half-eaten. What do you mean, you don't like the crusts? Well you're not having another until you've finished that one. We don't waste food in *this* house."

Sooner or later, a sandwich, sausage or jam tart fell to the floor. Mum bent down to retrieve it and placed it back on the child's plate.

"I can't eat it now it's been on the floor."

"Why ever not?"

"It's dirty."

"Oh don't be so ridiculous. The floor's not dirty."

"Mummy says I shouldn't eat things that have been on the ground," says the child, dangerously close to tears.

"Catherine, Christopher, you eat it then, or I will. I'm not letting good food go to waste."

"Eh? What's that?" asks Granny, alerted by the word 'waste'. "Och, what nonsense, there's nought wrong with a bit o' good clean dirt. Here, pass it to me."

Then there was Dad. Inevitably, he would burst into the living room pretending to be some character or other and address us in strange voices. Oh no, we groaned inwardly. We were on tenterhooks as he dramatised and told bad jokes, anxious that he was embarrassing or alarming our guests, afraid that he would get tetchy if the children did not respond as he wanted. Plus there was always the danger of him flaring up angrily and leaving the room. Sometimes that was exactly what happened.

Mum ticked our friends off for calling her 'Auntie'. "I'm not your auntie, my name's Elizabeth." The children were nonplussed. Every mum who wasn't your own was 'Auntie' when you went to tea or birthday parties. Mum told us it was ridiculous to call a friend's mother and father 'auntie' and 'uncle' when they weren't. We should call them by their proper names, she insisted, which was difficult, as we did not know what they were. We were also instructed not to say 'Thank you for having us'. For some reason, Mum and Dad thought it vulgar.

"You haven't been *had*," said Mum.

"Then what do we say? Everyone says thank you for having me. It's polite." They laughed in a way that excluded us and shook their heads.

"You could say 'It's been very pleasant to meet you'," Dad suggested, "or 'Thank you for inviting me' or 'We enjoyed the party very much' – any number of phrases come to mind, but not 'Thank you for having me'. The sentence is incorrect and meaningless."

When it was time for our friends to leave, we winced when we heard one of them utter the dreaded phrase, and silently beseeched our parents not to take them to task about it. In an attempt to avoid the awkwardness, we told our friends *not* to say, "Thank you for having me". But then their mum or dad would arrive to pick them up and give them a nudge: "What do you say to Auntie Elizabeth, Susan?" they would prompt, unwittingly delivering a double faux pas.

If any further proof of our non-conformity was required, Mum did not hand each child a slice of birthday cake wrapped in a paper serviette as they left. "They should have taken a piece when it was offered to them. I'm not giving away Granny's good chocolate cake if I think it will end up in someone's dustbin. We'll eat it ourselves."

12
FOREST SCHOOL CAMPS

To provide each child with the opportunities to meet the challenges which his forebears met is, in our view, the best way of equipping him with the skills and the enterprise to meet the challenges of the future.

extract from the Forest School Camps programme of 1970

Dad took his four weeks paid holiday each year to coincide with the school breaks. He, Mum and we children, from our earliest years, went on holiday together, leaving Granny to look after the cats. Apart from one trip to Cornwall and a couple of visits to Mum's brother and family, we always holidayed in Norfolk. John and Margaret Comer, friends that Mum and Dad had met through their Communist Party connections, lived partly in Woodford, where their daughters went to school, and the rest of the time at Lenwade in Norfolk.

John Comer owned Walcis Farm in Lenwade, as well as Wensum house, where he and his family lived, and two cottages. On several occasions, Mum rented one of his cottages for our holidays. She began to wonder if it might be possible to buy a cottage herself. Dad made it clear that he had no intention of contributing any of his money, but Mum was excited by the idea. It was John Comer who encouraged her to go ahead and look. Property in Norfolk was cheap at the time – there was no demand for holiday homes then, and Norfolk was not the tourist destination that it later became.

John and Margaret Comer's daughter, Helen, was one of Mum's piano pupils. After the summer holidays, Helen would come to her lessons talking excitedly about tents, campfires, country dancing, Elves and Woodlings. Intrigued, Mum asked Helen's parents to tell her more, and that is how she found out about Forest School Camps. The camps were (and still are) run for boys and girls aged six-and-a-half to seventeen and held during school holidays at various sites around Britain. Two of the sites were in Norfolk – one was at John Comer's Walcis Farm and the other at Whitwell. By the summer of 1962, Izzy and I would be exactly six-and-a-half. Mum liked the sound of FSC, its emphasis on equality and its socialist ethos. She thought we would enjoy the experience of camping and it would be an ideal time for her to go cottage hunting.

FSC was an important element in our lives. Essentially, it is the same today as it was when Izzy and I were six. The original Forest School was situated in the New Forest, set up in the 1930s by teachers and parents who wished to educate their children in a more progressive and natural environment than was to be found in mainstream education. It was the first school of its kind, but the families were not able to continue their pioneering work during the Second World War.

I quote the following from the 2009 programme:

> Forest School, which ran in the 1930s, drew its philosophy from progressive educators, from the Woodcraft movements and the Native Americans, from Quakers and others. Special importance was attached to the experience of boys and girls, children and adults, learning to work and play together close to nature.
>
> Forest School Camps began in 1947 when former pupils and staff came together, anxious to develop and pass on the ways and values of Forest School, which by then had closed. Our approach to education is about discovering for oneself how to do something, rather than being told in the abstract. Children and staff find themselves in situations that foster this; the outdoors demands and encourages learning. We remove unnecessary authority and, with due regard for safety and legality, encourage children to take responsibility and to reach their own decisions on small and not-so-small issues, individually or as members of a group. At camp we aim to teach ourselves how to live with independence and responsibility; concern and care for ourselves, other people and the environment; resourcefulness and self-confidence; tolerance and respect. FSC is determined that all people be treated equally regardless of age, gender, sexual orientation, ethnic origin, religion or disability. These are high ideals – we don't always succeed. A Native American belief is that you will only be in touch with nature if you "sit and sleep on the earth". This feeling for the wholeness of life on the planet is expressed in some of our rituals and the names we give things at camp.

Every Forest School Camp is built from scratch. An ideal site is one near woods and rivers that will provide a source of fuel for fires and water for drinking, cooking and washing. Not every site is perfect. Sometimes timber has to be bought or drinking water supplied by hose. A small group turn up in advance to get the site ready. A kitchen is prepared; turf cut out for a fireplace; pits dug for disposal of waste; large tents erected for food storage, tools, shelter and first aid. Latrines, or lats, are dug and hessian screens put up around the trenches to provide some privacy. A dining circle is formed with logs and a campfire site decided upon. Food supplies are ordered by the caterer, delivered from local shops and arranged in the kitchen tent. The size of a camp varies. In the early days they were small, but now there may be as many as 130 children and staff. All members of staff are volunteers. The children camp in age groups, each group having a separate site away from the communal area. The youngest group of six- and seven-year-olds are called Elves. Next are Woodlings (aged eight to ten), then Trailseekers (eleven to twelve), Trackers (thirteen to fourteen), and the oldest are Pathfinders (fifteen to seventeen). Nowadays there are also Pixies – babies, toddlers and under-sixes who camp with their parents; and Waywardens – adults with learning difficulties. Izzy staffs this group year after year.

Food is cooked over an open fire. Sturdy iron grids support ten-gallon dixies, frying pans the diameter of dustbin lids and a double-boiler the size of a water-butt. The camp is divided across the board into five 'clans'. Each clan takes its turn in the kitchen, preparing, cooking, serving and clearing up the meals for the whole camp. Elves only get to peel potatoes, butter bread, or pour milk onto bowls of porridge, while the Trackers and Pathfinders cook over the fire, swing axes and saw logs in the woodpile. The dining circle is the meeting place for the 'Lodge', the collective name for the camp. We meet there for morning rally – a time when each group has a chance to report what they have been doing and the day's activities are outlined and discussed.

Two nights before the end of camp an evening's entertainment is staged – an event known as 'Merrymoot'. Each group has to come up with sketches, jokes or songs and perform their items to the rest of the camp. It is the Pathfinders' job to create the theatre. Some sets are amazingly inventive; others are more obviously extended lat screens. The previous day-and-a-half is spent trying to come up with ideas, writing scripts, rehearsing, assembling props and costumes. There is a buzz about the place. Birthday tea precedes Merrymoot. A giant cake celebrating children's birthdays at camp and another year of FSC is carried into the middle of the dining circle, cut and distributed. As soon as everyone has had a slice, there is a rush back to group sites to don costumes. The camp assembles, the fire is lit, a few songs sung by way of an overture, and the cabaret begins. The Elves' contribution is usually the best. Woodlings get into lavatorial humour, Trailseekers throw water, Trackers try to be clever and Pathfinders get too quasi-intellectual for comprehension. The staff group has to come up with a finale, which the children have all been waiting for. Then the show is over. On the last full day, clearing-up begins. Dixies and mess tins are scoured, lats filled, group fires re-turfed and tools returned to the store tent.

The final evening is Lodge Common Council, which is a serious event. A ceremonial fire is laid. Before it is lit, the camp-chief sprinkles it with ashes saved from last year's fire to symbolise renewal and continuity. (I have often wondered if they are really last year's ashes or just a jarful from the previous night's embers.) Burning torches are carried from the kitchen to light the Lodge fire. All those who have sat too close soon move away as the flames leap into life. When we were young, it was on this night that children received achievement awards. Later it became a forum to discuss feelings about the camp, to make suggestions, praise achievements and say farewell. There are songs and tributes, tears and hugs; then we stand and link hands in a full circle. At this point, our favourite Camp Chief, Leslie Holden, would always say, "Our time here has ended but our circle will go on." After a few moments' silence, somebody might start to sing softly:

> It's time for man to go home,
> It's time for man to go home,
> It's time for man and it's time for beast,
> It's time for man to go home.

When we arrived at our first camp, the Elf leader, Greta, wasted no time in introducing us to the lat. She took us behind the screen of hessian to explain how the lat worked, demonstrating how to cover up whatever you had produced with earth. She lifted a tin to reveal a toilet roll suspended on a stick. Outside the lat was a bucket full of water, reeking of bleach with dead flies floating on the surface. Were we supposed to dip our hands in it? Everyone had to be called by his or her first names, which then was as disconcerting as calling our Mummy 'Elizabeth'. Izzy and I shared a tent, an ex-Army bivvy that was dark inside and smelled of mildew.

We queued up for our meals and held our plates out to be served. On several occasions I lost the whole meal before I made it to the dining circle. Sometimes the plate became too hot to hold or I didn't realise I was carrying it at a tilt and the contents slipped off the plate onto the ground. We soon became aware of the rule that the dining circle must be walked around, not across: if someone started to cross the circle accidentally, we all shouted 'tablecloth' to remind them of the rule. It was scandalous if anyone ran into the circle deliberately. We liked being 'on clan', because we could sit around the kitchen fire and serve the food at meal times. If we were lucky, we could ring the gong for teatime.

In those days there were tent inspections after breakfast, when everything had to be pulled out on the groundsheet, sleeping bags aired and items arranged neatly. Our waterproofs were kept handily at the entrance to the tent and our wellington boots upended on two sticks outside. At about ten o'clock, the gong sounded for rally and we gathered around the dining circle. Each group would give a short report about their activities of the day before. As I was the only Elf ever willing to volunteer, it was usually I who spoke. Inside I felt nervous and self-conscious, but I pretended not to be. Already I was convincingly confident. At the end of the meeting the post was given out. We listened for our names to be called, delighted when they were, disappointed when they were not.

Our favourite activity was country dancing. We changed into our skirts and skipped down to the field in readiness. With music billowing from a tape recorder and a member of staff calling the steps, we learnt the routines for *Pat-a-cake Polka*, *The Dashing White Sergeant*, *Strip the Willow*, *Circassian Circle*, and my favourite, *Cumberland Square Eight*. One part of the dance involves two couples meeting in the middle, the men joining arms and whirling the girls around in the air, skirts flapping and feet flying. We soon knew to pick one of the Pathfinders or a member of staff for a partner to get extra high swings. At last I had found a type of dancing that I could do – no finesse required, just the ability to skip and keep in time.

In the evenings we sang songs around the campfire, mesmerised by the flames, eyes streaming when the smoke blew in our direction. When it was bedtime, the rest of the camp sang a song to us:

Goodnight Elves, goodnight Elves,
Goodnight Elves, it's time to go to bed.
Merrily you roll along, roll along, roll along,
Merrily you roll along, on your way to bed.

Then we made our way to the kitchen for a mug of cocoa and a biscuit, washed our hands and faces, brushed our teeth, got into our pyjamas and wriggled into our sleeping bags. I couldn't wait to be eight-and-a-half when I would be able to hear the goodnight song for Woodlings. It was such a disappointment to discover that the Woodling song was exactly the same as the Elf song. All they did was substitute the word 'Elves' with 'Woodlings'. The staff kissed us goodnight, held our hands, read us stories and listened to ours.

We enjoyed camp and hardly suffered from homesickness. Mum and Granny told us that this was because we came from a secure and happy home and were well-adjusted children. Homesickness only affects those who come from disturbed backgrounds, they said.

The next year, we were enrolled at Whitwell camp in Norfolk. Before going, Mum decided that we should have our hair cut. We had come home from our first camp with our hair so matted and tangled, it had taken hours of tugging and yelling to comb out the knots. Un-plaited, it was so long we could sit on it. Izzy and I were delighted by the idea of short hair, but Dad was not.

"I don't want them to have their hair cut," he said grumpily.

"But Derek, the staff don't have time to comb and plait their hair every day, and you remember what a mess it got into last year."

"Why do they have to go camping at all? I don't like them to be away for so long."

"They enjoy themselves and it's good experience."

"Oh, but their lovely hair," he cried. "Must you really cut it?"

"They want to have it cut, don't you, girls?"

We nodded eagerly. "Come here then," said Mum, scissors at the ready.

"Oh, no, no," Dad howled, hopping from foot to foot, reaching out distractedly to touch our heads.

"Derek, I can't understand why you're so against it. It's only hair. It will grow again." She took hold of one of Izzy's plaits. Dad sobbed pitifully. Chop, chop. Oh, oh. Then the second plait was off. Dad picked them up, grief-stricken, while Mum, trying to ignore his anguish, brushed out the remaining stubs and trimmed the ends neatly. Izzy skipped off to look in the mirror while Dad whimpered as I lined up for the guillotine.

"Oh for heaven's sake Derek," said Mum exasperatedly. My two plaits were quickly severed. Dad lifted them tenderly, looking at the four blonde lengths, still bound at the ends with elastic bands, as if they were dead and he had just witnessed their murder. He grieved for days, maybe longer.

Izzy and I enjoyed camp as much, if not more, the second time. From then on, we camped with FSC every year, until we too became Pathfinders, and later staff. Perhaps what changed the most over the next decade of FSC was the gradual disappearance of 'Tests and Trials'. These were designed to teach children camping and woodcraft skills. Every day was programmed to include some woodcraft activities. Elves were considered too young, but Woodlings were encouraged to pass four basic tests – to pitch a tent, make a wooden tent peg, light a fire, and, the one that was so difficult, to remain silent for an hour (I feel sure this was thought up to keep Woodlings quiet). Trials were more demanding – map reading and orienteering; whittling with a penknife; naming trees and flowers; keeping silent for twenty-four hours; going off unaccompanied to light a fire and cook a meal. I remember doing this last trial myself when I was an eight-year-old Woodling. I set off at about eleven o'clock carrying my rucksack packed with provisions, and stopped in the woods by a stream. After many failed attempts, I managed to get my fire going, peeled my potato, put it in my billycan of water and waited for it to boil. Apart from pangs of hunger, I was happily absorbed in my own little world, until a member of staff broke the spell. Out of breath and cross he said, "So there you are! What have you been doing? It's nearly dark; you should have been back hours ago."

"I'm cooking my lunch," I replied defensively.

"What – all day? Come on; clear up quickly. It's time for campfire."

"But I haven't eaten it yet," I cried.

"Why ever not?"

"It's not ready." He looked at the large potato in my billycan.

"Why didn't you cut it into pieces?"

"I didn't know," I wept.

He simmered down, found my fork and prodded the potato.

"You know, I think this is cooked to perfection," he said, smiling. "Why don't you sit over there and eat it while I douse the fire."

It was the best potato I had ever tasted, not too soft, not too hard, delicately flavoured with ash. "Would you like some?" I asked. He declined.

If all the Trials were successfully accomplished, the child was dubbed a 'Deft Woodling' and presented with something that resembled a curtain tassel. As an Elf, I thought this very strange. Why would a Woodling wish to be deaf? Perplexed, I asked Izzy.

"Deft, D-E-F-T, not deaf, you daftie," she informed me, but as I didn't know what deft meant, I was none the wiser.

Trailseeker, Tracker and Pathfinder Tests and Trials went up in degrees of difficulty. Some were extremely challenging – real endurance tests that required levels of camping and survival skills that Pathfinders of today would find hard to believe – not only what they entailed, but that any Pathfinder would bother to attempt them. By the mid 1970s, despite attempts by older campers to keep what they saw as the traditions of FSC alive, Tests and Trials had gone. Children no longer wished to take them and it wasn't FSC policy to force them to do so. Woodcraft and camping proficiency was instead picked up by demonstration, suggestion and experiment.

Over the years we learnt the songs of Woody Guthrie, Ewan MacColl, Pete Seeger, Alan Lomax and other social activists – in their words, "Hard hitting songs for hard-hit people". To begin with, we didn't have a clue what the words meant. They were just songs with good tunes, often led by excellent singers and guitarists, but we gradually absorbed and began to understand something of 'man's inhumanity to man', learning of the heroic martyrs, humanitarians and civil rights campaigners who tried to bring about change.

It was at FSC where we first heard the word 'Hiroshima'. There are several occasions I remember when the whole camp gathered to mourn the day that the first atom bomb was dropped. We stood in silence around the campfire holding candles, branches and hands. After a few minutes, an older child or member of staff spoke a few words to inform those younger ones, who might not yet know, what was done to Hiroshima on August 6th 1945 and to Nagasaki three days later. Sometimes a poem was read or a muted song sung, and then we would be silent again before dispersing quietly in small groups back to our sites – for how can one speak of the unspeakable?

13
SUNFLOWERS

No sunflower is bent on making event
Of its yellow centre

Jean Lipkin

One morning before school, Izzy was in the music room practising her violin with Mum, when she burst into tears. "What ever is the matter?" Mum asked. Izzy shook her head, unable to explain why she was so distressed. Now she can put it into words: "It was the whole atmosphere in the house that overwhelmed me – the rows between Dad and Granny, Mum's deep unhappiness, the pervasive despair and foreboding that hung like a black cloud over our lives."

Granny kept her stockpot of antagonism simmering on the back burner while Dad percolated his grounds of resentment. Mum tried her best to placate him. What could she do to make him happy?

"Well, for a start you could wear some make-up."

"Oh, Derek, what would I want to wear make-up for?"

"For me! All wives wear make-up for their husbands."

I watched Mum joylessly and inexpertly apply blue shadow to her sad eyes and pink lipstick to her downturned mouth in a futile attempt to please him.

"And here's another thing; why don't you phone me at work?"

"Well, I'm busy all day, Derek. It's not something I'd think to do."

"My colleagues' wives phone every day to see how their husbands are. How do you think that makes me feel? Eh?"

"Well, alright, I'll try to find the time." So Mum pretended and Dad knew it wasn't real.

Mum and Dad never went out together, even with Granny there as a full-time babysitter. Looking back, I am struck by the realisation that I didn't ever hear Dad say Mum's name. Mum often said "Derek", but Dad managed to exclude "Elizabeth" from every conversation, if one could call the stilted exchanges they had conversation. It was a peculiar cruelty; by avoiding her name, he refused to acknowledge her.

It is very hard for a child to behave unnaturally and even harder when receiving conflicting and confusing signals, but we too did our best to please Dad, tried to anticipate his moods, acted out the roles of dutiful children – anything to make him happy. For instance, we thought he would be glad if we went to meet him at South Woodford station on his way back from the office. For a while, we tore ourselves away from children's television and waited by the ticket barrier from five-thirty each evening. He was pleased to see us, but it wasn't much fun. Often we waited for half an hour before his train came in and were soon bored. Izzy and Chris dropped out of the contrived ritual, and after another week or so, feeling guilty, I also gave up waiting for him. All we had done was to make matters worse.

"You never come to meet me from work these days," he complained.

Sometimes he sent me out to buy him twenty Players, but he wasn't allowed to smoke cigarettes in the house. He used to smoke a pipe in the evenings, until Granny banned that too. The upstairs lavatory turned into his smoking room and reeked of tobacco.

Father's Day, Mother's Day and Valentine's Day were considered to be "stuff and nonsense, manufactured by commercialism". As for weddings: "a dreadful waste of money; better used to put a deposit down on a first home," said Granny. "Better not to get married at all," added Mum. Our birthdays were acknowledged, but the adults' birthdays came and went without notice or comment. Surely though, Dad would be pleased if we made him a birthday card? We presented our crayoned offerings to him. "You've made me a birthday card? Well, what a surprise. Thank you, thank you, my dear children. How about a birthday kiss for your old Papa?" We hadn't bargained for that. He jutted his chin towards us and we placed a peck on his bristly cheek while he patted our backs and said, "There now. Oh, what a lucky father I am." He said no more. We stood beside him in awkward silence.

"Happy birthday, Dad," I said, the enthusiasm in my voice not sounding at all as it should.

"Happy birthday," said Izzy and Chris uncomfortably. We turned and left the room, feeling that we had somehow got it all wrong.

When I was ill, a bed was made up for me on the couch in the living room. The wireless was switched on and I listened to music while my eyes wandered over the wallpaper. Its pattern was created with brush strokes in blues, greys, browns and black with a little touch of ochre and jade. It depicted a scene in a Chinese paddy field – small oriental people with black pigtails, lampshade hats, blue tunics and black trousers, all occupied in various tasks. There was a figure that carried buckets suspended from a yoke across the shoulders, one who filled a basket, some bending over in the fields, others squatting or walking, and children standing on an arched bridge waving. It was a picture of active harmony, imprecisely painted – an artist's impression of some foreign land. It might not have been China at all; perhaps it was only an abstract design, but it seemed to me that all over the wall the same happy scene repeated; children waving to other children, a multitude carrying baskets of rice to their homes.

On one occasion, when my skin felt hot and prickly and my ribs ached from coughing, I heard Mum and Granny talking. I saw that there were several cumbersome wallpaper sample books open on the table.

"What do you think, Mammy?"

"Aye, that one's nice – and this too. Och, it's awful hard to choose."

"Well, I'll mark these," said Mum, placing strips of torn paper between the pages, "and see what Derek thinks."

"Huh, what's it to do with him? He'll not be paying for it."

"We haven't discussed that yet, Mammy, and I'd like to have his opinion."

"Aye, well whatever you think," she said, not meaning that at all.

The little Chinese families were going to be scraped away. I felt sad about that. I looked at them intently, determined to remember the pattern forever.

"Derek?" Mum called cheerily, when he came home from work, "Come and look at these wallpaper samples and tell me which one you would choose." He met her smile with a scowl. "The wallpaper we have now seems fine to me."

"Oh Derek, we have to redecorate. This paper's been up since we moved here!" Her tone was playful. What fun this is – we can choose together! What a cosy, intimate thing to do!

"Come and see what we've picked out so far," she said, in a perky voice.

"Oh, very well," Dad replied irritably. He moved stiffly towards the table, his jaw clamped. What was the matter with him? Why did Mum pretend not to notice?

"See, dear? I was considering this one, perhaps – or maybe this?"

He barely glanced at them. "Oh, I don't know," he said, anger spiking his words.

I thought; Mum, just leave it, will you? Dad's cross, can't you tell?

She ploughed on. "I'm sure you're good at imagining what would suit a big room; something abstract maybe – or more traditional? What do you think?"

He refused to cooperate, reminding me of an obstinate child. Then suddenly, the book flopped open on a page of big sunflowers.

"There," he said, "that one."

Dad! The book just fell there accidentally. You can't possibly choose that!

"This one?" asked Mum, nonplussed. "Oh. Well it's not one I'd picked out, but if you think so? Derek? There are others here you haven't... seen... yet..." Her voice trailed miserably away as he left the room.

"Well," she said brightly, snapping efficiency back into place, "time for you two to be having your bath. Isabel? Go and turn on the taps. Christopher? You can start getting undressed." She walked over to me and put her hand on my brow. "How are you feeling now?"

The three of us often went out to feed the ducks. Chris and I munched pieces of stale bread as we meandered up the road. "Don't eat so much – we won't have any left for the ducks," Izzy complained. We crossed the High Road, weaved through the chestnut trees on the green and started to walk along The Drive, a wide road that boasted the grandest houses in the neighbourhood. Each was detached, well separated from its neighbours, with large front gardens and extensive grounds to the rear, which we glimpsed through side gates and driveways. One of our games was to choose the house we were going to live in when we grew up. I had no doubt which was my favourite. Before reaching it, we passed its splendid coach-house with wide wooden doors, which would once have opened for horse drawn carriages to enter and depart. The house itself was Victorian, with ornate soft red brickwork, mock-Tudor timbers and gabled windows. One corner of the house was built in an octagonal shape, the rooms within it on the ground and first floors having five windows, making up five sides of the octagon. Above was an eight-sided turret with a weather vane at its tip. It looked a bit like a castle, which suggested all sorts of fairytale scenarios to me: an imprisoned princess waiting for a brave knight to come to her rescue and carry her away on his white stallion; Rapunzel tossing her long tresses out of the window; Sleeping Beauty pricking her finger on a spinning wheel. I liked to imagine how it would feel to be inside looking out of the upstairs windows. Chris often chose the biggest house in the road, which had a rather off-putting crucifix built into the brickwork. Apparently, it belonged to a bishop and within its walls was a chapel. We spooked one another with tales of séances, sacrifices and black magic and decided it would be too scary a place to live. Izzy usually chose a house at the other end of the road, which was my second favourite. Having walked the length of The Drive, we turned back into the High Road, then right at the Eagle pub towards the lake.

The Eagle Pond is a man-made lake in Epping Forest, its northern side bordering Snaresbrook Road, the water lapping right up to the pavement. We found our favourite spot under the weeping willow tree where we could stand near to the edge of the water and tempt the birds with our stale titbits. Ducks and greedy geese arrived first, jostling for prime position, but we waited for the beautiful swans to glide over unhurriedly, refusing to compromise their dignity by rushing forwards too eagerly. Chris told us that swans are unusual in that they mate for life. It was nice to think of those serene creatures falling in love forever.

"They're monogamous, then," said Izzy – she knew lots of big words.

Situated on the opposite side of the lake is an elaborate stately home with private gardens inclining downwards to the waterside. It was built in 1843 as an Infant Orphan Asylum. The romantic aspect viewed across 'Swan Lake' belies the severe Dickensian regime that governed the displaced children. When the orphanage was closed in the sixties, it became the Royal Wanstead School for some years before being revamped into what we know today as Snaresbrook Crown Courts.

By the west side of the lake, within Epping Forest, there once stood a carving of a larger-than-life-sized swan, painted white. A poor male swan fell in love with the wooden impostor and courted her tenderly. He built his nest by her side and brought her food to eat. Her rejection of his offerings compelled him to search for tastier morsels, but nothing he found would tempt her. Year after year he wooed his beloved, unconcerned that she refused to swim on the water with the other swans. Perhaps it was her rigid disdain, her haughty indifference, her self-centred vanity that he worshipped, or maybe it was the curve of her neck, her unruffled feathers and the constancy of her expression. Without doubt, he loved her, rested happily by her side, protected and cared for her as if it were his undivided devotion that kept her rooted to the spot.

Our lovesick swan became known as Siegfried, the name of the Prince in the story of *Swan Lake*. I wonder, though, who was his wooden sweetheart – Princess Odette, the spellbound swan-maiden, or Odile, the bewitched duplicitous daughter of the evil sorcerer, Baron Rothbart? Swan Siegfried's obsession with his idol grew stronger. He was constant and faithful to the immovable love of his life; but as the years went by, she started to disintegrate. Her body rotted and her neck fell sideways. The forestry commission decided to remove the decomposing effigy to avoid a possible accident. Siegfried was distraught. He searched for her everywhere and flew distractedly around the lake honking pitifully. He stopped eating; his plumage lost its sheen; he became thin, bedraggled and hopeless. The foresters realised his misery and arranged for a new carved swan to be placed on the same spot. But Siegfried knew at once that this was not his own true love and swam away to die grief-stricken, alone and broken-hearted.

14
WORTLEY

The WMA is an association of various musical organisations, choirs and individuals who believe that music has a bearing on social life and that it can be one of the means of attaining a brighter and better society.

statement from the WMA membership leaflet of 2006

Dr. Alan Bush (1900-1995) founded The Workers' Music Association in 1936. He became its president in 1941 and remained so for the rest of his life. The music of Alan Bush was the voice of the British Labour movement from the general strike of 1926 through the Hunger Marches in the depression of the 1930s. He joined the Communist Party in 1935, convinced that Communism was the only way forward for society and a better world.

His operas are unashamedly political: *Wat Tyler* stages the Peasants' Revolt of 1381 when one hundred thousand peasants marched to London, led by Wat Tyler and John Ball, to demand that the King to put an end to feudalism. Wat and John were murdered, but their martyrdom marked the beginning of the end of feudalism; *Men of Blackmoor* is about the struggle of the Northumbrian miners of the early nineteenth century; *The Sugar Reapers*, set in 1953, tells of the African and Indian sugar workers of Guyana trying to overcome the oppression of the British; *Joe Hill – The Man Who Never Died* is about the life and death of the American proletarian revolutionary. Alan's songs call for workers to unite; an end to war; freedom, equality and peace. Having sung his compositions myself in the WMA chorus, they do indeed succeed in rousing courage and optimism. Aubrey Bowman, late president of the WMA wrote:

> The deep humanity with which Alan's music is imbued was integral also to his personality. He was a person equally kind, interested in and sympathetic to whomever he came in contact with, no matter from which walk of life.

Alan was a fine person and I was privileged to work with him, giving first performances of some of his compositions, including in 1979 a rhapsody for cello and piano (he playing the piano) called *Pro Pace et Felicitate Generis Humani* (For the Peace and Happiness of Mankind).

Pure Communism is a high ideal, which I do not believe human society will ever be capable of realising. In simple terms, the theory is that a civilisation works together for the greater good, sharing the fruits of its labour equally amongst a society where all people work to the best of their ability and the extent of their capacity. There is no exploitation, discrimination, unemployment or profiteering. All citizens benefit from collective cooperation; the sick, old and young are looked after, talents nurtured, education, healthcare and transport freely provided. Why should there be war, or crime, or even currency, when in this Utopia there is no conflict and everyone has what he or she needs?

The flaw is human nature: there has never been a true Communist society. The megalomaniac leaders of 'communist' countries utterly corrupted communist ideals. In my opinion, the major mistake that British Communist Party members (like Mum and Dad) made was to believe that the Communist governments of the Eastern Bloc were models of working communism. My parents refused to consider any negative reports, believing all exposés to be Western propaganda. The USSR and her minions were irreproachable. It took a very long time for Mum to accept that the 'communist' regimes were dictatorships of the worst order. Without safety nets or moderation, it seems that human greed and its quest for power, riches and supremacy knows no bounds. Winwood Reade, the nineteenth-century novelist and explorer, writes in his book *The Martyrdom of Man*:

> The human race is not placed between the good and the bad, but between the bad and the worse.

He goes on to say:

> There is nothing so certain as the natural inequality of man… as long as men continue unequal in patience, industry, talent and sobriety, so long there will be rich men and poor men – men who roll in their carriages and men who die in the streets. If all the property of this country were divided, things would soon return to their actual condition, unless some scheme could also be devised for changing human nature; and as for the system of the Commune, which makes it impossible for man to rise or to fall, it is merely the old caste system revived.

– and doesn't one need motivation to work, a certain friction to think, stimulation to create, some recognition of achievement, a goal to strive for? If our individual uniqueness ceased to matter, our differing thoughts had no platform for political discussion, would it not be a dull, barren world in which to live? If our lives were too comfortable, our intellect too complacent, would humankind perhaps fall asleep? Communist ideals are not bad; in principle, they are noble; unfortunately, they are unrealistic.

Mum met Alan Bush in 1951 when they were both involved in an extraordinary experience on their way to a youth festival in East Berlin. Their ordeal, which they shared with three hundred others, is described in a published pamphlet titled *The Innsbruck Story*. Here are the opening paragraphs:

> The World Youth Festival, which opened in Berlin on August 5th 1951, was the third of its kind since the end of the war. It was organised by the World Federation of Democratic Youth and the International Union of Students, two bodies set up to unite youth and students all over the world in their common desire for a peaceful future in which to build their countries anew after the destruction of war.
>
> This is the story of three hundred young British people who set out on that first

> day in August for a World Festival of peace and friendship in Berlin. It is the story of the obstacles placed in their way, of subtle diplomacy and brute force, and of how they overcame all these obstacles and finally arrived in Berlin. Not least it tells something of the courage and self-sacrifice of those many people in Austria who made this possible.

Briefly, the US military would not allow the party to travel through the American zone of Austria to get to Berlin. There was no apparent legal right to refuse the bearers of British passports entry, but the US military decided, without evidence or grounds, that a group of youths travelling to a festival of peace must be 'Commies' and instructed their troops to prevent the party from proceeding. There *were* one or two Communists in the group – Alan Bush being one – but most were young people of differing or no political persuasions who wanted to celebrate peace at a World Youth Festival. The British Consul in Innsbruck refused to help, telling them to go home – an order that bore no relation to the words in their British Passports: "to allow the bearer to pass freely without let or hindrance, and to afford him every assistance and protection of which he may stand in need."

On principle, the group refused to turn back. They were held at gunpoint by US soldiers at Innsbruck station, brutally treated, denied food, water and lavatories. It was an experience that turned Mum against the politics of the USA and also prejudiced her against Americans. She always saw them as mean, gum-chewing, brutes. Before setting off to Berlin, she was not a member of any political party. She wrote: "I went as a pianist, having won a scholarship to compete in the International Cultural Competitions which were to be held at the Festival. I was naturally interested to see for myself what life was like in East Berlin, but I was particularly looking forward to the opportunity of playing in the British concerts at the Festival and of meeting and competing with other pianists with whom I would normally have no chance of coming in contact. I arrived too late to take part. The events in Austria were my political baptism – being on the wrong side of an American bayonet really concentrates the mind!" Soon after her return to Britain, she joined the Communist Party.

In 1951, Wortley Hall, a derelict stately home in Yorkshire, was bought by the Trade Union, Labour and Co-operative movements and voluntarily repaired and restored by the workers of the surrounding area. The cost of refurbishment of individual reception rooms was paid for by Trades Unions and the rooms then named after those Unions. Bedrooms were grouped into areas identified by past members of socialist political groups – Keir Hardy, Robert Owen, Tom Mann, Abe Moffatt, Vin William and George Lansbury. The 'Home of the Labour Movement' was opened: for sixty years it has been hosting residential courses, conferences and international delegations from all over the world.

The Workers' Music Association ran a music school at Wortley Hall for a week every summer and Mum decided that we should all go. When we went for the first time in 1963, the accommodation was still rather basic, with dormitory-style bedrooms of up to eight beds. Izzy and I were seven-and-a-half. We had only been playing for a year, but as the school claimed to offer music making to people of any standard or age, Mum thought it was worth trying. She would play her cello, Dad could join the folk music course – country dancing and Morris dancing were on the agenda, which he enjoyed – and Chris – well, he was five years old and hadn't begun to learn an instrument yet, but Wortley Hall was set in twenty-six acres and there would be plenty of people to keep an eye on him. The Hall itself was a children's paradise, with a network of corridors, staircases, dark passages, attics, cupboards and secret doors.

The garden contained secrets too – hidey-holes in walls, large bushes with spaces in their middles where nobody would find you. There was a lake, a bowling green, woods, spinneys, formal gardens and statues. We had the run of the whole place. While Izzy played her violin and I played my cello, Chris explored the grounds and collected beetles and insects in tins and boxes, which he brought back at mealtimes to show to anyone willing to look.

One afternoon, we all went for a walk through the woods. The path we had taken came to an end at the perimeter of the grounds. Chris ran ahead to look at the sheep grazing in the field beyond. In his haste, he stumbled on a cattle-grid and both his legs slipped between the bars. Immediately, he started screaming. Mum rushed to pull him out. She was horrified to see that the space beneath the grid was full of vigorously growing nettles. Chris's bare legs were ablaze with stings. Izzy and I choked back our tears and searched in vain for dock leaves. Mum hugged him tightly as he writhed in agony. Dad flared up, blaming Mum for allowing Chris to run off and Chris for not looking where he was going. Mum told him it was nobody's fault. She picked Chris up and ran with him back to the hall where she managed to find some cream to rub on his flaming skin. He was soon fine again.

Izzy and I had a marvellous time. Len Davis, our tutor, found chamber music simple enough for us to manage and put us in trios or quartets. He did not talk down to us, but treated us in the same way as the other students. "If you can't hear what everyone else is playing, you're too loud," he would say, encouraging us to concentrate on rhythm, intonation and sound production. He had the gift of being able to get more than the best out of everyone, which was just as well, as he had to shape an orchestra out of a motley collection of instrumentalists. Some years the standard of students was high, other years far from it, yet somehow Len turned us into a passable orchestra and our performance in the final concert was consistently a huge success. The brass band always stole the show, however. They were outstanding – many were miners, steelworkers and railway men who had been given scholarships by their Trade Unions. Other lads and a few lasses came with financial support from their hometown bands. The northern tradition of excellent brass band playing held fast at Wortley.

There was country dancing on the lawns on fine afternoons, talks and recitals in the early evenings. The jazz students played in the bar every night and provided the music for dancing in the ballroom. All students were invited to sing in the choir, and most did. In the library, the home of the orchestral course, instrumentalists got together outside the official timetable to play chamber music. That was where we learnt so much of the repertoire. Groups and individuals rehearsing and practising could be heard all over the building, the one rule being that between the hours of midnight and eight o'clock in the morning, music must cease.

Mum thoroughly enjoyed herself. She had not had an opportunity to play her cello for years – the last time she had played in an orchestra was when she was a student at the Academy. She was thrilled to have the chance to play some of the great chamber music repertoire. She made friends; she was well-liked; she became involved; she was in her element. The only person who did not enjoy himself was Dad. He was critical of the folk music course, he did not like the people, he found fault with the accommodation, the staff, and the meals. He spent his evenings drinking in the bar with the locals and resented Mum spending her evenings attending lectures, socialising with the other students and playing chamber music. When we got home I heard Mum say to Granny that Derek hadn't fitted in, that he had seemed determined not to enjoy himself.

"Aye," said Granny, "the whole world's out of step but him. Cussed, that's what he is."

He did not go to Wortley again. But we did. For Mum it was the one week in the year when she could be herself. They were the happiest weeks of her life. For us, Wortley and camp were the highlights of our year.

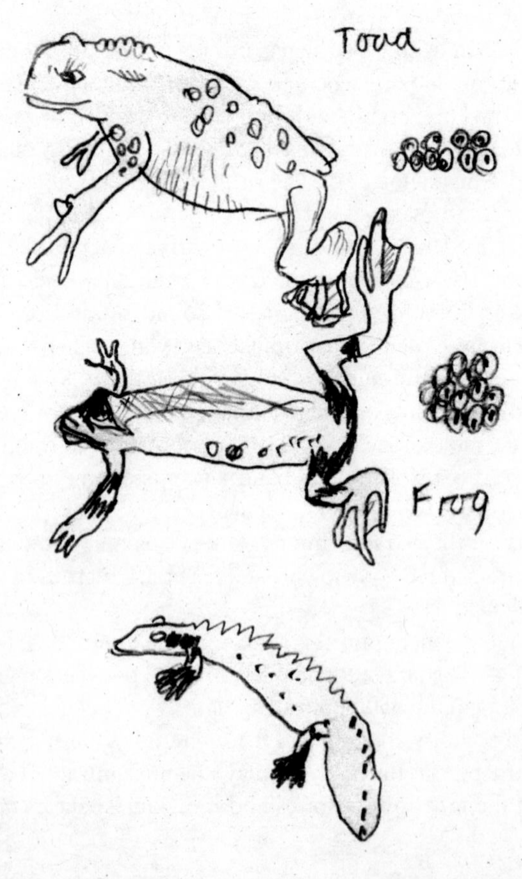

LEFT:
At Wortley Hall aged eight.

BELOW:
Rehearsing in one of the Wortley bedrooms, aged nine, with Len Davis, the orchestral and chamber music tutor of the WMA Summer School.

ABOVE: Chris, an Elf, at Forest School Camps, Summer 1964.
BELOW: Izzy, a Woodling.

15
BUGS AND BONES

The world is so full of a number of things,
I'm sure we should all be as happy as kings.

Happy Thought – Robert Louis Stevenson

Chris was a born naturalist. Everything he saw had to be minutely examined. He found ants, worms, beetles, spiders, centipedes, snails, and was happy to have them crawling over his hands and arms before collecting them in jars and matchboxes. His Infant School 'News Book' indicates his enthusiasm:

> I was trying to get some nature under stones and I found a few of them.
> I went to Norfolk and found six nests, a thrush, a white throte, two blackbirds and a front of a motor boat and 50 snale shells and one musle shell.
> I bort a new I-say book yesterday about Butter Flies and Mothes in the sweet shop in Gorj-Lane.
> I went to F.S.Camps with my sisters for Two days. I found a catapiller and a snale shell.

Clearing up after a Sunday dinner, Chris looked at the remains of the joint of meat.

"What's that?" he asked.

"A bone, stupid," I replied mockingly.

"No, I mean, what kind of a bone?"

"It's called lamb when we eat it, but actually it's mutton which is a grown-up sheep."

"It's the shoulder blade," commented Izzy, without looking up from her book.

"Can I have it?" he asked.

"What for?"

"Well, it's interesting, that's why."

We scraped off the meat scraps, scrubbed the bone in the washing-up water and Chris took it to bed with him.

"I'd like to have a whole skeleton," Chris confided after we were in bed.

"You've got one – your own," I pointed out. I could be quite haughty sometimes.

"No, I mean one to look at." He was serious. He was five years old. From then on, chicken, cattle, sheep and pig bones were saved from roast dinners and Chris worked out which part of the skeleton they came from. At twelve years old, he described his early interest in natural history:

> When I was about five I used to go with my parents to visit friends in Norfolk. One of the girls was called Helen Comer. She had a collection of animal skulls and skeletons, including an almost completely mounted Badger Skeleton with a wired up backbone. I was inspired by this. When I got back home I began keeping the bones of the Sunday joint, and I remember distinctly going to the butcher's and asking for a left handed shoulder blade of a pig! At about this time our pet hedgehog died, so I buried it, kept its skeleton and started collecting seriously.

He found the dead body of a squirrel in Epping Forest and brought it home to bury.

"When can I dig it up?" he asked excitedly.

"Next year, maybe," said Mum, thinking he would have forgotten all about it in a few days; but then he found dead birds and buried them too.

"You'd better make markers for them or you'll forget where they're buried," I suggested. Before long, the garden became a graveyard for mice, voles, weasels, rabbits, and to Chris's delight, a fox that somebody had found in the forest. When he was older he wrote:

> When collecting, often funny things happen when you are trying to get specimens. I remember obtaining a duck's head from the butcher's. I buried it, unfortunately too near the surface. The very next day I saw a large dog from next door digging it up and walking away with its prize.

The first graves were exhumed. Chris sorted out the skeletons on a table in the garden. The bones of the small animals had been lost in the earth, but he saved the skulls. From then on, he buried the bodies in shoeboxes or plastic bags punched with holes so that all the bones could be retrieved. He became skilled at mounting small skeletons by gluing them onto card and learnt the scientific name of every bone and animal. He went to the Natural History, British and Science Museums whenever he could and questioned the museum curators ceaselessly about every aspect of animal life. They came to know him, as did the keepers at the London Zoo. He exhibited his collection of skulls and bones in his bedroom along with fossils, shells, stones, birds' eggs, nests, butterflies and moths.

16
3, BRIDGE COTTAGES

In that country of luminous landscapes and wide horizons where the wind runs in the reeds and the slow rivers flow to our cold sea, a man may still sense and live something of the life of the older England which was uninhibited, free and natural.

Norfolk Fowler – Alan Savory

Mum's cottage search was successful. 3, Bridge Cottages, in the village of Great Ryburgh, was in a dreadful state, but the asking price was a reasonable £500 – within Mum's reach. It was mid-terrace, but large for a cottage, with one big room and a kitchen, three bedrooms and a good-sized garden – ideal for the family. John Comer helped with the purchase negotiations, advising Mum to put in an offer of £440. She was nervous to do so, afraid she might lose it, but John's instinct was correct. Mum's offer was accepted and the cottage became hers in May 1964.

Two months later, when it was time to go to Forest School Camps, I was ill with asthma. Chris, as had been arranged the year before, stayed at home with Granny and the cats. The rest of us drove to Norfolk. Izzy was dropped off at Whitwell camp, but I went with Mum and Dad to the new cottage to recover before going to FSC. I couldn't understand why Mum was so excited about the place: it was dilapidated. Dad, in bad temper, hacked through five-feet-high weeds to get to the front door. There was lichen on the clay-tiled floor, mould growing up the walls, no bathroom, no toilet, no mains drainage and no hot water. Mum set to, cleaning and scrubbing enthusiastically, while Dad started on the jungle. I thought everything about it was awful, particularly the tumbledown shed at the bottom of the garden that housed a chemical toilet. The smell was so noxious, I found myself longing for a camp lat. Mum gave me a basin of water and set me to work cleaning the windows. I sat on a ledge upstairs, smearing a damp cloth ineffectually through decades of grime, feeling dejected. My asthma was no better – in fact the damp and dust at the cottage probably made it worse. I pleaded with Mum to let me go to camp, making enough of a nuisance of myself for her to take me to Whitwell the next day.

I wheezed at night, worrying the staff, but already I knew there was nothing anyone could do. There were no effective drugs for children with asthma, and doctors were dismissive. When I had asthma, I learnt to keep away from other people if possible, to endure it and hope that nobody would ask me if I were alright, for I had no breath to reply. I found that if I hunched my shoulders and leaned forwards, it gave me some relief. If I scratched the skin on my sides in an upward movement from hip to armpit, this also helped. It became a habitual reflex: at times I drew red welts in my flesh. The bones in my upper chest and ribcage became deformed over the years that I fought for breath – asthma's retained legacy.

Mum put all her efforts into making the cottage habitable. She scrubbed the floors, hung curtains and paid local workmen to mend the roof and decorate the rooms. Granny and Mum went to auction sales to bid for beds, furniture and kitchenware. How much Dad helped, I don't know. Izzy remembers him laying a path in the back garden one summer with very bad grace, but it was Mum who dug the vegetable patch. I can't remember him doing much more than getting the fire going (which in fact Mum did far more efficiently) – but then, we children were out roaming the countryside.

Opposite the cottage was an area we called the wasteland, which we explored as far as the banks of the River Wensum. We picked bull rushes, climbed trees and got stung by nettles. There were plenty of dock plants around and we knew to squeeze the leaves and rub the sap onto the white nettle bumps to soothe the stinging – although it didn't seem to make any difference as far as I could tell. Just up from the cottage, the road bridged the river. We clambered down the bank with jam jars on lengths of string to dip for minnows. Beneath the bridge was a narrow concrete pier, a little dangerous to crawl onto, but once we were there, sitting in a row with our feet dangling inches above the rushing water, our voices echoing in the arched chamber, we were in a secret place of our own.

When Mum bought the cottage there was still a passenger train service running from Wymondham to Wells, which stopped at many stations along the way, including Great Ryburgh. To many people's regret, in October 1964, the service ceased. For us it meant that we could get onto the railway cutting at the level crossing and walk for miles down the disused track, leaping from sleeper to sleeper or balancing like tightrope walkers along the metal runners. Rabbits and hares hopped across the tracks in the distance and pheasants sometimes startled us by running out suddenly from the hedgerows. In the late summer we picked brambles, eating them along the way. Occasionally, Mum and Dad came with us, but mostly it was just the three of us, joking, telling stories, making up games, having to rest from time to time while I caught my breath.

One of our games started along these lines: "What do you prefer; custard or gravy?" We would consider this from all aspects, imagining what apple pie with gravy might taste like, or sausages with custard. Other foods were compared: Marmite or jam; porridge or semolina; milk or orange squash? Then we might ask: "What do you prefer; cats or dogs?" Usually, we agreed upon cats, but we didn't agree about everything. I liked the smell of petrol whereas Izzy and Chris preferred the smell of hot tar. Chris would ask us more distasteful questions such as, "Would you prefer to be kicked or punched?", or, "If you had to, would you rather eat pus or snot?" Then, inevitably, his questions sunk to a lavatorial level and Izzy refused to answer. If we asked, "Whose driving do you prefer; Mum's or Dad's?", Mum's was the unanimous answer. The question, "Whose smacks do you prefer?" only really applied to Chris and me, as Izzy was never naughty enough to warrant a smack. However, we all thought about it and concluded that we would have to choose Dad's. Mum smacked us very rarely, but when she did, it was swift, delivered smartly and it hurt. When Dad raised his arm to us, it looked threatening, but he would lose impetus mid-swing and by the time his hand reached us, the slap had become an ineffective pat. It didn't leave a mark on us, whereas we could see the pink imprint of Mum's hand on our skin. Dad's smacks were an embarrassment. We didn't know what to do afterwards with Dad looking apologetic, regarding his hand as if it didn't belong to him. Once, the game came to a confusing end when one of us asked, "Who do you prefer; Mum or Dad?" Mum and Dad were different, but how could we choose one and not the other?

In the middle of the village was a dairy farm. We entered the farmyard with caution, fearful of the angry white geese that hurtled towards us from the mucky pond, necks stretched out, honking and flapping their wings. The farmer, an affable, red-faced man, swore at them, brandishing his stick until they returned to the pond. Every morning and evening the farmer rounded up his cows and herded them past the cottage up to the farm to be milked. We followed the lumbering creatures and listened to the farmer rambling on in incomprehensible Norfolk dialect.

He knew all his cows. Each one had a name beginning with D – Daisy, Dora, Delilah, Dotty, Dinah and so on. Into the milking stalls they crammed, moaning to have their full udders emptied. The herd supplied the milk to the village. By mid-morning, the farmer was in his milk cart delivering pints. When compulsory pasteurisation came in he was forced to send his milk away and had to deliver pasteurised milk received from a central dairy. He hated the system and kept a churn or two back after milking, so those who knew could ask and buy fresh milk straight from Daphne, Diana or Dyllis.

Next to the row of cottages was the church, built of flint stone, with a round tower, which was ancient, probably dating from Saxon times. The church was small, but seemed cavernous when we were taken in to look. It smelled of incense, old books and forest mould. As the heavy door swung shut behind us there was an eerie feeling that we were entombed forever. Izzy wanted to leave and even Chris and I were reluctant to linger. Surrounding the church was its graveyard. I found it sad reading the gravestones, particularly the little ones encrusted with lichen telling of beloved children who had died when only a few months or years old. It seemed even more heartbreaking that they had died such a long time ago. Why did they die? Who were they? What did they look like? How must their parents have felt? What about their brothers and sisters?

Walking in the other direction, away from the church, we crossed the bridge over the Wensum and headed towards Little Ryburgh. A narrow road on the left, with grass growing in the middle, led up the hill to a ruined church and a large graveyard, which was still used for burials. An enormous stone angel mounted upon a pedestal and enclosed within cast iron railings towered over the site. Its marbled eyes seemed to stare at us with cold condemnation and follow our every movement. It wasn't a place to play. Further along the road were some derelict cottages that looked as if they had been built for dwarves. The doorways were so low, no ordinary sized adult would be able to enter without stooping. We wondered who had once lived there. Just beyond the cottages was a larger dwelling with a yard adjacent to it that was occupied by hundreds of garden gnomes. In garish costume they regarded us with salacious vulgarity, so out of place in the hushed, deserted village that we guessed the adjoining cottage must be a garden gnome factory.

If we turned right instead of left, we were on the rutted dirt track that wound upwards towards the barn and Sennowe woods. The barn was old with a pan-tiled roof. Sometimes it was full of bales of hay, which we climbed and leapt off from more and more daring heights. Then we lay at the very top, hay stalks scratching our bare legs and arms, looking up at the sky through holes in the roof and making up stories. We were slightly scared of being found, not sure if we were allowed to be there. Once, a dog appeared, barking ferociously, as we were on our way out. We were terrified until a man with a walking stick rounded the corner and told the three of us to clear off. We ran away in relief as he called his dog to heel. Walking on from the barn, the track petered out and became a footpath. Now we were on high ground in open fields. A few fields further on, the land dipped down again and we came to the edge of a forest. By the gate was a sign that read 'Sennowe Woods. Private Property. No Trespassing', but there was nobody to be seen, so over the gate we climbed. Under the canopy of trees, the temperature dropped suddenly and goose pimples rose on our skin. Nobody came here but the gamekeeper and poachers. The forest was a perfect setting for Hansel and Gretel, Little Red Riding Hood or Goldilocks. Maybe there were wolves and bears hiding behind trees and witches in gingerbread cottages. We were more frightened of the gamekeeper than of coming face to face with a wolf, but thankfully we didn't meet either.

On one occasion, Chris gave a shout of distress. In the undergrowth was a stoat with its back legs clamped in the metal jaws of a shark-toothed snare. The bloodied creature looked at us with pain-filled eyes. "What are we going to do?" Chris cried.

"There's nothing we can do," I said. "Even if we could get the snare open, its back legs are crushed and it wouldn't survive."

"We can't just leave it in agony. We have to do something," he pleaded.

"I suppose the best thing would be to put it out of its misery. Bash it over the head with something."

"Kill it, you mean?" asked Izzy in alarm.

"It's the kindest thing to do, isn't it, Kate?"

"Well don't look at me," I said, "I'm not doing it."

"Please, Kate, please," implored Chris tearfully.

"We're going to have to find something very heavy first," I said firmly.

We wandered away from the pitiful sight, looking for something suitable. Chris picked up bits of wood, which I rejected as not being weighty enough. By the time a large flint stone had been dug out of the soil and we had returned, the stoat had mercifully closed its eyes and died.

From then on, Chris searched for the snares by beating the thick undergrowth with a stick, snapping shut the ones he discovered and leaving splintered wood in their jagged clutches. Further into the woods was a clearing, to one side of which was a long barbed-wire fence. Beyond it, up a lightly wooded hill, stood Sennowe Hall, an impressive brick and stone building. We didn't dare to venture near it. Once, when we reached the clearing, we were shocked to see well over a hundred black carrion crows strung up by their necks along the barbed wire fence. Chris called it the gamekeeper's gibbet, explaining to us that the birds were hung there deliberately to scare other crows away. Despite the intimidation of Sennowe woods, we went back time and again. For Chris, it was a rich source for his collection.

In springtime we looked forward to seeing the recently born foals, calves and lambs. Leaning over gates and fences, we called to the horses, holding out handfuls of grass for them to eat from our outstretched hands. We watched the ducks, moorhens and swans with their broods of babies swimming on the Wensum.

Up at the playing field, the village children eyed us warily, but we were grudgingly given our turns on the swings and slides and formed brief, transient friendships. Once, a travelling circus arrived in Great Ryburgh and pitched a round tent in the playing field. Mum and Dad took us to the show, where we sat on narrow wooden benches to watch the troupe perform. There were only three of them – two men and a woman, whom we had already seen outside in different costumes selling tickets, drinks and popcorn. The woman seemed too old, bony and brittle to be dressed in not-so-sparkling leotards. She swung rather arthritically from the trapeze, but succeeded without accident in catching the proffered hands of her equally aged partner as he caught her mid-air. She inched her way along a tightrope, wobbling shakily on the points of her toes, and the men unicycled and clowned. The younger man performed more daring athletic feats; somersaulting on the tightrope; leaping through flaming hoops. There was juggling, knife throwing and stilt walking, all a little lacklustre and unspectacular. For the finale, they brought on two plumed and braided ponies and rode around the ring, closing the show by forming a human triangle upon the mounts – the two men standing on the ponies' backs with the scrawny woman balanced stiffly on their shoulders. There was something rather pitiful and desperate about the act; the faded costumes and frayed ropes, whitened faces and grease-painted smiles – even the ponies looked worn out. At the end, the applause was meagre, although we did our best to boost it by clapping until our palms stung. As the audience melted away, Dad stayed and struck up conversation. The threesome was husband, wife and son. They had been on the road for as long as they could remember. In their youth they had belonged to a large travelling circus. Now they were the only ones left and were struggling to survive. The following morning, Dad took them a box of food and sat in their caravan drinking mugs of sweet tea. Part of him, I thought, yearned to go a-roving with them.

If the weather promised to be fine, we drove to the seaside town of Sheringham with our buckets and spades, towels and sandwiches. On the way down to the beach, we were always hurried past the amusement arcades and souvenir shops and told not to look. Once, Mum did not make sandwiches. For a treat, we were taken to a fish and chip restaurant. As soon as we were seated at a table, Dad started to tell us off: Be quiet. Sit still. Behave yourselves. Keep your voices down.

"Oh Derek," said Mum mildly, "They're not doing any harm. This is a family restaurant. They're used to children."

"I will not have them misbehaving in a public place," Dad hissed.

"They're not being naughty. They're hungry, that's all. Ah, here comes the food."

A cheerful waitress placed enormous platters in front of us. Dad picked up the bottle of tomato ketchup and shook it vigorously from side to side. The top came off, showering blobs of sauce over people sitting on either side of us. Izzy, Chris and I clapped our hands over our mouths to hide involuntary smiles. Dad was both furious and distraught. He and Mum apologised profusely to the two people who had been splattered, both of whom took it in good humour.

"I must give you some money for cleaning," wailed Dad.

"Wouldn't hear of it," said the woman, laughing her head off. "Worse things have happened."

"What *idiot* left the cap unscrewed?" Dad demanded angrily of the waitress, who arrived with cloths in her hand.

"Everyone cleaned up now?" she asked.

"We're fine, love," said the woman. "No harm done. Go on; see to your other customers."

"OK, Sir?" she asked Dad.

"No. I am not."

"Derek, sit down and eat your meal, dear," Mum soothed.

He sat, embarrassed and agitated. With subdued appetite, we continued to munch our way through our giant portions. Dad stared at his food, not touching it. Suddenly, he pushed his chair back, stood up and walked stiffly out of the restaurant. Mum watched his retreating figure. She looked at us distractedly.

"I'd better go and find him. Finish your dinner. I'll be back in a minute."

The remaining cold chips defeated us. Dad was in a foul temper for the rest of the holiday, blaming us for the misfortune. "I'm never taking the three of you to a restaurant again," he said.

On wet days we tackled jigsaw puzzles, played cards, Scrabble, Ludo, Monopoly and 'The Merry Game of Floundering'. This last game consisted of variously coloured cardboard flounders, each one in six numbered pieces. The object was to assemble a whole fish of uniform colour, which was achieved by throwing the die to match the numbers. Another favourite was the 'Tell Me Quiz Game'. Questions about various topics were printed on cards. A small metal spinner, similar to a miniature roulette wheel, was set in motion with a deft flick between thumb and forefinger. When it stopped, a letter of the alphabet was revealed and the quizzing began. "Name a flower beginning with D; a river beginning with O; a city beginning with Y; a sport beginning with K..."

We formed the Sevens Club, for children only, which tested our skill at playing 'sevens' – a card game based more on luck of the deal than skill. Scores were kept, certificates prepared and formally presented – by me, I have to admit. While the adults perused the *Daily Worker* (which became the *Morning Star* in 1966), *Comment* (the bulletin of the Communist Party), *Labour Weekly*, *Czechoslovak Life* and the newly launched *Private Eye*, we devoured the *Dandy*, *Beano* and *Bunty* comics – even Chris read *Bunty*, lamenting at its girlishness. We read books and wrote stories, leaving them at the cottage with the games and comics for the next time we visited. They are still there, held in a time warp. My children have also played The Merry Game of Floundering and completed the same jigsaw puzzles, but for the two or three pieces that have always been missing. Some years ago, we visited a newly opened museum at Gresham, a few miles away from Great Ryburgh. In we walked to a reconstructed home of the early 1960s. "This isn't a museum," my children complained, "it's just like the cottage."

During the October half-term, when we were eight, Izzy and I saw some dolls in the Woolworths in Fakenham, the nearest town to Great Ryburgh. The dolls had rubber arms from elbows to hands and rubber legs from knees to feet. Their plump fingers were slightly closed, with adorable dimples on the knuckles, and their toes curled sweetly inwards. Their heads were also rubber, with golden hair and cute, chuckling baby faces. Their bodies and upper limbs were soft, sewn from flesh-coloured material and stuffed with a fabric that made them huggily squeezable. Clothed in infant dresses, they were like real babies.

"Aah, aren't they lovely, Mum?" we cooed.

"They are very realistic, I must say."

Back home, she saw the same baby dolls in Woolworths in George Lane. Rather extravagantly, she bought us one each for our ninth birthday. Anticipating our delight when we opened our presents in the morning, she was rather surprised by my silence. Izzy was thrilled with her doll, but I looked at mine with sinking disappointment. I knew I ought to be smiling and saying thank you. I was aware that Mum had done something very special for us – actually bought us the dolls she knew we wanted. Except it wasn't the right doll.

"What's the matter, Catherine?"

"Nothing," I said, my voice cracking. Then I burst into tears.

"What's wrong, dear?"

"It's the wrong doll," I sobbed.

"They're exactly the same as the ones you saw in Norfolk."

"They're not. The ones in Norfolk had more laughing eyes and different smiles and golden hair."

"Isabel, does your doll look any different to you?" Mum asked.

"No. Well, maybe a bit, I can't tell."

"So you're happy with it?"

"Yes," she said positively.

"Catherine, dear, it was months ago when you saw them. You've probably forgotten what they looked like."

"I haven't," I wailed.

"Don't cry. If you don't want it, I'll take it back to Woolworths and you can have something else. How's that?"

"OK," I agreed. But all I wanted was my own baby doll, the one with the face I would never forget.

Mum, to her eternal credit, drove all the way to Norfolk. In the Woolworths in Fakenham she found the dolls we had seen and made an exchange. Comparing the two, she had to agree that the Norfolk version did indeed have a slightly different expression and a darker shade of hair. Why it mattered so much to me, she had no idea. I rewarded Mum's efforts by being utterly overjoyed when she presented me with the doll I had thought I would never see again. I called her Tara; Izzy called hers Bridget. We were happy for our dolls to be different. Like us, they were not identical twins.

17
GAMES

Sherbet lemons, hard against the palate,
vicious yellow. Strong sucking
made them spurt, fizz, foam,
sugar splinters lacerate
the inside of my cheeks,
surprising as ice crystals in the wind
that cut my legs through my socks.

Mouthfuls – Carole Satyamurti

In the shed amidst sun-faded deckchairs, garden tools, shelves of old paint tins and mud-caked wellington boots, we formed a secret club. Dares and challenges were thought up, which had to be undertaken to become a member and prove commitment. One of these involved creeping into the living room, getting through to the kitchen and out the back door without being spotted. The adults must have pretended to ignore us because we usually succeeded. It was I who assumed the role of 'president' and drew up certificates, which were formally presented when a mission had been executed successfully. Chris described one of these tasks in his Infant school News Book:

> I was playing hiding upstairs. Each time you are seen you knock off a point from twenty. I was seen five times. I had fifteen points when the game stopped.

Although Izzy and I are twins, I was designated the role of older sister. Perhaps it was because I was bigger, taller and bossier (a word that was often, to my distress, used to describe me), or maybe because of an ability (often a curse) to organise. Izzy and I didn't argue, but Chris and I sometimes quarrelled and bickered, winding each other up to screaming point.

"Och, wheesht, the pair of ye. I cannae hear myself think," Granny would shout. We would reduce the volume, but continue to squabble, occasionally ending up actually fighting. If we went too far, causing real pain and tears, we were suddenly remorseful. Then there would be a last wallop by the injured party to settle the score and all was well again.

Chris thought it fun to startle me, and hid behind doors waiting to say "BOO".

"You didn't scare me at all," I would say contemptuously.

"Yes I did. I saw you jump."

"No you didn't." "Yes I did." "You didn't." "Did." "Didn't."

Once he really did scare me. I was coming downstairs, walking along the hall towards the living room, when he leapt out in front of me, arms outstretched, a hideous look on his face and shouted a loud, staccato BOO. I shrieked in pure blood-curdling terror, not once, but over and over again.

"It's only me," said Chris, horrified by my reaction. "Kate, stop. It's me."

Mum came hurtling out of the music room.

"What on earth's going on?"

"It's OK," I gasped, "Chris scared me."

She looked at both of us angrily and in one swift movement slapped Chris hard on the back of his bare leg. As he ran out into the garden, she turned to me: "And don't you ever make such a noise again. I thought someone was being murdered."

I went into the garden to find Chris propped against the wall in the shed crying. I sat beside him, hugging my knees. "Are you OK?"

"Why did you scream so much?" he asked accusingly.

"You frightened me. I thought you were a burglar. Does it hurt? Where Mum smacked you?"

"Not much," he sniffed.

"I'm sorry."

I saw a smile gathering. "Oh, it's alright. You can't help it – your brain's eighty per cent water."

"It's not," I said, accepting the insult in good humour.

"Actually it is: so's mine. Everyone's brains are eighty per cent water."

Two second-hand bikes were purchased for Izzy and me. Mum and Dad took us up to the forecourt of Harvey Hudson's garage on the High Road to practise. The bikes did not have stabilisers, so Dad pushed us up to a speed then let go. We tumbled and grazed our knees and knuckles, but could cycle within an hour or so. Soon after, we wobbled our way up Broad Walk towards Epping Forest. Mum and Dad followed us with Chris pedalling furiously on his tricycle. By the time we reached the forest, he was worn out, moaning that he had 'bent legs'. Mum and Dad suggested he leave his tricycle concealed in a bush for us to pick up on our way back. Izzy and I cycled merrily up and down the bridle paths across bumpy stretches of grass, enjoying our newfound speed and freedom. When we returned, Chris's tricycle had gone. We must be looking under the wrong bush, I insisted, but Mum and Dad knew that it had been stolen. I couldn't take this in.

"But why would anyone take it if it wasn't theirs?"

"Some people are like that," Mum sighed. "We shouldn't have left it there."

"Maybe they'll bring it back when they realise it doesn't belong to them?"

"No," said Dad sorrowfully, "it's gone forever."

"But it must be somewhere," I persisted.

We walked back, pushing our bikes, Chris trotting along tearfully.

"I've got bent legs," he bleated. Dad carried him home on his shoulders. For months afterwards, I searched the bushes of Epping Forest, hoping to find the tricycle and be able to give it back to him.

A couple of years later, Chris had his own bicycle. He and I used to go out for bike rides. Izzy preferred to read, so rarely came. We cycled round and round the roads on the other side of the High Road, which were laid out in grid form. I led and Chris followed. After dozens of rights and lefts, I stopped for a breather. Chris came to a halt behind me.

"Oh dear, I think we're lost," I said dramatically.

"Oh no," Chris whimpered, "what are we going to do?" His brow puckered and his little face crumpled. I couldn't believe he actually thought we were lost – we had just been going round in circles. Anyone could find the way back to the main road.

"Only joking," I said, "don't cry. It's easy to get home."

"Are you sure?" he asked anxiously.

"Follow me!" I said confidently, turning the bike around.

"Wait, wait," he cried.

"I won't leave you behind," I reassured. When we reached home, Chris ran breathlessly into the house and told Mum that we'd been completely lost, it was terribly frightening, we hadn't known what to do, but Kate had managed to find the way home. Mum eyed me suspiciously.

The following week we went bike riding around exactly the same roads. When we stopped, at a different place this time, I again announced that we were lost, thinking that he would know I was joking. Poor Chris – he was immediately close to tears and as alarmed and worried as before. I felt awful that I had upset him again with my stupid joke. Chris's anxiety made him fragile – that part of him had to be handled with care.

At weekends we were each given eightpence to buy sweets. We walked up to the shop on the High Road to make our selection. Large jars of loose sweets lined the shelves behind the counter: sherbet lemons, fruit bon bons, pear drops, Fox's glacier mints, jelly babies, butterscotch, pink shrimps, dolly mixture and so on. We asked for two ounces of this or that, watching as the shopkeeper brought down the jars, unscrewed the wide lids and shook the contents into a teardrop-shaped metal bowl until the scales balanced. The sweets were funnelled into paper bags, which the shopkeeper twirled around with a flourish to twist the corners. Izzy liked walnut whips and Chris liked Fry's mint chocolate; my favourites were Caramacs, Turkish Delight and Milky Bars. We all bought packets of Refreshers, Love Hearts, wine gums, Opal Fruits and Trebor fruit-salad chews at four a penny. There was a Trebor building near us, on the Woodford Avenue by Charlie Brown's roundabout. Mum pointed out to me that Trebor was Robert spelt backwards. I told Izzy, hoping to impress her, only to be informed that she had worked that out ages ago. Sometimes, on a Sunday afternoon, we were allowed to move the chairs and table in the living room and make them into a den. Mum would provide us with old sheets, which we would drape over the arranged furniture; then we would crawl in, taking our sweets with us to share out.

One very hot day, I had the bright idea of buying lemon sherbet, which was sold loose, and mixing it with water to make fizzy lemonade. We spent every penny of our sweet money on the stuff, and bought so much that we were soon sick of it: so my next idea was to sell it. Mum didn't seem too enthusiastic about our plan, but allowed us, grudgingly, to go ahead. We took as many cups and glasses as we could find into the front garden and arranged them on the wall, together with our jugs of fizz. I drew some notices: 'LEMONADE 2d a glass'. Children playing nearby came over to see what we were doing and ran home to beg for tuppence. Soon we had attracted quite a crowd, including an elderly gentleman who gave us sixpence each. This seemed a little excessive, but I duly poured out nine glasses for him. To my bafflement, he left them on the wall untouched and walked away smiling, telling us to enjoy ourselves. In the end we gave all that was left of the lemonade to a small boy, who drank the lot. We counted up our takings and found that we had made a shilling each!

Our garden-market thrived for a few weeks until the day of the jumble sale. We pooled together a few old toys, including some that Chris was quite reluctant to part with. Displayed on the wall, our collection seemed rather feeble, so we raided the cellar and the shed, adding old paint tins and flowerpots. Still not satisfied, I went around the house picking up bits and pieces to augment our assortment of items for sale. It all went reasonably well, although we were left with the broken toys we didn't want whilst other things that we had rashly included were snapped up. As we were clearing away, an unmistakable shriek came from indoors. "Where's my wool?"

"Catherine?" called Mum, "Have you seen Granny's wool?"

I gasped. It was one of the first things we had sold. I was in big trouble, especially when Granny found out that I had sold it for thruppence a ball. "That was brand new wool, Cath-er-reen. It cost a shilling and sixpence." We were all sheepish, but it was I who took the rap – only Catherine could have thought up such a hare-brained scheme.

Soon after our first trip to Wortley, Izzy and I, aged seven, moved to Oakdale Junior School, a short walk down the road from the Infant School. There we were streamed, the pupils divided into 'A' and 'B' classes not very cleverly disguised as 'M' and 'K'. Izzy, always top of the class, and I, usually third or fourth, went into the 'M' stream. Our first teacher was Miss Coyne, but we only had to endure her for one term: the headmistress, Miss Wallington, realised that Miss Coyne's severity was too extreme for seven- and eight-year-olds and moved her to the older age groups. Mrs. Birchill was the replacement – an elderly, vapid woman; short, stout, heavily girdled and topped with a light-mauve perm. Pronunciation was not her strong point: taking the register every morning, she would repeatedly read out Penelope Runnicles as 'Penny-lope Runny-clees'. She plastered herself with face powder and played the piano for assembly. Her head nodded unrhythmically up and down as she bashed out wrong chords with gay abandon and sprinkled the keys liberally with peach-coloured dust.

My school News Book from that year reveals my interests and observations. Here are a few extracts:

> **April '64:** In the morning I woke up and heard all the birds singing and flying about. I looked out of my bedroom window and watched the birds picking up all the bits of coloured wool that my Granny put out in the garden after finishing the cardigans that she had been knitting. In the garden I saw all the daffodils and Great [*grape*] Hyacinth blowing backwards and forwards in the wind. On the way to school it was a sunny dry morning. We saw some pink almond and some beautifull tulips. There was a lovely beautiful excuisite Magnolia tree. In the weekend I did some weeding in my garden and planted some seeds. We have lovely forgetmenots. They are blue with little yellow spots in the middle. I have got some red and yellow tulips in my garden and some very nice bluebells and some London Pride.

> **May '64:** In the morning when we went out of the front door we saw a mouse on the step. My brother giggled a lot. Our cat came out of the front door as well and sniffed the little dead mouse. We put the mouse out on the wall. We saw Nickolas coming along the road. We called him over and said 'Look at our pet mouse'. He giggled and carried on his way to school. Then Mummy came out and we had to go to school ourselfs.

> **June '64:** On Sunday Auntie Marther came over to our house. She listened to us playing the piano first and then she had a cup of tea and some biscets. After tea we played our cello and violin. Isabel and I go swimming at Harlow New Town and we have lessons as well. I and Isabel go there everey Sunday but today I cant go because I have got a veruca. I am 8 and you can go for lessons when you are 8. Swimming is one of our best hobbies. Music is my very best hobby. It is my brothers birthday on 24th June. I have brought him a tool set and 2 puzzles. My sister has brought him some army men and some lego.

> **July '64:** On Saturday afternoon we went over to play with Pamela. She lives next door. We have been practising for a play. We are going to do the play in the garden. The first thing we do is to dance round the maypole. For the may pole we have got a long pole which is stuck into the ground. We have tied beautifull coulerd ribbons onto the pole and it really looks like a may pole. We all curtsy in front of the audience. After that we do a dance on our own and then a dance together. We have got a curtain on the clothes line and we pull the curtain along the clothes line at 4.0 when the play starts. At the end, Pamela asks the audience some puzzles. The first one to guess gets a sweet. At the end we give the audience all 3 sweets and then they all clap. They give us 3d to come in and they give a penny for the program. We are going to practice at 5.0 to 6.0 because we need a lot of practice. There are going to be 8 people in the garden watching us and they each

> pay 4d. We will have 2s 8d by the end of the day if they all come!
>
> On Saturday we had our tea in the hut. We called the hut a cafee. I was the serva who gave Isabel and Christopher their tea. It was nice having our tea in the cafee. On Sunday morning we saw a little bird who had broken its wing, In the afternoon one of the cats caught it and we were sad. We could not stop it from getting caught because we knew it would die in the end.

My spelling was consistently inaccurate, but phonetically inspired. Mum was always amused by 'socj', my attempt at 'sausage'. In holes at the top right of our lidded desks were ceramic inkwells filled with permanent blue-black ink. We were issued with wooden pen handles to which we attached metal nibs, the indelible ink staining our fingers and often our clothes as well. We scratched, smudged and blotted our letters onto lined paper as we tried to get to grips with joined-up writing. Parents who could afford to do so purchased fountain pens for their children. We were given ours a couple of years later as a Christmas present. They were incredibly messy to use, with a rubber ink tube within the pen shaft that had to be refilled manually. Mrs. Kernahan took us for our second year – an energetic teacher whom we all liked. She called me 'Sweet Kate' and Izzy, 'Isabella'. We flourished in her happy classroom.

Pamela, an only child, lived at 30, Cleveland Road. She was about a year older than us and went to a private school, but as she lived next door, we often played together. Her bedroom was adorned with posters of Cliff Richard and other contemporary pop stars, whose names and music were unknown to us. Pamela's knowledge of their lives and records was extensive, but our ignorance prevented us from sharing her enthusiasm. In the hot weather, her mother used to bring us jugs of lime cordial clinking with ice accompanied by interesting selections of biscuits, which we consumed outside in a wigwam-shaped play tent. Her father was a keen philatelist and encouraged us with our stamp collections. Mum's piano recordings were requested from many foreign parts: Malaysia, Hong Kong, Singapore, Trinidad and Tobago, Kenya, Ghana, Mauritius, Tanzania, to name but a few, so our stamp collecting was off to a good start just from the post that dropped through the door. We steamed the stamps carefully from the envelopes and stuck them into albums, but our interest waned after a few years. I have no idea what happened to the books.

On the other side of us in the upstairs flat lived Mr. and Mrs. Tappenden and their two children, Julie and Roy. Julie was about six years younger than us, a cute, shy little girl whom we all liked to mother. When Roy was born, Izzy and I must have been about nine. We would have loved to look after Julie and baby Roy more often, but I have a feeling that their mother found us, particularly me, rather too boisterous. I remember charging around the garden with Roy in his pushchair, Roy screaming with laughter as I ran faster and faster, until I realised that his shrieks of laughter had turned to cries of pain. I came to a halt and saw to my horror that Roy had cut his head. I untied him from the pushchair, hugged and comforted him, and carried him upstairs to confess to his mother. By the time I handed him into her arms, he was laughing again. It was just a scratch, but I felt dreadful about it. No amount of apologising, or Mrs. Tappenden's forgiveness, made me feel any better. I had injured a baby: it was awful.

In the long summer evenings, when we were sent off to bed before the sun had set, I would hear Mr. and Mrs. Tappenden in the garden and peep through the edge of my curtain to watch them. Sometimes they played a type of squash. Mr. Tappenden bashed a post into the grass with a mallet. Attached to the post was a length of elasticated string with a tennis ball at the end. He struck the ball, which hit the wall and bounced back for Mrs. Tappenden to play. They laughed and smiled; he hugged her and she put her arms around his waist. I could tell that they loved each other. Then I felt a bit guilty about spying on them, straightened my curtain and climbed into bed, feeling the thumps of the ball against the wall and hearing their distant, melodic conversation. I hoped that when I married I would be as happy as they were.

At the rear of our garden was a vegetable patch, and along each side of the lawn were flowerbeds. I asked if we could have our own gardens – a little plot each. "Well, I suppose so," said Mum doubtfully. Undeterred, we took her reply as a yes and divided the flowerbed on the right into three. Chris had the piece nearest the house, Izzy the middle section and I took the third, which adjoined the vegetable patch. Each plot was about seven feet by three. I set to work at once, digging, weeding, raking and removing stones, sacrificing sweet money to spend on bedding plants and seeds. Soon my garden was filling up with primula, aubrietia, lobelia, nemesia, pansies and marigolds. Izzy didn't seem very interested in maintaining her garden. Foxgloves and bluebells already grew there; I gave her a few marigolds, but before long it was a bed of weeds. With little difficulty, I persuaded her to hand her allotment over to me. Chris planted a few bulbs and was pleased to see them appear the following spring, but otherwise he gave up bothering. He knew I was angling for the last third of the flowerbed, but flatly turned down my takeover bid of a week's pocket money. Even two weeks' money failed to bring him to the negotiating table. I had to rethink my strategy. At last I had a brainwave: I offered to keep his stick insects supplied with privet. There were no privet bushes in our garden, so the stick insects' staple diet had to be harvested by cruising nearby streets and swiping leafy stems from neighbours' hedges. He agreed and the deal was struck. My garden became my pride and joy. Bit by bit I encroached into the vegetable patch until Granny called a halt when I reached the rhubarb. My garden did become the prettiest view from the back windows and I kept it well stocked and tended until I left home.

In the middle of the lawn was a cherry tree, which produced edible cherries. We picked the ones within reach and looked longingly at the plump, dark-red fruit hanging in the topmost branches, cross that the birds could so easily steal them. Izzy was particularly fond of cherries. She would put her book down, uncurl herself and risk life and limb to pick them. Chris and I held the ladder while Izzy, nimble and light, wove her way through the branches and threw down the fruits, which we caught and gathered in a bowl. With her safely back on land, we shared out the haul, Chris and I trying hard to be generous in letting Izzy select the best ones first. We had a strong sense of fairness, although when it came to 'licking the bowl', it was the fastest who took the most. We didn't actually lick the bowl, we scraped it. When Granny had finished blending and beating the ingredients for a cake and emptied it into baking tins, she handed each of us a teaspoon. We eyed the spoons critically, checking that they were of the exact same size, and then sat on the floor in a circle. With our spoons poised, we waited for Granny to place the mixing bowl in front of us, and then we scraped and ate frenetically until there was nothing left but the bowl. I once asked Granny whether she could just give us the cake mixture to eat and not bake it. She told me not to be so ridiculous.

War games were discouraged. Toy guns were not bought for Chris. Even water pistols were considered to be aggressive weapons. In the playground the boys pretended to shoot one another, pointing two extended fingers at their targets and shouting, "Bang, bang, you're dead." With hands pressed against chests, the victims howled in staged agony, falling dead or wounded to the tarmac. However much the adults lectured about the horror of war – the reality of killing, the evil of guns – nothing was going to stop little boys from playing soldiers, cops and robbers or cowboys and Indians. Chris borrowed from his friends, who had whole boxes of guns, pistols, swords and daggers.

Meanwhile, Izzy and I looked longingly at our friends' Sindy dolls. We even plucked up the courage to ask if we might have one for Christmas.

"You've been watching those dreadful adverts at your friends' houses, haven't you?" Mum jumped on us.

"No, we just like Sindy dolls."

"Don't be silly. You've been brainwashed by advertising. You don't really want to play with such ridiculous, artificial, stick-like things. They're not proper dolls at all – and the price of them!"

There was no point trying to persuade her further.

In the toyshop at the bottom of George Lane, Izzy and I spotted Tammy dolls, inferior versions of Sindy. Nevertheless, they had long arms and legs, protruding bumps on their chests, face make-up and long gingery-blonde hair. A slight plus was that they also had gold-coloured metal hair-bands. They were much cheaper than Sindy, so Izzy and I decided to save our pocket money and without letting on to Mum, buy each other a Tammy doll for Christmas. We would pretend to be terribly surprised when we unwrapped our presents to find that we had coincidentally bought the same thing. Our plan went well.

"Have you bought 'you know what' yet?" I whispered to Izzy a week before Christmas.

"Yes," she replied, "Have you?"

I nodded conspiratorially. We placed our identically shaped packages with the other presents. When we opened them, we feigned amazement, but Mum was not fooled. She glanced at the dolls derisively. "I don't know why you wanted to waste your money on such daft things. Did Catherine put you up to it?" she asked Izzy.

"No, it's what we both wanted," replied Izzy, truthfully.

Cathy, "Christine" and Izzy.

Chris loved to dress up.

18
INDEPENDENCE AND HOMESICKNESS

I strive to search wherefore I am so sad,
Until a melancholy numbs my limbs;
And then upon the grass I sit, and moan,
Like one who once had wings.

Hyperion – John Keats

When Izzy and I were nine-and-a-half, I went to FSC by myself. The brochure and enrolment forms had arrived at the beginning of the year. For some reason I decided to go to a camp that was not in Norfolk, perhaps because the description of that particular camp in Wales appealed to me. Izzy wanted to go to Whitwell again, and Chris, who was seven, would go with her.

As the summer holidays approached, I looked forward to going away by myself. Mum drove Izzy and Chris to Norfolk and Dad took me to Paddington station to meet up with the FSC escort party. When we arrived, I didn't recognise anyone I knew. My stomach lurched as the train started moving away. I slightly regretted my decision, but there was no turning back: I was on my own.

It was strange being without Izzy. I found myself making things up – inventing far-fetched tales about my family, pretending that Dad was a famous scientist; that I went to boarding school; that we lived in a huge house by a river, kept horses, travelled abroad and other such wild fantasies. Izzy wasn't there to keep me in line, so nobody would know. The funny thing was, when I told my tent partner that I was a twin, she didn't believe me. I spent the rest of camp trying to convince her, but she became dubious of everything I said.

There is one thing that sticks out in my memory. A Pathfinder girl befriended me. She sat beside me at mealtimes, held my hand when we walked to the campfire and took me under her wing. I thought she was wonderful. We had grown-up conversations and even talked about music and parents and feelings. One glorious evening we were sitting together on bales of hay watching the country dancing when she turned to me and said, "What's it like being so pretty?" I looked around to see which girl she was referring to.

"Who do you mean?"

"I mean you."

"Me? Oh, I'm not pretty. You should see my sister – she really is pretty."

"I'm looking at you and I think you are the prettiest girl I've ever seen." I stared at her in astonishment, but there was no doubting her sincerity.

"Oh, look!" she said, "They're going to do *Cumberland Square Eight*. Will you be my partner?"

"Yes please!" I replied. Exhilarating though it was to be twirled through the air, I soared higher with the happiness I felt inside. When the Woodlings were called to bed, my Pathfinder friend said, "Goodnight, pretty girl." I hugged myself to sleep with sheer pleasure.

Chris was not doing too well at Whitwell:

> Dear Mummy I hope you are well and I hope Daddy's chaff is better. It is very nice at whitwell and I have lost my knife. love from christopher giles
>
> Dear Granny I hope you are well. I like it at whit well camp and I have lost a fork and spoon
>
> Dear mummy plees cood you give me 2s for some tooth paist
> Love from Christopher
>
> Dear mummy I hope you are allright. Last night my tent fell down and I was soaked and my knife is lost and a letter has arrived from Catherine.
> love from Christopher
>
> Dear daddy today I went to ling and I had a swim and all the elves have had a bath and Mark refuse to take off his swimming trunks and I went in last because I had direar.
> Love from Christopher
>
> Dear Mummy I am having a verry bad holiday and I want you to visit me again and Isabel has been on trek and I was crying
> lots of love and kisses from Christopher
>
> Dear mummy and daddy I am feeling home sik and I want to go home
> love from Christopher
> XXXXXXXXXXXXXXXXXXXX
> XXXXXXXXXXXXXXXXXXXX

Izzy writes:

> Dear Granny,
>
> I hope you are having nice weather at home. I arrived at camp at about quarter-to-five. I am on clan two. Today was my clan and I grated some cheese, peeled everso many potatoes and washed up.
>
> Today we are having COUNTRY DANCING, it is nearly time for it. I sleep with Nadia Dixon. Our leader is called Robert, he is very nice, he is Scotish and he is on my clan. There is a horrid girl here called Elizabeth.
>
> GOOD LUCK LOVE FROM ISABEL XXXXXX
>
> Dear Mummy,
>
> Thankyou very much for the letter you sent me, I got it at rally. I hope you can stay to dinner on Sunday, I havn't spent any of my 2s 6d yet. It is getting very hot here and I wear my bathing costume a lot.
>
> Yesterday Christopher was feeling rather homesick and he cried at mealtime, and had to be comforted by his leader, (Nadeline)
>
> Lots of love and kisses from Isabel

Dear Mummy and Daddy,

Thankyou very much for the letters you sent me. Just before we went on our trek I slept with Christopher for two nights, and when I left for trek he cried because he didn't want me to go. We went swimming in the river at Lyng. Yesterday we walked there and arrived at about 3 O'clock. The first night we went to bed at 11 O'clock and the second night we raided Clarissa's group when they were in bed, and on that night we got to bed at about quarter to twelve.

LOTS OF LOVE FROM ISABEL

From me to Chris:

Dear Christopher,

I am enjoying myself a lot. The weather isn't very nice but it doesn't matter much. I am reading a funny book at the moment. The book is Jane's. She sleeps with me. Sometimes silly sheep come into the field we have camped on. But they don't disturb us. Last night when the rain was pouring down a tent fell down and in the morning the children were soaked.

With love from Catherine

From me to Mum and Dad:

Dear Mummy and Daddy,

I can't find any stamps in my ruck sack. Please could you tell me where to find them. I had a nice journey. On the way I made friends in the train. While Daddy and I were on the way to Paddington a man said "Hallo Cath" and he told me that he knew my name because of the badge I wore. I am sorry I can't write more,

LOVE KATE XXXX

Dear Mummy and Daddy,

Today we lit some fires with Kate our leader, and many a time we tried to get them going but failed because of the terrific wind. Please do you think you could send me some more stamps because I only have two left. Our tent nearly fell down this morning because the tent pole went squint. I have spent 6d of my money so far on a bar of chocolate which I ate up almost immidiately.

LOVE Catherine

Dear Mummy, and Daddy

At camp the weather is horrible, but still I am having a nice time. I am sleeping with a girl called Jane. Every day so far we have played at least four games. I am on clan three. I am not sleeping in a forest school tent, but are sleeping in Janes own tent. From my tent there is a most beautiful view. I have done many sketches. We have been climbing a very big hill. When you get to the top you get even a better view. We have found many sheep skelitons. My leader is called Kate. She is a nice girl. There is a great deal of hay in the field and a lot of boys nearly always have hay fights.

LOVE FROM CATHERINE XXX

Why, we wondered, was Chris so homesick when he came from a secure and happy home? Granny supplied the answer: "Och, he wasnae really homesick; it just takes longer for wee boys to grow up. Girls learn to fend for themselves earlier."

19
DOWN YOUR STREET

Never did I behold a vision so horrible as his face, of such loathsome yet appalling hideousness.

Frankenstein – Mary Shelley

One day in June 1966, a reporter from the *Woodford Times* rang our doorbell. He explained that he wrote a weekly feature called 'Down Your Street'. The idea was to select a road in the Wanstead and Woodford area, knock on a few doors at random, go into the houses and interview the occupants. No doubt it was Mum's plaque on the garden gate that prompted him to pick number thirty-two. Mum was well-used to the press. She tended to treat all journalists with suspicion, sure that they would get the facts wrong, and then think up some dreadful pun for a caption. Indeed, in 1963, the same *Woodford Times* had printed a photo of Izzy playing the violin, which was identified as 'Susan, 7, Hits the Right Note' – so perhaps she had some justification. However, the reporter was invited in. His name was Mel Rolfe.

"Of course, it will be my daughters you'll want to hear about," she stated, as the young man followed her upright figure down the hall to the living room. "They're twins, both very talented, particularly Catherine. They auditioned for the Menuhin School, you know, and were offered places, but I turned them down. To send seven-year-olds to boarding school is an act of cruelty. I wouldn't have dreamt of letting them go. This is my mother, Annie Fraser. She keeps the household running to schedule – I couldn't keep my teaching practice going without her." Granny gave a wary nod in his direction. Chris was sitting at the table. He had been drawing, but now swivelled around to regard the stranger. Their eyes met with interest.

"And who is this?" asked Mr. Rolfe.

"Oh," laughed Mum, "that's Christopher doing some of his daft drawings."

Chris grinned: Mel Rolfe smiled back. "Would you like to show them to me?" he asked, pulling out a chair to sit beside the boy. Immediately, the two were engrossed in conversation. Mum hovered. This was not going to plan. She would have to wait until he had finished talking to Christopher, and then he would surely want to spend some time with the girls. Still, he seemed very amused by Christopher, which was nice to see. She often wondered what possessed her funny little boy to draw such gruesome characters, which were usually depicted with severed limbs, ripped flesh, blood-dripping fangs, oozing scars, warts, carbuncles and similar disfigurements. His output was prolific, but there was no sense in keeping such things when dozens more would appear the next day.

To Mum's surprise, the reporter decided to take some shots of Christopher and his cartoons. That done, he at last turned his attention to the rest of the family, taking notes as Mum expounded on her musical beginnings and brought her daughters back into the conversation. She would have liked to say more, but Mr. Rolfe decided that the interview was concluded. He asked if he could take a photograph of the whole family before he left. Dad emerged from somewhere, possibly the cellar, and we assembled in the music room. Mum set out a chair for me to sit upon to play the cello, but that wasn't required: Christopher was to be the centre of attention, the only one of us to be pictured playing an instrument. Mum protested mildly, pointing out that Christopher was not a particularly proficient player, but it seemed churlish to raise further objection. So it was that Chris found himself in the limelight as a violinist for once in his life. The following week, 'Down Your Street' devoted a disproportionate amount of space to him. Here are some of Mel Rolfe's words from the article:

> Christopher Giles sat in front of the mirror. He jerked, twisted and screwed his face into a series of grotesque masks. His eyeballs protruded. His mouth hung sadistically. His hair was awry. Strange rumblings came from his throat [*see picture on page 145*]. An Academy Award performance. Refreshed by sudden inspiration, Christopher took up pad and pencil and produced another horror picture. Which is remarkable, because Christopher Giles is only eight-years-old.
>
> Christopher was, in fact, eight on Friday. He has been drawing pictures like this for as long as his parents remember. Note the macabre touch of the bolt neatly inserted in the throat. Young Christopher lives at 32, Cleveland Road, South Woodford, with his parents, grandmother and two sisters. They are a talented family. Yet I have a feeling that the exuberant Christopher will really take the world by storm. He looked at me with wide blue eyes. His first reporter – my first mini-cartoonist. I suspect Christopher did not let my visit go without eagerly making something out of the situation. A hideous drawing, doubtless inspired by me, has been added to the Giles junior collection.
>
> 'Giles', the national newspaper cartoonist, with his host of scavenging, mischievous children, would have a rare treat watching Giles junior pencilling out an army of outer space morons.
>
> At Oakdale Junior School his drawings are hung on the wall. I can well believe it. He can draw un-ugly pictures, but prefers the sabre-toothed, claw-handed, hysterical-to-meet-at-night type. He told me, 'I often start to draw at seven in the morning. I can't remember when I first began. I just like it.' Christopher has an un-grotesque, boyish face, with which, his mother told me, he likes to make people laugh. His drawings make a few people shudder. But in his list of the top four jobs he is at present aiming for when he leaves school, Christopher does not include anything remotely connected with drawing: 1. Vet; 2. Comedian; 3. Zoologist; 4. Stunt Man. Quite a mixed bag. But not an artist. Christopher just shrugged and didn't really know why, but his list is unshakeable.
>
> Christopher's father, Mr. Derek Giles, 45, works in an overseas accounts department of a London insurance company. His mother is Mrs. Elizabeth Giles, better known locally as Miss Elizabeth Fraser, music teacher. The two sisters are ten-year-old twins, Catherine and Isobel. Grandma is 73-year-old Mrs. Annie Fraser. Catherine plays the cello; Isobel the violin. Catherine, says her mother, has the makings of becoming a professional. And Christopher plays the violin. Elizabeth has given concerts and broadcast for the BBC. Yet to become a concert pianist, apart from the ability, you also need influence, money – or both. The young Elizabeth Fraser who came from Glasgow to study had neither influence nor money, but she had a reputation of being a first class music teacher, and has not needed to advertise for pupils since 1947. She qualified at the Royal Academy of Music. It is difficult to detect Elizabeth's Scottish accent, with good reason. When she came south,

> she determined to get rid of it.
>
> 'People are very rude', she said. 'They imitate you, then stare back and smile, as if it's a big joke. I didn't like being laughed at.' She added, scathingly: 'People in the south are very arrogant and conceited. They have a very high opinion of themselves.' Elizabeth does not only teach. She runs an advisory service for music teachers, with gramophone recordings. Quite a family.

Mum was annoyed that 'Isabel' had been spelt with an 'o'. Newspapers always got it wrong. She felt her clever children had been slightly misrepresented. It was a bit of a joke to make it appear that Christopher was the violinist in the family. She was pleased, though, that the journalist had been so taken with him. Chris could draw, certainly; he was a comic, there was no doubt about that; but were his cartoons worthy of such admiration? Perhaps so: still, her opinion about southerners had been printed. Quite right too, she thought. I am sure the word 'prejudice' did not cross her mind.

In June 2008, I tracked down Mel Rolfe to ask him if I could quote from his article. Did he remember Christopher Giles, I enquired? I received this reply:

> I must say I was staggered and moved to receive your email with one of my cuttings from forty-two years ago almost to the day. And yes, I remember Christopher. I imagine he was a lad who would be difficult to forget by anyone who had met him, even for the short time I spent with your family. I remember Christopher because of the talent and intelligence which I saw instantly whirring behind the intense concentration of those eyes. I also remember wondering if it was fair to single him out as someone I thought was special. But having met many scores of people – young and old – while involved with writing this feature and other articles and reports I did for the newspaper, I had not spoken to anyone quite like your brother, so took a chance. Certainly I remember Christopher's Frankenstinian monster, pictured in the newspaper, and he showed me some of his other drawings. What a pity he threw so many away. Presumably plenty survive for your book.

Sadly, almost none of Chris's monster-cartoons survive. Mum didn't keep his 'daft drawings'. It wasn't because she thought they were rubbish; she just had no idea how brilliant they were, so facilely did they pour from Chris's imagination onto reams and reams of paper. He couldn't help but draw them – they were doodles that made him and others laugh.

When Mel Rolfe wrote his article, Chris's first year at Junior School was nearly over. He had been put into the 'A' stream because of his obvious intelligence, despite the fact that he had been slow learning to read and couldn't make any sense of maths. There were two boys in his class with whom he was particularly friendly – Ross Pearlstone and Steve Cladingboel. Ross remembers Chris fondly, but can't recall anything specific. Steve, however, has many clear and detailed memories of Chris, their schooldays, and the times they spent together. Of Chris's ability to draw, he wrote: "He was a really good artist, which caused me, perhaps for the first time, to feel a sense of competition since I could also shoot a reasonable pencil. However, he had really bad handwriting: I remember a teacher asking him in an exasperated way why he couldn't write more neatly – after all, she said, handwriting is just another kind of art." But Chris's handwriting was his own: it didn't change much and was never neat.

Chris continued to spend a great deal of his playtimes rolling on the tarmac, and dropped dead several times a day. He wasn't too bothered about soccer, preferring to be involved in imaginative games rather than kick a soggy stuffed sock around – the only type of 'ball' allowed, but he joined in when he was asked. Steve told me, "Chris had a novel way of blowing his nose in the playground – he would depress one nostril with a finger and blow heartily out of the other, producing an awesome spray of snot. Then he would do the same with the other nostril. Today every footballer does this as routine, but back then I was mightily impressed and it was Chris's showpiece for a while."

His class teacher, Mrs. Wallis, remembered by Steve for riding a Moulton pedal bike, gave her end-of-year appraisal:

> Christopher can work very well at times. His reading has improved greatly. Lack of concentration, however, has shown itself in Arithmetic. Answers well on oral lessons. Very interested in the world around him.

His next teacher, Miss Cheatle, failed to recognise anything exceptional about the blue-eyed comedian in her classroom, and wrote a miserable report:

> General effort: Spasmodic. Christopher is capable of much better work. He has the ability, as he sometimes shows. He does not like Maths and consequently does not make much effort to master it. Let's hope that in the near future Christopher will realise that in order to be a vet one must have working knowledge of other subjects besides Natural History.

However, the headmistress, Mary Wallington, adored him. She always added an encouraging remark at the bottom of every report. For example: "Christopher is one of the youngest in his class and when his written work is as good as his oral work he should do extremely well." To Miss Cheatle's comments, she added, "I am confident that with determination Christopher is going to overcome any difficulties he encounters."

DOWN YOUR STREET

MEL ROLFE MEETS…

Monsters (on paper) and their creator

Woodford Times June 30th 1966

Mel Rolfe wrote the following captions for these photographs:

ABOVE: "Aaaargh! Christopher's really done it this time. Imagine meeting something like this at the top of the stairs on a dark and stormy night. On second thoughts, let's just NOT imagine it."

RIGHT: "A few flashes of pencil and Christopher Giles has completed another cartoon character. Christopher's output is vast, and unfortunately he throws much of it in the dustbin."

Woodford Times June 30th 1966: Mel Rolfe wrote: "The talented people who live at No. 32: Left to right: Mr. Derek Giles, Isabel, Mrs. Elizabeth Giles, Mrs. Annie Fraser, Catherine and Christopher."

BELOW: At Thaxted, where we danced with the Morris men. Izzy and I are eight, Chris nearly six.

20
PIERRE

Start not – nor deem my spirit fled:
In me behold the only skull
From which, unlike a living head,
Whatever flows is never dull.

Lines Inscribed Upon a Cup Formed from a Skull – Byron

My asthma was keeping Izzy as well as me awake at nights, so Mum and Dad moved into the spare room, Izzy was given the big front bedroom, I had the bunk beds to myself and Chris stayed in the back room beside me; and that was the little room I coveted. It was private – furthest away from the rest of the house, with a window that overlooked my garden. It was small and cosy and the only bedroom with a washbasin.

"Chris? Would you like to swap bedrooms with me?" I asked sweetly.

"No."

"Why not? Mine's a much bigger room and you'd have more space for your collection."

"I like my room."

"What if I gave you my week's pocket money?"

"No."

"Two weeks?"

"No."

"Oh Chris, please."

"No."

"You can have the bookcase – and the chest of drawers. You can have all the furniture – I'll move it for you."

He considered this.

I thought I might be getting somewhere.

"And I'll help you exhibit your collection to look like a proper museum."

"Would you?"

"Yes – I'll type the names of all your skulls onto cards – it'll look much better than the bits of paper you're using at the moment, and there'll be so much more room – we can arrange things in categories."

"Alright then."

I'd done it! We shifted the furniture and true to my word, I helped in every way I had promised. Izzy typed as well, both of us assisting with the displays. In fact, it was stimulating work for us all. Chris wrote out lists of his collection and we went into Mum's office to type the cards. It took ages because we made so many mistakes and binned dozens of failed attempts, to Mum's annoyance. Chris wanted the cards to display the animals' common and scientific names.

For example:

Fox: *Vulpes Vulpes*
Sheep: *Ovis aries*
Hare: *Lepus*
Cat: *Felis*

For his ninth birthday, Chris asked for a human skull. It was Grandad, Dad's father, an inspector of surgical instruments, who somehow managed to find a way of purchasing one via his connections in the medical profession. The skull was smallish – perhaps that of a young woman or adolescent, as it didn't have a full set of teeth. On the top of the skull were three obvious scratch marks. Chris invented ghoulish stories to explain them. The one he often repeated was that it was the skull of a teenage boy who had gone hunting. In the forest he came face to face with a brown bear that mauled him to death, digging his massive clawed paw into the boy's head and ripping off his scalp. Chris called the skull 'Pierre'. Soon after Pierre's arrival, he made a list of his collection so far.

SKULLS: Human, pig, ox, sheep, ram, hedgehog, mole, house mouse, wood mouse, cat, dog, fox, crow, rook, owl, German sea bird, blackbird, rat, black headed gull, pigeon, guinea pig, rabbit, hare, tawny owl, thrush, weasel, vole, seabird.
BITS OF SKULLS: Fallow deer jaw, goat jaw, goat upper jaw, Scottish sheep upper jaw, roe deer antlers, red deer antlers.
MUMMIFIED ANIMALS: Shrew, lizard, crow.
STUFFED ANIMALS: Mongoose, snake, fox head.
FURS: Mink/rat, pine marten, fox, fox tail, arctic fox.
TREE BARK: Birch
SHELLS: Sea snail, cowry, cockle, mussel, razor, limpet, whelk, edible snail, scallop, ear snail, winged snail, winkle, shells from Spain – unidentified.
SKELETONS: Duck, hedgehog, pigeon, cat, rat, weasel.
PARTS OF SKELETONS: Fox, cat, whale, owl.
FOSSILS: Scallop shell, sea urchin, graptolite, rhynchonella, plicatilis, belemnite, ammonite.
STONES: Marble, coloured marble, pudding stone, rock from the Alps, solid lava, cave-man tool, coloured stone, iron pyrites.
FISH: Angel fish, red tailed shark (preserved).
OTHERS: sea urchin, cuttle fish bone, crab shells.
BIRDS' EGGS: Domestic fowl, great skua, arctic skua, sparrow, house martin, pheasant, partridge, French partridge, starling, lapwing. Five unidentified.

Some of Chris's specimens were donated, like the big case of stuffed birds, a smaller one of a fox and stoat, a fox head, a deer head and a large pair of antlers. Occasionally, the keepers at London Zoo gave him specimens, including skulls, skins shed by snakes, dead insects, spiders and butterflies. The zookeepers were as fascinated by

Chris as he was with animals. Chris read up on taxidermy and had a go at skinning a dead rabbit, but was disappointed with the result. Nevertheless, he kept on practising and became more successful with each attempt. He invited anyone who came to the house to view his collection, and provided a running commentary whilst showing his visitors around. Before they left, he asked them to write their comments about The Cleveland Collection in the Visitors' Book. The first entry is from our house cleaner at the time:

A most interesting display of bones, beasts and bugs – don't attempt to move any skulls or you may find the lower jaw falls off!
Barbara Kemp.

I like all the bonse and things and I like the dirds mests and the eggs and I like your bunc bed.
Frances Kemp. (6)

I like it very much,
But it has a gloomy touch.
Isabel Giles
P.S. I like helping Chris to type out the notices for the collection. I also think it is very good for a very young boy to take interest in such things. I.G.

This is a very interesting collection. A lot of time and care has obviously been given to it. The supervised instruction and interesting talks given to visitors while "inspecting" the collection are most enjoyable and the charming way of telling them all adds to the impact.
Catherine Giles.

A most interesting collection with plenty of variety and well displayed.
Elizabeth Fraser.

Almost as good a collection as I would have made myself, had I ever started one.
D.C.F. Giles.

There is no entry from Granny; I do not know why.

21
GRANDAD

A truth that's told with bad intent
Beats all the Lies you can invent.

Auguries of Innocence – William Blake

On Sunday mornings Dad took us to visit his father – our Grandad – and a woman we knew as Auntie Lilian. She had moved in with Grandad soon after the death of Dad's mother. That was in 1951, before we were born, before Mum and Dad had even met. Grandad and Auntie Lilian lived in Roding Lane North, a bland suburban road connecting Woodford Bridge to South Woodford. Number fifty-two was a meanly-dimensioned terraced house. A narrow garden path led to the front door, which opened into a tiny hall. The front room, darkened by swathes of nets and curtains, and overfilled with looming furniture, brass candlesticks, china figures, plates and vases, was rarely entered. Auntie Lilian polished and dusted it daily – a showroom where important visitors could be received when circumstance demanded. There was no occasion when we encountered an Important Visitor, but we did not question their existence. The second door on the left led into a pokey back room, fuggy with smoke from Grandad's cigarettes. The airless, dingy house, with its worn carpets, saggy brown armchairs and cracked linoleum was ugly, cramped and chilly. We climbed the steep staircase to use the loo, but that was as far as we ventured upstairs. Beyond the hall was a small kitchen. From there the back door opened onto a few concrete steps, which led into a surprisingly long garden that sloped downhill. Dad was expected to cut the grass and prune the gnarled apple tree, a hated obligation that was the subject of many angry exchanges between him and his father. This had been Dad's home for many years before he moved in with Mum and Granny. He had been just as miserable there as he was at Cleveland Road.

Lilian was another woman whom Dad detested. He talked uncivilly to her, made snide comments to her face and described her as a stupid, gossip-mongering snob. True, she made valiant attempts to conceal her working-class accent with what she imagined to be genteel intonation and vocabulary, littering her sentences with grammatical clangers that made Dad cringe, but it was more than her ignorance that infuriated him. His antipathy towards her was as strong as the hatred he felt for Granny; but Lilian was made of softer stuff, which gave Dad the upper ground to vent his meanness openly.

We couldn't have explained it, but Auntie Lilian wasn't like Granny or Mum. She dressed differently, wore jewellery, sprayed herself with flowery perfume and painted her nails. Her white hair was set in curls with mauve or pink tints, her face powdered, her mouth smudged with bright lipstick. She sometimes sang in a high soprano voice with a vibrato that wobbled wildly from the pitch, which made us smile – not unkindly: we liked her cheerful trilling, although we did wonder how it was possible to sing so out of tune. She had been widowed before she met Grandad. As I remember, she had three children; Vera, Iris, and Victor; and a number of grandchildren – Colette, Clare, Julie, Vivian and Alix being the names I recall. Although we didn't meet them, we prompted Auntie Lilian to update us with the latest news or tell us stories from her past. One granddaughter was training to be a nurse, which gave Auntie Lilian a plethora of wonderfully gruesome hospital dramas to relate. She knew little about medical conditions and even less about anatomy, which exasperated Dad. I remember her describing how a man almost died from a hernia, but a brilliant doctor, with the help of her granddaughter, of course, removed it just in time. "It was so big," she said, "that he kept it and put it in a jar."

"Really?" we asked, wide-eyed with wonder.

"Oh yes, dears. My granddaughter says this doctor has shelves of hernias on display in glass bottles."

"You're talking utter nonsense," said Dad. "A hernia isn't a tumour. I wish you wouldn't tell the children such rubbish – and I wish you three wouldn't encourage her with her ridiculous gossiping."

We ignored him and asked for more. She told us about the man who swallowed his false teeth, the boy who arrived at hospital with a chamber pot stuck on his head, mothers going home with the wrong babies, patients nearly having a leg amputated when they were only in for an ingrown toenail – but the heroic granddaughter sorted out the muddles, rushed to the rescue, saved lives and received numerous letters of gratitude. It didn't matter if the stories weren't true – we knew that storks did not deliver babies, that eating carrots did not help you see in the dark and that you would not 'catch your death' if you went outside with wet hair. She usually rounded off her anecdotes with the phrase, "So, you see dears, it only goes to show."

"Goes to show what?" demanded Dad.

Apart from hospital stories, there were weddings. We heard which little ones were going to be bridesmaids and pageboys and what they were going to wear, Auntie Lilian describing the dresses in detail. Izzy and I sighed ecstatically. We knew we would never be bridesmaids, but oh, how romantic! Just think of it – wearing a special bridesmaid's dress with sticky-out petticoats and white patent shoes.

It didn't cross our minds to ask why we called her Auntie Lilian: we always had. Yet clearly, she was not our Auntie, but our step-grandmother. She would, I realise, have liked it if we had called her Nana. In our birthday cards, which she, not Grandad, chose and sent, she wrote "lots of love from Nana and Grandpa. God Bless." I puzzled over it. Why Nana, when she was Auntie Lilian? Why Grandpa when he was Grandad? Why God Bless? The truth was that Dad would not agree to us calling her Nana. Apart from his snobbery about 'Nana' being a common, working-class term, he would not allow her to claim us as her grandchildren. But if he thought this would marginalise her from our lives, he was wrong. She was our Auntie Lilian; a person who cherished us, whom we trusted and liked. She attended our concerts, even though she knew nothing about music, and was the only adult in the family who told us repeatedly how clever, talented, brilliant and special we were. To her, anything we did was wonderful. She sent us cards for every occasion – Good Luck cards for exams and concerts, Congratulation cards for successes, Thank You cards just for visiting her on our own and of course Birthday, Christmas and even Easter cards – with love from Nana.

She knew that I liked to sew and make things. She bought me skeins of embroidery silk and showed me how to decorate tablecloths and napkins. She taught me how to work needlepoint, how to sew a hem with invisible stitches on the right side, how to tack, backstitch, chain-stitch and blanket-stitch. She was sensitive to us, which was just as well, because Grandad was not. He was a big, intimidating man with no empathy for children. We were wary of him, his gruff voice, his unpredictable temper, the smile we couldn't trust.

Grandad moaned incessantly at Dad and called him Colin. It seemed odd to us, when we knew Dad's name was Derek, and we could tell that he didn't like to be called Colin. We were too young to analyse the dynamic between Dad and his father, but we felt their antagonism, could see Dad's clenched jaw and the darts of anger that Grandad shot towards him. Grandad criticised Dad about our behaviour and disapproved of the fact that we were not being brought up as Christians. I remember him quizzing us about our knowledge of God.

"What's up there in the sky?" he asked.

We knew this to be a trick question by the sly twist in his voice.

"The Universe," answered Chris after a moment.

"No, no, no", said Grandad, his voice rising. "Who *lives* up there in the sky?"

We looked fearfully to Dad for guidance, but he didn't meet our eyes.

"Might it be God?" asked Izzy tentatively.

"Yes! That's right!"

Dad turned away uncomfortably.

"And where does He live?"

There was a long silence.

"It's heaven, dears, isn't it?" offered Auntie Lilian helpfully.

"I wasn't asking you, woman!" he roared.

"Father, just leave it, will you? Let's get down to the Cocked Hat."

"I'm telling you, you're not raising those children properly – just look how they behave! They'll turn into good-for-nothings, the lot of 'em, you mark my words."

"Put your coats on," Dad ordered.

We helped Chris into his duffle coat.

"He's old enough to do that himself," Dad snapped.

The three of us and Auntie Lilian climbed into the back of the car, Grandad sitting grumpily in the passenger seat, Dad, purse-lipped and dismal, driving in his usual nervous, hesitant manner, braking erratically at the sight of every moving vehicle. We were left to sit on the bench outside the pub, whatever the weather. After a while Dad would appear with pineapple juices. Auntie Lilian came out with him and sat on the bench with us, sipped her sherry and took Chris onto her lap to resume her captivating tales. Dad complained at us all the way home, saying he could not take us to Grandad's again if we didn't learn to behave.

When Grandad was in a reasonable mood, he produced the chess set and showed me how the pieces moved. I learnt quickly. He played competitively, chuckling when he defeated me. There came a day when he made one or two wrong moves, I saw my chance and took his queen. He glared at me with hatred. With as much subtlety as I could muster, I endeavoured to lose the game.

"Ha, ha. You see, you can't get one over on yer old Grandad!"

He delighted in teasing. On Chris's fifth birthday, he gave him ten shillings. This was a fortune to a child in 1963. None of us had ever held one of those crisp brown notes in our hands. In all our seven years, he hadn't given anything to Izzy or me.

"See, girls, I'm giving this to Christopher because he's such a good little boy. Not like you two, eh?" he chuckled. "Now, you take care of it, son."

Chris saw our crestfallen faces. "I'll share it with the girls."

"You'll do nothing of the sort," said Grandad. "Your sisters don't deserve anything. It's a present from your Grandad to you." Chris looked dejectedly at the note in his hand. Either Izzy or I started to sniff, which set the other off.

"I don't believe it, Colin. It's Christopher's birthday and those girls want to take his money away from him! What did I tell you? They've no manners; they're ungrateful and spoiled and old enough to know better. Look at them!"

Now we were both weeping, and Chris's little face was puckering too.

"Stop it at once," Dad barked, "I'm taking you home."

"Yes, you do that. I don't want bad children in my house. What dreadful behaviour. Poor Christopher, and on his birthday too."

Crying, the three of us were pushed out of the house. Halfway down the garden path Grandad called out, "I was going to give the girls five shillings each as well, but they're not getting it now. Not after showing how jealous and spoilt they are!" He was smiling.

"See! See what you've done?" yelled Dad. "If you'd behaved yourselves you'd have some money too. You've only yourselves to blame. Stop that awful howling and get in the car."

Dad didn't try to soothe us on the journey home. No, he vented his pent up rage on us. For he had been rebuked and manipulated too, just as he had been subjected to countless incidents of emotional foul play as a child.

So often, people who suffered unpleasant and disturbing experiences in their early years foist the same upon their children. So it was with Dad. He found cruel pleasure in teasing us. "Hey, look up there!" he'd say. During the two or three seconds that we looked away, a cake vanished from our plate or some similar hoax was performed. You would think we would grow wise to his tricks, but he was adept at fooling us. "Look out!" he'd cry urgently, "behind you!" While our back was turned, he had hidden the thing we were playing with. The more het up we became, the funnier he found it.

One Saturday, we walked to George Lane with Dad. He made a few purchases and we were on our way home. "Who'd like a treat?"

"What sort of treat?" we asked in anticipation.

"A very special treat, but only one of you may have it."

We jumped up and down.

"Me, me, me," we clamoured.

Obviously, I shouted the hardest.

"Very well, Catherine. Here you are."

He handed me the bag of shopping to carry.

"Hee, hee," he chuckled, "we fooled her didn't we? What a good wheeze!" Izzy and Chris laughed too, although they didn't mean to hurt me, I'm sure. They walked off, leaving me feeling humiliated, foolish and ashamed of myself for being so gullible.

Chris looked back. "Come on, Kay," he called.

I dumped the bag on the pavement, turned on my heels and walked in the opposite direction, eyes stinging, throat burning.

ABOVE: Outside the Cocked Hat pub with Grandad and Auntie Lilian.

Grandad and Izzy

Grandad in his back garden

ABOVE: Chris showing off 'Pierre', the human skull he was given for his ninth birthday.

BELOW LEFT: With our cat, Sally. RIGHT: At the cottage removing feathers from a dead crow with the visiting cat asleep beside him. Chris had an affinity with animals. He seemed to attract cats wherever he went.

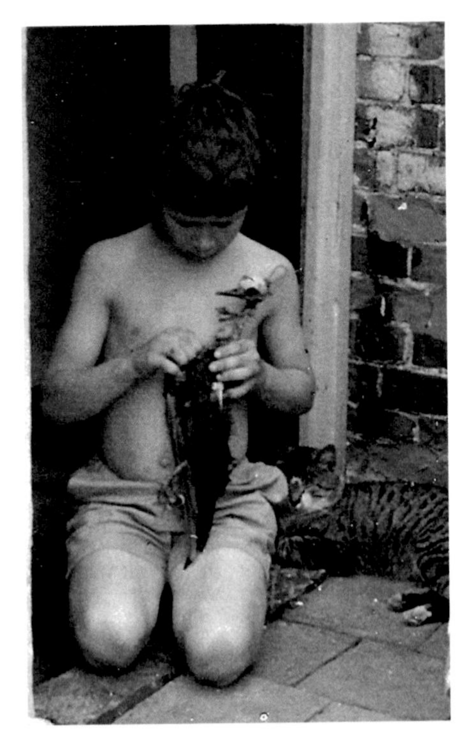

DAD'S STORY

They think not but that every eye can see
The same disgrace which they themselves behold,
And therefore would they still in darkness be,
To have their unseen sin remain untold.

The Rape of Lucrece – Shakespeare

22
INDIAN EMBROIDERY

When I began to research my father's mother's family, I had no inkling of the labyrinth I was about to enter. I knew very little about Dad's mother. When, as a youngster, I pressed him for information, he seemed reluctant to discuss the subject. He did tell me this, though – a story that left me with lasting impressions and unanswered questions.

"Her name was Georgina May Anstruther. She was born and lived her early childhood in Bengal, which is in India, during the heydays of the British Empire. She and her parents enjoyed a life of luxury, waited on by a multitude of native servants. Everything was done for the little girl. She wasn't expected, or even allowed, to lift a finger."

Having read *The Secret Garden*, I found this thrilling. Georgina could be Mary Lennox herself, with her own Ayah to dress and serve her. I imagined heat, silks, spices, tropical plants and tea plantations. I pictured mosquito nets draped over brocaded beds, barefoot native girls, white-suited servants, sprawling villas, shaded verandas, pavilions and exotic vistas. I saw Georgina's wealthy parents reclining on divans, the servants fanning them with large palm leaves; their little girl free to do as she pleased, playing games with her Ayah and drinking iced lemonade.

"Her father was Colonel Robert Anstruther," Dad continued. "He and his wife, Mary, would have lived, partied and socialised within the elite and privileged circles of the British Army, which occupied India during the late nineteenth century. This was the world that Georgina, their youngest child and only daughter, inhabited. She was a very pretty girl and became a strikingly beautiful woman. Alas, when I knew her, she often wore a sad, troubled expression. Yes, she had a tragic life, my poor mother."

"Why was she sad?"

"Ah well, it was a long time ago; before you were born, before I was born, even. I shall tell you what I know. I should say from the start that she was a Roman Catholic. That was her greatest handicap. All religious creeds are dreadful, but Catholicism is one of the worst."

"They don't allow contraception, do they?"

"That's just one of a whole range of rules the Catholic Church uses to control and repress the human mind and spirit – but we won't go into all that right now."

"What about Georgina then, Dad?"

"It was her father who brought his family to ruin; unintentionally, I presume – he couldn't have envisaged the outcome."

"What happened?"

"Well, my dear, he had an affair with a Bengali girl, probably one of his servants. No doubt plenty of his fellow British officers did the same. They were in a position of power, you see. They could have clandestine affairs without consequence to themselves. However, Robert Anstruther made two fatal mistakes – he fell in love with the girl and he was found out. What's more, she was pregnant. You can imagine his predicament. He found himself in the centre of a scandal, facing a destroyed career, a shattered marriage, public disgrace and ostracism. The realisation of utter ruin overwhelmed him. He took the only way out."

Dad seemed to become lost in his own thoughts and stopped talking. I had to prompt him. "What did he do?"

"I'm afraid he shot himself."

"Oh no."

"Suicide. Terrible." He fell silent again.

"Then what happened?"

After another pause, he went on: "His wife and children were sent back to England with nothing. There was no pension or widow's benefit for a man who had committed suicide. Mary, her sons and daughter arrived in London impoverished and destitute."

"What happened to the Indian girl and her baby, Dad?"

"Oh… I don't know."

How could he not know? It was the saddest part. Did the young woman survive? What happened to her? Was the baby born? My father did not repeat the story. Mum and Izzy had no recollection of ever having heard it. I sometimes wondered if I had dreamed the whole thing up.

I had to find out more. Having successfully traced back several generations of Mum's ancestors, I naively entered 'Colonel Robert Anstruther' into an Ancestry.com search, expecting to track him down without too much difficulty. How wrong I was! As this book goes to print, the man is still unidentified. But I did find a posting on the Ancestry message board from somebody called Mark Elliot Anstruther Heal, titled: "Colonel Anstruther with a skeleton in his cupboard?" It read:

> I should welcome help with this elusive great grandfather, possibly named Colonel Robert William Anstruther, but this might be an assumed name… the seven offspring knew very little of their father and were not encouraged to ask. Their birth registrations have not been traced and they came to assume they were the illegitimate family of a well born father in India, whose sudden financial demise and possible suicide plunged the mother and children into extreme and unaccustomed poverty back in London.

This was obviously the same story that Dad had told me. I contacted Mark Heal. We worked out that he and I are second cousins: his grandfather and my grandmother were siblings and we share the same elusive great grandfather. We met up a few days later and since then have spent many years trekking through our family's maze of mystery and intrigue together. As the story unfolds, it might be helpful to refer to the 'Anstruther, Lupino and Giles' family tree printed at the end of the book.

Although our search did not begin here, I will start with our great grandmother, Mary Henry, supposedly Colonel Anstruther's wife. Her parents were Dominick Henry (c1806-1873) and Ann (c1812-1883). Mary was born c1838 in County Sligo, Ireland, a devoutly Roman Catholic country. Catholicism dominated and governed the lives, minds and identity of the Irish population. It is important to remember this: Mary was as Catholic as she was female. I have already mentioned the potato famine in *Granny's Story*, but will expand upon it a little here.

In 1845, when Mary was a child, a fungus called *Phytophthora Infestans*, commonly known as 'black rot' or 'blight' attacked the potato crops of Ireland. It had struck before in localised areas, but in 1845 and over the following few years it hit every part of Ireland, bringing widespread famine in its wake. The starving population headed for the cities and crowded into disease-infested workhouses seeking relief and shelter. Cholera and typhus spread rapidly. The dead lay everywhere, too great in number to bury with any decency or speed. Some landlords paid for their tenants to resettle in America, Canada and other English-speaking countries, but even emigration was hazardous. Thousands of desperate passengers were crammed onto ramshackle vessels labelled 'coffin ships', sometimes as many as a third on board dying of disease and hunger. Starvation, disease and emigration depopulated the island from eight to five million in just a few years.

Whether by choice or decree, Dominick Henry, his wife and seven children, left Ireland in 1851, arriving in New York in October. Mary was then aged thirteen. Some of the Henrys settled there permanently, but in about 1863, Mary, her parents and other members of the family sailed back across the Atlantic to Liverpool. Mary's trail is difficult to follow here, but we do know that she lived in Liverpool for some years and gave birth to a son, Edgar, in September 1866 when she was twenty-eight.

However, long before we had come this far, we were embroiled in the hunt for our mysterious 'Colonel Anstruther'. I had been enthralled by the colourful tale Dad told me, enticed by the spicy flavours and exotic scent of a far off land and egged on by a photograph [*see page 165*] supposedly taken in India of young Georgina in the arms of her Ayah. The snake charmer did not have to play his flute all that beguilingly to lure me to India. I didn't go there, but I wasted a lot of time in fruitless research and found nothing that helped.

All we knew was that our great-grandmother, Mary Henry alias Anstruther, bore at least seven children, whose names, we thought, were Edgar, George, Frederick, Gilbert, Melgund, Dominick and Georgina. The first helpful clue came with Mark's discovery of Mary Anstruther and her four youngest children living in Southwark in the 1891 census. Mary's birthplace is given as Sligo, Ireland; her son Gilbert's as Southwark, London; Melgund, Georgina and Dominick as having been born in Hanwell, Middlesex. India didn't feature. On closer inspection, the Indian photograph looked very odd – as if the child and the Ayah had been grafted together from two different images. What ghastly secret might demand the extraordinary subterfuge of faking a photograph?

Then I had a breakthrough. I searched the 1881 census using just first names and found Mary and her six children living at 3, Clifton Villas, Hanwell, Middlesex. The only child missing was Dominick – Mary was pregnant with him when the census was taken. The combination of their unusual names had at last given them away. But what was a complete revelation was finding a 'Robert G. Bennett' listed as the 'Head', Mary as his 'Wife' and all the children with the last name 'Bennett'.

The name 'Bennett' meant nothing to anyone in the family, but it enabled us to trace four civil birth registrations: George, Mark's grandfather, was born George Elliot Carnegie Bennett on September 14th 1870 in Southwark; Melgund was born Robert Herbert Bennett, on June 4th 1876; Georgina, my grandmother, was born Mary Georgina Anstruther Bennett on March 4th 1879; Dominick was born Dominick Compton Anstruther Bennett on September 30th 1881, the last three in Hanwell, Middlesex. On all four certificates, the father is registered as 'Robert George Bennett' and the mother, 'Mary Bennett, formerly Henry'. But despite years of searching and employing professional genealogists, no record has been found of a marriage between Mary Henry and Robert Bennett.

However, we knew that Mary was a devout Roman Catholic. She might have been willing to keep the birth certificates hidden, but she could not have conceived of sentencing her children to eternal hell and damnation: they must have been baptised. Mark's persistent rooting found Catholic baptism records for Mary's youngest six children, all registered with the last name 'Bennett' and a father called Robert George Bennett. Melgund, named Robert Herbert Bennett at birth, was baptised Melgund Robert Anstruther Bennett.

Edgar's civil birth registration and Catholic baptism were traced just a few weeks before this book went to print. He was born on September 10th 1866 in Liverpool and baptised at St. Nicholas Roman Catholic Church (which no longer exists). However, this new information raises more questions and presents further mysteries, for Edgar's last name on both documents is Crockford, which is as much of a surprise to us as Bennett. Edgar's father is recorded as 'Frederick Crockford', and his mother, 'Mary Crockford, formerly Henry'. Who was Frederick Crockford? Again, no marriage record has been found between Mary Henry and Frederick Crockford, and it seems that all trace of him disappears after Edgar's birth. By the time of the 1871 census, Edgar, aged five, had become Edgar Bennett. Who, then, was Robert George Bennett? We have not found a birth or death registration for him. His name appears on two censuses and some of the children's birth and baptism documents, but this is insufficient evidence to substantiate his identity or existence. Did Frederick Crockford change his name to Robert Bennett? Are they one and the same, or two separate individuals? Presently, there is no proof that Mary Henry was ever Mrs. Crockford, Mrs. Bennett, or Mrs. Anstruther, come to that. Everything we have learnt points to the fact that the children had no idea that their last name was

Bennett, or in Edgar's case, Crockford. They were all brought up believing that they were Anstruthers, and their father was Colonel Robert Anstruther.

The story that Dad passed on to me is almost certainly complete invention, as probably are others that have filtered through the generations. For example: that Colonel Anstruther brought himself to financial ruin in India by running up colossal gambling debts; that he was cashiered[1] for gambling and cheating at cards; that he committed suicide by either shooting himself or cutting his throat; that he was not married to Mary, already having a wife and another family. It does seem abundantly clear that 'Colonel Robert Anstruther' was a fake name, or a bogus character, possibly invented to obscure the true identity of the children's father. And maybe the children's mother had a big secret to hide too. If Mary was not married to Frederick Crockford or Robert Bennett, was she already another man's wife? Had she married in New York and deserted her husband when she returned to England? To live with and have sex with a man who was not her husband was a mortal sin; a sin so heinous and shameful to a Roman Catholic that Mary would have gone to any lengths to keep it hidden. It is one explanation why the children never saw their birth certificates, but not a satisfactory one. For how were they persuaded that they were legitimate Anstruthers without evidence of birth certificates? And why was the name Anstruther chosen? Moreover, how did the story evolve that the children were born in India? Which of our ancestors were the deceivers, colluders and collaborators?

There is a theory, which at times I find compelling, that Gilbert John Elliot-Murray-Kynynmound, who later became the Fourth Earl of Minto, might have fathered the children. He was born in 1845 and given the courtesy title of Lord Melgund in 1859. It was not until June 1883, when he was thirty-eight, that he married Mary Caroline Grey. Soon after the honeymoon, the couple departed for Canada. Here is the crucial fact: the wedding was nearly two years after the birth of Mary's last child. It would be perfectly feasible for Lord Melgund to have had a long-standing mistress from the age of twenty-one – 1866, when Edgar was born – to around 1881 when Mary's youngest, Dominick, was born. The dates fit, many of the names match those of the Elliot/Minto clan – Melgund, Gilbert and Elliot are particularly persuasive, as are Carnegie and Compton (middle names given to George and Dominick respectively, which also appear in the Elliot lineage). But illegitimate children do not make heirs. Family and social pressure might perhaps have coerced Lord Melgund into legal matrimony, at which point, it could be plausibly argued, Mary and her seven children were discarded. How convenient to allow the myth to grow about financial ruin, adultery and suicide to explain the disappearance of a father and 'husband'. How clever to stage the action in India, keeping everyone's heads turned in the wrong direction. It would take too long to go into all the research undertaken on the Elliot/Minto tribe here: suffice to say, it has been extensive, but I have not been able to establish any hard facts to prove my hypothesis. Placed within the complex web of concealment and deception, it is probably just a neat solution that has no connection with the truth.

1. 'Cashiering' was a punishment severer than dismissal for army or naval officers in that it disqualified the offender from entering the public service again in any capacity. The punishment was not abolished until 1970.

Interestingly, though, Lord Melgund *was* in India in 1879, arriving in Bombay in January and returning to his family's estate in Minto, Roxburghshire about six months later. Georgina was born in March 1879 while Lord Melgund was away – could it be that Georgina was told her father was in India at the time of her birth and this is a clue as to why she imagined she had been born there?

My father knew none of the above. It is possible that his mother, Georgina, knew a great deal more than she ever told, was instrumental in spreading some of the rumours and sparing with the truth. For example, she was not the youngest child, being two-and-a-half years older than her brother, Dominick, yet she persuaded everyone that she was the baby of the family. Those who knew she wasn't protected her secret or just forgot the facts. She successfully lied about and adjusted her age throughout her life. However, if Georgina was a skilled deceiver, her mother was a virtuoso. All evidence suggests that even Georgina did not know that her name was Bennett.

Georgina Anstruther, as I shall call her, was born in 1879 in Hanwell, now the W7 district of London. By the time she was four her father had vanished. With his disappearance came financial hardship. Mary and her seven children had to leave Hanwell, and moved to 82, Quinn Square, Waterloo Road, a very poor area just south of the Thames. In July 1886, the eldest son, Edgar, now nineteen, joined the Royal Marines in Portsmouth. Mary missed him dreadfully. A copy of a letter she sent to him soon after his departure reveals something of the family's circumstances (try hearing it with an Irish accent):

> Dear Edgar,
>
> You must have thought me very unkind not to have replied sooner to your welcome letter – it was such a relief to my mind to get it, as from your silence I imagined all sorts of things. On the day you left, George returned home very ill and was so bad I had to go to Rumbold for a bottle of medicine for which he charged me a shilling – was it not mean after all he had from us – I need not tell you how I felt that night – you gone and all – the next morning I sent Fred up to Mr. Geldom to say that George could not attend the business & as usual Fred got into conversation with the Chief Cashier who asked him how long he had been from school etc. & the upshot is that, thank God, they have taken him into the office of the Chief Cashier at 8/- a week, not as manager but to take the numbers of cheques & use the telephone – if he were competent they would have given him twice as much as that. So I must work him up – the same old man came to see me as calls at the Square & he says they think highly of George & that I may make my mind easy about the boys. I know this will please you. Fred has been three days & likes it, with the exception of the stairs – he has to climb ninety steps to go up several times a day.
>
> I miss you so much Edgar. Little Dom cried after you the first night we told him you had gone. How do you like it. The change at all events is good for you. Have you a Church near. I hope you have, as God has been so good to us, I hope He will be to you too & never forget Him nor his blessed Mother – for I am sure it is in answer to our prayers Fred has got the place. Out of Freddy's money next week he must have a pair of boots, but the week after, please God, I will do well. The boys all send love & Gina & Dommy send kisses.
>
> My dear Edgar. With much love your Mother
>
> P.S. I had not a penny for a stamp till last night. Pollock is out of work & Bradshaw ditto, so that up to the present I am the richest on this landing.

What I find conspicuous by its absence is the fact that there is no reference at all to a 'father' in Mary's letter. If he were dead, one might think she would have written something like, "Your father, God rest his soul, would have been proud of you." But perhaps she knew that he still lived.

Not long after Edgar had enlisted, George, who worked as a clerk for the railways, left home and moved a few streets away to York Road. At this point, he became immersed in Catholicism. He began to write as a freelance journalist for Catholic newspapers and spoke passionately at Hyde Park Corner, where Father Philip Fletcher, the founder of The Guild of Ransom, spotted him.[2] Father Fletcher was so impressed by George's fervent outpourings that he invited the young man to move into Ransom House, Catholic lodgings in Peckham, where he was introduced to the Church Militant. Bede Bailey, O.P., in his essay *Table Talk* writes:

> He [*George Anstruther*] began his Catholic career with his fellow lodgers in combating the traducers of Catholics, in persistently heckling them at their meetings, in interrupting and speaking whenever the chance came.

This fundamentalist group later formed part of what developed into the Catholic Evidence Guild, George reportedly its most zealous member. Describing the activities of the group, Father Bede Bailey goes on to report:

> – how, in the parish of St. Mary and St. Michael in the East End, during one of the Catholic processions of witness, someone was so ill-advised as to spit on the procession from a top window. Several burly Irishmen slipped away from the hymn-singing cavalcade, entered the building, went upstairs to the room from which the spittle was dispatched, and threw all the furniture out of the window. They then returned to the procession, proclaiming to friend and foe alike that they would remain faithful through dungeon, fire and sword.

Mary's third son, Frederick, also left home and became a travelling agent for Suttons Seeds. By 1891, the widow Mrs. Anstruther, as Mary Henry now called herself, was still living at Quinn Square with Gilbert (16), Melgund (14), Georgina (12) and Dominick (9). Melgund worked as a bellboy at the Savoy Hotel and Gilbert as an assistant waiter at Scott's Supper Rooms. The late hours that Gilbert worked meant that he often slept overnight in staff rooms above the restaurant. One such night was May 9th 1892, the very night that a fire broke out in the premises, raged through the building and took the lives of Gilbert and three other employees. The *Times* reported the incident under the heading 'FIRES AND LOSS OF LIFE' and the Catholic paper, the *Tablet*, printed an account a few days later. Below is a cut down version.

> The Haymarket of London was the scene, in the early hours of yesterday morning, of a very disastrous fire, which resulted in the loss of four lives and in the partial destruction of an old established restaurant known as 'Scott's Supper Rooms'. The upper floors were used as bedrooms by the numerous employees of the firm. On the third floor, four young men, who were especially attached to the refreshment and oyster saloons, slept entirely

2. The Guild of Our Lady of Ransom was founded in London in 1887 by the Reverend Philip Fletcher and Lister Drummond with the aim of restoring England and Wales to the Roman Catholic Church.

> apart from the others. The fire broke out under the staircase leading up to the first-floor refreshment rooms and spread with great rapidity. The police in the immediate neighbourhood discovered the smoke curling through the cracks of the door at about 1.35, and raised an alarm. They blew their whistles, knocked loudly at doors, and in every possible way endeavoured to arouse the inmates. Eleven occupants awoke to find the place full of suffocating smoke, rushed terror-stricken downstairs and made their way to the street, but the four lads were quite away from reach or hearing, and from first to last they gave no sign of life. The engines arrived at the same time and found a fierce fire raging in the centre of the restaurant and up the staircase, while the flames were bursting through the roof. The escape had been placed against the front of the building, and officers and men at once ascended and forced their way in. The smoke was so dense that the lamps they carried went out immediately. They would have gone further but a mass of flames was bursting up between the front building and the back, the staircase acting as a flue. Directly the premises had cooled, a search was made and the dead bodies of the unfortunate lads were discovered. It was evident from their appearance that three of the bodies had been suffocated, and had struggled a good deal in a semi-conscious state to make an escape. The fourth lad had evidently been burnt to death. The arms were uplifted as if in agony and the flesh had been completely burned from the bones.

On May 21st 1892, a column appeared in the *Times*:

> Yesterday afternoon at St. James's Vestry-hall, Piccadilly, Mr. John Troutbeck, the coroner for Westminster, resumed and concluded his enquiry into the circumstances attending the deaths of WILLIAM DENNING, 17, cashier; GEORGE HENRY HUGH BARKER, 16; GILBERT ANSTRUTHER, 17; and THOMAS PHILLIPS, 15; assistant waiters who lost their lives in the fire at Scott's Supper Rooms, Coventry Street, Haymarket, early on the morning of the 9th inst… Mr. Edward Carstonsen Segundo, a consulting electrical engineer, under the Coroner's instructions, visited the premises… his conclusion was that it was probable that the fire was caused by a leakage in the electric wiring, more especially if rats and mice had been gnawing at the casing… the jury, after some deliberation, returned a verdict to the effect that the boys died from suffocation, and that the cause of the fire was unknown. They added that they considered the firemen and police to have done their utmost at the fire and to be deserving of praise.

One cannot imagine how disturbing an effect the horrific death of Gilbert must have had on his mother and his siblings. Georgina was thirteen at the time. I assume she attended a school – census information gives her occupation as 'scholar', but this was a general term used to describe most children. It is probable that she was taking dancing tuition, as a few years later she embarked upon a career on the stage and began to travel the country with touring theatrical companies.

In 1899, the Boer War began. Dominick was stirred to join the 5th Royal Fusiliers in June 1900. Bizarrely, he gave his name as Frederick Shaw and supplied an incorrect address. I think the reason for this subterfuge was simply because he thought he was not yet eighteen. None of Mary's children knew their dates of birth, and it seems that Dominick believed he was born in September 1882 and therefore not old enough to enlist (in fact he had turned eighteen in September 1899). He was sent to South Africa in January 1902 and served in the Boer war until July.

ABOVE: Mary Henry, Dad's grandmother, and mother of the seven 'Anstruther' children.

ABOVE: Gilbert Eliott-Murray-Kynynmound (1845-1914). He was known as Lord Melgund from 1859 and became the Fourth Earl of Minto after his father's death in 1891. He is pictured here in 1885. It is possible that he might have been the father of Mary Henry's children, but so far there is no conclusive evidence to support the hypothesis.

BELOW: The baffling photograph, allegedly of Dad's mother, Georgina, in the arms of her Ayah in India.

The Anstruther brothers. The quality of the images is poor, but nevertheless it is interesting to have some idea of their looks. I have no photos of Edgar or Gilbert.

ABOVE: George (1870-1940) Frederick (1872-1942)

BELOW: Melgund (1876-1944) Dominick (1881-1937)

For Mary Anstruther, the only child still living with her was Melgund. The two of them moved to Fulham, SW6. Melgund is described in the 1901 census as a 'salesman of fancy goods' and Mary a 'caretaker', possibly of the building in which they were living. But I must leave the Anstruther boys now and move on with Georgina's story. As you might expect, it is not the least bit straightforward. By now Georgina was in her early twenties. She had probably been on the stage for some years, working as a chorus girl. One of her fellow actors was a young, talented man called Barry Lupino. It is here that he makes his entrance.

Whilst searching for clues about Dad's past, I came across a copy of a twenty-one-page letter written by Barry Lupino to his daughter, Florrie. Barry wrote it in December 1961, eight months before he died. The first paragraph responds to a letter he must have received from Florrie. The rest can be read as his memoirs. Some of it is informative, much of it wildly inaccurate, but he writes entertainingly. Dad's mother, Georgina Anstruther, was Barry's first wife. Florrie was their daughter, Dad's half-sister.

Barry Lupino was born George Barry Lupino Hook in 1884. Lupino was not the family name. His father, George Hook, appropriated it and grafted the antecedents of the real Italian Luppinos [*spelt with twp p's*] onto the Hook family tree. Barry's reminiscences begin when he and Georgina met and fell in love. He tells us that they were both teenage members of a small touring company playing in a musical comedy *Admiral Jack* in Bootle, near Liverpool, in 1901. Barry was the principal comedian and Georgina, using the stage name of May Gordon, was a chorus girl. (May was the name by which she was known for the rest of her life, but for clarity I shall continue to refer to her as Georgina.) However, they were not both teenagers. Barry was seventeen; charming and entertaining, with an irresistible twinkle in his eyes; Georgina was in fact twenty-two. She had already deducted a number of years from her age, her pretty face and youthful figure allowing her to get away with it.

Barry wanted to believe he had high-status family links. He convinced himself that he was truly descended from the Italian Luppinos, the "oldest and most famous family in the Theatrical Profession". A gentrified name was all it took for the impressionable man to claim connection with the aristocracy. Now I know better, but this next passage sent me off on a wild goose chase:

> It was not until I applied for a marriage license that I discovered that my bride-to-be was Georgina May Gordon Anstruther-Anstruther, of Anstruther, quite a mouthful wasn't it. Apparently she was the descendant of an ancient Scottish family from Fifeshire that dated back to the 1400's and the head of the family was a Sir John Anstruther. When I had recovered from my surprise I asked her what she was doing in a third rate Theatrical Company. She told me that her Father had been a Colonel in the Scots Guards, at one time a Constable of the Tower of London and had left her Mother practically penniless. So to help her Mother out, May [*Georgina*] obtained permission from her family to go on the Stage – providing she did not use the name of Anstruther.

It is true that there is a titled Anstruther family whose genealogy can be traced back for centuries. There is even a Colonel Robert Anstruther amongst them, but he died in 1833 and is not our man. The Fifeshire Anstruthers seemed promising to start with, but ultimately led us nowhere. However, there is one phrase in the above extract that is of interest and may prove significant in establishing a connection with the Elliot clan. In 1867, Lord Melgund joined the Scots Guards and remained in the Army for three years.

Georgina, as we know, was a Roman Catholic. Barry was a Protestant, of sorts. In the summer of 1903, Georgina found she was pregnant. She must have been desperate to marry quickly, but this was not to be. Myth has it that Barry and his sweetheart were forced to elope because Georgina's family would not give their consent, which was then a legal requirement if under the age of twenty-one. In fact, Georgina was twenty-four. It was Barry who was under twenty-one, not coming of age until January 1905. The elopement story was probably concocted by Georgina to sustain the fallacy of her tender age. To Liverpool they headed, taking lodgings in Everton, both of them very likely working there. In February 1904, by which time Georgina was seven months pregnant, the couple married in a Register Office in West Derby, Liverpool. Their marriage certificate shows that she only deducted a modest two years from her age, but Barry added three years to his for good measure. They returned to London, possibly tweaking the date of their marriage, where their daughter, Florrie, was born in Camberwell in April. Barry writes:

> Neither of us thought that when we got married the difference in our religion would cause any trouble. How wrong we were – as soon as the news reached the ears of her family, 'Merry Hell' broke out. At the time of our marriage, her brother, George Elliot Anstruther was the editor of the 'Catholic Universe', 'The Catholic Tablet' and the Organising Secretary of 'The Catholic Truth Society'. Calamity – Calamity – Calamity! Not only had his sister married without permission, but to an illiterate actor of dubious Italian descent, and thus blotted the aristocratic escutcheon of the Anstruthers of Anstruther.

Barry's memory of 1904 was not serving him well. George was certainly making a career out of Catholicism, but he held none of the above positions until years after Barry and Georgina's marriage. George married Lydia Richardson in 1896. They had four children. Their third, Philip, born in 1903, entered the Dominican Order when he was seventeen and was ordained priest six years later. Known as Father Godfrey, he became a professional researcher of Roman Catholic history and spent many hours during his lifetime trying to investigate his own provenance. Using his skills and experience, he left no stone unturned, but his grandfather, 'Colonel Anstruther', evaded detection. His notes are interesting, however:

> I have been through to Army Lists but could never find a Col. Robert Anstruther that fitted. My father, George Elliot Anstruther, had many talents, good looks and good breeding. He was artistic and musical, playing the piano by ear. He had never been to a public school and was largely self-taught. He had a smattering of Latin, good tourists' French, and quite impeccable English. He never spoke to us of his background or encouraged us to ask. My mother knew very little, though was full of curiosity and spoke to us quite openly. She said that before they married, Dad had taken her round the National Portrait Gallery & pointed out a number of distinguished people, saying, "He's supposed to be one of

> my ancestors and I couldn't care less." But I don't think he knew a great deal himself. I remember when I was in my teens he went to look for the registration of his birth and was surprised when he never found it. He told Mother, I'm probably a bastard and I don't care, or words to that effect.
>
> Another interesting clue: Elliot. It is the family name of the Earls of Minto. Gilbert Elliot runs through several generations. The courtesy title of the eldest son is Lord Melgund. And I have an Uncle Gilbert and an Uncle Melgund! Yet I can find no intermarriage of Elliot and Anstruther.
>
> A skeleton in the cupboard should be introduced to the children as soon as they can walk. Otherwise they will exercise their own vivid imaginations.

Barry, Georgina and baby Florrie moved into a three-roomed flat in Peckham "with use of bathroom, furnished on the H.P., rent 15/- per week". They did not live there for long, as Barry's star was rising:

> I had begun to be a successful comedian – eventually the Catholic Anstruthers accepted me as a type of Morganatic relative albeit of common clay... and then, practically overnight, my financial position altered and I became what is now termed a 'Starlet'. Their entire attitude changed within a few months. I was enabled to leave my semi-slum Peckham Flat and move to a district that was then much favoured by the Stars of the Music Halls – Brixton. I leased in Loughborough Road a Victorian double-fronted detached house with gardens back and front and stabling in which I garaged a 4.5 De Dion Two Seater.

Mary Anstruther moved into Loughborough Road with her daughter and son-in-law. According to Barry, Georgina's unmarried and improvident brothers, Frederick, Melgund and Dominick, were quick to take advantage of their sister's improved circumstances and moved in too. Along with the Anstruthers came Catholic artefacts. Barry complains:

> Scattered around the place were plaster statues of male and female Saints and on the walls colour prints of Stations of the Cross. These of course clashed with my collection of Play Bills and my Dad's oil paintings... at times, in addition to the aroma of Theatrical Props, greasepaint and Costumes, a strong perfume of Incense Sticks permeated the atmosphere and in every bedroom there was a Crucifix. All this led to my brother Mark calling the house 'The Lourdes of Loughborough Road'.

Barry also states that there were "numerous rows". He and Georgina were often away with touring companies performing in theatres around the country. With them went their young daughter, Florrie. Almost as soon as she could walk, she appeared on stage, following in the footsteps of her parents.

In late 1907, the Lupinos were booked to play a pantomime season in Liverpool. Mary Anstruther went with them. Whilst there, she fell ill. Mary Henry, alias Crockford, Bennett and Anstruther, died on February 2nd 1908. Barry was the informant, giving his mother-in-law's details as 'Mary Elliott [*sic*] Anstruther, aged seventy'. She was buried in Liverpool, probably at St. Nicholas Roman Catholic Church where her beloved son Edgar had been baptised. Her secrets were buried with her.

In September 1908 Barry, Georgina and Florrie travelled to New York to undertake a three-month theatrical contract. When they returned to Loughborough Road, Barry was appalled to find that his wife's brothers had run up enormous bills on the Army and Navy credit account. The De Dion car had to be sold and an accountant brought in to straighten out the financial mess. The boys were turfed out temporarily. However, in May 1910, Barry, Georgina and Florrie once again set sail for America and would be away for over two months. It was reluctantly agreed that Melgund should be reinstated as caretaker.

Later that year, Georgina found that she was pregnant again. It was not welcome news, as her marriage was on the rocks. By all accounts, Georgina was a tempestuous character with a fiery temper. Barry, I feel, was more easy-going, inclined to see the funny side of life and quick to turn his observations into theatrical comedy. He was only seventeen when he met Georgina, twenty when he married her, at which time he was a young player struggling to make ends meet. A decade later, he was a music hall star, admired, well-paid and successful. For Barry, the teenage passion that had flared so hotly had burnt itself out. He had fallen in love with another woman, an aspiring actress by the name of Gertie Latchford.

It must have been a very difficult time for Georgina. Her baby girl, Elsie Iza Mary Lupino, was born at Loughborough Road on July 25th 1911. Barry was not around to give Georgina, little Elsie or his seven-year-old daughter, Florrie, the care and support they needed. Gertie had just broken the news to him that she was pregnant and he could expect to become a father again in early March. It does not take long to calculate that she had conceived about six weeks before Georgina gave birth. Elsie did not survive: she died twenty days after her birth from severe gastroenteritis and exhaustion. Poor wee mite; and poor Georgina, who must have been completely exhausted herself. It was heart-rending to read the death certificate. I found myself weeping as I experienced Georgina's sorrow and despair. And here is an example of the deeply affecting part of biographical research: the dead, it seems, are woken: accumulated evidence, reflection and empathy invest cold bodies with feeling; their blood warms; their hearts begin to beat. Georgina was no longer just an ancestor on my family tree, a grandmother I had never known. Her life had become mentally tangible. She inhabited my mind, as did Elsie, for many more than her twenty days in this world. Elsie's brief life was erased from family history. Georgina never spoke of her. My father knew nothing of her. Only Florrie kept the secret memory of a little sister who had come and gone.

So it was that Barry Lupino deserted Georgina. She had once been a bright-eyed, vivacious girl kicking her legs in the chorus line – an attractive redhead with whom he had fallen head-over-heels in love. Ten years later she was left with his name, his seven-year-old daughter and a baby she'd had to bury.

It appears that Barry tried to find a way to divorce Georgina and marry Gertie, but did not succeed: in this country he and Gertie were never lawfully man and wife. Divorce was possible in England at the time, but it was expensive, and grounds for procuring it were few and discriminatory. For Georgina, divorce was impossible, the position of the Roman Catholic Church being that marriage is a sacrament that is indissoluble and endures until one spouse dies. Barry and Gertie, unmarried, but travelling as Mr. and Mrs. Lupino, emigrated to Australia in October 1913. Barry simply used his own passport, which included his wife Georgina, and passed Gertie off as Georgina – conveniently the two women had the same initials. Their seven-month-old son was left behind in England, given away for adoption.

Georgina picked up her fragmented life, locked her grief away, deducted a few more years from her age, put on a brave face and went back to work. She and Florrie had to earn a living. The theatrical world gossiped, but not, I think, maliciously; she wasn't the only wife to lose a husband to another woman. The music halls were where Georgina and Florrie belonged and thrived. They were not stars, but nevertheless, when the curtains rose, they shone, they smiled, they danced and they performed. The stage was their arena; backstage their home.

To conclude this chapter: Edgar died suddenly in his early forties just seven months after his mother. Frederick died in London aged sixty-nine. George also died at the age of sixty-nine. Melgund married Ethel Cleaver in 1921 and spent most of his later life living in Oxford under the assumed name of George Anderson. Of all the Bennett children, Melgund's names changed the most: born Robert Herbert Bennett; baptised Melgund Robert Anstruther Bennett; known as Melgund Anstruther; married as Melgund Eliot [*as spelt on his marriage document*] Anstruther, lived in Oxford as George Anderson and named on his death certificate, confusingly, as George Anstruther.

Dominick married Violet Hurst in 1920. She had six children, but only two of them were her husband's – the first, Terence, and the third, Diana. Dominick and Violet spent much of their marriage living apart, although Dominick returned to his wife towards the end of his life when he was terminally ill. He appears to have accepted all the children as his, even though he knew that most of them were not. Indeed, Violet was pregnant with her sixth child whilst nursing Dominick during his last months. He died in June 1937 aged fifty-five. The baby was born a month later.

Florrie enjoyed a brief but impressive stage career as a dancer at Les Folies-Bergère in Paris, the Winter Gardens in New York and the Dominion Theatre, London. She met her husband, Sydney Poole, when she was performing at the Derby Hippodrome. By the age of twenty, she'd had her first child and given up her career. She and Sydney settled in Kirkby-in-Ashfield, Nottinghamshire, when Sydney became the electrician at the Regent cinema. Florrie had six children, the eldest only four years younger than Dad. Sydney was a most unreliable husband. He had affairs with at least two women, both liaisons producing illegitimate children. In an act of extraordinary generosity and forbearance, Florrie took one of Sydney's 'other' children into her home and brought him up with her own after his mother declared she didn't want him and virtually left the baby on the doorstep.

There are still umpteen unanswered 'Anstruther' questions. Whether Mark and I shall ever find out the true identity of our great-grandfather or solve any more of the riddles remains to be seen. However, we have uncovered far more than our great-grandmother, Mary Henry, ever wanted anyone to know. She must be turning in her grave! Our research and sleuthing continues.

Drawings by Dad, aged about seventeen.

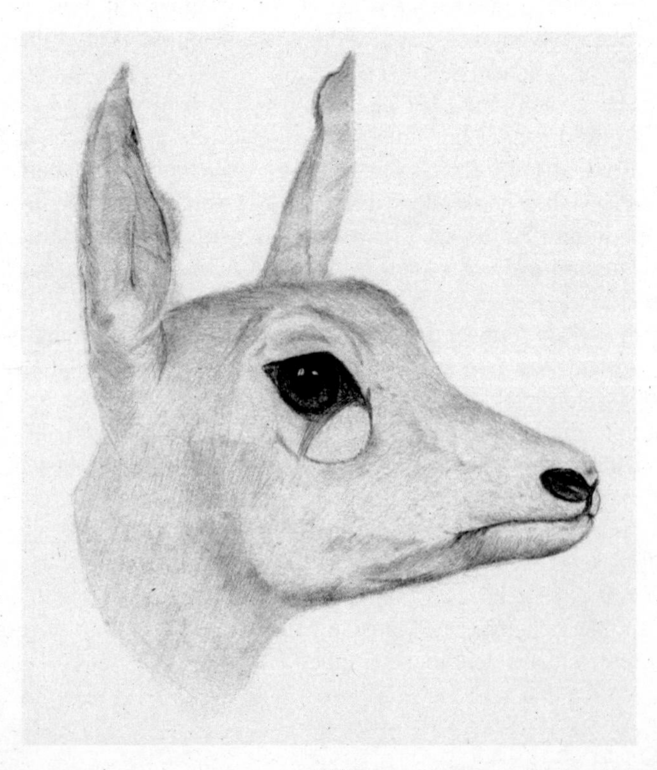

Dad's mother, Mary Georgina Anstruther, born in Hanwell, Middlesex in March 1879, not in India in 1887, which was the story she told Dad.

She was a Music Hall Artiste, calling herself May Gordon for the stage. She worked in the theatre for more than twenty years.

In 1904 she married Barry Lupino, who became a star of the Music Halls, famously known for playing the roles of pantomime Dames. He was also a celebrated comedian.

ABOVE: A studio photo of a theatrical company, probably taken between 1901-1903
Barry Lupino is standing on the far left, Georgina is seated on the right.
The girl in the middle is not Florrie, as I originally supposed.

BELOW: Georgina on the right and her daughter, Florrie Lupino.

23
BEHIND LOCKED DOORS

In about 1917, Georgina met Frederick Giles, a man who was thirteen years her junior, although he never knew it. Frederick Eli Giles, my grandfather, was born in 1892 in Kennington, a poor area of south London. He served in the army during most of World War One. When he was discharged, he worked as a motor mechanic. Later he became a hospital theatre assistant, and then an inspector of surgical instruments (it was Frederick's connection with the medical world that facilitated the acquisition of a human skull for Chris's ninth birthday). Georgina and Frederick moved into 82, Dumbarton Road, a ground floor flat in Brixton, pretending to be husband and wife. As a Catholic, Georgina was burdened with guilt – she had already fallen from grace when she committed the mortal sin of fornication and fallen further by marrying a Protestant. Cohabiting with Frederick meant that she was now living permanently in sin. The shameful secret tainted her life. She lived in fear of the truth being discovered along with the pervasive knowledge that her wickedness could not be hidden from God.

On October 4th 1918, Georgina gave birth to another girl, who was registered as Betty Iris Lupino. The father is not named on her birth certificate, but there is no doubt that he was Frederick Giles. Exactly two years later, on October 4th 1920, my father, Derek Colin Frederick Giles, was born. Throughout his childhood he was known as Colin. He did not reclaim the name Derek until he was in his twenties. On both birth certificates, Georgina states her occupation as 'Music Hall Artiste'.

That Dad remembers his mother as melancholic is understandable, for Georgina was dealt another tragic hand: on April 15th 1924, her young daughter, Dad's sister Betty, died at the London Hospital. The little girl was five-and-a-half years old. Her father, Frederick Giles, informed the registrar of her death, the cause of which was tuberculous meningitis, which one has to assume was true. I remember Dad once showing me a photograph of him and Betty and standing side by side outside a house – probably their home in Dumbarton Road. What became of that photo, I don't know, but it made a deep impression on me. I looked at it closely, particularly at Betty, a little girl who had died. How was it possible? There she was, alive; her hair was straight, cut in a bob with a side parting, a Kirby grip pinning it back from her face. She was smiling, holding her brother's hand, her skinny legs sticking out from a dress that was too small for her. Dad was half her size, with lighter, curlier hair, a round-cheeked, serious-looking toddler wearing wide shorts that reached his knees. I could sense the shape of Betty's fingers clasped around her brother's plump hand, the warmth of their flesh. A moment after the camera captured the image, she would be moving, talking; maybe she would hunker down and give her brother a hug. Her life would continue for a while longer; a life that was inextricably related to Dad's. Imagining her was sad. I felt very sorry for Dad and asked him if he remembered her. He said he did. Then he told me this, a story that will always perplex me: Georgina, Betty and Colin had just reached home, having been out shopping.

Georgina was in an irritable, aggravated mood. She laid down her bags to unlock the front door, looked back over her shoulder and saw Betty and Colin playing 'jump' off the doorstep of the opposite flat as if they hadn't a care in the world. "Stop that nonsense," she shouted angrily. "Get over here and help your mother."

The children did as they were told, but as Betty reached the door and stepped into the hall, Georgina struck her. Betty stumbled backwards and fell, cracking her head on the path below. Dad remembered his sister being carried unconscious into the house and being told not to tell anyone what had happened. He never saw Betty again – another loose end; another secret – or more probably a three-and-a-half-year-old's rationalisation of the disappearance of his sister. Her death was not explained to him. Perhaps his parents thought he was too young for it to affect him and he would soon forget her. What he knew was that his sister, the big girl he played with, had gone. Betty's head had smashed on the pavement – he had heard the sound of the impact, seen her limp body and thought she was dead. The incident triggered a connection with her loss and became so imprinted in his mind that it turned into the truth. I feel sure that Dad did not know that his sister had tuberculosis of the brain – certainly the story he told me about the cause of her death was the one he believed, and therefore what I also believed until I bought a copy of the death certificate. What a terrible thing for Dad to carry through his life – the suspicion that his mother's furious wallop had killed his sister.

Dad described his childhood in curiously opposing ways. One was through rose-tinted glasses, the other spoke of cruelty. Reminiscing, he writes of Dumbarton Road:

> Here we lived our placid days and years. If adequate shelter, clothing, love and wholesome food be luxuries, then indeed my childhood was one of luxury. My parents must sometimes have felt the pinch of penury but, with a kind of stubborn pride, they managed to keep such conditions from my knowledge. They accepted that life consisted largely of hard work, long sustained, punctuated by occasional periods of leisure, most usually spent in hearty enjoyment of that abundant and varied vitality in which our neighbourhood abounded.
>
> When I was a very little child it was my great pleasure to squat beside the scullery waste pipe outlet to watch drips of water falling into the drain. That was my first remembered adventure. But the garden and the street soon became the places where adventure was to be found. Our back garden, so safe, so near, contained much of interest to a lone child. To one with a natural bent for detailed examination, blades of grass, insects, stones, shadows, leaves and much more, were an everlasting cornucopia of fascinating objects.
>
> Halfway along our hall passage was a cupboard beneath the stairs to the flat above. The door to this was held by a spring catch. No doubt I would have opened the door had the lock been within reach. But one day I saw that the door had been left ajar. I tremulously and excitedly peered inside. I could see dusty gilt frames of some large oil paintings, some smaller pictures, apparently executed with pen and ink, some wooden boxes which seemed to contain crumpled paper, a child's cot, Mother's 'Ewbank' carpet sweeper and, right at the back, wedged between a side-ended scullery table, a little girl's toy pram. From this I was able to extract a small floppy object made of some hard material. I was shocked when a little later on, Mother, seeing what I was examining, showed some distress. Tears, even. I was very sorry. I didn't know it was wrong to go

> into the hall cupboard. I would take the bead purse with its penny back to the cupboard. Perhaps Mother wouldn't cry any more if I did that? Mother stroked my head. It was All Right. She was just a Little Off Colour. It was true, I mused. My parents were indeed sometimes inexplicably sad, and when they were like that it made me sad too. Did Grown-Ups have problems which boys and girls didn't? I would certainly never look in the hall cupboard again.

I doubt that Colin was treated quite so gently for looking in the cupboard. A sharp telling-off and a smack were probably closer to the truth. When he asked his mother where babies came from, she told him that they grew under gooseberry bushes. Colin asked where he might find a gooseberry bush. "Don't go looking for trouble," was her cryptic reply. When he discovered that a neighbour had some growing in his garden and asked if he could search underneath the bushes for babies, both the neighbour and his mother laughed at him.

Occasionally he would be given a penny, which he saved in his piggy bank. He had managed to collect nearly five shillings when his father, broke and in need of a drink or a smoke, asked his son to lend him the money. To Colin's dismay, it was not returned, but he was too afraid to ask for it back. His father used to tell him that he was once a beautiful little girl with golden ringlets and a dimpled smile, until the gypsies stole her away and left a horrible, dirty little boy in her place, called Colin.

His mother wouldn't let him bring friends home in case they saw the threadbare carpets and empty grates. She let the cold water run for five minutes after the bath water had drained away, imagining bizarrely that the neighbours would be listening to, and taking note of, the quantity of 'hot' water pouring down the waste pipe and think them well off. Visitors were actively discouraged: no prying eyes would see into her house, no intruders would be allowed across the threshold to take loose gossip away with them. When, as a youngster, I heard these stories from my father, I thought that Georgina's experience of a wealthy childhood in India was the explanation for her embarrassment of poverty. Now that I know differently, I suspect that Georgina had illusions of grandeur. She thought she had blue blood running through her veins – and maybe she had every right to think so. The brief encounter with extravagance that she – and her brothers – had enjoyed at Barry's expense had suited her very well.

Dad's sister, Betty, was buried in a churchyard in Bow:

> One day I was surprised to be taken by my parents on a bus journey which seemed to last interminably. Mother and Father were solemn, yet readily reacted with smiles and good humour to any of my trivial remarks. At last we left the hard seats and placed our feet upon pavement again. We were in Bow. We walked down several streets of sullen aspect, lined with high, blackened, tenement flats. Forlorn looking children played in the gutters. "Oh, I should not like to live here! I wish we could go home!" Seen from the end of the street was a pair of large decorative iron gates, of which one hinged leaf stood open wide. We entered. My spirits sank further as rows of incised Gravestones, iron railed Tombs, drooping Angels, Christ Figures, Crosses, Mausoleums and low weed-grown mounds closed around us. Why had they brought me here? A looming prescience

of something Wrong seized my consciousness.

When Mother and Father stopped, we were by one particular plot defined by a low wooden surround painted green, and by a very small gravestone upon which appeared the opening words "Sacred to the memory of Our Darling Betty"... Mother was weeping, Father standing hatless. I perceived that the key to the mystery was here being vouchsafed. I watched. During the homeward journey, Mother explained. Yes, yes! Now I remembered, I really did! A little companion who used to play with me? Share my toys? Talk to me? Was that her beneath the soil upon which Mother had laid the flowers? Was I only three when it had happened? Was that why Mother had cried when she saw the bead purse? Was it? Was it?

Full understanding of irreparable loss, full understanding that I had once had a sister, that my parents had once had a Daughter, but that we had one no more; full understanding of that and much more besides, was not to come crushing down until many a long year had passed. Forty years later I returned to Bow. No trace of the little grave could be found. A German bomb had torn into that part of the cemetery and nothing remained but a shallow depression. I placed my flowers upon an unknown grave as I left.

Colin was left-handed, which, when he was a child, was considered abnormal. At school his left arm was tied behind his back, forcing him to use his right hand to write. If caught using his left hand, a ruler would be struck sharply across the knuckles. Yet, via a rosy filter of wistfulness, he describes his schooldays thus:

New Park School was my social incubator. Here I learned how to relate to other children, how to carry out a number of simple manual and mental tasks, how to behave toward a number of powerful figures called Teachers and how to understand that concept called "pecking order". Notwithstanding certain often-repeated ceremonies, incantations and songs, they did not succeed in conveying to me (or perhaps to any other mite there assembled), any notion at all of what was in their minds. We knew, however, when these matters were in hand, that if we wished to be thought well of, we should adopt a solemn and humble demeanour. Yet it was a friendly, homely place, a community of children and teachers. We were neither pressed too hard, nor punished unduly, nor deprived of laughter or kindness.

His father was critical, dictatorial and bad tempered. He took his son to visit his father, Colin's grandfather, just as Dad took us to visit him, our grandfather, decades later. Dad writes of one visit:

All was dormant, shut, closed, almost silent. This was a Sunday morning, gratefully enjoyed by some men in Church, but by very many more in their beds or the pub. The Women, as always, would be hard at work in their kitchens. Quite severe restraint was imposed by parents upon their children. Perhaps it was that constraining influence which impelled Grandfather one Sunday morning, to protest against my whistling a popular air within earshot of his house. We were approaching the back door when he appeared, irate.

"Don't do that," he said. "This is a respectable house. We don't have whistling or singing, or shouting outside, so just stop it, now." We entered, crushed. But Grandfather was merely being on his best behaviour. Dressed in his best suit, with gold watch and chain, he was going to Take Us Out. We strolled gently along Brixton High Road, Grandfather tall, slightly stooped, with his stick and square crowned bowler hat, Father

> with more fashionable rounded bowler and me with lightweight Panama hat. Perhaps we went to the "Crown and Anchor", or further afield to the "White Horse"?

He also wrote a less romantic version:

> When I was a small boy my father used to call weekly to his parents' house, taking me with him. My grandfather was vaguely affable but never expressed any real interest in the boy before him, while my grandmother kept out of the way entirely. Bloody fools! They could have had a loving grandson in their neglected last years. So that's another bent family to ponder over! [*The underlined words are as the original*]

Dad often hinted that there were terrible secrets in his past. I feel sure now that he was waiting for us to ask what they were, but his every insinuation suggested the revelation of something awful and was spiked with such ominous implication that we were afraid to hear what he had to tell. His writing is full of innuendo:

> In later years I was to wonder whether, had the two men [*his father and grandfather*] then stood firm together against the crushing powers of Convention, they might have dispersed and conquered the shadows of circumstance slowly taking shape around us.

What "powers of Convention", what "shadows of circumstance"? In another passage, he describes a childhood accident. He was certain that the physical damage it caused was the reason why people treated him with hostility and judged him negatively:

> One day, when little older than five years, walking with Mother, I suffered an accident. A boy sitting upon the curved copingstones of a front garden wall decided to slide from his perch at the same time as we were passing by, landing upon my shoulders and bearing me to the hard pavement. Mother picked me up, staunched the bleeding, dusted me down, smacked the boy and took me home.
>
> I soon recovered, Mother much relieved that her son had collected only bruises from the episode. She did not know that the Septum had been displaced, partly blocking both nasal passages. Breathing thereafter became difficult. I was obliged to clear an air passage by a lift of cheek to the left, thus altering the facial expression for the worse, for it seemed to wear a perpetual sneer. Later, I could not, for want of air, indulge for long in the rough horseplay in the school playground, soon earning myself the reputation of a sissy.
>
> What misunderstandings were to arise in later years from that unfortunate legacy! What tentative friendly approaches rejected because of appearance, what aggressive stances displayed against imagined challenge, what sad awareness that lots of people didn't like me, although I didn't know why. The fault was partially corrected over thirty years later by a simple surgical operation.

Colin was a lonely child; introspective, shy, small for his age, and consequently bullied at school. Georgina's mothering was unpredictable and emotionally confusing. His father was insensitive and intimidating, and quashed Colin's gentle, artistic nature. Colin was also, I am sure, far more intelligent than either of his parents. They had no understanding of their quiet little boy. He struggled to make sense of what he heard, felt and saw, but his questions were not answered. He was, however, allowed to go to the library:

> Brixton Public Library was founded by Sir Henry Tate (1819-99), the man who gave the Tate Gallery to the nation. The children's section was in the basement. It was exciting to exchange returned books for tickets, thence to wander among the free treasure so well displayed upon the shelves. At the 'Tate', I was to find in books my lifelong friends and advisors, although one had to learn (painfully at times), that all which is in print is not necessarily true, or of worth. There also I found Love. Respectfully, earnestly and mutely, I loved the lady behind the counter who date-stamped the borrowed books. How often I would think of those dark eyes, those busy hands, that neat figure in green overall coat. Sometimes she would bestow a faint smile and then I knew that no other lady would ever receive even the smallest portion of that devotion which I was so anxious to lay at her feet. We never spoke.
>
> Walk up the stairs again and you were back in the pillared and arched entrance hall. Pass through one easily opened glass panelled door and you were in the Reading Room. Smell of leather-bound book, sound of foot on parquet flooring, odour of beeswax and turpentine, lustre of table top, rustle of newspaper, muted cough, murmured comment – this was the very stuff of the Academic atmosphere, Here I learned to revere Learning, although (most strangely), no such attitude was ever to be applied to my schoolwork.

Nevertheless, Colin did well at school and gained consistently high marks. In one report he was placed second in a class of forty-five. Attendance and Conduct are described as "excellent". His head teacher comments: "Colin has done remarkably well. I consider him a potential scholarship winner." Colin left school in May 1938, aged seventeen, to take a job in the insurance company with which he was to remain for the rest of his working days. When war broke out, he joined the Royal Navy. A pretty, blue-eyed boy, physically slight, naive and inexperienced in the ways of the world, his sheltered, repressed childhood offered him little preparation for the Forces. It was during his time in the Navy that he was introduced to brothels and alcohol. I have the impression that his boyhood innocence was wrenched from him, the green film wiped rather roughly from his eyes. His time at sea was spent on board a minesweeper. Minesweepers, as the name implies, were small naval warships designed to detect and neutralise moored mines. He was in constant fear of being blown up, living under military discipline in dangerous waters and tough conditions. Yet he sentimentalised his wartime years with glowing nostalgia, liking nothing better than to remember the 'good old days' in the Navy. As yet I have not been able to find out the name of the vessel on which he served. It may have been one of the twenty-one Halcyon-class minesweepers; perhaps he had every reason to recall his time at sea as the halcyon days of his life, but it was probably just as well that the starker aspects of those years were blotted out of his memories.

When the war was over, he went back home to live with his father and mother, who had moved from Brixton to 52, Roding Lane North, Woodford Bridge, the house we later knew well from our childhood visits to Grandad.

Georgina Anstruther died in January 1951, aged seventy-one, of uterine cancer. Frederick Giles, in all honesty, gave her age as sixty-four and named her, not so honestly, as his wife on the death certificate. Florrie wasn't standing for that. She insisted it must be changed. Heated arguments ensued, causing Florrie, in a fit of pique, to reveal to her half-brother the fact of his parents' unwed state. A month later, the document was corrected by a Statutory Declaration signed by Florrie and Frederick, making it clear that Georgina had always been the wife of Barry Lupino. Dad was devastated by the revelation, appalled to discover that he was a bastard – a reaction that Mum, when she later heard about it, thought irrational and extreme. Yet it was something that Dad dwelled upon morbidly, believing that the "gruesome secret" had brought "much heartache and calamity to fall upon the shoulders of my parents and myself." In a letter to his cousin, Sallie Anstruther (one of Dominick Anstruther's children, or so it was thought at the time – Sallie only discovered that he was not, in fact, her biological father in 2001 when she was seventy), Dad wrote:

> Had I known as a boy what I know now, how different would have been life's pattern. I should have understood my parents more. I should have understood the curious attitude adopted by relatives towards me. I might have understood some of the mysterious undercurrents of secrecy; why my parents always insisted that I should "Never let other people know your business." Clearly I would not have felt out on a limb and inexplicably odd. Does one not shudder to think of all the careful obscurantism, lies and destruction of personality which must have gone into the fashioning of the "official" version of our family history?

Not long after Georgina's death, Frederick met Lilian. She moved in with him to Roding Lane North. It was assumed that Lilian and Grandad were married, but I have found no record of a legal union. Florrie and Dad kept in touch sporadically. I discovered a card from her congratulating Mum and Dad on the birth of their twins. There are also photographs of her in the garden of Cleveland Road with two of her daughters and another of her with Mum. However, soon after that, she and Dad must have fallen out irrevocably. The first paragraph in the long letter to Florrie from her father, Barry Lupino, maybe explains the rift between half-sister and brother. It begins:

> My dear daughter Florrie,
>
> During my stay in the Hove Hospital I once again tried to decipher your letter about your dispute with Colin. But my eyesight and your handwriting defeat me. I gather the trouble seems to be about the Ownership of the Furniture, Pictures and other Goods and Chattels I gave your mother in 1911…

The dispute is not referred to again, the rest of the letter devoted to family reminiscences, extracts from which I have quoted in the previous chapter. I can only assume that it was never resolved. Dad writes of the contents of his childhood home:

> On entering number 82, Dumbarton Road, one was at once face to face with that large, oval, gilt-framed oil painting of a roaring lion, which Mother liked to have hanging there because no other wall space was suitable (our house was crammed with large oil paintings). As the visitor turned left along the passageway he could, provided there was enough light, examine Man Trapped by Bear, Woman Plucking Goose, Old Lady Reading Bible and Lady on Beach. These pictures were much too big for our small flat, but they were a legacy from Mother's past and were very precious to her, indeed, to us all. The chairs upon which we sat were elegant, high-backed and caned; another legacy from Mother's past, as were many other artefacts in the home.

None of the items Dad describes ever found their way to Cleveland Road, not even to its cellar, so perhaps there was good reason for the disagreement with Florrie. It seems a shame that a materialistic quarrel led to Dad cutting himself off from her, thereby severing the only connection that we may have had to his mother's side of the family. In a letter that has recently come to light, Dad wrote this:

> When Barry Lupino and my mother parted, certain of the furniture, pictures and bric-a-brac remained in my mother's possession. When she "took up" with my father this formed the major part of the furnishing and décor of their joint home in Dumbarton Road, Brixton Hill. Sister Florrie had noted this, as also had she noted (either then or later) that neither my father (no relative) nor myself (a bastard) would have right of inheritance should mother predecease my father. So, after mother's death, Sister Florrie set her well prepared plan of attack into action… But I'll write no more on this just now; it's too sordid a tale by half, and also, for various reasons, I think it inadvisable to commit it to paper.

By nature, Dad was a diffident character with an introspective inclination. The parenting he received did nothing to boost his confidence or nurture his self-esteem. His mother was forty-two when he was born, worn-out by the punishing life she had already lived, steeped in guilt, grief and disillusionment. His father was narrow-minded and selfish. Neither of them related to their little boy. Dad was starved of straightforward, generously-given love. What he grew up with was deception, unreliability, cynicism, ignorance, insecurity, unkindness and bullying. His inherited history and upbringing could not have been more different from Mum's. Her family had their tragedies, their illegitimate children and their losses to bear, but they were, in general, honest, open, down-to-earth people who didn't change their names or pretend to be anything other than who they were. Mum's childhood was happy, wholesome and secure. Dad's was rooted in secrets and lies. Nevertheless, many people have suffered deprived childhoods: it does not follow that they will inevitably live out that damage. Dad, though, carried it all with him for his whole life. He always saw himself as the victim.

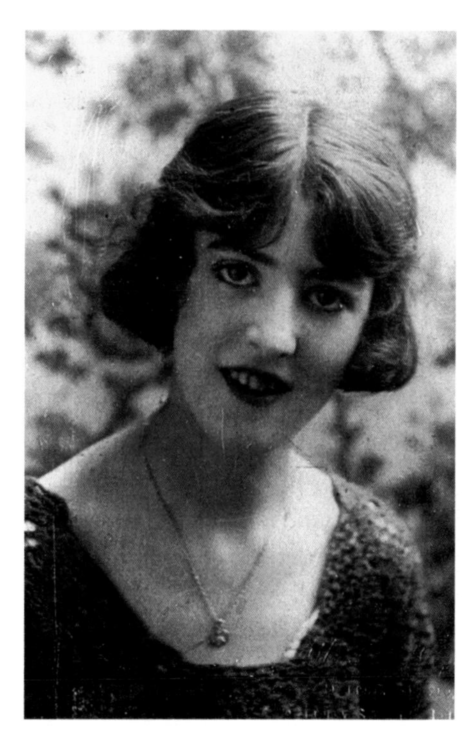

ABOVE: Barry Lupino and Florrie Lupino as a teenager.

BELOW: Georgina on the left with her son, Colin (Dad). The other woman and man are unidentified.

ABOVE: Dad with some of the crew on board a minesweeper during WWII when he served in the Royal Navy. Dad is pictured in the centre wearing a white sweater. "Skipper Reeve and his staff" is written on the back of the photograph.

LEFT: Dad aged about eighteen soon after he joined up.
BELOW: Dad during his 'halcyon days'.

ABOVE: Dad at his office desk in the City.

LEFT: Mum and Florrie. This was very probably the last time Florrie visited her half-brother at Cleveland Road before a dispute over the ownership of their mother's furniture caused her and Dad to fall out.

BELOW: A passport photo of Dad.

Drawing by Derek Giles

24
DAD'S MATES

Not every hand extended
Has intention of goodwill.

Jean Lipkin

Near the churchyard in Bow, where Dad's sister had been buried, lived the unsavoury Bert Jackson. Half-blind, one eye immobile and off centre, the other appearing to twitch, with stained, crooked teeth, a slack mouth and greasy flesh, Bert was not the most attractive of men. His clothes wouldn't have sold in a jumble sale. Bizarrely, he never wore socks, which led Dad to refer to him affectionately as 'The Sockless Wonder'. Bert smelt bad, talked obscenely and beat up his wife. He was also a member of the Communist Party, which is where Dad had met him. Dad enjoyed Bert's irreverence, bad language, dirty jokes and brash confidence. I don't suppose he approved of the wife-beating, but nevertheless, he admired Bert's authority over his wife. Bert could tune pianos (although Mum didn't let him near hers), but made little effort to earn a living. The dole, disability benefit, petty crime and soft touches like Dad, provided him with beer and fags and funded his gambling.

Izzy, Chris and I kept our distance from Bert. We were left in his flat in Bow with Gail, his wife, and their four children while he and Dad went out, sometimes with Bert's barrel organ, to grind out some tunes and drink the afternoon away. The flat, on the second floor of a run-down building on the Bow Road, was foul. It stank of urine, stale cigarettes, booze and decay. Gail didn't seem to clean or tidy. Dirty nappies spilled out of a bucket; stale food, beer bottles, newspapers and discarded clothes littered the floor. Feeding bottles lay dripping amongst the filth, which the youngest child, Malcolm, picked up, sucked and dropped back on the floor. To us, it was an alien environment.

Gail chain-smoked and screamed at the children. She had a thin, haggard face, hollowed cheeks where teeth were missing and wore glasses with incredibly thick lenses. Like Bert, she was partially-sighted – they had met at a school for the blind. Unabashed about the state of the flat, she welcomed us in, gossiping to Izzy and me as if we were her pals. She complained, in a strident cockney accent, about men, the landlord, varicose veins, the cost of living, the broken cistern, bedwetting and Bert gambling away the child benefit. This was novel – an adult talking to us about grown-up stuff. I relished the feeling of inclusion and liked Gail as a result. Despite the squalor and din, there was vitality in the Jackson household.

The children appeared to ignore their mother's yelling and were remarkably cheerful. Susan, the eldest, was about the same age as Izzy and me. I found I could make her laugh, a delightful bell-like giggle. Next were the twins, Neil and Nina. They were skinny with pale complexions, particularly Nina who had delicate blue tracings of veins showing through her paper-white skin. The girls wore ill-fitting plastic shoes and gaudy, synthetic clothes, which Izzy and I thought rather trendy. Mum would never let us wear skirts so short, or shoes with even a suggestion of a point or heel. Our Clarks sandals, hand-knitted woollen cardigans, neatly plaited hair and grey pleated skirts were a clear indication that the Jackson children were not like us. Even Chris, with his scabby knees, scuffed shoes and untucked shirt, looked well dressed by comparison. Still, they had open smiles and we were all up for having fun.

One room in the flat was full of junk – broken bikes, prams, furniture, mattresses and so on. Its smashed windows were patched with cardboard. That and the lack of a light bulb made the room perpetually dingy and cold. Amongst the rubbish was a wind-up gramophone that played old seventy-eight records. Our record collection at home consisted of *Peter and the Wolf* with *The Young Person's Guide to the Orchestra* on the reverse side, the *1812* overture, Jimmy Shand and his orchestra playing Highland dances and a whole record of Bagpipes, which became a little wearing on the ears after a while. Apart from those, Dad had a recording of *I Dream of Jeannie with the Light Brown Hair*, which he played sometimes. I heard it as 'Genie', imagining Aladdin singing to the lamp, trapped in his cave of treasure. The second line, 'Borne like a vapour on the summer air' confirmed my notion. The only other 'light' music we had at home was a small 45rpm record that had been delivered free to every house as a promotional campaign to encourage the purchase of ESSO paraffin. Izzy, Chris and I listened to it over and over again. I still remember the words, sung to the tune of *Smoke Gets in Your Eyes*. This is how it went:

> They asked me how I knew, it was ESSO Blue…
> I of course replied, the lower grade one buys
> Smoke gets in your eyes.

It was obviously an inspired method of advertising, as we have not forgotten it, even though paraffin is not used for heating many houses nowadays. Unfortunately for ESSO, it was the children of 32, Cleveland Road who became hooked on the jingle, not the adults. On the Jacksons' old gramophone we listened to *My old Man Said Follow the Van*, *Daisy Daisy*, *The Lambeth Walk* and other Music Hall favourites, as well as popular songs from the Second World War and what was probably Dixieland Jazz. We jived for a few minutes until the record came to an abrupt end. Then Susan turned it over, wound up the gramophone and the music started again. The fun stopped when we heard Dad and Bert stumbling up the stairs. After a shout-up between Bert and Gail, Dad would take us home, he in good spirits, laughing to himself at Bert's amusing behaviour.

Mum did not come with us to visit Bert and Gail – Dad would take us when she was teaching. But the Jacksons came to visit us. Mum and Granny felt great sympathy for Gail and nothing but contempt for Bert. Granny baked huge quantities of cakes and scones when she knew they were coming and Mum sorted out all the clothes that we had outgrown. Gail was always given something to take away with her. When the youngest Jackson child was about three, Gail found the courage and resolve to take the children and escape from Bert. I don't know how she managed it, as there were no women's refuge houses then. She and the children continued to visit us occasionally. The last time I remember seeing them, Izzy and I were about fourteen. As for Bert – well, Dad still sought him out in pubs in Bow, looking for him grinding his barrel organ.

Bert was an unpleasant lout, but Ken Booker was worse, and had quite an influence over Dad. He reminded me of the fox in Beatrix Potter's *Jemima Puddleduck* – a sly, scheming, sinister character. Izzy thought him odious – she said he gave her the creeps. Chris wasn't too enamoured either, calling him "one of Dad's parasites". Ken fancied himself a philosopher and pretended to be terribly clever. Dad responded with quotes from Dickens and Shakespeare. They showed off to each other and expected us to be impressed by their pretentiousness.

I remember going to Woodford Bridge with Ken and Dad to search for horseradishes. We found quite a few, dug them up and took them back to Ken's place. He washed and grated the white roots, added some other ingredients and mashed it into a sauce. He told me it was delicious then roared with laughter when I tasted it and the top of my head nearly blew off.

His living room was full of paintings he had done of nude women. I thought them gross and vulgar. All nude paintings made me distinctly uncomfortable, but these were particularly obscene. Dad, grinning idiotically, appeared to admire them. Ken made a lewd comment that I wasn't meant to understand, about the models coming to his house to pose for him, which made Dad snigger. Then Ken selected a folder from a high shelf and the two of them ogled over its contents. They spoke in a coded language, chuckling and tittering. Expressions I had not seen before animated Dad's flushed face. Standing in Ken's smutty room with a deliberately blank expression, I felt as if maggots were crawling over my flesh and wriggling in my stomach. I had not yet heard the word pornography and did not fully understand what I had witnessed, but the effect it generated in me was clear enough. There was something repellent about Ken. I didn't like Ken and I didn't like Dad when he was with Ken.

25
SCARS

And suddenly we see
that love costs all we are
and will ever be.
Yet it is only love
which sets us free.

Touched by an Angel – Maya Angelou

I have a three-inch scar running from my thumb down into the fleshy part of the palm on my right hand. When I was about nine, I wondered for the first time what had caused it. Curious, I asked Mum. She said that my thumb wouldn't straighten and I'd had to have an operation when I was very young. "The doctor told me you had a 'trigger thumb' and you'd need surgery to correct it. I asked if it could wait for a while, but he insisted it should be done as soon as possible. You were only fifteen months old, just a baby. I had to take you to the hospital and leave you there. I wasn't allowed to see you until visiting hour the following evening. When Dad and I arrived, we found you soaked in sweat and urine. You were in an awful state. So I changed you and held you and asked the sister in charge if I could take you home – after all, you only had a bandaged thumb. She wouldn't hear of it. Oh, it was unbearable to leave you screaming."

("Yes," Dad later told me, "it was the only time I ever saw your mother cry.")

"Isabel missed you. 'Where's Caagy?' she kept asking. By the third evening, you were worse – running a high temperature, almost delirious. Well, that was it. I wasn't going to leave you there a moment longer. I picked you up and walked out of the ward with you. The nurses came running after me and told me to bring you back at once. I took no notice of them. I said I was taking you home where you'd be properly looked after."

I imagined her rushing out of the ward, tearing along the corridor, through the doors and into the open air, hurrying across the hospital grounds, then slowing her pace to button me inside her coat and walk home. She rescued me, my brave-hearted mother.

"When you were home, you asked for water – not that you could really speak then, but I knew what you wanted. Well, you drank a cupful and asked for more and drank that too and still needed more. Poor wee thing; you were completely dehydrated."

"Did I get better?"

"Oh, you were soon playing happily with Isabel. You were thrilled to see each other again. A couple of days later you were right as rain. You wouldn't remember anything about it, but the experience must have had a deep effect on you. When you were about three, I took you both to the dentist for the first time. You were as happy as Larry on the way there, but when we entered the dentist's surgery, you screamed and screamed. We left straight away. I'm sure something about it reminded you of the hospital. You were fine the next time we went to the dentist – it was just that once."

Contemplating what Mum had told me, I realised that I did have flashbacks of my hospitalisation. I remembered opening my eyes and seeing a white ceiling high above me. I was lying on my back, unable to move. When I turned my head to the side I saw metal bars. Then I tried to sit up – struggled, kicked and strained, but to no avail. Across my chest was something tight. I didn't know it then, but it was a broad piece of canvas-like material that stretched from under my arms to my waist and tethered me down so rigidly that I could not move. I remember feeling defeat and despair. Perhaps it explained why sometimes at night I woke up thrashing my limbs, terrified that I was trapped. There were other memories: one was being carried by a woman (a nurse presumably) through the length of what must have been the ward, past high barred windows and rows of beds. She took me to a fish tank, where she turned her face to me and smiled, pointing to the fish swimming around. The fish did not make me feel any better, but I realised that she was trying to cheer me up. I remember distinctly feigning interest to please her. And this: in the aisle of the ward was a long table with benches on either side. I was picked up and placed on one of the benches. The table was so high I could barely see over it. Opposite and beside me were rowdy children tucking into food. I sat with my hands in my lap, too scared to move.

"Mum?"

"Yes dear?"

"When I was in hospital, was I strapped into my cot?"

She looked at me strangely. "Yes, you were. It was so cruel. They put a harness across you and buckled it to the sides of the bed. To stop you from falling out, they said. You were in a children's ward, you see. Although the beds had bars around them, they weren't high cot bars. Why you weren't in a babies' ward, I don't know."

"Was there a fish tank?"

"I believe there might have been."

"Then I do remember, Mum."

I described my memories. She was astonished, but she believed me. After all, nobody could have told me those things – I was there alone. Another memory surfaced: I was in a pushchair, Mum behind me; we came to a green wooden door and went in. Mum lifted me from the pushchair and I sat beside her on a long, dark, polished wooden seat, my legs swinging above the linoleum floor… and then she and the pushchair were gone.

At the top of George Lane is a pub called The George. Back then it had a side entrance door, painted green. I used to walk past that door quickly. Something about it filled me with dread. Talking to Mum, I made the connection.

"Was the door to Wanstead hospital green?" I asked her.

"Green? I've no idea."

I went to look for myself, and there it was, still green.

The scenes in my nightmares were explained. My scar was more than skin-deep.

26
KIPPERS

The weak in courage is strong in cunning.

The Marriage of Heaven and Hell, Plate 9 – William Blake

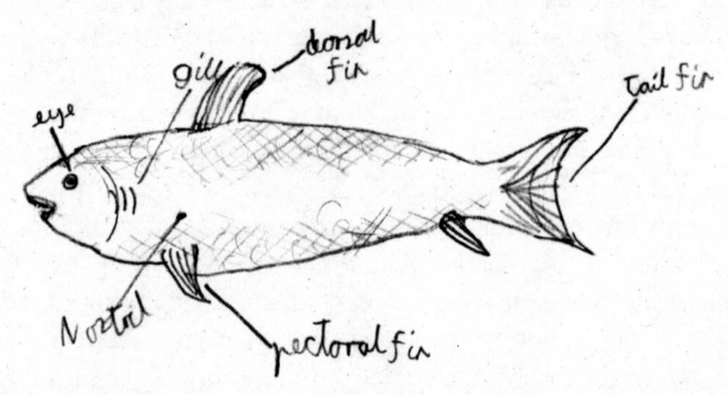

Granny and Dad hated everything about each other. They built up a catalogue of resentments, one of which concerned kippers. Dad liked them. Granny did not. Mum endeavoured to divert confrontation by trying to find out when Dad was intending to cook kippers and doing her best to keep Granny out of the living room at those times, but she wasn't always successful. One Saturday, Granny was still in the kitchen when Dad came back from the shops carrying a parcel wrapped in newspaper. Granny eyed the package suspiciously and picked up the scent.

"Och, you've not bought those awful kippers again have you? I can't abide the smoke or the smell of them and nobody else likes them." Anticipating another row, I blurted out, "I do."

"You do?" Dad asked in surprise.

"Och, don't be ridiculous. You've never tasted them," said Granny scornfully.

"Well, I'd like to try some," I said evenly.

"Then you shall, my dear, you shall," said Dad.

Granny shook her head at me and left the room, issuing instructions in her wake, "and keep the windows open and the doors shut and make sure you clean the grill pan properly."

Dad's voice rose over hers. "Clear off, will you – and shut your door too."

When she was out of sight he added, "and your mouth, and stay in your room and rot in hell. Bloody interfering woman."

We went through to the kitchen where he unwrapped the fish.

"There we are; a nice pair of kippers. Smoked herring. Delicious!" He lit the grill, laid them skin up on the tray and under the flames they went. A minute or two later, he flipped them over and they started fizzing, spluttering and smoking. Hastily, I closed the kitchen door.

"Go and fetch some plates, dear."

"Are they ready?"

"Cooked to perfection."

We took them, steaming, through to the living room table and sat down together. They tasted good, but the bones were impossible, each mouthful the texture of horsehair. I had to spit out a matted bone-ball.

"Here," said Dad, "allow me." He separated some meaty flakes for me.

"Mmmm. Really nice."

"Well, how about that? We've found something we both like. You shall eat kippers with me every Saturday and to hell with that woman. Smoke be damned. We'll enjoy ourselves!" Every Saturday? Dad's delight at sharing a supper together was as nothing compared to his wounded disappointment when I declined, and was left to pick up the pieces of guilt. He was like a gambling machine; default set to 'no win'.

I was eating toast one morning when Granny told me off for making so many crumbs. Then she turned her accusing tongue on Dad – "and you're not setting much of an example are you? Just look at the mess you've made."

Dad slammed his knife onto his plate with such force that the plate broke. He rose to his feet and his chair crashed to the ground.

"Eeee – now look what you've done, you clumsy fool," shrieked Granny, as Dad shouted furiously, "That's the last breakfast I'll ever eat at this table," and raged out of the house.

"Oh, Mammy," cried Mum, "why did you have to say a thing like that?"

"What did I say? Eh? It was nothing."

"It upset him. There was no need to say anything."

"Huh," she retorted, "Men!"

It was the last breakfast he ate with us. The sunflowers, relentlessly cloned, nodded their mocking heads from the walls.

Life continued as usual – dinner on the table at six o'clock, Granny and Dad throwing poisoned darts at each other, Mum losing all trace of herself, Izzy escaped to the world of books, Chris immersed in his collection and the horn, I in music, writing, making clothes and gardening. We children had great fun together but we also occupied ourselves in separate pursuits. Although we were close, the perplexing behaviour we witnessed between Mum, Dad and Granny was not something we talked about. We were on our own; isolated individuals having to deal with nameless apprehensions. I was sometimes overcome with feelings of dread, and I worried about Izzy and Chris, for, strange though it may seem, I felt responsible for them.

Dad took me to the Jubilee Hospital summer fête – just the two of us for some reason. We headed for the white-elephant stall where Dad browsed through second-hand books and I rifled through a box of jewellery. Dad bought some tarnished bone-handled fish forks for himself and a chipped glass swan and a small brass pot for me. "It will polish up beautifully," he said as we walked away, "and look at these forks! Solid silver. They'll shine like new pins when I've cleaned them."

I heard a man shouting, "Bingo about to begin. Take your seats ladies and gentlemen. Prizes galore. Bingo." Laid out on tables were coloured chequered boards with numbers in some of the boxes. It was a game I didn't know.

"Dad? Can I play? Please?" He stopped and frowned at me, tutting.

"I mean, *may* I play?"

"That's better. When will you learn to speak correctly?"

"Are you joining us, sir? Come on, the little girl can play too. Two seats right in front of you, sir. Two bob each."

"Oh, very well," Dad conceded. We sat down.

"How do you play?" I asked him.

He sighed. "How does *one* play. Well, the man calls out numbers and if they correspond with the numbers on your board, you cover your number with one of these counters. See?"

It seemed too easy to me. The game began. The man spoke animatedly through a microphone. "And the first number, ladies and gentlemen. Two fat ladies. Eighty-eight." There it was on my board, but not on Dad's. I covered my square with a counter.

"And the next. Half a crown, two and six, twenty-six." I picked up another counter.

"Unlucky for some, number thirteen."

The players laughed, tittered or groaned at jokes I didn't understand, the sun pushed at my back and I continued to pick up counters until all my numbers were gone. I waited, wondering what would happen next. The caller's voice boomed on.

"Dad?" I whispered. "What do you do when all the numbers are covered?" He looked at my board.

"Are you sure you heard every one of your numbers called?"

"Yes, I'm sure."

"Well then, you call out Full House. Go on. *Shout*."

"Does it mean I've won?"

"Yes. Yes, now shout before someone else beats you to it."

"FULL HOUSE," I bellowed, thrilled with myself.

There was a moment of quiet. The woman next to me pursed her lips. The caller laid down his microphone, walked over and took my card away.

"He's checking your numbers," said Dad.

"All correct," he confirmed. "Come and choose your prize, girlie. Don't go away ladies and gentlemen: another game coming right up. Take your seats for Bingo."

We looked at the array of prizes. A canteen of cutlery, a lacy tablecloth and napkins, a pressure cooker, a set of golf balls, a book on fishing, a bottle of whisky, a cut glass decanter, a basket of fruit… how disappointing, I thought. I supposed I had better choose the fruit.

"Take the whisky," urged Dad. "I'll buy you something else."

We wandered from stall to stall until I spotted an enticing cellophane-wrapped box of coloured pens and pencils. It was two shillings and elevenpence – far too pricey, I knew. To my surprise and delight, Dad bought it for me.

"Thank you, Dad!"

"A pleasure, my dear. There's no need to go telling your mother and that woman about my whisky, though, eh?"

27
DESOLATION

In winds that blow me weary
And heavy drops that follow,
Let me know what salt and sorrow
Turn the sea and fling the swallow.

Condole – Jean Lipkin

Camp was not always a happy experience. When Izzy and I were ten and Chris eight, we were all Woodling age, which meant that the three of us would be in the same group. We chose to camp together in the New Forest. FSC maintains an Aid Fund, available for children whose parents cannot afford the fees, and to fund holidays for children in care on the recommendation of Social Workers. In theory, only the staff leaders know who has been specially enrolled, but it was obvious within a group who the disadvantaged children were. Their camping equipment was supplied by FSC; the clothes they brought with them were not quite suitable; but the most striking difference was their behaviour. We were not supposed to notice any disparity and kept our observations to ourselves. They in turn did not broadcast their circumstances, but during conversations we would hear disturbing descriptions of lives that bore no resemblance to our (in general) middle-class backgrounds. Put a group of children together and the naughty boys will immediately gravitate towards each other, the most popular girl will assume her position of superiority without election, and a pattern of hierarchy emerges that appears to have been established before anyone met. The misfit is clocked, the fat boy noticed, the bully eyed warily, and the children in care might just as well be wearing T-shirts saying so.

FSC aims to integrate each camp, encouraging children to work together, to be tolerant, caring and co-operative. The staff group meets regularly to discuss any difficulties that arise, seeking diplomatic solutions to resolve problems. However, the success or failure of this strategy depends entirely upon the quality of the staff and in turn upon the camp-chief. He or she must direct and support, listen and consider, and be aware of individual personalities and feelings within groups.

The camp-chief of this particular camp was known by the name 'Beefy', and revered throughout FSC – not only an experienced camper but also one of the founders of Forest School. One would have thought that we were in safe hands, but Beefy gravely failed one child on his camp – me.

The site was within Purlieu Farm, near Fordingbridge, in the heart of the New Forest. We shared the land with the wild New Forest ponies, sheep, cattle, badgers and rabbits. The Woodlings were camped at the top of a hill, which looked down onto the communal area of dining circle, kitchen and shelter tents.

From the start we were aware that Lydia and Haydon were 'specially enrolled'. They also had an older sister, Lynda, who was a Tracker. We put up FSC bivvys, not yet having tents of our own. Izzy and I shared one and it happened that Chris shared a tent with Haydon. Haydon was unpredictable and defiant. He would not follow instructions from the staff and delighted in breaking rules. Running across the dining circle was an obvious way to gain attention. To shouts of "tablecloth" he romped in the middle, annoying everyone, challenging the staff to stop him. He also caused havoc by tearing through the roped off kitchen area and deliberately barging into people around the fire. He laughed if anyone gave chase, kicking and punching when a member of staff tried to restrain him.

On the first morning at rally, Beefy talked to us about the wild ponies. We were warned to keep our distance, to respect their space, to be aware that the New Forest is their home and we the intruders. He told us to stay within the boundaries of the camp site and explained the dangers of leaving the site without permission. Haydon took no notice and persuaded Chris to go with him to find some horses. Later, he reappeared without Chris. Staff located the abandoned Chris in tears trying to find his way back to camp, having been kicked in the stomach by a pony. Haydon had deliberately tormented a group of ponies and provoked one into kicking Chris. There was a mark on his tummy, but he wasn't badly hurt, more distressed that he might be in trouble.

From the start, Chris was dreadfully homesick. Now he was desperate to go home. Izzy and I tried to comfort him, but he was inconsolable. Meanwhile, the Woodlings had measured one another up. Lydia was cast as the misfit and ostracised. She was partially deaf and wore a hearing aid in one ear. Her speech was difficult to understand, and the other children mimicked her cruelly. I tried to help her fit in, showed her how to use the lat, queued up with her for meals and sat beside her at rally. The girl who had shared a tent with Lydia on the first night moved into a tent with two other girls the next day and refused to return. I offered to move in with Lydia to keep her company. Chris moved out of Haydon's tent and shared with Izzy. Chris was still extremely unhappy. Izzy wrote to Mum and Dad: "He keeps on asking me when we go home. But I think he will last out."

The Woodling group-chief was a man called Chris Lee. Other members of staff were Veronika, Suzanne and Jane. It wasn't easy sharing a tent with Lydia. She slept restlessly, rolled into me during the night and wet her sleeping bag. I made up a game to play when we were supposed to be going to sleep. We had to draw words on the sides of the tent with the light from our torches and guess what they were. I soon realised that the words I was spelling were too difficult for her, so I simplified them. But she didn't get any of them. Even C-O-W was beyond her. Then she drew the letters G-A-S.

"Gas," I said.

"No." Perhaps I hadn't seen clearly. I asked her to do it again.

"It *is* gas," I insisted.

"No, it's not."

"OK, I give up. What is it?"

"Grass!" she said, delighted to have caught me out.

I told her that G-A-S was not the way to spell grass, but she didn't understand

and started to write the letters again with her finger on the canvas.

"Don't do that! The rain will come in," I warned, too late. Water started trickling from the G.

"Never mind. Let's go to sleep," I sighed.

On the fifth morning, the gong sounded for rally. The Woodlings rushed off down the hill to find the best logs. Izzy took Chris by the hand and I waited for Lydia. She was still inside the tent.

"Come on Lydia, it's time for rally. What are you doing?" I called from outside.

"Getting changed."

"Hurry up, then."

By the door of our tent was a clump of flattened thistles. I kicked at them absent-mindedly. Then something awful happened. Just as I was aiming another kick at the thistles, Lydia stuck her head out of the tent and my booted foot slammed into her ear. She screamed and screamed. I gasped in horror. "Lydia! Are you alright? I'm so sorry. I didn't mean to. It was an accident." Thank goodness it wasn't the ear in which she wore a hearing aid. I knelt beside her, wanting to comfort her, but she pushed at me with all the force she could muster, clasped her arms around her head and screamed in a way I had never heard anyone scream before – long howls interspersed with short, fast, piercing staccato shrieks. As soon as her first scream was heard down at the dining circle, members of staff came running.

"What happened?" they asked.

"She kicked me, she kicked me," Lydia bawled.

"Where, Lydia?"

"My ear." She howled; she screeched.

"Did you kick her?" asked Chris Lee accusingly.

"Yes, but I didn't mean to," I wailed.

"How can you *not mean* to kick someone?"

"It was an accident," I explained fearfully.

Lydia was hugged, held and examined by several people and I was led away. Chris Lee made up his mind then and there that I had deliberately kicked Lydia in the head: "And in her ear, when you know she's deaf. What kind of a person are you?"

My protests were in vain. It was difficult to describe exactly how the accident had occurred, and Chris Lee, having already decided I was guilty, muddled what I was trying to say. It was tricky to work out how it had happened. If she had put her head out of the tent a second later my foot would have missed her, and if it had been a moment earlier, I would have avoided the impact. Fate had colluded with Time to connect two unrelated actions into an appalling collision. Again and again I attempted to clarify what had happened, but my words were received with hostility, accusation and incredulity. My belief structure collapsed. It offered me no protection at all. Judge Chris Lee blew it down as easily as the little pigs' straw house. I was given no materials to build my defence, no fair trial and no right of appeal. I gave up trying.

A short time later, another FSC bivvy was pitched on the Woodling site, far away from the tent Lydia and I shared. Who was it for, I wondered, and then realised with sickening clarity that it was for me. Chris Lee told me to get out of Lydia's tent and moved all my belongings into the conspicuous new one. I sobbed my heart out and wrote to Mummy and Daddy, begging them to take Chris and me home, and Izzy should probably leave too, as this was a horrible camp. Worse was to come. Lydia seemed to be entirely recovered. I tried to apologise again, but she screamed every time I went near her. Haydon pushed me or shoved me off logs whenever he saw an opportunity, but the score was to be settled by Lynda, their big sister.

"There you are, yer fuckin' bully. Fink yer can fuckin' kick me sister's 'ead in do yer?" I was terrified. The staff diverted her away from the Woodling site.

"I'll fuckin' get yer. I'll kick yer fuckin' 'ead in til you wish you'd never bin fuckin' born," she threatened over her shoulder.

I clung to Izzy and Chris, and hung around the kitchen, terrified of Lynda finding me alone. I was beset with diarrhoea for the rest of the camp. The following day, less than twenty-four hours after the incident, Chris Lee hauled me into his tent for further questioning.

"OK," he began, "let's talk about this. Tell me the truth. Why did you kick Lydia?"

"I've already told you. It was an accident."

"Oh, come on. Don't lie. Be honest then we can talk about why you did it and try to help you."

I kept silent. *I didn't mean to. Why won't you understand*? I stared at a point on my knee, noticing abstractedly that the fabric of my trousers was torn. I could see my dirty skin underneath.

"I'm waiting, Catherine. Did Lydia do anything to make you kick her?"

He was trying to trick me into admitting that I intentionally hurt her. I picked at my nails. *It was an accident.*

"You kicked her, didn't you?" Silence. "You've already said so." Silence. "Why?" Silence.

"OK. If you're not going to talk about it, perhaps you can explain the meaning of this to me."

Horrified, I saw that he was holding the letter I had written yesterday to Mummy and Daddy. He pulled the pages out of the envelope. "Do you recognise this?"

I nodded expressionlessly. *But I'm sure I put it in the camp post box. How can you have it? Oh no, no. Did I drop it on the ground*?

"Catherine, we can't let you send this to your parents. Think how much it would upset them! Christopher has been a bit homesick, but he's fine now. Children are occasionally homesick at camp but we help them to overcome it. Just as he's beginning to enjoy himself, you're trying to spoil things for him by asking your parents to take him home. It is not up to you to make those kind of decisions. Thankfully, I found your letter before it was posted, so you're lucky, no damage has been done. I'll throw this on the fire where it belongs. I'm also here to help you, you know. Think about what I've said, think about what you've done and come and talk to me."

I made a move to leave.

"I haven't said you can go yet. There's something else to tell you. Hike starts tomorrow and we're splitting the Woodlings into groups. Isabel, Christopher, Lydia and four others will be in my and Veronika's group. Haydon will be in the second group and you plus the remaining six will be with Suzanne. Jane has left, so a new member of staff called Pat will be joining you. She knows all about the situation."

I had never felt so alone – not just removed from everything around me but also detached from my physical self. I retreated into a solitary place deep inside to find some solace with music. Coiled into my shell, I listened in my head to Bach's double violin concerto, trying to hear it clearly; I sang Saint-Saëns's *The Swan* silently and longed for my cello. I wanted to feel the pressure of my fingers on the strings, my bow drawing out its sound. In my tent I read Noel Streatfeild's *Ballet Shoes*.

On hike I plodded along mechanically on my own, watching the ground. I sat apart from the group and couldn't eat. Pat, the new member of staff, didn't pry, but stayed near me, waiting for me to catch up when we walked. She was concerned that I wasn't eating; I remember that. I endured the rest of camp; so did Chris, ever homesick, who continued to ask when we were going home. I counted the minutes. At last it was over. There was Mummy waiting for us on the station platform. Tears of relief and happiness overflowed as I ran to her, threw my arms tightly around her waist, and wept.

"There, there. You'll see all your friends again next year," she said sympathetically, patting me a couple of times on my back before disengaging herself from my clutch. She would never know the source of my tears. I kept my ordeal to myself. When the FSC brochure arrived in the New Year, I said I didn't want to go camping.

"Why ever not? You always enjoy camp."

"I just don't want to go."

She enrolled us all anyway, sure that I would be persuaded to camp when the time came. I was, but none of us ever went on another camp run by Beefy. Chris Lee stopped staffing on FSC; we never saw him again.

28
THE HORN

To sound my horn I had to develop my embouchure.
I found my horn was a bit of a devil to play.
So artfully wound to give you a sound,
a beautiful sound so rich and round.

Ill Wind – Michael Flanders/Donald Swann

Chris continued to do battle with the violin, taking his grades I, II and III, which he passed with merit. The comments given by the examiner for one of his grade III pieces described Chris's inimitable style rather well: 'Tone a little scratchy and your staccato notes rather bounce off the string, but a vigorous and musical performance'. Then in April 1967, when he was eight and in his second year at the Junior School, an opportunity arose for somebody in his class to learn a brass instrument.

"Would anyone here like to play the trumpet?" asked Miss Wallington, the headmistress. Chris looked around the room. Seeing no sign of interest from anyone else, he thought, "Oh well, why not?" and stuck up his hand obligingly. It wasn't quite the right instrument for him, but luckily, he had found the right teacher. John Ridgeon had just left the Royal Academy of Music and been appointed Supervising Brass Teacher in the new London Borough of Redbridge.

In 1965 the Borough of Ilford amalgamated with the Borough of Wanstead and Woodford, of which South Woodford was a part. The new borough's Music Advisor, Malcolm Bidgood, was determined that every schoolchild in Redbridge would have the opportunity to learn a musical instrument. His vision seemed far-fetched, but he worked ceaselessly to overcome problems and remove obstacles. Until this time, the only children to have instrumental lessons were those whose parents could afford it. Mostly, those parents were musicians themselves or had some knowledge or interest in music that they wished to foster in their children. Mr. Bidgood believed that financial restrictions and musical ignorance should not deprive any child from learning to play an instrument. He managed to persuade the Borough to invest money and established the 'Instrument Bank'. This was a unique and innovative way to provide instruments to children, which they could rent at small cost with options to buy in instalments, upgrade, or trade in. He then appointed a full-time instrument repairer and administrator, and the Instrument Bank began to function. To begin with, there were only a couple of peripatetic teachers, but within a few years, there were over sixty. Three schools were utilised on Saturday mornings where four orchestras, four bands, a wind band and choirs rehearsed, and theory classes were held. During the week, the peripatetic teachers visited the schools in the Borough, giving instrumental lessons to every child who wanted to learn. The school music teachers were also closely involved, arranging the peripatetic timetables and forming their own school orchestras – previously impossible. Furthermore, Mr. Bidgood established *Musici*, an orchestra made up of the peripatetic teachers, senior students and other local musicians, which visited the schools and gave all children in the borough the opportunity to hear a symphony orchestra.

John Ridgeon had wanted to play the trumpet when he was a young boy, but his parents could not afford music lessons. Instead, he joined his local Salvation Army band, was loaned a trumpet and virtually taught himself. At ten he won a Junior Exhibitioner's scholarship to the Royal Academy of Music and was made principal trumpet of the Essex Youth Orchestra. However, when he went on to the RAM as a senior student, his embouchure collapsed. Nobody could help him. He had to solve the problems himself. He learnt about the muscular structure of the mouth, lips and face, observed different physiognomies and patiently built up a full understanding of the physical aspects of brass playing. He worked out how best to utilise and strengthen the muscles with maximum control and minimum pressure on the mouthpiece and put his knowledge, which was second to none, into practice as a teacher. Rather as F. M. Alexander was forced to solve persistent vocal problems that threatened his career as an actor (which evolved into the acclaimed Alexander Technique), John Ridgeon developed his specialised teaching method from having to solve his own embouchure problems.

Taking up the trumpet with John Ridgeon was a turning point in Chris's life. Mum hired a trumpet from the Instrument Bank at ten shillings a term and his lessons began. With John's exemplary teaching and Chris's natural physical set-up for brass playing, he raced ahead. Mum wasn't too keen on the sound of the trumpet, but it was preferable to the sound of Chris's violin, which was practised less and less. Chris kept his trumpet polished, the valves oiled and the crooks greased, caring for it as fondly as one of the cats.

A few weeks later, John phoned Mum. "Hello, am I speaking to Mrs. Giles? This is John Ridgeon, Christopher's trumpet teacher."

"Please call me Elizabeth. And I use my own name, Elizabeth Fraser, professionally. I'm a music teacher myself. So, how's Christopher faring with the trumpet?"

"He's doing brilliantly. I have never come across anyone so naturally able or so instinctively musical. He has real talent. The reason I'm phoning is that Christopher could do with longer lessons than the ten minutes or so he gets at school. I'm wondering whether you would consider him having private lessons from next term?"

"Yes, of course," said Mum, "but do you think Christopher might be capable of playing the French horn? I know it's a difficult instrument, but I do much prefer the sound of the horn to the trumpet."

"I'm quite sure he could play the horn. It requires a different embouchure and is a demanding instrument to play, but I can't see him having too much of a struggle. The problem is that there are no horns available from the Instrument Bank – would you be able to buy him one?"

She scraped the money together and bought him a second-hand Paxman Studenti. In September 1967, Chris had his first lesson and a horn player was born. John Ridgeon came to Cleveland Road every weekend thereafter to teach him. The violin was packed away forever. The sound of the horn added to the musical voice of our house and the horn repertoire soon became familiar to our ears. Mum did not have to badger Chris to practise. He was smitten, and tended his horn even more lovingly than the trumpet.

Mum paid for all our music lessons and bought us anything we needed. It must have been tough finding the money for Chris's horn. She didn't once refer to the cost, but we knew that money was not plentiful. When I was nine, she bought me a very good three-quarter-size cello. I don't know how much she paid for it, but I was aware that she'd had to save and borrow to buy it. Dad was tight with money and moaned about every penny Mum asked him to contribute. Quite how they worked things out financially is a mystery. His wages must have gone somewhere (on booze and tobacco, like all men: plenty to spend on themselves, I hear Granny say), but he didn't put his hand in his pocket for our lessons or instruments. On the whole, he was uninvolved with our musical lives. He tolerated us practising, but didn't encourage it. Yet he was keen to listen to me making up pieces on the piano – perhaps because when I did, Granny complained that I wasn't practising properly. He was particularly fond of one tune, which he called 'English Autumn'. Then he spoiled that small scrap of empathy by asking me to play it for him when I didn't want to and getting aggrieved by my refusal. Worst of all, when people came to the house, he expected us to perform to them.

"Catherine, come and play your cello."

"Daaaaad," I'd moan, squirming with discomfort.

"They'd like to hear you perform – wouldn't you?" he'd ask, turning to the guest.

"Well, yes, if Catherine would like to."

"Come on then," he'd say with false jollity whilst his eyes conveyed: don't let me down in front of my friends.

I suffered the indignity and hated the exposure. Dad sat there smiling proudly, tapping his feet irritatingly. Couldn't he tell how awful it was, how I detested it? Sometimes I protested.

"Oh Daaaaad, not now."

"Just one piece – a little Bach perhaps?"

"Derek, she doesn't want to," Mum intervened.

"I wasn't asking you."

It all became miserable, fraught and confusing.

"Now you're going sulking up to your room, I suppose?" he called angrily after my retreating figure.

LEFT: At the sink in my bedroom, scene of so many tortured hours when I battled with asthma.

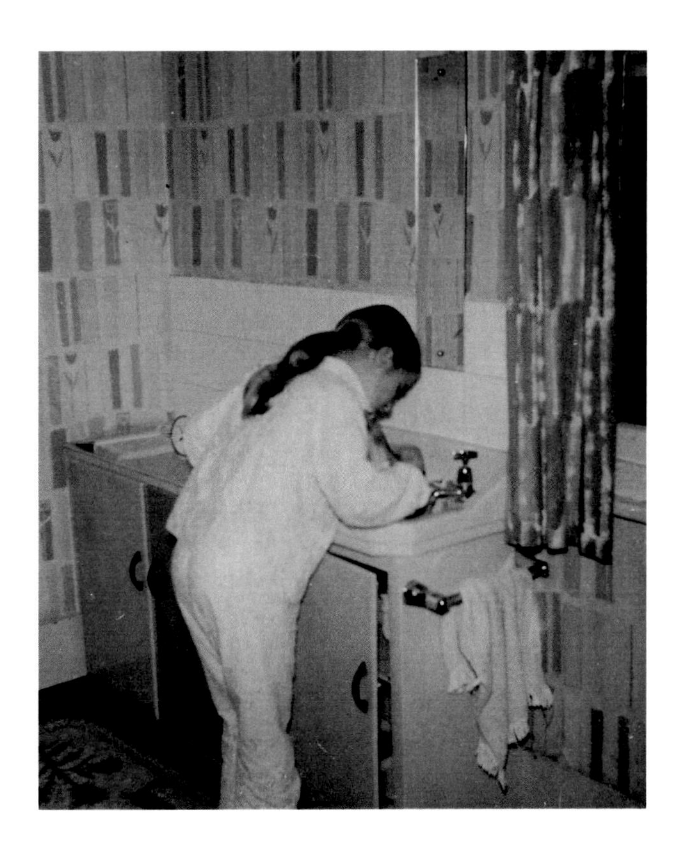

BELOW: Izzy and I performing at a concert in July 1966 when we were ten.

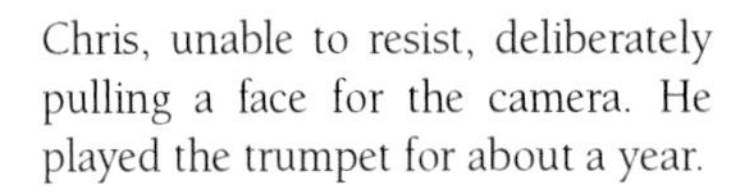

Chris, unable to resist, deliberately pulling a face for the camera. He played the trumpet for about a year.

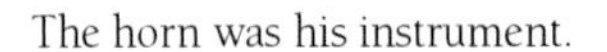

The horn was his instrument.

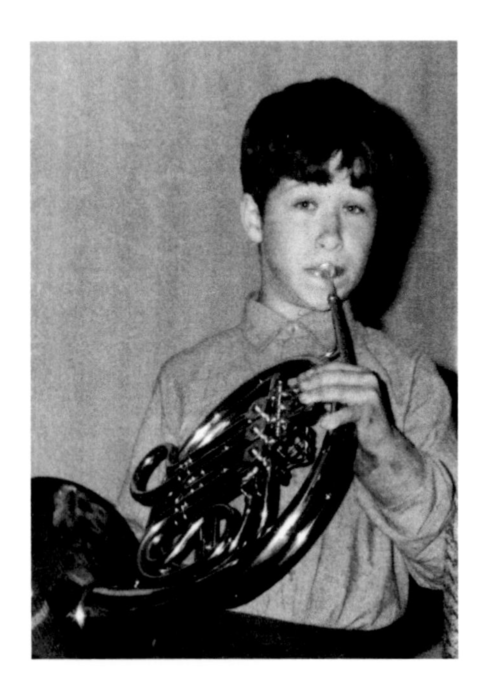

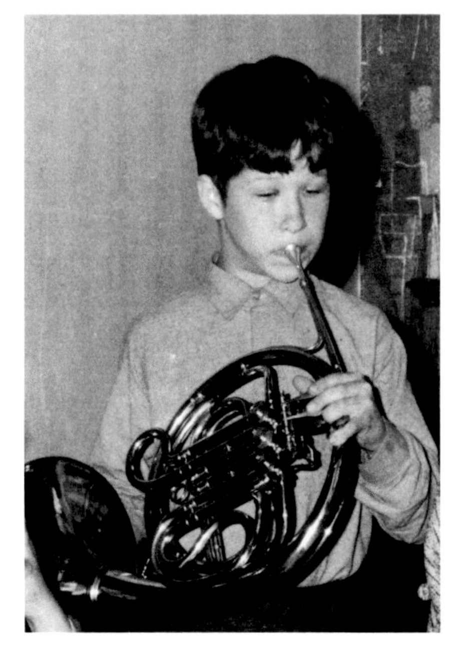

29
THE KISS

The night that holds
The door ajar
For you to enter
Narrows as you go.

Fragments i – Jean Lipkin

Stan Gillick came to Wortley summer school for the first time with no knowledge of chamber music. He was a very good pianist, largely self-taught, and an excellent sight-reader. Although music was not his profession, in his hometown he played in dance bands. I was nine that year. He asked if I would play piano trios with him and a violinist called John. I thought Mum would say it was time for bed, but he said, "Leave it to me. I'll have a word with Elizabeth." To my surprise, she agreed.

We browsed through the pile of piano trios. I had to confess to Stan that they all looked much too difficult. "Nonsense," he said, "you can do it, Cath. Come on, have a go. I don't know any of this either. We're all sight-reading." We set up the music stands and opened the parts. It was a trio by Schubert in E flat major. Stan and John decided on a tempo and we began. I played the first note and immediately lost my place. Stan shouted out bar numbers, but by the time I found the bar, they were miles ahead and I had missed the cue. I searched the music for clues, but it was all very bewildering. "Coming up to letter C," called Stan. "Get ready. Four bars to go. I'll bring you in. Three, two, one. Play *now*."

I managed to get in! It reminded me of the skipping game when two people are holding the rope at either end, turning it over and over and you have to watch the rope, count the rhythm and leap in at the right moment to jump clear and keep skipping. I kept going for about eight bars. The music sounded wonderful and I was part of it, chugging along on E flat crotchets and quavers in the same rhythm as the violin, while the piano played a lilting tune. Then the notes became complicated and I was lost again. Stan didn't stop. "I'll shout out the next letter. Join in if you can. Great stuff, Cath."

By the end of the long first movement I had probably played less than one percent of the notes, but I was exhilarated by the music, and Stan made me feel that I had done well. The following day, he asked if I would play again that evening.

"Are you sure?"

"Sure I'm sure."

"What about John?"

"He asked me to ask you. Eight o'clock in the library. Don't let us down."

John was a good player himself – what generous people they were to give a nine-year-old such enthusiastic encouragement. We played the same piece, Stan shouting out the letters. I was able to play a few more notes and began to find my way in the music, which now sounded familiar. I missed loads out, but managed to keep more or less in the right place.

In those days, Stan chain-smoked. He played with a cigarette hanging from his mouth and when it had burnt down, he upended the butt on top of the piano, as there was no time to stub it out. By the end of the evening a row of burnt out cigarette ends stood lined up on the piano lid. Amazingly, the varnish was not damaged. No doubt it was a technique he had learnt in the dance bands.

Mum also let me stay up to listen to a lecture by Dr. Alan Bush, in which he talked of the historical reasons as to why the Workers' Music Association had been formed and the role of music in the fight for equality, peace, freedom and social justice. He was so convincing, rousing and inspiring that I decided to join the WMA immediately. At nine years old I must have been the youngest member.

The next year, after my bad time at camp, I was ten. "Eight o'clock tonight?" said Stan as soon as he saw the Giles family arrive. "I've booked the library." Peter was the violinist this time. Stan found another Schubert trio in B flat and decided we should have a go at that. The first movement was completely beyond me. I sat watching the notes whizz by unable to catch a single one. But then we came to the second movement. It opens with a slow theme on the cello in 6/8 time accompanied in quavers by the piano. I could just about manage some of it and was enraptured by the sublime melody. My playing erred more towards the ridiculous than the sublime, but by the end of the week it was at least recognisable.

That year at Wortley I witnessed something I knew I was not supposed to see. Mum and the three of us shared a family room. Mum put us to bed, made sure we were settled, and told us she was going down to the ballroom for a little while. She switched off the light, said goodnight and closed the door. The corridors were always lit; we knew our way around the building, so if any of us had needed her, we could have found her. Much later, I heard a noise at the door. The Schubert trio had been going round in my head for hours and I was still awake. I opened my eyes and saw Mum silhouetted in the light from the hall. There was a man beside her and I could see she was whispering goodnight to him. Then he took her in his arms and kissed her. I watched, surprised but not shocked. The kiss went on for a long time before Mum pulled away. I could tell she was saying to him that she must go to bed and was afraid that the children might wake. I kept absolutely still, hardly daring to breathe. He didn't want to let her go and kissed her again, but then Mum separated from him and stepped into the room. As she closed the door she gave him a last quick kiss on the lips, then all was dark. I could tell who the man was and thought he was very nice. I knew that it wasn't quite right for Mum to be kissing him, but it was OK by me. She looked so elegant in her evening gown, standing in the doorframe, her body yielding with pleasure into that nice man's arms. I wanted her to have that pleasure – I wanted her to be loved. "Don't worry about us," I thought, "go and enjoy yourself. Stay with him all night." But I also knew that she wouldn't. I heard her get into bed and make herself comfortable. I spoke to her silently through the darkness, "I won't tell a soul what I saw, Mum. I hope he'll kiss you again and you'll be happy."

At breakfast the next morning I watched them both carefully, looking for any signals that passed between them, searching for signs of their passionate embrace. They were just friendly, as normal, and didn't even sit on the same table. I was rather disappointed. I tried to stay awake the following nights, but sleep denied me another glimpse of my mother as I wished she could always be. It was the only true embrace I was ever to see her receive.

Over the years at Wortley, Izzy, Chris, Mum and I played all the major chamber music repertoire with Stan – sonatas, trios, piano quartets and quintets by Brahms, Dvořák, Schumann, Beethoven, Schubert and so on. Long after I had stopped going to Wortley, Stan came to stay with me from time to time, as eager as ever to play. He brought his compositions to try out, and we played until I had to insist we stop for a break. Izzy joined us and the piano trios would get an airing. We always played the Schubert E flat (and I still know exactly which eight bars I managed to play when I was nine) and the B flat. The last time Stan visited, we also played piano duets. When Izzy arrived, he produced a piece by Rachmaninov called *Romance* written for six hands at one piano. Rachmaninov wrote it in 1890 for three sisters, but Stan told us that he composed it so that he could sit in the middle with a girl on either side, in order to "have his wicked way".

"Come on you two," said Stan, "I'll pretend to be Rachmaninov, one of you on each side and I'll demonstrate. You'll recognise the tune." Sure enough, it is almost note for note the *Adagio* from his second piano concerto. In fact, he used his *Romance* as the melody for the slow movement, which he wrote ten years later. We began to play. It soon became apparent that in order to reach the notes, the player in the middle has to cross both right and left hands over the hands of his partners, the music written in such a way that a little contact with the sisters' breasts was unavoidable. Perhaps there were also moments when it was easier, surely, to put his arms around their backs to stretch for the more distant notes? We could hardly play for laughing and it ended with both of us in Stan's arms.

"See what I mean, girls? Naughty boy, eh, that Rachmaninov."

My asthma was getting worse. Attacks were more frequent and I wheezed most of the time. The London Chest Hospital in Bethnal Green Road, right beside the Museum of Childhood, became a part of my childhood, I went there so often. It was a grim and grimy place that smelt of surgical spirit, boiled cabbage and disinfectant. More than anything else, I remember sitting for hours in the corridor learning how to pass time. After the first marathon wait, Mum and I took sandwiches and flasks. She annotated music and I knitted, crocheted, wrote stories and read. I don't recall any other children being there. The corridor (there was no waiting room) was filled with old people, some in striped hospital dressing gowns, others in wheel chairs, all of them wheezing, coughing and gasping, incapacitated with emphysema and bronchitis. Their haggard faces and crippled bodies reflected chronic suffering. If their eyes met mine, they held the connection intently, seeming to plead for help and release. I looked with pity and helplessness and was the first to glance away.

The consultation itself lasted no time at all. I stood in my underwear while a stethoscope was pressed to my chest; then I had to blow into a tube, which measured the strength of my exhalation. I was told I could do better than that, but there was little improvement on the second try. At one visit, a noughts and crosses grid was drawn on the inside of my arm, each square grazed with a needle and drops from phials dripped into the abrasions. Within minutes, my arm was red, swollen and burning. 'Allergic' was written in my notes. I couldn't follow much of the conversation between the doctor and Mum, but knew that Mum was concerned that so little could be done to help. "There's no cure; she'll grow out of it," Mum was told. I began to think that in some way asthma was my fault – like wetting the bed or sucking one's thumb – just a phase that, if I put my mind to it, I could stop.

I was given a chart to keep. On a scale of one to five I had to indicate in boxes how bad I considered my asthma to have been during the day and at night. I had to write down the number of hours I had wheezed, whether I was coughing up phlegm, what colour it was (white, yellow, green, grey, bloody) and the drugs I had used. Before the age of twelve, the only drugs that could be prescribed were Ventolin syrup, which did not help much, and Orciphrenaline. I was too young to take Orciphrenaline orally, but could take it as a suppository if my asthma was very bad. The side effects of the drug were awful. Five or ten minutes after insertion, nausea would set in and get worse. As I felt sicker and sicker, my mouth went dry, my colour changed to greyish-white, my lips looked almost blue; I became cold and shaky; sometimes I vomited; my hands shook; I felt dizzy and had diarrhoea. Eventually the trembling wore off, but the nausea continued and I would feel limp, weak and exhausted. However, Orciphrenaline gave me relief; and sickness and nausea were far, far better than asthma. Unless I had a high fever and couldn't get out of bed, I went to school, I did my practice and carried on. Illness was normal, and also isolating. Asthma and bronchitis became a lethal mixture – it was hard to distinguish between the two, because I would often have both at the same time. Every cold went to my chest and my temperature rocketed. I was given penicillin injections and sweated and shivered it out on the divan couch in the living room, listening to Radio Three and the Home Service, coughing and spluttering my way to some sort of recovery.

Mum didn't have time to take me to the chest hospital again, so I went on my own. She met me from school, gave me my train fare, a bag containing sandwiches, Granny's buttered scones and pancakes, another with my knitting and books and off I went. I handed over my chart, which would be scrutinised critically – surely my asthma hadn't been *that* bad; I couldn't have coughed up phlegm *every* night, and how could I have wheezed for *twenty-four hours*! Why, I wondered, was I asked to fill it in if the consultants refused to believe me? I started to downgrade my measurements to please them. The cold weather was bad for my asthma, and the autumn months particularly awful. Summer time was a bit better. Izzy used to get hay fever, but pollen wasn't too bad for me. Izzy also had quite bad eczema and went to consultant dermatologists, but again, there wasn't much that helped. Chris was remarkably free from everything apart from homesickness and an underlying, subtle anxiety that he carried with him all the time.

30
THE FIREBIRD AND MARNIE

In her long white dress, with the reeds standing up all around her, and the moonlight shining on her pale hair, she looked more than ever like someone out of a fairy story.

When Marnie Was There – Joan G. Robinson

Every week we visited the library – Izzy sometimes twice a week, she read so much. We knew to avoid books by Enid Blyton, aware that Mum and Dad disapproved of her writing; but even when we stole a glance at them, the illustrations put us right off: the stories seemed bland and the children superficial. The novels we chose were by authors such as E. Nesbit, Noel Streatfeild, C. S. Lewis, Frances Hodgson Burnett, Anna Sewell, Susan M. Coolidge and Joan G. Robinson – writers who managed to create wholly believable characters to which their young readers could relate. In the stories we recognised ourselves and learned about the complexities and mysteries of adult behaviour. Our family might be strange, but others were stranger. On the other hand, that ours was not a normal, happy family was also confirmed. We could empathise with children who were lonely, rejected, abandoned, betrayed, misunderstood, falsely accused, secretive or friendless. A well-paced adventure would structure the book, but the great stories were the ones that explored and questioned feelings and beliefs. These sensitive authors credited their readers with maturity and intelligence, managing to facilitate the young mind's imagination and insight. Any hint of condescension would have turned us off instantly. There had to be a happy ending, though, riddles solved and questions answered satisfactorily. *Black Beauty* almost didn't fall into that category; Izzy was inconsolable when Ginger died.

There is one book I remember above all others: *When Marnie Was There* by Joan G. Robinson. The story is about Anna, an orphaned, solitary girl with whom I empathised from page one when I read: "It was impossible for her to say goodbye naturally, with the spontaneous hug and kiss that other children managed so easily." I learned that she tried to look "ordinary" to avoid being noticed and "things like best friends and parties were fine for everyone else, because everyone else was 'inside' – inside some sort of invisible magic circle. But Anna herself was outside." She had asthma, couldn't go to school for nearly two weeks and was sent to Norfolk to recuperate near the sea. I knew asthma, and Norfolk. Wandering alone, she discovered an old house beside the creek and had the strange feeling that it had been waiting for her. She glimpsed the shadowy figure of a girl in one of the upstairs windows; the baffling, enchanting and elusive Marnie: I was hooked.

The library loaned records as well as books. The music I chose was entirely random, as I selected it according to the appeal of the artwork on the record sleeve. A colourful painting of fabulous plumage introduced me to Stravinsky's *The Firebird*, which I borrowed on the same day as *When Marnie Was There*. I put the record on and began to read. The music was the most fantastic I had ever heard, the book was captivating, but combined it was as if the two had been designed to go together. I read: "A small bird flew over the creek, uttering a short plaintive cry four or five times running, all on one note. It sounded like 'Pity me! Oh, pity me!'" At that moment, the music imitated the bird's lamenting call. This was too amazing to keep to myself. I had to share it with Izzy and Chris. Izzy was engrossed in another book, so it was just Chris who curled up beside me to listen. I put the record back to the beginning and started to read the story. We entered an atmospheric world of magic and fantasy that was ghostly and shimmering, emotive and powerful. We were both enthralled. *The Firebird* was played over and over until the music was so familiar that it became associated with characters in the book.

Marnie's melody was the theme that starts with a simple rising major triad with the sorrowful addition of the minor seventh, then falls in haunting minor thirds; a perfect *leitmotiv* for the fey, waif-like, ephemeral girl. Stravinsky artfully introduces parts of the recurring 'Marnie' melody on single instruments (clarinet, flute, horn) then extends it using solo violin and cello, gradually drawing the whole orchestra into a rich, passionate outpouring. Anna we associated more with the gentle sound of the string section, her moods resonating with the differing musical emotions. The oboe, cor anglais, bassoon and horn conjured up the deserted windswept dunes and marshes, marram grass and sea lavender. In the scary bits, the heavy brass and percussion jumped out to frighten us and when the story was eerie and unfathomable, tuned percussion and celesta made weird and supernatural sounds. To finish, there is a gorgeous, transcendent, triumphant closing melody; everything is going to work out, it says, we are on our way home and all will be well: the all-important happy ending.

In this way, I read the whole book, Chris my companionable audience of one. I suppose the rest of the family must have been coming in and out, as the record player was in the living room, but we were unaware of any interruption, so involved had we become in the music and story. It must have been read in several sittings, but I know that Chris was there beside me for the duration. I worked out 'Marnie's theme' on the piano and played it frequently so that I wouldn't forget it, as the record and book had to be returned to the library.

Anna wasn't exactly the same as me; I wasn't entirely rejected by my peers, nor was I orphaned or fostered, but I knew about solitude and isolation. I too had an inner dialogue of worries and anxious feelings I couldn't explain. As Anna begins to make sense of who she is through her friendship with Marnie (who is really a reflection of Anna's inner self), so a child like myself learns that loneliness is not strange or unusual. Near the end of the book is this passage:

> He was the loneliest person she had ever known. And yet he had been one of eleven children! She had been lonely because she was one. And Marnie had been lonely because she was one. It was raining harder now and she was beginning to get wet, but it did not matter. She was warm inside. She turned and began running along the dyke, thinking how strange it was – about being "inside" or "outside". It was nothing to do with there

> being other people, or whether you were "an only" or one of a large family – it was something to do with how you were feeling inside yourself.

Never patronising, always sincere, Joan G. Robinson found a way to talk about human psychology with children. For the next Christmas or birthday, I asked for a recording of *The Firebird*. I was disappointed not to see the fiery red and orange feathers on the cover, but far, far worse, Marnie's tune had disappeared. I listened again, but it simply wasn't there. Like Marnie herself, it had vanished. The ghostly girl had spirited the music away with her. I puzzled about it for years, playing the haunting refrain on the piano, and wondered sadly if I had imagined the whole thing.

31
PRINCE CHARMING

I should think there never can have been a man who enjoyed his profession more than Mr. Creakle did. He had a delight in cutting at the boys, which was like the satisfaction of a craving appetite.

David Copperfield – Charles Dickens

For our last two years at Junior School, between the ages of nine and eleven, Izzy and I were back with the dreaded Miss Coyne. She did not wear the tippity-tappity court shoes that the other women teachers wore, which gave pupils fair warning of their approach – no, her feet were laced into flat, crepe-soled Hush-Puppies, which enabled her to sneak up on us unawares. After playtimes, we were expected to sit quietly behind our desks awaiting her arrival. As the seconds ticked by, our silence could not be contained. Before long, we were all talking. As if on cue, Miss Coyne loomed into the doorway, triumphant at having caught us out, terrifying us with thunderous words.

Those who could keep up without difficulty were largely exempt from her cruelty, but children who didn't immediately understand were taught with the slipper, the ruler and the malicious lash of her tongue. Roland Mortlock struggled with maths: a tremor of trepidation fluttered through the class when Miss Coyne, standing over his desk at the rear of the room, sent him up to the front to work out a long division sum written starkly on the blackboard.

Roland, white-faced, held the chalk in a trembling hand and stared at the numbers in petrified confusion. We felt his fear and vulnerability, and sent thought-waves of help through the air. Then, to our horror, Miss Coyne began to creep slowly and stealthily from the back of the classroom towards the blackboard. We held our breath as she edged nearer and nearer to Roland, positioned herself right behind him and waited. Poor Roland was entirely unaware of her presence. Suddenly, she shouted "YOU STUPID BOY". We all jumped, but Roland almost leapt out of his skin, uttering a terrified yelp as she slapped him on the head. The chalk dropped from his hand and shattered into pieces on the floor.

We witnessed the administration of the slipper several times. The occasion I remember most vividly was that of Richard James, a sweet-looking, likeable, blonde-headed boy. I have no idea what he had or had not done, but there was no doubt as to what was about to happen when Miss Coyne ordered him to fetch his slipper bag. Every child had a slipper bag – a cloth pouch drawn together with cord which hung from our designated hooks in the cloakroom and contained shorts, a T-shirt and a pair of rubber-soled, slip-on black plimsolls.

With our eyes, we followed Richard's steps out of the classroom. I wished he would run away and not come back, but he returned obediently. Miss Coyne made him pull open the bag, extract a plimsoll, place it on her desk, unzip and drop his shorts and lie in his underpants across her lap. Clamping him firmly across the shoulders with her left arm, she raised the slipper in her right, poised it in mid-air for a suspenseful moment before bringing it down, sole first, with vicious strength and accuracy on Richard's bottom. She lifted the shoe above her head again. I gritted my teeth and squeezed my eyes shut as she repeated the assault five more times, counting out every number relentlessly, each hit more ferocious than the last. Then she released her grip, told Richard to stand up, pull on his shorts, hang his slipper bag in the cloakroom and return to his desk.

When he came back into the classroom, his face was flushed, his expression a complex grimace of humiliation, pain, and bravely attempted nonchalance. We averted our eyes in deference as he walked stiffly past us, biting back the tears he was determined not to shed. We heard the scrape of his chair as he sat down; then the whole class waited, immobile, suspended in a dense, suffocating silence. Into it came the unmistakable sounds of stifled sobbing. Richard was crying. Miss Coyne told us icily to get on with our work. I kept my head lowered, gripping my fountain pen tightly. A tear rolled down my nose, dripped onto the blue-black ink and stained my exercise book.

Our reading ability was measured using a chart of specifically selected words. On each new line, the words increased in difficulty and were printed in progressively smaller type. Every term, Miss Coyne placed the same dog-eared card on her desk and one by one we were called up to stand beside her and take the reading test. She held a ruler under the top line, moving it gradually downwards towards trick words designed to catch us out:

right flour below weight integer comb
sign hymn doubt choir orchestra misled reign

The last three words, in the smallest typeface of all were:

pneumonia sepulchre idiosyncrasy

Izzy recited them perfectly. After a few tries, I managed to figure out every word except for the last one. Iddy-oss-yin-crazy was the best I could make of it. I knew I wasn't pronouncing it correctly, but it was such an odd word. I asked Izzy. "You know that word on the card – sounds like idiot-something? Can you say it?"

"Yes – it's iddy-oh-sink-rr-see."

"Iddy-oh… but what does it *mean*?"

"It's a peculiar way of behaving."

The definition was satisfying – an odd-sounding word that actually meant 'oddity'. However, the next time I was called up to read the word card, I didn't dare to pronounce idiosyncrasy correctly in case Miss Coyne thought I was cheating. I stumbled through iddy-oss-yin-crazy as usual, hoping she wouldn't notice any difference. Chris, thankfully, did not have to suffer Miss Coyne; she retired before he reached his third year.

In our penultimate year at Junior School, when we were ten, Keith Donovan took a liking to me. We used to meet outside the sweet shop by the station in the early evenings. He bought 'Kojak' lollies and offered them to me like cigarettes. Feeling cool and grown up, we propped ourselves against the wall, copying the awkward postures adopted by teenagers, sucked our lollies and tried to think of things to say to each other. One time, a window above the shoe shop opposite was thrown up and a girl of about fifteen stuck her head out.

"Oi, Keef, that yer girlfriend then?"

He didn't look up.

"Who's that?" I whispered.

"Just me sister, don't take any notice of 'er"

"Keef, didn't you 'ear me? I said is that yer girlfriend?"

"Yeah, she is, now get lost will ya?"

"Oi, you, wot's yer name?" she shouted, addressing me.

" 'Er name's Caffryn, now leave us alone."

"She ain't got much to say for 'erself 'as she?"

"Come on, let's go," he said, taking my hand.

"Oooo! Look at yer, 'oldin' 'ands. Where yer goin' then?"

We turned left into Marlborough Road and walked along hand in hand. It was the first time I had felt claimed, protected and looked after by a boy. He had positively stated that I was his girlfriend and I felt elevated, viable, valued. Naming me as belonging to him had given me an exclusive place in his life and less concern at that moment about my own. We sat near each other in the classroom, made sure we shared the same table for school dinner, and walked home together, holding hands if other boys weren't around to tease. In the playground, Keith played football and hoped I was watching. Somehow I was always looking the other way when he scored a goal.

Keith was one for getting into trouble. Nothing all that serious, but if there was a fight in the playground, Keith would be in the middle of it. He talked in class, was told off for not paying attention and couldn't resist having water fights in the swimming pool. Once he ran naked into the girls' changing room and dared me to do the same back. I nearly did, but the shrieks of the other girls brought Miss Coyne running, and Keith was caught streaking down the corridor. I pulled on my clothes hastily.

Towards the end of that school year, the class voted for Head Boy, Head Girl and six Prefects who would assume their positions at the beginning of September, our last year at Junior School. The election duly took place and the results were announced. Izzy was voted Head Girl, Paul Chaplin Head Boy, and to my surprise I was voted in as one of the Prefects. Keith, to his disappointment, was not selected. He turned to me and whispered, "I voted for you. Did you vote for me?" I hadn't. I was intending to, but Miss Coyne had given us a stern talk, saying that the Head Boy, Head Girl and Prefects would be undertaking roles of responsibility; they would be Ambassadors for the school and should be dutiful, well-behaved and able to set a good example to the younger pupils. We must therefore vote for children, who, we felt, already possessed these qualities and would be capable of carrying out their duties with the utmost dependability. With all conscience, I had to admit that Keith didn't quite fit the bill and felt duty-bound to vote for others. I looked at Keith, not knowing what to say.

"You didn't, did you? You didn't vote for me!"

"I'm sorry, Keith," I said quietly. I tried to explain my reasons, but he wouldn't listen: he was hurt, humiliated and angry.

"I wish I'd never voted for you. You're a stuck-up pig."

"Oh, Keith…"

"Go to hell."

It was horrible. Why hadn't I immediately said yes, of course I voted for you? But he would have known I was lying. Bloody Miss Coyne: why had I listened to her? I wished I had voted for him, my favourite boy in the class; then we might have been Prefects together. We both thought it was entirely my fault. There were no more Kojak lollies for me, but I did watch him scoring goals.

Another election took place that year – the General Election of 1966. The Communist Party of Great Britain put up fifty-seven candidates – twenty-one more than had stood in the 1964 General Election, when Labour had gained a majority control. Mum and Dad roped the three of us in for canvassing. During the weekends leading up to polling day, visits to Grandad were curtailed and instead we piled into the car with both Mum and Dad and drove to a local constituency. We were sent down streets and into blocks of flats with bundles of leaflets to push through letterboxes. It was fun to begin with. We set off with alacrity, proud to be helping with such important work, but after a while our legs ached and the mission palled. Worse, sometimes doors opened and people shouted rude things at us. Izzy was most distressed to be told that our parents should be in gaol.

"Mum? How much longer do we have to do this?" I moaned.

"Just another couple of streets then we'll call it a day."

"Will our leaflets make any difference?"

"They might persuade a few more people to vote Communist."

"Enough for them to win?"

"Oh no, I shouldn't think so."

Then what are we doing this for, I thought? At last it was polling day and our canvassing duties were over. It was quite exciting the next morning to see in the newspaper how many votes our candidate had won. More than a thousand!

"You see?" said Mum, "I'm sure some of those people voted because of our leaflets." But as I studied the paper more closely, I saw that the Labour candidate had won more than twenty thousand votes and decided it had all been a waste of time.[1]

1. The fifty-seven Communist candidates of 1966 collectively gained 62,112 votes – 0.17% of a 75.81% turnout. In the 1970 general election, fifty-seven Communist candidates again stood for election, but the number of votes they gained almost halved. Since then the numbers and percentages have continued to fall. Just six Communist candidates stood for election in the 2001 General Election, gaining only 1,003 votes in total – 0.002% of a 59.38% turnout. Maybe our canvassing in 1966 had not been completely in vain.

Before we became pupils at Oakdale Junior School, the Parent Teacher Association had raised enough money to build an open-air swimming pool, so we had the benefit of swimming lessons at school twice a week. The water was very cold most of the time, but on the whole, we enjoyed swimming. I was reasonably good, but not fast, as I couldn't master front crawl. I did gain one prize, though. It meant swimming a quarter of a mile. You didn't have to win; you just had to finish. Keith and I tried for it. We were taken to Loughton swimming baths and had to swim seventeen-and-a-half lengths of the huge pool. He finished long before me. After ten lengths, I was ready to give up, but Keith urged me on. Standing at the side of the pool, he kept on shouting, "You can do it; just a few more lengths. Don't give up. You're nearly there." With a supreme effort that took me almost to the point of collapse, I made it. Gasping, I got out of the pool and smiled at him; he smiled back, but he never held my hand again. We were both presented with the 'Ribena Award'. Izzy could swim quite well, but despite the twice-weekly lessons, Chris never became a proficient swimmer – a few widths of inefficient doggy-paddle were about his limit. Izzy and I often went to local pools with groups of friends and learnt to dive and swim underwater, but Chris rarely came with us, preferring to spend his time working on his collection or practising.

The highlight of the last year that Izzy and I spent at Oakdale Junior was our production of *Cinderella*. Izzy was Cinderella, Keith was one of the Ugly Sisters, Penelope Runnicles was Prince Charming and I had a very small speaking part as a town crier, which opened the play. I had to walk on stage left, ring the school bell and announce to the assembled townsfolk, "Hear ye! Hear ye! His Royal Highness the King proclaims there is to be a Grand Ball at the Palace where his son, the Prince, will choose his Bride. Hear ye! Hear ye!" then exit stage right. Izzy was a perfect Cinderella, playing it so well that when we performed it to the Infants, some of them started crying when they saw Cinderella sobbing by the hearthstone unable to go to the Ball. Best of all, the chosen music was *The Firebird*. The last movement was played for the grand finale when Cinderella weds Prince Charming. I listened for 'Marnie's tune', but as usual it didn't appear. I was so nervous that I fluffed my lines or forgot them at every performance, but hopefully nobody noticed over the din of the school bell.

32
THE CLEVELAND COLLECTION

Hurrah for positive science!
Long live exact demonstration!

Song of Myself – Walt Whitman

Chris, aged nine, began his third year at Oakdale Junior School. His friend, Steve Cladingboel, was absent, as he had been taken ill with meningitis and was in hospital. Everyone in the class wrote to him. Steve kept all the letters. Here is the one that Chris sent:

> Oakdale Junior School
>
> September 13th 1967
>
> Dear Stephen,
>
> I hope you are better. When I was on holiday I got two sheep skulls and a rabbit skull and a cat skull. At school we have two new teachers and the dinners are in three groups instead of two. We are swimming every day for three weeks and I can swim with a rubber ring. Julie Howes is our form captain and dick is our vice form captain. On holiday I went to our cottage twice to camp once and to a music summer school once it was at the summer school I found the rabbit skull and the two sheep skulls. Christine bigby gave me my cat skull. Our class is upstairs but I don't like it as much as downstairs.
>
> Love
> Christopher

And here is an extract from the letter that Julie, the new form captain, wrote:

> Mrs. Speedyman has started telling us the story of the Kon Tiki, and Christopher Giles keeps bringing sculls. So far he has brought a cat scull and a mouses scull.

Steve Cladingboel was a frequent visitor to Cleveland Road – "a big old house that I thought looked rather grand. I particularly remember viewing the contents of Chris's bedroom. He was especially pleased that he had managed to get a human skull (I think it was for his birthday). I was struck by how much smaller it was than I had imagined. Chris was very matter of fact and scientific about the skull, never regarding it as in any way macabre." On a number of occasions, he and Chris went off on day trips. Steve told me: "Back then it was perfectly acceptable for two young boys to travel alone across London and spend a day in the museums – and this was long before the days of interactive displays, computer simulations or hands-on activities for children. Chris's fascination with wildlife, nature and bones led us inevitably to the Natural History Museum, a place full of wonder. Bizarrely, the most vivid memory I have of our visits is not the stuffed animals, plaster-cast bones, or respectful, hushed conversation but standing at the top of the huge building, having climbed the grand staircase, listening to Chris describe what the human condition would be should one fall to the solid floor below, explaining how the legs would crumple and buckle backwards on impact. He didn't set out to frighten, but he was brilliant at visual imagery. I hung on to his every word."

Chris had finally grasped the concept of reading and was devouring books with nearly the same greed as Izzy. Maths, though, was still a muddied blur – a subject that would always be his stumbling block. His class teacher, Mrs. Speedyman, had this to say in his end-of-year report:

> Christopher is a lively intelligent boy but he is an erratic worker. His general knowledge and vocabulary are exceptional and he is a lively contributor to all class discussions. More hard work is still necessary in mathematics.

Chris's collection now included skulls of the badger, red and grey squirrel, pine marten, goat, red deer, otter, dozens more types of vole, mouse, bat and bird. Someone by the name of G. C. Scott donated insect specimens from the Rothamsted Experimental Station in Harpenden, where he worked. The bugs (*Hemiptera*) and beetles (*Coleoptera*) were preserved in 70% alcohol and 5% glycerol and labelled with their common and scientific names. Chris bottled whole creatures in jars of Formalin and became practised at skinning animals and 'carding' the skins, which involved stretching the skins onto thick card shaped to the size of the animal.

Chris loved animals and couldn't bear to see one suffer. He didn't kill any of his specimens – they were found dead. Butterflies and moths were the exception. I thought it was rather horrible – so did Chris, to an extent, but he reasoned that the life-span of butterflies and moths is very short, and putting them into a jar with a cotton wool ball soaked in ether didn't hurt them – it just sent them to sleep before they died. He collected caterpillars, which he kept in tanks or makeshift containers with supplies of an appropriate leaf diet, and waited for them to become chrysalises. He also ordered pupae of specific *Lepidoptera* from a company that supplied such things. It was amazing to watch a butterfly or moth struggling to emerge from its cocoon, or to find that one had hatched during the night. As soon as the wings were fully unfolded and wrinkle-free, into the killing jar the creature went. A second or two later it was all over. Chris would remove the specimen carefully, and then mount it in a display box, identify and label it.

He went for long walks with his binoculars, observing birds and learning to recognise and name them. He wanted to know everything he could about natural history, and because he was so interested he retained every scrap of information. The Natural History Museum ran a series of talks, which Chris attended. Each lecture was about a different group of vertebrates. Chris kept a notebook. He began by writing this:

> All things on earth are either living or non-living. Living things are divided into two groups: Plants and Animals. Animals are divided into two groups: Vertebrates and Non-vertebrates. Vertebrates are divided into five groups: Amphibians, Reptiles, Birds, Mammals and Fish.

Throughout the book are drawings of animals, many of which have been included in this one. More comments were added to The Visitors' Book.

From his teachers:

A fascinating collection if a bit scaring to the uninitiated. I particularly admire the small skeletons. Goodness knows how Christopher knows one from the other. The lectures given by the curator are most instructive and enjoyable but I advise the audience to find a comfortable chair before the lecture begins! M. B. Sprakes

Here was a bedroom that produced a gasp – not at untidiness that I often see, but at incredible order and organisation. I loved the delicate paleness of the ancient bones and no shoe box has contained more fascinating treasure. Every time I see a bird now I shall be more aware of the shape beneath the feathers. I would like to see the collection in ten years time.
K. Aldridge.

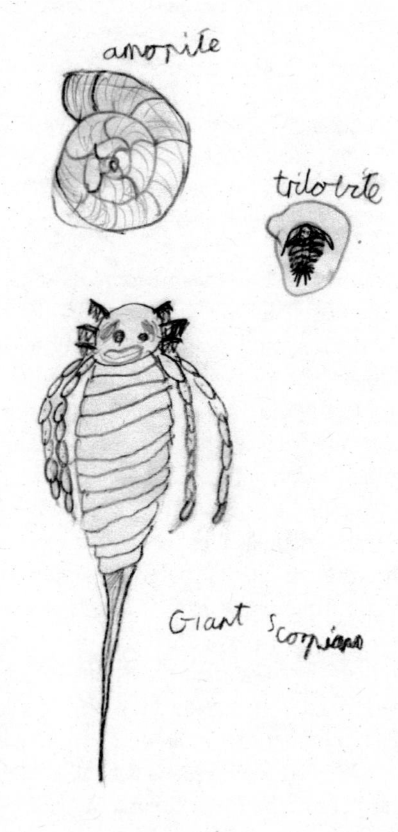

I should like to leave you with this thought. Composition or decomposition?
John Ridgeon.

From his school friends:

I like the ornaments in your bedroom especially your carpet. Lesley Fisher.

Very interesting and fascinating collection. Must come again. Robin O. Gerlis

A very breath-taking sight. Very good indeed. S. Cladingboel

I think your collection is good as it is the only kids one I've seen. I think you could make it better by putting insects in the catalogue. Apart from that I think it is excellent and I like coming to your house to see it. My favourite is it all. Stephen Hudson.

I do like the skulls what Chris collects. Richard Everett

I don't really know allot about Bones and fossils but seeing Christopher's collection I think it is good and he has put allot of work into it. Michael Browne.

I think that Christopher has worked terribly hard on this wonderful collection.
David Ranson.

From family members:

A very nice show, Professor. I cannot improve upon the remarks made by Lady Catherine. I am not quite sure about the skull – is it Pre-Adamite? Keep it up, Professor. Grandad 5/9/68

Very impressive display! Ailsa Land 9/9/68

Very nice. Richard Land

What bones! Let Granny have them for soup. Lily Fraser

From our house cleaner, who was about to leave, and her four-year-old son:

Yours is the best collection I have ever seen in a bedroom. I shall miss dusting them on Fridays. With so many bones, fossils, shells and stuffed animals, will you still have room for the bed by the time you're 20? Love Maureen and Adrian. P.S. Adrian likes the fox best and calls him Fred.

Meanwhile, Chris was progressing rapidly on the horn. One of the first tunes I remember him playing was *On Wings of Song* by Mendelssohn. His apparently effortless sound really did seem to be carried on heavenly wings. He worked diligently through exercises: long notes, lip slurs, articulation, sustained pianissimo and fortissimo, but I cannot recall a time when he struggled with the instrument. He had only been learning for a year when John Ridgeon entered him for Grade IV. He gained a distinction. He was also entered for two classes in the local music festival – the Wind and Brass Instrument Own Choice class, age sixteen and under, and the Wind and Brass Concerto class, age eighteen and under. When he climbed onto the platform, he had forgotten which piece he was supposed to play in which class. As both pieces he had prepared were concertos, he realised it didn't much matter which one he played first. He turned to the adjudicator and asked, "Would you like to hear the Mozart or the Strauss?" Something about the way he asked, or the way he looked – an untidy little boy – made everyone laugh. The adjudicator covered his amusement and told Chris to play whichever he wanted. He won both classes.

One Saturday we saw a small group of instrumentalists playing jazz, of sorts, on the steps of the Plaza cinema in George Lane. We stopped to listen and Chris started chatting to them. When they discovered that he played the horn, they invited him to join them. We stayed while Chris went home to fetch his instrument. He soon returned, took his horn out of the case and stood beside them, playing along by ear and improvising without thinking about it. They were obviously not expecting what they heard. Izzy and I listened in amazement. Where did he learn to do that? How could he play without notes in front of him? Dad, who usually had the camera with him, took some photos. After a while, Chris put his horn away and we wandered home. He couldn't understand why Izzy and I were impressed – the band wasn't much use and as for playing along; well, that wasn't difficult.

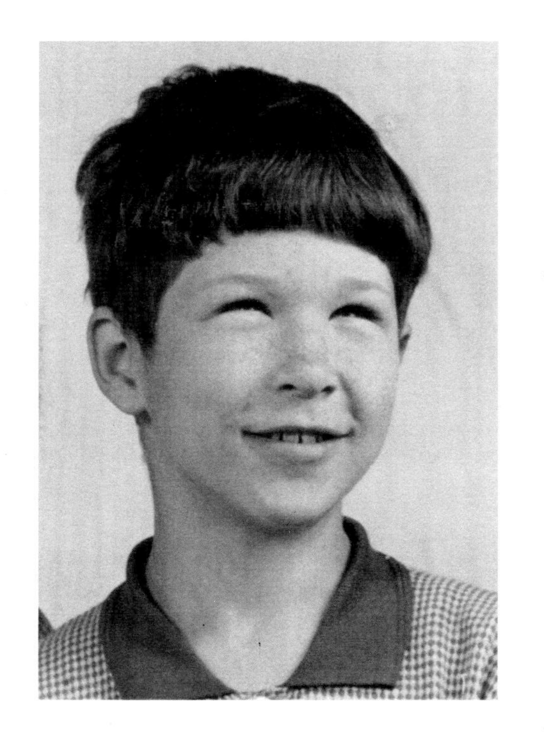

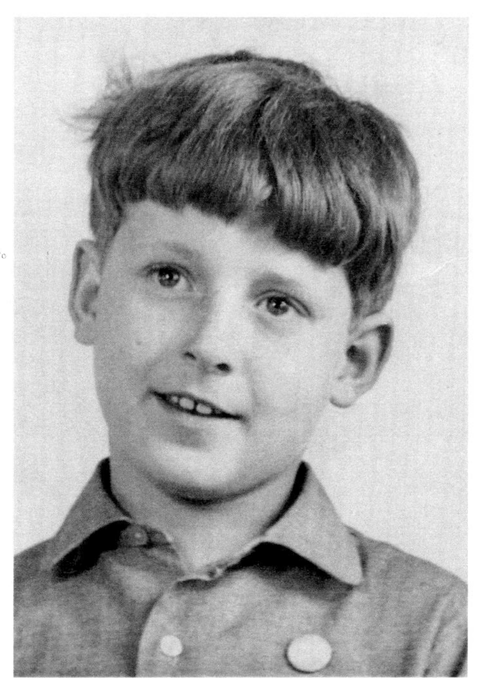

ABOVE: Chris aged nine and his schoolfriend, Steve Cladingboel, aged ten.
The two boys often travelled unaccompanied into central London to visit museums.

ABOVE:
A part of Chris's Natural History Collection, which he displayed in his bedroom.

LEFT:
Chris improvising on the steps of the Plaza cinema in South Woodford.

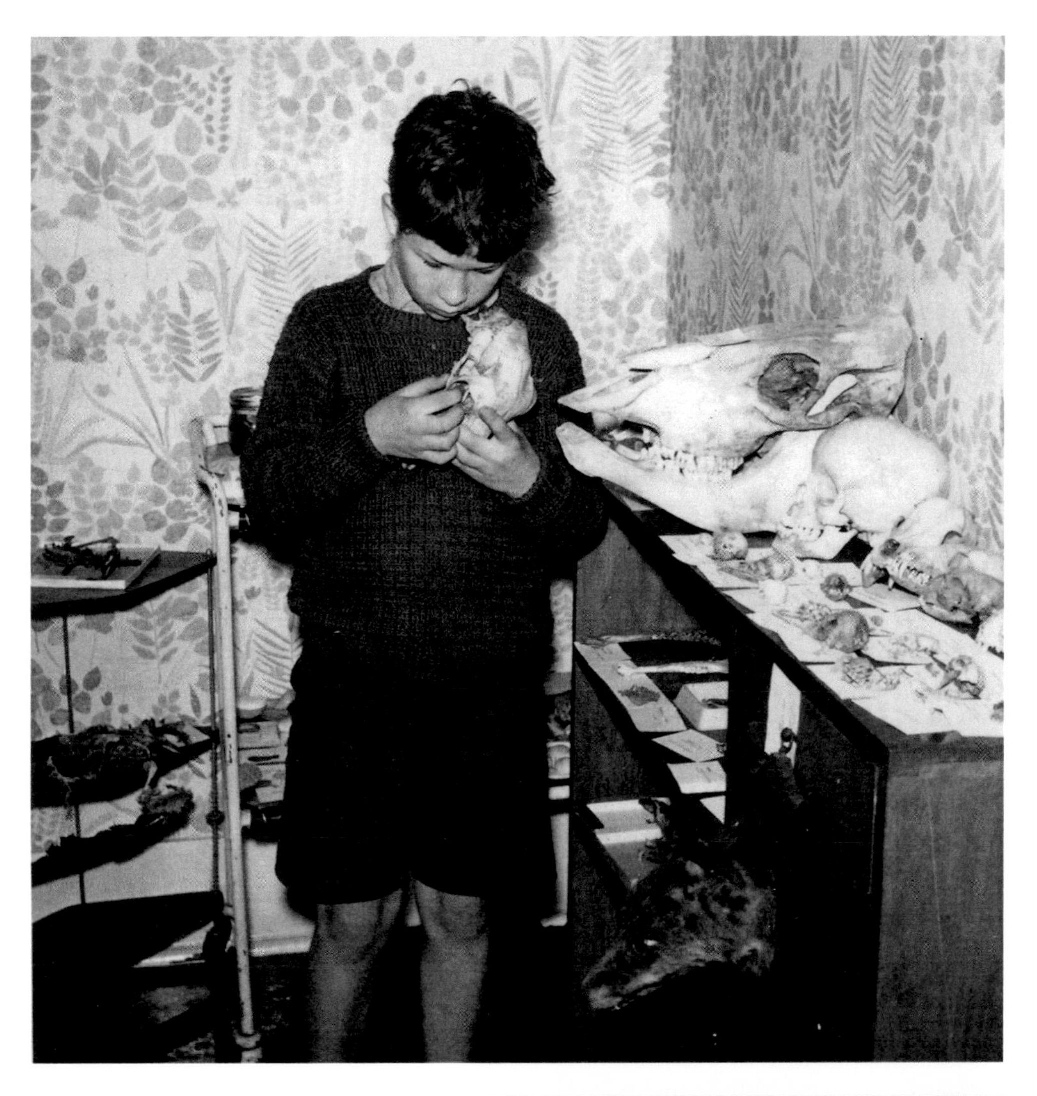

ABOVE:
This is the only other photograph I have of Chris's extensive Natural History Collection.

RIGHT:
Chris in the back garden holding a ram's skull.

ABOVE: Cathy reading with Chris.
BELOW: Oakdale Junior School pantomime, Christmas 1966
LEFT: Izzy, aged eleven, as Cinderella with her Prince Charming, Penelope Runnicles.
RIGHT: Dressed for my walk on part as a town crier with Izzy, the belle of the ball.

33
GIRLS' GRAMMAR SCHOOLS

It was always said – she
was the strong one,
the emphasis implying
something not quite natural.

Partners – Carole Satyamurti

Izzy and I passed the eleven-plus and schools had to be chosen. Mum decided it would be good for us to go to different schools, where we would be viewed as individuals and not compared as twins. Loughton County High School for Girls was selected for Izzy, but Mum needed to find somewhere for me that would accommodate my musical commitments. Now that I was eleven, I would be going to the Junior School of the Royal Academy of Music one afternoon a week to have cello lessons with Florence Hooton. My secondary school would have to accept a weekly half-day's absence. Mum's research led her to Beal Grammar School for Girls in Ilford. Unusually, it worked to a six-day timetable. If Monday was Day One the first week, the following week it would be Day Six, Tuesday becoming Day One, and so on. Conveniently, this meant that I would miss a different set of lessons every Thursday afternoon when I went to the Academy. Mum arranged an appointment with Miss Evans, the headmistress, who agreed that I could have an afternoon off a week, but Mum went further. She wanted to find a way for me to have free time during school hours to do my homework so that when I came home all my time could be devoted to practice. Mum scrutinised the timetable: "I'm not having her doing sport of any description. Too many of my own pupils have broken their fingers and arms playing hockey. General music – there's no need for that; she's far more advanced. RK? Religious Knowledge? No, I don't want her wasting her time with that nonsense. So, let's see: by cutting out those subjects, she will have seven free periods a week. That should be enough for the moment." I cannot imagine Miss Evans' side of the conversation: she was so strait-laced and conventional; it is a wonder how Mum persuaded her to agree.

I was taken to Henry Taylor Ltd., school outfitters in Ilford, to buy my uniform – a ridiculous array of unnecessary and expensive garments in the hideous colours of 'Brownie' brown and yellow. The saleswoman brought a skirt and blouse to the changing cubicle. I reached to draw the curtain. Mum held it open. She saw my aggrieved look. "Don't be silly;" she said in a loud voice, "you've nothing to hide." Hot and embarrassed, I turned my back, stripped down to my underwear and folded my arms across my chest to hide the two lumps that were beginning to show through my vest. Mum handed me the garments, watched me dress then told me to step outside so she could see. The saleswoman hovered. Mum gave her appraisal. "No; too small. She needs at least the next size up. She's a well-covered girl – a big frame, broad-shouldered, as you can see. She can hardly get the buttons done up around these cuffs. Mind you, she has wide wrists and large, strong musicians' hands, like mine."

"The buttons can easily be shifted, Madam."

"No, there has to be room for growth. Would you mind bringing a larger skirt, please? She'll not be able to get into this one in a few weeks."

Mum scanned the uniform list, ticking off our purchases. At least I would get the regulation school cardigan and V-necked jumper, with yellow stripes around the cuffs and neck. The PE kit was a yellow aertex shirt and voluminous thick cotton brown drawers. I needed a tie, a blazer, a dark brown gabardine coat, a brown science overall, a summer dress and a school hat – brown velour trimmed with brown and yellow ribbon. I tried on the one handed to me.

"Oh, I'm sorry," said the saleswoman, "that's the smallest size."

"She has a big head," said Mum, "I hope you have a hat large enough. She's a twin, you know, but the pair of them couldn't be more different. Her sister's a dainty little thing. I can't find a uniform *small* enough for her."

Oh Mum, please stop going on.

"She's not so big," the woman responded, smiling at me. "Smaller than average, I would say. I have much bigger girls to fit."

"They're quite the opposite in character too." I knew what was coming now. "It's perfectly obvious, having had twins, that people are born with their personality. Here are my two, brought up in precisely the same way, yet they have entirely individual natures." She flicked her head towards me. "This one's the boss – aren't you Catherine?" Her voice was indulgent, affectionately conspiratorial. If she had been someone else, she would have winked at me. I glared at the carpet.

"I shall never forget an occasion when I was taking the twins for a walk in their pram." *Oh no, here we go.* "They must have been about eight or nine months old – sitting up, anyway. I started chatting to a man who had stopped to admire them. After a few minutes, he pointed to Catherine and said, 'that one was born first.' Why yes, I said, but how can you tell? He told me he was a dog breeder and explained that it's always the boisterous, bossy puppy that pushes its way out first, not necessarily the largest. Catherine here weighed less than her sister at birth – mind you, she soon overtook," she laughed, "so there you are – he spotted immediately which one had the stronger, dominant character."

I felt as if she had dug an ice-cream scoop into me and hollowed several semi-spherical dollops out of my intestines. The saleswoman gave a polite, noncommittal smile.

"Shall we make sure you have everything you require?" she asked, changing the subject. "Ah, you don't yet have a cardigan or V-necked jumper."

"Goodness me, we're not wasting money on those flimsy things. My mother will knit them in the same colours."

I should have known better. We followed the retreating back of our assistant to a glass-fronted counter, where she prepared a handwritten bill. Mum continued dauntlessly, "She's a marvellous knitter, you know, my mother. She knitted this suit I'm wearing and Catherine's Fair Isle cardigan. Catherine? Come here. Look at the work in that, the blend of colours. Of course she was taught to knit by her grandmother from Shetland ..." Mum was interrupted.

"Would you please take your bill to the cashier to settle up? Just over there, Madam."

Izzy's school colour was navy blue and she had to wear a gymslip in her first year. At least I didn't suffer that indignity – Beal girls were in skirts from the start. On the other hand, Loughton girls did not have to wear hats. Off to school we went, encased in our stiff, oversized uniforms. Izzy had a satchel, which she could hang from her shoulder, but I was encumbered with an old brown leather briefcase that Dad brought up from the cellar. I opened my mouth to protest and shut it again. What was the point? I had to take three buses to get to school; Izzy went by tube to Loughton station.

Upon arrival at Beal, first years were shepherded into the school hall, our hats making us conspicuously distinguishable from the other years. None of the older girls were wearing them. We realised we'd been had. How were we to tell our mothers that we needn't have bought them after all? On day two, only a spattering of veloured heads were to be seen. By day three, they had vanished, many, like mine, crushed into the bottom of school bags where they remained for months until, ink-stained and shapeless, they were stuffed into a street litter-bin.

Miss Evans attempted to maintain the formalised structure, traditional values and conservative ethos of an old-style Grammar School for Girls. It was compulsory to wear the correct school uniform, but of course there were deviations. Many of us flouted the regulations by wearing white socks instead of beige. Our excuse was that our mothers couldn't find any beige ones in the shops. After a few weeks, when the majority of girls were parading white socks, Miss Evans sent a letter to our mothers, stating that if beige socks were not available, white ones could be successfully dyed by steeping overnight in a strong brew of tea. She even made girls remove their white socks and sent them to the staff-room to stew their hosiery in a heavily tanninised pot of tea she had prepared herself. We were also dispatched to the secretary's room if our hair was loose and made to pay sixpence for a rubber band. She prowled the school in academic gown, maintaining discipline and order. She would, no doubt, have preferred all the teachers to wear gowns and mortarboards, but none wore the latter and it was only on the occasion of Speech Day that black capes swished along corridors leaving the smell of camphor in their wake.

On the whole, Beal wasn't too bad, but I was different and not just because of Granny's knitwear. I was absent from RK and games and had a half-day off school every week for cello lessons, which cast me as an oddity. Beal, however, had a flourishing music department. I found friends there, particularly Sue Eversden, a bassoonist in the year above me. The Head of Music was Michael Crombie. More than a third of the school sang in the choir. He taught singing individually and formed a vocal ensemble, which won all the local music festivals. The school orchestra was good, since every member had the advantage of tuition under the Redbridge instrumental scheme set up by Malcolm Bidgood. Peripatetic teachers visited Beal and taught in the disused sports pavilion, which had been converted into two music studios. Sue

Eversden and I practised in the pavilion studios when they were free. We could hear each other through the wall. Sometimes the bassoon fell silent. A minute later, Sue would appear at my door to ask if I could give her a cello lesson. I am sure she would have made an excellent cellist had she been given the chance.

Mum, I am sorry to say, was musically prejudiced. She believed that only 'classical' music was worthwhile: pop music was banal and vulgar – we were not allowed to listen to it: Radio One was utterly banned – we wouldn't have dared to find the station on the wireless at home. I remember smuggling in a borrowed Beatles album, which I kept hidden as furtively as pornography. We played it when the adults were out, with one of us on watch at the front room window.

A photograph of Mum and the three of us playing, or rather, pretending to play our instruments, appeared in a local paper, the *Express*, on October 4th 1968. Mum took the opportunity to air her views:

> POP music takes a pounding this week from a Wanstead music teacher, housewife and mother, Mrs. Elizabeth Giles. Mrs. Giles, or as she is known professionally, Miss Elizabeth Fraser, considers that young people are 'being deprived of the opportunity to develop an appreciation of good music'. In the Giles' home, pop music plays no part, and Mrs. Giles has strong opinions about the detriment to young people generally, which 'a continuous background cacophony of pop music is bringing'. She explained: 'none of us at home here could possibly tolerate the radio just droning on and on in the background of our lives. Personally, I think there is a conspiracy going on to get the money out of the youngsters' pockets in return for absolute rubbish which is completely lacking in any value whatsoever.' And neither Catherine, who attends Beal Grammar School, Ilford, Isabella, a pupil of Loughton High School for Girls, nor Christopher, who is still at junior Oakdale Road School, rate radio and television pop-shows anything but a 'miss'.

How could we protest against our misrepresentation in the face of such fervour?

Mr. Crombie chose all types of music for the school orchestra. As well as the classical repertoire, we played selections from Rodgers and Hammerstein's *South Pacific* and *Oklahoma!*; extracts from Gilbert and Sullivan operettas; Negro Spirituals; songs from *Carmen;* pieces by Percy Grainger, Eric Coates and others. The music captivated me: it was such fun to play, instantly accessible and emotionally stirring; but when I described what we were playing to Mum, she threw a wet blanket over my enthusiasm, dismissing the music as populist nonsense and criticising Mr. Crombie for programming such trash. She decided that playing in the orchestra would be of no musical benefit to me, and furthermore, after-school rehearsals were a waste of my practice time. It is possible that Miss Evans intervened here, perhaps pointing out that as the school was being so accommodating with my 'special needs' it wasn't unreasonable to expect me to play in the school orchestra. Mum agreed reluctantly, but said I could only go to a minimum of rehearsals. Mr. Crombie used to get very fed up with my lack of attendance and couldn't resist taking a dig at Mum. Any 'non-classical' pieces would be handed out with the comment "of course, your mother wouldn't approve of *this* would she?" Sometimes, to please him, I would risk it, go to orchestra practice and be late home, making up tales of bus delays – but deception is an unwieldy tool and I could never hold it comfortably. Caught up with politics and prejudice, it wasn't easy for me to find a comfortable position.

Single sex schools often breed abnormal behaviour. It may be almost undetectable, but any imbalance in natural order will create some distortion. For girls (or boys) of eleven to eighteen, with hormones running riot, passions must find subjects to desire. I had crushes on several girls at school; my classmates drooled over pop stars – David Cassidy was one of the favourites. There were a few male teachers at Beal, but only one became a target of adoration – Mr. Crombie. No wonder so many girls joined the choir – the majority were in love with him. I fell into the minority, instinctively keeping a wary distance. I respected him as a musician, but he could be moody and manipulative; friendly and charming one day, critical and cutting the next – not just with me, but with other girls too. Yet he was usually helpful in finding me practice space. If there was nowhere else to go, he let me practise in the stock cupboard – a windowless storeroom annexed to the music room, which housed the record library and the school harp. I had fallen in love with the sound of the harp years before. Practising beside one, I developed a yearning to play it. I knew that it was out of the question to ask Mum if I could have lessons, but when I thought nobody would hear, I ran my fingers up and down the strings, picked out a few tunes and tried to work out the functions of the pedals. My secret longing to learn the harp never diminished.

I had been at Beal for about six weeks when Mum entered into a vigorous battle. Mr. Crombie, an excellent pianist, assumed that he would accompany me in my performance of Cyril Scott's *Lullaby* at Junior Speech Day. Mum wasn't having that. She had always accompanied me. It would, she thought, put me off if someone else played for me. I had the onerous task of explaining this to Mr. Crombie.

"Does she think I'm incapable of playing for you?"

"I suppose she thinks it would be better for me to play with someone I'm used to," I said, struggling with diplomacy.

"What about you? What do you think?"

"I've always played with Mum and she wants to play for me."

I wouldn't have minded if he had accompanied me, but I couldn't say so – Mum would have been hurt and furious. Mr. Crombie took umbrage. "Well, I've never heard anything like it – a parent taking over from the school's music teacher and laying down the law! Your mother will have to talk to Miss Evans." Oh why couldn't Mum keep out of it – I hated all this fuss, offending Mr. Crombie and causing disruption. And I would look so babyish at Speech Day with 'Mummy' stepping out from the audience to accompany me, but that is what happened.

I liked our English teacher, Miss Joynes, and enjoyed her lessons. Many people complain that school ruined Shakespeare for them, but Miss Joynes brought Shakespeare to life. Roles were shared amongst the class and we read quite a number of the plays during my years at Beal. I particularly remember *Othello*. At the point in Act V Scene II, when Iago's evilly sown seeds of jealousy compel Othello to murder Desdemona, the girl taking the part of Desdemona broke down, granting license to the rest of us to delve into our bags for handkerchiefs.

At the end of my first year, one of my stories was printed in the school magazine. Miss Joynes had encouraged me to submit it months earlier, but I had not expected it to appear. It was titled 'First Day at a New House' and was about a girl moving with her mother to a neglected country cottage (not dissimilar to the one in Great Ryburgh) after the sudden death of her father. When I saw it in print, I was overcome with embarrassment, ashamed of every word I had written. To my surprise, girls who had never spoken to me before told me they thought my story was good, and asked with some concern if my father had really died. I assured them it was all made up, but obviously something in it had sounded too convincing. I was a little concerned that they might think I was a liar. I didn't submit any more original entries to the magazine for the rest of my schooldays.

As well as attending Beal Grammar School for Girls, I was also a student at the Junior School of the Royal Academy of Music. Mum picked me up from Beal every Thursday at the end of morning lessons and drove me to South Woodford station. From there I travelled, with my cello, via Liverpool Street to Baker Street Station and walked along the Marylebone Road, past the Planetarium and Madame Tussauds, to the Academy. When I joined the Junior School, Florence Hooton had seven senior students and I was her one junior. She decided to put on a performance of Villa-Lobos's *Bachianas Brasileiras* No. 5, a piece for eight cellos and soprano. I was enlisted as the extra cellist and given the seventh part. In those days, female students had to wear long white dresses for concerts. I had a short white dress for junior concerts, but not a full-length one. Miss Hooton told me not to worry; I could borrow the one that had been made for her daughter, Nina, when she was a student at the Academy. Although the dress fitted me reasonably well from the waist upwards, it was about four inches too long and could not be altered in case Nina wanted to wear it again. The day of the concert arrived. We made our way onto the Academy's Duke's Hall platform in seating order. There were six cellists in front of me. Behind me, the eighth cellist saw that I was having difficulties climbing up the stairs and carried my cello for me, so I could hold up the heavy satin material of the skirt. I was doing fine until the last step, when I trod on the hem, tripped and slid horizontally onto the stage. That was my first appearance in a senior concert at the Academy.

As Redbridge was contributing generously towards the cost of my lessons, it was expected that I should be involved with music in the borough. Izzy and Chris were not in the same position, but we all attended the Redbridge Saturday morning music school. The music making was occasionally good, often indifferent and sometimes bad. Nevertheless, it was an invaluable introduction to the orchestral repertoire. We also benefited socially, made friends for life and met some fine musicians. There were those who shone out, whose characters and flair gave the Redbridge music scene its unique personality. There are too many to name, but I must mention Bramwell Tovey, an outstanding talent, charismatic and entertaining, and Paul Hart, whom I first met when I was seven, a striking individual and extraordinary musician, infamous for his idiosyncratic style of clothing and extremely long hair.

34
GROWING PAINS

It scalds, remember,
to realise your gaucherie's been on parade.
Such blatant inexperience, when the present
sizzles like fat on a hotplate, and when time
aches like a wisdom tooth in the gum…

In Time of Famine, number II of *Six Misapprehensions* – Gregory Warren Wilson

On the day before my twelfth birthday I went with Mum to a Woodford Music Society concert at the Sir James Hawkey Hall, the same venue where Izzy and I had once skipped on stage as forget-me-nots. The Alberni quartet was appearing with an additional performer, nineteen-year-old Anthony Pleeth, who was to play the second cello part in the Boccherini and Schubert quintets. He walked onto the platform, self-assured and smouldering. Sitting in the middle of the front row, I took one look at him and was instantly smitten. The group played the Boccherini first, a lovely piece, but it was Anthony who took my breath away. At the end of the first half, I turned to Mum, and couldn't help but ask, "Don't you think that cellist is amazingly handsome?"

"Which one?"

"The young one," I replied, wondering how she could have failed to notice what was so blatantly obvious.

"Oh. Well I wasn't particularly looking at him, but I suppose so."

She went off to buy a coffee. I stayed in my seat in a daze. Mum seemed oblivious to my besotted state when she returned after the interval.

The performers came back on stage for the second half to play the Schubert quintet, already one of my favourite pieces of chamber music. That night I thought it the most fantastic music ever written. My ears locked into the marvellous second cello part and my eyes followed Anthony's every movement. Oh, how I wished I could be up there playing the cello with him!

As always, I went backstage to collect autographs, but on that occasion I only collected four. Tongue-tied and self-conscious, I couldn't bring myself to talk to Anthony. Later, I berated myself severely for such lack of initiative. For months I daydreamed about him, imagining wonderful scenarios when by chance we would meet, he would fall madly in love with me and whisk me off into some fairytale happy-ever-after future.

At school, my mind wandered during lessons. I drew "Anthony" decoratively all over my exercise books and entwined our two names together in heart shapes. Once, a stern voice interrupted my reveries: "Catherine! I've asked you the same question twice! Will you please pay attention?"

What a wrench to find myself back in a geography class.

Later that year we camped again at Whitwell in Norfolk. Izzy and I were second-year Trailseekers, the group of eleven- and twelve-year-olds, and Chris was a ten-year-old Woodling. In our Trailseeker group was a tall, gangly French boy whose limited English and, to us, unusual social behaviour, singled him out as different. It upset me to hear some of the others laugh at his mispronunciations and trick him into using rude words. My attempts to shield him from the teasing and help him with English resulted in his seeking to be with me all the time. It became too much. At bedtime he was egged on to call out, "Good-night Catty, I love you," from his tent, which was followed by uproarious laughter from all the other tents.

When it came to the Trailseeker's contribution to Merrymoot, it was decided that I was to be cast as the 'bog roll' Princess. The French boy (my boyfriend, they sniggered) would be 'lat-man'. He would be dressed in a hessian cloak, would rescue me from the lat with sword and shield (a tent pole and trowel), we would fall in love by the hand-dipping bucket and get married. I was appalled.

"I don't want to be the Princess."

"Oh, don't be such a spoilsport, it's only pretend."

"I don't care; I don't want to be in the play."

"But I do, Catty," said 'lat-man'. "I want to marry you." Everyone laughed. He was being ridiculed too, but didn't seem to mind.

Merrymoot began. I was dressed in something that represented a wedding gown. Flowers were stuck into my hair; a posy put in my hand. I had no choice but to go through with it. On stage I concentrated on trying to feel nothing. The French boy led me through the routine, turning to me with beaming smiles that received no response. "I do," he proclaimed joyfully, when asked if he would take me, bog-roll princess, to be his wife. He grabbed my hand and squeezed it when the words, "Do you take lat-man to be your lawfully wedded husband?" were spoken.

I mumbled something incomprehensible in the direction of my feet, pulled my hand out of his grasp and heard the awful words, "You may now kiss the bride!"

There were hoots and catcalls. He kissed me softly on each cheek, French style. I stood lamppost-straight, my body rigid, my head switched off.

"Aw, come on, a proper kiss," the crowd clamoured.

He stepped closer, held my shoulders and kissed me on my lips with what I registered as tenderness: and it was that which so alarmed me. As soon as we had taken our bows, I fled to my tent. He ran after me.

"Catty, Catty, wait for me," he called. "I sleep in your tent tonight."

"Leave me alone," I shouted viciously.

I reached my tent and worked desperately to untie the flaps before he caught up with me.

"But Catty, I love you."

I spun around to face him. "Go away!" I screeched. He came to a halt, staring at me with a look of hurt incomprehension. As I glared at him, ready to attack if he came any closer, I knew that he had acted out the stupid marriage ceremony wholeheartedly. He hadn't been fooling; he hadn't been teasing me; nor had he been unkind: it was I who was being cruel.

"Why you not like me?" he asked. I didn't reply. He turned and headed for his tent. I crawled into mine, curled up and cried. I kept seeing the wounded expression on his face and wondered if he was crying too. I hated myself for rejecting him, but I couldn't go near him again: the emotional landscape into which I had fallen was way beyond my understanding.

At Wortley I fell into another forlorn place. The youngsters on the brass band course were a high-spirited, sociable crowd. We gravitated towards them, larking about together as children do; but we weren't quite children any more. Innocence had lost its clarity; thoughts mushroomed into confusion. On the cusp of adolescence, the games we played developed new interpretation. Richard was friendly and funny. Chris and I fell about at the jokes he told in his broad Yorkshire accent. On the second evening, we congregated in the billiard room watching some of the older lads playing. One of the tables became free.

"Want a game?" he asked.

"I don't know how to play."

"I'll show you."

He set up the table, putting the balls at one end in a wooden triangular frame, which he then lifted away and placed the white ball at the other end. He handed me a cue and asked if I would like to break.

"Break?"

"Take the first shot. Here, I'll show you how to hold the cue."

As he adjusted my hand and positioned my arm, I received the first inkling of an ulterior motive beneath the mechanics of the game. The others drifted off to listen to the jazz, leaving Richard and me alone. I was hopeless at billiards and soon gave up, anxious to return to the safety of the crowd. Richard followed me to the bar and sat beside me, meaningfully close: I edged away; he shifted nearer. I stood up.

"Where are you going?"

"I'm tired. I'm going to bed."

"I'll walk you to your room, then."

"I know where it is!"

"So? I'll walk you anyway."

"See you later, Rich," said one of the other boys, laughing. I walked off quickly, Richard running to catch up.

"What's the hurry? How about a stroll outside first?"

"No, thanks," I squeaked, increasing my pace. At my door, I fumbled with the handle, desperate to get inside.

"Goodnight then," he whispered, "see you tomorrow." He hovered beside me. I was afraid he might attempt to kiss me, but the door suddenly gave and I plunged into the safety of the room, uttering a hasty goodnight as I shut myself in. For the rest of the week I attached myself to Mum and followed her around like a duckling. I clung to her every time I saw Richard.

"What's wrong with you, dear? Go on, off you go and play with your friends."

"I want to stay with you," I said.

It was at the end of those summer holidays that Dad disappeared. Nothing was said about his absence.

"Where's Dad?" we asked. Mum didn't answer straight away. She seemed to be considering our question.

"Well," she said cautiously, "he's in hospital."

"In hospital?" we queried anxiously. "Is he having an operation?"

"No," she reassured. "It's nothing for you to worry about. He just has to be in hospital for a little while. He'll be fine."

"How long is he going to be there?" we asked.

"I shouldn't think it will be for long."

"But what's wrong with him?"

"I've told you, it's nothing to worry about." Her voice had a finality to it that put a stop to any more questions. We puzzled over it together. I concluded that he must be having an operation on a private part of his body that Mum couldn't discuss with us. Maybe Dad was embarrassed and didn't want us to know.

"His willy, do you think?" asked Chris.

"Something like that."

We decided to write to him, to cheer him up. Chris's letters survive.

> Dear Dad,
>
> I Hope you are well and I Hope the meals are good. The last two days, Catherine has been making our tea. Our cousins sent a post card and amongst other things it said they had a sheeps upper Jaw. The Jaw is larger and different than the other two skulls.
>
> LOVE Chris

Mum took us to the cottage. Chris's next letter is written from Great Ryburgh.

> Dear Dad,
>
> When we went to sheringham Izzy found a spotty eel about three inches long and the tide was out so much that at the end of the beach it was nothing but hard white rock. When we first came the garden was full of weeds. Cath cleared half of the front garden but she hasn't got round to doing the other bit.
>
> On one of our walks I found (well Mum did really) a skinned rabbit and it was inside out. First of all I thought it was a bat, but I changed my mind when the shoulder blades were at the finger end and I couldn't find the feet. At the farm fluffy is expecting kittens and I saw a ginger and white cat on the pan-tiles.
>
> LOVE FROM Christopher

It was years before I worked out that Dad had spent some time in Claybury Mental Hospital. He and Mum kept his clinical depression under wraps. Our intuition that it was something they thought shameful and embarrassing was not wrong – that, I think, is how they felt about it. They lived in a place of emotional avoidance. Mental illness could not be faced. It was sealed into isolation, given sanitising drugs and treatment, but the stain of depression could not be removed. Dad blamed his wife and mother-in-law as the main causes of his illness, and there was no curing that. It wasn't the only occasion when he was a voluntary patient at Claybury.

Two or three times a week, I went straight to Oakdale Infant School from Beal. After the children had gone home, Oakdale turned into a cello academy. While Miss Sprakes taught, her other pupils and I practised, socialised, listened to one another's pieces, and at the end of the day played together in cello ensembles. I ran a theory class for a while, which taught me that I had no ability as a class teacher. Within a few minutes the children sussed out that I was incapable of keeping order and messed about, to my rising frustration. Izzy, on the other hand, wanted to be an Infant School teacher. She had the gift of knowing how to keep the attention of a group of young children and a quiet authority that commanded good behaviour. I despaired of my theory group, and after a couple of terms my pupils defeated me.

Every term, Miss Sprakes took her senior students out for a meal at Wood's fish and chip shop, and once took us all, including Izzy, to Kew Gardens. She went way beyond being a committed teacher. She promoted companionship, consideration and respect between her pupils. I was grateful for all of that and liked Miss Sprakes's students – several were very good friends – yet part of me didn't belong. Privately, I was finding much of the music making uninspiring. I felt guilty thinking such things, but I was becoming increasingly aware of Miss Sprakes's limitations. She loved music, but she didn't realise her own or her pupils' inaccuracies – rhythmical errors, bad timing, even wrong notes. Occasionally, in ensembles, I made suggestions, and tried to correct rhythms and bad intonation (which I found unbearable); but however tactfully I put it, Miss Sprakes did not always appreciate my 'help'. The last thing I wanted to do was to annoy or upset her, for she was one of the nicest people I knew.

She gave both Izzy and me more than our fair share of her love. Once, she took us on holiday to Wiltshire, where we went horse riding for the first and only time. She gave us presents for our birthday and at Christmas, which she chose with care. When I was ill, she brought me flowers – usually freesias with their sweet apricot perfume. Her garden was filled with colour the whole year round, which was exactly how I wanted my garden to look. She gave me cuttings and advised where best to plant them, and when she came over she voiced her admiration. It was Miss Sprakes who helped me to make my first dress. She bought the material, invited Izzy and me to her house, helped us to cut out a simple dress pattern, sew the shapes together, turn the hem, and finish the edges of the collar and arm holes with bias binding. It was the only dress Izzy made, but I went on to make dozens.

Sometimes I wished I could talk to Miss Sprakes properly about how I felt, but I wasn't able to. I didn't have the words to explain what it was that bothered me, even to myself. My internal world was filled with anxiety and contradiction. I was perplexed and ashamed by my thoughts. I had to keep my feelings secret; pretend to be the girl I was supposed to be; act my part, meet expectations, be good, follow the rules, please everyone, say thank you, conceal the tears, block the mind with a smile – that extrovert one that they thought was mine, polished against the grain. I couldn't integrate how I felt with how I appeared: my inside did not tally with my outside. It seemed to me that I was a fraud. Nobody knew the real me, and I was scared about being found out.

I was also unable to talk to Miss Sprakes about the times when Miss Hooton, or

Florrie as we called her, upset me, for in Miss Sprakes's eyes, Florrie could do no wrong. True, Florence Hooton was an exceptional teacher. She knew I tried hard, was generous with her praise and excited by my improvement. I was her protégée whose progress she directed and whose future she planned. I had to consult her about any performance I was asked to give and gain her permission before I could accept. I knew she had my best interests at heart, yet she could also be daunting, not just with me but with all her pupils. She particularly detested her students playing in orchestras, believing that it damaged the technique and ruined the intonation. I think she saw herself as a teacher of potential soloists, not rank and file cellists, and her opposition to orchestral playing put many of her pupils into awkward situations. She didn't know I played in Redbridge Orchestra One on Saturday mornings, and I kept it quiet – so, indeed, did Mum and Margaret Sprakes. I did not set out to deceive Florrie, and was not even aware that I was doing anything terribly wrong – as explained earlier, Redbridge was funding a substantial part of the cost of my cello lessons at the Academy, and it seemed there was an unstated obligation that I should participate in the Redbridge Music School. What was not made transparently clear to Florrie was that my participation included playing in the orchestra.

For two years all was fine until, by some accident, Florrie found out. She was furious, accused me of disobeying her, not taking my playing seriously, and reduced me to tears in moments She forbade me ever to go to Redbridge Music School again. I opened my mouth to try and tell her that I went to a theory class as well, and couldn't I just go for that, but she held up her hand before I had managed to speak a word. "I'm not listening to any excuses," she said imperiously. "You're not going again and that's final." Mum withdrew me from the school at once. Devastated in every way, I wrote Florrie a profusely apologetic letter, which only succeeded in making matters worse. The incident marred the weave of our relationship. We moved on, but the pulled threads left a flaw in the fabric. Later, Florrie agreed that I could return to the Redbridge Music School, and even rejoin the cello section, when Malcolm Bidgood asked me to play as a soloist with the orchestra. She understood that having the opportunity to perform, or even just play through, cello concertos with an orchestra was not something to pass up.

On one occasion, Florrie was engaged to adjudicate the string classes in the local festival. Margaret Sprakes entered her pupils as usual, as did other local string teachers. The red carpet was metaphorically rolled out and Florrie welcomed as royalty. I sat through the whole day with Mum, Granny and Miss Sprakes. After Florrie had announced the results and summed up the day's playing, she invited all the cellists in the hall to gather round, as she had an exercise to show them. There was a shuffle of chairs as people made their way to her table.

Mum gave me a dig in the ribs. "Go on up, then," she said. I had been considering this, but thought that as I had been studying with Florrie for years, she would have taught me the exercise, and anyway, there was a crowd around the adjudicator's table. It would be better to leave room for those who weren't Florrie's pupils.

In all innocence I replied, "Oh, I expect I know the exercise already."

"Catherine!" exploded Mum.

"What an appalling attitude," reproached Miss Sprakes, "I'm surprised at you."

"Get up there now," Mum commanded, pushing me in the back.

"She thinks she's a cut above the rest," added Granny spitefully.

Red with shame and confusion, I edged past them while Mum and Granny continued to discuss my high-and-mighty, know-it-all arrogance. It was one of many occasions when I was slapped down and entirely misunderstood.

Miss Sprakes tried to rescue the situation by saying, "I'll come with you. I'll probably learn something myself." But I felt wounded and wretched.

By now, my life was structured around cello lessons and cello practice. In general, I looked forward to my cello lessons; they were my reward after a week of practice – and as I went to my lessons with everything well prepared, Florrie was usually pleased with me. But cello practice was a different matter. There were times when it was stimulating, absorbing and energising and I felt a real sense of achievement; but there were other occasions when it became monotonous, loathsome and punishing. Sometimes I felt enslaved by its demands. Every single day it seemed as though I had to pay my penance to an unforgiving deity, and if I didn't, I felt awful. That was the funny thing – I could not enjoy a moment of life until I had practised. Worse, Mum was my conscience, which I hated. "You haven't done any practice yet today," she would say in a tight, accusatory voice. I knew that only too well: it had been eating me up all day and I resented her criticism intensely. Pablo Casals, the great Spanish cellist, tells of a time when he was climbing, fell and damaged his hand. His first thought was: thank God, I won't have to practise. Sometimes, coming down with bronchitis, I felt the same.

It was different for Izzy. She says herself that she wasn't a high-flyer. Although she did well on the violin, it is true that she didn't have the same sort of ability as I did. She practised a bit and improved quickly, but said from a very young age that she wanted to be an Infant School teacher, which is exactly what she became. Her life wasn't programmed for her in the same way as mine. She played in the Redbridge orchestras, competed in local music festivals and spent the week at Wortley every year, so we were involved in some of the same things, but from the start it was accepted that music was not going to be her career. Chris, with his consuming interest in natural history seemed set to do something in that direction. He considered joining the Natural History Museum as a classifier of animals, becoming a vet or working in the London Zoo.

This is how things stood in 1968 as I bring this first part to a close. Our early childhood was over: Chris would soon be leaving Oakdale Junior School; Izzy and I were nearly teenagers. We were about to enter the next phase of our lives. Music was to become more central to Chris's life, and as it turned out, to Izzy's. Before continuing with our story, I am going to begin the next section by returning to Mum's youth, picking up from just after the death of her father.

"A Pirate" by Chris Giles aged eight

END OF PART ONE

PART TWO

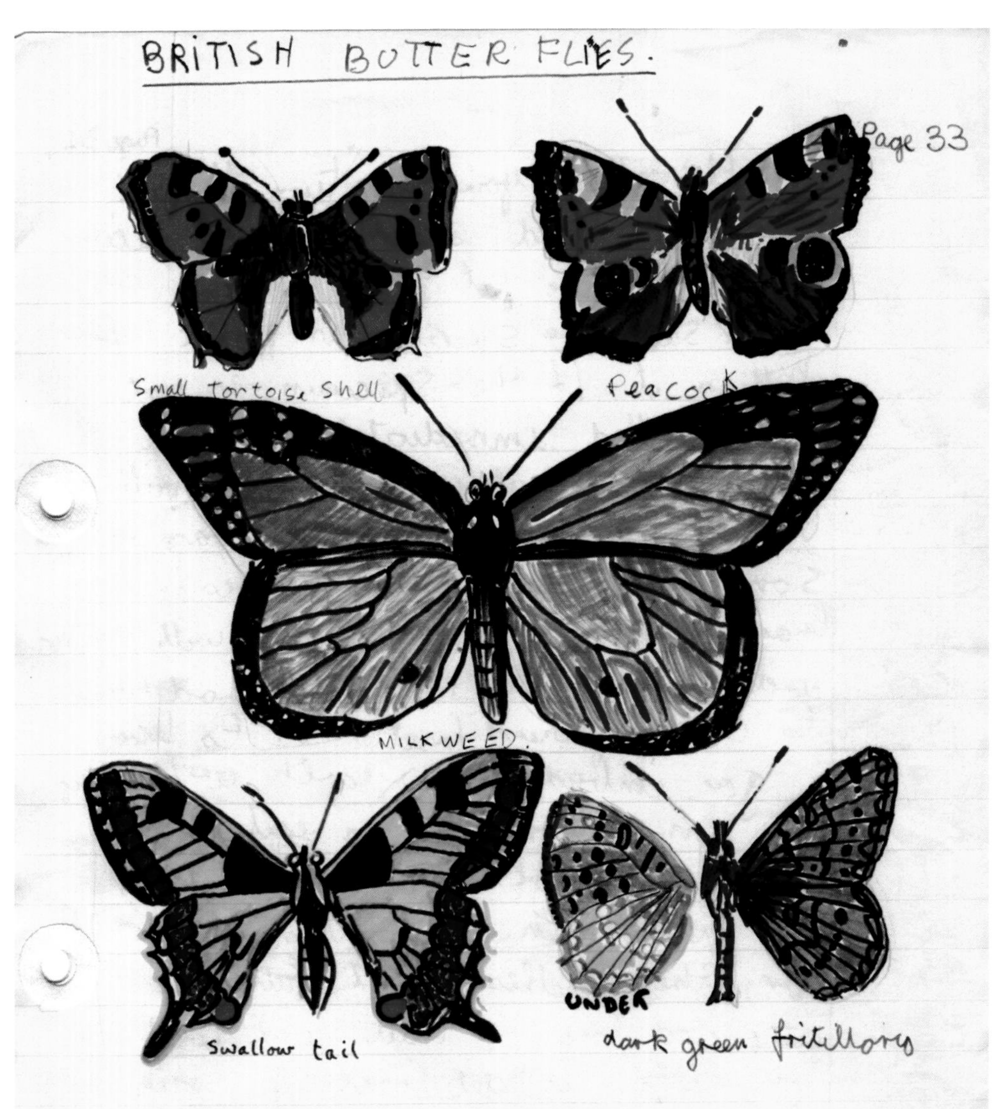

all of these butterflys are natural Size. The true colours are Slighty darker than the colours in these.

Chris, aged eleven, in his first year at
Buckhurst Hill County High School for Boys.

MUM'S STORY

Man's inhumanity to Man
Makes countless thousands mourn!

Man was Made to Mourn – Robert Burns

35
LAST YEARS IN SCOTLAND

"When Daddy was ill," Mum told me, "he and Mammy were careful to protect us from the distressing aspects of it. We were sent to stay with Auntie Martha for a few days when Mammy knew it was the end. When we came back home after Daddy's funeral, I burst into tears because Mammy looked strange and unfamiliar all dressed in black, and it frightened me. Everyone assumed I was crying about Daddy, but I wasn't. I didn't really grieve for him as such."

After Davie's death, Annie returned to her old job at the Post Office. Work was scarce at the time, and even though she was a skilled telegraphist with more than ten years' experience, and her late husband had been an employee of the GPO, she felt lucky to have the job. At the same time, Annie's father, William Greig, retired. He helped with the meals and kept an eye on Robert and Betty when his daughter was at work. Annie missed Davie deeply, but her grief was private and unsentimental. Her sorrow did not descend into depression. She not only got on with life, she enjoyed it. She gave her children a secure base from which to grow, and did everything she could to help them in their endeavours and give them a happy childhood. For herself she wanted very little. She had no great personal ambitions or creative yearnings: her talents lay in her homemaking skills and her strong sense of family. When talking of this time, she told me there were occasions when she had to put cardboard in her boots to cover the holes in the soles, "but there was food on the table every day and my children always had shoes on their feet."

She had been a mother to Martha, a housekeeper for her father, and had nursed her Davie for years. In many ways, it had been Annie who, from a young age, had held the family together. She was not remotely interested in finding another husband. It wasn't just because Davie was the only man she would ever love, but also because she recognised the advantages of being a single, independent woman who could organise her family, manage her finances and make her own decisions. Her natural feminist and socialist feelings became strongly held views.

Annie, her sister Martha and their children enjoyed two more carefree summers by the sea before the Second World War broke out. On September 3rd 1939, Great Britain and France, followed by India, Australia, South Africa and New Zealand, declared war on Germany. Robert and Betty were evacuated, he to Ayr and she to

Prestwick. Betty was miserable. Although there was a piano on which she could practise, she missed her lessons, her school and her Mammy. After a few weeks she was wretched enough for Annie to agree that she should come home. Robert, happy with his foster family, was enrolled at the Ayr Academy, a good school where he did well. After six months he returned to Glasgow to sit his Highers, the Scottish equivalent of A levels. His results gained him a place at the West of Scotland Agricultural College.

Archie McKillop, Martha's younger son, was also evacuated from Edinburgh to Macduff, a fishing town a long way away on the north coast above Aberdeen, but he was back in Edinburgh a few weeks later. Many evacuees soon returned home, as nothing much seemed to be happening, to the extent that this period was referred to as 'the Phoney War'. Archie had by this time taken up the clarinet and developed a keen interest in jazz. He joined a jazz club and played in various bands, becoming friends with the clarinettist Sandy Brown, who was already quite famous. Archie's nine-year-old sister, Marie, was sent to her McKillop grandparents in Oban.

Bessie's husband, Hal Dicken, rejoined the RAF as a catering officer. In April 1939, Bessie and her daughter Ailsa sailed to Vancouver, travelling on to Lynn Valley to stay with Aunt Maggie Glass, Aunt Hannah and her husband, Jim Davidson, who had emigrated from Scotland almost twenty years earlier. When the war began, Hal persuaded his wife to extend their stay. In the end, Bessie and Ailsa spent five years living in Canada. They both voluntarily enlisted into the Canadian Women's Army.

Billy McKillop, the eldest of the cousins, left school in 1937 and started to work part-time as an apprentice with a firm of printers, whilst also studying commercial art at the Edinburgh College of Art. In the same year, he joined the Peace Pledge Union, took up the study of Esperanto and became a vegetarian. He was happily occupied, but in 1940, a few months before his twentieth birthday, he was drafted into the Armed Forces. He turned up to enlist, but stated that he was only prepared to serve as a non-combatant, declaring himself a conscientious objector on moral grounds. Conscientious objectors who refused to contribute in any way at all to the war risked imprisonment: what happened to Billy, though, was arguably worse.

On September 25th 1940, two months after he was enlisted into the Pioneer Corps, the city of Bristol was severely bombed and would be bombarded repeatedly throughout the war. Bristol was a strategic target for the Germans as it was a port where sugar, tobacco, grain, coal and other essentials were docked and stored and where the Bristol Aeroplane Company was constructing warplanes. Billy was sent to Bristol to dig bodies out of the rubble. What he experienced shocked him so utterly that he was sent into a state of catatonic disturbance. He was discharged from the Army to a mental hospital where he underwent treatment, which included electroconvulsive therapy (ECT). With no sign of recovery, he was sent back to Edinburgh and admitted to a psychiatric hospital suffering from what was termed 'severe depression'. Martha and Archibald visited Billy to find him horribly changed. Their high-spirited, tearaway son had been traumatised away. His cheeky grin and shrieks of laughter were gone. They could no longer recognise the boy who used to run panting into the house with the excitement of an adventure to tell. It seemed the doctors could do nothing.

Billy's brother, Archie, left school to work as an office boy in the Scottish Command section of the War Office at Army Headquarters. He turned eighteen in April 1942, but as he was already working in the War Office, he wasn't drafted. His parents did not want him to join up, hardly surprisingly, and did their best to dissuade him. But the war was into the second year: everyone now knew something of the Nazi atrocities. Most British men felt that they must fight. Not only did Archie enlist, he volunteered as a paratrooper and joined the Army Air Corps Parachute Regiment in January 1943. He was sent to Norwich in England for training and later to Salisbury Plain.

Robert, Betty's brother, was eighteen and eligible to be called up. However, as he was acquiring useful skills studying agriculture, the War Office expected him to stay to complete his course. He remained in Glasgow, attended college and did his duty with the Home Guard.

Betty attained distinctions in all her piano exams, resulting in the Associated Board awarding her a Special Certificate for achieving the highest marks in Scotland. She won every prize at the Glasgow Music Festival and the gold medal for the best piano playing at the Edinburgh Competitive Festival. Not yet seventeen, she also gained two professional qualifications – the ARCM and LRAM performer diplomas. To be able to continue with her studies at a music college she would need a scholarship, as her mother could not afford the fees. She auditioned successfully and was awarded a full Caird scholarship to the Royal Academy of Music in London. This would pay her tuition fees and give her a small grant on which to live. The Academy wrote to inform her that her piano teacher would be Frederick Moore. She had hoped to study with Harold Craxton, but it didn't occur to her that she had any choice in the matter. She was overawed by the thought of going to the Royal Academy of Music; an institution where many famous musicians had studied, where renowned professors taught. London itself was a city that she had only heard about, since she had never been south of the Scottish border.

She wrote to Frederick Moore to express how much she was looking forward to studying with him. She thought her new teacher would be pleased to know that she had already gained her ARCM and LRAM diplomas, and would like to hear of her recent successes in the Glasgow Festival. It was an innocent letter, written in an unsophisticated way. She enclosed a newspaper cutting from the *Glasgow Herald*, which contained a small article about her. The cutting was returned with a curt reply, in which Mr. Moore made it plain that in London she would be a small fish in a big and illustrious pond. He implied that the Glasgow Festival was a laughable, provincial set-up that nobody in London took seriously, and that her achievements were inconsequential. Betty was absolutely crushed. Mr. Moore's arrogant manner was not unique. His condescension merely reflected the superior attitude at the core of the London musical establishment – an elitist, upper-class, public-school consortium. One has the impression that working-class scholarship students were tolerated, but not welcomed. Betty, as Frederick Moore clearly pointed out, was 'a nobody'.

36
1942-1945

In September 1942, Annie saw her daughter onto the London train at Glasgow Central station. Betty's trunk had been sent on ahead, but she had to take her cello, a small suitcase, a food parcel for the journey, and, most importantly, her ration book. Betty was seventeen, leaving Scotland to live in the capital city in wartime. Whatever concerns Annie may have had, she kept them to herself: she had every confidence in her daughter: it would all be good experience. She waved goodbye with optimism and encouragement. Betty would be living in student digs in St. John's Wood, fairly close to the Marylebone Road where the RAM building stood. Arrangements had been made to transport her piano, the one her Daddy had bought for her, down to London to have in her room. Her father's cousin, David Bradford, and his daughter, Audrey, who lived in London, met her at Euston Station. Audrey and her twin brother knew Betty and Robert from childhood holidays in Dundee [*see photo on page* 68]. I met Audrey in 2006, when she was in her eighties. She remembered Betty's arrival in London, in particular having to manoeuvre the cello into a taxi. To my delight, she found her 1942 diary with an entry on Saturday September 10th: "To Euston with Dad to meet Betty Fraser from Glasgow. Train 50 minutes late. Car to St. John's Wood." The taxi took them to Marlborough Place, a turning off Abbey Road. David and Audrey saw Betty up the front steps of number forty-three and left her to move in.

43, Marlborough Place was substantial, with a communal lounge and dining room on the ground floor and a large room in the basement known as 'the playpen', which housed a table-tennis table and a gramophone. Each bedroom was equipped with a gas ring, which the students could use to make simple meals. Betty's fellow lodgers were mainly girls, as most able-bodied young men had volunteered or been called up for the war. The students took their breakfast and evening meals with the housekeeper, Doris Davison, and the landlady, Daisy Tresauer, a retired actress who had trodden the boards in her youth. The lodging house did not provide bed linen or any proper clothes washing facilities. Betty could hand wash her underwear and stockings in the sink, but she sent her dirty sheets and linen home to Glasgow. Her Mammy would get them washed at the steamies and post them back clean. Annie also sent food parcels of pancakes, scones, tablet, cheese, oranges, tinned milk, meat rolls – anything she could manage, forfeiting her own allowances to give extras to her daughter. Occasionally she sent eggs, but despite careful packing they sometimes broke en route. Throughout Betty's student years, her Mammy's food parcels, laundered linen and letters arrived regularly.

Betty found her piano teacher, Frederick Moore, cold and formal, but she did not allow his indifferent teaching to diminish her love of the piano. She practised hard and maintained her own high standards even though her efforts were barely recognised. Mr. Moore didn't seem the slightest bit interested in her. Fortunately, this was not the case with her cello teacher, Alison Dalrymple (who later taught the young Jacqueline Du Pré). She was a kindly, vivacious person who not only encouraged Betty's cello playing, but also recognised her talent as a pianist and accompanist. Betty played frequently for Miss Dalrymple's pupils in prizes, exams and concerts, and often appeared on the Academy's Duke's Hall stage as an accompanist. At the end of her first term, Betty performed the first movement of a Goltermann cello concerto at Miss Dalrymple's pupils' concert, which took place at the London Violoncello School.

Betty was home in Glasgow for Christmas and her eighteenth birthday on December 30th. On January 1st 1943 she started to keep a diary in which she wrote nearly every day for the next five years. I didn't know of its existence until she told me on her seventieth birthday that she had spent a nostalgic day browsing through her old diary. Intrigued, I asked if she would allow me to read it. Her response was that it contained some "purple bits" which she wasn't sure she would want me to see. I didn't press her further. Months later she handed me a stack of hard-backed notebooks: "My diary," she said, "you wanted to read it."

I anticipated a fascinating account of Mum's past and so was disappointed to find it dull – too dull to glance at more than a few pages. However, in order to write this section, I read it – all seven volumes. I have selected what I feel to be the most interesting and poignant entries from her journal and have identified the main characters and relationships that appear in the pages. What follows is my impression and interpretation of her account, together with the reminiscences she shared with me. Here are some short extracts from the first pages, to give an example of her style of writing:

January 1st 1943: In the morning baked shortbread and apples for dessert. Mammy home at 12.30. She bakes gingerbread. The three of us go to Cinema to see 'King Arthur was a Gentleman'. The plot was weak. It was a cold, drizzly day with sleet in the morning.
January 2nd: Made the dinner, Mammy home at 2.00. Robert goes to the concert with a girl, I think. Mammy and I go to Mayfair to see 'Son of Fury' with Tyrone Power. It was good. I finished reading 'The Little Minister'. I enjoyed it. Have started 'The Whalers' by J. J. Bell. It was cold and damp and froze at night.
January 3rd: Freezing this morning. One siren went off about 7.00. Must have been a false alarm. Finished 'The Whalers' – very exciting. Played the Dvořák with Robert. He is still on all-night guard with H.G. [*Home Guard*]
January 4th: Frosty and slightly foggy. Went to book for washhouse. Went to see Miss Ommers [*Julia and Elsa Ommer, Betty and Robert's music teachers*]. Julia has been very ill. This is the first day the doctor has given Elsa any hope.
January 5th: Practised in the morning. Ironed my clothes for going away. After tea some cello practice. After supper I played to Miss Elsa. Julia is a little better. It has begun to snow.
January 6th: Robert makes a music stand out of the Meccano set. I pack my case and send my underclothing by post. I go to Joyce's for supper and then we go to Embassy to see 'The Young Mr. Pitt'. Joyce smoked 3 cigs, I smoked 2. Home about 10.15. I am reading 'Gulliver's Travels'.
January 7th: Finish packing my case. Take it to the station. At 7.30 go to dance with

> Robert. I danced with Robert most of the time. We nearly won the elimination[1]. There was us and another couple left. First the boys had to propose to their partners, then they had to sing. Robert sang 'Home on the Range' and the other boy 'Loch Lomond'. The prize was awarded to the one who got the most applause.
> **January 9th 1943:** Some snow lying. In morning got messages [*shopping*]. In afternoon went to see Julia. She is a lot better. Robert went to the concert. Mammy and I left the house at 7.30. The train was at 9.10. In the carriage were a soldier, an ATS, a sailor and me. On the other side a sailor an airman and a WAAF. The sailor and I were wrapped up in his greatcoat. It was beautifully warm.
> **January 10th:** We all shared our sandwiches and we had ½ an orange each. We were in complete darkness all the way except that the soldier had a torch. The train arrived at 8.20. I arrived at St. John's Wood at 8.45. After breakfast I went to bed until 12.45. After lunch I went down to see the playpen. It was damp all day.

Back in London, Betty discarded her childhood name and started to call herself Elizabeth. She also made a conscious effort to lose her Glaswegian accent, as she was sick of being teased about it. She appears to have been on friendly terms with all the lodgers at 43, Marlborough Place. They had lunch and tea in one another's rooms, played ping-pong down in the playpen and listened to the radio in the lounge. Their favourite programmes were Victor Sylvester and his dance band, and 'ITMA' [*It's that Man Again*] starring Tommy Handley, but they also listened to concerts and tuned in to the news for the latest war reports.

Of her studies with Frederick Moore, she simply enters "piano lesson" every Friday and lists the pieces she is learning. Once she writes: "He was quite pleased", but she received virtually no praise. She auditioned for the RAM Second Orchestra and succeeded in gaining a place on the fifth desk of the cello section, which, as she explained, was second from the back. She writes: "I'm not very good at sight-reading on the cello but I expect I'll get better." It was the first symphony orchestra she had ever played in. At the end of term there was to be a concert for which all girls were required to wear long white dresses. With clothing rationed and no money to spare, this posed quite a problem.

> I go to a little shop in Regent Street to ask the price of white dresses – 7, 8 and 9 guineas. In Dickens and Jones they are 16 guineas. There is a lovely dress in Bourne and Hollingsworth for £8/5/6d.

She hadn't that sort of money to spend, especially as she had just bought a new set of strings for her cello, which cost £1/4/6d. Fortunately, the Academy kept a selection of ex-students' discarded white frocks, so Elizabeth was able to borrow one, a scheme that she continued to take advantage of throughout her student days. She did, however, have to purchase three yards of five-inch wide red grosgrain ribbon for the sash, to be worn over the left shoulder to just below the waist on the right.

1. The "elimination" was adjudicated dancing, where the judges progressively eliminated couples, leaving the best pairs on the dance floor. I was quite impressed to think that Betty and Robert were accomplished dancers. In those days, everyone learned to dance at school, going 'jigging' most Saturday nights.

This white/red ensemble remained compulsory Academy concert wear for women until 1970. By the time I was a full-time student, long black had become standard, except for the end of year prize giving ceremony when long white dresses slashed diagonally with red were *still* mandatory.

In a letter from home, Elizabeth's Mammy wrote that there had been an incendiary raid on Glasgow, which had burnt out the church in Langside Road. The German Luftwaffe targeted Glasgow, along with all major cities, but London was constantly under attack.

January 18th 1943: Sirens go at 4.30. I open my curtains and watch the gunfire and shells bursting in the sky. I hear the whistle and the flash of a bomb that falls in St. John's Wood somewhere, which makes the house rock. The all clear goes about 6.30. The bus to Baker Street takes a very roundabout route to avoid an unexploded bomb.
January 20th: Sirens go about 12.30. There is some gunfire and we watch the shells bursting in the sky.

Many young men in the Allied Armed Forces stopped for a few days in London on leave. Most were a long way from home – Canadians, Americans, French, Norwegians, Belgians, and lads from all over Britain. They were homesick, lonely and tired. Some had not yet seen active service, but were undergoing gruelling training in the tough regime of military life. Those who were back with first-hand experience hoped to blot out the scenes they had witnessed, to forget for a while the war they were fighting to which they must soon return. They needed entertainment and distraction, company and comfort. Some wanted only to chat, share a drink, dance and be merry; others hoped to lose themselves in a movie or sex. The hearts of the girls in town beat with a fervent tenderness for their brave boys dressed so dashingly in military uniforms. War altered reality: barriers fell; social conventions were redefined; women enjoyed a freedom from restraint they hadn't before experienced. Life was on the line, taut with possibility; time was precious, passions unchecked.

Elizabeth's closest companion at this time was Nancy Wyllie, perhaps because she was also from Glasgow. Whenever they went out together, they met young men on leave and struck up conversation. One evening they walked to the buffet at St. John's Wood station for coffee. An airman came to sit beside them:

March 13th: Nancy offers him a light and we start talking. His name is Douglas Hird age 21. He is just my height, light ginger hair and blue eyes. He walked part of the way home with us. We are to see him tomorrow at 2.30. Joke: Have you heard about the new 1943 dress? One Yank and it's off!
March 14th: He [*Douglas*] brings his friend Syd, whose real name is Ivan Horler with him and we go for a walk in Regents Park. We take them home and sit talking, drinking and smoking and have some tea and toast, then go out for a drink. I have a gin and lime which I quite like, then a beer, which Douglas has to finish for me. They are leaving tomorrow. We go for a walk in the moonlight and he has his arm around my waist. When he kisses me goodnight he gets rather unpleasant, which spoils the day for me but otherwise it was great fun.

There are other similar stories:

> **March 20th 1943:** An airman came over to us. He and his friend have a bet. If we are nurses he has to stand us drinks, if we are not, he still has to stand us drinks, so we get a gin and lime. They are Taffy, an ex-policeman, and Robin, a terribly nice boy age 20. They see us home. Taffy wants to kiss me but I won't let him.
> **March 28th:** After supper go up to St. John's Wood buffet. Meet Barney and Jack. Barney is in the RAF and Jack, the Ordnance Corps. Barney would have kissed me goodnight but I didn't let him.
> **March 29th:** Meet Jack and Barney at the station. Barney walks down the road with his arm round me and kisses me goodnight very passionately. He seems crazy about me. He implores me to write to him and I get his address. He says, "Gosh! I wish I had known you at the beginning of my leave."

Barney began to write regularly and she replied dutifully. The next day, Elizabeth's brother, Robert, came down from Glasgow to see her. It was his first visit to London. Elizabeth took him to museums, art galleries, the Royal parks, St. Paul's Cathedral and Buckingham Palace. They went on a boat trip up the River Thames to Hampton Court, and to an agricultural exhibition in Regent Street. But the place Robert admired most was Kew Gardens, which he saw at its springtime best when the magnolias, camellias and rhododendrons were blooming magnificently. A week later, he, Elizabeth and Nancy Wyllie boarded the train home to Glasgow for the Easter break.

> **April 7th:** Two Canadians sit beside us. Mine is Jim – he is of Swedish parents. Nancy's is Floyd who's Irish. They have nothing to eat with them, so we share our lunch. At 3.30 we have tea by which time Floyd has his arm round Nancy and Jim is holding my hand. By the time we arrive at Glasgow, he has his arms around me and is holding both my hands. I am seeing him tomorrow afternoon.
> **April 8th:** Meet Jim at the Paramount at 2.30. We go to see 'The Moon and Sixpence'. He holds my hand. Take car [*tram*] to Clarkston. Walk through Busby and along the little road past the waterfall. We sit down for an hour – perhaps it was longer – it didn't matter.
> **April 10th:** Nancy keeps me waiting and I am five minutes late for Jim. He was getting quite anxious. We go to see 'George Washington Slept Here' with Jack Benny. Meet Nancy and Floyd and have tea at Cranston's. The boys go to shave and then we go to The Albert and book a table on the balcony. Jim isn't a good dancer but we get on OK. He kisses me.

Two days later, she saw Jim off at Glasgow Central station and handed a food parcel of sandwiches she had made for him through the carriage window. They kissed goodbye. He promised to write as soon as he returned to camp. True to his word, a letter arrived from him a week later. It coincided with a visit from Archie McKillop, Elizabeth's favourite cousin, who was home on leave and seeing his Auntie Annie and cousins in Glasgow before returning to Edinburgh to take his Officer's test.

> **April 25th:** Show Archie Jim's letter. He says any boy would be glad to take me out. I feel quite pleased.

This would have been a lovely compliment for Elizabeth, who adored Archie and looked up to him. Archie was a handsome boy, an attribute that Elizabeth could hardly have failed to notice, but it was his personality that was so endearing. Mum described him as "someone with no prickles or jagged edges, a warm-hearted, sweet-natured boy." Jim did not write again. There is no explanation in the diary as to why this was.

Nancy Wyllie passed her LRAM and left the Academy. With Nancy out of the way, another lodger named Margaret Whittlestone attached herself to Elizabeth. Margaret was, in Mum's words, "a poor creature; unprepossessing, insecure, and rather feeble." She sought Elizabeth's company whenever possible. Soon they were travelling to the Academy at the same time, eating together at the cheap British Restaurant, going to films and concerts and having tea in each other's rooms. Margaret complained of stomach upsets, which rewarded her with Elizabeth's sympathy, yet when she went to the doctor, nothing was found to be wrong. Elizabeth made mugs of Ovaltine for her before seeing her to bed, and when air-raid sirens screamed in the night, Margaret climbed into Elizabeth's bed for comfort. However, when they went out together there were no stories of picking up boys.

Elizabeth signed up for Fireguard Duty – it was not compulsory to do so, but most civilians volunteered willingly, as did Margaret, who engineered to be on call for the same shifts as Elizabeth. The two had to report for duty to number fifty, across the road, where they were issued with regulation tin hats and gas masks and instructed to watch for fires, alert the emergency services and offer assistance. However, there was no occasion when they had to deal with a crisis. Occasionally, they bedded down to snatch a doze between air-raids, but more often they drank coffee and smoked cigarettes until the all clear sounded.

In July, Barney wrote to say he had two days' leave, and asked to see her. Elizabeth had met him only once four months earlier. She confided to her diary: "I don't know what to do."

> **July 17th 1943:** Barney rings up at 10.15. I decide to go with him tomorrow. To meet him at 10.30 at West End Lane station.

Reading between the lines, the day out was not a success. Elizabeth was back home by ten o'clock with no mention of a kiss goodnight. Later she wrote a letter "trying to explain my feelings for him" and received a "very short" reply. They had no more contact. Barney, I hope, found another girl to love.

Frederick Moore was away for a few weeks and arranged for Elizabeth to have piano lessons with Victor Booth during his absence. She writes: "He [*Victor*] spends an hour on the 'Chromatic Fantasia' and says my fugue is very well planned. I have not to change it one iota." It was the first praise she had received for her piano playing since she started at the Academy. After her second lesson, she reports: "he is pleased with my Bach. Says I have a quick mind and have remembered everything he told me. I play him the beginning of the Brahms 'Paganini' variations. He says it is one of the most difficult pieces for piano and I am doing well with it." When Mr. Moore returned, she comments: "he tells me to do some of the things Mr. Booth told me not to." Before the term ended, Frederick Moore asked if she would like to change teachers and study with Victor Booth in her second year. Her reply was a quiet "yes." She passed all her first year exams, was placed in the Blakiston piano prize, and gained full marks in aural training.

At the end of July she was back in Glasgow. Robert had finished his studies at Agricultural College and was for the moment training and serving in the Home Guard. With her own piano in London, Elizabeth had to make arrangements to practise on a neighbour's piano or at the Ommer sisters' house. Never once does she complain about having to practise, nor does she make any other comments about it, apart from noting the times – usually three or four hours a day. Her dedication to the piano – and the cello – is evident throughout her diary. Later in the summer, she went to visit her Auntie Martha and Cousin Marie in Edinburgh. Once there she was able to practise as much as she liked on Auntie Martha's piano, a very good upright almost identical to her own. However, Archie McKillop was home on embarkation leave – and when there was an opportunity to spend time with her much-loved cousin, her practice took second place.

August 23rd 1943: Archie and I sit in garden talking. After supper, play piano a little. Archie and I go to the Empire – quite a good variety show.
August 24th: After breakfast, practise, then go with Archie to art galleries to see Greek exhibition. We discover it doesn't open till twelve o'clock, so go up Calton Hill. It is very warm and sunny. We want to go to London Phil. Concert at the Lyceum but miss the bus. Arrive in middle of Rossini's 'Semiramide' overture. They play Beethoven 8, Rimsky-Korsakov 'Capriccio Espagnol', conductor Anatole Fistoulari. Cyril Smith plays Chopin.
August 26th: Lovely sunshine this morning. Archie and I go up Corstorphine Hill. Lie in the sun till 1 o'clock.
August 28th: Archie & I go to Arthur's Seat. We get home at 2. We all go brambling.
August 30th: Archie leaves at 9.15 for the 10 o'clock train. I give him my London address.
September 8th: It is a nice day. Mammy & I go to Rothesay. Train from Central at 10.40. Boat from Wemyss Bay. Walk round to Port Bannatyne then back by top road. Come back by Loch Fyne. Home at 7.10. Marvellous news. Italy capitulates!
September 9th: A lovely day again. Robert, Mammy and I go to Loch Lomond. We walk over to Arrochar on Loch Long and have tea in the hotel. When we come back to Tarbet, the sun has gone and the Loch is quite choppy. Get boat back.

Before the start of her second year at the Academy, Elizabeth spent a week in Wakefield with Margaret Whittlestone and her family. Mum told me that it was clear to her then why Margaret was so insecure; her father was a bully – a schoolmaster of the type who terrorised his pupils. Mr. Whittlestone had sent his daughter to the Academy expecting her to achieve: at home, she was made to practise and perform, and constantly criticised. She was a competent enough violinist and pianist, but not exceptional. Mum said she felt sorry for her. But Margaret was not stimulating company and the entry "I am bored" appears in the diary.

September 29th: Post card from Archie. He is in London this weekend.
October 2nd: Archie rings up at 3.45 – says he is in Euston. I meet him at Baker St. at 5. We go to see 'Mr. Lucky' at Odeon, Swiss Cottage. A very good programme.

October 3rd 1943: Change into my pink blouse and black skirt. Meet Archie at Hyde Park Corner, tube to Charing X. Walk to Adelphi Theatre. Cheapest seats 7/6 (we don't go!) Walk to St. Pauls. Buy some apples and eat them. Bus to Trafalgar Square. Go to National Gallery. Velasquez' 'Venus and Child' is up. Bus home from Piccadilly. Go into lounge. There is a dead silence because of Archie. Tea in my room. Very hilarious. M, June, Archie & I play ping-pong. Archie leaves at 7.30. June thinks "He's sweet; I hope he comes back again".

Archie visited Elizabeth in London whenever he had a short leave, as there wasn't time to get home to Edinburgh, a journey that took all day. From Salisbury it was about three hours to London by train, and Elizabeth was his contact with home. On several occasions Robert was in London at the same time. The War Office had posted him to the Vale of Glamorgan where he was employed as a Horticultural Officer. His job was to advise farmers how to achieve the best yield from their soil and encourage ordinary people to turn their gardens over to the cultivation of vegetables as part of the War Effort. It was at 43, Marlborough Place, Daisy Tresauer's lodging house, where both boys stayed. Daisy was tight-fisted about food rations, but she charged very little, or nothing at all, for accommodation for lads on leave. This could have been because they brought their short-leave ration books with them, which for the troops were generous. A few days later, Elizabeth listened with admiration to Douglas Cameron playing the Elgar cello concerto (interrupted by a siren) and went to the Albert Hall to sit in on an LPO rehearsal of the new Vaughan Williams symphony (his fifth). She writes: "Dr. Williams was there giving directions."

October 11th: Letter from Robert. He is coming this weekend.
October 15th: Robert arrives from Glasgow. Tea in my room. Take him to the lounge where we talk till 9.30. Play ping-pong. Robert beats me.
October 16th: Archie rings up at 3.30. He and his friend John come for tea. Archie, John, Robert and I go into West End to see a Robert Donat film at the Empire, Leicester Square. Archie and John give me their photos and I give them mine. I get to bed at 11.30. Sirens go at 1.25. Get up and dress and go to no. 50 for fire duty. Nothing happens. All clear in 25 minutes.
October17th: Robert and I meet Archie and John at the National Gallery at 10.15. Go to a fun fair. Robert wins 2 cheroots. Wander around making batty conversation. Home at 6. The boys get ready and go. It's all too soon. Archie is back – he has forgotten his hat. Make sandwiches for Robert tomorrow.
October 18th: Air-raid. I heard the warning and gunfire but no all clear. Percy[2] was very near and making a lot of noise. Robert leaves at 7.40. Train at 8.55 from Paddington. I feel very tired today I have had such a hectic weekend. Go to bed at 9.15. Air-raid at ¼ to 11. M. comes down. We watch searchlights and gunfire. M. comes into bed with me.

When Elizabeth went dancing, it was with Valerie, a fellow student who lived in the same digs. She was a fun-loving, flirtatious Welsh girl from Bangor.

November 1st: Go to Astoria Tottenham Court Road. I dance with a soldier from Vienna. A Norwegian soldier watched Valerie for ages. They dance together. We sit talking to him. His name is Canute. Afterwards we feel like kicking ourselves for not encouraging him to take us home. When we get home Daisy's living room light is on so we go and sit on the seat on the corner of Blenheim Ter. outside the pub. When we go back the light is still on. We get in and up the stairs without her hearing us. She switches on hall light. We run along passage to my room. Lie low for 10 minutes.

November 2nd 1943: Daisy heard Valerie last night and gave her a lecture this morning. She didn't mention me and V. kept my name out of it. M. goes to doctor at 12. Her stomach has been upset since Sunday night.

November 5th: Have bath and get dressed in blue summer dress. Betty and M. come along to see me. They say I look very nice. Go for Valerie. We arrive at Astoria at 7.30. Meet Canute again and his friend Willie. Willie & I and Canute & Valerie sit & talk on the couch. They bring us home at 11.15.

November 6th: Valerie is meeting Canute at 7. Go to see her before she goes. Tell her she has a date next time Archie comes. M. & I are just going to bed when there is gunfire so we go on duty. There is no-one at no. 50 so we go for a walk and come home. We have just got to bed when the siren goes. The man on duty gives us cigarettes & a cup of coffee. It is very cold & windy tonight. Moon shining brightly.

November 11th: (Armistice) Piano lesson. Victor talks to me about cultivating my musical sense. Gives me a book on Aesthetics.

November 17th: Practice piano. Play Chopin Scherzo to M. and Valerie. After dinner do a little cello practice then up to M's room. Read "Foundations of Musical Aesthetics" while she practises.

November 19th: I give Val a lesson on Chopin Waltz. Have bath. Put on my blue dress. After dinner go dancing. A little Pole dances with me. He says, "You please me. I like you meet tomorrow" I say "No thank you". Talk to a Norwegian called Sverre. Home at 11.15. Val comes to get bread from my room. I go up to M's room to wash my face because my sink is blocked with tealeaves. Parcel from home today with 2 oranges, choc biscs. & almond cake.

November 27th: I get home and am just making tea for myself at 5 when bell rings for me and there is Archie. He has a short weekend leave. We go to see Laurence Olivier in 'Demi-Paradise' at the Odeon. Come home and make something to eat. Sit till 11.

November 28th: We rush to the Albert Hall only to find we haven't enough money to get in. Go home and sit in lounge. Listen to Brains Trust and news, play spelling game. Daisy comes in and asks if Archie would like to stay to supper. He can't because his train is about 9. He leaves at 8. Archie gave me his Paratroop badge today.

Elizabeth and her Mammy spent the Christmas holiday mending clothes, knitting gloves, going for walks and to the theatre and cinema. They were content in each other's company. Although she doesn't state it as such, it is clear that Elizabeth had the greatest respect for her Mammy and was happy to be with her. Sadness catches me, knowing that Izzy and I were not able to achieve the same easy mother/daughter rapport with Mum. The bond of kinship between Annie Fraser and her daughter never faltered.

Back in London, Elizabeth auditioned for the RAM First Orchestra. She played a Marcello sonata and had to sight-read passages from the cello part of Wagner's *Die Meistersinger*. The result was a promotion from the Second Orchestra to the back desk of the First. To begin with, she found the rehearsals challenging: "I make a hopeless mess of 'Tannhäuser' and 'William Tell'. Beethoven 5, 'Symphonie Espagnol' and Mozart A major piano concerto are not so bad." Mum was quite proud of the fact that she played in the Academy's First Orchestra when Sir Henry Wood, or Timber, as he was affectionately called, conducted.

January 15th 1944: After dinner sit in lounge till 7.45. Siren goes, some gunfire. All clear 8.45. Sew pyjamas. Play 'Buzz and Fizz', 'I went to Market' and Spelling game. Invent two new words – whirsting (talking aimlessly) and ghoso (baloney). Foggy all day today.
January 16th: Archie rings up at 12. I meet him at Marble Arch at 2.15. We go to see Ann Sheridan in 'Naughty but Nice' – not very good. Walk back and the fog is very thick. Flares in the middle of the road. At St. Johns Wood we are behind a man with a torch so are all right. Archie stays for supper and M. and I walk back to the station with him.
January 28th: Val comes in to show me silk stockings and Coty powder she got from an American. After supper Betty, Roger, M. & Val go to Wuthering Heights. They want me to go but I practise instead. Val comes back because she's afraid she will cry too much. We have a serious talk about Val's life.
January 29th: Val goes out for walk just as sirens go. M. & I go up to my room to watch the flak. The gunfire is very loud and near. A lot of shrapnel falls. Val comes back and shows us a piece of shrapnel that fell just beside her.
February 19th: Siren goes at 12.30. There is a very loud barrage of gunfire – Percival[2] is closer than he's ever been. I stay in bed until two bombs drop very near and the house shakes. We all gradually assemble in the basement with Daisy, except for Val who hasn't come home. Daisy imagines she is on Fire Duty and we don't enlighten her. In the morning, M. and I go for a walk. There is a bomb at the end of Clifton Hill and an unexploded one in Abercorn Place. An anti-aircraft shell exploded outside St. Mark's and blew in all the rectory windows.
February 20th: Archie turns up at 1.45 just as I am starting dinner. I knew he'd be coming this weekend (telepathy?) We go for a walk in Regents Park then to Trafalgar Square by tube and have tea at Strand Palace. Back in the lounge we play games and give Archie supper and coffee. The siren goes, so M. and I leave Archie in the lounge and go to Fire Duty. Pretty bad tonight but not too close. A big fire somewhere near Paddington. It is light as day with all the searchlights, flares and fires.
February 21st: Sirens 3.25 till 3.55 this morning. Go to village to spend a short-leave ration card Archie has left me. Get 4 mutton chops, 2oz sugar, 1oz butter, 4oz marg, carrots and ¼ stone potatoes. The man asks me if that is how we buy them in Scotland. I prepare the veg and put stew on. Archie comes in at 11.45. Have dinner at 12.30 – it is very good indeed. Finish with buns, coffee and ⅓ an orange.

Elizabeth played the piano for Archie before walking back to the station with him, picking up bits of shrapnel along the way. She and Margaret ventured to the Albert Hall for an afternoon concert only to find that it had been cancelled because of bomb damage. She writes: "The Royal Geographical Society building is in a dreadful mess and the windows are out all along High Street Kensington." Buses had to take detours around roads made impassable with rubble, but the people of London continued to go about their daily business, taking life as it came. Even Elizabeth's diaries convey an almost blasé attitude to the German air strikes. There was nothing they could do if their number was up. By ignoring fear and feigning indifference to danger, it was possible to carry on as usual.

2. Percival ('Percy') Proctor and Percival Q.6 Petrel were British reconnaissance planes.

March 2nd 1944: M. and I go to the Academy and I bag 2 seats for us in the balcony. The Duke's Hall is cluttered up with cameras, reporters and arc lights. The ceremony begins at 11.45. Leslie Boosey [*of Boosey and Hawkes*] presents to Sir Henry Wood a cheque for 1,000 guineas and a carnation. Dr. Vaughan Williams gives him a book autographed by over 1,000 composers, conductors and soloists. Sir Adrian Boult says a few words on behalf of orchestral players and Sir Henry speaks. We decide to skip aural. We line the entrance hall and wait for Sir Henry to come out. We sing, "For he's a jolly good fellow". Among people there were William Walton, Richard Tauber, Arnold Bax, Edwin Evans and Granville Bantock.

In the lounge one evening, a discussion arose about character and every student received a personality assessment from the others. Elizabeth reports: "I am told I am very difficult to understand." But one girl went further: "...finding fault with my character, her main objection that I was lacking in emotion and sense of humour." The rebuff must have upset her, as she reacted by taking out her hurt on Margaret: "M. and I continue conversation in my room and I tell M. some of her faults and tell her how I felt about her intrusion on me at the very beginning two terms ago."

March 11th: Archie comes for tea and we go out to the Empire, Leicester Square to see Greer Garson and Walter Pigeon in 'Madame Curie'. We have an egg for supper.
March 12th: Archie and I listen to a concert – Beethoven overture, Bach double, L'Après-Midi d'un Faune and something from Wagner's Parsifal. We twiddle the knobs on the wireless and get lots of jazz programmes. Make a nice supper of salad and pilchards and talk till 10.30.

On Thursday March 23rd it was Robert's twenty-first birthday and, as luck would have it, both Robert and Archie had weekend leave. Annie sent a parcel of one-and-a-half dozen oranges and a registered letter containing £5. Elizabeth's female housemates were over the moon that the two boys were coming. Robert was an attractive young man too, with his blue eyes and open smile, which hadn't gone unnoticed. Archie was already the house heartthrob.

March 26th: Get up early and M., Val and I go to meet Archie at Piccadilly. We walk through St. James's Park and Green Park, round by the Serpentine Lake, through Hyde Park and Kensington Gardens and get the tube back from Lancaster Gate. M. is on dinner duty and we don't get back till 1.15 – Doris is furious. After dinner I help M. clear up and go down to the garden where Archie, Val and Robert are lying on the lawn. I change into a summer dress, it is so warm. Stanley and Christine come at 4. Stanley looks immaculate in his uniform and Archie looks slovenly – a hole in his sock and his tunic off.

Unconcerned about his socks or his appearance, he probably just wanted to feel the sun on his body and relax in his cousins' company. His training with the Parachute Regiment must have been exhausting. On leave, he needed a rest from it all. They were so young – Robert, twenty-one, Archie not quite twenty and Elizabeth, nineteen, all a long way from home. At least for this one precious day they could be together in London. The happy-go-lucky holidays they had shared on Arran must have seemed a long time ago.

March 26th 1944 contd.: We have tea in my room then come down to the lounge. Valerie and Archie disappear and I get suspicious, but when they come back we discover they have gone back to my room to do the dishes. Borrow gramophone and records and dance. Archie leaves at 8.15.
March 28th: Put on blue dress. Go dancing with Val. I get 5 partners. I finish with a Canadian and Val with a Norwegian. Come home together. We stay outside the house until nearly 2. He wants to make love to me and it takes all my willpower to control myself. I'm seeing him 6.30 tomorrow. Got in at last. I can't think how they got home.
March 29th: Lunch at BR [*British Restaurant*] with M. & Val. I don't feel very hungry. I can't stop thinking about my Canadian. Go to Baker St. station at 6.15 to meet him and wait till 7.35. He doesn't come & I go home. I am in tears. I get ready for bed. Val comes up & I tell her what has happened. She is terribly sorry for me.
March 30th: Val comes in & tells me her Norwegian said my Canadian had every intention of coming last night – in fact he talked about me all the way home on Tuesday. I write down as much as I know about him & she is going to try and trace him for me.

But Elizabeth never saw him again and never found out why he stood her up.

April 1st: Back home to Glasgow. Mammy meets me.
April 5th: Mr. Downes is home on sick leave. He was torpedoed and broke his spine and leg and has shrapnel wounds in his shoulders. His wife Edith is an utter mess.
April 18th: A letter from Archie arrives in an Active Service envelope. He says his chances of leave are rapidly diminishing.

Thank goodness for Annie's food parcels, as the meals that Daisy served were ghastly – macaroni *without* cheese followed by bread pudding, for example. There were mutterings that Daisy was filching their rations, either selling them on the black market or indulging herself. She used the majority of points on the students' ration books to buy food for the household, which inevitably aroused her lodgers' suspicions. On the other hand, they sneaked marmalade, jam, sugar and milk from the table when Daisy's back was turned.

May 6th: Archie rings up at 6.15 to say he's in London on overnight leave and comes straight over. Doris invites him to supper, then we play card games, give him a coffee in my room and he goes at 11.
May 8th: We have a row with Daisy about the milk rations at breakfast. As usual she talks her way out of the tight corners.
May 9th: Doris announces with the utmost coolness that there will be a jug of milk per day from now on. Daisy kept my dinner for me in the kitchen. While I am having it, she consumes about 1 pint of milk with shredded wheat and a cup of tea with 2 lumps of sugar.
May 14th: Decide to reform No. 43 by having a deputation to Daisy about the food.
May 15th: Lunch in my room. M's stomach is upset. She only has toast. Meet Nicky coming downstairs as I go up. She tells me to hurry – Archie had come about ½ an hour ago. I cook some potatoes for him and open a tin of beans. After dinner we all gather in lounge and fetch Daisy. She gets a terrible shock when she sees the whole house collected and is very annoyed because a stranger – Archie – is there. We ask her for 4 points, more tea, sugar and vegetables. She takes it quite well but also talks her way out of it easily. She says she will consider the question of points but can't offer us any hope.

The next day Archie met Elizabeth at the Academy at two o'clock. He sat in the Duke's Hall listening to her playing in a First Orchestra rehearsal. Afterwards they had tea together in the canteen before he caught the train back to Salisbury. It was the last time she would see him.

May 29th (Whit Monday) 1944: Margaret tells me to look out of the window to see Daisy sunbathing in a pink and white striped costume and a little flowered parasol. She looks like one of those doubtful holiday picture postcards. Val's undies have flown off her windowsill into the next garden and one of the boys climbs onto the wall to retrieve them from the creeper. Daisy comes out to see the cause of the unseemly mirth.
June 6th: At breakfast, Doris tells us the Invasion has begun.

Allied preparations for the greatest amphibious invasion of all time had been in the planning for years. During the months immediately preceding D-Day, the build-up of allied troops and equipment in the south of England was massive. By May, the area was a vast armed camp with military vehicles parked in every available space. Airfield resources were strained to breaking point, as the mighty force of aircraft was crammed as close to France as possible for the attack. The scale of the invasion plan, known as Overlord, was colossal. Going ashore on D-Day from the sea were 57,500 American and over 75,000 British and Canadian troops, plus 900 armoured vehicles and 600 guns. This required a transport fleet of 4,126 vessels manned by almost 200,000 sailors. A remarkable total of 13,743 aircraft took part, including those that landed the 27,000 airborne troops on the night of June 5th/6th by parachute. The US 82nd and 101st Airborne Divisions were landed north of the mouth of the River Vire in the west of Normandy; the British 6th Airborne Division, north of Caen to the east.

Within this British division was the Army Air Corps Parachute Regiment to which Archie had enlisted. The AAC were a body of specially trained infantry who could be air-landed from plane or glider by parachute to precise locations. Archie's seventeen months' training had been intense. His regiment, who wore distinctive red berets, assembled on Salisbury Plain during the latter part of May 1944 in readiness for action. On the night of June 5th/6th, Archie flew to Normandy on his first World War Two mission. He and his compatriots, entrusted with protecting their Army's flank, had the following objectives:

1. To capture intact the bridges across the Orne and its canal between Benouville and Ranville.
2. To destroy the German coastal battery at Merville, close to the mouth of the Orne.
3. To destroy the Dives Bridge between Troarn and the coast.

The capture of Pegasus Bridge across the River Orne was one of the first engagements of D-Day. It was a crucial mission, considered by many to be the turning point of World War Two. It is not known exactly where Archie landed that night, but he dropped safely and fought to secure positions essential for the success of the invasion. Early on June 10th 1944, he was shot and died from his wounds. He had just turned twenty.

Later that day, a telegram was delivered to Mrs. M. McKillop. Marie remembers hearing her father say, when he read the telegram, "How about this for a birthday present," but she didn't understand the implication at the time. She explained, "We did not 'do' adults' birthdays in our family, and I had never known when my parents' birthdays were." The neighbours, Marie's friends and Archibald's work colleagues learned straight away of Archie's death, but strangely, Martha did not immediately tell her father or sisters; nor did she and her husband talk about it with each other or with their daughter. Marie told me, "I did not find this surprising at the time. It just seemed impossible to say anything. But we were together in it. I did not feel isolated." Martha's silence, though seemingly hard to fathom, makes sense to me, for that was her nature. When she had been abused and then found she was pregnant, she had run away, unable to talk about it with her family. Now she escaped into herself and waited, for a delay would change nothing. Her son was dead.

Annie sensed that something was very wrong with Martha. Although the two sisters often visited each other, Annie felt that Martha needed her and decided she must move to Edinburgh to be nearby. There was no reason for her to remain in Glasgow, and she was sometimes lonely with just the company of her father – the move might be of benefit to them all. (This was another defining piece of evidence to support the notion that Granny possessed the Highlanders' sixth sense: Granny claimed that she knew Archie was dead before Martha told her, and it was that conviction which prompted her to move to Edinburgh. I suspect she guessed – it was, after all, so terribly likely.) Annie asked Martha to keep an eye out for a suitable house. Perhaps it helped Martha to be occupied, as she put her energies into the search and found an ideal house in the Portobello area of Edinburgh. Annie withdrew her savings from the Co-operative Bank to pay towards the deposit, and Martha was able to repay her debt to Annie by making up the remainder. The house was a detached, double-fronted property that Annie eventually ran as a boarding house.

Elizabeth's diaries continue in ignorance of Archie's death. There was a huge increase in air-raid warnings, gunfire, bombs and plane crashes over the next few weeks, during the day as well as the night. The Proms for the time being went ahead. Margaret and Elizabeth queued for many of the concerts and used the tin helmets they had been given for Fire Duty to sit upon in the arena. On one side of the conductor's rostrum was a red light, which flashed for air-raid warnings; on the other side a green one indicated the 'all clear'. The audience mostly ignored the red alerts: presumably the orchestra had no choice but to play on.

Germany launched the first V-1's into London on June 13th 1944. Two days later, 144 crossed the English coast, 72 exploding in Greater London. V-1's were pilotless bomb-carrying planes and the first guided missiles used in war. They became known as buzz bombs, robots or doodlebugs, the most terrifying moment being when the audible buzz of the engine stopped, at which point the missile went into its terminal dive.

June 18th 1944: We spot a pilotless plane being chased by a spitfire. We rush into the garden and get a marvellous view of it before it goes over the house. It is flying quite low and has flames coming out of the back. We rush to the front door and hear the engine stop and the explosion, which is a long way off. Listen to news reports – first live broadcasts from Normandy – thousands of Germans are trapped in Cherbourg peninsula – German radio is giving terrific prominence to the dreadful havoc caused by the pilotless planes. Collect sandwiches, blankets, cushions etc. and M. and I go on duty at 11. M. and I make a bed on the billiard table. We have just settled when Mr. Lerchenfeld comes and shows us the camp beds in the basement. We shift all our stuff downstairs and are nicely settled when we hear someone coming down the stairs. "It's only me!" booms the voice of a hearty young man who chats to us about pilotless planes, then leaves saying, "If you want any trouble I am just upstairs."
June 19th: A few explosions in the night. I learn that a plane fell in Tottenham Court Road at 12.50. We hear three robots coming over and rush between rooms to see them.
June 20th: Am awakened at 3.00 by a plane crashing and feel the house rock. Margaret comes into my bed and says it sounded as though it stopped right over the house. Gunfire wakes us later. There is a notice downstairs telling people to leave the top floor. M. brings her bed into my room. Another plane crashed in Kilburn.

Margaret received a letter from her mother asking that she and Elizabeth come home for a long weekend. Everyone who knew anyone living in London was becoming increasingly worried for their safety as the German air strikes escalated. The girls arrived in Wakefield late on Thursday night. In the morning, Margaret slipped into bed with Elizabeth. There were no sirens there. Elizabeth felt uncomfortable about Margaret getting into bed with her, but could not turn the poor girl away when she was "feeling very miserable and shivering all over." Margaret's need for comfort and protection – and perhaps something less definable – had been bothering Elizabeth for some time, but she could not find a way to put a stop to it. With little or no psychological understanding of those who were not straightforward, she was always bemused by complicated, unstable behaviour. Her response was to ignore it, hoping, I think, that patience and kindness would make it disappear. When Elizabeth and Margaret returned to London, the bombing was worse than ever. Here are some diary extracts from the next four days:

Siren goes while we are in the taxi. We have just got back to 43 when a buzz bomb drops. There were two or three bombs during my harmony lesson.
A buzz bomb comes over. M. and I duck between the beds. A bomb falls. The blast makes the front door rattle. Another bomb comes over. It is very near. After the explosion we see a cloud of black smoke rising. It fell in Finchley Road.
There is a traffic diversion and a cord across Finchley Road from Circus Road to the next crossing. We walk round the back. It's still smoking and the firemen are at it.
At 7.50 we hear a buzz bomb coming over. It sounded as though it was flying in circles around the house. It eventually fell and the black-out curtains are blown into the middle of the room and the door comes open. I go to the window and see the puff of smoke rising from Clifton Hill direction. My legs are wobbling so much I can't stand up. All windows out of flat opposite.
Quite a few of the shops have lost their windows as the result of the Mortimer Court

bomb. Go for a walk down Abbey Road to West End Lane and look at the damage. It is dreadful – very widespread with windows out a long way away.
I was wakened by buzz bombs. There were quite a lot and not very far away.

The bombardment continued and so did the Promenade concerts, until June 30th, when Elizabeth and Margaret turned up at the Albert Hall to discover that the Proms had been cancelled indefinitely.

At the beginning of July 1944[3], Martha received this letter:

No. 3/AAC/1/1. Army Form B. 104—82B.
(If replying, please quote above No.)

ARMY AIR CORPS Record Office,
EAST CLAREMONT STREET, EDINBURGH 7
1 July 1944.

Madam,

It is my painful duty to inform you that a report has been received from the War Office notifying the death of :—

(No.) 14515843 (Rank) Private

(Name) McKILLOP, Archibald,

(Regiment) ARMY AIR CORPS

which occurred in NORTH WEST EUROPE

~~on the~~ Date not yet known.

The report is to the effect that he was Killed in Action.

I am to express the sympathy and regret of the Army Council at the soldier's death in his Country's service.

I am,

Madam,

Your obedient Servant,

Mrs M. McKillop
18, Corstorphine Park Gardens,
EDINBURGH

[signature]

Major,

for Officer in Charge of Records.

(26738) Wt.52900/605 25,000 2/44 A.& E.W.Ltd. Gp.698 [P.T.O.

3. It was not until August 8th that a final communication from the AAC arrived containing the following words: "A further report has now been received stating that the soldier Died of Wounds on 10 June 1944 in North West Europe."

It was only then that Martha imparted the news to Annie. Just after lunch on Wednesday, July 5th, Daisy summoned Elizabeth downstairs to take a telephone call. Elizabeth's diary entry for that day matter-of-factly reports the chronological order of events. She describes her morning routine as usual until this extract appears after a siren is heard at half past twelve:

> Mammy telephones – she hasn't heard any word since I wrote from Wakefield and is terribly worried and asks me to come home as soon as possible. Archie has been killed. I tell Val. She is quite upset. I can't play Gwen's accompaniment. M. comes to the Academy with me to tell her. I ask Joan Hughes to do it for me. Walk in Queen Mary's gardens with M. till 2. They are glorious. All clear 1.45. Back to Academy. Wait for Victor. Tell him I am not coming to Monday lesson and may be going straight home. I start crying when I think about Archie and M. comes into my bed.

She was shaken to the core by the news. Archie, her fine and bonny cousin, her lovable, cheery, openhearted companion was dead; but she did not write of her feelings. Mum remembered the summer of 1944 as the one time when Londoners became demoralised. On July 6th, Winston Churchill reported to Parliament that 2,754 V-1 bombs had so far been launched against London, that "a very large proportion of these have either failed to cross the Channel, or have been shot down and destroyed by various methods" and that "2,752 casualties had been sustained" – the latter being war-speak for "people killed".

The RAM cancelled all the end of term concerts and distribution of prizes, and shut down after exam week. Everyone wanted to get away from London. The trains going out of the Capital were crammed to bursting point. Elizabeth and Margaret went to see Robert in Wales, who did not yet know of Archie's death. I can only assume that he could not be contacted by telephone, or perhaps Annie considered it better for him to hear the news from his sister rather than by telegram. The girls had to queue an hour for tickets and just managed to find a space in the corridor of the train where they were able to perch on their cases.

> Robert meets us at Cardiff and takes us home in his car. I tell him about Archie. We go out in the car to the top of Caerphilly Mountain where we get out and look at the view. We see across the Bristol Channel to Weston-super-mare in Somerset and Devon farther West. M. and Robert play the Bach double, then Paganini caprices and the Devil's Trill.

For the rest of their visit they accompanied Robert on his rounds. In the evenings, when Robert did not have office work or Fire Guard duty, they played and listened to music. At the end of the week Robert drove them to the station. Margaret departed for Leeds while Elizabeth headed back to London, tidied her room, and then took a taxi to Euston to catch the overnight train to Glasgow.

> There is a mad scramble for seats during which I am shoved on top of some cases and graze my leg. I get a seat by pure good luck. The carriage is packed from door to door in a few minutes. There are eight adults and seven children on eight seats and a sailor and soldier on the floor and another on top of the seats. I take a little girl on my knee and later on a baby. He is as good as gold and sleeps peacefully all night.

Annie was relieved to have her daughter home and spoilt her with breakfast in bed whenever she was not on the early shift. Marie arrived by herself from Edinburgh and stayed for ten days. Bombs fell on several occasions. Marie remembers getting up and sheltering in the "close mouth" – the ground floor entrance passage. The London air-raids must have affected Elizabeth. She writes: "It is very warm and sultry and neither of us can get to sleep – the windows rattle and aeroplanes make me imagine buzz-bombs. We take aspirins at 12.30." (She would still shudder when she heard the sound of air raid sirens in the 1970s TV comedy series *Dad's Army*.)

Elizabeth and Marie went for long walks together, taking flasks of tea and a 'piece' [*sandwiches*]. They visited a "very beautiful" Chinese Art Exhibition and went to the Embassy cinema to see 'The Sullivans', "at which," Elizabeth writes, "I weep more than I have done for a long time." At a fun fair on Glasgow Green, they "go on a plain roundabout, then the flying ships and the Waltzer. We are quite sick then and spend the rest of our money shoving pennies." But they did not talk about Archie. Marie told me: "It was just too awful. We didn't discuss Billy either – that was almost worse. It was good to be in Glasgow, though, and I loved being with Elizabeth, but she didn't tell me that she had spent time in London with Archie. I would have been happy to know that." Perhaps by being together, sorrow and heartache were wordlessly communicated. Maybe they remembered the best of times they had all shared on holiday before the war stole both Marie's brothers away.

When Elizabeth returned to London for her final year at the RAM, her lodging house was still standing and much the same, as were the sirens, splitting the air with their fearful, swooping howls. Coastal guns were succeeding in shooting down many V-1's over the Channel, whilst the Allied armies' rapid advance eastwards through France reached the launch sites, putting an end to the worst of the V-1 attacks. However, a potentially more serious threat was looming. In early October 1944, Germany fired their first two V-2 rockets, which arrived within sixteen seconds of each other, the first in Chiswick, West London and the second in Epping, north of the Capital. Unlike the V-1, the V-2 could be launched from any location using a small firing platform. Mobile carriers transported the missile horizontally to the chosen launch site, and then turned it to the vertical for firing. The V-2 could be launched within an hour and a half and the mobile unit on the move half an hour later. Once fired, the rocket took less than five minutes to reach its intended target. V-2s achieved speeds of 3,000mph, several times the speed of sound. They fell from the sky without warning and caused major destruction. Of the 1,190 that succeeded in leaving the launch pads, more than half fell short of London, but the five hundred that did drop in the Capital killed 2,724 people and injured 6,476 more.

Margaret's instability was more evident than ever before. She had not done well in her end of year exams. Her father, bitterly disappointed with the results, had harassed her all summer to work harder, insisting that she go back to the Academy and enter for the LRAM diploma. His refusal to acknowledge that his daughter was an unexceptional girl of average ability denied her the possibility of even moderate success. Elizabeth advised her not to take the LRAM, but Margaret had no choice but to submit to her father's wishes. Her anxiety was causing insomnia.

October 13th 1944: Siren about 12 and two more about 5 & 6.30. M. comes down about 6. She hasn't slept at all and has had three attacks of ague in the night. She lies in bed with me till 7.30
October 14th: Get ready for bed at 10.45. M. comes down ¼ of an hour later. She is in a panic about not sleeping and she has ague. She goes down to Doris who gives her 4 bromides. She comes into bed with me. I tell her that her ill-health is caused by her father and that something should be done about it before her sister Helen goes the same way. Daisy is giving her a cup of milk every night so I make her Ovaltine.
October 17th: Parcel from home with apple tart. M. nearly breaks down. She is feeling terribly depressed – we think it is the effect of the bromide.
October 22nd: M. is having a slight attack of rigor so stays in my room till it passes. Three V-2 rockets explode in the night, waking us all up.
October 30th: I am sound asleep when M. comes down about 12.30. She has rigor and can't sleep. She stays all night.
October 31st (Hallowe'en): A rocket in the night which wakes us up. Up at 7.30. Another rocket at 7.45 and siren about 8 during which there is another crash.
November 1st: M. goes down to fetch her milk and tells me Doris wants to see me. I go down and we talk about M. for 35 minutes. She says "M. will be lucky if she gets through the Graduate year without a breakdown". She tells me I must use my influence to make her more independent and bring out the fight in her. I have not to tell M. we have been talking about her. When I go upstairs, M. is as white as a sheet till I tell her we were talking about the Christmas party.
November 3rd: Jenny, Betty & I talk about M. They think it is most unfair the way M. clings to me and is so jealous of me.

Elizabeth travelled home to Edinburgh for the first time, now that her Mammy and Gran had completed their move to Portobello. The GPO agreed to transfer Annie to their Edinburgh site, where she continued to work shifts as a telegraphist until the house was ready to take in boarders. Gran was hardly ever mentioned in the diary, but he was there. His granddaughter became a bit fed up with him at times when he took over 'the room' and she had to wait for him to leave before she could listen to the wireless or do her cello practice. He annoyed her when he was "too lazy" to fetch the milk or bread and she was pleased when he was out on the bowling green or at whist drives. Robert arrived home from Glamorgan on December 22nd in time to enjoy a Christmas Eve dinner of gosling and dumpling cooked by Martha.

Gran arrives late when we have all finished. I play for Mammy and Robert. Before I play the Chopin Ballade, I ask Gran to stop turning his pages so noisily while I'm playing. He didn't and I am furious.
Christmas Day 1944: Mammy is home from the early shift at 12.15. Marie and Uncle Archie come about 12.30. Auntie Martha comes later because she has been to see Billy. Dinner at 1.30. Mutton, mince balls and peas, apple tart, plums and custard. We play knock out whist and Pelmanism and go along to the pictures to see 'Come and get it' starring Edward Arnold and Frances Farmer.
December 30th My birthday (20): Marie comes and we go for a walk along to Musselburgh. Auntie Martha arrives and we sit in the room talking about Psychology. I give them the Introvert/Extrovert test. Auntie Martha is very extrovert, Mammy is nearer the medium mark and Marie is too young yet to judge.

Marie had turned fourteen in October. I pick up from the diary that she was very unhappy at this time. On the last day of 1944, Elizabeth writes: "Marie feels sick and is terribly low and depressed." The whole family must have been silently, separately grieving for Archie, and also for Billy.

Billy had been in hospital for several years with no noticeable relief or improvement from profound depression. His parents were advised that he might benefit from surgery. Frontal lobotomy, it was explained, is an operation on the brain whereby the frontal lobes – the parts of the brain that trigger emotional response – are severed from the rest of the brain. It would cure his depression, they were told, and allow him to lead a normal life: well almost. With no clear information available as to the effects of frontal lobotomy and wanting so desperately to see Billy free from depression and to have him back home, they agreed to the operation. At the time, frontal lobotomy was the last remaining option available that could, they hoped, release Billy from his terminal nightmare.

The Billy who materialised from the anaesthetic had to be cared for ever afterwards – by his mother, Martha, until her death in 1974, and then by his sister, Marie. The surgery did succeed in eliminating his depression, but it removed a great deal more besides. Yet, as Marie reflected, was it not worse to be incarcerated in a psychiatric hospital, suffering in a way that most of us are incapable of imagining? At least he was back with his family, and later able to take simple jobs. A few years after his operation, encouraged by his mother, Billy started to paint again. It was different from his earlier work – much looser and more impressionistic. His technical ability to draw seemed to be the connecting factor between his two selves. To me, his paintings convey an expressiveness, sensitivity and touch of emotion that defies the surgical destruction. But of course it was war that destroyed Billy and war that deprived him of the life he could have lived. Billy died aged eighty-nine in 2009.

By the New Year of 1945, the Allies were becoming increasingly confident of victory. With the German forces irreparably damaged by Hitler's last great show of strength in 'The Battle of the Bulge', the British, American and French armies pushed onwards into Germany, while the mighty Soviet armies, after their massive drive into Poland, were poised to attack the Eastern frontier. The V-2 attacks on London ended in March 1945 as the advancing Allied armies forced the missile transporters to retreat deep into Germany. This put London out of range of the rocket, but V-2s were still targeted on other cities such as Antwerp and Rotterdam while the Allied armies continued relentlessly in their goal of defeating Nazi Germany.

January 18th 1945: Lunch in my room with M. Talk till 2 about what M. is going to do next year. Her father wants her to use her State Scholarship and go to University. M. knows exactly what she herself wants to do but she lets her father take the upper hand all the time. Practise piano before and after dinner till 9. M. comes down at 9 & we make timetables for ourselves. I again try to impress upon her the disadvantages of coming down to breakfast at 8.45. She loses 2 hours work per week but it doesn't worry her. Her mind seems more and more childish.
February 14th: A rocket falls just as the bus turns into Baker St. It sounds quite close.

March 3rd 1945: Sirens and bumps in the night which I hear vaguely.
April 26th: All this week the Russians have been gradually encircling and occupying Berlin.
May 2nd: HITLER IS DEAD
May 4th: News gets better and better. Capitulation any day now.
May 5th: The Germans have now completely surrendered to British and American troops. Denmark, Holland and Belgium are free. The last "war report" is broadcast.
May 7th: It is a marvellous day – just right for Victory. The wireless says tomorrow is VE day.
May 8th: Watch the flags being put up from my window – a Union Jack on each bathroom balcony, a Russian flag on J's and an American one on mine. Daisy lends me a big bowl and I make the trifle (cake, dried peaches, plums, raisins, prunes, custard and milk chocolate). Listen to Mr. Churchill at 3 followed by descriptions of the crowds in London, Edinburgh, Belfast and Cardiff. King's speech at 9.00pm then we all depart by tube to Trafalgar Square. We join a procession heading for Admiralty Arch towards the Palace. We arrive and wait till 10.50, shouting "We want the King" and sing and cheer when they put the floodlights on and groan when they turn them off. A Canadian perched on top of one of the statues leads the chant "1-2-3-4-Who are we waiting for G-E-O-R-G-E, George!" The Royal family come out and the cheering is terrific. We walk down Birdcage Walk to Westminster. Central Hall is in lovely orange lights and Big Ben looks marvellous. Onto Westminster Bridge. The County Hall is lit in green and white. Back up Whitehall, across Piccadilly and up Regent Street. People are dancing on top of air-raid shelters and any vehicles are almost invisible for people. Along Oxford Street, to the Academy and home through Regents Park. M. asks me to take her upstairs – she has worn herself out. I get her off to bed and go down to lounge and dance 'Dashing White Sergeant' and quicksteps.

It was Victory in Europe, but defeat for Margaret. She had failed her LRAM.

Students at 43, Marlborough Place, St. Johns Wood.
ABOVE: Mum, Kathleen, Margaret, Ivor
RIGHT: Margaret Whittlestone and Mum
BELOW: Margaret BELOW RIGHT: Val

Archie McKillop
April 2nd 1924 - June 10th 1944
Paratrooper in the Army Air Corps
Killed in action in WWII aged twenty.

BUCKINGHAM PALACE

The Queen and I offer you our heartfelt sympathy in your great sorrow.

We pray that your country's gratitude for a life so nobly given in its service may bring you some measure of consolation.

George R.I.

BELOW: Archie's grave in Ranville British Cemetery, France. This photograph of the temporary cross marking his grave was sent to Archie's parents soon after their son's death. A few years later, all of the servicemen's graves were set with engraved headstones.

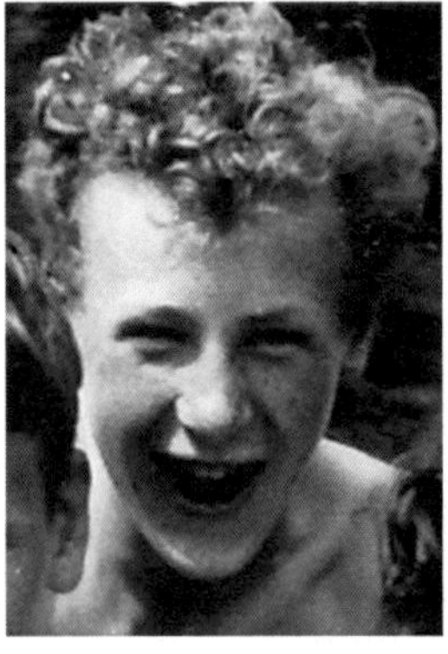

37
JENEFER CARLYON

I am the tide forever returning
Over these long yellow sands.

Jenefer Carlyon

In June 1945, towards the end of Elizabeth's final year, Jenefer Carlyon moved into Marlborough Place. The Carlyon family owned a substantial estate on the Cornish coast near St. Austell, which encompassed long stretches of coastland, including Carlyon Bay, said to be one of the finest beaches in south Cornwall. Jenefer grew up on the estate, which had belonged to the family since 1565, and lived in its magnificent house, Tregrehan. She was the third of five children. The youngest was the only boy, the son her mother doted upon, who was simply called 'Boy'.

Jenefer immediately befriended Elizabeth. Margaret Whittlestone she ignored. Margaret had been Elizabeth's faithful companion for more than two years. She not only depended on Elizabeth but also, it seems clear, worshipped her. That they were friends, lived in the same house and shared a daily routine was perhaps happiness enough for Margaret. Jenefer's arrival put an end to it.

> **June 13th 1945:** Meet Jenefer at June's room. She wants to know what to wear to go to Franny Osborne's. I make her change into a dress then we go together in bus. M. comes home about 8.30 tired out. Jenefer bounces in to say she will come 'in a jiff' to hear my Brahms. She comes at 5 to 9. Play Brahms and most of 1st mvt. of Emperor to please her. M. feels sick – she goes up to her room and brings up all her dinner. She goes to bed. Jenefer showed me a lot of her poems – they are absolutely marvellous. I get ready for bed & read her poems till she comes back just before 11. Make Ovaltine & talk till 12.15.

Jenefer lost no time in informing Elizabeth that Margaret was in love with her. Elizabeth was quite taken aback. It hadn't occurred to her that Margaret's feelings for her were anything more than fondness. As Mum told me, "Jenefer put me straight about Margaret. She could see at once what was going on." Jenefer's apparent worldliness, her knowing, enigmatic comments about lesbianism and sex dented Mum's self-assurance. From the way Mum conveyed this incident, I believe that she felt suddenly gauche; embarrassed that Jenefer saw her as gullible and naive. Margaret had deceived her and she, Elizabeth, had been taken for an ignorant fool. I wonder if it occurred to Mum that Margaret was probably just as innocent about lesbianism as she was. Her feelings for Mum could, I think, be better described as an adolescent crush. Forgetful of Margaret's devotion and the occasions when her company had been of comfort, Elizabeth all at once saw Margaret in a different, sullied light.

> **June 14th:** M. comes home in a worse state than last night. Jenefer comes up to hear my Brahms. M. visibly stiffens when she comes in – she is quite green with jealousy. Play Brahms and Chopin Polonaise. Jenefer goes and M. has an attack of rigor and clings to

> me like a lover. I get her upstairs and leave her to go to bed. Have a bath. I ask Jenefer in & we talk about M. & me & her.
> **June 15th 1945:** M. is home earlier tonight. She comes into my room and stays for a while putting me off. She has a bath & I go into Jenefer's room & take her a drink. She shows me a lovely book of modern poetry with wonderful illustrations for 'The Ancient Mariner'. To bed at 11.30.

Within a few days, Elizabeth was calling Jenefer by her nickname, 'Batty'. Margaret's tummy upsets and shivering attacks no longer solicited Elizabeth's sympathy: instead, it was Jenefer who received her undivided attention. The routines changed. Lunch and tea was now taken with Batty. Elizabeth not only made Jenefer night-time mugs of Ovaltine, but also pandered to her needs by tucking her into bed. The diary is full of comments about her:

> Batty interrupts my practise and I give her a lesson on Solfeggietto. Give her some help with harmony until 7. Batty comes back from concert. Have Ovaltine & read till 11.30 while she draws a cat for George's birthday.
> To Augener's for music for Batty. Get tea ready and have it in garden with Batty.
> Batty washes her hair in my room & listens while I practise piano. Give Batty lesson on Brahms G min Rhapsody & she practises in my room till 6. Out to buffet with Batty & sit watching people till 10. She starts telling stories about herself & family & Cornwall.
> Play Chopin Polonaise to Batty & give her a lesson. She does ironing & I finish it for her.

After just two weeks' acquaintance, Jenefer proposed to Elizabeth that they should leave Marlborough Place and share a bed-sit together after the summer holidays. Elizabeth accepted.

> **June 26th:** Daisy calls me down and has a tête-à-tête with me. I say I shall be leaving. She asks about M. but I don't know and care less what she does. She also discussed Batty.

What was said about Batty is not disclosed. Maybe Daisy was not so taken with her. Elizabeth, however, seems to have been almost mesmerised. Perhaps Jenefer's fascination with telepathy, mysticism and psychic phenomena was part of the magnetism. Mum told me that Jenefer confided "strange and unaccountable" things to her – things Jenefer had experienced that defied explanation; visions she saw of the future that turned out exactly as she had predicted.

Spiritualism was in vogue at the time and Elizabeth had gone along with fellow students to several Spiritualist meetings. To her diary she declared, "of course it's all nonsense", but there was something about Jenefer's premonitions that she could not dismiss so easily. Disturbingly, Jenefer was convinced that she would die before she reached the age of thirty-five. She was certainly not a straightforward character. Her personality drew people she needed to her, but she was capricious and egotistical. She showed little sensitivity towards others, but demanded a great deal of attention for herself. There were occasions when she arranged to meet Elizabeth and then failed to turn up: or asked her out and then changed her mind at the last minute. She often let Elizabeth down. Perhaps because of this, it wasn't long before Margaret was back in the picture. Although she never again climbed into Elizabeth's bed for comfort, she must have found a way to deal with the situation to ensure that she was not entirely cast out of Elizabeth's life. All three went together to the RAM Club meeting. Elizabeth sat next to her cello teacher, Alison Dalrymple, who pointed out Pablo Casals to her:

> – a sweet little man with a pipe. Sir Stanley welcomes him and he makes a little speech in broken English. The Griller quartet play Bloch and Haydn – absolutely perfect! We stay a long time afterwards watching Casals congratulating the Grillers. It's all terribly thrilling.

They waited outside the Academy to watch Casals get into his car just as Mr. Churchill and his entourage happened to be driving along the Marylebone Road. Everyone stopped to wave. When they looked around, Jenefer was standing right next to Casals, shaking his hand.

> Daisy kept supper for us. Up to my room and we compose a letter to Casals & enclose our programme to be autographed (M, Batty & I). I go out and post it. Get ready for bed. M. goes and Batty stays talking. I make her some Oxo. I have to kiss her goodnight when I tuck her in.

It seems clear that Elizabeth was as uneasy about Jenefer's need to be mothered as she was about Margaret's. Both were unstable and needy – the type of person whom Elizabeth would repeatedly attract. But as usual, she went along with it, reluctant to cause disappointment and too well-mannered to protest.

> **July 1st**: After breakfast Batty comes in with a book on palmistry which she and M. and I read till 11.
> **July 3rd**: Go to Albert Hall with M. and Batty. M. and I are in 21/- complimentarys right opposite the orchestra. Charles Münch conducting – Overture Egmont, Brahms violin concerto (Ginette Neveu)[1], Ravel Tzigane (violin and orch.) and Bolero. Band of Royal Horse Guards play some fanfares. Queen Mary is there. We join the crowd and watch Queen Mary leaving. Round to the artist's door. Pluck up courage and go in. Stand outside artist's room for a while watching Ginette changing her shoes. Go in and get her autograph.

Elizabeth heard that she had won the Henry Eyres Aural Training prize, having gained full marks at the highest level. She writes: "I couldn't believe it till I went down to notice board." (Mum told me that an Academy professor looked at the results and commented rather dismissively, "Well, you must have perfect pitch." She replied, "No, I don't." "Then how did you do it?" he asked. "I used Sol-fa," she told him. Apparently, he laughed in a sneering sort of way, implying, Mum thought, that Sol-fa was a joke and she must be lying. It was an incident which, when remembered, would always rouse her indignation.)

1. Ginette Neveu was a brilliant French violinist. After winning the Wieniawski Competition in 1935 when she was sixteen, she toured Europe, the Soviet Union, the USA and Canada, until the Second World War halted her international career. The concert she gave on July 3rd 1945 at the Albert Hall was her London debut. It was also the only performance she would ever give in Britain, as she and her pianist brother, Jean-Paul, both died in a plane crash on October 28th 1949 on their way to the USA.

July 6th 1945: Out with Batty. Up to buffet and sit till 10. Talk to woman beside us – Mrs. Hickmott from Oxford – who reads our hands. I am going to be happily married to someone who will be very fond of me. I have a very good hand and a fine character.
July 8th: Tea in my room. We sit talking till 7.40 when M. comes and interrupts our serious discussion in her usual childish way. Have a bath and then brush Batty's hair.
July 10th: Batty enthusiastically tries to 'do' something with M's hair. It is the usual dismal failure. Daisy is on the prowl just after 11. She catches Priscilla in Jean's room. Batty is in my room and hides under the bed but Daisy doesn't come in.
July 16th: M. & I have tea in my room. Practise piano. Batty comes in and washes her hair & we do Times crossword. We are going dancing. I comb my hair out. To Astoria after dinner. Get quite a lot of dances and do some jitterbug with Batty. A Frenchman asks me to dance then we have lemonade. He says we must get out and have a proper drink. The pubs are closed so go to his flat. I look at his drawings and we have a glass of wine and talk about music and art. He is a Professor. He makes love to me [*flirts*] but doesn't actually seduce me as I don't want it. Talk till nearly 1. He rings up for a car. I creep upstairs. Daisy and Doris are still up and Daisy's living room light is on, but I am sure they don't hear me. I can't sleep very well for thinking too much. Wake at 7.00 and go into Batty's room at 7.30. She is very sceptical about my Professor, but I enjoyed it and don't care what the others think. Doris calls me down to her room after breakfast and her first words are "Where did you sleep last night?" I felt furiously angry, but couldn't convince her I wasn't lying because she said I still wasn't in at 2.30. She gives me a lecture about murderers, drug fiends, prostitutes etc.

The Frenchman's name was Claude Happé, although whether he was a Professor is questionable. She met him for lunch the next day at the Cara Prada in Euston Road, before allowing herself to be taken back to his flat. And then they did make love, which for Elizabeth was the first time.

July 17th: He loves me and I love him. It is wonderful. I go out for rolls & he makes coffee. I tell him about M. & Batty. He says they are only two of many neurotics in this country as a result of lack of sex or bad lovemaking.

I suspect that Batty was rather miffed by Elizabeth's sudden infatuation. Claude, unlike Margaret, was serious competition. Batty's course of action was to get involved. When Elizabeth next met Claude, Batty went too.

July 19th: We arrive at last about 4. Claude and Batty argue for ages about all sorts of things – most amusing. I ring Daisy to say we are out for supper. He says he will sketch us in the nude. I undress first and he draws me. After a lot of persuasion Batty also undresses. Then he sketches us lying together – it is the best one. We all lie on couch together. He has marvellous control. He caresses us both but goes no further. I can't stand it much longer and at 10.00 we go into the bedroom and make love. Batty disturbs us at 10.30 and we go home.

A strange, three-cornered affair ensued, with Batty and Claude goading each other into the rousing heat of argument and Elizabeth seemingly supplying the demands of both. This part of Mum's diary was obviously the "purple bit" that she had been reluctant to let me see. It certainly revealed an aspect of Mum that I had not imagined.

Her lack of inhibition surprised me – she appeared to be self-assured and at ease – someone without hang-ups. Yet despite her apparent sexual confidence, she was, I feel, an innocent. Her gameness to undress showed an almost childlike unawareness of her own vulnerability. Mum's instinctive kindness, her trusting, helpful nature, her sense and capability, exposed her time and again to manipulation by others.

The following week it was Prize Giving Day and Elizabeth's last day at the Royal Academy of Music. Margaret had failed her degree, but went faithfully to watch her friend graduate and receive her aural training prize. Elizabeth took one look at the certificate, saw that her name had been spelt incorrectly – Frazer instead of Fraser – and promptly gave it back to be altered. It was the last time that she would have to borrow a long white dress – in fact she would never wear such a garment again. She kept the sash of broad, red ribbon – which she would one day give to me to wear. Straight after the ceremony, she rushed off to see Claude. He made love to her and then they had supper at the Shanghai restaurant in Soho.

Term ended. Margaret went home to Wakefield, Batty to Cornwall. Then it was time for Elizabeth to say goodbye to Daisy and Doris and leave 43, Marlborough Place for good. She spent her last two days in London at Claude's flat, before departing for Edinburgh on August 3rd.

> Claude is very tired and doesn't get up. He is almost too sleepy to open his eyes and say goodbye. Leave at 8.55. I'll miss him terribly.

Back in Edinburgh, she missed her period. In her diary she always wrote an 'X' to indicate when each period began. By August 28th it was two weeks overdue.

> **August 30th 1945:** The fear of pregnancy is awful. Decide to tell Robert my fears & see a doctor tomorrow. Can't eat much supper.
> **August 31st:** Wake at 4. Can't sleep much more for worrying. X. What a blessed relief!

Margaret visited Elizabeth in Scotland for the last time. It feels from the diary that they enjoyed their final episode together, that their mismatched friendship was still possible in as far it had ever been. I sense that Margaret had harvested some strength from somewhere, as there were no more references to nerves or sickness. She remained at the Academy for another year, passed her degree and graduated. Courageously, she went against her father's wishes for the first time and refused to go to university. Instead, she applied for a job as a music teacher in a girls' boarding school in Surrey and was given the position. She and Elizabeth corresponded for a while, but after a few years lost touch. I hope that Margaret was fulfilled in her work and found some happiness. She may have been rather pathetic, but it was she who walked with Elizabeth in Queen Mary's Garden after the awful news of Archie's death, she who attended Elizabeth's graduation and she who, throughout their relationship, maintained a steadfast loyalty and endured unrequited love. Through Mum's diaries, I grew to like her and I respected the dignity she found at the end. Oddly, I wish that Mum had shown more sensitivity, more passion, but I realise I am being unfair: Mum was Margaret's carer and companion by default more than by choice: she showed patience, even tenderness, to a rather lost person who had little to offer back. It seems to me that Mum was not a lead character in the play of life. She took the supporting roles, while others took centre stage. It wasn't she who received the attention, nor was it she who threw tantrums or had nervous breakdowns. She was passive about friendships; she did not create or direct them, but adapted to others' needs and demands, yielding to their moods and personalities. She was not submissive, but at the same time did not make an impact on people. Mum said of her student days: "I was largely ignored at the Academy. Once I met a woman who had been at the Academy at the same time as I was. She barely recognised me, then she remembered – 'Oh yes. You were the one who was *always* practising!' Well of course I was: isn't that what music students should be doing?"

That summer of 1945, the USA dropped two atomic bombs on Japan. The first, a Uranium bomb known as Little Boy weighing 9,000lbs, was delivered by parachute above the city of Hiroshima on the morning of August 6th. In his photographic documentary book, *World War II*, the author Ivor Matanle writes: "The blast, equal to 17,000 tons of TNT, and the firestorm that it raised, completely flattened almost everything for 4.7 miles around the point directly below the explosion. Two thirds of the buildings within 9.5 square miles were either destroyed or seriously damaged. Between 60,000 and 80,000 people died either immediately or in the weeks that followed. Another 70,000 suffered terrible injuries. Over 20,000 children were killed." The second, a Plutonium bomb known as Fat Boy, was dropped on Nagasaki on August 9th. The blast was even greater than that of the Uranium bomb, with an equivalent explosive force to 20,000 tons of TNT, but because of the more hilly geography of Nagasaki, it did slightly less damage. I quote Ivor Matanle: "…but it should not be forgotten that the real total killed and injured for both nuclear attacks was very much higher than the figures for immediate casualties suggest. The subsequent radiation sickness and high incidences of cancers, congenitally abnormal births, spontaneous abortion and other conditions greatly increased the total casualties over a period of twenty or thirty years and even now, the final genetic effects cannot be fully known."

I quote again from Winwood Reade's *The Martyrdom of Man* published in 1872:

> It is not probable that War will ever cease until science discovers some destroying force, so simple in its administration, so horrible in its effects that all art, all gallantry, will be at an end, and battles will be massacres which the feelings of mankind will be unable to endure.

38
MARRIAGES

In September 1945, Elizabeth, her piano, and Batty moved into a bed-sit in Belsize Square, Swiss Cottage. Elizabeth had taken a part-time job as a music teacher at Beltane Boarding School in Melksham, Wiltshire. In London, she continued with some of the jobs that had supplemented her student grant by playing piano for ballet classes and choirs and accompanying singers and instrumentalists. She also began to have private piano lessons with James Ching, at last finding somebody who could really teach. It made her realise how mediocre the piano tuition she had received at the RAM had been. James Ching recognised Elizabeth's considerable talent and gave her the praise and encouragement she so rightly deserved. Her playing matured and flourished, unlike her relationship with Claude, which rapidly cooled. He was invited over for a meal, but Elizabeth reports:

> I feel very tired and can't be bothered with him. I play the piano a bit. Claude barely speaks and eventually goes off with hardly a word. He behaves like a spoilt child. I don't know what's wrong with him except that he's jealous of Batty.

Claude disappeared from their lives. Batty and Elizabeth settled into their room, getting used to living together. It seems that Elizabeth did all the accommodating:

> Batty comes back with an awful youth, Stan, who she picked up on Hampstead Heath. He doesn't say a word and I feel very uncomfortable as well as annoyed.

Elizabeth's diary stops for some unknown reason three weeks later with no more entries for a year. I have the impression that she became a little disenchanted with Batty, whose neurotic, demanding personality was probably too much to endure in a shared bed-sit. By the following summer, Batty had moved out, but the two remained friends and Elizabeth spent several subsequent holidays with her in Cornwall.

Elizabeth went home to Edinburgh at the end of the academic year. In August 1946, aged twenty-one, she gave a broadcast on the Scottish Home Service of the BBC, performing a recital of Bach and Debussy, which was well received. On September 19th 1946, she resumed writing in her diary. She was still renting the bed-sit in Belsize Square, but now her cousin Ailsa was her room-mate. Ailsa and her mother, Bessie, had been compassionately demobbed from the Canadian Army (as Bessie's husband Hal was to have a thyroid operation) and returned to England at the end of 1944. Ailsa, entitled to an ex-service grant, applied to the London School of Economics. A few days after arriving in London, she went for an interview and was offered a place. The cousins decided to move house, as the landlady had begun to object about Elizabeth practising and threatened to put up the rent. They soon found a nicer room nearby in Eton Avenue. Ailsa writes:

It was in the autumn of 1946 that I came to live with my cousin Elizabeth in Swiss Cottage when I was a first year undergraduate at LSE. We had one large room with a thin pink carpet, a gas fire, two divan beds, a couple of chairs and the main feature – Elizabeth's piano. On the floor beside the fire was a gas ring for cooking. Rationing was still very much in force. As a matter of tactics, I had a vegetarian ration book. This produced a significant lump of cheese each week and some cashew nuts. Elizabeth's ration gave us one (or was it two?) lamb chops. I think we each had one egg a week, and perhaps one or two sausages. The biggest food problem was the half-pint of milk every other day, which was the meagre entitlement. I was deputed to do the food shopping while Elizabeth did the cooking. We had a household purse into which we very scrupulously put the right number of pennies every week. Elizabeth was a genius at preparing meals on the one small gas ring. With a few bones from the butcher, which were off ration, she would boil up a stock every week and prepare a large Scotch broth with lots of vegetables. She also made sure that we cleaned properly. We didn't run to luxuries like a vacuum cleaner; we kept our tealeaves and sprinkled them damp on to the carpet before getting down to sweep with a dustpan and brush.

That winter of 46/47 was very bitter. I remember that it was still snowing in April. The whole British economy was in crisis as transport of coal from the mines broke down. The gas fire was reduced to a little row of blue flames along the bottom. Fortunately for me, the LSE seemed to manage to have some heating, so I survived most of the week by staying there during the day and eating in the refectory, or at the Lyons Tea Shop on the corner of Lincoln's Inn Fields. Elizabeth was doing a part-time teaching job at a school in Wiltshire and was away from Sunday till mid-week. When she was home, she had to do her piano practice with a hot water bottle on her lap under a rug, taking turns with left and right hand playing.

Elizabeth's Diary: Go with Ailsa to Piccadilly theatre to see Vivien Leigh in 'Skin of our Teeth'. Very funny. Most unusual play I have ever seen. Thoroughly enjoyed it. Sit talking about telepathy, the Universe, flying to the moon etc. Listen to the BBC Dancing Club and show Ailsa some steps. Give her a music lesson on keys and harmonics then we do our French lesson together. Parcel from Mammy with tin of marmalade, dates and oatcakes. Do the Times crossword together, cook dinner and listen to 'Week in Westminster' while we wash up. Hear Mr. Attlee's speech at the Lord Mayor's Banquet. We sit talking. Ailsa tells me she has a feeling she is in the world with a mission and expounds some of H. G. Wells' and G. B. Shaw's ideas. Mammy writes that Robert wants to be married at Christmas.

Robert was still living and working in Wales and had met Lily Waters, a girl in the Land Army. They married in January 1947 in Penarth near Cardiff. Robert took a job as head gardener at Dale Park, an estate near Arundel, where a cottage in the grounds came with the job. Their daughter Anne was born in October 1947. Soon after, they moved to Huntingdonshire, where Robert worked at a Borstal institution. Later he was the gardening instructor at a Boys' Approved School in Warwickshire. He and his family lived there for many years. They had one more child, a boy called Huw David, born twelve years after Anne.

It was through Ailsa that Mum met her first husband, Bill Stewart, who was also a student at the LSE. She and Bill went out together for the first time to the Leicester Square Theatre and queued to see *The Best Years of our Lives* starring

Frederick March, Myrna Loy, and Dana Andrews. The following Friday they visited the National Gallery, walked in St. James' Park and had tea at the Lyons Corner House in Piccadilly. The next day she wrote in her diary:

> Walk along to Drury Lane Theatre for 7.00 to see an American musical, 'Oklahoma!' We hold hands. I've never been so much in love before. Have gin and orange in interval. Walk along Embankment hand in hand. Tube to Swiss Cottage from Charing X. Walk around streets and finally sit at top of Lancaster Grove. He kisses me and holds my breast. Says goodnight in porch at 11.50. I don't sleep very well for thinking of him. Bill arrives at 10.15 the next morning. We have coffee then sit on the couch. I suggest going to bed. He is impotent still after his operation, but I love him so much it doesn't matter. We lie on my bed for a while then sit on the couch in each other's arms. We would be utterly happy if I didn't have to go to school and Bill wasn't going home to Scotland a week on Monday.
>
> I can now hardly believe it is true that I am loved and in love. We have the same feelings about things and the same attitude to life. We were both brought up in Scotland and lived 'up a close' [*in the tenements*], he with even more accent on care with money. His roots are in the Clyde and Scotland, but he feels its limitations, especially with his own people. He has a great fear of poverty, as his father was unemployed for 9 years. He is more nervous and temperamental than I am and gets depressed probably because of an unsettled home. His parents used to fight and his father got drunk. He is conscious of lack of breeding and 'savoir faire', which I have acquired – and he will also with a few more years in London. He has a sense of inferiority because of his impotence but I feel sure I can help him in that. His only experience of women is in the army in brothels but now he is changing his attitude since he has known me.

On Friday evening, June 27th, less than two weeks after they had first met, Bill asked her to marry him.

> He gets me all passionate and excited but he still can't satisfy me… We go to Regent's Park and sit in deckchairs in the rose garden till 7.30 making plans about our marriage and telling each other about our families. Bill tells me in French his various experiences with prostitutes. His French accent is very good and he also talks a bit in German.

On Sunday evening they kissed goodbye at the ticket barrier and she boarded the train back to Wiltshire, engaged. Bill went home to Scotland. They did not see each other for two months.

> My first letter from Bill with his passport photo in it. I have his photo always beside me when I practise, cook and go to bed. I feel like crying because he is so far away.

Mum pinpointed Bill's weaknesses immediately – nervous, temperamental, socially awkward, depressive, and sexually insecure. She knew he had lived an impoverished, deprived childhood and had grown up in a violent home, yet she didn't heed the warning signs.

While Elizabeth was absorbed with love, Ailsa was considering the idea of buying a house. It seemed economically defeating to pay inflated rent to a landlord if an equivalent or lower sum could instead become a mortgage repayment. She wanted to find somewhere big enough to house seven or eight people. Ailsa writes:

> On the floor above us were a newly married young couple: John was a Jamaican and his wife, Sylvia, an English girl. Sylvia was expecting a baby, and the owner of the house had warned them that they would not be acceptable there after the baby was born. I had been to visit some friends who lived near Leytonstone. At the time, Leytonstone was the terminus of the London Central Line. It occurred to me that if one were prepared to move out of central London to the end of the tube line one might be able to buy a cheaper house requiring a smaller deposit. I felt that my parents might be cajoled into purchasing such a house on which we could pay rent and would also be able to offer accommodation to Sylvia and John.

Marie arrived for a holiday in London at the end of July and stayed with her cousins in their one room. Elizabeth was now twenty-two, Ailsa just twenty and Marie, sixteen. Together they travelled by tube to Leytonstone to look at houses. They viewed 133, Whipps Cross Road, priced at £1,150, and were so taken with it that they walked back to the agents and put down a holding deposit of £10 then and there. Ailsa's parents came up with the purchase deposit and within a week, the house was bought.

A month later, Elizabeth's diary came to an end. Her last entry was on September 3rd 1947. Why did she keep a diary? What prompted her to so conscientiously and truthfully report the details of her days? Did she imagine that one day it would be read and its contents would inspire speculation? Unable to evaluate her feelings, she perhaps hoped that her words would supply enough clues to lead a reader to discover the Elizabeth that she herself did not know, and to empathise with her. I suspect there is some truth in this for most diarists – a desire, whether conscious or unconscious, to be known, to be seen and accepted. Her diary was like a message in a bottle, and through reading it I absorbed an understanding of her.

Ailsa, Elizabeth and Bill, Sylvia and John, and another couple moved into 133, Whipps Cross Road. Elizabeth and Bill married at the Essex Register Office on June 19th 1948 followed by a small reception at the house. Guests included Elizabeth's and Bill's mothers and Jenefer Carlyon. Margaret Whittlestone was not present. Marie remained in Edinburgh to finish her schooling. Encouraged by Ailsa, she too gained herself a place at the London School of Economics and lived at Whipps Cross Road during her second undergraduate year of 1949-50. In 1950, Ailsa met and fell in love with Frank Land. It wasn't long before he too moved in. They married in 1952 and are still enjoying their lives together. After Marie graduated, she met her future husband, Mike Smith. They married in 1954 and continue to have a successful, happy partnership.

Elizabeth's wedded bliss did not last long. Her attempts to help her husband gain confidence only highlighted his insecurity; her capability magnified his inadequacy; his sense of powerlessness resulted in verbal aggression and physical violence. Jealous of the time she spent practising, he dictated that when he was in, she was not to play. But no matter how hard Elizabeth tried to compromise, it made no difference. Bill's violence escalated. Elizabeth fought back. Never imagining that her physical strength would be put to the test, she found she could land a few punches herself; but it was degrading and undignified. She was appalled that her marriage had reached such a level of debasement.

Despite the domestic strife, she maintained her practice and gave a number of piano recitals: a Brahms programme in 1949 at the Wigmore Hall, which included the virtuosic *Variations on a Theme of Paganini*, a performance of works by Chopin at Chowdray Hall, a Bach concert at Toynbee Hall in 1950 (marking the bicentenary of Bach's death) and a Scarlatti recital at Canterbury Cathedral.

It was at the end of 1951 that our Granny, well aware that her daughter's marriage was a failure, made her move to London. She stayed at Whipps Cross Road while she looked for a house to buy. Her father, Gran, who had lived with her since she married Davie in 1922, moved in with his middle daughter, Martha. He had been unwell for some time. On February 4th 1952, a few weeks before 32, Cleveland Road was purchased, he died, aged eighty-five. Through writing this book I feel I now know something of my great-grandfather – a boy born to Protestant parents who thought his way out of religious dogma; a lad who played the Irish fiddle, who started working for the GPO when he was fifteen; a young man who fell in love with Annie Glass, but enjoyed only five years of her companionship before she died; a widower who had to relinquish his baby daughter, Bessie, to be brought up by his brother and sister; a desperate father who searched high and low for Martha when she ran away pregnant, who found and rescued her; and a well-read man who delighted in solving crosswords and chess problems, played golf, bowls and cards.

Mum remembered him trying to teach his grandchildren how to play Whist and getting furious with them for larking around. She also remembered being scared at night and Gran comforting her, telling her that Mammy would be home soon. For Robert, he was a grandfather who stepped in for the missing father. Marie described him on holiday, swimming in the sea with his large belly sticking out above the water and his grandchildren laughing and calling him the Loch Ness monster. He was rather too fond of his drink, there was a slightly selfish side to him, but he had a good heart, a cheerful nature and even photographs of him in later life show a sparkle in his eye, the residue of the dashing young man he once was.

As has already been reported at the beginning of this book, Mum left Bill Stewart as soon as Granny moved into Cleveland Road – only to trap herself in another utterly miserable marriage a few years later.

When we were four and Chris, two, Mum and Dad took us on holiday to Cornwall. We stayed at Tregrehan with Jenefer and her two children – Nicola, aged seven, and Tristram, aged four. I can't remember whether we took to one another or not: there is a photo of us in the garden looking friendly enough. I do remember waking one night to find that I had been sick in the bed. I didn't have to call for Mum. She was there, getting me up and taking me to the bathroom to wash my hair. Izzy and Chris were already in the bath. We had all picked up a bug or reacted violently to the different water. Dad was also up, in a fussing, wringing-of-hands state, but between them, the sheets were changed, our hair washed, teeth brushed and we were carried back to bed in clean pyjamas.

We took a picnic down to Carlyon Bay. I wandered off alone to paddle in the rock pools while the adults spread out towels and blankets between boulders and huddled together chatting. It was a blustery day, not very warm, but as Mum said: nothing like sand and sea to keep children happy. I could hear their voices drifting through the air between gusts of wind, even though I could no longer see them. Izzy and Chris were a little way off. I shouted to them to come and see a baby crab I had found, but they were out of earshot. Stepping out of the water to join them, I was surprised to see red trickles running down my legs. I wiped them off, but the rivulets reappeared. It must be blood, I realised, although strangely it didn't hurt.

"Mummy, mummy!" I cried as I ran back to the picnic group.

"Oh my goodness!" exclaimed Mum, "What's happened?"

Jenefer peered over. "Leeches," she announced, "haven't seen them for a few years, but in the right conditions, they breed in the rock pools."

"You might have warned us, Batty."

Izzy was on her way over, Chris toddling along beside her howling, blood dribbling down their legs too. Mum seemed more upset than we were. She washed our stings with drinking water and wrapped us up in towels. We sat beside her eating gritty sandwiches through chattering teeth, then everything was packed away and the excursion abandoned.

Jenefer was thirty-three at the time of our visit. Did she still believe that she would die before she was thirty-five? A year and a half later, there was a telephone call, which I think I remember, perhaps because of the way Mum gasped, saying in a low, peculiar voice, "I'll take this upstairs." I didn't know it then, but Jenefer was dead. It was her lover who found her. He told Mum that Jenefer had been in bed with a very bad cold. When he went up to see her that evening, the room was full of gas. The official version was that due to her cold, she hadn't smelled the gas escaping from the unlit fire and had been overcome by the fumes. She was thirty-four and nine months old. Mum remains convinced that it was an accident. There are others who say it was suicide. Rather strangely, four months before Jenefer's death, 'Boy', her only brother (whose real name was Tristram), had also died. I do not know the circumstances of his death.

Many years later, Mum's reflective memories of Batty enabled her to make an attempt at a tentative closeness with me. I was fourteen or fifteen. She came into my room and asked if I would like to see some poetry that Jenefer Carlyon had written.

"Your friend Jenefer who died?"

"Yes. She wrote these when we were students and gave them to me to keep. I don't know why she wanted me to have them."

"She probably trusted you."

"Well, we were good friends. She was a couple of years younger than me, and I suppose she saw me as somebody who was ordinary and reliable. They're quite strange, some of her poems and, well, I don't know – ethereal, perhaps. I just thought you might be interested as you write yourself, don't you?"

I was ill at ease with Mum sitting next to me; it was so unexpected. She must have had to jump several emotional hurdles to come to me with an offering of poetry from a dead friend, although all I understood at the time was that she was nervous.

"Will you read them to me?" I asked hesitantly.

"Oh, I can't read them all, there are too many." She shuffled through the pages. "Maybe this one: it's called Sunday Morning."

Morning comes barefoot
up the street
with dawn winds
in her long pale hands,
while day, like some drab ghost
sits on the roof-tops
watching the thin smoke melting
in the sombre skies.

Like some huge goddess
London lies,
blankets of mist
still pale upon her sleeping eyes,
as soft her river glimmers by
with musing waters caught in
diuturnities of thought.

The Sunday silence falls
sweet as our lost content
upon the city's walls,
as remotely now we hear
each fainting chime
crumbling down the winter air,
as diamonds hung
on fragile threads of prayer.

(London, December 1947)

"Mmm. Read me another."

"Well, I can leave them here for you to look at, if you like."

"OK, thanks." Mum leafed through a few more, then stopped, and laughed softly.

"She wrote this one when I was practising Chopin's broken chord study. She liked to write while I played and she'd ask me to play pieces again and again. I don't suppose it ever occurred to her to get her poems published, but I've often thought they deserved recognition."

Now where are you my love?
Down through the tight-stretched darkness
Your arms swan-white no longer move
As though demanding my flower-wind caress
No more, no more, only forgetfulness!

Now where, oh where, the swallow-swift grace,
The selfless sweetness of you

Your mind-lovely face,
Your eyes half-hidden grey-blue?
No more, no more, my eyes must close too.

Now where, oh where, in a thicket of dreams
Will I find your bloomless flower?
In lakes of love your likeness gleams;
Now sleep-flakes are falling in feather soft shower –
No more, no more, only hour must follow each hour.

(September 1945)

I visualised Mum playing the piano, her swan-white arms and grey-blue eyes.

"Did she love you?"

"Me? Oh. No, the poem's not about me."

Why shouldn't it be? Mum and the music. Hadn't I, as a little girl, been drawn out of bed to sit as far down the stairs as I dared to listen to her play? A few days later, I gave the poems back, thinking we might talk about them more.

"Oh, those," she said, taking them from me without another word.

I read all the poems Jenefer gave to Mum – some thirty of them, most of which she wrote in her late teens. Here are a few lines, which speak of loneliness and sorrow:

I am the one who wanders here
In shadows of clouds and rain…

I am the dagger darkening your dreams…
And I am the one who never sleeps,
Who stole the tears from your eyes –
Ah, my beloved, forget the ghost who weeps,
Once-loved, now lost, the one who cries:
"Death, my darkling, my last release,
Lend me your lullabies…"

Jenefer Carlyon: born April 6th 1927, died January 4th 1962

I have come to the end of the section *Mum's Story* and will now continue with family life at Cleveland Road. The rest of the book follows chronologically.

ABOVE: Elizabeth

ABOVE: Jenefer Carlyon

BELOW: Ailsa Dicken, when she served in the Candian Women's Army.

BELOW: Marie McKillop

After graduating from the Academy, Elizabeth shared a bedsit in Swiss Cottage with Jenefer (Batty). When Jenefer left, Ailsa moved in. Marie visited her cousins in London in July 1947. It was during Marie's visit when the three girls travelled to Leytonstone to look at houses. In the academic year of 1949/50, all three cousins lived at the house in Whipps Cross Road: the daughters of Annie, Martha and Bessie Greig.

ABOVE: Mum and Bill Stewart.
BELOW: Mum with her brother, Robert.

ABOVE: Martha and her son Billy, after his operation.
BELOW: Granny with her new son-in-law. His volatile behaviour shattered Mum's happiness.

ABOVE: Last holiday on the Isle of Arran 1939
BACK ROW: Archie, aged fifteen, Billy, eighteen, Robert, sixteen
MIDDLE ROW: Marie, aged eight, Annie Fraser, Archibald McKillop
FRONT: Betty, aged fourteen
BELOW: Betty and Marie, Archie and Robert in 1938

A FAMILY GATHERING 1961

BACK ROW, LEFT TO RIGHT: Frank Land, Dad, Robert Fraser

MIDDLE ROW: Ailsa Land, Mum, Granny, Bessie Dicken and Lily Fraser

THE CHILDREN: Richard Land, Anne Fraser, Frances Land, me, Izzy and Huw David

Chris is in the foreground surrounded by his favourite cars and lorries.

39
51, PRIMROSE ROAD

The Friend will become bread and springwater for you,
a lamp and a helper, your favourite dessert
and a glass of wine.

Green Ears – Rumi

Towards the end of the summer holidays of 1968, when Izzy and I were twelve, we were walking up George Lane when we happened to meet a school friend, Melanie Turner. She and Chris were in the same class at Oakdale and we were the same age as her brother, Jonathan. Music was a connection, as Jonathan had played the violin when he was at Oakdale, and Melly, or Mel, (as Melanie was also known) learned the cello with Margaret Sprakes. Melly invited us back to her house and Izzy and I stepped into 51, Primrose Road for the first time. As soon as the door opened, an alarmingly large alsatian leapt all over us, barking, licking, sniffing and panting. We tried to shield ourselves from the rapturous attack until to our relief Jonathan pulled him away.

"He won't hurt you, will you, Frankl, you old softie?" he said, dragging the excited dog into the living room, where the two of them wrestled playfully on the floor.

"Mum, I've brought Kate and Izzy home," Melly called. We already knew Melanie and Jonathan's parents, Patricia (Pat) and Desmond (Des) Turner, from school functions and musical events, so they were not strangers.

"Hello girls, it's lovely to see you," said Pat. She hugged Melly, and then, to our surprise, she hugged us too. "Come on in. I'll put the kettle on."

Melly introduced us to their cat, rabbit, gerbil, hamster, guinea pig, and the blackbird in a cardboard box with a broken wing that Pat was nursing back to health.

"Are you staying for supper, girls?" asked Pat. "We're having eggs, ham and chips."

"Oh goody," said Melly, turning to us, "you don't have to go do you?"

I phoned Granny.

"The dinner's all ready and now you're telling me you'll not be having any – and what about your practice, eh?"

"I'll do some later."

"Och aye. I don't know what your mammy will have to say about this."

I decided that permission had been granted and we stayed. When Des came home from work, he took Pat in his arms and kissed her thoroughly. Jonathan rolled his eyes at us as if to say, "Don't mind them". There were more hugs all round. I felt as if I were in the middle of a romantic movie. Des started playing the piano in the living room – Chopin and Rachmaninov, which I knew, then Scott Joplin, Gershwin and other tunes that I had never heard Mum play. Pat came through, which prompted Des to launch into a Charleston. Pat laughed and danced.

"That's my girl," said Des, admiringly. Supper arrived a few hours later. We were soon to find out that there were no set times for meals in the Turner household. Melly and Jonathan walked us home. Dad was cross with us for getting back so late, Granny annoyed we had missed dinner and Mum irritated that I had not practised. We hardly registered their ill temper. Our lives had perceptibly shifted.

Despite a lack of space, the Turners bought an enormous Christmas tree, which swamped the living room. Pat asked us over to make some decorations to hang on it. We spent a happy afternoon creating stars and angels out of coloured tissue paper, silver foil and pipe cleaners. Pat rescued our failed attempts, identifying the strange shapes as moons, fish or ducks, praising each and every one.

After Christmas dinner at home, we walked over to Primrose Road. To our surprise, Des handed each of us a present. Chris received a book on Natural History; Izzy and I were given little boxes.

I opened mine to find a piece of polished jade on a gold chain.

"It's to match your jade green eyes," Melly told me.

"I don't have green eyes!" I laughed.

"Yes you do," she insisted. In their bathroom I looked in the mirror to check. Sure enough, my eyes really were pale green. How extraordinary that the Turners had noticed something that I had no idea of myself. In Izzy's box was a nugget of turquoise, also on a gold chain. Her eyes were not that colour, but Des had not been able to find a stone to exactly match Izzy's eyes, which were a light, cornflower blue.

We often went to the Plaza in South Woodford to see films together, but in April, Des took us to the Empire, Leicester Square to see *Gone with the Wind*. Apparently, Melanie was named after Melly Hamilton, which I couldn't understand – the Melly of *Gone with the Wind* was such an insipid character. Pat disagreed, pointing out that she was loving, trusting, loyal and brave. Yes, we reluctantly conceded, but it was the feisty, flirtatious and fabulously pretty Scarlett O'Hara we all adored. True, she was scheming, self-willed and treacherous, but wonderfully passionate, courageous and endearing nonetheless.

The Turners took a keen interest in Chris's collection and kept their eyes open for new exhibits for him. If one of their pets died, the body would be presented to Chris to bury in the back garden. Des gave him a number of fossils and whenever they went on holiday they would usually come back with something. Here are their entries in the Visitors' Book:

> You should do very well in the future, Christopher, with so much patience and thought.
> I think it all very grand and exciting. Bless you!
> Pat Turner. 20/4/69

> The potential extent of this collection, now in its infancy, staggers the imagination. I would suggest an early application to the Rockefeller Foundation for suitable housing in the future. Each aspect of animal life is represented. The presentation is clear, occasionally brilliant, the re-assembly of components meticulously done, the variety of subjects amazing. I am considerably impressed.
> D. B. Turner 29/5/69

It's fantastically good. Jon Turner.

I think that Christopher's collection is fantastic but I wouldn't like to sleep with all those skulls hovering over me. I like the butterflies very much and Chris has done a very good job. Melanie Turner 2/9/70

Des first met Pat one Saturday evening at a dance in Walthamstow in 1944. It was wartime, when dances or socials were held every week in church halls, assembly rooms or any venue where people could get together. Des was sixteen and went along with his friend Ken. There she was – a gorgeous girl wearing a gold frock, with movie-star looks, rich wavy brown hair falling to her shoulders, an eighteen-inch waist and, as Des put it, "every curve in the right place." She was seventeen. Des fell in love with her at first sight. I was reminded of the heart-fluttering moment in *West Side Story* when Tony sees Maria for the first time across a crowded dance floor. I imagine it was the same for Des. He went home in a state of euphoria, telling his mother that he had just met the girl he was going to marry. "Does she know yet?" she asked.

Pat lived above a tobacconist, newsagent and sweet shop that was managed and run by her mother. The shop opened early and shut late – there were similar tobacconists on every street corner, so Pat's mother had to be more attentive to her customers than she could be to her family. Pat's father worked long hours and when he was home he helped in the shop; her sister was seven years older than she was, the age gap too wide for them to be playmates. Consequently, Pat had a lonely childhood. When she was six, she was admitted to Great Ormond Street hospital with a serious kidney infection. In the days before antibiotics, the treatment was to starve the bacteria out. She survived on barley water and glucose and became so weak that she was in a wheelchair until she regained strength and learnt to walk again. She was evacuated early in the war and placed on a farm in Cornwall with an illiterate couple who made her work for them, treated her unkindly and didn't give her enough to eat. When she went home three and a half years later, she was suffering from malnutrition. She stayed in London for the rest of the war and attended a technical college where she received training as a milliner. Soon after she met Desmond, she started work with Madame Rita, milliner to Queen Elizabeth, the late Queen Mother, and travelled to Berkeley Square every weekday to make hats. Pat received her calling-up papers just before the conscription of women ceased. She had her preliminary interview and was sent to evening classes to train in first aid and nursing. The skills she learned proved invaluable, but she was not in the end required to tend the war-wounded.

Desmond courted his beloved Pat ardently until he was called up at eighteen. The war was officially over, but he joined the Third Regiment of the Royal Horse Artillery and was posted to Verden-Aller in occupied Germany. He operated tanks and guns and was involved in some gruesome action. When it was discovered that he could play the piano, he was employed to entertain the regiment and given time off to practise. To improve his transposition and harmony skills, he practised *All the Things You Are* by Jerome Kern, a melody with a complex chord sequence: he felt he was getting somewhere when he could play the song fluently in any one of the twelve possible keys.

After twenty-eight months of service in Germany, Des returned to England. He worked at Connaught Hospital in Walthamstow as a trainee radiographer and ECG operator for £4/10/- a week whilst also attending evening classes in accountancy in order to improve his job prospects. In one year he took twenty-seven exams, gaining his National Certificate, Royal Society of Arts exams (receiving the gold medal for maths) and ACCA (Association of Chartered Certified Accountants) qualifications.

Des and Pat married at St. Paul's church, Leyton, in 1951 and moved into a two-roomed rented flat in Hackney. They lived on Des's wages and saved all of Pat's. Two years later, Des was given a job as assistant accountant in a wines and spirits company, Saccone and Speed. His increased earnings and Pat's savings meant that in 1954 they were able to buy, with mortgage, 51, Primrose Road in South Woodford. Having settled in, they acquired Vincent, an alsatian from Battersea Dogs' Home.

When she found she was pregnant, Pat handed in her notice to Madame Rita. As a result of her rather neglected childhood she had already decided that when she had her own children she would not go out to work. Jonathan was born in January 1956, a month before Izzy and me. After his birth, a black tomcat known as Timothy Turner moved in, and Des bought a motorbike and sidecar. Pat, with baby Jonathan in her arms, the cat on her shoulder and the dog sitting upright at the back, all squeezed into the sidecar for rides to Epping Forest and beyond. The menagerie continued to grow when a baby sparrow was found abandoned near the house. After he was nursed back to health, he learned to fly, but wouldn't leave Primrose Road. Every evening he called to be let in. The sparrow also took his place in the sidecar for the family outings. It seems incredible, but dog, cat, bird, parents and baby enjoyed picnics and going for walks together, the animals returning obediently when called for the ride home. The sparrow lived for about a year, until one day he was hopping around in the garden and his body exploded. Des thinks he must have had a growth in his stomach.

Melanie was born twenty months after Jonathan and the Turner family of children was complete. However, the animal intake continued to rise. Chickens were next. Des built a hencoop at the bottom of the garden for six hens; then he dug out a pond, which he filled with goldfish and carp. Queen Sophie, a she-cat, took up residence and Frankl, another alsatian from the Battersea Dogs' home, was adopted after Vincent died. Pat's first-aid training proved handy when it came to mending birds' wings, bandaging wounds and setting animals' broken legs, but I don't suppose even she was expecting to give the kiss-of-life to a chicken.

One of the hens was white, which prompted Melly to name her Angel. Angel was small and henpecked by her larger, brown-feathered companions: she also had a penchant for blackberries. Having stripped the bushes at ground level, she was desperate to reach the higher ones. She must have tried again and again to leap up for them. In a last frantic effort she managed to propel herself right out of the pen. As she went over, she caught her head in some string. Hearing a commotion, Pat and Jonathan went into the garden where they found Angel dangling from her neck. Pat supported the bird's weight and tried to untangle it while Jonathan rushed indoors to get some scissors. Angel was cut free but she was limp and inert. Pat was not one to give up easily. She placed her mouth over the hen's beak and blew in gently whilst rubbing its chest. After a few minutes, Angel opened an eye and blinked. The hen was resuscitated and Pat swears that Angel was a changed personality after her near-death experience. No more did she suffer bullying from the other chickens.

When Melanie was weaned, Pat wanted to find something she could do for one evening a week away from the children. She decided to take up ballet and enrolled into Francesca Highfield's 'Del Sarto' ballet school. Pat had an instinctive feel for dance. Francesca was amazed to hear that her new pupil had not had any previous ballet training. Melanie, when she was three years old, started joining in the classes, revealing a natural aptitude that took her to the threshold of a professional career. But music had by then become more important to her and ballet fell into second place. After the children started school, Pat, already a member of the Labour Party, became more actively involved with politics. She was a passionate socialist and campaigner for social justice. Later she was elected to the local council and served for many years as a Labour councillor.

Melanie was talkative, ebullient and vivacious. She greeted everyone with a hug and a kiss. I admired her ballet dancing enormously and dreamed of being a ballerina myself. I imagined wearing pointe shoes, tying pink ribbons, executing pliés, grand jetés, pirouettes and arabesques, and gliding gracefully through the air, lifted effortlessly by my partner. In my reveries I was almost weightless, slim and delicate-boned. How I wished it were true. I saw myself as fat, broad-shouldered, big-footed and ugly-handed; too much of a lump ever to leave the ground: but in my fantasies I was a dancer, imagining it so convincingly as to almost experience the bodily feeling.

Francesca Highfield did not have any hair. She wore a wig and painted in her eyebrows. Melly informed us that her dancing teacher had lost her hair when she had pirouetted off the stage into the foot-lights. How tragic, we thought, and told Mum the awful tale. Mum scoffed, saying it was complete nonsense: Francesca had never had any hair – some people just didn't, and she was one of them. But Melly insisted the story was true and Pat confirmed it, so the dancing accident held. Francesca's garden almost backed onto ours. In the summer months, when the French windows of her studio were open, we could hear the sound of the piano bashing out music for the classes and Francesca's voice – one, two, three and *four* – drifting across the fence. When Francesca's 'Del Sarto' ballet school celebrated its twentieth anniversary, Des wrote the music for a new ballet called *The Swallow and the Prince* based on Oscar Wilde's heartbreaking tale *The Happy Prince*. Melanie danced the lead part of the swallow to her father's lyrical music.

Melly was our immediate friend, but I soon found Jon (as Jonathan was also known) a sympathetic companion. He too suffered from asthma and supported me when I was badly affected. "Game of chess, Kate?" he'd suggest, setting out the board, not expecting me to use my short supply of breath to reply. Des was also an asthmatic. They both understood what I was going through.

Pat and Des chose to become involved with our family. During the writing of this book, I asked them why they had taken us under their wings. "You were three wonderful kids," Des told me, "and you needed help. We could see that you were emotionally deprived and we did what we could." I guess Pat and Des saw that we could do with some tender loving care and took us into their animal sanctuary with their usual compassion.

"We wouldn't have done it if Melanie and Jonathan hadn't been all for it too," explained Des. "They were aware that your home life wasn't happy, in as far as children can be, and anyway, your companionship was important to them. It worked both ways."

Des befriended Dad, but he had no desire to leave his family and slink off to the pub with him, although that is what Dad would have liked. When we were children, it had seemed that he and Dad got on well, but even then I wondered if Des extended his friendship towards Dad for our sakes.

"Did Dad offer any kind of friendship to you?" I asked him.

"No, not at all. He bore a lot of grudges and was not a giving person. But you know that."

"Yes, I do." It was good to hear him speak in his familiar, forthright manner.

"Looking back, Des, how would you describe him?"

"Hmm: he was a needy, self-absorbed, materialistic man: and a poseur. He considered himself intellectually superior to me, tried to belittle me by quoting Shakespeare and showing off his literary knowledge, which was actually quite limited. He looked down his nose at our humble dwelling, which was neither here nor there to me. But anyway, once I'd levelled the playing field and pointed out that he was just an ordinary sailor and I an ordinary soldier, we were able to rub along."

"Did he talk about his home life?"

"Incessantly: his evil mother-in-law, his cold-hearted wife, the terrible suffering he endured. I'd heard all about the women he lived with before I met them. When I did, I liked Elizabeth. She was friendly and kind. I was fond of her, although I could tell she had troubles she kept to herself. Granny was a domineering, outspoken woman with a strong loyalty to her daughter and grandchildren, but she wasn't evil. I respected her even though I couldn't warm to her."

"If Derek had thought about it though," said Pat, "he should have realised that he was lucky to have Granny at home to look after the children and the house. How could he have managed without her? She cooked the evening meals and did all the baking and was there when you came home from school and Elizabeth was teaching."

"I'm afraid that wasn't how Dad saw it at all," I responded, almost smiling at Pat's simple reasoning, "mainly, of course, because Cleveland Road was Granny's house." The flow of conversation came to a halt until Des broke the silence.

"How extraordinary," he said. "I never knew that. He always led me to believe that he owned it."

I was as astounded as they were. I had thought that everyone who knew us was aware that we lived in Granny's house, but now I ask myself why I should have assumed so. Back in the 1950s and 1960s it was almost impossible for a single woman to get a mortgage. Indeed, in 1952, Granny was refused a mortgage to buy Cleveland Road on the grounds that she was sixty years old and, more significantly, a widow, which defined her as a single woman. The mortgage and the title deeds had to be secured in Mum's married name of Mrs. William Stewart – the fact that she had a husband (whom she was living with at the time) being the crucial factor. Granny did not broadcast the fact that the house had been purchased with her capital; Des was unaware of the situation, and Dad not only failed to enlighten him, but also, it seems, kindled the misconception.

Pat and Des walked with their arms around each other and held their children's hands. Melly even went so far as to hold Dad's hand once – not that he proffered it, she just took it. Her example did not encourage us to try. I wondered how Melly could bear to touch him, and was then ashamed of my disloyal thoughts. I knew that Izzy felt the same way. It was fine when Des held our hands, though. He walked briskly, sometimes reaching his arms around our waists to lift us over kerbstones or swing us up steps. I worried that he would notice how heavy I was in comparison to Izzy. Melly always held our hands (mine and Izzy's anyway), which we found a little disconcerting to begin with. Self-consciously, we worried that passers-by might think it odd, but Melly was unconcerned and would have been puzzled and probably hurt if we had let our hands drop.

Our visits to Grandad improved enormously, as Melly came with us. While Dad and Grandad downed their pints and scotches at the Cocked Hat, we raced to a nearby swing park. Up and down we would swing, Melly chattering non-stop. One Saturday, she took my arm and walked me a little away from the others.

"Kate," she began seriously, "what do you think of Jon?"

"I like him very much."

"Is that very much or *very* much? He really likes you, you know. Why don't you two go out together?"

"Oh Mel, we're friends, that's all."

"But you've got so much in common. You've both got asthma, you play chess together; you're always having deep discussions. I think you'd make a good couple." Melanie was a matchmaker even then.

"I don't think I feel that way about Jon."

"But Jon's lovely, Kate! He'd be very good to you."

"I'm not saying he wouldn't."

"Well, then. You *have* to fall in love with Jon and marry him, to keep us all together. I've thought about it, and Izzy and Jon wouldn't suit each other. It has to be you because, just think, if you won't marry Jon, then I'll have to marry Chris!"

One pursuit that both Jon and I enthused about was driving. Izzy and Melly were not interested and Chris was, I suppose, too young. Des decided it would be good for Jon and me to learn to drive, despite the fact that we were only thirteen. He drove us in his Vanden Plas 3-Litre Princess (Mark II) to a disused airfield in Debden where he could teach us. We visited the airfield most weekends for several months and both became confident drivers.

Pat and Des supported and encouraged all three of us with our endeavours, whatever they were. I had become quite good at knitting little things for dolls, and was able to follow Fair Isle patterns that needed two balls of wool, using a hand for each colour as Granny had shown me. I crocheted blankets, ponchos and scarves and started to make clothes from remnants of cloth bought from Hedges, the drapers and haberdashers in George Lane. Over the years I learned how to sew. I copied shapes from my clothes onto newspaper, cut out patterns and tried out my own designs. I made everything by hand, which took ages. Pat Turner had a Singer treadle sewing machine, so she suggested I bring my cut out material over to Primrose Road to run up the seams. My dressmaking became quite prolific as a result. In my diaries I drew the designs and pinned samples of the fabric into the pages. I still have some of the garments I made.

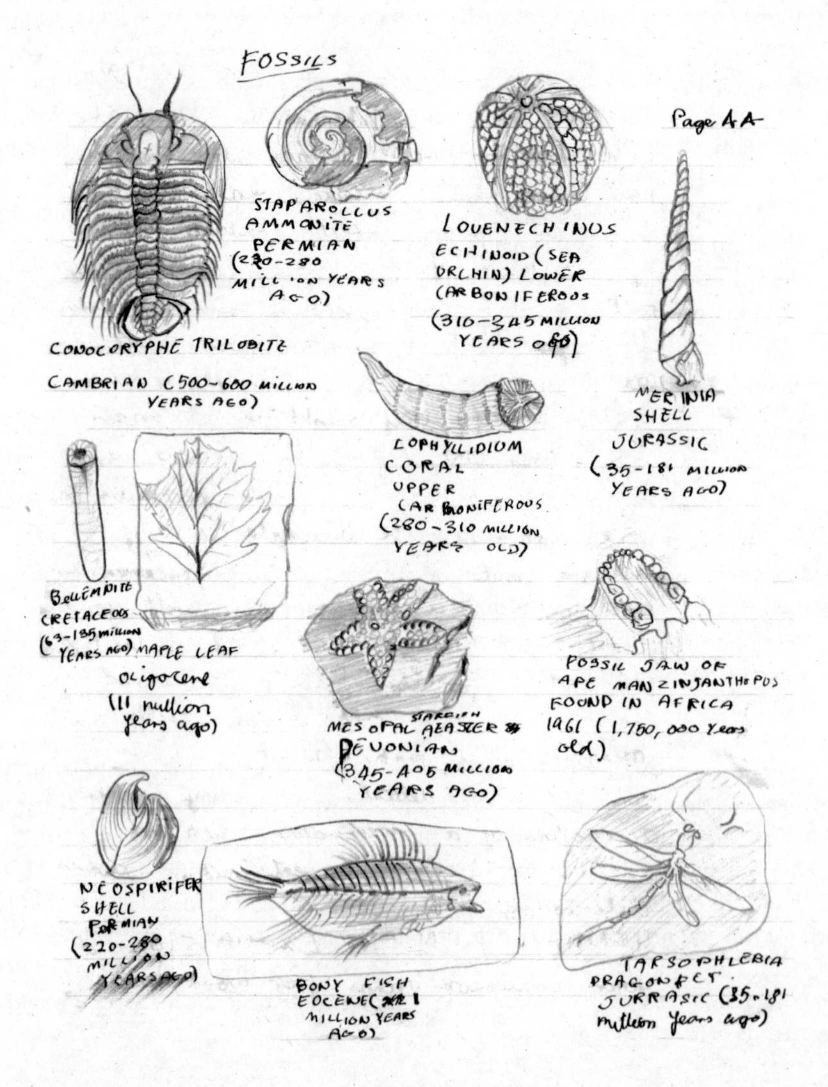

The Turner family
ABOVE: Pat and Desmond
RIGHT: Melanie
BELOW: Jonathan with the cat, Queen Sophie

TOP LEFT: Dad, Izzy, me and Mum.
TOP RIGHT: Margaret Sprakes RIGHT: me aged thirteen

LEFT: Melly choreographed her own dance to Saint-Saëns' *The Swan*, which I played for her on the cello and she danced at Mum's annual pupils' concert in 1968. Here we are on the day of the performance. I am wearing Nina's long white dress.

BELOW: Malcolm Bidgood

40
REDBRIDGE YOUTH ORCHESTRA

I don't play accurately – anyone can play accurately – but I play with wonderful expression.

The Importance of Being Earnest – Oscar Wilde

Malcolm Bidgood's pioneering work to give every school child the opportunity to learn a musical instrument began with his appointment as Music Advisor of the Borough of Redbridge in 1965. In 1966, he established the Redbridge Youth Orchestra. I wonder if there has ever been another youth orchestra like it. During the Easter holidays of 1967, Mr. Bidgood took the RYO on its first residential course to Aldeburgh, a town on the coast of Suffolk. The orchestra took over all the available accommodation in the two best hotels, the White Lion and the Wentworth. Sectional rehearsals[1] took place in the hotels' largest rooms, the lounges and the White Lion ballroom, and full rehearsals were held in the local Jubilee Hall. The course finished with a concert at The Maltings in nearby Snape. The RYO was the first youth orchestra to perform in the newly opened International Concert Hall.

The Maltings was built in the mid nineteenth century on the banks of the river Alde. It had been one of the largest barley maltings in East Anglia, but by the 1950s it was becoming uneconomical. In 1965, malting stopped completely. The owner agreed to lease the building to the Aldeburgh Festival, which had been established by the composer Benjamin Britten and the tenor Peter Pears some years earlier. The Festival engaged Arup Associates to design the conversion of the malt-house into a concert hall. Much of the existing structure and original character of the building was retained and most of the new material used was wood – even the audience seating was made of wood and wickerwork.

I joined the RYO for the Easter course of 1969. On the first evening the entire orchestra gathered in the White Lion, rushed the bar staff off their feet for half an hour, and then filed into the dining room. The hotel manager and employees greeted familiar faces from previous years and welcomed new guests with open arms – either they were looking forward to another five days of huge bar profits, or they genuinely enjoyed the novelty of a youth orchestra under their roof – or maybe both. Wine was ordered, food selected from the menus, the buzz of excitable conversation and eruptions of laughter filling the room. Towards the end of the meal, Mr. Bidgood rose to his feet to give his opening address. With much shuffling of chairs and clearing of throats, those who knew prepared themselves for what was to follow. I had been warned, but nothing could have primed me for the actual length of the speech. (One

1. The orchestra is made up of 'sections' of instruments. The main sections are the strings, woodwinds, brass, and percussion. But these can be further divided into specific instruments – e.g. the violin section, the oboe section, the horn section. Sectional rehearsals are ones in which sections of the orchestra rehearse separately. 'Full' rehearsals involve the whole orchestra.

of the waiters, I was told, was heard to comment "We'll be serving the cornflakes soon.") I remember part of it: he said he would start the course without any rules, trusting us all to behave appropriately, but if it became apparent that rules were needed, he would make them up as necessary. I was impressed by such a laissez-faire approach.

When the talk ended, people rushed back to the bar, and then drifted into the lounge where there was a piano. An impromptu music session began, inevitably involving Paul Hart and Bram Tovey. I mentioned Bramwell Tovey in an earlier chapter as charismatic, entertaining and one of the most outstanding musical talents in Redbridge. He was a key figure in our lives, and as he will be appearing in the pages that follow, I would like to tell you a bit about him.

Bram was born in 1953 to parents who were members of the Salvation Army. He was named after Bramwell Booth, the son of the founders of the Salvation Army, William and Catherine Booth. By the age of seven, Bram was learning the piano and playing various brass instruments in the local Salvation Army Band. In the Redbridge Youth Orchestra and the Redbridge Brass Band, he played the tuba and was a virtuoso on the instrument. He was also brilliant at improvisation, an excellent pianist, composer and conductor. Although he came from a Salvation Army background, intellectually he could not accept their beliefs or doctrines. Amongst other things, the Salvationists' commitment to complete abstinence from alcohol was not something that he wished to embrace. He did not want to upset his parents, but at the same time, he found it impossible to live by the Christian Mission's rules. Bram's engaging personality made him well liked by everyone. Mum admired him enormously. On more than one occasion she asked me speculatively what I thought of Bram, hoping, I think, that she might claim him as her daughter's boyfriend. I disappointed her, I am sorry to say.

Just thirteen, I was a little too young to join in with the parties and illicit goings-on. In the evenings, I went to bed early, too shy to hang around in the lounge with such awesome, grown-up people. I enjoyed eating in the hotel dining rooms, where we chose from menus and were waited upon. Mealtimes also gave me the opportunity to observe the interaction and behaviour of the older members. The boys, lanky and hairy, joked and laughed in deep voices; the girls wore high-heeled shoes and carried handbags, from the depths of which they whipped out small mirrors, holding them in front of their faces to reapply lipstick and eye-shadow. They seemed so sophisticated and confident.

The Redbridge Youth Orchestra was of a much higher standard than any orchestra I had played in before, and the conductor, Charles Farncombe, was excellent. The programme for that particular course included *The Flying Dutchman* overture by Wagner. I couldn't play it at all – the notes flew by faster than the Dutchman. I had to stop, feeling embarrassed and incompetent. It was then that I received my first piece of orchestral advice. One of the other cellists asked me why I wasn't playing. I said that although I'd practised, I couldn't play it at that speed. He laughed and said, "Neither can I. But don't sit there doing nothing and drawing attention to yourself. Fake it like everyone else. Nobody's playing all the notes. Try to get the first one in every group and fluff the rest. Just keep going, stay vaguely in the right place and it'll all add to the general effect." Also on the programme was Mahler's *Kindertotenlieder* with the singer Anne Wilkens. It was the first time I had played Mahler. The markings in the part were in German as opposed to the Italian I was used to seeing. I didn't understand a word of it. Even the way the music was printed seemed complex and unfamiliar. But what I heard was a revelation – sounds, textures, colours and harmonies that transformed the orchestra into a new multi-dimensional instrument. How was it possible that I had only just discovered Mahler? He went straight into my amazing composers list, along with Stravinsky, Bach and Beethoven.

Every year the orchestra put together an evening's entertainment at the Jubilee Hall to which the residents of Aldeburgh were invited. Individuals gave solo performances – my contribution that year was Saint-Saëns' *Allegro Appassionato*. The programme in 1969 was fairly serious. Towards the end, the jazz group played an arrangement by Kenny Ball of *Midnight in Moscow* and Bram Tovey and Paul Hart performed *Ill Wind*, the marvellous Flanders and Swann arrangement of the *Rondo* from Mozart's fourth horn concerto. However, in the years that followed, the latter half of the Jubilee Hall concerts became legendary for musical slapstick. The combined compositional, comedic and performing talents of Paul and Bram produced some hilarious items. Roderick Elms, Chris Stearn and Russell Jordan were also key players, as later was Chris.

By the time it came to the final concert at Snape Maltings, I was managing to play more of the notes and was getting to grips with the technique of faking. Appallingly, a few months after the 1969 RYO concert, a fire broke out in The Maltings. The roof and interior burnt to cinders along with Benjamin Britten's piano. No time was lost in rebuilding the venue. A year later, Snape Maltings reopened. Unfortunately, it was not completed in time for the Easter 1970 RYO concert. The course was still held in Aldeburgh, but the orchestra returned to Ilford Town Hall for the final concert.

41
SUMMER of 1969

And through the glass window shines the sun.
How should I love and I so young?

anonymous (16th century)

On July 16th 1969, the spaceship Apollo 11 blasted off from the USA carrying three men to the Moon. Four days later, Neil Armstrong and Buzz Aldrin became the first humans to land on the Moon, while Michael Collins orbited above. The Apollo 11 mission was given massive television coverage, which did not please Granny. Dad and Chris watched avidly whenever they could. Izzy and I watched less, partly because it was so scary – the astronauts could have died at any moment and we didn't want to see that happen. Mum avoided it completely as she couldn't stand the American accents. Dad harboured a niggling resentment that the USA was receiving worldwide acclaim and attention. "Don't forget," he lectured, "it was the Soviet Union who put the first Man in Space – and a long time before America. 1958 it was, when Yuri Gagarin orbited the Earth. What a momentous achievement *that* was."

A week after the Moon landing, we were on our way to camp in Ratlinghope in Shropshire. FSC had this to say:

> For the Child to know and understand the routes by which Man reached the Moon, he must know and understand and feel for himself the situations and circumstances which made it possible for Man to develop the skills and the enterprise to overcome his environment. These skills and this initiative, we believe, did not largely come from reading books and passing examinations, but from the ceaseless struggle with the natural elements.

Chris was eleven, a Trailseeker, Izzy and I thirteen-year-old Trackers. Mum and Dad went to the cottage for the first week we were away, Mum and Granny for the second. A large number of letters were exchanged during the fortnight, the style and content of which are revealing of our characters. Chris's are full of mishaps, ailments, and descriptions of animals, dead or alive; Izzy's are eloquent and unwittingly funny; mine, informative and lengthy. Both Izzy and I give reassuring accounts of Chris's well-being, seeking to allay Dad's anxiety. Dad writes with schoolboy humour, Mum describes her economy measures and Granny discusses the weather.

From Chris:

> Dear Mum and Dad,
>
> I have made friends with a boy called Mathew Pia. This morning I trekked up a mountain (well, nearly one) and found a dead sheep. I am sleeping in a Forest School Camps tent with a boy called Andrew but on the first night I didn't sleep, because he

snored! Today I found a dead carrion crow, but it stank, so I'm leaving it til the end of camp. Instead of logs round the camp fire, the Trackers have made seats that look a bit like Stone Henge.

Lots of love, Christopher

P.S. (Excuse the writing, I didn't have anything to lean on)

Dear Mum and Dad,

I have changed tents and am now in with Matthew. I have picked up a sty, two scratches and a horsefly bite. Today I thought I lost 5 shillings, but I found half a crown by my tent and half a crown on the other side of the field. I was on clan and as I was kept awake by snoring, I slacked, but the food was O.K.

Love from Chris XXXXX

(P.S. excuse writing, I had nothing to lean on)

From Dad to Chris:

Dear Chris,

Please excuse the writing even although I do have something to lean on. We have received your two letters and are glad to hear you are keeping your end up at camp. The way to stop people from snoring is to get them to turn over, or else cut their throats. I hope you have forgotten all my good advice.

Love from your venerable papa.

From Chris:

Dear Mum, Dad and Granny,

Today the Trailseekers went Rock Climbing (it made me dizzy). Now I have a girl friend called Ruth, and she has a funny accent. I am feeling constipated and slightly ill, and I hope Rusty, Tinker and the stick insects are all right. Last night I slept well and was not woken up by snoring. Both my sandles are broken so I have really nothing to wear.

Love, Christopher XXXX

From Granny to Chris:

Dear Christopher,

All the animals are going fine. I have been looking after your stick insects and they are thriving. Rusty and Tinker would send you their love if they knew how to do that. The weather seems to be good in all of England and Wales according to the forecast, so I hope it is being kind to you.

Lots of love, Granny

From Chris:

Dear Mum, Dad and Granny,

We are sleeping in a barn and it is great fun, but there are sheep in the other half of the barn and they keep you awake. The only shoes I have to wear are my boots and my plimsoles. So next year I want to have proper walking boots. I have not found any skulls at all, but it is marvellous countryside. I am feeling a bit homesick.

Love from Christopher

P.S. then we watched the shearing, and it was very interesting.

From Mum to Chris:

Dear Christopher,

I am sorry to hear you are feeling a bit homesick. Perhaps it's because the girls have gone off on trek. Granny and I came to the cottage yesterday evening. This morning we went to Fakenham to do some shopping in the market and I bought you three pairs of shoes in a sale. I should think that will keep you going for a year, don't you? I hope your feet grow the right amount to fit them. They had all been reduced in price from £2/12/11 to £1/8/11, so I think that was quite a good bargain.

With lots of love, Mum

From Chris:

Dear Mum, Dad and Granny,

I received the letter and the ten shillings, but the nearest shoe shop is 4 miles away. Now my flip-flops have broken, so I have only plimsoles and Wellingtons if it is rainy. I don't know whether to send the ten bob back, by post now, or keep it here just in case I get the chance to buy shoes. In Desmond's reply to Cathy's letter, it said they had got a specimen for my collection. I still have not found any skulls, but one of the Elfs, on hike, found a ram skull with curly horns, but he did not think to bring it back here. If you find any exhibits for me, keep them as a surprise for when I get home.

Lots of love from Christopher Giles

Dear Mum, Dad and Granny,

This is the last letter I am sending because this is the last stamp. I am going to buy a song book, which gives all the words for camp songs, and it only costs half a crown. The straps on my rucsack are lost so I shall either have to give a lot to the girls, to see if they have any room in their rucsacks, tye it up with string, or carry it on the train, so don't be surprised if you see me stepping off the train at Euston station with a couple of blankets tucked under one arm. Weather is fine, hope all goes well with you.

Love from Christopher XXXXX

From Izzy to Mum and Dad:

Our leaders are called Marcus who has a black beard and a moustache, Rosemary who has very short hair and Robin, who has an electric razor. Christopher seems to have settled in well and has made many friends. Country dancing will be held in the farmyard, which has been specially scrubbed and cleaned for the occasion. I have been stung by a wasp but it doesn't hurt very much, so don't worry, Dad. In our tent we have millions of little insects, which jump when you touch them. We also have quite a few spiders, which I am not very pleased about. There are many cows and sheep dotted all over the hills, and you can hear them moo-ing and baa-ing practically all the time.

Love from Isabel XX

From me to Mum and Dad:

My sleeping bag is on a molehill and it is very lumpy. I had a little asthma attack last night but apart from that I'm fine. Christopher was lined up for breakfast at 7.30, and it wasn't until 8.30. He has found plenty of friends and is not in the least bit homesick. He played the bugle to call us for country dancing. It poured in the morning and on clan I had to try to keep cornflakes, weetabix, porage oats and bread dry and stop the milk getting too diluted with water.

We set off in the rain on trek to the Stiper stones and then down to a farm where we stocked up with clean water. The farmer was very nice and gave us a field to pitch our tents. After we had had our tea the farmer and his family came to our camp with a churn of drinking water. We then sat around the campfire telling ghost stories and shaggy dog stories. And this brings me to where I am now. It has poured all night and the rain is coming down in buckets. I may be going bivvying today – living in the mountains with no tents and wrapping yourselves in sleeping bags and ground sheets – but now that I have seen the weather I might change my mind.

We all walked to the Stiperstones and I took my sleeping bag. We found thousands of bilberries. At about four o'clock the others went back leaving me, Marcus and a few others behind. It was beginning to get very cold so we found a sheltered place and started pulling away the moveable stones so it wouldn't be too uncomfortable. We then cut piles of heather to put on top of the earth. Supper consisted of 1½ sardine sandwiches, ½ a banana, a weetabix, a handful of raisins and four cold prunes. It was now as cold as a winter's day. My hands and feet were like blocks of ice and my teeth were chattering. We found a convenient place to do our torch signals back to camp (we'd arranged this beforehand). I then climbed up to the triangulation point, 1,700 feet above sea level. We were sleeping just below the triangulation point. We signalled to camp and they signalled back then got into our sleeping bags and huddled up to keep warm. It started to rain. We covered ourselves up with our ground sheets but by now it was really cold. We slept in our clothes. I was so cold my teeth were really chattering. We got up at six o'clock as we had to be back to camp for breakfast. A thick mist had fallen and it really was very cold. We packed up our sleeping bags with numb fingers and made our way back. You could hardly see a foot in front of you so we all stuck close together. We stopped on the way and drank some water and ate the left-overs from yesterday. My hair was soaking from the mist. At eight o'clock we arrived back at camp. Robin had bet me a bottle of Corona I wouldn't stay up there so he went off to buy my corona. Izzy hadn't gone to the Stiperstones – she was too scared. Anyway, it was quite an experience.
I will have to help Chris pack as he has lost the straps of his rucksack.

Lots of love, Cathy XX

P.S. Please will Dad excuse my grammar and the excessive use of "got" (ta).

From me to Granny:

There is a boy here called Barnaby. He is very nice and is our sort of ringleader. Our best staff leader is Robin. He has very tender skin and when he goes in the sun he gets blisters. Our group has dammed the stream and made a waterfall and swimming pool. We are also going to make a rope bridge across it. Are the animals all right?

Lots of love, Catherine

A subtle transition took place at that camp for Izzy and me. As mentioned in our letters, we met two brothers, Barnaby and Matthew Pia. I was drawn to Barny and Izzy to Matthew. The attraction seemed to be returned. It was a new experience for Izzy and me, perhaps for all four of us, to find that liking somebody was extending into uncharted areas of growing-up feeling. During country dancing, it seemed that their arms encircled our waists more fully. We continued to hold hands after the music had stopped, guarding our partners for the next dance, reluctant to let go. When Barny called to me across the dining circle and patted the space on the log next to him, a thrill of pleasure washed through me. At supper time he made jam sandwiches for two while I stood at the urn and filled our metal mugs with tea, that delicious camp brew flavoured with wood-smoke and camaraderie. I liked his tousled, shoulder-length, dusty-blond hair and noticed the way he raked his fingers through it to keep the overgrown fringe out of his eyes. He was sure-footed, well-coordinated and bursting with physical energy. It was he who rallied the Tracker group together, spurred us on to dam the stream, initiated the construction of a Tracker Grotto, lit the group fire and kept our spirits burning. He was the one who urged me to spend the night at the Stiperstones, who set the pace on hike, who impelled us to walk further. I admired his casualness, the way he seemed to do everything just right, his pealing laughter and his abundance. He led without being bossy and we followed willingly. For me, it was a relief to be out of the driving seat with someone else at the wheel: maybe that was an element of the attraction. When the gong rang for campfire, we raced to get there first to claim our favoured Tracker area before the Pathfinders arrived. One evening towards the end of camp, my wheezing slowed me down. I had to walk, gauging my breaths, stopping occasionally to lean forwards with my hands on my knees. I wasn't worried – Barny would save me a place. From afar I heard his voice calling, "Cathy! Come on!" I looked up. The rest of the group had gone, but he was waiting for me, a small figure in the distance. I shook my head and waved him on. He stood where he was for a few seconds, then suddenly he was sprinting towards me. I could feel the thud of his feet through the ground as he drew closer, nearly as out of breath as I was.

"Are you alright?" he panted.

"I'm fine," I wheezed.

"You sound like a bloody steam engine" – "bloody" now a word every Tracker dared to say out loud.

"Here," he said, stretching his arm towards me. Our hands met. He clasped mine firmly, sending warm, shivering tingles through my bone marrow. I was unexpectedly overcome with shyness. Barny pulled me along over the lumpy ground through thistles and cowpats. For a second I was afraid that he was letting go of my hand, but no; he was just loosening his grip so that he could entwine his fingers through mine in the intimate boyfriend/girlfriend way – the real thing. He fell into step beside me. Neither of us spoke, but everything had been communicated. How disappointing that he had left it so late: camp would be over in two days. Time ran out for Matthew and Izzy, who parted with only the memories of country dancing to remind them of their love from afar.

Chris, as was usually the case, came up with the ideas for the sketch that his group presented at Merrymoot. Naturally funny, unconcerned about standing up in front of an audience and willing to play the clown, he was the obvious choice for the lead part in the Trailseeker version of *Romeo and Juliet*. His ardent courtship of Juliet, the delivery of his lines, the melodramatic acting of his prolonged, excruciating demise was the highlight of the evening.

Later in the summer, we went to the cottage. Walking up to the barn, we began our 'What do you prefer?' game. Over the years it had progressed to such questions as: "Would you rather freeze to death or burn to death?" These questions required serious debate, helped along by Chris's graphic descriptions of, in this case, the effects of freezing and burning.

"What do you think would be worse; to be blind or deaf?" This too needed careful consideration, as did the question, "Would you rather lose an arm or a leg?"

"I don't want to lose either," said Izzy.

"But you have to choose," I reminded her.

"What would you prefer; to be able to fly or to swim underwater without needing air?" asked Chris.

"To fly," I said at once. Flying was one of my favourite fantasies. In my daydreams it came close to reality – I could almost experience the sensation of leaping from the ground, becoming airborne and soaring through the sky. I felt I knew what it would be like to have a bird's eye view of the world, to fly over the tops of mountains, to perch on the highest buildings. "Imagine not having to walk to school," I said excitedly, " – you could just fly there. And you could rescue cats from trees and pick the best cherries."

"I'd choose to fly too," Izzy decided. "Sometimes in dreams, I do fly and I can float upstairs and if someone's chasing me, I take off into the air and escape. I could be like Tinkerbell in Peter Pan."

"Mmm," Chris reflected, "I think I'd choose to be able to swim underwater, explore the depths of the oceans and go to places nobody's ever been before."

Chris, unlike Izzy and me, was well aware that the majority of the Earth beneath the sea was unexplored and unreachable. Scientific research indicated that within that unknown world, there might be millions of undiscovered species; strange sea creatures and plants that people had never seen. He dreamed about living with dolphins and learning how to communicate with them in their language. Despite the horrible things that man has done to them, he would say, they're amazingly forgiving and still welcome human company.

"You know, girls, there's a theory that humans originated from the sea, and the reason our hair grows so long on our heads is that babies hung on to their mother's hair while she swam. That's why babies have such a strong instinctive reflex to clutch with their fists and why women don't go bald. Yes, I think it would be more interesting to live in the oceans than the skies."

"But it would be so cold!" I said.

"Yeah, but if you could really swim like a fish, you'd have gills to breathe and you'd be cold-blooded. Anyway, it's very cold in the sky too when you get high up. You'd need feathers to survive."

"It would be nice to be able to do both," said Izzy. We agreed, but the rules of the game did not allow it.

Lying on the bales of hay in the barn, we contemplated the future. "When I grow up," I said, "I'm going to have four children – two boys and two girls."

"I'll have two," said Izzy, "a boy and a girl. I'd like to have a boy first, so that when they're older, his friends will be the right age to be boyfriends for his sister."

"And her friends could be his girlfriends," I added. "What would you call them?"

"Matthew for a boy and Louisa, Megan or Amy for a girl," she replied.

"I quite like the name Barnaby," I said, lingering over the name, "or Benjamin. Maybe Dominic. Eleanor for a girl, or Jemima."

"Jemima! That's revolting – it's the name of a duck – you can't call a girl that," Izzy complained.

"Well, I like it. Do you know, if we'd been boys, Mum was going to call me Roderick and you, Robert?"

"Roderick – yuk."

"And Chris would have been Rosalind."

"Our names would all have begun with R-O, then," Chris realised. "Rod, Rob and Ros… like the cows whose names all begin with 'D'. It's funny, isn't it? Life is completely arbitrary. We're all here by chance." After a moment, he said, "I'd like three children; two girls and a boy. Preferably twin girls."

"Like us," said Izzy.

"Well, it's nice, isn't it? It's good being the only boy."

"What would you call them?"

"Diana and Helena. I don't know about a boy's name. Hey, look at the skylarks circling." We lifted our heads.

"They make their nests on the ground," he informed us. "They drop from the sky in a straight line, but land some way from their nest to fool predators then run across the ground to reach it." We talked about camp, sang songs and danced. Chris re-enacted the death of Romeo and we called one another Roderick, Robert and Rosalind for the rest of the day.

At the start of the new school year, John Ridgeon asked Chris to join the Redbridge Band. As the French horn is not considered a brass band instrument, he played the tenor horn with a French horn mouthpiece. The band rehearsed twice a week. All the members were John's pupils, most of whom would never have played at all had it not been for Malcolm Bidgood's introduction of the Instrument Bank and peripatetic teaching scheme. It wasn't long before band members came to Cleveland Road to be shown round Chris's bedroom. They left their comments in the Visitors' Book:

You show more industry than
I have ever possessed. [*no name*]

When I die, my body to you.
Clive Miller 15/10/69

In 6,000 years time you can
have my prehistoric teeth.
Ruth Miller 15/10/69

I think you make the best skull.
Martin Koch 8/11/69

Chris was the type of pupil whom teachers find stimulating and rewarding to teach. He listened attentively, practised with intelligent application and soon developed a robust embouchure. John taught him to use the minimum pressure of the mouthpiece against the lips, so that he could relax and contract his muscles with finely controlled precision to make the most delicate and the most full-bodied sounds. When he played, the horn became the instrument through which his emotions resonated; yet in his lessons, he kept his innermost feelings to himself.

John remembers giving Chris Ravel's *Pavane Pour une Infante Défunte* to learn, a hauntingly plaintive piece that mourns a dead princess. The music was so sad that Chris found it almost too painful to play. Then one day he understood it for himself, found the courage to expose an introspective grief, and out poured Ravel's intimate lament; seamlessly phrased, emotionally controlled and so poignantly heartbreaking.

Chris had an insatiable appetite for music. As with his interest in natural history, he approached music with an all-embracing enthusiasm. He took to searching record and music libraries for rare, out-of-print or unusual horn pieces. He listened intently to all sorts of music, learning to play every orchestral horn solo he heard. It seemed he only needed to hear something once and he would know it. In his head he stored his own music library and amassed an extensive catalogue.

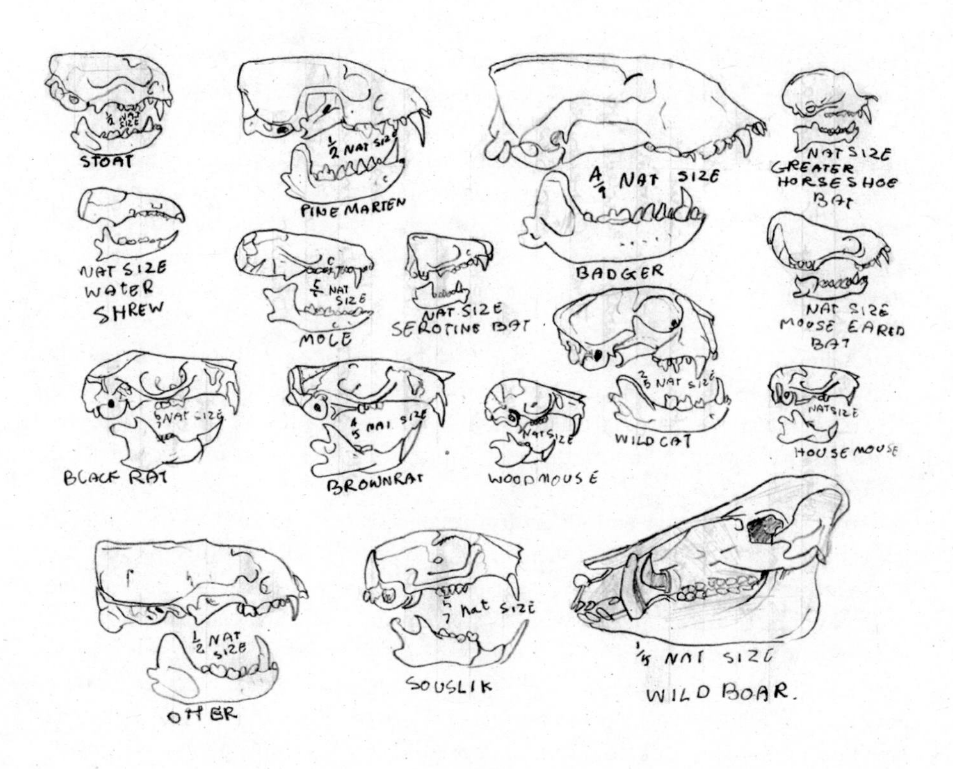

42
BUCKHURST HILL COUNTY HIGH SCHOOL

Firm set above the Roding Stream,
By wide and grassy leas,
Our house stands firmly to the winds,
'Twixt Essex lanes and trees.
While we within its walls are found
Like loyal sons we rest,
Contriving how our varied gifts
May serve the school the best.

The School Song (1940) – R. Steele / S. Campbell

When Chris left Oakdale Junior School he received the following comments from his class teacher, Mr Phillips, in his final school report:

> Christopher works extremely hard at any subject in which he is interested and can become completely absorbed. He is intelligent, untidy and unpredictable; capable of very good work; interested in all that goes on around him; likes to experiment and is independently minded.

Despite a general ability grade of A, Maths was still his bugbear. He was given a C+ for the subject. In September 1969, he entered Buckhurst Hill County High School for Boys, where he was placed in the same form as Steve Cladingboel, his friend from Oakdale. Buckhurst Hill was a grammar school that aped the public school system. The pupils were divided into four 'houses' (as they were in my and Izzy's school), which were named and coloured: Forest – green, Roding – red, Hainault – yellow and Chigwell – blue. Chris was assigned to Chigwell house. Boys were addressed by their last names, and masters, most of whom wore academic gowns, had to be called 'sir'. Yet for all the posturing, the headmaster, Mr. Colgate, adopted a fairly liberal attitude. He was not an advocate of corporal punishment, and whilst insistent on correct uniform, did not mind too much if boys wore their hair long. The major difference between BHCHS and a true public school was the fact that it was not fee-paying, which meant that pupils came from a broad range of social backgrounds.

A number of boys played musical instruments, enough to form an orchestra. In Chris's year, four boys stood out: Chris himself, Martin Koch, Martin Wheatley and Cliff Oliver. Chris already knew Martin Koch, a trombonist, as they both played in the Redbridge Band. Martin Wheatley, or 'Nitram', as Chris called him, played the saxophone and guitar. He took up the oboe when he realised that he would need to be able to play an orchestral instrument in order to gain entry to a music college. Cliff Oliver played piano and viola. He was an instinctive musician who could improvise at the piano. From the age of fifteen he supplemented his pocket money by playing in pubs, encouraged by his father, who sang. His father was a member of the Communist Party, a fact that Cliff did not hide. Cliff even encouraged Marxist debates at school, in which Nitram and various other boys with left-wing leanings participated, but Chris did not become involved, keeping quiet about Mum and Dad's Communist Party membership. The secrecy our parents imposed upon us caused some discomfort. Was it not cowardly to deceive, dishonest to pretend? If they believed in communism, why behave as if they were ashamed of it? Not that we asked such questions out loud; like Chris, Izzy and I kept our mouths shut.

Mum's rather conservative tastes in musical genres had no effect whatsoever on Chris, who was eager to listen to, explore and experiment with music, whatever its description. Nitram and he became good friends, not just because of their unpretentious, eclectic approach to music, but because they shared a similar off-the-wall, wacky sense of humour. The music department was run by Mr. Rippin, a shortish, balding man, fast-spoken, with a dry wit, who welcomed the talents of Giles, Koch, Wheatley and Oliver. A week before the end of each school year, when the examination period was over, Mr. Rippin organised a School Music Festival. He engaged an outside adjudicator and invited entries from any boys who could play, compose or sing. A large number of pupils responded, including Steve Cladingboel, who entered the novice piano class and submitted a composition. The school also had a first-rate drama group, which staged *Hamlet* during the time Chris was there.

Although it appeared that some of the masters were appointed via the 'old-boy network' and lacked academic qualifications, there were some good teachers at Buckhurst Hill. Mr. Rooney, for example, was unanimously respected for his inspirational teaching of English. The boys felt secure enough with him to ask why he wore a gown. He replied that its purpose was to keep the chalk-dust off his clothes. Mr. Downey, known as 'Fluff', was also an excellent English teacher, and was Chris's form master in his second, third and fourth years. Mr. Leek and Mr. Loveridge taught Geography so well that most boys chose to take the subject at O level. Steve Cladingboel described Mr. Leek as the very best teacher he ever met, an aged but active man with the look of an adventurer, who commanded attention and impeccable behaviour without ever being fierce. Mr. Loveridge was a younger man, flamboyant in personality, with a passion for Wagner. He used the word 'Buxtehude' as an exclamation of horror. On good days he could be heard singing arias in a falsetto voice as he bounced along the corridor.

Maths continued to prove difficult for Chris. It seems odd when he was so mentally alert, but he simply could not latch on to it. The subject did not enthuse or captivate him; he could not make any sense of it and fell so far behind that he knew he would never catch up. His BHCHS report book contains numerous negative comments from his maths masters. For example:

> More effort required. He is forgetful and must try to really learn the work.
> Very confused. Jumps too easily to the wrong conclusions & finds the pace rather quick.
> A disappointing examination mark (21%). A greater effort required if he is to improve the standard of his work.

Yet he did try, as is evident from the following:

> He has worked well and is making steady progress.
> Shows interest & is anxious to please, but must revise thoroughly.

He was put into the lowest set, never managed to achieve higher than a 'D' grade, nor ever passed an exam. His highest mark in five years was 43%. Chris's consistent failure in maths indicated conclusively that he would be excluded from a scientific career: to work as a researcher and classifier of animals, to become a Zoologist or anything of a similar nature, required maths O level. He had given up on the idea of veterinary work after he discovered that he was too squeamish when he fainted during the dissection of a frog in biology. Sadly, he was forced to realise that any career in which he could utilise his scientific mind was closed to him. His aspirations for the future naturally turned towards a professional career in music, and would probably have done so anyway. Nevertheless, he always remained deeply interested in the first passion of his life.

Miss Cecilia Hynes-Higman, one of the few female members of staff, taught French. After explaining something to her students in French, she would ask, "Do you get my gist?" Chris's response to the oft-repeated phrase was, "j... j... gist about." Grins spread and shoulders shook, but the joke was 'perdu' on Mademoiselle. Chris, taken with the descriptive sound of words wrote 'A dollop of mottled sputum' next to a stain on the cover of Nitram's notebook.

There were a few hated teachers: Chris particularly loathed the PE instructors; sadistic, bullying types, who thought it necessary to push boys beyond their pain threshold. Nothing pleased them more than snow, rain, sub-zero temperatures or heat waves – ideal torture conditions for cross-country running. Various routes were deployed, but the one most favoured by the PE staff involved going over the River Roding via a metal sewage pipe several feet in diameter. The river flowed sluggishly some distance beneath the pipe, slushy pats of brown dung-like matter floating on its surface. The pipe's cylindrical surface provided insecure foothold; with nothing to hang onto, getting across was plainly dangerous. Week after week, trails of mud-splattered, barelegged pupils followed the compulsory cross-country course and made their way precariously over the Roding, hounded across by the PE teacher.

On one occasion, a boy in Chris's year fell from the pipe into the river. The boy was taken by ambulance to hospital, where his stomach was pumped to rid his body of the contaminated water he had swallowed. Chris was shaken by what had happened and appalled when it became clear that there would be no investigation. Such was the power of authority, the incident was washed away as swiftly as the water under the bridge. It didn't wash with Chris: the thought that the boy could have drowned or been seriously injured preyed on his mind. The attitude of the PE staff disgusted him – not just the facile way in which the accident was covered up, but the fact that they bull-headedly refused to alter the route. Steve Cladingboel told me, "I can remember having to cross that pipe – once we had to do cross-country when the River Roding was actually in flood. Although we took the other route rather than the pipe route, it still involved us having to splash around in water, unable to see the bank! Can you imagine?"

Chris often went to visit Steve at his house in Buckhurst Hill. Steve wrote: "We would go for long walks in the woods. I don't know what we used to talk about. I wish I could remember – conversations with Chris would always be different and interesting. We were very close friends in junior school and in the first two or three years at BHCHS. Sadly, from my viewpoint, we began to drift apart: we were never strangers, but as we grew up, our interests divided. He was turning into a fine musician and had friends who were similarly blessed. My musical prowess was more emotional than actual. I dabbled in composition, but my limited ability to play meant that I wasn't destined to be taken seriously. Suffice to say, Chris was one of the good guys; a gentle, unconventional person who saw things logically and would not tolerate unfairness. He didn't judge people and never, ever set out to do any harm."

David Long, a pupil four years below Chris at BHCHS, echoed Steve's sentiments when he told me: "What I mostly remember about Chris was that unusually for his year he didn't pick on we younger boys or give us a hard time."

43
A NEW DECADE

I know that the twelve notes in each octave and the variety of rhythm offer me opportunities that all of human genius will never exhaust.

Igor Stravinsky

Although my cello teacher, Florence Hooton, disapproved of my playing in orchestras, she decided that I should audition for the National Youth Orchestra of Great Britain. The NYO was, and still is, considered to be the finest youth orchestra in the country. It would be an achievement to get in and good for me to meet and play with other accomplished young musicians. I auditioned in October 1969 and was offered a place. The first course would begin on December 27th. I was sent a large package containing the cello parts of the music we would be playing, six pages of general instructions and a three-page inventory packed with rules, warnings and restrictions. After the fun and freedom of the Redbridge Youth Orchestra, the NYO sounded intimidating and austere. Mr. Bidgood's instructions to members of the RYO were brief:

> Please try to contain all your luggage in one suitcase and remember the course is only for five days. What to bring is in the main rather obvious and I shall leave this to your own good sense. Do not forget to bring your music with you and spare reeds, strings etc. if likely to be needed.
> POCKET MONEY: The amount of spending money you bring is of course an individual matter, and will in any case depend upon personal wealth.

That was it. The NYO directives read like a prison rulebook. To give you an idea, here is the NYO's inventory of 'Suitable Day Wear' for girls:

> **Shoes:** Sensible walking shoes or boots for outdoor use (NOT sandals and NOT boots of the high variety). They should be flat heeled with no iron tips or studs. Stiletto heels are NOT PERMITTED
> **Indoors:** White gym shoes must be worn at all times with white, green or red soles only. Substitutes are not accepted.
> **Coat:** This should be tidy and of a sensible length (not a half-coat, maxi-coat or cloak) and in a dark, plain colour. Bring a plastic mackintosh to wear over your coat and a rain hat or weatherproof headscarf.
> **Girls:** Suitable dress (not sleeveless) or skirts and blouses. MINISKIRTS are NOT permitted. Cello and harp players should ensure their skirts are of a suitable length and width.
> Cardigans or sweaters (plain colours), Stockings – neutral shades, not white or patterned.
> TROUSERS ARE NOT PERMITTED

On it went – pages and pages of regulations, the word NOT appearing in every sentence. It was so dated as well. Nobody wore stilettos in 1969 – they had gone out in the fifties. Miniskirts, though, were in. Mum was not going to buy me a new wardrobe to go to the NYO, as it was costing her enough already. What, we puzzled, was wrong with trousers?

I left for the first course feeling that I was about to spend time at Her Majesty's pleasure. The director of the NYO was Ivey Dickson. Ivey held the auditions and hand-picked her orchestra, which numbered twice as many boys than girls. She discriminated openly against her own sex, promoted boys over more able girls and barred females from principal positions, apart from one or two notable exceptions. Fraternisation between the sexes was actively discouraged, boys' and girls' dormitories well-separated, and house-staff quick to admonish couples seen holding hands. But how could they possibly have kept us apart? No restrictions have ever quelled the magnetic force of attraction.

However, the petty regulations could not diminish the unforgettable musical experience of the NYO or the highs, and lows, of an intense social interaction. The NYO became the focus of my life, not just the three residential courses each year, but also the vast correspondence I maintained between-times. I enjoyed the taste of boarding school life: sleeping in dormitories; gossiping after lights out; sharing secrets and woes. In later years, I joined with other girls in night escapades for secret rendezvous with boys – creeping along corridors; stifling hysterics; breaking out in cold sweats as a stair creaked outside a member of staff's room; feeling our way in the dark down to basements; shivering in our nightdresses, suddenly conscious of how scantily-clad we were – assignations of such daring and terror that the satisfaction of being with the opposite sex was tempered by thoughts of the hazards of returning to our dormitories without being caught. I think the pleasure lay more in the telling and re-telling of our intrepid missions.

The first course I attended was Christmas 1969, held at South Croydon School. The classrooms were turned into dormitories, each room containing a dozen or more camp beds. My initial task was to make the bed. Wrestling with the collapsible canvas stretcher next to mine was a girl whom I admired at first sight, not for her bed-making skills, which were worse than mine, but for her beauty, grace and sophistication. She looked helplessly at her bed, turned to me and giggled. "I'm Louise by the way. Who are you?" So it was that I met Louise Williams at my first NYO course and idolised her from then on. I was in awe of her superior intellect and remained so, aware that she existed on a higher plane and would always be out of my reach. My inferiority, real or imagined, never quite allowed us to be bosom buddies.

The orchestra had to assemble half an hour before every full rehearsal to tune up. The procedure, which was directed by the leader (the principal violin), took twenty-five minutes, each section tuning separately, every wind player tuning individually. It was an extraordinary process peculiar to the NYO. For the last five minutes we had to remain completely still and quiet, a period of time that was famously known as 'The NYO Silence'. When the conductor walked into the hall, we all stood up, waiting until he had taken his place on the rostrum and indicated that we might be seated.

The programme was Stravinsky's *Rite of Spring* and Debussy's *La Mer*: our conductor was Pierre Boulez. I was one of the youngest and was placed on the back desk of cellos (desk nine) next to another young novice, Keren. She and I stuck together for the first couple of days while we familiarised ourselves with the routine. Douglas Cameron coached the cellos – an elderly, rotund, Scottish gentleman with a partiality for whisky. In his prime he was one of the great British cellists. Although he often forgot our names, he was proud of his NYO cello section. He received our unanimous loyalty and we felt protective towards him. Often, he would sit behind the back desk during full orchestral rehearsals uttering inebriated grunts of praise to Keren and me. He was kind and lovable, and we cellists adored him. We smiled to one another when he swayed unsteadily into the cello room after lunch, red-faced and half asleep. At that time of the day, he often abandoned the set works and produced pieces written for massed cello ensembles, which were marvellous to play.

The 1960s came to an end during the course. Predictably, we were sent to our dormitories with lights out well before midnight – not that it stopped us from staying awake to whisper Happy New Year to each other in the dark. Izzy and I had been given page-a-day 1970 diaries for Christmas presents. During the evening of January 1st, we made our first entries. From here on, I will be quoting from the pages we filled. What I have selected is a tiny percentage of our output, but I have to say that the discarded material was far less mundane than the bulk of Mum's diaries. Yes, we did record the trivia of daily life, and there were many times during the writing of these chapters when I felt that our teenage scribble was far too embarrassing, mediocre and pointless to include at all: but nevertheless, the social history of the early seventies and the atmosphere in which we lived leaps from the pages. Our words describe our lives as they were happening. Reading them, it seemed as though I were watching a documentary about Cleveland Road, seeing holograms of us all. Our diaries only go so far, yet we write words that were not spoken. It was interesting to read Izzy's parallel account of those years for the first time, to compare our reports of the same events. Neither of us possessed the maturity to articulate our feelings adequately or the fearlessness to divulge our deepest thoughts, but we reveal ourselves all the same.

This has been one of the most awkward sections to bring together. I have found it difficult to decide how much of our diaries to include, which sentences to use and where best to place them. As Chris was not a diarist, it has been problematic to keep his voice audible in the mix. It has also been hard to strike a balance between Izzy's words and mine. I do not intentionally give her extracts less space – she simply did not write as much as I did. Never one for excess, she used the allotted space and stopped. A page a day was often insufficient for me, so I continued on loose paper, which I clipped into the book. As with Mum's diaries, ours are useful historical references and have helped to place events and rouse memories, but they are certainly not works of literary merit. For clarity, extracts from Izzy's diaries are printed in italics; extracts from mine are printed in plain type. I haven't dated every extract, but have grouped them chronologically. Each new line indicates a separate extract.

Whilst I was at my first NYO course, Izzy and Chris were with the Redbridge Youth Orchestra. Their week ended with a concert at Ilford Town Hall.

IZZY: January 1970: *Everything went very well but during the Schumann piano concerto, Kelvin Little climbed up into the rafters above the stage and threw something down onto one of the drums, which made a large thump.*
Mum, Granny, Chris and I left for the Fairfield Hall Croydon to hear Cath playing in the NYO. The concert was smashing – we were sitting right behind the percussion.

CATHY: January 1970: The concert went wonderfully. Pierre Boulez was called back seven times. Auntie Lilian listened to the concert on the radio and phoned to say, "The Rite of Spring is so nice, dear. It really gives one the feeling of Spring coming." It actually sounds dissonant and aggressive – like a sacrificial ceremony.

Our diary entries indicate the huge amount of time we were engaged with music. Chris and I practised for hours every day, Izzy rather less so. Izzy had violin and piano lessons; I travelled to the Academy every week for my cello lesson, with extra lessons on Sunday afternoons. On Friday evenings, Mum, Chris and I rehearsed with *Musici*, the Redbridge teacher/student orchestra founded and conducted by Malcolm Bidgood. *Musici* gave three public concerts a year and a day of concerts in schools every term, known as the 'Day Series'. Saturday mornings were spent at the Redbridge Music School. On Saturday afternoons we travelled to Goldsmiths College in south London, where we played in the Goldsmiths Youth Orchestra – a group that Len Davis, the Wortley summer school tutor, ran and conducted. Chris had band practice on Tuesdays and Sundays as well as his horn lesson. Hardly a week went by when we were not performing in at least one concert. There were music festivals, prizes, competitions, school orchestra rehearsals, school concerts, as well as many one-off concerts in which we were asked to play. Each of us had to remember what we were doing and when, but it was Mum who managed the family diary and kept track of the timetable. Her commitment to our activities was a full-time job in itself, but she also taught some forty pupils a week, ran the Professional Service, did her recording sessions and took on umpteen other responsibilities too.

CATHY: January-March 1970: Dad went up the wall at us for eating sweets. Bitterly cold. Dad had forgotten to put the heater under the car so I had to walk to the bus stop. Made Chris a hot-water-bottle.
Went to the Doctor's. I still have this damned verruca. He froze it with CO2 snow and says it should do the trick. Des and Melly came to collect me as I can't walk properly. Pat is wearing false eyelashes. She looks so pretty.
Got to the Academy and waited around for Miss Hooton. She was late for my lesson, but seemed very pleased with me and said I was 'growing up' (one usually does).
In science, boiled copper filings in dilute Nitric Acid. Then had dinner. In biology we dissected – a pea!
Listened to New World symphony, played the Pathetique sonata and listened to Mum playing a Hindemith fugue (yuck).
Went to Musici rehearsal with Mum.
The car has broken down again – this time the fan belt's gone. In the evening went with Miss Sprakes to the Fairfield Hall to hear Jacqueline Du Pré – she was fantastic.
Went to hear the Aeolian String Quartet at the Hawkey Hall. During the concert, a man had a heart attack. He was on a machine for 10 minutes, but died.

Went straight upstairs to practise, came down for dinner, then retreated my steps upstairs again to work on my skirt. Hell! Absolute Hell! My skirt isn't wide enough for me. I must slim as I never have before. Then Dad came snooping into my room. I wish he wouldn't. Dad had a row with a woman at work and she reported him to the boss. The boss said he'd see him tomorrow and accused him of 'un-gentlemanly language'. When Dad came back from work, he looked so pale and tired and came home so early that my heart missed a beat and jumped to the conclusion that he'd got the sack. Oh what a big weight off my mind when I found he hadn't. In fact, he's just been put into another department and will be getting a 7½% increase!
Izzy, Chris and I went shopping to Ilford with money Mum gave us for our birthday. Got a nice pair of patent plastic shoes, a navy and white dress and a bra. Izzy got a dress and 2 bras. Bought some material in Bodgers for me to alter Izzy's dress she needs in the school play.
I was playing around with the stapler and a staple went right through my first finger. Oddly enough, it didn't hurt much. I pulled it out and washed my finger. Luckily it didn't happen to my left hand.
Mum drove me to Florrie's and I did a complete performance of the Shostakovich sonata.
Izzy went to a barn dance. I stayed at home and finished her dress.
Met the Turners at the Queen Elizabeth pub with Grandad and Auntie Lilian. The clutch is going on our car. Des trailed Dad all the way home from the pub in case he broke down and needed a tow.
Had to heat the water for our bath in kettles – the boiler had gone out.
Went to see West Side Story at the Plaza with Miss Sprakes. So terribly sad at the end. Couldn't sleep with all the tunes going round in my head.
Practised NYO music – Tchaik 4 and Brahms 2.

IZZY: January-March 1970: *Mum did some fiddle practice with me. We watched the first episode of Forsyte Saga.*
We had a Latin test and I got it all right, surprisingly enough. In Hockey I was goalkeeper. The field was like a marsh and since the ball never came in my direction, I was freezing. The boring game was livened up by the arrival of a playful black dog. In RI we had a discussion on birth control of all things. I auditioned for the middle school play – Pride and Prejudice – got the part of Kitty. We're reading Jane Eyre and Oliver Twist in English. Bought a drink from the new Robo-Serve but the machine forgot to put in any sugar. Lunch was suet pudding like concrete.
I went to Chigwell School for the Henry Riding competition. Mum accompanied me. I played quite well.
I did a long typing session for Christopher. I am reading Sons and Lovers by DH Lawrence. Des gave it to me.
I have won the Henry Riding memorial prize which is £20! I paid it into the bank. Cathy and Mum went to a Musici rehearsal. Chris and I watched 'Oh! Brother' and 'The Golden Silents'.
The Bishop of Barking took a 'birthday' service. His prayer was so long that I practically fell to sleep. We went to the Plaza with the Turners to see 'Topaz' and 'The Life of a Woman'. Topaz was bloodthirsty but the other film was very good. All through it I was thinking of Matthew Pia, I don't know why but it made me feel sad, probably 'coz I'll never see him again.
Dad, Chris and I went to the Turners. I had a glass of wine. We saw some sweet little pups at Club Row, the Henry VIII exhibition at the Bethnal Green Museum, then Des drove us back and we had champagne. Dad says it's the last time he's ever going to the Turners'. He says Melanie and Jonathan are too cheeky.

On one occasion Des took Izzy to Club Row, a pet market in the East End, on her own. For some reason the rest of us were busy or away. Izzy was particularly taken with a ginger-haired guinea pig. Des bought him for her, complete with hutch. She was delighted and called her new pet Gingerbread. But when they brought the animal home, Mum was affronted that Des had impulsively bought Izzy a pet without first asking if it would be OK. Des was astounded. To avoid conflict, he said he would keep Gingerbread at Primrose Road, where Izzy could visit him whenever she wanted. Sometime later, I persuaded Mum to let me have guinea pigs, which I kept in the hut. Her condition was that I had to look after them – she was not going to clean out the hutches or buy their bedding and food. Unfortunately, I became more and more allergic to them. They made me sneeze, wheeze and brought me out in a rash. In the end, Mum was lumbered with the care of them, until Miss Sprakes said she would keep them at Oakdale.

> ***IZZY: April 1970:*** *Chris and I packed for RYO Easter course and Cathy packed for NYO. Went on the coach to Aldeburgh. I changed for dinner which was very long and drawn out. I sat next to a very homesick girl who was crying all through the meal, poor thing. Bramwell Tovey is playing the Vaughan Williams tuba concerto with the orchestra. We went to see the Maltings in its present state. Chris has found some human bones!*

I shall pause for a moment to elucidate Izzy's last comment. It was true – Chris did find some human bones. Izzy recalls that during the week in Aldeburgh, Bram Tovey and Chris became firm friends. Although Chris was only eleven and Bram sixteen, the age difference was irrelevant: there was something extraordinarily mature about Chris. He was comfortable conversing with anyone on virtually any subject – what he didn't know he enquired about, not at all afraid to ask questions. Bram and Chris were well-matched in intellect and humour, enjoying a companionship that stretched their minds and sharpened their wits.

When Chris heard that a graveyard in Dunwich, not far from Aldeburgh, was falling from the cliffs and that it was possible to find human bones on the beach, he had to get there. His enthusiasm charmed an older member of the orchestra with a car into driving him and Bram to the village to investigate. As they walked along the sands, they looked upwards to the cliffs to see the macabre sight of hundreds of human bones sticking out from graves that had been stripped away by the elements. Chris did not find a skull, as he had hoped he might, but he did return with a few human bones. I will be writing more about Dunwich in a later chapter, as this was not the only time that he, or Bram, went there.

> **CATHY: April-June 1970:** Izzy & Chris are in Aldeburgh with RYO and I am in Ramsgate with NYO. Our conductor is Fjeldstad who is rather sweet but not half as good as Boulez. Douggy Cameron (our cello coach) was rather drunk. Chris Waltham (leader of cellos) took the sectional. We were playing a lovely piece by Klengel for 12 cellos when Ivey barged in and spoilt the whole thing. Poor Douggy was very offended and upset. We all felt dreadful after that and in sympathy with Douggy. We gave him a tie and a bottle of Scotch to express our regret for the insults he received yesterday.
> Said goodbye to Chris Waltham who I really admire for his casualness and the way he

does everything just right.
Apollo 13 has gone wrong and there isn't enough oxygen left for the astronauts. They might die. I read the 39 Steps and watched The Expert – a tragic story about two children who die from carbon monoxide poisoning.
My garden is looking lovely at the moment with daffs and tulips and the wallflowers are all in bud. Found out that Izzy and I are almost illegitimate.
Apollo 13 has landed safely and the men are OK. Watched Steptoe and Son.
Went to Beal in the evening for the concert. It went very well really. Intonation was pretty atrocious, but I think I played my solos well.
Miss Sprakes came over and we watched Klemperer conduct Beethoven 6.
Dad has just this minute come nosing about in my room, going on at me about leaving Grandad's too soon and telling me it was my fault.
Did end of year exams at the Academy. Douggy examined me – he was wearing the tie we bought him at NYO! Afterwards he bought me something to eat – he's so sweet.

IZZY: May-July 1970: *Mum drove me to the Dance. I 'got off' (as my friends so delicately put it) with a boy called Ray. He is quite nice but not so nice as Matthew. He saw me to the station and kissed me goodbye.*
We did our play in English class and it was an absolute flop. I was covered in tomato ketchup, which stank to high heaven. In art we had to draw a shrimp. They had been bought on Saturday and smelt a bit.
I'm reading Gone with the Wind again. Even though I knew how it ended, I still cried buckets.
Des fixed up Chris's new case of stuffed animals. I helped Chris paint the back of his fox case.
I've been given the part of Viola in Twelfth Night. I am the tenth smallest in the third year.
We had to do another drawing of the shrimp and then paint it.
At BHCHS fair, Cathy won 25/- on Chris's stall.
In Biology we did genetics and saw a dissected rat and its embryo. We also saw pictures of a Caesarean birth, which didn't look very appetising.
I found a dead fly in my school dinner, which quite put me off. I got A- for my 'embossed' shrimp.
My friends and I went swimming to Loughton pool. Ray (boy I met at dance) was there, (unfortunately) he is revoltingly spewy.
In biology we did about twins and then did alcohol and smoking.
First lesson was RI. We gave in our Methodist projects, and are now doing the Salvation Army.
The Tories won the General Election, pots to them!

44
A CHESTFUL OF DRUGS

All the truth of my position came flashing on me; and its disappointments, dangers, disgraces, consequences of all kinds, rushed in in such a multitude that I was borne down by them and had to struggle for every breath I drew.

Great Expectations – Charles Dickens

CATHY: January-July 1970 re: Asthma:
Took my pills. I'm worried about my Ventolin inhaler – I'm getting to rely on it too much. Went to the chest hospital and waited one hour 20 mins before I was seen. Have more pills to take – Phenergan to make me sleep. Had bad asthma at school and sat in the cloakroom (a common practice of mine as I feel so out of place in the library) reading David Copperfield.
Bad asthma and another layer of snow on the ground. I wasn't going to go to school, but when Granny and Mum started telling me off about various things, I left and trudged through the snow to school.
I felt very queer in the night, probably because of the mixture of Ventolin, Orciphrenaline, Phenergan and Aminophylline in my blood. At school I went all dizzy and faint and stayed in the medical room till lunchtime.
I had a very bad night of asthma. My back aches. Asthma always makes it so. I don't know what it is that's causing this. I'm getting fed up with it being so bad. I felt pretty grotty all through my practice – weak, wobbly and shaky with a slight pain across my tummy. Asthma bad after dinner so didn't go to rehearsal. I tried to sleep in the afternoon but couldn't.
I woke up very tired… Asthma as bad as ever. Dad came up to my room fussing. I wish he'd leave me alone.
Had assembly, maths, French, asthma attack, break, double English, another asthma attack, dinner, double needlework, when I finished Izzy's skirt all but the hem. Asthma bad.
Another grotty night and went to school. My cough is really very bad. I have a load of phlegm in my chest. Stayed after school for orchestra. I just coughed and coughed and coughed, felt very tired and grotty. I thought I had a temperature.
I had quite a bad night and one really nasty attack, but I think I'm getting better. Up at 6.15 because of asthma. Sunbathed until I came out in a sun rash. Des phoned. He confirmed that he's sure our asthma is psychosomatic.
This asthma is supposed to be psychosomatic, but it has been bad with me. I think it could be because I have such a lot of fluid on my chest. At the First orchestra concert I felt sick, shaky, faint and ill during the performance because of pills.
Walked through the park to the Chest Clinic. Dr. Turner-Warwick was away. I saw Dr. Price. She was a bit worried about my asthma. She looked at me accusingly and asked me if I smoked. Smoked! The smell of smoke is enough to give me an attack. She asked again, saying I had to be honest. I told her I was. I've lost 9lbs in weight. Went back to school. Felt grottier than ever, probably because of new drug, Franol.
Another appointment at the Chest Hospital, only a week after the last one. I went alone.

There were some poor old people there and one particularly poor old man who was upset because they'd decided to put him into hospital again and he'd only just come out. I now have Intal spincaps.

Tired again. Took my pills and potions. The spincaps I'm taking 4 times a day taste revolting – a mixture of salt, petrol and manure! It was while I was in the library that a terrible pain started. I felt faint and really awful, so I went and lay down in the medical room. The pain was so bad that I cried. I cried on the way home, then lay down. After dinner it miraculously stopped so I played in the school concert after all – 'Hiawatha's Wedding Feast' and 'In Windsor Forest'.

Absolutely exhausted after a rather restless night. I now have a barky cough and a very sore throat. My bronchitis is quite bad really and I'm getting asthma from it.

I felt weak and a bit faint when I went to school, very sleepy and rather depressed. Oh my feet were so heavy to drag along the ground.

Still feeling awful. I didn't do much practice because I felt so odd.

I woke up feeling weak and odd again and couldn't go to school. It's the terrible feeling of being heavy, as though my feet weigh a ton and I can't lift them.

Went to the Chest Hospital. As I walked, my feet felt heavier and heavier and I was pleased to sit down when I arrived. I now have some red and black anti-biotic pills. My cello case felt terribly heavy with all the pill bottles in it. I was worn out when I eventually arrived at the Academy. I had a reasonable lesson except that I was exhausted. Went straight to the Infant School to rehearse. It's a terribly hot day and very humid. The heat had made me even droopier and I was decidedly wobbly. I felt rather faint. Chris and Mum went to Musici but I didn't – Mum reckons I'm ill. P.S. I've lost more weight.

I wish I saw more of Mum. I hardly see anything of her. I somehow don't feel part of my parents – least of all Dad, he's so crotchety nowadays. Izzy and I bought Chris a Texan cravat for his birthday and Mum bought him a pink shirt.

Oh, that interminable wheezing, the wracking coughing, gasping and snatching for air. I hated a fuss being made and did not want to draw attention to myself, but asthma is not a silent affliction. I propped myself over the washbasin in my bedroom at night, shoulders hunched up to my ears, and coughed and coughed, spitting green and yellow gunge, my mouth stretched to suck oxygen into lungs that were already full – the distress of asthma is in part the inability to exhale. I scratched my sides, while every short breath I forced out carried a monosyllabic word – no, no, stop, no, don't, no, stop, please, no, no.

My Ventolin inhaler went everywhere with me. It rescued me from attacks, but the asthma persisted. Nothing was going to knock it out. Desperate, I puffed the inhaler more frequently than I should. My hands shook. My temperature was consistently higher than normal. When I packed my bag in the mornings, I had to sort out my drug supplies for the day. The spinhaler was a problem to take at school. Inside the contraption was a small propeller, which whizzed when you breathed in, expelling the powder from the capsules into the lungs. The problem was that it sounded like a silly party whistle. I hid in a cubicle in the toilet block, home to secret smokers and swarms of Daddy longlegs, hoping to conceal my identity as absurd whees and zooms poured forth.

The six drugs I used to take daily were a combination of bronchodilators, short-acting Beta Two agonists and antihistamines. I have now discovered that side effects include shakiness, nervous tension, dizziness, confusion, blurred vision, dry mouth, increased sensitivity to sunlight, nausea, abdominal discomfort, insomnia, heart palpitations, tachycardia (faster than normal heartbeat) and hypokalaemia (low blood potassium level). No wonder I felt ill.

I started itching under my right breast and around my side to my back. In the mirror, I saw a line of red spots and decided that some sort of midge or mosquito had become trapped underneath my bra and bitten its way around. Having had plenty of insect bites at camp, I assumed they would go away. Instead, the itching became worse and the spots got bigger. Mum asked me why I was scratching.

"Oh, just some mosquito bites. I've had them for weeks. They're quite annoying because they're directly under my bra line."

"Mosquito bites? They can't be mosquito bites."

"Horse-fly bites, then."

"Don't be ridiculous. Let me see."

"They're OK, really."

"Come on, show me."

By now they were quite painful, with little heads all over them. Reluctantly, I undid my blouse and lifted the edge of my bra.

"Those are definitely not mosquito bites. Come and show them to Granny."

"Oh Muuum." Granny took one look and said peremptorily, "Shingles. That's what she has."

"You'd better see the Doctor," said Mum.

I phoned and made an appointment for the next day.

CATHY: I've had a rash for a while. It's rather painful and has little heads all over it. I went to the Doctor's. He said the rash is shingles – the thing like chicken pox, and it would have been worse but Phenergan, my sleeping pill, has some kind of substance in it that kept it at bay.

I looked up Shingles and found this: 'Shingles is an infection caused by the chickenpox *varicella-zoster* virus. It causes the sufferer to feel extremely debilitated and exhausted. Aches and pains, a mild fever and depression are other symptoms. The rash starts off as red spots, which turn to blisters and crust over. It is extremely itchy and usually very painful. May need up to three weeks off work. The disease generally affects the elderly, although it can occur in younger individuals whose body's immune defences are affected by stress, nervous tension, other infections or certain drugs.' The description ticked all the boxes for me. I didn't have three weeks off school, however; not even one day.

At around this time I missed a period. I had only been menstruating for about a year, but I was concerned. I couldn't take my worries to Mum. I don't know how it was for Izzy, but this was my experience: when I realised I was having my first period and, hot with embarrassment, told Mum, the first thing she did was to broadcast the fact to Granny. "Aye, well," Granny responded, "ye'd best get used to them, for ye'll be having them for many a year yet."

There I was, standing in the kitchen by the toilet with a pair of soiled knickers screwed up in my hand. I whispered to Mum, "What shall I do with these?"

Granny waded towards me. "Let me see," she demanded, snatching the offending article from my hand and inspecting the stain, "Och, that's nothing."

Drenched with humiliation, I whimpered, "Muuum."

Mum told Granny to put my knickers in the bag-wash and said, "I'll go and find Catherine a sanitary towel." I fled to my room intent on shutting myself in forever.

I would never again speak to Mum about periods, nor did I feel able to broach the subject with Izzy; we both wanted privacy. But I could talk to Chris, in a roundabout, hypothetical way. He seemed to know everything. I found him in his room dissecting an owl pellet.

"Look at this, Cath. You can tell what this barn owl has eaten from the stuff it's regurgitated."

I watched him loosening little bones with tweezers from a matted mass of fur and feathers.

"See, that's a jaw bone – probably a shrew – and here's a foot."

"They're so tiny. How can you tell?"

"Well, the shrew is the smallest mammal. I'll know better when I've separated the bones out. Do you know where the smallest bones in the human body are?"

"Yes, the ear."

"Hmm. *Incus Malleus Stapes*: the anvil, the hammer and the stirrup. Amazing, isn't it?"

"Just out of interest, Chris, is it possible to get pregnant without having sexual intercourse?"

He told me about hermaphrodites that are both male and female and can reproduce by themselves – stick insects, worms, barnacles or snails for example, moving on to the unusual reproductive behaviour of the seahorse and duck-billed platypus. Then he revealed that the word *parthenogenesis* means to reproduce from an unfertilised egg.

"Do humans ever reproduce in that way?" I asked nervously.

"I think it's impossible. On the other hand, millions believe in the Virgin birth. Christianity is based on parthenogenesis, if you think about it."

"I suppose you're right," I replied, thinking about it.

"There's something I'd like to ask you," said Chris.

"What's that?"

"Have you ever eaten your own shit?"

"Of course I haven't," I answered indignantly.

"*Incus Malleus Stapes*! Don't get narky! I didn't really think so, but I've been reading an interesting book about adolescence and it says that in some rare cases, pubescent girls have been known to eat their own excrement – something to do with hormonal imbalance. I was just curious, that's all."

"Well, no I really haven't, and I'm sure Izzy hasn't either. In fact, Chris, you'd better not go around asking girls – they might get offended."

"I wouldn't do that. I'm not daft; but I can ask you and Izzy – I wouldn't go telling anyone else, you know… if you *had* eaten your own shit."

CATHY: I hope my missed period is just an unusual thing this month. Otherwise, it must be parthenogenesis because I certainly haven't had intercourse with anyone. Dad brought someone called Steve back from the office and he stayed to dinner, then Dad got very cross with me because I wouldn't play English Autumn to him. I'm getting to hate the piece anyway – the middle section is so bad.

Dad hung two pictures in the living room. The one above the upright piano was of a nude woman. "Don't you think she's beautiful, Catherine?"

"Erm, no, not really."

"But it's Art! Renoir! One of the greatest impressionist painters! You should learn to appreciate Art."

How could he think her beautiful with her bruised-looking skin, fat arms, podgy hands, huge breasts and matted hair? She was an insult to Mum, a daily embarrassment, and a place on the wall from which to avert one's gaze when practising the piano. Yet she was always there, an amused, conspiratorial look in her eye as we struggled with scales and arpeggios.

The other print, clashing crazily against the sunflowers, was also a Renoir – *La Petite Irène*. It was a semi-profile painting of a young girl with what looked like a turquoise fish gasping for breath clipped into her long chestnut-brown hair.

"Such a beautiful child," Dad lyricised. "She reminds me a little of Melanie Turner."

"Melanie!" I protested, "Melly's far prettier than her. I'd much rather have a framed photo of Melly on the wall."

"Oh you – you have absolutely no appreciation of beauty, do you?"

He huffed out of the room, shaking his head exasperatedly.

45
THE PACT

Now that my ladder's gone
I must lie down where all the ladders start
In the foul rag-and-bone shop of the heart.

The Circus Animals' Desertion – W. B. Yeats

My bedroom was my sanctuary, the place where I kept my secrets, diaries, letters and private thoughts, and also the space that contained my suffering – where I wrestled with asthma, fighting for every breath. But it was not always a place of safety. I have a memory of a disturbing incident that happened in my bedroom; something I did not speak about until my late thirties in the safety of a therapy room after many years of sessions. To write about it, I find it necessary to use the present tense.

One evening, writing cross-legged on my bed, I hear unwelcome steps crossing Chris's room towards mine, followed by Dad's loathsome knock on the door.

"Yes?" I say, wishing he would leave me alone.

"May I come in?"

"Just a minute," I reply. I want to say "No", but don't. Shoving the pages I've been writing under my pillow, I call, "OK then." The door opens slowly and he shuffles in.

"What is it?" I ask uncomfortably.

"Oh, I'd just like to spend a little time with my Caagy," he says, using the baby name that Izzy used to call me. "We don't get much time alone, do we? Ahh, Caagy and Diddiga – do you remember?"

"Yes, Dad," I reply, unable to disguise my irritation. It was sweet that Izzy and I called each other Caagy and Diddiga when we first began to talk, but it got on our nerves when Dad used our baby names with such indulgent sentimentality.

He comes and sits beside me on the bed, reaching out his hand in a gesture of approach. I fear he is going to put his arm around me and inch away. My discomfort intensifies. He looks at me with a tight, stretched smile that is not a smile. His eyes bore into me, pleadingly, devouringly. I feel hunted. My mouth is dry. He smells of alcohol.

"Ah, my Caagy," he croons, "you're the only one who understands what it's like for me here. Living with those dreadful women, those witches." He spits out the last words. Mum and Granny. He hates them. I pretend he is joking.

"They're not witches, Dad!"

"What would you call them, then?"

"Well – er –" I feel my heart thumping.

"I heard her having a go at you today. And you answered back. Good for you. You tell her what you think of her."

Granny did tick us off occasionally. She had criticised me about something and for the first time I had retaliated with a nasty rejoinder. As the words came out of my mouth, I experienced a surge of satisfaction, followed by instant remorse. Sometimes it seemed that everyone in the house was cross and moody. It happened more and more these days.

"I didn't mean to shout," I say.

"No, you go ahead. Shout. And I'll back you up. We must stick together. They're too much for me alone. And you need me to stick up for you too – don't you?"

"No – well, I know it's difficult sometimes," I say, in a pinched voice.

"Difficult! You don't know the half of it. I could tell you some things –"

"Dad, I –" *I don't want to hear any of this.*

"Your mother, she – and her mother – the way they treat me. Well, I'll tell you, they're wicked, evil –"

He stops speaking. I stare into my lap, willing him to go away. Silence sucks the air out of my lungs. Dad sighs and breathes in heavily. "Oh, my dear," he says. "We must support and protect each other. Could we do that? It would help so much to know that you are on my side."

His eyes cling to me like burrs, searching my face. "I've wanted to have this conversation for so long. Yes, for so very long. Tell you what," he says, his voice brightening, "we can form an alliance!"

"An alliance?"

"Yes, that's right. But this is just between you and me, you understand? That's what an alliance is. We'll know, but they won't. You promise to be on my side and I promise to be on yours. You will promise, won't you? Eh?"

"Er, I suppose," I mumble miserably.

"Well, you know, when people make an agreement, they form a pact."

"A pact?"

"Yes; a commitment – a promise that can never be broken. What we must do is to conduct a little ritual. Have you something sharp here?"

He looks around; goes to open my private drawer.

"Only some nail scissors," I say hurriedly, putting my hand against the drawer.

"What about a needle? You must have a needle."

"What for?" I ask nervously.

"Don't worry, dear. Just get one."

I breathe in little snatches through my nose and nearly whimper. I stand up and go to the cupboard. Hands that seem to no longer belong to me rummage in my sewing basket. I give him a needle, my heart walloping in my chest.

"This will do fine. Now usually people use knives, sharp ones, and make a deep cut, but I think it will suffice if we just prick our thumbs and hold them together to mix our blood."

Far away, I register that he is enjoying this.

"I'll go first," he says.

Horrified, I watch as he digs the point into his right thumb and squeezes until a drop of bright red appears. He hands me the needle. I feel my heart thumping like a bass drum.

"I can't do it, Dad. I don't want to."

"Go on. It doesn't hurt. I'm sure you've pricked yourself many times when you've been sewing."

If I do this, I think, he will go. I clench my jaw, command my nerve and push the needle into my left thumb. I feel it puncture the skin.

"There's a good girl. Now squeeze. Here, like so."

A scarlet drop appears. I turn away. I don't want to look. He takes my wrist, holds my thumb and I feel him apply my bloodied thumb to his, pressing the two firmly together. His hands feel like sandpaper.

"Now we are as one," he pronounces, "and this is between us, our secret, only we shall know. It's us against them. It will give us strength to live on." He smiles and laughs a little. Then without warning, he draws me into a hug. I think he is going to kiss me. I jerk my head away. He holds it to his shoulder. Inside I am screaming.

"There, there," he says soothingly, stroking my head, "My dear Caagy."

I am as stiff as a board. He releases me, walks across the room with a bounce in his feet and leaves. I wait until I am sure he has gone, shut my door and lean against it. Then I go to the sink, run the hot tap and hold my throbbing thumb under the scalding water. I raise my head and with utter shame confront my mad-eyed, mirrored self and whisper, "How could you? How could you have sided with Dad against Mum and Granny? What have you done? I hate you. I hate you. I hate you."

In my diary I do not allude to the 'pact'. There are many entries that state combinations of the following: "Dad came into my room – fussing – moaning – I wish he wouldn't – he interrupted me writing – he left in a huff –" The only one I have identified as possibly referring to the above is this: "Mum took Izzy and Chris to the Town Hall for their concert. I stayed at home, had a bath, went upstairs to write letters and Dad came knocking at my door. It was awful." For some time, I panicked as to what Dad might ask of me now that he had me on his side. If there were an argument, would he call for my support or worse, reveal me as the Judas I was to Mum? Would he say to Granny that he wasn't the only one in the house who hated her? I had nightmares about it. During the day I felt as if I were on death row, waiting for the moment when I would be exposed; Dad would publicly claim me as his ally and Mum would never speak to me again. I steered clear of Dad, fearful that if he found me alone he would remind me of the pact. I knew that he knew I was deliberately avoiding him. I caught him looking at me with pained, accusing expressions. I had failed him; I had broken the promise. My responses to him were wrong and unnatural. I pleaded guilty to crimes I could not name and stood in the dock of judgement. I felt that all of it was my fault, but I couldn't put it right.

He didn't mention the pact again: and sometimes I wonder if it actually happened. Could I have imagined it? Was it not so bad – or worse – than I recall? I am not sure; yet the image of the needle, the blood, the fear, the horror, the sour-breath smell of alcohol, the helpless entrapment, the sense of being manipulated – I have carried those feelings since that time.

Dad's behaviour towards Izzy was not so directly invasive. As I have mentioned before, even though Izzy and I are twins, the role of older sister fell to me. My feelings of responsibility made me vulnerable. Izzy is quieter, more reserved, outwardly less emotional. Her method of self-preservation was to enclose herself, shut herself away in her world of books and appear to be indifferent and impenetrable.

She reminded me of an occasion when Dad decided to take us to 'the office' to meet his work colleagues. We were about eleven. He would not let us go as we were, in our holiday clothes. No, he selected our outfits, insisting that we dress identically in our grey pleated school skirts, freshly ironed blouses, white knee-length socks and polished shoes. Our hair was neatly plaited and he wanted ribbons tied at the ends. During the train journey he instructed us as to how we were to behave. We must shake hands with every person he introduced us to and say, "I'm very pleased to meet you." We were to be shown off as his beautifully groomed, perfectly mannered twin daughters. The whole day was unnatural and contrived. We were shy and uncomfortable. Dad put on an embarrassing performance. Needless to say, we failed to follow the script of his charade. On the way home he made it clear to us that we had disappointed him. To our relief he did not plan to take us to the office again.

For all Dad's supposed free-thinking, he was deeply conventional and prudish. He hankered after a bygone patriarchal era in which he, the head of the household, would dictate to his wife and children and would receive absolute obedience and acquiescence. Izzy and I were to play the roles of the dutiful, virtuous daughters and Chris was to play the part of the loyal, reverential son. Dad treated Chris like his 'son and heir', which Chris could not stand: he loathed the antiquated father/son posturing. Dad sought to live his lost boyhood through Chris and expected him to find schoolboy pranks and jokes from a long-gone generation amusing. Chris found it insufferable. If Dad was disappointed in Chris's response, Chris was disdainful of Dad's childishness. All three of us agreed that Dad was a pain.

46
SEPARATION AND INTERVENTION

I thought how unpleasant it is to be locked out;
and I thought how it is worse, perhaps, to be locked in.

A Room of One's Own – Virginia Woolf

When we were fourteen and Chris had just turned twelve, we camped at a site in Merionethshire, north Wales, not far from Harlech. Izzy and I were Trackers and Chris a Trailseeker. Steve Iliffe was one of the Tracker staff and he and I were also on the same clan. Although he was the clan-chief, he relied on my efficiency in the kitchen, whilst I admired the way he kept up his clan's spirits, sometimes literally. He sneaked me small shots of whisky in the catering tent "to keep you going – can't have you flagging, I need you too much!" I hated the taste of it, but savoured the thrill of being included in a staff secret.

Leslie Holden was the camp-chief. The three of us agreed that he ran the camp better than any other we had attended. Quietly-spoken, unobtrusive, thoughtful and compassionate, he kept his finger unerringly on the pulse of the camp and dealt diplomatically with issues before they became problems. No doubt he observed exactly what was going on in the Tracker group and in his wisdom left well alone. Izzy paired up with a boy called Ian Yellowlees while I tumbled into a swamp of abandonment and jealousy. I didn't want Ian for myself, but I was peeved that he liked Izzy better than me, and worse, that Izzy wanted Ian's company, not mine. I sulked, and for the first time there was a rift between my twin and me.

CATHY: Oh, I'm so jealous but also I'm pleased for Izzy. It's so difficult to explain. I've never been like this before. I really hate myself for feeling jealous of my own sister. It isn't exactly jealousy, it's the fact that I never see her, never speak to her and when I do she seems cross with me and that's unbearable.

Izzy settled between Ian's legs by the campfire while I sat beside them staring into the flames. I had a strong urge to kick Ian solidly in the thigh, to pull his arms away from Izzy's body, but I contained my feelings of spite and rage. I couldn't understand how Izzy had learned those lovers' postures – the way she kissed him and wrapped her body around him as if she had been practising for years. It seemed that she had crossed a wide river and left me stranded on the opposite bank. I sought out Chris in the Trailseeker group and admired the ram's skull he had found, which was now spiked onto his tent pole. His homesick days were over. Unintentionally popular, he attracted a crowd wherever he went, keeping them entertained with his encyclopaedic collection of astonishing facts. If one heard peals of laughter and spotted a ring of captivated people, it was more than likely that Chris would be in the centre. Unfortunately, I couldn't decamp to the Trailseeker group. I was stuck with the Trackers.

We went on a long, arduous hike, climbing Snowdon via the Watkin path. I was at the back the whole way, wheezing badly. The last stretch seemed to go up at a forty-five degree angle and had a sheer drop on one side. I felt sick with vertigo, but Steve Iliffe pushed me onwards to the summit, which was a huge disappointment, the ground strewn with litter and orange peel and clouds obscuring the view. We didn't stay there for long. The descent was just as treacherous. I could only do it in a seated position, inching cautiously down the rocky path with Steve reassuring me from behind. Once we were beneath the clouds, though, the views were spectacular. We came to a waterfall with a deep pool beneath it. Some of the others were already swimming. I dived in with my clothes on – a rare moment of pleasure. For most of the five-day hike, I trudged alone. Way ahead, Izzy and Ian walked hand in hand together, never giving me a backward glance.

IZZY: *We came to a crater-pitted track infested with brambles, horse flies and midges. Cathy had worn shorts so her legs were a real mess when we eventually got out of it.*

Back at main camp I stared miserably at my midge-attacked, bramble-lacerated skin. For want of anything better to do, I counted the bites – four hundred and forty-seven on my legs alone. Steve sat beside me. "Those bites look bad."

"Midges always go for me."

"You must be very tasty. Why don't you wear trousers? Keep yourself covered up?"

"The zip's broken, and anyway it's too late now."

"Come on, cheer up. Let's go and get you some calamine lotion from the first-aid box and see if we can find someone to lend you some trousers."

I departed from camp four days early to get to the NYO and travelled back to London alone, glad to have left FSC behind.

IZZY: *I'm afraid Cathy had rather a hard and jealous time at camp. I was rather mean to her, spending all my time with Ian, but I bet and hope that she has loads of admirers at the NYO.*

The NYO course was held in Plymouth and I missed Wortley for the first time. I can't say that the boys were lining up for me, but one of the older boys boosted my spirits.

CATHY: I can't tell you how nice he is. He talked to me while we were folding programmes. He is very flattering, saying that I am extremely attractive and the most attractive things about me are my green eyes, my small nose (that's a laugh), my hair and my nice figure (equally laughable). He's so sensible and thoughtful and a fabulous composer. We talked about all sorts of things and later he came and sat next to me to continue our conversation.

Six brass players were caught in a pub drinking. Ivey chucked them out of the NYO and sent them home. It was intended as a severe warning to all members that such behaviour was absolutely forbidden and would not be tolerated. The disgraced boys became NYO heroes. Those who remained raised their glasses to them.

Izzy gathered several admirers at Wortley, but they did not impress her:

I'm being pursued by a couple of boys in the band. I really miss Ian. It doesn't feel like just three days since I saw him, but three years. I played a game of draughts with a drippy boy, who probably thinks I like him, but he's got hold of the wrong end of the stick. All the boys here are so stupid, but maybe I'm rather biased.

Chris spent most of the week in the company of Bruce Fox, a horn player from Lancashire. They had met the previous year and become firm friends. Bruce wrote to me recently: "I was fourteen when I first went to Wortley Hall in 1969. Chris was eleven and you were somewhere in-between. My earliest recollection of Chris actually dates from before meeting him. I had started taking piano lessons with one of the summer school tutors during my lower fifth year at grammar school, just before my first trip to Wortley. I asked him if there were any other horn players likely to be at the summer school, and he told me about a 'small boy called Christopher Giles, who disconcerted his mother by collecting a variety of beetles, spiders and other creepy-crawlies in the Hall gardens and bringing them back in matchboxes'."

That summer of 1970, Bruce introduced Chris to *Monty Python's Flying Circus*. He recalls: "We managed to get permission to book the jazz room, the only place in Wortley Hall where there was a telly, and ended up rolling about in fits of uncontrollable laughter, with tears pouring down our faces and stitches in our sides." Chris was immediately, incurably, addicted. It gave him such unequivocal pleasure, merriment and mirth for the rest of his life that it has to have a place in this book.

The first Monty Python episode was broadcast on BBC2 on October 5th 1969. By the time the series ended thirteen weeks later, the bizarrely titled TV programme had begun to make its way into the English language. We had heard about *Monty Python's Flying Circus* from school-friends with enlightened or unconcerned parents who did not mind their children staying up until 11.30 on a Sunday evening to watch it. The name of the programme alone persuaded Granny to ban it, but the titles of the episodes left her in no doubt. 'Whither Canada?' and 'Owl Stretching Time' were plain silly, while 'Sex and Violence' and 'Full Frontal Nudity' smacked of obscenity. In May 1970, a repeat of the series began showing on BBC1 at an earlier hour. Granny still refused to switch it on. There was so much TV we were not allowed to watch, that we didn't fret too much. Intrigued though we were about the programme, we hadn't seen it so had no idea what we were missing.

When Chris returned from Wortley, that was no longer the case. What's more, he insisted that it was essential viewing for Izzy and me too. For a few weeks, Chris took us to watch it at a friend's house nearby in spite of Granny's chiding. Then Granny relented. "If ye insist on going out at this time of night, ye may as well watch your daft programme here." To our amazement, Granny, Mum and Dad watched it too. They were won over before the episode had ended, despite Granny's comment, "Och, this is awful silly." It wasn't long before Chris, with his talent for mimicry and recall, could recite entire sketches verbatim. I thought Monty Python was brilliant, and still do, but it was far more for Chris. Everything about it appealed to every part of him – he had an open ticket to Monty Python's Circus and flew with it.

By the time I was back from the NYO my jealousy attack had evaporated and Izzy and I were back in empathy. But I was not happy in the inharmonious atmosphere at home. Having been away for nearly four weeks, I had forgotten how depressing it was. I escaped to the Turners every day after I had practised, until Melly suggested I stay for the last week of the holiday. She and I slept top to tail in her little bed; we practised together, she danced; I played chess with Jon, and Pat fed us enormous meals at unusual hours.

Des was working in Edinburgh at the time. He was chief accountant of the company Charles Kinloch, and had been sent to their Scottish branch, Melrose-Drover, to streamline, restructure and integrate it into the parent company, Courage – a job that was to last more than a year, during which time Des would drive up to Scotland every Sunday night and return very late on Friday. Yet he was up early on Saturdays. With unflagging stamina he packed our weekends with outings and entertainment.

Whilst staying with the Turners, the phone rang. From bits of the conversation I could tell that the caller was Dad. I tensed as I heard Des saying pleasantly that he couldn't meet him at the pub, explaining quite firmly that this was family time, which must have annoyed Dad. Des's replies became more clipped and my anxiety rose. Des called me. "Kate? Your father wants to speak to you." He shot me a wink as he handed me the phone. Dad was in a foul mood, furious that I was not at home, irascible and accusing. As soon as I hung up, I burst into tears. Des put his hands on my shoulders, guided me into the living room, sat me on the couch and put an arm around me.

"Kate," he began, handing me a handkerchief, "you're not responsible for your father's feelings or the way he behaves."

"But he's so inconsiderate towards you."

"It's up to me to deal with Derek. He's a challenge sometimes, but he doesn't upset me. You mustn't worry about your parents. They have problems, but they're not your problems."

"It feels as though they are; especially between Dad and Granny."

"There's nothing you can do. They're adults, honey; you don't cause their arguments and you can't solve them."

"I just wish Dad wasn't so miserable and crotchety. He's so difficult to please."

"You can't carry his burdens for him, Kate, and he shouldn't lean on you. It's not good. Not good for your relationships with boys and bad for the asthma." He squeezed me, hugging me for the first time. "I know you're wary of male company and I haven't wanted to frighten you by cuddling you too soon, but you do know I love you just as much as I love Izzy, don't you?" I thought: how does he know of the discomfort I feel with boys? Not all boys; but some, sometimes. What have I said that has informed him? It is as if he can see inside me, has heard my inner voices when I thought they were so well concealed.

"You're a complicated character, Kate. Asthmatics often are. It's what makes you interesting and lovable. But we can do without the asthma. We have to sort it out; you can't go on like this."

"It hasn't been too bad recently," I replied, bemused by hearing myself described as interesting and lovable.

"Well, good, but I want you to see somebody – a doctor I've met in Edinburgh who's done a lot to help me. I'm going to speak to your parents and see if I can arrange to take you up there with me."

"To a hospital?"

"No, it's called the Kingston Clinic; nothing to do with the NHS. The man I want you to see is Alec Milne. He believes that asthma is a psychosomatic illness that can be treated without resorting to drugs. The man talks a lot of sense. You'll like him."

"Will it cost money?"

"It's not free, but that's not your problem. You need help. It doesn't matter what it costs if it can make you better."

I thought: it does matter. It will be seen as a waste of money, an extravagant shot in the dark: and what if it doesn't work? Granny will think a huge fuss is being made about nothing. When I've tried to talk to Mum about the possibility that anxiety might play a part in asthma, she says it doesn't apply to me. Granny says it's all this psycho nonsense that Des puts in my head that's making me anxious. I'm sure they won't want me to go. It would be best not to ask.

Des did speak to Mum and Dad, or more likely Mum and Granny, and persuaded them to let him take me to the Kingston Clinic. We left for Edinburgh late one Sunday evening, stopping for two hours' sleep on a lay-by. Des worked in the morning while I was taken on a guided tour of the brewery. In the afternoon he drove me to the clinic – a large house set in several acres of well-tended grounds. We were early and walked around the gardens, while I fretted about the expense, feeling apprehensive about my appointment. Des and Alec Milne shook hands and I was shown into a consulting room while Des waited for me outside. This is what I remember:

Mr. Milne asked me what drugs I was taking. I reeled off their names.

"Do you have them with you?"

"Yes, in my bag."

"Let me see." I placed my bottles of pills and inhalers on his table.

"Anything else?" he asked.

"Just penicillin for bronchitis when I have it."

Then he lifted the rubbish bin from under his desk and to my horror swept the whole lot into it. I gasped, feeling tears prickle the back of my eyes. "Give them back," I wanted to cry out, "they're mine; I need them." He watched me, gauging the effect of his dramatic gesture. I stared at the point on his wide polished table where my medicines had been. I could not look at him.

"Let me tell you something: asthma can't kill you: those drugs can. Drugs don't cure asthma, they mask it; the asthma has to come out. The more you suppress the natural function of asthma, the stronger it becomes. The drugs will have less and less effect and the attack will force its way out anyway. Your asthma is trying to teach you something and you have to learn to work with it, not against it."

Mr. Milne implied that my subconscious had conjured up a demon that manifested as asthma. He seemed to suggest that I was responsible for creating it – but how could I begin to work out what it was supposed to be telling me? He went on to quiz me about my life-style and diet and asked if I exercised. I didn't, not specifically. He told me to walk to school instead of taking the bus, to join in PE lessons and to go swimming at least three times a week. I hung my head, knowing that every suggestion was impossible. It would take hours to walk the eight miles to school, Mum would not let me do games, nor would I be able to waste practice-time swimming – apart from which, I had a verruca.

He was not impressed with my diet. He handed me a list of 'good' and 'bad' foods and a booklet of simple recipes giving suggestions for breakfast, lunch and supper. I already knew that I might as well throw it in the bin with my medicines.

"I'd like to see you again next month," he said, "find out how you're getting on."

"OK," I said, "thank you. Erm, do you think I could have my pills back?"

"You don't need them, you know."

I wanted to protest, but couldn't open my mouth to say: "I do need them, I rely on them. I must have them even if I don't use them, just in case." A wall of silence grew between us. We held our positions. At last he yielded, fished the bottles and inhalers out of the bin and lined them up with ostentatious precision.

"Reject them," he said, "it will be your first major step towards a new understanding of asthma. Remember, you won't die without them." I wished I hadn't brought any of my medicines with me, but left them safely in my suitcase at the hotel. Here I was in the all-too-familiar adult/child, teacher/pupil, doctor/patient scenario, feeling overpowered and paralysed, afraid he would be disappointed in me, concerned that I should not let him down.

"Could I just take the Ventolin inhaler, please?" I asked. It was the one that gave me instant, if short-lasting, relief.

"If you feel you must. But try not to use it."

Des asked how it had gone. I tried to tell him, but I was confused. He suggested I let it sink in and we could have a chat later. He whisked me straight off to see the film *The Battle of Britain*, which took my mind away from asthma, then out for a Chinese meal – the first Chinese food I had tasted.

That night as I sat hunched in bed wheezing, Des sat beside me helping me through it. He taught me far more than Alec Milne. He explained his understanding of Alec Milne's theories, which began to make some sense, but I was unconvinced that any of it would help. I doubted that my thoughts would be strong enough to banish my asthma. The wheezing did not progress into an attack that night, but it was relentless and in the end I took a puff of Ventolin. The relief was wonderful, but I felt I'd failed. Des encouraged me by pointing out that I hadn't taken any other drugs for twelve hours, which was a minor victory. The next afternoon I caught the train back to London, thinking of my drugs lying uselessly in a wastepaper bin in Edinburgh.

Back home I showed Mum and Granny my food list. Derision rained down.

"What is this rubbish? There's nothing wrong with the food you get here. Good, nourishing, wholesome meals. I'm not wasting my time cooking up special things for you. As if we haven't enough to do already! You'll eat like the rest of us."

"Just a minute, Mammy; let's look at what it says. Well, you already have plenty of fruit. You can eat your carrots raw if that's supposed to be better for you, but no milk or butter? That's nonsense: everyone knows milk is essential for good teeth. Look how good your teeth are – you've never needed a filling."

"I'm not having margarine in this house," stated Granny vehemently.

Mum read from the leaflet: "Avoid all fried food, pork, fish, fowl, game, tea, coffee, alcohol, white bread, porridge, vinegar, mustard and pepper."

"Porridge!" exploded Granny, "Why, it's the staple food of Scotland. The Scots have lived on it for centuries. This Doctor's a quack if ye ask me." I sighed and left them to it. The following morning, having not slept at all, I made myself a packed lunch of salad. Clutching my inhaler protectively, I walked to the bus stop.

The Consultants at the London Chest Hospital prescribed me a panoply of drugs and left me to get on with it. The effects were barely monitored. My blood potassium levels were not checked, no blood tests were taken at all. The asthma charts I so conscientiously filled in were given no more than a glance. I was asked a few routine questions, re-stocked with chemicals and dismissed. Rash though it may have been to prescribe them so liberally in the first place, I had become accustomed to them. Now, suddenly, they were withdrawn. Mr. Milne had banished them. Incidentally, his sweeping statement that asthma cannot kill is untrue: it can be fatal. At the time, I did not doubt his words. As I fought to breathe through my attacks, I told myself that however bad it became, I would not die.

It was obvious to me right away that the drug to which I had become most addicted was Phenergan, the one prescribed to make me sleep. I told Mum that I hadn't been able to sleep since I came back from Edinburgh.

"Oh don't be ridiculous. That was weeks ago. Of course you've slept since then, you just don't realise it." She did not believe me, but in truth, the insomnia I suffered at that time was diabolical. I still have bouts of insomnia today. The other drugs were perhaps not so addictive, but nevertheless, the asthma went out of control. On the other hand, I persuaded myself, it had been bad even with the drugs, so I was no worse off. It was not an option to go to the London Chest Hospital to re-stock. In fact, I did not visit the hospital again, although I did still have a few spare bottles of pills that I had not taken to Scotland with me; a little stash of security. My new regime was to do without drugs. Guiltily, I puffed the inhaler when I could not endure any more and sometimes I resorted to taking Orciphrenaline, feeling like a thief and a cheat. I did not see Alec Milne again. It wasn't until I was clearing out some drawers in Cleveland Road after Mum had moved into a care home that I came across this letter from him:

September 29th 1970

Dear Mrs. Giles,

I don't suppose there is anything I can tell you about Catherine's condition which you do not already know. Obviously, having only seen her for a short time I feel I am not in any position to do other than make a few simple suggestions to her.

I presume that like many other asthmatic children, her difficulties rest in the feeling of not being sufficiently valued by her parents for herself alone. Usually it is the pole relationship, i.e. with her father, which is the crucial, reassuring one. One notes the obvious trap; that she endeavours to seek approval through her cello playing.

The point of view I put to Catherine is similar to that in our leaflet: the possibility and method of getting over an attack of asthma without using drugs; the development of deep breathing exercise and control over ribcage movements; as much general exercise as she can be encouraged to take; the importance of diet. With this combination, Catherine should at least feel she is doing something to help herself.

The more subtle points take time to develop, such as the need to make independent decisions based on what she feels is right for her, and to try to avoid the feeling of responsibility she seems to have. The asthmatic situation is where you feel consciously impelled to do something through a sense of duty, loyalty or responsibility, but which is in fact counter to one's instinctive need.

I hope to see Catherine again in the near future, and of course we would love to have her here for a period of 2/3 weeks if at all possible and certainly if she fails to show progress. We do feel her asthma is trying to say something, to which a response must be made.

Mum replied as follows:

September 30th 1970

Dear Mr. Milne,

Thank you for your letter and for the suggestions about Catherine's diet. I am interested in your mention of the feeling of responsibility she seems to have. Even at a very young age and many years before the onset of the Asthma, Catherine showed a compulsive need to 'organise' others. I remember her at about three years old coming into the house after playing with a small group of neighbouring children. She was emotionally exhausted – rather than physically exhausted – with the effort of directing the game of make-believe they had been playing. She seemed to feel that everything would go wrong if she were not there to control the situation. I don't think she was simply being aggressive or bossy.

She is a very intelligent person and much more mature and responsible than most of her contemporaries at school. She is emotional and inclined to dramatize, which of course is why she is such a fine interpretive musician. When she gives a performance, one is not aware that this is a child; she is a highly sensitive artist. I am a professional pianist and always play for her when she gives a performance so I am very much aware of the quality of her talent; not, however, as a doting parent (I hope!)

I very much hope that the talk she had with you will help her and I am sure that she would be very pleased to see you again in London when you are here.

Mum did not show me Alec Milne's letter, nor did she discuss its contents with me. Four further appointments were offered, all of which Mum turned down, as they clashed with musical commitments. I do not believe that I sought approval through my cello playing, but it was certainly where approval was given. For Mum, the family's musical diary was undoubtedly more important than my asthma and I am sure she felt it was more important to me too. Her last letter to Alec Milne in April 1971 reads: "As I'm sure you realise, Catherine has a great many commitments, which make it difficult to arrange appointments at short notice. Her asthma has in fact almost cleared up since the consultation which she had last September."

Sadly, that was not true.

47
LAST MONTHS OF 1970

Will someone glance inside my notebooks?
All the lines and fragments – will they leap out
like clowns, assassins, suitors, militants?
Or, malnourished orphans, slip the page?
Words, the last skin; beyond them, nothing.

Leasehold – Carole Satyamurti

Pat Turner stopped coming out with us when Dad decided to come too. She told me recently that it was because he made it obvious that it was Des's company he sought and she saw little point in being there.

"Didn't that upset you, Pat?" I asked, "I mean; weekend time with Des must have been precious."

"Well, I had a lot to do at home and it was important that you children had time together. Des was able to ease the situation with your father, which all helped."

Des told me that the main thing Dad talked about was 'those evil women'. He found it distasteful, but tried to remain impartial, realising that Dad did not want advice, only somebody who would hear his grievances.

"I was also aware that your father was jealous of the relationship I had with Pat and with my children," he explained, "and I think he was probably jealous of the relationship I had with his children. I can't remember whether it was just before or after I took you to Edinburgh, but I received two very peculiar anonymous letters in close succession. They were written on pieces of card and the author implied cryptically that I was sexually interested in young girls and then went on to make veiled threats. There was an odd bloke at work who might have been responsible, but Pat and I both thought it could have been Derek who sent them. We couldn't be sure so I didn't challenge him about it, and as no more arrived, we chucked the sordid things away and let it go."

CATHY: October 1970: Asthma has been rather bad recently. I think too much fuss is being made over it. Granny is going to make Mel a poncho to thank Des for taking me to Edinburgh. We talked about asthma, but judging from what Des says, I think it's being made out to be much worse (emotionally) that it really is. They're inventing all sorts of causes for it. It's all very well, this asthma business but honestly, asthma isn't the only thing in life. Since I've been to the clinic it has not been brilliant. I think it would be better if I used the inhaler more. Oh, well, I expect things will sort themselves out.
I asked Mr. Crombie whether Izzy and Chris could come to see 'The Gondoliers' with the school party. He said yes so I signed all our names under the list. I ate two packets of toffos. I feel awfully fat.
Had a very good cello lesson – Florrie was pleased with me. I'm having three lessons in one week to prepare for the NYO audition, but I'm not at all happy about the pieces I'm playing – I don't think they're nearly good enough to get into the NYO again.

Picked some flowers from my garden and arranged them in 12 different pots in my bedroom. Picked two carnations, one for Miss Sprakes and one for Mum.
Made the pattern for my midi skirt-to-be. Bought 4 yards of turquoise needlecord corduroy, which cost £3/4s/10d altogether – a hell of a lot – I feel rather bad about it. Practised, then cut out the pattern. After dinner sewed all 3 seams, waistband & joined it to skirt – all by hand in one evening. I'm hoping to finish it by Saturday so I can wear it to the WMA concert. Did some crocheting and took it to school to do during music appreciation lesson. Started on a poncho for my large doll – don't think I'm stupid – I'm only doing it for practice as I want to crochet one for myself.
In English we're reading The Importance of being Earnest by Oscar Wilde and George Orwell's Animal Farm, which was discussed. I think it's bad that schools should bring politics into lessons, talking along the lines of "those evil Communists" and using Animal Farm to exemplify what we're told will inevitably happen to all socialist countries. I have to keep quiet. I really must learn to concentrate more in French. My mind wanders all the time and when I'm asked a question I don't know what they've been talking about. I told Mr. Crombie I wouldn't be able to play in Harvest Festival because of my lesson. He was rather annoyed.
Had drama with Miss Dymott. She's terribly old but very nice. I have a feeling she's a bit mad – she shouts at us one second and the next she's calm again and she makes us do the most ludicrous things like staring into your partner's eyes for 5 minutes.
Mum pinned the hem of my skirt and I sewed like mad till it was finished and wore it to the RAM.
Helped Chris write out 500 lines "I must not talk in lessons".
Izzy lent me her turquoise pendant that Des gave her, which is exactly the same colour as my skirt. I started on a shift dress for her, which is getting on well. I had terrible trouble putting on my mascara, nearly poked my eyes out, then Izzy, Chris and I went to the Hawkey Hall to see The Gondoliers. It was fantastic. Mr. Crombie admitted to really liking Izzy. He thinks she's "a smasher".
Did quite a good practice but I know I'm not practising as well as I ought to and although I do have time to do more, I just can't get down to really concentrated practise on my pieces but spend all the time on technique which is easier.
Chris has been ill for 5 days and now I'm ill. My temperature is 103.5. Feel awful as I go to bed. Have stayed in bed crocheting between sleeps, Mum bringing me up soup, apples and yogurt which I don't eat much of. Dad comes in and fusses a lot. I went downstairs, temperature lower, and listened to The Gondoliers with Tinker on my lap and Izzy acting all the parts at once, which was very funny.
Went to the library and got out Brahms' 2nd symphony. Dad has painted the posts of the fence orange! It looks disgusting. Went with Melly to see Doctor Zhivago – very good.
Clive Miller came to practise trumpet with Mum for his NYO audition.
Ripped out my poncho again to use wool to make dolls clothes for the Morning Star bazaar.
Got to Holborn Central Library for NYO audition. Ivey listened to all of the first movement of the Shostakovich but none of the second. She thinks it would be much wiser for me to do A levels before I go to the RAM as a senior. Anyway, the playing went well & I'm almost definitely IN next year. Chris's NYO audition went extremely well – Ivey was very impressed with him but Chris was not impressed when she called him 'poppet' and even 'baby horn'. Yuk. Sue Eversden, bassoon, also auditioned for NYO. I do hope she gets in.
The cleaners are on strike so there's no school. I started on a dress for myself. I think it's going to look quite nice. Dad said he fancied a sweet so I produced some of my saved up ones. I was pleased about it – it's these little things that help to make the world go round.

IZZY: *Went round to the Turners'. We picked some brambles for Granny to make into jam. Jonathan and Chris did shooting and target practice with air guns.*
Melly has got her dancing scholarship! One year's free tuition from famous ballet teachers. Went over to the Turner's and drank wine and other intoxicating liquor.
Mum had to borrow John Stokes' car as ours has finally conked out.
We had an idiotic fire practice – absolutely pointless but it cut the History lesson short, which is about the only good thing. In English we are doing 'Romeo and Juliet' – of course Mrs. Watson picked me to read Juliet!
Granny went to visit Auntie Martha.
Our head, Miss Heald, says that no-one ever sings in assembly, it's very bad and we all have to pull our socks up. After prayers, during which hardly anyone sang, we saw two boring films on digestion. In biology we had to make blood slides from our own blood. Half the girls were too scared so I had to donate some of my blood to them. We cut up a sheep's heart – very good. In my report I got A for Music, A- for English, History, French, Latin, Biology and Art, B+ for Geography and Maths, B for Games and B- for Physics (which I expected) – overall A-.
The Turners came round and we took Melly to her dancing practice, Jon went fishing in the Serpentine and Des took us to Harrods, a very posh, expensive shop. Chris bought a guinea fowl egg, I bought ½lb of plums and Cath bought two carrier bags.
Daddy and I went to Grandad's. We came back and watched a programme, 'Are you a good husband?'
We watched 'Top of the Pops' (generosity itself on Granny's behalf!) because a girl in Cathy's class won the prize for being the best dancer. Cath finished making my 'jumper of many colours'.
We've got our new (second-hand) car – a Hillman Minx Estate – £690!!!!
Daddy found a little kitten – it was lost. It has adopted us and we have advertised about it.
Went to Wimpole Street to see Mr. Roger. He says my teeth are making good progress. The half cheap day return ticket now costs 4/-!!
I wish Ian would write. I doubt if I'll ever see him again.
The little cat, Spot, has been claimed.
I bought a zip for a dress Cathy's making me – Empire line, blue cord, really nice. She's also making me a midi. Talked to her about Wortley. Wrote to Ian.
Redbridge Band have won their section of the National Finals at the Albert Hall.

In 1970, John Ridgeon decided to enter the Redbridge Band to compete in the National Youth Championships of Great Britain. The group had only been together for four years, but John believed that the competition would be good experience even if they didn't get anywhere. He entered the band for the Junior Section, but as there were no rules against it, decided to also put them in for Section Three, Section Two and the Championship Section, which required the performance of some phenomenally difficult championship set pieces. The south of England regional finals were held at Watford Town Hall for one long Saturday, starting at nine o'clock in the morning. Bands from all over the south turned up to play their competition pieces. At eight o'clock that evening, the chairman of the judging panel rose to his feet to announce the results of each section. "Winners of the Junior Section – Redbridge Band; winners of Section Three – Redbridge Band; winners of Section Two, Redbridge Band." They could barely contain their excitement as they held their breaths for the last result: "And finally, the winners of the Championship Section – Redbridge Band." They had won the lot.

Their win in the Regional finals meant that the next weekend they competed in the National Youth Championships at the Royal Albert Hall. They won, beating the Black Dyke Mills Youth Band, a long-established group from the north of England. It was a remarkable achievement. John Ridgeon was a young man of twenty-six, few years separating him from the oldest members of the band, yet he commanded their absolute respect. He also had the measure of them. On Sunday mornings, when they rehearsed at Loxford School, John arranged with the school caretaker to open the swimming pool so that the lads could take a sobering plunge before the rehearsal to cure the Saturday night hangovers. There are several entries in Chris's diaries for Saturdays: "Rehearsal pm, Concert eve, Party after, Don't get hangover, Band tomorrow." Word of the extraordinary Redbridge Band spread around the music business: on Tuesday nights, professional players often turned up just to listen to the rehearsals.

CATHY: November 1970: Hi there! Here's your famous friend once more speaking as usual from her bedside. At long last I've found my pen again.
Mum, Dad, Chris and Jon Turner have gone to the cottage for a long weekend. Melly came over and we watched TV – the Basil Brush Show, Dad's Army, Not only but Also and a crappy thing called 30-minute theatre about Helen of Troy. Mel stayed the night. Must practise more tomorrow.
Des came over and took Izzy, Mel and me on a long walk. Practised loads and then played piano for a long time and tried to really learn the last movement of Beethoven's Pathetique sonata and Bach 2 part inventions.
I gardened for about 2 hours – dug up all the gladioli & dahlias & transplanted various things. Weeded everything. All I have to do now is to clear up the leaves.
I actually managed to answer three questions correctly in French. Miss Joynes was very pleased with my essay on Oscar Wilde's use of social satire. She was going to read it out but I was saved by the bell.
I've just found out that Dad's firm, the Guardian Royal Exchange, is moving to Ipswich next year.[1] It'll mean that Dad'll be out of a job. I hope he'll be able to find another one at his age.
Mr. Bidgood has asked me to play the Saint-Saëns concerto with Musici and wants to run it through next month. I haven't started learning it yet and I'll never be able to manage it with Grade VIII and NYO as well.
I've just been given the school exam timetable. I'm really worried about French. In the test, I got 1 out of 10 for French dictation and 2 out of 30 for comprehension. Oh well, I shall just fail.
I eventually persuaded Mum to come with me to Prize Giving in the evening. I was awarded a 10/- book token. I fed and watered two rows of mums and dads and one row of teachers. Had a group photo taken. Mum enjoyed herself – very successful I think.
Made some Christmas cards out of sweet papers and foil.
I do wish I could get to sleep. It's dreadful. I turn from side to side, can't get comfortable and rarely sleep. Then when I'm nearly asleep, Rusty comes and scrapes with his paws on my bedroom window to be let in and I have to get up, open the window, carry him downstairs and quite often he's back half an hour later having climbed out of the kitchen

1. Part of The Guardian Royal Exchange Assurance Company did relocate to Ipswich, but Dad kept his job in the London offices at the Royal Exchange Building.

window. The result is I'm worn out most of the time.
I've got to slim. It's ridiculous, I'm getting so fat, I'll not be able to fit into any of my skirts. I tried to accidentally 'forget' to eat my breakfast but Mum told me to eat it.
Clive Miller came to practise trumpet with Mum for his NYO audition.
Dad was in a terrible mood. He was going up the wall at Mum about everything – he's so mixed up and very bloody minded about Granny. Watched Graham Kerr (the galloping Gourmet), Z Cars and Steptoe & Son. Had a bath during which Izzy made me laugh so much that it brought on asthma. Has been bad again.
Went for a walk with Des and Dad then I started making a dress for myself out of the navy & white crepe material Miss Sprakes gave me – have finished the bodice already. It's going to be very nice with large puffy sleeves, maxi length, gathered at the waist.
Revised madly for the French exam. Miss Chadwick said the paper would be difficult but I found it worryingly easy so I must have done a lot wrong.
I don't feel quite so depressed and seem to have found living much easier today. Mind you, there's still a lot to be desired about my life – I seem so false, nasty and unkind. It's so difficult to explain. A terrible gloom hangs over me and I drive myself silly with worry.
I hate my journey to school. It's so long and boring. Nothing interesting ever happens and I'm usually freezing to death.
Mum dithered around so much that we were almost late for the Musici Day Series. First concert really awful, second concert pretty ropey. Went home for dinner (1 lettuce leaf and a pilchard). Dad came to the third concert – he's taken the day off work.
Went to Chris's school bazaar. Some terrible boys there – one asked me out to a party and another squirted me with a water pistol. I bought a ring and a pendant for Izzy's Christmas present and a fantastically large jotter for 1/-.

IZZY: *I wish Ian would show some sign of life.*
Mum, Dad, Chris and Jon came back from the cottage. Chris has lots of new specimens. Melly and I did our homework and drank the sherry that Mum and Dad won in a raffle at Gt. Ryburgh.
We played for the Goodmayes Gramophone Society. I didn't play particularly fantastically but Cath and Chris made up for it. We earned ourselves £1 each. I wrote to Ian.
Dad came home with all the jargon about Ipswich. I hope we don't have to go.
Miss Sprakes took us to 'Dido & Aeneas'. Melly was dancing. The singing sounded like strangled cats and castrated canines – bloody awful.
I wrote another letter to Ian. I hope I see him in the Christmas holidays.
Dad and Chris went to the J. C. Galleries in Marble Arch to get Chris's Christmas present – 5 butterflies and the world's largest moth, the Giant Atlas moth. Chris is very pleased with it.
I got 121 for my grade VII piano.
I sent Ian a birthday card. I wonder if I'll see him? I hope so but very much doubt if he'll bother to phone.
Wonder of wonders, I actually got a Christmas card from Ian. I thought he might have written me a letter but no such luck. Still, it's enough to know he hasn't forgotten I exist.

CATHY: December 1970: Bought Mum & Dad a joint Christmas present – a lovely blue Wedgewood plate for 17/-.
Came 1st in English language, 1st in History, 1st in music, 3rd in English lit with 73%, 74% in Maths and nowhere in French – 5½ out of 10 for dictation, 8½ out of 10 for aural comprehension and 42 out of 80 for the paper – 56% altogether, but at least I passed.
Went to Loughton School to see Izzy play in Noye's Fludde. Production was very good but the bugles were so out of tune you couldn't decipher which note they were supposed

to be playing.
The lights went out on the way to school. The electricity workers are on strike – good for them, I hope they get their rise. Electricity went off at 11.00 and stayed off until 3.00 by which time the school was like a fridge. Reminded Mum to fill the petrol tank – pumps won't work without electricity. At the moment I'm trying very hard to see what I'm writing by the light of one tiny candle. Unfortunately, all my beautiful candles and candlesticks that I've had arranged in my room have been sequestered for the house.
Chris, Clive Miller and Sue Eversden all got into NYO. Told Mr. Crombie I wouldn't be at music tomorrow because of my lesson. He put his arm around me and kissed me! You just never know how he's going to respond.
Told Sue not to bother with a flu vaccination, but I think she's taken all the NYO instructions rather to heart and is having one tonight.
My complexion is very bad – tried to clear it up succeeding only in making matters worse.
Lights out at 4.00. Held rehearsal at Beal for carol concert in darkness – only torch and candlelight. Izzy's playing in it too.

There were several musical highlights for me at Beal. Perhaps the most exhilarating were the two performances we gave of *Hiawatha's Wedding Feast*, the text by H. W. Longfellow and music by Samuel Coleridge-Taylor. Scored for women's voices, solo soprano and orchestra, it was perfectly suited for a girls' school. I thought it wonderfully inspiring and rousing. Mr. Crombie trained and rehearsed the large school choir and boosted the school orchestra with some RYO members, including Izzy and Chris. In the choir we sang *Pedro the Fisherman* – a favourite that Izzy, Mel and I knew every word to. Izzy remembers Beal concerts as a real treat – they were always packed and we often did two or three consecutive shows. Mr. Crombie worked very hard indeed.

CATHY: Well, it's Christmas Eve but it doesn't really feel like Christmas. Then it started to snow and turned into a truly white Christmas – about 4" deep. Asthma is terribly bad again. I hope it's not like this at NYO.
This is what I was given: In my Stocking: 1 pr. Tights, a 2" Christmas tree, sugar mouse, chocolate pennies, pencil case, comic, nut, orange, ball and pencil (no surprises there), a black blouse from Granny, a coat and a 1971 diary from Mum and Dad, some green and blue eye shadow and a lipstick from Izzy, white tights from Chris, Green and Gold material and box of black magic from Turners, 10/- from Miss Sprakes, 10/- from Grandad, and lots of cards and bubble bath from my friends at school. Watched lots of telly, ate lots of fab food, Des, Mel, Pat and Jon came over and we all played monopoly and cards. Boxing day we trudged over to the Turners' in the snow. Asthma dreadful.
Sue Eversden arrived and she, Chris & I went to Charing Cross station and got to Croydon, Stockwell College for NYO course. I've been promoted from back desk to 5th. Rudolph Schwarz is the conductor. I can't make out his beat at all – looks as though he's prodding something. We're doing Bruckner 7, Walton Partita for Orchestra and Mendelssohn Ruy Blas overture but also having sectional rehearsals on La Mer and Bartók's Music for Strings Percussion and Celesta because Boulez is conducting them on the summer course. Schwarz is rather odd in the way he tries to make us do things, his conducting is weird, but he does talk sense and the Bruckner is fantastic. Douggy is really keeping it up this course – normally by now he's reverted to the Klengel and Villa-Lobos, or is letting us out hours early.

48
NATURAL HISTORY COLLECTING

For the future generations the union of technology and biology will be what Prometheus' torch was for our ancestors.

Animal Travellers – Igor Akimushkin

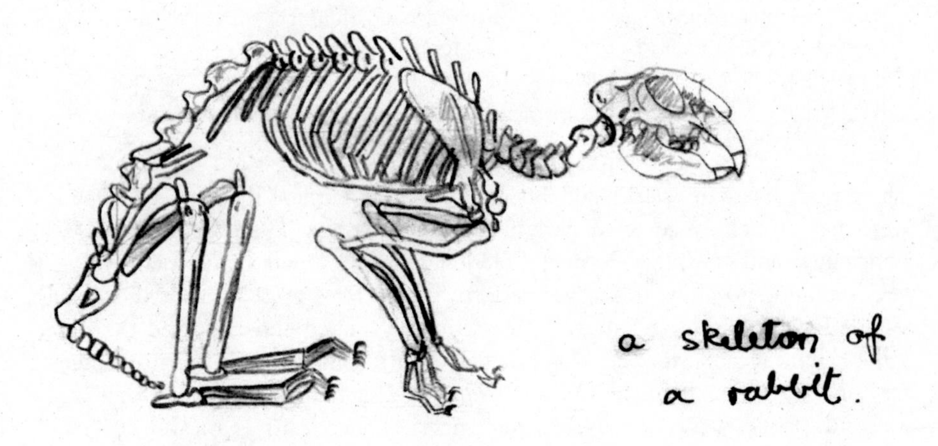

Chris was twelve, in his second year at BHCHS. His English class was given an assignment. Each boy had to choose a topic in which he was interested and produce a comprehensive article on the subject. Chris didn't have to think twice: his project would be Natural History Collecting. It resulted in a sixty-page booklet divided into six chapters full of scientific facts, illustrations, diagrams, practical advice and enthusiastic encouragement to would-be collectors. The chapters are titled 'Skull and Skeleton Collecting', 'Wet and Dry Preservation', 'Bird Egg and Nest Collecting', 'Insect Collecting', 'Fossil Collecting' and 'My Collection'. I have already quoted from it in an earlier chapter *Bugs and Bones*. Here is another extract:

> The best places to find skulls and skeletons are on country walks and in woods. Pigs, rabbits, sheep and ox you can often get from butchers. If you keep a pet cat, mice and bird's bodies will be found in abundance all over your garden! Some small weasel and rodent skulls may be found complete with other bones in owl pellets. These are lumps of bone and fur that are coughed up by owls and other birds of prey like Herons and Kingfishers, and found at bottoms of trees. After collecting the pellets, boil them for a few minutes till the hair floats to the top to form a matt and the bones fall to the bottom. Pour the hair off and rinse the bones in cold water. Soak them in bleach solution (dilute) and after drying them, display in glass-topped boxes. When a buried body is dug up, it is best to put it into diluted bleach to kill the germs. When mending or sticking teeth into skulls, polystyrene cement is the best glue to use.

In the final chapter he writes:

> When I was away camping, I found the pelvic girdle of an ox. When I arrived back, I was met by my parents at the station. My Dad had to carry the bone home by slinging it around his shoulders. My collection became so large that I had to move into a bigger bedroom, and even the bedroom I am in now is cramped.

He ends by writing a full list of the contents in his collection, adding in brackets: "The following contents are at the time of writing, so when you, if you do, see my collection, it might have been added to."

There is an earlier inventory of his collection in the chapter *Pierre*. I am not going to list every individual item again, but this should be sufficient to indicate how much more extensive his collection had become.

30 WHOLE SKELETONS (Including skulls) of different (mainly British) mammals and birds as well as parts of several domestic animals found at an Archaeological dig by a Saxon village.
More than 40 SKULLS of (mainly British) mammals and birds, including a human skull.
Also plenty of half skeletons including a few human bones and incidental extras.
Two dozen STUFFED ANIMALS
6 FURS
INSECTS: Nearly Five Hundred Butterflies, Moths, Flies, Dragonflies, Beetles and Cockroaches.
FOSSILS: Too many to name.
BIRDS' EGGS: 27 land and sea bird eggs, rare and common, ranging from a sparrow to a Great Skua.
BIRDS' NESTS: Bullfinch, House Marten, Four Blackbird's, Yellow Hammer, Two Thrushes, Wren. I also have lots of mummified/dissected birds, bird's wings and nine owl pellets.
GEOLOGICAL SPECIMENS: 51 minerals ranging from Amethyst and Jade to Flint and Pebbles.
MARINE SPECIMENS: Nearly 200 shells, Sea Urchins, Crabs, Marine worm casts, too many to name.
ANIMALS PRESERVED IN FORMALIN: 20 Cockroaches, Beetles and Bugs, Two still-born Rabbits, Three Pheasant Chicks at different stages of development inside their eggs, Five Tropical Fish, a Bat, a Frog, Three Earth-worms, a Silkworm.
SWAPS: Two drawers crammed full of bad, broken or swap specimens.
EXTRAS: Ranging from Honeycomb to Desiccated Birds.
BOOKS: 29 reference books.

On the next page is a plan Chris drew of his bedroom. In the top right hand corner he has written, "door to next room". This was the door to my bedroom.

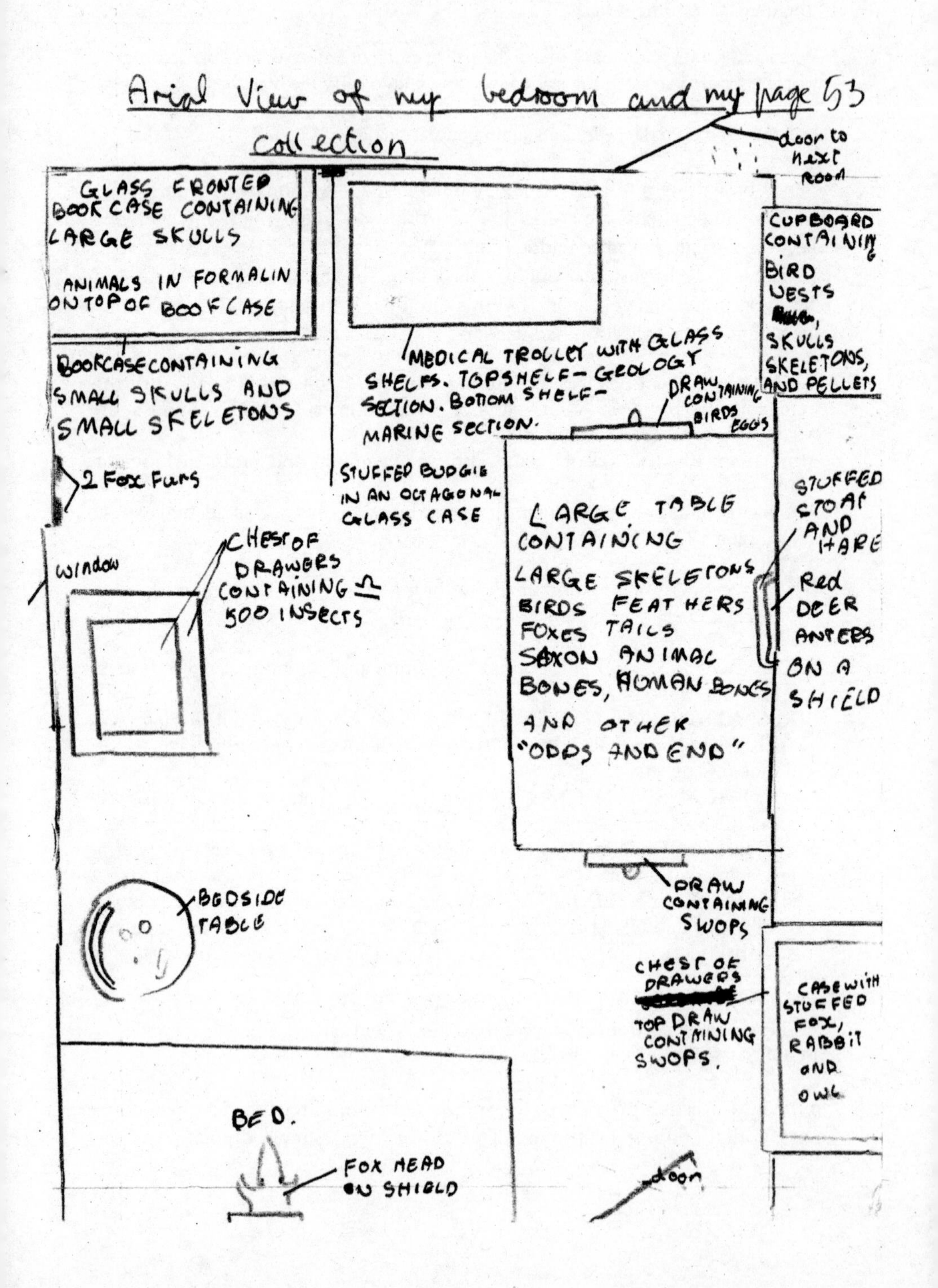
Arial View of my bedroom and my page 53
collection
door to next room
GLASS FRONTED BOOK CASE CONTAINING LARGE SKULLS
ANIMALS IN FORMALIN ON TOP OF BOOKCASE
CUPBOARD CONTAINING BIRD NESTS, SKULLS SKELETONS, AND PELLETS
BOOKCASE CONTAINING SMALL SKULLS AND SMALL SKELETONS
MEDICAL TROLLEY WITH GLASS SHELFS. TOPSHELF – GEOLOGY SECTION. BOTTOM SHELF – MARINE SECTION.
DRAW CONTAINING BIRDS EGGS
2 FOX FURS
STUFFED BUDGIE IN AN OCTAGONAL GLASS CASE
STUFFED STOAT AND HARE
LARGE TABLE CONTAINING
LARGE SKELETONS
BIRDS FEATHERS
FOXES TAILS
SAXON ANIMAL BONES, HUMAN BONES
AND OTHER "ODDS AND END"
window
CHEST OF DRAWERS CONTAINING ± 500 INSECTS
Red DEER ANTLERS ON A SHIELD
DRAW CONTAINING SWOPS
BEDSIDE TABLE
CHEST OF DRAWERS TOP DRAW CONTAINING SWOPS.
CASE WITH STUFFED FOX, RABBIT AND OWL
BED.
FOX HEAD ON SHIELD
door

Chris working on one of his animal specimens in the garden with Rusty keeping him company.

Beyond the fence is the dance studio where Melanie took her ballet classes.

Chris holding a dead fox cub found in Epping forest, which he is about to skin.

ABOVE: Chris skinning an animal in the back garden. I am not sure what it is.
BELOW: The Giant Atlas Moth that Chris chose for his Christmas present in 1970.

49
ACCIDENTS

The missed opportunity
Plummeted like a shot bird
And the moment passed.

Jean Lipkin

CATHY: January 1971: Well, here we go on yet another diary. I'm still at NYO. It's such a shame that just as you're beginning to really enjoy the course, it ends. I'm dying for the next course already. Chris and I played our NYO parts of the Walton Partita with the recording – sounded pretty awful – I don't realise how badly I play those parts, especially the quick bits.
Set books for English O level are 'The Lord of The Flies' – very gory, 'The Day of the Triffids', 'Wuthering Heights' and 'Pride and Prejudice' (which I've already read). Mum bought Chris a cabinet in the sale for his ever-growing collection.
Woke up in the night screaming – I'm not sure why. Went to the British Museum with Mum and Dad to see Beethoven's manuscripts – very very untidy but interesting. Dad bought me a BM reproduction of the Gorgon's head in a pendant on a gold chain. Don't know what I did to deserve that.
At school, Jackie was in the music room mooning around. Sue cracked some remark to Mr. Crombie saying, "She's got it bad too," referring to the fact that Jackie fancies him. Being sarcastic, Mr. Crombie said, "You don't fancy me, do you Catherine?" I said "No" with such emphasis that I hope it didn't sound rude.
Wore my newly made black maxi and green & gold blouse at the Turners'. Des took a photo of me and Izzy. Then followed a bad evening. Des played jazz all the time and everyone danced – except me. Oh I do like dancing, it's just that I can't stand doing it in front of other people or with Dad, so I wasn't in a good position. Des tried to tell me that I should dance but I just don't want to. I don't know what I'll do when (or if) someone does ask me to dance – I'll be in a bit of a fix.
Well, here we go again on one of my fantastic illnesses. Very bad night coughing, sneezing, sore throat and temperature. Mum phoned Mr. Crombie to say I wouldn't be able to play in concert at Beal tonight, but I was determined to play. Changed into school uniform and staggered to school. I played with a temperature of 101. It went quite well, considering. The Americans are sending up another rocket tonight – Apollo 14.
Miss Sprakes didn't exactly tell me off but warned that people were beginning not to like me because I was too hasty and expected everyone to mould round me and my way of doing things. I'm very ashamed if that's what it's seemed like. She said "always be nice to everybody even if you don't like them. Swallow bad feelings and be nice." Am I really so bad? I was very upset and cried. I'm so worried – my life is in fragments about me. I feel like a hypocrite when I'm all nice to someone I don't really like. I don't know how far one can extend 'niceness' until it becomes hypocrisy. I feel terribly out of everything nowadays. All I do is play the cello and never seem to talk to anyone. I'm just getting rather depressed about my whole way of life and I lack friends.
Bruce Fox and Alistair, Chris's friends from Wortley, have come to stay. We all went to the WMA Wortley reunion. I played Bach D minor suite reasonably well. Sold raffle tickets

and danced with Bruce (in a kind of a way) and talked with him for ages. We got home and Chris, Bruce, Izzy and I chatted and laughed in the living room till 12.30.

Bruce was passionate about music to the point of obsession, but there were few people in Southport with whom he could share it. After the Wortley reunion he wrote to me:

Dear Catherine,

After having what I found to be a most interesting and enjoyable conversation at the reunion on such subjects as Pierre Boulez and 'Le Sacre Du Printemps', I decided that it would make a marvellous change to be able to converse with someone who is intelligent even to the extent of actually knowing what she's talking about! – i.e. You. Previously I had never found anyone with whom I can hold a sensible conversation on music, as musicians in and around Southport are few and far between (proved by the fact that for the last three years I have been considered, except by myself, to be the undisputed "best" orchestral instrumentalist in the school!) So by setting pen to what the packet describes as 'writing paper of exceptional quality' I will proceed to bore you with whatever 'pseudo-intellectual' ideas come into my mind during the course of the next 'n' pages.

His letter does extend to 'n' pages! Every word about music – the records he's bought, concerts he's been to, what he's heard on the radio etc. Here are a few extracts:

Which of Bach's unaccompanied suites did you play at the reunion? – I was highly impressed, both by the work and its wonderful performance, and would like to obtain a recording of it.

It's a pity that I didn't hear your recording of the Rite of Spring with the National Youth Orchestra. I would have liked that very much indeed. Actually, I did hear it on the radio, but that was at a time when I could tolerate neither the Rite of Spring nor Pierre Boulez – yet now I admire both of them.

I saw Michel Tabachnik conduct his own work 'Fresque' for three orchestras. Modern music, such as 'Fresque' is most interesting, and often highly amusing. The trombonist in the Third orchestra (who incidentally is called Stephen Wortley) couldn't stop laughing at the trombonist in the first orchestra – he was so busy grinning at his colleague that he forgot to insert one of his two mutes – I've never seen anyone move so quickly as he when he realised. Another marvellous modern work performed at the Phil. [*Liverpool Philharmonic Hall*] was Gordon Crosse's 'Changes' for soprano, baritone, mixed choir, children's choir and orchestra. After this, one of the percussion players said to me "Did you notice we got lost for three pages in the middle?" – quite frankly, I didn't. Roberto Gerhard's 3rd symphony caused the remark from the principal oboist "The score's great, but the film for which it was composed has been banned!"

I notice that your two inferior colleagues, Jacqueline Du Pré and Pierre Fournier are appearing with the Israel Phil and the London Phil shortly.

Ah well, I think I've bored you sufficiently now, but please remember that I don't mind receiving letters, boring or not, so please write back!!

Yours (I won't commit myself to putting any adverb!!) Bruce

(Little did either of us know that in years to come, I would study with both Pierre Fournier and Jacqueline Du Pré and become a friend of Jacqueline's during the last years of her life.)

IZZY: *Double biology – dissected a herring.*
The new decimal coins are terribly small – I don't know how you're supposed to use a public loo. A Methodist bloke came to preach to us – as usual trying to put us off the permissive society and fashion – it's all they ever talk about. Had maths. Miss Echley said I was weak and lazy – the feeling's mutual.
School dinner was foul – the meat was like flavoured leather.
Listened to Bruckner 7. Accidentally dislodged a butterfly wing, but Chris managed to stick it back together. Listened to Bruckner 7 again – Cath and Chris are mad about it.
At music school we're playing Rhapsody in Blue – it's great. Talked to Chris Stearn. He plays bass trombone. He's a nice bloke.

CATHY: February 1971: The country's in a bad way. 10,000 Post Office workers are on strike (couldn't phone Mum because there are no telephone operators working), 5,000 workers at Ford's are on strike, Rolls Royce has gone bankrupt which will mean another 25,000 unemployed.
D Day today – change over to decimal currency [*15th February 1971*]
Since going to Edinburgh I've been trying to do more exercise. Decided that I really ought to go to PE. Well, had a good go on the trampoline, but as I was getting off I caught my foot and I literally did a dive into the floor. I was stunned and very surprised. Anyway, the result of the fall was pretty drastic. My left elbow won't bend and it's very painful. Mr. Crombie was very kind to me. Phoned Mum who came and took me to King George Hospital. Had two X-Rays – they bandaged it up and this will mean no practice for three weeks. I can't even lift my arm without support and actually I'm very worried. I'm taking my Grade VIII in March. Mum has to help me wash and dress and I feel so guilty doing nothing. Pain excruciating. Florrie has told Mum to take me to an osteopath, Mr. Miller. Mum phoned and very luckily was given an appointment at 5.00. We left immediately for Baker Street. He massaged and manipulated my arm – says the elbow is dislocated. Gave me an injection to ease the swelling and bruising and said to come back in three days.
There was a great demo on Sunday. The Government's planning to put through a bill that will make Trade Unions illegal again. 140,000 people went to Trafalgar Square to protest with the slogan 'Kill the Bill'. There were so many people, the meeting extended onto the embankment. I wish I could have gone. Had a lesson at RAM with Florrie entirely on right arm and bow technique then went to Mr. Miller who massaged my arm and got it to move a bit more then suddenly clonked it back into place. It doesn't hurt so much but still feels very odd, as though my hand's in the wrong position.
Izzy and I are 15. Chris has given me a lovely woven litter bin! (I did need one). Miss Sprakes gave me £1 and this weekend I'm looking after a gorgeous baby guinea pig that some kid found in his garden, called Scruffy. He's so small he has to be fed milk and water from an eyedropper.
Granny tells me that as a result of a dance Izzy went to last night, she now has another boyfriend, Paul. She's going to a party tomorrow night with him. I'm afraid I'm jealous. I never get a chance to go to anything – my life is just music, music, music – so much so that I've got myself into a rut – I've no boyfriends, and girlfriends amount to about 3. There must be something wrong with me. The stupid things I say are enough to put any boy off me from the start.

IZZY: *We had a foot inspection in PE. The staff are sadists chucking us out on frosty freezing pitches! Our play is Pygmalion.*
Chris has got another cabinet for some of his collection – only £2/10s.

Mum, Dad and Chris went to the cottage and Des took me & Cathy to the King's Head in Chigwell. We drank cider and Des gave us our birthday presents – mine is a gorgeous suede bag with long tassels and a shoulder strap – it sounds stilted, but it really was the very thing I wanted. Cath got some lovely gypsy-style material.
I'm doing a sponsored walk of the 19 bridges of London. Met up with girls from school at station. Got to starting point at 9.15. Tim, Dave, Ivar and another bloke came with us on their scooters. Got to finishing point at 5.15. Got a coach home, Dave & Tim followed it all the way. I can hardly walk, I'm aching so much. Couldn't go to school, my legs hurt too much.
I got a letter from Ian! I couldn't believe he'd actually managed to put pen to paper. He can't come on the same camp this year. Talked to Cath about blokes. Wrote to Ian.

CATHY: We went to the RFH for the Morning Star Rally. The rally was very good but the singers were not much use. Mum and Izzy went home (Izzy to her party) but Chris and I went on the march, walking at the front alongside the Morning Star banner, with police escort – had plenty of photos and film taken of us. We left before the march reached the US embassy and went home. Oh God – While I was away, little Scruffy died. Mum & Dad think he probably choked himself to death by swallowing too much milk at once and some getting in his windpipe. I'm so upset, especially as Miss Sprakes trusted me to look after him. It's absolutely dreadful. How am I going to tell her? I feel sick about it. I cried for half the night over Scruffy. I don't think I've ever felt so dreadful about something.
Ill again – asthma and bronchitis. Very bad night. Coughing all the time. Had to take inhaler several times. Too ill to play in school concert. Cancelled cello lesson and appointment with osteopath.
At the Musici Day Series, Chris had to play the Oberon overture by ear as there was no music and sight-read Sheherezade because Colin (first horn) forgot to turn up! Chris is so brilliant – sounds miles better than Colin.
Mum and Granny, Chris and I went to Aldeburgh for the Musici weekend. Dad's not coming – he said he dreaded the idea. Went for a long walk along the beach with Chris – we found a revolting dead fish about 18" long. Thankfully Chris left it where it was after he'd inspected it. At dinner, Bev asked me to sit at his table and I found myself with all the gang leaders. I had 3 glasses of wine and in the lounge afterwards, Dick Tyler bought me a martini, Bev improvised on the violin, a jazz band played, Dick bought me another martini and asked me to dance (I must admit I was rather tipsy). Mum and Gran went to bed, then Mr. Bidgood asked me to play the cello! I started playing a Bach suite, found myself at the end and didn't have a clue what had gone on in between. It was rather peculiar. Stayed up talking to Dick Tyler and others. Anyway, I'm really pleased because for once I felt part of something.
Dick called round to ask if I'd play at the Jubilee Hall concert in Aldeburgh this Easter with RYO. I'm sure I told him I was in NYO, but as Chris so bluntly put it, "He probably just came round to see your pretty face!" I wish really that I'd asked him in or something but I didn't.
There's something wrong with Mum. She was sitting in the front room in the dark on her own.

"Mum?" I called from the hall one evening. "Mum?" She must be in the office, I thought. I went upstairs to find her, but she wasn't there. Puzzled, I returned downstairs. "Mum?" There was still no response. I pushed open the door to the music room and peered around it into the darkness. There she was, sitting in the armchair behind the door. Her head was bowed. She seemed to be staring at her hands, which were lying limply in her lap. She didn't look up, just went on sitting in the gloom; immobile, silent, a shaft of light from the hallway falling onto the swan-patterned carpet. I retreated, pulling the door carefully back to the nearly closed position in which I had found it. Her despair seeped into me. I crept upstairs and lay on my bed, numbed by what I had accidentally seen. I knew without a shadow of doubt that Mum was deeply unhappy.

Much later, we talked about those years; the stress and unhappiness she had privately endured; the emotional abuse she had suffered. She told me that when Dad looked at her, she sometimes saw such intense hatred that she experienced it as evil. When I asked why they didn't separate, she told me, "I felt sorry for him. I couldn't chuck him out. Where would he have gone?" Guilt, fear and subjugation rendered her powerless.

I believe that Dad's self-pity, depression and bitterness, and his pathological hatred of Granny, stunted Mum's growth as a woman, incapacitated her sensuality and damaged her mothering. Habitual despair rendered her unable to engage with us in a straightforward way. How could she be relaxed, open and affectionate within a miserable, constrained relationship? She could not be natural with him, so she could not be natural with us – and that is how it always was: we could not change what had been established before we were born. Her life would have been so much happier without the burden of a debilitating, stultifying marriage, and so, I am certain, would ours. But in her music room she was able to shut the door on the rest of her life. It was her emotional connection to music that restored her over and over again. When she played the piano she escaped into her own world. When she taught she formed unfettered relationships with her pupils; relationships where she could be herself, show her love and express her feelings. Izzy remembers overhearing a conversation between Mum and a parent who had phoned to say their son was ill and unable to come for his lesson. She was startled to hear Mum say "give him a hug and a kiss from me". In some ways, her pupils enjoyed the best of her.

CATHY: Dad came home in a hellish mood. He said that no-one says hello to him when he comes in and then went up the wall at me for it!
Dad bought me a jewel box and a painting from a jumble sale.
Asthma getting very bad again.
Izzy went to a party last night and met this boy called Dave. She's so popular – I'm not. She goes to parties – I don't.
Went with Chris to BHCHS to see Hamlet. Was V V good. Even there, a boy said to Chris, "Where's your other sister?" HELL what can I do about it? I know it's my fault for being just what I am. Shy in an odd sort of way and afraid of boys. While I was upstairs I heard Mum complaining about me. Chris and I left for NYO – St. Lawrence College, Ramsgate.

At the NYO I tortured myself with incapacitating crushes on boys. There was one who preoccupied me for an absurd length of time. He was, I thought, beyond my wildest dreams, enthroned unreachably upon Olympian clouds. From an almighty height he dropped me morsels of hope occasionally, but mostly he mocked or humiliated me, or worse, ignored me altogether. There was so little chance with him that I swivelled my need for attachment onto lesser mortals, flirting unsuccessfully with boys I fancied and attracting the attention of those I did not. Every day I received countless confusing messages and could feel elated or suicidal, excited or mortified a dozen times a day. I wasted so much time hankering after boys who were indifferent to me. If I received the tiniest indication of interest – a smile, a few words – I would spend hours trying to decipher its significance, pulling petals from an over-picked daisy "he loves me, he loves me not, he might like me a bit, he hates me..."

Chris was there, but I didn't see much of him, except when I hung around by the horn room hoping to bump into one of my infatuations 'accidentally'. I was quite impressed when I heard he had been to the pub with the brass players – he was only twelve.

In those days, boys liked to wear their hair long, some (like Paul Hart) down to their waist. NYO, in public school spirit, stated in the rules:

> The National Youth Orchestra has a reputation for a high standard of personal appearance. This reputation now depends on you. Boys must be clean-shaven and are expected to have had a very short, neat haircut and a shampoo immediately before the course. Make sure that the back and sides are as tidy as possible. Hair must not touch the back of the collar and must be no more than a half an inch below the ear. Sideburns are NOT permitted.

Mum had cut Chris's hair exactly to the specifications, so he was annoyed when the housemaster pointed at him and told him to report to the NYO barber. I tried to help by cutting his hair a bit shorter with my nail scissors, but whatever I did would not have made any difference. Chris had been deliberately singled out. His self-containment, independent spirit and unassuming popularity rankled the NYO staff. They could see that he was well behaved and perfectly courteous, yet they felt strangely undermined, as if their authority were being mocked. The length of his hair was not the issue; it was Chris they wanted to cut down to size. In measured tones he protested against the injustice, but his objections fell on blocked ears and he had no choice but to endure the hacking of the barber's scissors. Afterwards it was apparent that the overall length of his hair was no shorter – it had simply been chopped and thinned – badly. He didn't say a word, but I could tell from his set expression that he was boiling with fury. He maintained a studied composure, brandishing looks of absolute contempt upon the staff. I found his dignity quite awesome. Clive Miller was also subjected to the barber. He knew that his hair was indeed longer than the rules dictated and accepted his fate, but he was incensed about the way Chris was treated. He told me, "As you know, everyone who played in the NYO liked and admired Chris. To see him being punished so unjustly for simply being himself – this person for whom we had such respect and fondness – was appalling."

> **IZZY:** *Went to cottage with Mum, Dad and Melanie. Melly and I walked to Sennowe Woods and Little Ryburgh and bought some carrots from the shop to feed the horses – a foal we've called Bulgaplod and four horses we've named Florence and Dougal, Caspian and Destrier.*

Mum wrote to me at NYO:

April 8th 1971

Melanie danced for us. It has been a great success having Melanie here. She is such a happy person that she makes everyone around her feel happy. It has been very good for Isabel because she has been very quiet and subdued at home recently. Melanie has brightened her up and they go out for walks together and have long talks.

IZZY: *Dad drove to Aldeburgh to take me to RYO. I'm sharing a room with Carolyn Wilson – the one who gets homesick. Found a fossil for Chris on the beach. Bev Wood and Paul Hart were showing Charlie Chaplin films in their room.*
Cath and Chris are still at NYO. Got a letter from Chris saying he can only play from mf upwards.
The Jubilee Hall concert was hilarious. Bram sang Mozart's horn concerto.[1] *Frank Mizen did a duck obligato and the jazz band was great. Chris Stearn had a fire extinguisher put in his bed and it leaked causing quite a bit of damage.*

The NYO course finished with a concert at the Festival Hall. Chris and I at last performed Bruckner 7, which we had worked on and listened to for months. It was an exhilarating experience. Bruce Fox, the horn player we had met at Wortley, came down from Lancashire for the concert.

IZZY: *The new Maltings Hall looks really great and smells all woody inside, but it's a funny hall to play in – it feels as if you can only hear yourself playing. Mum, Gran, Chris and Bruce came to the concert – NYO have chopped off Chris's hair! Everyone was making fun of him. Apparently Ivey's dyed her hair blonde! Chris and Bruce did Monty Python sketches all the way home in the car. It really was hilarious.*
I'm having packed lunches as the dinners cost too much.
I got another letter from Ian Y – nearly fainted with shock!

CATHY: Up at the dreadful hour of 7.10, dressed in drab school clothes – I've had my skirt since the first year and it's shiny and worn thin with a hole in it. The sleeves of my blouse are all torn. Mum, Gran, Chris and his friend Ross have gone to the cottage. Izzy cooked dinner and left the potatoes on too long and I made gravy that was so repulsive we had to chuck it away. Melly stayed to dinner (what there was of it).

Jon Turner belonged to a shooting club. Dad had an old air gun, which he lent to Chris, so Jon and Chris practised target shooting together. This led to an upsetting occurrence. Chris looked out of his bedroom window and saw a sparrow perched on the gutter of the house next door. "Hey, watch this," he said. He aimed the gun at the bird, not thinking for a moment that he would hit it. Bang went the gun and the little sparrow dropped like a stone to the ground.

"Oh, my God, I've killed it," he gasped. He rushed down to the garden and lifted the tiny body from the earth. It was dead. He was utterly shocked and inconsolable. He hated himself for what he had done, despised his stupid bravado and would

1. *Ill Wind* – Michael Flanders and Donald Swann – see words on page 603

never again hold a gun in his hand. He buried the sparrow and wept bitterly. I don't think he ever forgave himself.

IZZY: *Chris has joined the RSPB. He got 131 for his grade VIII and Cathy 140 – everyone's very pleased as the examiner, John Railton, told Mum over lunch that he never gives 140.*

CATHY: Showed Mr. Crombie my grade VIII report. He said well done but I could have done better.
Went to the medical room to practise. Mr. Crombie came in. He said, "Do I moan?" I said, "Yes, all the time." Then he said, "You have doubts about me, don't you?" He put his arm around me (as he always does) and said that whatever they were, they weren't true. Then Mr. Crombie talked to me on my own. "You don't really have doubts about me do you?" I said in as nice a voice as possible "No, not really." He then said that he'd never done anything to help me because I was so well looked after at home, which is true. I suddenly understood him for a moment and thought he was nice.
Chris and Izzy have Scabies. My goldfish has died. He was never very healthy.

Chris had been playing the horn for three and a half years when he took his Grade VIII. One of the exam pieces was Schumann's *Adagio and Allegro*. Chris's musical interpretation and technical mastery of that work was breathtaking. I have never heard any other horn player come close to matching his seamless, expansive phrasing of the *Adagio* or the flair and exuberant vitality he brought to the *Allegro*. Mum accompanied him, playing the demanding piano part of the Schumann brilliantly. John Railton may have been mean with his marks (he gave Chris twenty-eight out of thirty for a performance that deserved nothing less than full marks), but his comments were otherwise:

Adagio: Played with a most lovely, natural, easy tone. Most sensitively phrased. Splendid low notes. *Allegro:* An astonishing performance. Brilliant and assured.

Chris and I practised in our bedrooms, but such was our individual concentration, noise from the neighbouring room was not off-putting. Both the cello and horn have a wide pitch range from the bass to the treble as well as the luxury of a richly warm middle register. Consequently, cellists often appropriate music written for the horn. The Beethoven horn sonata in F is frequently played by cellists, as is Schumann's *Adagio and Allegro* (both of which sound infinitely better on the horn). Horn players are fortunate to have four concertos by Mozart (who wrote none for the cello) and although Richard Strauss gave the cello a major role in his *Don Quixote*, he honoured the horn with two substantial concertos.

We were in Chris's room placing newly typed cards beneath recent specimens.

"What's happened to your stick insects?" I asked, eyeing the empty tank.

"I let them loose on that big privet hedge down the road."

"You didn't!"

"Yeah. I was fed up with them multiplying so fast and anyway I needed the container for more pupae. I know, I know, it was a bit horrible, but what else could

I do? I sold some and gave loads away, but nobody else wants them. I couldn't bring myself to squash them or flush them down the loo. At least they had a good meal on the privet before the birds ate them."

"Poor stick insects. You used to be so concerned about them."

"Yeah, well, things change." Then he changed the subject completely.

"Hey girls," he asked, "Can you roll your tongues?" He pushed his tongue, curled up at the sides, out of his mouth.

"Yes," I said, doing the same.

"And you, Izzy?"

"Yes."

"Well go on then."

"There."

"Hmm. You know, not everyone can do that. It's odd, isn't it, as all babies curl their tongues to suck?"

"Maybe only breast-fed babies can do it?" I suggested.

"No. All babies must suck, whether from the breast or a feeding bottle. It's the strongest natural instinct, but some people forget how to do it when they pass the baby stage." Then he demonstrated another ability – flaring and contracting his nostrils, like a rabbit.

"Can you do it?" he asked us. Yes, we were both able to expand our nostrils. "I think if you can roll your tongue, you can also flare your nostrils," he said, "but if you can't do one, you can't do the other. At least, that's my theory. I'm testing it out."

"Ah, but can you do this?" I challenged, going cross-eyed then moving one eye outwards and back into a squint.

"Easy," he responded, copying me. "Bet you can't do this, though," he boasted, opening his mouth, jutting out his lower jaw, pushing it to one side, squeezing it half-shut and squirting out a spray of saliva.

"I wouldn't want to. It's vile."

"No, it's great. I can direct it on target now. I had to teach myself to do it. Like raising one eyebrow or waggling your ears. You could do it; you just have to learn to access your muscles."

"But what's the point?" asked Izzy.

"It's just surprising how many muscles we have that don't get used. There must have been a reason for them once. The toes are another funny thing; lots of people can't move the big toe independently, or flex their toes, yet nearly a quarter of the bones in the human body are in the feet. I'm working on trying to achieve independent movement in every toe – supposedly not possible, but we must have been able to do it once. Then there are the parts of the body that are becoming obsolete – eventually human beings will be born without tonsils or appendixes. Life is evolving all the time."

50
IZZY'S QUIET REBELLION

I know, and that is certain,
Flowers do not care
And this which so involves me
Is not for open air.

Pandora – Jean Lipkin

The day we turned fifteen was a Friday. Izzy went to a dance and got off with a boy and I went with Mum and Chris to *Musici* and rehearsed *Scheherazade*. From then on, Izzy went out every Friday night with girls from her school to a youth club held in a church hall in Loughton, where they met boys from neighbouring schools. She had fretted about Ian Yellowlees for months, written numerous letters to him to which he had not replied, but by March it was Izzy who had forgotten about his existence.

IZZY: *At the dance got off with a smashing bloke called Paul Betts. We walked arm in arm to the station, kissed and he gave me his phone number. Mum says I can go to the party on Sunday. Paul didn't speak to me once! He got off with Elaine and looked right through me every time I happened to catch his eye. Walked home with Yvonne and we talked about how nasty some blokes can be.*
Went to Jan's party and got off with Dave Evans. He rides a motorbike and smokes. I'm not sure if Mum and Dad approve. My clothes pong of fags – everyone was smoking last night – I wasn't, I don't even want to start. He's picking me up at 3.00 tomorrow.
He didn't turn up. He phoned at 6.00 saying he'd gone to some motorcycle place – he didn't seem very sorry about it.

CATHY: Watched a film about VD at school – it was horribly frightening. I wasn't really sure before what VD was. Talked to Mum about it. She's terribly worried about Izzy and thinks she'll end up pregnant or catching VD or both. I was quite shocked that Mum was thinking such things. I'm sure Izzy's being sensible but she wants me to talk to her.

IZZY: *Got off with Graham. Took Cathy along to Club. She saw all my friends and we had a séance – nothing serious. Went to the pub, then Cathy went home – she didn't like some bloke who was chasing her.*

CATHY: Izzy rather abandoned me, but I saw a few girls I knew. Izzy went off with Graham and was kissing and hugging etc. Then I unfortunately got mixed up with some 4th years from BHCHS. One put his arms around my waist and walked with me to the pub. I was not enthusiastic. I went home early. I really just went to see what was going on and I'm satisfied. Izzy's a bit sexy with Graham, but he's a nice bloke so she'll be OK. I ought to be depressed, but I'm not. I wasn't really myself there. It's all rather false.

IZZY: *Graham was in a funny mood and I knew something was wrong. He said, "I think this has come to an end." He was really everso nice about it, but I just started crying and couldn't stop.*

On thinking it over, maybe Graham chucked me because he thought I was getting to like him too much. Had another cry and felt a bit better. Told Cath about it.
At Colin's party, I got off with Bill. He's a boarder at Bancroft's School. Went to Bancroft's and met him in the common room. The headmaster told him to "take that wench somewhere else", so we went into the forest and got absolutely covered in leaves. I really do like Bill a lot better than Ian, whom I don't really want to see again. That sounds very nasty but I'm afraid it's true. Cathy came to Club again – she got off with Fee – I'm glad coz I rather deserted her last night. She thinks Bill's sweet.

CATHY: Izzy went off to Theydon Bois with Bill and I stayed behind feeling v. v. left out. Thought I'd go home at 8.30, then this guy called Fee went after me, put his arm around me and took me to the pub. He's far too over-sexed – what revolting kisses – tongues in yer mouth, eugh, and his hand right up my jumper and almost right down my trousers. I didn't like it. Then he walked me to the bus stop and gave me two revolting kisses. I felt like throwing up.

IZZY: *Cathy cooked tea and I did the washing up. Talked to her for a long time. Seemingly, Mum's been talking to her and is worried that I'd go the whole way with a bloke. I told Cath that I wouldn't be so daft, which she already knew.*
Des woke me at 11.30 and talked to me for a while about not getting into trouble etc. It's everso nice and kind the way he worries about me – not that he needs to.
Played in the music festival – I actually won!! Got 91 marks!

CATHY: Went with Izzy to Deb Jones' party. Fee was there. At first I didn't talk to him, then he said "Coming to the pub?" Got chucked out of the pub so went to another. Back to party, lay on the floor, kissed. He gave me a love bite, not a pleasant feeling, and put his hand right down my drawers. He's so randy. I kept pulling his hand out but he kept putting it back. Then a copper came round. The neighbours had been complaining about the din. We all left and got on the same train and they behaved awfully, taking out all the advertisement cards in the carriage. Back home, looked in the mirror – what a shock when I saw how huge the bite was! And so high up! Looks as though a vampire's attacked me. Izzy had a good idea – cover the bite with a plaster and say that my choker scratched me. But it's so big and red – Fee's vicious. I feel depressed now and worried.
Wore a polo neck jumper, but it didn't cover the bite, so I put a plaster on it and went downstairs with my chin down. Mum asked why I was wearing a jumper on such a hot day, and in the end I was so hot, I had to change. Went to the Turners and told Mel the truth about the love bite. She gave me a proper plaster, as the one I was using was an old one stuck on with selotape.

IZZY: *Had a discussion about sex before marriage in R.I. Of the 19 girls in our class, 5 have already lost their virginity – it all seemed a bit pointless.*
Miss Echley went really mad at us in Maths saying we weren't very nice people (little does she know). I suppose we do take rather a carefree attitude to life, especially as O levels are coming up, but as Mary says, "At least we're happy".

CATHY: I don't really want to go to Club any more because I haven't liked anyone. That's the trouble – nobody loves or even much likes anyone else – they just flit around from one boy or girl to the other. So shallow-minded. Fee scared me. Occasionally I suppose it's enjoyable to mix with the sort of people who, when you were little, hung around in teenage gangs and scared you.

This was the Club that Izzy went to every week. 'Getting off with a bloke' meant, in basic terms, that you let the boy grope you. The girls were openly provocative and the boys physically intrusive. Both sexes bypassed every courtship procedure, preamble and subtlety. It was a bizarre sexual dance, swapping partners each time round, devoid of emotional connection, conversation, sensitivity and intelligence.

Izzy flirted outrageously, but so did all the girls, while the boys felt them up with a hard, cynical detachment. It was empty, meaningless and dangerous – teenagers intent on slapping social convention in the face and sticking two fingers up to adult authority. I was alarmed by the overt behaviour, disturbed to realise that to be a part of the group I would have to sacrifice my body to molestation, switch off my brain and pretend to be the same as the rest. Was it only I who objected to the mauling, who felt uneasy, troubled and different? How far did they go? Did the boys expect the girls to have sex with them? Did the girls want it too? I hated the way the boys shoved their hands into your knickers as if it were their right to do so. You pulled their hands away and they would be back seconds later.

It seems odd to me now that such heavy petting went on unchecked in a youth club. There was no supervision. The doors were unlocked, the strip lights switched on and the kids (who promptly switched them off) left to their own devices. Mum and the Turners were getting worried about Izzy. She was often home late from school, was out at Club every Friday and going to parties every weekend. They would have been apoplectic if they had seen what actually went on, yet both Izzy and I were utterly responsible about sex. We were not going to risk pregnancy, nor would we have contemplated sex at that stage. When the time came that we did, we made sure we were protected.

Although Izzy refused to have sex with any of the boys, plenty of the other girls did. It is a paradox that the young want to grow up as fast as possible, snatching every experience, rampaging through life as if it were a supermarket and you have five minutes to fill your basket. Try it all, do it all, have it all now. In older age, when one wants to savour and engage with each moment, reap every grain from the fields of knowledge, flow slowly in the tides of sensuality, time is speeding up, hurrying us on, years flying by as fast as the weeks of teenage frenzy. We couldn't wait when we were young.

I only went a few more times to Club, much preferring *Musici* rehearsals, but Izzy went every Friday and was frequently out on Saturday nights too. Occasionally she missed the last train and had to walk home, arriving back in the early hours, much to Mum and Dad's consternation. Yet it appeared that she took no notice of their disapproval.

51
BREAKING THE RULES

Fool that I am
I do not learn restraint.
Eagerly towards love
I turn. And burn
And burn and burn.

Young Girl – Jean Lipkin

> **IZZY:** *Everyone's away. I asked Dad if I could have a party tomorrow. He said Yes!!!!!!!!!! Got the living room ready and went down to the station to meet everyone and millions of others turned up. Collected money for booze, walked to the pub and got loads of it. All managed to squeeze into the living room. Ken Booker came round so Dad went off to the pub with him. Everyone left about 11.00. Dad and Ken came back from the pub. Dad was in a good mood. He made me a lovely breakfast.*

It seems extraordinary that Dad agreed so readily to Izzy inviting an "uncouth mob of long-haired louts and yobbos" into the house. It must have been because Granny and Mum would not have allowed it. When Izzy's friends arrived, he went off to the pub with Ken Booker, no doubt enjoying the pleasure of defiance.

There were a number of times when Mum, Granny and Chris went to the cottage, leaving Izzy and me with Dad. His relief was palpable as the car pulled away. He turned back into the house with a smile, rubbing his hands with glee.

"Isn't this marvellous, girls? Nobody telling us what to do! Oh, what larks we can have now!" Izzy and I, indifferent to his excitement, switched on ITV; Dad went out with a spring in his step, bought whisky, wine, beer, kippers, horseradish, pickled onions, rollmops, smelly cheese, and lamb chops for us. He invited Ken Booker over for homemade curry. The house filled with nose-stinging smells of hot spices and garlic. He peeled potatoes, cutting them lengthways into boat shapes the way *he* wanted, roasting them without parboiling first, declaring that his method was far superior to Granny's. He pretended to be a waiter, bringing our dinner through to us in the TV room on trays with a tea towel draped over his arm.

"Mesdemoiselles, your supper is served," he announced, bowing deeply. We accepted our meals without comment; he poured us wine and raised no objection to the programme we were watching. Later, he donned his smoking jacket, an article of clothing ridiculed by Granny that he had picked up at an Oxfam shop. He and Ken settled into chairs in the living room, lit their pipes and sipped whisky and water from cut-glass tumblers that Dad kept hidden in the cellar. Izzy and I stayed up watching late films and went to bed when we felt like it. In the morning he grilled kippers, chuckling when the kitchen filled with smoke, and brought us tea in bed. There were cornflakes for breakfast.

IZZY: *Des brought me presents back from Italy – a leather powder compact and an onyx egg – really great.*
Chris got all the gear for collecting butterflies for his birthday. (He's 13)
Dad's going to hospital today for about a week to get his nose done.
Ken Rosewall beat Cliff Riche 3 sets to 2 – lasted 4 hours – great match. Evonne Goolagong beat Billie Jean King 6:4, 6:4 (hoorah)
Mum and I went to see Dad in Mile End hospital. He seems OK. Three blokes in his ward have had their legs amputated! Newcome won the men's singles.
Rehearsed Pygmalion – I'm Eliza, tons of lines to learn. Amazingly, Mr. Rodger, the dentist I go to about my brace practises at 27, Wimpole Street – the same house as Henry Higgins has!

Izzy remembers going with Mum to visit Dad in hospital. When visiting time was over, Mum kissed him goodbye – a kiss that was given out of obligation to Dad, but also, Izzy sensed, was a tragic attempt by Mum to reassure her daughter that everything was fine and normal between her parents. It made Izzy feel sad and sorry for Mum.

CATHY: May 1971: Bought 3 dozen bedding plants, 2 yards of amber coloured ribbon, 3 birthday cards, a packet of rubber bands, a pair of tights and some brown leather sandals for £1.99 from Freeman Hardy Willis'. What a gorgeous day it is – the cherry tree has been in bloom for about a week now.
Went to a concert at the Hawkey Hall and started to feel sick, faint, hot & cold and an awful pain. Mum brought me home in the interval.
I'm so tired all the time. It's so awful when the birds start to sing and I'm still awake. Had a very bad asthma attack – haven't had one for a while.
Paid 3/- for postage stamps – the cheapest is now 2½p.
I'm getting so fat. Granny has just knitted me a jersey and I look enormous in it. My feet are in a terrible state – I've got this awful verruca (that I've had for 4 years) and Dad tells me I've got bunions!
At long last Mum bought me a new school skirt and blouse.
Mel's going out with rather a drip of a boy called Stephen. He's only 14.
At the Redbridge concert, Dick asked me if I was going to Bram's party – I'd have loved to but of course I had to get home. I must cut down on bread and potatoes.
Chris & I went to the RFH together – fantastic concert.
Chris is in a real state. Tinker (one of our two cats) has been peeing all over the house and Mum wants her put down. V. cruel I know, but I can see it's a problem. Chris is promising Mum that he'll clean up all the messes she makes. Her life remains in the balance.
Saw Mr. Crombie at the Wanstead and Woodford Music Festival. He said, "Doesn't she look gorgeous", referring to me. Then he put his arm around me. Fortunately Mum didn't see. Maybe he doesn't dislike me quite so much at the moment, but I never take him seriously. He is definitely leaving at the end of the term and going to Wanstead County High School.

Chris's plea for Tinker's life was successful. His distress at the thought of her being put down was so extreme that Mum had to pacify him by promising that it wouldn't happen. She continued to clean up after Tinker without further complaint.

CATHY: June 1971: Watched 'Face the Music' and a programme on depression. We're hiring a new TV – about time too. I've decided to slim.

Miss Sprakes is going to give me singing lessons. I think I'll be hopeless, but I suppose it'll be OK if nobody else is listening.
I enjoyed my singing lesson. My voice is very weak and small. Miss Sprakes was telling me how to produce sound by opening up my throat as though I was yawning. I sang scales in Chees and Haas and she gave me two lovely songs by Vaughan Williams to sing.
Mel was here and we had a long chat – she's still going out with Stephen. She's lucky to be so popular so young. Took an eyedropper over to Primrose Road for Mel to feed her baby bird. I was too late as the bird had died.
Went to Musici with Mum and Chris – a good rehearsal. Shostakovich 5 is fantastic and Bev played the Brahms violin concerto beautifully.
Asthma bad. Was breathless and wheezy for my singing lesson. Took my grade VII theory exam. Mel's not going out with Stephen any more.
Mum bought me a gorgeous maxi dress, all gathered and flouncy. Showed it to Dad – he doesn't like it. Chris said I looked fat in it, so I took it off and refused all potatoes. Gran told me off & said I was ridiculous and that I wasn't fat.
Mel phoned – she's got herself another bloke. I don't think she likes him that much – just going out with him for a laugh.
Entirely mucked up my French and maths exams. I managed English comprehension OK, but answered the questions far too fully – filled 14¼ foolscap pages in a 2-hour exam. English Lit was OK – 11½ pages, I write far too much.
Went to Covent Garden with Mel. Absolutely dreadful seats, on a precipice at the very top of the theatre with about ½ of the stage obscured. Even so, it was absolutely fantastic. There were three ballets – Apollo (music by Stravinsky), Song of the Earth (Mahler) and Marguerite and Armand (Liszt). Nureyev and Fonteyn were dancing. I lost count of the number of times they were called back – at least 12. The choreography of the first two was very clever, unclassical, but quite marvellous. The last was really beautiful.
Feel really awful. Ill again. Temp. of 104.4. Mel came over & tried to comfort me & sponged my face. Mum just took ages to get home. When the phone rang I thought she was dead. Then Mum came back and persuaded me to get the Doctor. He gave me a penicillin injection. Mel stayed with me for hours. I love her for that. Terrible dreams. Slept with Mum. Miss Sprakes brought me some lovely flowers. Des came round with some roses, raspberries and lettuce.
Dr. Franklin came again – temp. 102.5. Wrote loads of letters. NYO instructions have arrived. I'm playing in everything, but Chris is not going to Edinburgh. Hair regulations have been further enforced – he's livid and so am I. It's so pathetic.
One of Chris's pupae is hatching. He came home from school, as his teachers are on strike. He lost one pupa – Rusty probably ate it.
Very tragic – the three Soviet astronauts have died on re-entry to the Earth's atmosphere. Watched ITV – Peyton Place (which I'd never seen before) – God, Gran didn't even complain, perhaps because I'm ill, so watched more.
Gave my lunch away and just had a tomato and an apple. I've given up sugar in coffee. No potatoes at dinner and no pudding. So tired and depressed. Just can't sleep.
Went to practise in the medical room and for the first half hour just cried. Nobody came in. I felt so queer – as if I were several different people – one wanting someone to come in and offer sympathy, one wanting to hide and be on my own and another observing myself with contempt. I felt in a strange way that I was a fraud – merely PUTTING ON my frame of mind. I watched everyone else and felt as if I were an intruder in a world in which I don't belong. I don't think I do belong anywhere. Sue is collecting money for Mr. Crombie's leaving present.

CATHY: July 1971: Janet phoned to say I came 1st in history & came 1st in English Lit. Got 70% for maths and 61% for French! I'm so surprised, was sure I'd failed. I have so many blackheads, it's sickening.
Went with Des to look at pianos. There was a lovely Bechstein, which Des was almost sure about, but then we went to pick up Melly and Pat and looked at the pianos in Harrods. I tried them all, but there was an absolutely fabulous 6 ft 3" Blüthner for £718 – Des had tried it last week, but it had had a Sold sign on it. But today the Sold sign has gone, replaced by a Sale sign, so Des bought it! We've called it Julius.
Mel phoned to say that Thomasina has had four baby guinea pigs – unfortunately one of them was still-born, so Chris went round to get it to preserve in Formalin.
Dad hasn't been to work since Whitsun. What an awful day – this morning I played the Saint-Saëns through with Redbridge Orchestra One – Rod Elms conducted. The orchestra managed fantastically and Rod was great & we kept together, but I played very badly. I was drowned half the time, technical passages were awful & I just scraped my way through it and at the end mucked up the last run AND failed to come in. Oh Hell. Bram said he enjoyed it very much. Back home I moped around and ate far too much, then went to see 'Cromwell' at the Odeon. A good film, but in the middle of it, Dad shouted out across the audience "Pack up that bloody gossiping over there!" and quite honestly I hadn't noticed anyone talking.
I only did about 1½ hours practice interrupted by phone calls and little bouts of daydreaming, I was so fed up and couldn't be bothered – I can't play any of it anyway. I'm in a funny sort of mood and don't like it. I dream about nearly committing suicide by taking an overdose of my asthma drugs to make people help me and feel sorry for me. I just take enough to pass out and look as though I wanted to kill myself, but not actually taking enough to die. I often daydream things like that – if not suicide then having some terrible car crash or accident and landing up in hospital near death's door but eventually recovering and frightening people into loving and protecting me. It's terrible to *know* that you're feeling sorry for yourself. The trouble is, I see all sides of everything I do and it makes me feel that I'm false. I *am* false. I don't know who the genuine *me* is. This is the first time I've had the courage to state this in this diary – I don't actually say anything that is untrue, but I often exaggerate or dampen down happenings to avoid appearing stupid or immature. And when I know I'm in the wrong, I never admit it fully. I write in my favour, trying to convince people that I'm a nice, agreeable, kind girl – which I'm not. I write in this way to mislead myself into believing my worth. Oh it's all so queer – I don't really know what I'm talking about or what's gnawing at me. I must stop now – I'm getting my whole mind and life muddled up and I don't understand myself or the world in which I live, but most of all, I don't understand or know my Mummy or Daddy. I don't seem to make any contact with them at all. Something in my life has gone very wrong.
The first Beal school concert went jolly well. Miss Evans made a speech in the second half about Mr. Crombie leaving and some girls burst into tears.
Went to school for second concert. Signed Mr. Crombie's card. Concert went even better than last night. Then Miss Evans spouted again and more girls burst into tears again. Afterwards we presented Mr. Crombie with an attaché case and diary and Mrs. Crombie with chocolates. By now everyone was crying – I mean that. I and one other girl were the only two who weren't. I was accused of being hard-hearted. While practising in medical room, Sue came in to tell me that Mr. Crombie and Miss Evans were quarrelling – she was telling him off for exciting too much emotion last night.[1]

1. In 2010, Michael Crombie, aged seventy-three, was arrested, tried and found guilty of thirty-four child abuse charges dating from 1991. Since the trial, twenty-three more victims have come forward. He is presently serving a seven-year jail sentence.

Chris said "Martin Koch doesn't half fancy you" (he goes to Chris's school). I think he's nice and I'd go out with him if he asked – mind you, he's two years younger. Russell Jordan is being jolly nice to me, but I'm flattering myself too much by writing this down.

That summer we camped in the Lake District. Izzy and I were Pathfinders for the first time. Marjory Guillen, our camp-chief, proved to be humourless, unfriendly and headmistress-like. Immediately, Izzy teamed up with another Pathfinder, Jonathan Hollis. He slept in our tent on the first night and Izzy spent subsequent nights with him. The arrangement did not meet with staff approval.

***IZZY:** Slept out with Jon in his sleeping bag – a bit of a squash but very nice. Justine, our group leader, found out that Jon and I were both sleeping in his tent and said that we were to stop sleeping together. After campfire that night, Jon and I went back to his tent and a quarter of an hour later, in storms Justine, blows her top off and sends me back to my tent. Silly old cow. Cath got off with Dave, the Woodling leader. He's only 19 so that's OK, but I doubt if Marge or Justine will approve. Jon and I moaned to our other leader about Justine's unfair treatment. "We're not having sex, we just want to sleep together."*

The person I fell for was Dave Rannie, a nineteen-year-old staffing the Woodling group. He played the guitar and introduced me to the songs of Joni Mitchell. I fell for him and for Joni. He taught me chords on the guitar and I learnt the words by heart. We sat on the same log at mealtimes and walked to the campfire together. At Woodling bedtime, I helped Dave to get the children into their tents. Later, we sat around the Pathfinder fire and he put his arm around me. My hand slid round his waist. He sang his songs – melancholy Irish ballads, old modal tunes a cappella, Simon and Garfunkel, Bob Dylan, Woody Guthrie and Joni Mitchell, the firelight dancing on his guitar and on his face. We lay on the ground talking quietly, finding each other's warm flesh beneath layers of bulky clothing.

"I don't know why I like you so much," he whispered.

"Do you really like me?"

"Yes. I do." I longed for him to kiss me. When at last he did, I understood something of desire. What stirred within me was so strong I was convinced that Dave must feel it too. Yet the next day, instead of seeking me out, he sought to avoid me. It didn't make sense. Alarmed, I went to find him on the Woodling site. He was sitting cross-legged outside his tent playing his guitar. He looked up and held my gaze as he continued to sing Joni Mitchell's *Circle Game*: *Yesterday a child came out to wonder, caught a dragonfly inside a jar, he was fearful when the sky was full of thunder, and tearful at the falling of a star...*

Mike Johnson, another of the Woodling staff, seeing me looking dejected, called me over. He told me that the camp-chief, Marjory, had had some stern words with Dave. His 'relationship' with me had been noticed and it must stop.

"But why, Mike?"

"Why? Because you're fifteen and FSC have a responsibility towards you."

"I'm fifteen and I'm responsible."

"I believe you are, but Dave's nineteen and a member of staff."

"So what? Does that make him less responsible? And what about our feelings?

What right does she have to dictate how people feel about each other?"

"You really like him, don't you?"

"Yes, I do."

"Oh Cathy. Life is tough sometimes, you know."

"I know."

"Our dreams don't always match reality."

"Mike, I didn't imagine what happened between me and Dave."

"I'm not saying you did, I just don't like to see you so sad."

"It's all Marjory's fault. What should I do?"

"I can't tell you what to do, but if you and Dave want to be together, you're going to have to play it cool. Keep a low profile."

Sadly, I knew nothing of subtlety or discretion, of patience or tranquillity. I contrived to be with or next to Dave at every opportunity. It was painfully obvious. It didn't occur to me that my intense yearning for tenderness – for love – might only have been a pleasant flirt for Dave. I couldn't let it go. I wanted his arms around me again, to feel the solace of affection, to be kissed, cherished and embraced. The small inner smile I had allowed myself disappeared. Once or twice he put his arm over my shoulder and said, "Come on, cheer up," treating me as if I were one of the Woodlings. I followed him around, if not physically, then with my eyes, but he kept himself distant. I made a nuisance of myself, unable to restore my equilibrium. It was to Mike that I poured out my heart. He listened with such attentive concern that I realised he liked me far more than Dave did. I was adept at falling for the cool, uninterested types, unable to fancy those whom I knew genuinely cared for me. After camp, I wrote long letters to Dave: he wrote back twice. I phoned him until he told me off for phoning too often, and that was the end of it. Only my love for Joni has survived.

Alas, it would not be the last time I felt desolate over a man. What wretchedly woeful times we cause ourselves to endure. We look for others to bestow value upon our worthless selves with their magic wand of approval and kiss of favour: we imagine that they can see right into our hearts and minds, can decipher every nuance of our emotions, and know us with a wisdom to which we have no access: we believe that they have the insight to explain us to ourselves. For a moment, we become Cinderella in her sparkling gown, the radiant belle of the ball, until the illusion is shattered and there we are back in our dirty rags. It is all too easy to attribute to people qualities that they do not possess. We go searching for a shell in a forest or a toadstool by the seashore and delude ourselves that we will find them if we only look for long enough; because we know that shells and toadstools exist, but we haven't a clue about context.

52
MEETING SIMON RATTLE

But if the while I think on thee, dear friend,
All losses are restored, and sorrows end.

Sonnet 30 – William Shakespeare

Back from camp, Mum, Izzy and Melly went to Wortley and Chris and I headed off to the NYO course. Boulez was there to conduct Bartók's *Music for Strings, Percussion and Celesta* and Debussy's *La Mer*. Boulez was inspiring and patient in rehearsals. Most of us had not played such complex music before and he insisted on accuracy. There was a new boy in the orchestra playing the solo piano part in the Bartók. He exuded such animation and rhythmical precision that my eyes and ears homed in on him. His name was Simon Rattle. I wish I could remember the first words we spoke to each other, but I can't. Every time I saw him, he was holding hands with a girl and I assumed they were together. I was wrong. He told me they were just friends who deliberately held hands wherever they went to protest against the nonsensical rule that forbade couples to do so.

"Don't they try to stop you?" I asked.

"Of course they do – it's hysterical! Look, here's one of them coming towards us. Quick, hold my hand." Simon pretended to be engrossed in intimate conversation with me as we walked past Mrs. Garland, whilst I spoiled the effect by giggling. She gave us a withering look but didn't say a word. His example caught on and others started to hold hands openly.

I was still infatuated with the boy-beyond-my-wildest-dreams and would have melted on the spot if *he'd* held his hand out to me. Getting nowhere as usual, my flirtatious displays sent out signals to Mike, a boy I had not intended to attract at all. He started to sit with me at mealtimes and wait for me after rehearsals. By the middle of the course he was grabbing my hand whenever we walked together. Inadvertently, I was 'with' him. He was eighteen. It was his last NYO course, after which he would be moving to London, having been offered a job in the BBCSO. He talked about what we could do in London and how grand it was that I lived there. He was as smitten as I was alarmed. He glued himself to me, staking his claim. I was unable to deflect his attentions and too scared to extricate myself.

Before the Albert Hall concert he took me by the hand and walked me across the road into Hyde Park. We wandered around the Serpentine lake then sat down on the grass. He lay back and pulled me down beside him. His kisses devoured, his hands sought greedily, squeezing my breasts painfully. My body tightened. I felt as if I were flailing in a sea of black treacle.

"I love you Cathy." Stunned, I laughed, trying to disguise my nervousness with light-heartedness.

"You can't possibly love me!"

"I do. I love you. Before this it used to be infatuation, but now I know the difference. I've fallen in love with you Cathy: will you marry me?"

"I can't," I yelped, panic mounting, "I'm only fifteen".

"I know, but it's alright, I'll wait till you're sixteen. It's only another six months, isn't it?" He moved to kiss me again. I turned away and sat up, picking at some blades of grass beside me, horrified by his words – so out of place, so alarming. He pulled my hand from its grass-picking, gripping it too tightly, and smiled at me, saying, "Oh, what will my mother say when I take you back home and tell her we're getting married!" I could not find any words to reply.

We returned to the Albert Hall for the Prom where I was relieved to see the familiar faces of Mum, Izzy and Granny. I barely remember the concert, so tangled up had my feelings become. Afterwards, Chris went home, as a smaller orchestra was going to Edinburgh. I wished I could go home too. Somehow I had to get through the next two days. I used every tactic I could think of. I tried to be blithe and carefree, but it only made him more serious. I larked about with the girls and flirted with the boys, which made him angry and jealous. I hung out as much as I could with other people, but he came searching for me. It seemed impossible to disentangle myself without brutally upsetting him, which I couldn't bring myself to do when the course was so nearly over.

On the train back to London he kissed me relentlessly, told me I was fantastic and fabulous and wrote 'I LOVE YOU' in my concert programme. I tried to tell him that I liked him but didn't want to get too serious. He refused to listen. "I'm going to miss you so much," he said, "but I'll be moving to London in two weeks and we'll see each other as often as possible. I can't wait." I couldn't wait for the two weeks respite. I escaped to go to the buffet car, and on the way Simon Rattle pulled me into the seat next to him and hugged me. What a joy. It was like sinking into a warm muffin having been gritting my teeth on burnt toast. He asked me what I thought about starting up an orchestra when he came to the Academy in September. Quite a number of NYO members lived in London and there were plenty of ex-NYO members at the Academy and the College. Did I think it would be possible to assemble enough players to form an orchestra that he could conduct? I thought it was a brilliant idea. We agreed to get in touch as soon as he arrived in London. He wrote in my programme: "With love and best wishes for a successful, ravishing musical career. Simon Rattle." Then Mike hauled me away. "See you next month at the Academy!" called Simon.

Back home, I anguished about the situation I had landed myself in, feeling wracked with remorse. Why hadn't I stopped it before it became so out of hand? Weakly, I had hoped Mike would lose interest, pick up my signals of resistance and let me off the hook, but he seemed unaware of my body language. I was acutely aware of his, though, and now I had no choice but to take responsibility for the situation I was in.

CATHY: Mike phoned and said to meet him as soon as possible at the Albert Hall for the Prom. Not looking forward to it. Went to the pub and had half a cider. Conversation very spare. The concert was good – Leningrad Phil playing Prokofiev 5. Didn't know what to say to Mike. He walked me to the station. Said the situation didn't seem the same but he still loved me and did I still want to see him? How could I tell him? It was so difficult and awkward.

Met up for another Prom and went for a walk in the park. I had to say something. I told him that it might be better for both of us if we parted now. He kept saying to give him a chance. I felt so awful. He was obviously sore about it but was very kind. He said not to be upset, that he'd get over it. It was so sad saying goodbye. Oh hell, it was dreadful. I hate myself.

Simon phoned to say he has arrived in London and will be starting at the Academy on Monday. On Tuesday I went into the RAM and met him. We decided to go to a concert at the Festival Hall on Sunday (26th September) at 3.15 to hear Shostakovich's 13th Symphony and he's coming over to Cleveland Road for dinner beforehand.

I walked down to South Woodford station to meet him.

"Are you wearing your brother's trousers?" he asked. I was – I never have anything to wear and thought Chris's trousers looked better than anything else I could find – obviously not! I find it so easy to talk to him. Chris gave Simon the tour round his museum and we had dinner – pretty foul actually. Granny wasn't too disgusting and Dad thankfully wasn't there.

We arrived at the RFH at 2.10 and bought tickets – I paid for mine of course – 75p. Then we walked along the embankment and talked and talked. We agree about so many things. The concert was fantastic. The Shostakovich – extraordinary. This is the third performance in the West, the first only two weeks ago. It was written in 1962, but the USSR banned it because the text used (Babi Yar by Yevtushenko) exposes and criticises Russia's anti-Semitism. It was quite incredible – a choral symphony with male voices only, the solo part sung by John Shirley-Quirk. It astounded us both. Afterwards we walked to the middle of Waterloo Bridge too stunned for a while to speak.

We watched the Thames flowing beneath us and discussed East/West politics – neither of us too well informed. We both found it disturbing that musicians and artists were imprisoned, literally and metaphorically, for their political views. I had my received opinions about Communism, but had begun to question. My parents believed the Soviet Union was a model that the rest of the world should aspire to. Everything written about the USSR in Western newspapers was, they insisted, propaganda. The *Morning Star* was the only paper that told the Truth. Communism was the way forward for humanity. Yet how could the USSR – the Eastern Bloc – deny composers and poets, writers and philosophers the right to express themselves? Ban the performance of music? Imprison those who didn't toe the Party line? How could there be anti-Semitism in a system of equality? And what about the extreme poverty and appalling living conditions we were beginning to hear about from those who had defected? It was unsettling. This was surely not the communism they believed in.

CATHY: Then we sat in a restaurant for two hours drinking coffee and I found myself talking about my family and fears. He has a happy family and I haven't. I feel so comfortable with Simon, not shy and nervous as I am with most people. We talked about so many things and seem to agree about everything. Simon is such a good friend. It's fantastic talking to him. He asked me whether I was still seeing Mike, and I told him no and how awful I felt about it. Now I'm concerned that Simon wants to go out with me, but I must steer him away from the idea. I am too afraid of it messing up our friendship.

I feel closer to him than any other boy. He's tremendously nice, considerate, thoughtful, kind and just plain fabulous.
At the Academy I met him in the common room and we played chess together, then he had to go. He asked if I'd wait for him while he had his lesson, but I had to get home for dinner. He said he'd phone and see me next week. It's such a drag having to go to school – another year before I can be at the Academy full time.

IZZY: *I'm going to get down to some work this term and not watch any television when I get home from school. We have Miss Fisher for RI. She's reading us some anti-communist stuff so I just go to sleep. Did some homework then watched telly.*
Cathy went to a Prom and I went to Club. It was really grotty. I've actually made an effort to stop biting my nails – they're looking quite nice now. Watched Monty Python – really hilarious.
In biology we had to do experiments on woodlice and blow-fly larvae – disgusting.
Didn't bother to go to Club because it's getting so bad. Chris went to some butterfly exhibition.
Cathy's writing millions of letters to millions of people. It takes her hours. She brought some bloke from NYO round today – Simon Rattle – quite nice, and went to a concert with him.
Chris, Cath and I talked in Cath's bedroom. Chris has brought an antelope thing back from Norfolk and Cath is making a dress for Melly.

Whenever I went to the Academy for my cello lesson I nearly always met up with Simon and looked forward to seeing his smiling face. Within a few weeks he had assembled his orchestra and persuaded the Academy officials to allow him to rehearse every Sunday afternoon in the Duke's Hall. It was a Herculean achievement, accomplished by his boundless energy, powers of persuasion and infectious enthusiasm. The first rehearsal took place in October 1971.

CATHY: Went to RAM. Talked to Simon. Knew some people from NYO, but quite a few RAM students are also playing. Four cellos. I sat number four. We played Beethoven's Eroica symphony. Simon conducted – he's very good but I don't think he's nearly positive enough.

I was soon to change my mind. Occasionally, Chris played in Simon's orchestra when the rehearsals didn't clash with Redbridge Band practice.

CATHY: Chris could go very very far with the horn. Compared to many so-called outstanding horn players, Chris outshines them all. He's a great bloke (even though I say it of my brother!) and he'll always be liked and I'm sure he'll be successful in anything he wants to do. Simon said to me that Chris is a really loved character and will be even more so when he's older; that he's about the best horn player in the NYO and has the most ravishing tone.
Phoned Simon to find out if there is orchestra this afternoon. There isn't, which is just as well as I don't have any money and Mum wouldn't give me any more for my train fare.
There were 5 cellists today at Simon's orchestra. We played Elgar Serenade for strings and a really beautiful Vaughan Williams piece, Tallis Fantasia. I like the way Simon rehearses – he isn't dictatorial but gains everyone's attention and makes even the 5th cellist (me!) feel that he values her contribution. He works on sound and tone quality until he gets what he wants to hear.

53
DIFFICULTIES WITH DAD

Misfortunes one can endure – they come from outside, they are accidents. But to suffer for one's own faults – ah! – there is the sting of life!

Lady Windermere's Fan – Oscar Wilde

I went to concerts at the South Bank as often as I could. It was possible to buy cheap tickets for the Festival Hall if one were prepared to sit on the uncomfortable benches in the choir stalls. Although it was odd hearing the orchestra back to front, I liked to be close to the players and to see the conductor's face, almost feeling as if I were part of the orchestra. There were some concerts, however, that I listened to from the auditorium. Mum bought me a season ticket for two to the Royal Philharmonic Society concerts, of which there were seven or eight a year. Chris sometimes came with me, but when he didn't, I chose my concert companion. On October 6th 1971, Rubinstein would be playing Brahms's second piano concerto with the LSO. Had the soloist not been Rubinstein, I might not have gone, because unexpectedly, Dad decided to come with me. He rarely attended concerts. Being with him alone was something I tried to avoid, but there was nothing I could do about it. He said he would go straight to the Festival Hall from work and meet me by the box office.

The reflection of coloured light danced on the surface of the Thames as I crossed Hungerford Bridge to the South Bank, passing the beggars playing their mouth organs. Dad, as usual, embarrassed me in front of my friends, and the discomfort I felt with him was as acute as ever. I didn't consciously work out a strategy as to how to be with Dad, but a method of self-protection evolved, which I shall describe: Keep alert; use your intelligence and intuition to pick up even the tiniest signals of danger; process and deflect; analyse and defend; do not lose attention for a second or you might make a wrong move. But beware: you should appear calm and natural; no indication of distress must be evident. When sitting beside him, be careful to maintain a safe distance without making him aware of any slight recoil if he gets too close. Chat and laugh at his unfunny jokes; direct conversation into neutral areas; manoeuvre away from any reference to Mum or Granny; but make sure you do not become too non-committal or indifferent. Remember to pronounce every word perfectly; avoid slang and use correct grammar. Be polite; attend to his needs. On the other hand, do not respond to his sighs or you will be drawn into the danger zone. Warning: this finely balanced defence system is very expensive to use. It runs on a fuel called fear, and the toxic emission is guilt. That is how it was for me, but I am sure it was far worse for Mum.

Haydn and Hindemith were performed in the first half of the concert, but it was Rubinstein most of the audience had come to hear. It was a joy to watch and listen to him, to hear Brahms's great second piano concerto with Dougie Cummings playing the sublime cello solo in the slow movement. I almost forgot the presence of Dad beside me. So accustomed was I to the Red Alert procedure, I had become practised at using it. In my diary I write: "Dad actually wasn't too bad. We all clapped for ages and eventually Rubinstein came back and played an encore – a beautiful Chopin Nocturne." The journey back home, though, was something else.

I had travelled to and from the Festival Hall so many times, I knew the route forwards and backwards. Yet when we arrived at Charing Cross station, Dad was worried we were on the wrong platform. I told him we just had to wait where we were, but he wouldn't believe me and wandered off to look at an underground map. Behind me, I heard a voice: "Are you lost?" I looked round to see a creepy man smiling at me. With as much brush-off as I could muster, I replied, "He is, but I'm not," and turned to walk away. I had learnt how to deal with pesterers: do not enter into conversation, clear off as quickly as possible and stand near other passengers. At that moment, Dad came back. The man approached again, asking where we were going. When Dad said Mile End, he said he was going to Mile End too.

Oh, no: please don't talk to him, Dad. Let's get away. Dad asked the man where he lived, and when he said, "Bow", Dad asked whether he knew such and such a place, then which pubs he visited, and then whether he knew Bert Jackson. My heart sank when he said he did. The man was leering at me the whole time. Surely Dad noticed?

The train arrived, crowded. There were two seats on one side and one opposite. If only I had sat in the single one, but I assumed Dad would sit next to me. To my horror, Dad indicated to the weirdo to sit beside me. Difficult though it was with Dad, right now I needed his protection. Yet he had deliberately manipulated it so that I had to sit next to this yucky man, who started telling me, in an odd high squeaky voice, about his cat and pigeons. Then he asked, "Do you have any boyfriends?" *Oh my God. Here we go.*

After a pause, I said coldly, "On and off."

"Yes, I've been out with a few girls, but I can never find the right one."

I kept stonily silent.

"Do you drink?"

"Not really." *Will you leave me alone.*

"Where do you go with your boyfriends, then?"

"It depends." I looked across at Dad, silently imploring him to come to my rescue.

"I reckon my cat will be getting hungry."

"Huh?" *How many more stops to Mile End?*

"My cat. Needs feeding. Do you have any pets?"

I sighed loudly. "Two cats and three guinea pigs."

"I like guinea pigs. You're very pretty. Do you live far away?"

I stared at Dad who was looking amused. *Save me from this can't you?*

"South Woodford," I said between my teeth.

"Ah. I've got relatives in Leyton. Do you ever come anywhere near Bow Road?"

"No."

"Stay around your part, do you?"

"Yes." *Counting the stops. Aldgate East; only three to go.*

"I'd like to see your guinea pigs. What colours are they?"

"Huh?"

"What are you doing this Sunday?"

"I don't know. Yes. Actually, we've got friends coming over."

"Is he your father?"

"Yeah." *Dad, will you please help me!*

"A nice chap."

"Hmm."

"Could I see you again? I don't think your father would mind, would he? Are you on the phone?" I glowered at Dad. He would not meet my eyes.

"Yeah," I answered unenthusiastically.

"Would it be OK if I phoned you up sometime?"

"I wouldn't if I were you," I said icily. *Thank God, we're at Mile End.*

I leapt up and rushed to the door.

"Well, it's been nice meeting you," he called.

"Thanks for all your help," said Dad, shaking hands with him. *What help?* I walked to the end of the platform to wait for the Central Line train.

"Do you reckon he was trying to get off with you?" *Oh, Dad, please!* "It was quite funny to watch. You looked so thoroughly bored all the time. He was trying so hard to talk to you and despite his cockney accent, I think he was quite a nice chap."

"Dad, he was really creepy. Why didn't you sit with me?"

"Ah, well, *he* wanted to, didn't he?" he smirked. "All very interesting to observe."

I stood there at Mile End station feeling deserted, longing to be in my room, away from him, away from the weirdo, hidden from everything.

"Isn't life sad sometimes?" Dad mused, "I used to try and get off with girls, although of course I'd never be so forward as he was." I was silent. Dad laughed. "Oh, come on, it was only a bit of fun!" My diary entry ends: "I feel strangely depressed – sorry in a way to think what that man must be thinking now. He didn't even ask me my name." Always my fault, you see. Those guilty fumes are poisonous.

IZZY: *Met Jon Hollis* [the boy Izzy met at camp] *at Brixton and went to his house. His two friends Ashley Redsell and Alan came round from playing rugger. I fancied Ashley as soon as I saw him. He may have a foul name, but the rest of him makes up for it. He's tall and gorgeous, cropped fairish long hair, bluey-grey eyes, a fantastic smile – really out of this world. Jon's Mum took us over to Blackheath for the party. At the beginning of the party, Jon said he loved me and I told him he didn't. He was drinking a lot – beer, cider, punch etc. I decided I had to get to know Ashley better. Jon got very pissed and spewed up all over the floor. I escaped to see Ashley and we started kissing. Cleared up the mess. Jon was getting jealous but was too pissed to do anything about it. I kissed Ashley for about 5 minutes and we stood by the door holding hands. Jon's Dad came to pick us up and Ashley said to Jon, "Thanks for Isabel." I do hope I see him again soon. If I could go out with him I'd be living in the clouds all the time. This is the most I've ever written about a bloke, which proves that I really like Ashley v.v.v.v.v.v.v.v. much.*

Cath went to her NYO orchestra with Simon at the Academy and Chris and I went to Turners', drank cherry brandy, listened to jazz, looked at photos and Melly and I swapped trousers.

Ashley phoned. I'm meeting him on Saturday 2.30 at Brixton. Gran doesn't approve of him and Mum says it's wrong of me to miss Goldsmiths Youth Orchestra rehearsal. I agree with her but I'd rather see Ashley.

Walked with Cathy to the station. She went to GYO, I went to Brixton. Met Ashley and passed Dulwich College where he goes. Got to his house, had coffee and stale sandwiches and went to his bedroom. Ashley's not randy, just plain sex-mad! But he's not crude or dirty. Took off my blouse and bra, didn't feel ashamed of myself at all. Got into bed but didn't do anything we shouldn't. Ashley really smokes a lot but he's the best bloke I've ever been out with. He's coming to the FSC ceilidh tomorrow with me and Cath though Mum doesn't know.
Ashley says he's in love with me and oddly enough I believe him. He's the first bloke I haven't said "don't be daft" to. I might love him but I'm not really sure.
Christmas Eve and Ashley came over with half a bottle of wine. Gave him something to eat and sat on his knee. He met Des and Melly who invited him over on Sunday. Dad came home. He's extremely cross every time Ashley comes round.
Chris went pupae collecting with Ross Pearlstone and Dad told me not to get involved with Ashley because I'm too young and not to sit on his lap and not to kiss in public. I'm definitely going to watch it with Ashley and not become his little slave and be dominated. I have some spots on my back and Dad said, "Ashley won't like that when he baths you."
"Why should he want to bath me?"
"When you're married."
"I'm not going to marry yet!"
"Oh, I thought it was all arranged. If his parents want a church wedding, I'm not coming."

CATHY: Went to Turners and talked for ages. It was great to see them all again – haven't been round for weeks because of all my rehearsals. Came home to find a cold dinner and cold expressions – oh well.
Chris and I went to RFH to hear BBCSO play Bruckner 7. Chris is so funny. On the train he was re-enacting Monty Python sketches and had me in fits.
Mum's great – she always brings my cello over to school when I want it and leaves it in the pavilion for me. She really does help.
My musical knowledge is appalling. I have a revolting essay to write on "The influence of the radio and the gramophone on our lives today" HA HA. 29 mistakes in French dictation – oh well, I shall just fail. As usual gave my sandwiches away.
Ivey has chucked Chris out of the NYO! Nothing to do with his playing but because he was about the only one (and the youngest) who had the gumption to object about the ridiculous rules and protest against having his hair cut. Chris isn't bothered at all and is looking forward to returning to RYO. Martin Koch, from Chris's school, and Alan Gulliver have both got into NYO – two more from Redbridge.
Practised til 6.00, had dinner, went upstairs again and wrote letters. At 9.30 when I went downstairs, Granny said, "Oh, so you've decided to put in an appearance, have you? You might just as well not be here at all for all we see of you." That rather hit me. I hope Mum isn't worried about me. I do shut myself in my bedroom every evening and get on with my own things. Ashley's nice but Dad has a real grudge against him – he just can't accept that we're growing up.

Ashley was Izzy's first steady boyfriend. She was aware from the start that he could be dominating and cautioned herself not to become his lapdog. Bullied and controlled by his father, he reflexively unleashed the same behaviour upon Izzy and could be overbearing and egotistical; but Izzy was not one to be manipulated. He tried every tactic, from the subtle to the blatant, to persuade her to have sex with him, but she held her ground. No meant no.

I decided to have my hair cut, which was a major decision, as it was thigh-length. A 'long crop' was what I wanted – something resembling the style of David Bowie or Linda McCartney – shorter on the top, but the rest still long. Mum was fairly confident that she could achieve the desired result. She did her best, but by the evening I was kicking myself for making such a rash decision and in tears over my folly. Ashley, however, thought it looked very nice. He had watched as my long hair slithered to the floor and asked if he could have some of it. "Sure," I said, "take the lot." He picked it up, put it in a carrier bag and took it home with him. Izzy went to stay the weekend with Ashley.

> **IZZY:** *We talked about religion. He used to be religious but isn't any more. He's having a very bad time with his father who won't let him do anything. We kissed all the way home, then went upstairs to Ashley's room. He has all Cathy's hair stuck on his wall!! Listened to music and kissed on his bed. His Dad came in and told us it was lunch – whoops! A bit embarrassing. Ashley's Dad wouldn't let him wear his Levi jacket at lunch, so he had to put on a jumper. All very formal. His Dad is constantly having a go at him and Ashley's really feeling very depressed. He's taken up chain smoking and is thinking of running away from home to see what his parents' reaction is.*

Our Dad was also constantly having a go at Izzy. If he wasn't moaning about her going out or voicing his disapproval of Ashley, he criticised what she wore. Once he went completely berserk over a vest-top. There was nothing risqué about it – it revealed no cleavage, showed no midriff; it was just a simple sleeveless T-shirt.

"You're not going out dressed like that," he spat.

"What's wrong with it?"

"It's positively indecent. I will not let you walk down the street exposing yourself." His voice sizzled with disgust; if she had been topless, she could not have been met by a more damning tirade. She turned on her heel and left the room, sickened by Dad's insinuations. There was no way she was going to change her clothes; if he wanted to think of his daughter as a whore that was up to him. She found him annoying, embarrassing and unreasonable, but blamed him, not herself, for his behaviour.

54
SIXTEEN

Sixteen springs and sixteen summers gone now,
Cartwheels turn to car wheels through the town,
And they tell him, "take your time, it won't be long now
Till you drag your feet to slow the circles down."

Circle Game – Joni Mitchell

CATHY: Late December 1971: Arrived early for NYO course – in Croydon again – got the biggest shock of my life – I'm on first desk! Not leading but sitting next to Rickman Godlee. There are such a lot of new people – 176 in the orchestra and 67 are girls. I immediately made friends with a zany girl from Bristol called Clare Ziman. Her mini skirts are even shorter than mine. Ivey has provided a smoking room for those who smoke – but girls are still not allowed to wear trousers. Rickman is everso nice to sit next to. Louise Williams is on first desk of first violins so we sit opposite and grin at each other.
Nick Terry, horn player, asked me to go to the pub with him. Snow still on the ground and he said,
"You'd better take my hand or I'll fall over."
"I'm sure you can walk quite well on your own."
"Yes – it was only an excuse to hold your hand."
At the pub he took off my scarf and coat (and almost my dress as well) showed off by drinking Scotch, Vodka and Guinness and on the way back he put his arm around me.
New Years Eve party – Martin Koch played jazz trombone – fantastic, then I danced with Nick Terry and he kissed me lots of times. He took my hand and we were going outside when Mrs. Garland told me to "Get upstairs immediately". He held both my hands and kissed me goodnight. "Sweet dreams, sweet Kate."
"Catherine! Upstairs!" shouted Garland.
Farewell 1971.

Nick Terry was a boarder at The King's School, Canterbury, as were quite a few boys in the NYO. True to form, I ran in fright from his attentions, feeling guilty that my flirtatious behaviour had encouraged him. But Nick was different. He did not attempt to pursue me. I felt foolish hiding from someone whom I actually rather liked, and I was concerned that he thought he had offended me. I wrote to him after the course to apologise and he wrote back.

Dearest Cathy,

Thanks very much for your letter. It's incredible really. I'd been trying to gather the courage to write to you to try and sort things out. Life last course did get really rather fraught in more situations than one – I just hoped that I didn't upset you in any way. As for that scene in the pub at Kings X, I was so sloshed it's a wonder I ever got home.

All my love,
Nick (Twaddle)

In February, Izzy and I turned sixteen, that magical 'age of consent' when sex and cigarettes are deemed legitimate. I saw it as something of a burden, or a challenge. What should I do with my newly granted liberty? Well, I had a whole year to work out what to do about my virginity. Smoking was a much easier option, and one I had taken up a week before my birthday, making a conscious decision to smoke. On February 20th I went out and bought myself ten Embassy Number 6 and a box of matches. I dragged on my first cigarette in my bedroom and exhaled the smoke out of the window. Unfortunately, I liked the dizzy buzz it gave me straight away. I wrote in my diary:

> Gosh, how easy to get addicted to them. Izzy would hate me. Why did I decide to try it out? So that if anyone offered me one I could take it and smoke it. Yesterday, for example, Ashley offered me a drag which I didn't take – I could now though. Amazing, I've done it. I feel rather guilty, an undercurrent of 'Oh, you idiot'. I don't want to start smoking loads of fags a day. Especially with my asthma.

Two weeks after my birthday there was a *Musici* weekend in Aldeburgh. It was there in the Wentworth Hotel that I spent my first night ever in a single bed with a boy whom I had admired from afar since I was thirteen. Russell was four years older than me and belonged to the elite, inner circle to which I had been invisible. Somehow, I had filtered through the magic barrier and was now orbiting in privileged realms. Now that I was visible, it was not such a mysterious place after all. I was pleased to receive his attention, but as he led me into his room – a scenario I had so often daydreamed – my heart was racing more with apprehension than anticipation. He stripped off his clothes and climbed into bed, naked. I went back to my room to fetch my nightdress and refused to go anywhere near having sex. It wasn't quite what he had in mind, but he didn't persist.

"Don't worry about it," he whispered, "I've come unprepared anyway."

It took me a few moments to work out what he meant. I lay with my head on his chest listening to his steady heartbeat while he slept, unable to sleep at all myself for the noise of sexual activity going on in the other single bed in the room. I wondered what would happen if Mum and Granny, just a few rooms away, were to walk in. It was so soothing to be held, to be this close to another person, to feel the warmth of his breath and the softness of his skin. I liked his male smell, the texture of the hair on his chest, his long legs and the contact of my leg tucked between them. I didn't want more than this. 'Going the whole way' was too risky to contemplate. Even part of the way made me nervous.

Sex was something I knew about, so I thought. That is, I knew the basic biological facts. Where babies came from was not a mystery. Everything else was. There was nobody I could ask, and anyway, I was far too inhibited to enquire. I didn't know whether Izzy was still a virgin. I thought she probably wasn't, although I was wrong there. We didn't talk about it, for we had no emotional language from which to draw, nor any experience of family intimacy. What I find so sad now is that a grandmother, a mother and two sisters never talked about being women. Yes, Mum and Granny talked of discrimination, equality, the feminist movement, the brutality of men, "the woman's lot" in a male-dominated society, but not about a woman's feelings, her sexuality, her intuition, her desires or her femininity.

I became more and more impressed with Simon as a person, a musician and conductor. Most people upped and left when the Sunday rehearsals were over, but I usually stayed to help him collect up the music. Sometimes we would go for a coffee afterwards and talk – what about, I cannot remember. I didn't flirt with him or even fancy him, but felt completely at ease.

On Sunday, March 19th 1972, Simon's orchestra gave its first concert. The poster described us as the 'New London Chamber Orchestra' – I had no idea that was our name. Actually, it might not have been, as in another programme we were called the 'London Student Chamber Orchestra', but the name hardly matters. The concert was in Bishop's Stortford and the programme was Beethoven's *Egmont* overture, Elgar's *Serenade for Strings*, Ravel's *Tombeau de Couperin*, Mozart's symphony No. 40 and *Dances of Galanta* by Kodály. I wrote:

> Simon is such a brilliant conductor – quite amazing in fact. I nearly cried after the concert but managed to control myself. He gave me a huge hug and held me for a long time and thanked me for playing and helping. He is so gorgeous.

My asthma had been troubling me less over the previous six months. Oddly, smoking did not appear to aggravate it, although there was no way I could smoke when I was wheezy. I kept count of the number of cigarettes I smoked. By March 20th I had smoked sixty-three. Mum confronted me.

> She came into my room and in a sort of disbelieving, disapproving, disgruntled voice (all 3 at once) said "Cathy, you're smoking aren't you?" I said gruffly, "Yes". Then she said something like "Well, I think you're MAD. It's so easy to start and so difficult to give up. Not only that but it's so expensive. Oh yes, you might say it's your own money, but I don't feel inclined to give you 15/- a week to go up in smoke. I would have thought you would have more sense. Anyway just think about it." All the time I was silent and didn't move or look at her till she'd gone out of the room, then I sat on the bed & stared at nothing for ages. I felt dreadful – & still do. So the game's up & suddenly I realised how bloody stupid it all is & have decided not to buy any more fags, though how long that'll last I don't know.

By the time the NYO Easter course at St. Lawrence College came around, Nick Terry and I were friends by letter and sought each other's company, as much as anything else to smoke cigarettes together. We found a door into the basement – a series of dusty, concrete-floored rooms, with water, gas and central heating pipes travelling like arteries along the walls and ceilings. Other smokers gathered with us. The exclusive ritual bound us together in an almost sensual way. Nick shared cigarettes with me by inhaling a deep puff then putting his mouth to mine and exhaling as I breathed in – the smoker's kiss. I found myself drawn to those willing to take a risk and enjoyed an inclusion through collusion that I hadn't experienced before.

Meanwhile, Melanie went with Chris, Mum and Dad to Great Ryburgh. Izzy decided to stay in London to spend as much time as she could with Ashley. At the cottage, Mel clowned around, keeping everyone entertained. She found a walking stick and an old cloth cap, several sizes too large, which she wore jauntily on her head. In her extremely short tartan mini-skirt and knee-length white socks, she danced along the country paths, twirling her stick, leaping over puddles in a Gene Kelly style, while Chris strode along beside her pointing out interesting birds and hedgerow plants. Behind them was a very unusual sound – Mum and Dad laughing.

One evening, an hour or so before sunset, Chris took Mel up to the barn to sit and wait for the barn owls. Sitting still and waiting quietly were not skills that Mel naturally possessed. Chattering away, Mel told me she was "somewhat crushed when Chris cut me off mid-sentence saying 'Sshh! You'll scare the barn owls', and proceeded to give me a lecture on the extraordinary aural awareness of the owl. As a romantic contender, he ruled himself out for me." However, his rebuke quietened Mel sufficiently for the barn owls to swoop soundlessly into the rafters above as the last light of day faded. Chris had the patience of a wildlife photographer and would happily wait for hours to see badgers or deer, owls or bats.

Mel, as you may imagine, had more than her fair share of romantic contenders. There were dozens of them and she broke a few hearts. Most were friends of mine and I received many letters from discarded boyfriends. For example: "Cathy, can you give my few words to Melanie on the enclosed piece of paper addressed to 'the love of my life'. Why was she so frosty on Sunday morning?" And here is another: "I still haven't got over Mel completely. Every time I see a girl with a hairstyle like Mel's or an Afghan coat, my heart misses a beat. I only realised why I got so hung up on Mel the other night; it's partly due to her family. I got on really well with Jon, and Des and Pat are such great people. I found I could talk with them about anything, something which I can't do with my own parents."

Yes, I thought, I know exactly what you mean.

In May, some NYO members gave a charity concert in Stevenage, in which Nick Terry was involved. He invited me to stay with him at his parents' house in Harpenden. They welcomed me as if I were a member of the family, receiving me as Nick's girlfriend – but was I? I wasn't sure that I wanted his parents, or Nick, to think of me in that way. I was amazed when his father offered us both a cigarette. It was a gesture that acknowledged us as young adults, as a couple, as being accepted. Perhaps I already suspected that I was going to disappoint them all. I was afraid of kindness, of being cared for and admired, fearful that I would not be worthy of such generosity. Who was I really? What part of me was genuine? How much did I make up? Should I trust my feelings? How could I know which ones to believe? Re-reading Nick's letters to me, I am humbled by his tenderness. After my visit, he wrote:

Cathy darling,

I had just about got over the fact that you had gone when your letters, all ten quadrillion words of them arrived. Many thanks – not only for the letters but also, and mainly, for having graced my humble abode with your, though you don't agree, lovely presence. Now Cathy, sorry if this next bit sounds a bit intense but I'm afraid that

Twaddle's customary non-involvement policy has got really rather badly dented by the Lady Giles. I felt that had to be said but never fear. Both my feet are still firmly on the ground, or would be except for the fact that I have my legs crossed.

If you can spare the time from your other correspondents it would be nice to hear from you occasionally – like twice every day. I ought really to be working but you are rather more important. The family this morning were all terribly excited by your epistles, especially poor little frustrated me. You think you've got problems? You can carry yours around with you to unload on poor fools such as myself but my major problem lives two hours away by train.

Sweetheart, all the best in your Academy auditions. Please give all that remains of my pitifully depleted stock of love to your charmingly wicked twin sister. XX

I hope to see you over half term and/or the minute my term ends, before NYO and then again after and anyway, why shouldn't I want to marry you? Don'ts are often far more exciting than Do's.

I love you very much despite all your peculiarities.

Your adoring Nick XX

Obviously, Nick's sweetly affectionate utterances of love sent me into panic once more and I must have written to him in alarm for his next letter is heart-breakingly reassuring:

Dearest, you need have no fears. I'm not in love with you or ever likely to convince myself that I am. I do love you, sometimes, quite a lot for all sorts of funny reasons that can't possibly be put down on paper, but I think you'll agree there is a subtle difference.

And his words created the space for our correspondence to continue. I regret that I wasn't sufficiently aware at the time of his sensitivity towards me, nor of his own emotional fragility.

Having gained distinction in my Grade VIII cello the previous year, I was eligible to enter the competition run by the Associated Board of the Royal Schools of Music, which awarded six scholarships to be taken up at any of the four Royal Schools of Music – the Academy or College in London, the Manchester College or the Scottish Academy. 184 candidates entered the competition, and after a preliminary round, I was one of about twenty selected to go through to the final, in which I had to perform a short recital of contrasting pieces to a panel of judges in the concert hall at the Royal College of Music. It was a nerve-racking experience, but Mum was there to accompany me on the piano and calmly supported me throughout. Although there was an emotional chasm between us, it wasn't a void. In unreachable depths there was love, hidden and inexpressible, but I did not doubt its existence. What she gave all three of us was her care and constancy, her kindness and unwavering dependability.

Another of Florrie's pupils, Corinne-Ann Frost was in the finals. It seemed unlikely that two cellists would both be awarded a scholarship, since the competition was open to all instrumentalists and singers. Back home, I felt deflated and gloomy, going over in my mind all the mistakes I had made in my performance – a memory slip, a badly timed shift, out of tune notes, poor phrasing – and convinced myself that it had been a disaster. Miss Sprakes phoned to ask how it had gone and could hear I had the blues. "I'm taking you out," she announced. "It's been jolly stressful for you these last few weeks and now you must just forget about it."

She took me to see the film of *Fiddler on the Roof*. I lost myself in the story, wept a bit and felt much better afterwards. At the end of April I came home from school to see an envelope lying conspicuously on the hall table addressed to me. Mum abandoned her pupil mid-arpeggio to watch me open it.

"Well, what does it say?" she urged. I was staring at the words, but could not make any sense of them – oddly, I seemed to have forgotten how to read.

"I'm not sure."

"What do you mean? Just read it out."

"Dear Miss Giles, I – am – pleased – to – in – form…" I handed the letter to Mum. "You read it." She glanced at the words and said, "You've done it! They've given you a scholarship!"

"Have they?" I asked weakly.

"'I am pleased to inform you'," she read, "'that the Board has awarded to you one of the six Scholarships offered as a result of the Competition in which you took part last week. The Scholarship, with cello as principal study, is tenable at the Royal Academy of Music for two years from September next, with the possibility of extension for a third year should the Board consider it desirable, upon evidence of satisfactory progress. I enclose an announcement giving the names of all the Scholars and take this opportunity of congratulating you on your success.' Well done, dear! You'd better go and phone Florence and Margaret right away and tell them the glad tidings. I must get on with my teaching." I looked at the letter again. The words began to sink in. Then I read the list of Scholars and was very pleased to see that Corinne-Ann had also been awarded a scholarship.

When I next went into the Academy, a boy of maybe nineteen came to sit with me in the canteen. He was tall, dark and good-looking – a cliché, but true. When he found out that I had never heard a Puccini opera, he took me to the Academy's record library, sat me down, found two sets of headphones and played me the last side of a two-disc LP recording of *La Bohème*.

We met in the canteen several more times, then one day he told me about an agreement he had with two sisters who used to come round to his house when his parents were out in order for him to make love to them. That was all they wanted, he said. He'd make love to one, then the other, and they would go home, satisfied. I was fascinated that they could be so forthright about their wants and curious that he could be so obliging. Why not be as outspoken as they? "Would you consider making a similar arrangement with me?" I asked. He said he would see what he could do.

My common sense and Mum's instilled fear of pregnancy carried me to a family planning clinic. I thanked the London magazine, *Time Out*, for listing such an essential place in their pages, and made an appointment at the Margaret Pyke Centre in Mortimer Street. Sitting in the waiting room, I felt exposed and apprehensive. My name was called and I was shown into a room. A female doctor with short dyed-blonde hair acknowledged my presence and directed me to a chair. She lined up some papers on her desk. "When did you first have sex?" she asked in a distinctly bored manner, pen poised to write.

"I haven't had sex yet," I answered. She looked at me in surprise or disbelief, commenting that most girls only go to a family planning clinic after a pregnancy scare.

"How long have you been with your boyfriend?" was the next question.

"About six months," I lied. Well how could I possibly tell her about my arrangement?

"How old is he?"

"Nineteen." Perhaps he was, I didn't actually know.

"OK, let's have a look at you. Take your clothes off and hop on the trolley."

There was absolutely no reason to examine me. I felt as if I were being cold-heartedly punished in advance for a crime I was about to commit. I left the clinic with a supply of bright yellow tablets and swallowed them conscientiously, but the arrangement was never fulfilled. For weeks I looked for him in vain, until one day I saw him leaving the building and called out his name. He turned around but didn't stop to speak. I wasn't unduly disappointed. I had been getting more and more anxious about my proposition becoming a reality, so it was quite a relief that he lost interest. My virginity stayed intact for a bit longer. I kept taking the pills.

It was around this time that I went to a party somewhere in Bayswater. I can't remember much about it, except that in one room there was a guy playing a guitar rather drearily. I sat near him and listened.

"Do you want a go?" he asked in a dull voice.

"I can't play, but I'd love to have a try."

I remembered the chords for *Circle Game* that Dave Rannie had taught me and attempted to sing the song.

"Doesn't sound as though you can't play," he said, without enthusiasm.

I strummed away for a bit longer, and then he stood up and made his way to the door.

"Hey, you'd better take your guitar with you," I called.

"No, it's OK. You can have it."

I laughed, getting up to hand it to him.

"I meant what I said. Keep it."

"I can't do that."

"Why not?"

"It's yours! Don't you want it?"

He shrugged. "Not really. Anyway, see you around."

When the party broke up and we were leaving, I couldn't find the guitar guy anywhere. Apparently, he had gone ages ago. Nobody knew his name and I didn't know what to do. "He said you could have it, so take it," my friend advised. "No point leaving it here for someone to pinch."

I left my phone number, sure that he would call to ask for it back, but he didn't. So I still have the instrument and thank the person to whom it belongs for lending it to me. I learned the basics and figured out enough to provide simple accompaniments to the songs we sang at FSC.

Izzy and I sat our O level exams. As soon as the last paper had been handed in, I walked out of Beal Grammar School for Girls, never to return. Of the thousands of letters I wrote, this one to Paul Mayes has survived. Paul was the leader of the NYO for seven years. Like me, he did not throw letters away.

Dear Paul,

I'VE LEFT SCHOOL & am in the process of tearing up all my old school books – a lovely feeling – one trouble though – I'll probably have to go back to re-sit all the O levels I've just failed! They were pretty awful – oh well. I still don't know if I'm doing the right thing – leaving school at 16, I mean, & trotting off to the Academy. In a way, I haven't had much say in what's happened to me – my parents (esp. Mum) & my teacher (Florence Hooton) both reckon it's a waste of time staying on at school & Florrie wants me at the Academy as soon as possible – says that the music world is so competitive that the younger you're in it, the better. So what can I do? Ivey's dead against me leaving school – every time I see her, she gives me a lecture. I saw her at the Academy the other week. Well, she started off by kissing me on my left ear to congratulate me on the scholarship – how nice!!!(?) – then said that she still thought it was a mistake to leave school. Makes me wonder myself – but ENOUGH of that boring subject.

Last weekend I organised an NYO party/rave up at my place – about 25 people turned up – I'll tell you those I can remember – Louise (Williams), Lowri (Blake), Steve Jones, Nick Terry, Steve Barlow, Martin Koch, Frances Eustace, Clive Miller, Sue Eversden, Trevor Ling, Joan Brickley, Johnny Martin, Jill Streater, Paul (from King's), Richard Lester, Matthew Bright, Irrita – oh & lots of others – quite a larf and great seeing all those people again. Louise, Nick, Steve Barlow & Johnny all stayed the night & we went for a walk at ¼ past midnight, got back about 1.30 & fell asleep on the floor to Brahms violin concerto! (wot a life!)

It's so awful that this will be my last course – I really love NYO & I'll miss it everso much – I wish I were staying on at school for that reason as well – 2 extra years in NYO would be greatly appreciated! Oh well, I really MUST go – mainly because I've written quite enough already to ensure your insanity. I'll leave you in peace – AND WRITE BACK QUICKER THIS TIME – that's an order.

Lots of love, your one and only (thank God!) Cathy

55
SUMMER of 1972

Like as the waves make towards the pebbled shore,
So do our minutes hasten to their end,
Each changing place with that which goes before
In sequent toil all forwards do contend.

Sonnet 60 – William Shakespeare

We went camping as usual, this time to the Isle of Arran. "It's a beautiful island," said Mum. She talked with nostalgic enthusiasm about her childhood holidays, but the three of us paid little attention, too preoccupied with the present to take much notice of Mum's past. We had chosen the Arran camp because Leslie Holden was the camp-chief. When we assembled at Euston station for the long journey, there amongst the throng was Ian Yellowlees, Izzy's boyfriend of two years ago. He bounded up to us, thrilled to see Izzy and obviously hoping to reclaim her. Izzy wasn't remotely interested. "I don't know what I ever saw in him," she said. I took the guitar I had acquired with me. By the end of the camp, everyone knew *Circle Game*.

The caterer of that particular camp was Brenda Hatcher, a woman who had honed camp cooking into her own unique school of discipline. She ordered the groceries and kitchen provisions long before camp began, making absolutely sure that she kept well within the budget. She issued precise lists of ingredients, recipes and methods to the clans, who received severe lectures if they did not follow her directions to the letter. She reduced me to tears on more than one occasion. Izzy remembers being handed a bowl of raisins and being told to cut each one into quarters to put into the muesli.

"Quarters!" she spluttered. "Why can't they go in whole?"

But there was no arguing with Brenda. When it came to serving, she decided the exact size of the portions, watching like a hawk to see that nobody received more than their allowance. For many, there was not enough to satisfy their hunger, but Brenda would not be budged into releasing a few more loaves of bread or ordering extra supplies. Several attempts were made to raid the kitchen tent at night, but most of the food was padlocked into wooden storage boxes. Out of shared adversity, though, came the funniest Merrymoot. Brenda was sent up mercilessly in sketch after sketch. The highlight was an inspired set of lyrics, written and performed by a member of staff, who played the guitar and sang. Unfortunately, I cannot remember the words, but Izzy recalls this small part of it, sung to the tune of *Whiskey in the Jar*:

As I was a-hiking over Kilmory mountain
I spied Brenda Hatcher and the cornflakes she was countin'
I counted out my baked beans and I found I'd less than twenty,
But when I asked for more I was told that I'd had plenty.

The Pathfinders called their sketch 'The Mad Hatcher's Tea Party'. The title was the best part of the script. Izzy described the Trackers' contribution to Merrymoot:

> *The Trackers, under Chris's leadership, did the Blue Danube waltz, during which they all gobbed up. It was really vile. They had mugs to spit into and had made some really thick green Angel Delight, which they spooned up with their fingers and ate! It was absolutely repulsive.*

Apart from going hungry, the weather was consistently bad and Izzy and I found one of our Pathfinder staff utterly obnoxious. On the plus side, Arran was indeed a beautiful place, and for once the Trackers and Pathfinders decided to amalgamate, so Izzy, Chris and I all went on the same hike. It rained continuously. Perhaps that was why we found ourselves one evening in a village hall watching *Carry on Cleo* – not exactly a laudable woodcraft activity.

The summer NYO course was held at the Royal Hospital School in Holbrook, near Ipswich in Suffolk. When Nick Terry and I met again, I once more shied away from his attentions, unable to offer him explanation or to understand my own shifting feelings, which swivelled towards a trombone player called Julian. Hormonal havoc, I suppose it could be called – those arbitrary surges of desire that suddenly swell up, often as short-lived as the life of a mayfly. For me it was also the unfathomable discomfort of being loved.

It was in Holbrook where more than sixty NYO members were caught in a pub. Ivey was in tears as she addressed the entire orchestra. Never had she felt so let down. She made it clear that she expected every culprit to apologise to her. Unhappily for her, she could not expel a third of the orchestra two days before a concert so had no choice but to allow the incident to come to an unsatisfactory close. Most did go to her with tails between their legs to beg forgiveness. I couldn't quite bring myself to do so. I am sure it did not stop members frequenting pubs on subsequent courses, but perhaps the staff had the sense to drink elsewhere.

The first concert was given at Holbrook on Wednesday August 16th. Mum, Izzy and Chris came to it, as they would be at Wortley on the day of the final NYO concert. I spotted Chris walking across the lawns towards me and realised for the first time that he was not a little boy anymore. He seemed to have grown a foot since I last saw him. He must have overtaken me in height long ago, but I hadn't noticed. Something shifted within me. My brother was a young man; tall, assured; more, he was handsome, amiable and fine. A mixture of pride, admiration and intense love welled up inside me, which translated into a huge smile. I was so pleased to see him. Perhaps he noticed me differently too, as he complimented me on my appearance, telling me that I looked lovely, and how beautifully my hair shone in the sunlight. I reached my hand out to him. It brushed his arm. He moved half a step closer to me. But we couldn't convert what we felt into an embrace. If I could replay that moment, I would hug him tightly and he would hug me back, and it would be the most inevitable thing in the world, even though we wouldn't be sure why we were smiling so broadly or quite what it was that filled us with such happiness.

The day before the London concert, the orchestra moved into the residential blocks of Furzedown College in Croydon, the girls in one block, the boys in two others, most of us with single rooms. After a great deal of seductive effort, I was beginning to persuade the trombonist to take notice of me, much to the annoyance of my short-skirted friend, Clare Ziman, who fancied him too. Over the evening meal, he told me, Clare and another girl that he was having a party in his room that night and dared us to come. This would be far more perilous than anything previously attempted. To get out of an unfamiliar girls' block and into the boys' after lights-out was a very risky undertaking, but the gauntlet had been thrown down.

"You're not really going are you?" asked Clare.

"Of course. Aren't you?"

"No, it's too crazy."

"I'm going," said the other girl.

"OK. Let's go. Clare? Are you coming? Last chance?"

"No. God, you're going to get into such trouble if you're caught."

The two of us left Clare and pattered barefoot down several flights of stairs to the outside door. I opened it gingerly and stepped into the night, walking swiftly across the grass to the dimly lit entrance of the boys' block. Halfway there, I looked behind me to see my accomplice retreating back to safety. I was on my own. My heart was thumping wildly, but I wasn't going to abandon my mission. I reached the building and peered inside. The foyer was empty. I let myself in, headed for the lift and pressed the ascend button. The doors opened with a thunderous shudder. Third floor, he had said. I hit number three, waiting for several interminable seconds for the lift to close. Up it went, leaving my stomach at ground level. The doors opened into an empty corridor. Right, right again, fourth door on the right, he had said. I could hear muted voices from inside as I knocked at the door. Julian opened it and I fell into the room, weak with terror.

"My God! I didn't expect you to actually make it," he said. There were two other lads in the room, both more shocked than pleased to see me, it seemed.

"Want a swig?" said one, handing me a half-bottle of whisky.

"Thanks." I took a sip, recoiling from the searing, bitter taste. How could anyone truthfully claim to like the stuff? We sat and talked.

"Keep your voice down," warned Julian. "If one of the Housemasters walks by and hears a girl's voice, we'll all be for it." I looked at him in astonishment. He seemed more scared about my being there than I was. The other two boys left.

"We'd best leave you two to it!" they said suggestively. Julian climbed into bed.

"What are you going to do?" he asked me.

"Well, now that I'm here, I'm staying. I'm still recovering from getting here."

"Come and lie down with me for a bit, then."

That was more like it. I hadn't risked life and limb for sex, but I was expecting a bit of approval. Watching him, I slowly pulled my nightdress up to my shoulders and lifted it over my head, dropping it to the floor. There I stood in my bra and knickers, waiting for some kind of response. He said nothing; not even a murmur of appreciation escaped his lips. Now I was a bit pissed off – or was my body entirely unworthy of comment? I certainly wasn't going to take off anything more. "Well?" I fished, "how do I look?"

"In this light it's hard to tell, but everything seems to be in the right place. How much longer are you going to stand there? For God's sake get into bed and warm me up."

Truculently, I obliged, but I didn't warm to his kisses. Before long he was snoring loudly and I was staring at the ceiling, wishing I had brought my toothbrush to scrub the taste of whisky from my mouth. It was not my most romantic encounter, and I still had to face the terrifying task of getting back to the girls' block. A few hours later, I fled barefoot across the lawns in the early light, unchallenged and unmissed.

It was my very last course with the NYO. I had been in the orchestra for three years and it had become a part of my life. I had progressed from new girl to veteran, from back desk to front, and didn't want to leave. My last concert with the NYO that Saturday evening, August 19th, was at the Fairfield Hall. The programme included Walton's *Johannesburg Festival Overture,* Tchaikovsky's *Rococo Variations* with Thomas Igloi as soloist and Sibelius's second symphony, conducted by Oivin Fjeldstad. I stayed for the last night in order to say goodbye to everyone. Perhaps I was a bit of a rebel, if a cowardly one, as I flouted the rules and wore trousers to that last breakfast, knowing that I could no longer be chucked out. There were hugs, tears and farewells all round. I had little to say to the trombonist. The escapade of the night before seemed rather foolish now, but Nick was there with open arms and kissed me passionately. "This isn't goodbye is it, Kate?"

"I hope not."

"Good. Then I'll see you in the pub later."

I vacillated between needing the confirmation of his adoration of me and being scared to accept what I was afraid I could not return. I was searching for something, but didn't know what it was. In the end, I let Nick down. Even then he was gallant, uncritical and considerate:

> Kate, thank you for writing. It was very sweet of you. You know I never expect you to write at all and was going jealously insane when I knew that Paul and Matthew had heard from you, therefore I was very pleased to get your letter.
>
> All this emotion from afar may be pure and noble or something but it's bloody inconvenient and makes it almost impossible to get a clear picture of the situation. Basically I want you now but there is damn all that can be done. Please be nice to me when we meet again. Despite the façade I am rather frail. Oh Cathy, it's quite impossible to say all that ought to be said on paper and in the cold light of day all this may look very silly, but no matter. It's a gorgeous lovely night. I wish you were here. Going back to you and me (dangerous ground), if you'll forgive me I think your excuse for not kissing me that other night is not quite true. Forgive me if I'm wrong but I think other factors were involved as well.
>
> Kings will have broken up, just about fragmented before the 16th, so I'd love to come to your concert if it can possibly be arranged. I must go –
>
> Look after yourself (it takes two to make any sort of relationship)
>
> Love to anyone
> and you, Nick XX

After the emotional whirlpool of NYO, I headed north for Wortley, two days late, to join Mum, Izzy and Chris. Paul Hart was there and we spent evenings playing chamber music before heading to the bar. That year we met Bill Worrall, who would became a life-long friend. Bill had taught himself the piano and guitar by ear, but had never had a formal music lesson. It was when he was at Redbridge Technical College preparing for an engineering course that he discovered a music O level course taking place and asked if he could sit in. Told that he didn't have a hope in hell of becoming a musician, he nevertheless applied to the newly established Leeds College of Jazz. The minimum requirements for entry were four O levels, which he had, and an Associated Board Grade V, which he did not have. At his audition he managed to play a Grade V piece adequately and also performed one of his own compositions, which is, as Bill puts it, "probably how I bluffed my way in." It was just before he took up his place at Leeds that he came to Wortley. He enrolled onto the composition course under the tutelage of Dr. Alan Bush. Alan recognised Bill's potential and gave him all the help he could from then onwards.

Chris played Mozart's fourth horn concerto in the final concert, a performance that Bruce Fox still remembers. After Wortley, Chris went to stay with Bruce for ten days before returning home. Bruce told me: "I think Chris must have come twice to our house in Melling Road. I can only recall lots of disconnected glimpses of those times, such as him describing Southport as a 'pukka' town. My clearest memory of his time in Southport was his visit to a tiny little shop called Tropical Shells Galore, tucked away down a narrow passageway off Lord Street. He came out of the shop the proud owner of a shark's jaw!"

Over the summer holidays, Ashley's life changed. His parents went to live in Italy and he was forced to board full-time at Dulwich College, which he hated. Deprived of his freedom, not allowed to stay out overnight, it was impossible to see Izzy and the connection between them shifted. When Ashley stopped coming over to Cleveland Road, Dad decided he was a decent chap after all. "Why don't you see Ashley any more? He was a pleasant boy – well spoken and civilised – a darned sight better than that yobbo you brought in from the gutter the other night. I don't want *him* in this house again."

Nick and I continued to write to each other and met up from time to time for another year or so. His last letter is dated 31st May 1973. He wrote as graciously as ever, promising to meet before he went up to Cambridge. This he did, staying at Cleveland Road for a couple of days in September. Then we lost touch. I tracked him down in 2005, living in Houston, Texas. He had kept all of my letters. He was going to copy and send them to me, but after a flurry of emails, I didn't hear from him again, which I found worrying and inexplicable. He did write this though: "You were a very special lady to me all those years ago. In truth you should know that I absolutely adore(d) you." Thankfully, I re-established communication with Nick in 2011, just before this book was printed. He had not been able to maintain contact with me in 2005 because his wife was gravely ill and very sadly died in 2009.

ABOVE: Me aged thirteen, a few months before attending my first course with the National Youth Orchestra.

ABOVE: At Primrose Road. I am playing on 'Julius', the Blüthner piano that Des bought in a sale at Harrods and Melanie is doing her ballet exercises.

BELOW: Louise Williams 1972

BELOW: Nick Terry

ABOVE:
Bridge Cottages in Great Ryburgh, a row of six with number six in closest view. Our cottage is number three.

LEFT:
Melanie and Chris in Norfolk, 1972

56
LOSSES AND GAINS

Willows do not weep
They let down their hair.

Jean Lipkin

My student days at the Academy began in September 1972. I was out of my foul 'Brownie' uniform and no longer a schoolgirl. I could reinvent myself, discard my shyness, enjoy a new independence and have fun. Pretty soon I had attached myself to the most irresponsible, wild, drinking, smoking and overdrawn students. As the Academy day ended, I did not queue for vacated rooms in which to practise, but left the building with a hairy, unkempt crowd and headed for the Rising Sun. I bought myself a half of lager and lime, making it last the whole evening, while the lads downed pint after pint. We commandeered the pinball tables, played the jukebox, smoked and joked. There was another girl inside me that didn't belong, that found her reckless counterpart distasteful, but she was too afraid to reveal herself: she kept quiet while the party girl joined in with the crowd that offered the least resistance. Tension rose at home as night after night I was late back.

"When are you getting home today?" asked Mum tetchily.

"I don't know."

"Well, are you going to be back for dinner or not?"

"I don't know. It depends."

"Depends on what?"

"I might have a rehearsal, or stay late to practise," I fibbed.

"What rehearsal? Why don't you come home to practise?"

I shrugged.

"Granny cooks a lovely dinner for you every night. It's very rude of you not to tell her whether you'll be here or not."

"I won't be here then, OK?"

"When are you going to eat?"

"I'll have something at the Academy."

She sighed exasperatedly.

I left the house, relieved to be out of it.

That evening in the Rising Sun, one of the lads suggested I go back to his place. He wanted me to spend the night with him, and I thought, OK, why not. He was several years older than me, a bit of a dropout, hippy in manner and dress, as we all were, with nothing much to talk about. Perhaps he was acting his part too. None of us really knew one another. We had just fallen into a group where we felt comfortably anonymous, unchallenged and free of parental shackles. I didn't fancy him, I had not considered going out with him or even kissing him. We put our arms around each other as we walked to the pub, but there was no special communication. I didn't feel threatened or intimidated by him, I didn't admire or look up to him, nor did I feel inferior or lacking. I liked him enough; that was all. I also figured that he had almost certainly slept with other girls, and as a novice I supposed it would be sensible to lose my virginity with someone who knew what he was doing.

The phone call home did not go down well. I woke Mum up, making the excuse that I had missed the last train, but it was OK, I could stay with a girlfriend who lived within walking distance. My lie sounded unconvincing. Mum was furious: I could hear the disapproval and doubt in her voice and felt bad that I had made her angry; but whatever she thought, I knew I was behaving responsibly. There was no risk of pregnancy; I felt safe enough with this friend and knew he wouldn't harm me. Although I was up to all the things that she was so afraid of, she had no need to worry.

He lived in the basement of a decaying house in a neglected, worn-out neighbourhood. I followed him down the steps, my foot sinking straight into a murky pool by the door.

"Sorry, should have warned you about that. Mind the puddle inside the door too." He wasn't joking. "Hang on to my hand. There's only one light bulb working and I can't remember which room it's in."

It would have been better if he hadn't switched it on. The whole room had been painted black. Someone had started drawing gold and silver stars and moons on the ceiling, but given up. There were half-finished rainbows on the walls, not a stick of furniture apart from an ancient looking bed with a sagging mattress covered in a soiled green sheet. The bare floorboards were littered with clothes, rubbish and the disassembled parts of a greasy oil-blacked motorbike.

"Well, what do you think?"

"Just great," I said.

"I might have a can of beer in the kitchen. I'll go and see."

"Where's the loo?"

"Oh, wait a sec; let me find you a torch. It's down the hall by the front door, but don't flush the chain because the cistern overflows. That's what causes the flooding."

I picked my way back through the debris and found the door. The weak torchlight shone into an entirely silver room, including the toilet. The floor was an inch deep in water and of course there was no paper. I perched above the seat, thankfully found a tissue in my pocket and splashed my way back. I removed my shoes and we sat on the bed sipping warm beer from a can. He found a couple of blankets, took off his clothes and lay down. I assumed I should do the same, although he gave me no encouragement. I could not have invented a less salubrious setting for the event that I imagined was to metamorphose me from girl to woman. Our naked bodies touched indifferently. I waited with bated breath as to what would happen next. It was uneventful and passionless. I put my arms around him, uttered a few moans and groans as I thought was expected, then he let out a strange grunt, shuddered a bit and rolled onto his back beside me. I thought; how extraordinary that people make such a big deal about that.

"Have you slept with many other girls?" I asked tentatively.

"Yeah, quite a few."

"What were they like? I mean, was I OK?"

"You were great, baby, one of the nicest screws I've had."

"Really?" There was some silence while I gathered the next sentence.

"So, honestly, would you have known that I was a virgin?"

That produced a reaction.

"Christ! A virgin! Why didn't you tell me?"

"I thought you knew."

"I don't believe it. I've deflowered you." *What? What's that supposed to mean?*

"Hey, babe, are you alright? You're not going to tell me now you're not on the pill are you?"

"Well, I'd say it's a little late to ask, but don't worry, I am."

"Thank God for that. Wow, a virgin. Far out, man. I mean; I've deflowered you." He fell asleep with his head on my shoulder. I didn't sleep at all, but lay there thinking about what had happened, trying to make sense of it, wondering about myself, what I felt, what it meant. I'd done it. I'd engaged in sexual intercourse, or plain intercourse as Mum termed it, 'sexual' not being part of her language, and I was none the wiser. I had so wanted to know what sex was like. As I lay there amidst the chaos of that black basement room, sweaty and uncomfortable, I somehow knew that I had been sold short. I felt sure it should have been more than that. I was baffled rather than disappointed, unenlightened but not about to give up. As morning dawned, I extracted my numb arm from under his shoulder, climbed out of bed and dressed. There seemed little point trying to wash in this place; I couldn't imagine I would find soap or a towel.

He half woke up. "Are you going already?"

"Yeah, I'd best get back. I'll catch the bus."

"I don't think I can offer you anything. We're out of coffee. There might be a half a jar of marmalade somewhere, but no, come to think of it there isn't any bread."

I smiled, feeling quite fondly towards him. "Don't worry, go back to sleep. See you around."

"Yeah, babe, see you soon."

I negotiated the puddles, stepped out into a new day, filled my lungs gratefully with the crisp morning air and walked happily to the bus stop. I watched everyone's reactions carefully. Did I look any different? Could they tell that I was no longer a virgin? What was the word for a non-virgin? A deflorist?

I was placed number three in the Symphony Orchestra, or First Band, as we called it. My desk partner, number four, was Melvyn Gale, a friendly, laid-back person who was to go on to become a member of the Electric Light Orchestra and would give me my first professional work. The conductor of First Band was Maurice Handford; a man who had a cruel streak and picked mercilessly on individuals to a point where they were so cowed that they could not play at all. It was ghastly to witness, but we all sat in silence, tense and agitated, quaking with fear that he might turn round and have a go at one of us next. I couldn't bear it, but nobody came to the victims' rescue. The only person ever to stand up to him, when I was there, was Bram, who had the audacity to challenge Handford's demands. We held our breath. It was as heart-stopping as the moment when Oliver Twist asks for more.

"Get out!" roared Handford. Bram rose to leave, and in so doing, accidentally knocked over a heavy music stand. It clattered down the tiered stage through the brass and woodwind sections and crashed to the floor at the back of the violas. We were too horrified to laugh, but it made a good story afterwards. People feared and worshipped Maurice Handford, stepping around him in awe while he enjoyed the hallucination of power. He may have been a good musician, may even have possessed a fine baton technique, but when it came to him being heralded a marvellous conductor, I could not go along with it. The use of tyranny, persecution and intimidation does not, in my opinion, get the best out of an orchestra.

In October, the Sonata Prize for Cello took place. The set work was the Boccherini A major, and almost every cellist in the Academy entered for it. Anthony Pini was the adjudicator. He spent all day listening to some thirty performances of the piece. I happened to be the last to play. When I had finished, I stood in the corridor with the other cellists until we were called back into the room for the adjudication. Mr. Pini spoke a little before revealing the results in reverse order. Third and second places went to two cellists in their final year, both of whom had seemed likely candidates to win. Nobody, least of all me, was expecting to hear: "And the prize-winner is Catherine Giles." I was stunned, especially when he went on to say that he had heard lots of good playing, had been finding it difficult to decide who should be placed first, until the last contestant started to play and it was obvious that she was the winner. A few people congratulated me. Then a cellist whom I recognised, but didn't know, came up to me and was effusive with his praise. He had also been competing, but had not had any expectation of winning, and was genuinely delighted that "a young, gorgeous, sixteen-year-old waltzed into the Academy and carried off the prize." He said he had been watching me ever since I'd arrived and could spot star quality a mile off.

"How about a celebration drink?" he asked.

"I don't even know your name."

"But I know yours. I'm François and you're gorgeous."

He was twenty and in his third year. I laughed – he always made me laugh – but declined the drink. He told me he'd get me to come out for a drink with him one day, kissed me on the cheek and we parted. I didn't feel so weird and deflated any more and felt able to go down to the canteen and face all the disappointed cellists. Then I remembered where I had seen him before. The previous year, I had heard him perform Bruch's *Kol Nidrei* with the Ernest Read Music Association Orchestra, and had been impressed by his expressive playing.

I was asked to play in the Academy's Opera Workshop with a small group of nine musicians, which Simon would be conducting. I agreed, in the same way as I might have accepted a local gig: "Oh, I think I'm free, yeah, that should be OK." It was Simon who pointed out to me that it was quite an accolade for a first year to be invited to play and I should have perhaps responded more enthusiastically. I had a lot to learn about protocol and hierarchy. One of the operas was *After the Wedding*, composed by Michael Head, who happened to be my second-study piano teacher, a sweet man, who I was delighted to discover was Dr. Alan Bush's brother-in-law. I have to admit that I remember very little about the opera, the rehearsals or performances. I was concentrating more that first term on going to the pub, playing pinball, staying up all night, smoking dope and losing my virginity. Simon was not amused when I turned up to a rehearsal late and hung-over. Seeing the disappointment on his face made me feel very contrite. I apologised.

"Are you OK?" he asked.

"I'm fine. Too many late nights, that's all."

"You don't seem quite yourself, Cath. Is anything bothering you?"

"No. No – I'm terribly sorry about today."

"That's alright. It's not like you. You're usually the first to arrive. Just take care of yourself, OK? And I *will* be seeing you at the rehearsal on Sunday, won't I?"

"Of course; I won't be late, promise."

I asked Mum if I could have a party and she agreed. I invited my NYO and RAM friends, Izzy and Chris invited school and Redbridge pals, and it promised to be a good do. Chris had recently started making his own beer from home-brew kits, so he would provide the beer, Izzy and I the cider and everyone was asked to bring a bottle. To begin with all went well, but the front door, as usual, was left on the latch for anyone to push open. I was in the kitchen doling out drinks in Granny's collection of empty jam jars – we had run out of glasses – someone was in the back garden being sick and the brass lads were drinking Chris's intoxicating brew out of mixing bowls and saucepans, when I saw Mum pushing her way through the crowd. She shouted at me over the din of the music, "Who are all these people, Catherine? You'd better come and see. They're everywhere and one of them has just been very rude to Granny. I'm not putting up with it any more."

I followed her through to the hall and saw that she was not exaggerating. People I had never seen before were sitting on every stair, smoking, rolling joints and snogging. I fell into someone cross-legged on the floor playing a guitar.

"Do you mind?" he complained.

"Yes, I do mind. This is my party. Who are you?"

There were others in the front garden; sitting in the porch; swinging their legs on the garden wall and more drunken strangers just arriving. I was aghast and didn't know what to do.

"Do something," said Mum, "and you'd better check the bedrooms."

I had to turn the new arrivals away, turf couples and threesomes out of beds and go around asking people to leave. It seemed that word of a party had spread through the Academy and beyond.

I can't remember how it all ended. Looking back, I think Mum was a saint to let us have parties – she wasn't pleased with me, but she didn't get angry. We had plenty of others. There were no more like that one, though.

At the Academy, I played the Haydn C major cello concerto through in an open rehearsal with the Repertoire Orchestra, otherwise known as Second Band. It went well, despite my nerves when I saw how many people had come into the Duke's Hall to listen. A few weeks later I gave a concert performance of it with *Musici* at Ilford Town Hall with Mum playing in the cello section and Chris playing horn.

When it came to concert dresses, my sewing skills proved useful. It is not easy to find something suitable off the peg, quite apart from the fact that long evening gowns are expensive. So I designed and made my own. The concerto I was to play gave me the inspiration. I spent sleepless nights dreaming up dresses, working out how to make them, and days searching for fabric. By this time, Mum's cousin, Ailsa, had kindly given me her old Singer treadle machine. It was excellent, with a number of ingenious attachments, some of which functioned in ways that no modern electric machine is capable of doing. I still regret that I gave it away.

Finishing a dress was far more crucial than practising the concerto, which annoyed Mum.

"You didn't do much practice yesterday and you've done very little today."

"I have to finish my dress."

"You could wear the green one, or that lovely orange one."

"They wouldn't be right."

"How much longer is this going to take?"

"Not long. It's nearly done." She would look in despair at the sections of material draped over chairs and bed, the chaos of scraps, pins, newspaper, ribbons, bias binding, scissors, rulers and cotton reels on the floor, and would leave the room with her reproof hanging in the air. Often I would be up until three or four in the morning the night before a performance giving a dress its finishing touches.

Mum pinned up the hems for me. To do this, I stood on the living room table wearing the shoes I would be performing in – all my dresses had to touch the floor – and turned around slowly until she was satisfied that the line was straight. I once made a dress from a stunning, pure-silk fabric in purple shot through with orange. It was a complex pattern that used yards and yards of material for the skirt. The colours shimmered and changed shade as I moved. After the recital, a friend asked me what I felt was the most creative aspect of performance. Without hesitation I replied, "Making this dress." She thought I was joking.

On Sunday, February 4th 1973, Simon put on his most ambitious concert to date at St. Giles' Church, Cripplegate, Barbican. The programme included Shostakovich's second cello concerto with Rod McGrath as the soloist, and Mahler's fourth symphony. It was another extraordinary concert. Again I was struck by Simon's ability to extract absolute concentration and commitment from every player. His eyes connected with each individual and when he looked directly into mine, I understood his burning intensity and felt sure that he recognised the passion I returned. He drew me into his mind like a hypnotist and each one of us responded to his musical demands.

Bram Tovey also conducted his own orchestra in Redbridge. During the years he spent in the Salvation Army Band, he met a horn player called Graham. It was

Graham who encouraged Bram to form the orchestra, suggesting the name *Concerti Allegri* (which approximately translates as 'joyful concerts'). Graham, having helped to set it up, wanted to play principal horn. At the time, Bram felt he couldn't refuse. The inaugural concert took place in November 1972, and Chris sat down the line. It didn't bother Chris whether he was first horn or not, he was simply pleased to be playing for Bram.

Two weeks after Simon's Mahler 4 performance, *Concerti Allegri*'s second concert was scheduled. Bram asked if I would come along and play, but I couldn't manage any rehearsals. He said he'd love me to play in the concert anyway, as he was conducting Beethoven 7, which could do with more cellos. The overall ability of the orchestra did not match the NYO, perhaps not even the RYO, but it was one of the most exciting performances of Beethoven's seventh symphony I have ever played. Bram was electrifying, charging the orchestra with such energy that he compelled us to play at maximum wattage.

> ***IZZY:*** *The concert was absolutely incredible. Bram is just the most fantastic conductor. It was the best concert I've ever been to. It was really moving. I felt part of the music. I felt like going away alone somewhere where I could relive it all, nothing else seemed to exist.*

The performance was marred only by the principal horn, and it was after this that, as Bram put it, "there was a coup and Chris stepped up to the plate." Bram felt bad about it at the time, but with so many excellent players in the orchestra, an inadequate first horn could not be accommodated. Bram was a magnetic character, an inspiring and innovative conductor. He had no trouble in assembling an orchestra of some of the best players in Redbridge. Chris was principal horn, I led the cellos and Izzy played in the violin section. Paul Hart, Chris Stearn, Sue Eversden, Chris Freeman, Clive Miller, Russell Jordan, Rod Elms, Melanie Turner and Martin Koch were some of the players, all characters who appear elsewhere in this book. There were others who now hold prominent positions in the music world, but too many to list here. It was a band of good friends who produced some amazingly good concerts.

Florrie decided I needed a better instrument. Reluctantly, I had to agree, although I was very attached to my cello. I had bought it for £50 with the money from my Post Office savings account (which Mum had saved weekly for each of us since we were born). But now, having won the cello prize, Florrie felt confident that the Academy would loan me one of their good instruments. Her request was turned down.

"Cathy, I have some bad news," she said. "The Academy has refused to lend you a cello. I asked why and was told that they consider you to be too irresponsible. They say it is evident from your behaviour that you are not taking things seriously."

My stomach lurched and I braced myself. "Oh no."

"I'm sorry; this must be a shock for you. It certainly was for me. I told them that this is not my experience of you at all. I am delighted with the progress you are making; you always come to your lessons well prepared and work very hard indeed. Now, I have to ask you if there is anything that might have given them this impression?"

Yes, I admitted to myself, probably a number of things. I had been trying to rouse support for the Students' Union, an organisation that the Academy did their best to ignore, which received little interest from the majority of students. One of the current campaigns was to endeavour to persuade the Academy to sanction the opening of a students' bar. There were forthcoming elections and I had been quite vociferous in my support for Bettina, the girl who was standing for Vice-Presidency.

"Well, I suppose I do lark about sometimes in the common room, and maybe I laugh too loudly and draw attention to myself –"

"Exactly! It's just youthful high spirits, which is what I told them. Goodness, you can't win the cello prize at sixteen without lots of hard work. I really don't know what they're talking about."

Oh, Florrie, I thought, thank you so much for sticking up for me.

"Who's been saying these things about me?"

"I can't tell you that, but I'm afraid nothing I could say would change their minds. So, Cathy, we'll just have to show them, eh? And maybe have your fun and games when you're outside the Academy – they can be a stuffy lot here – but don't lose your vitality over this, it's what makes your playing special."

Suddenly I was in tears, not because I had been refused a cello, or because someone had disapproved of my behaviour, but because Florrie was being so kind and supportive. After my lesson, I sat in a corner of the canteen weeping. Kathy Green, one of the percussion students, took charge of me.

"Come on. Let's go and sit in the medical room. Follow me."

I didn't know such a place existed, but she walked me to a door, opened it as if it were her own private office, made me climb onto the high, narrow bed and lie down.

"There now; have a good old cry and when you can speak, tell me what the trouble is. No hurry." She patted my arm, checked her make up in the mirror and handed me a towel to wipe my eyes. I sobbed out my tale of woe.

"Yeah, well I can guess who's been stirring up trouble."

"Mrs. Deller?"

"Who else could it be? You know what she says to me? 'I'm looking forward to the day when you display more sense and less cleavage'. And, 'I can see you've been overdoing the Baby-Bio on your eyelashes again, dear.'"

I laughed.

"There. That's better. Anyway, is your cello really so bad?"

"I like it. It just doesn't have a very big sound."

"Well, something else will turn up. Hey, don't let her or any of the other dreary bigwigs get to you. They're not worth it. They might take themselves seriously, but I certainly don't. OK?"

I nodded. "Thanks, Kathy."

"For what?"

"Looking after me; calming me down."

"All part of the course, love."

57
SCHOOL PERFORMANCES

Everyone was terrified of Doug. I've seen grown men pull their own heads off rather than see Doug. Even Dinsdale was frightened of Doug... He used sarcasm. He knew all the tricks; dramatic irony, metaphor, bathos, puns, parody, litotes and satire.

The Piranha Brothers Sketch – Monty Python

Izzy was in the Sixth Form preparing for her A levels. Since Junior School, it had been obvious that she had a gift for acting when she took the lead role in *Cinderella*. At Loughton County High, she was chosen for major roles in the school plays. Izzy asked Mum if she could join a drama group, but for some reason her request was overlooked, which always seemed a shame to me. However, in January 1973, she became involved in a production of *Oh What a Lovely War* at Bancroft's Boys school.

> **IZZY:** *It all began with Mrs. Caldow asking for four girls to be in the Bancroft's School play. Mary, Anita, Nina and I volunteered just for a joke. At the first rehearsals we were all petrified. We didn't know if we were any good, or what the blokes thought of us. However, Thursdays and Fridays soon became the highlights of our week. I've really enjoyed doing the play. This has been the most fantastic thing I've ever done in my whole life and I'll never forget it as long as I live.*

At the beginning of May, Chris Stearn asked Izzy out. He was soon spending a lot of time at Cleveland Road. He and our brother were already close friends. They were both taught by John Ridgeon, both members of the Redbridge Brass Band and played in the same orchestras. Conversing about horns, bass trombones and brass instruments in general was their favourite pastime. Together they pored over a book by Robin Gregory called *The Horn*, studying pictures and photos of horns and pondering the merits of different models. Izzy didn't complain that her new boyfriend spent more time talking to her brother than he did to her: she lay in the garden sunbathing and reading, while the two Chris's compared mouthpieces, crooks and valves. The boys also made frequent visits to Parkers, a brass shop in Soho's Chinatown located in a basement in Dansey Place, and to Paxman Horns, which was around the corner in Gerrard Street, chock full of Chris Giles's favourite instrument. Chris Stearn described his friend's excitement "like a boy with a sweet tooth being let loose in a chocolate factory – he hardly knew where to look first or whether he should even dare to blow a note into a new horn in case he liked it too much." Chris spoke in reverential tones to the Paxman staff and kept up to date with the latest developments. Sometimes he took his own Paxman horn in for minor adjustments and repairs, but more often than not, he would simply go to absorb the hallowed ambience of the shop and leave with a Paxman pencil to legitimise his journey.

Chris was fourteen, in his fourth year at Buckhurst Hill. His repertoire of strange physical tricks, particularly the 'saliva squirt', was well known amongst his peers. Steve Cladingboel told me: "Chris's talent for projectile saliva became an obsession with him for a while. He would do it constantly, like a habit you can't get out of. I seem to remember he got caught doing it inside the school (rather than in the playground) and didn't even realise he had done it." But Cliff Oliver almost upstaged Chris with the claim that he could breathe through his eyes. Cliff had discovered that if he blocked his nostrils, shut his mouth and strained to exhale air, bubbles came out of his tear ducts. Boys watched in fascination, too incredulous to consider whether the feat could justifiably be termed 'breathing'. It was something that Chris failed to emulate, though doubtless he tried.

One pupil remembers an incident "where Chris and a couple of other musicians were larking around and Chris somehow fitted a brass mouthpiece to the tubular frame of a music stand that had been dismantled and wrongly re-assembled and 'played' it, much to the amusement of others who were there."

Chris and his trombonist pal, Martin Koch, had become thoroughly fed up with the school orchestra, yet were obliged to attend rehearsals. They couldn't help but mess about, putting jazz voicings into classical pieces, swapping instruments or drawing cartoons into each other's music. To alleviate the boredom, they decided to take up the double bass. There was one school instrument, which Martin and Chris shared, taking lessons with a specially appointed peripatetic teacher who thought they were marvellous. For a while they enjoyed struggling as much as anyone else in the orchestra, until they realised that it hurt to play the double bass. Their arms ached, their fingers throbbed and the instrument was heavy and awkward to lug around. After a couple of terms, they gave it up, much to the devastation of their teacher, who declared they were the best students he had ever had.

In the school music festival that year, Martin Koch entered an original composition. The entry forms had to be submitted the day before at the latest. Martin, still writing his piece and running out of time, gave his entry form to Nitram to hand in.

"But what's the title of your piece, Martin?" he asked.

"Oh, I don't know," he replied. "You think of something to call it."

"OK, then," said Nitram.

The festival ended with the composition class. Mr. Rippin, with no hint of satire, announced that Martin Koch and his group were going to perform a piece entitled *Dinky Toy with All Its Paint Scraped (Apart From a Little Around the Driver's Door)*. Apparently, not a muscle in Mr. Rippin's face so much as twitched. The hall erupted with laughter. All eyes swivelled to Martin Koch, who was staring incredulously at a nonchalant, innocent-faced Nitram. Nitram's own composition was called *A Further Facet of Spanish Mike's Mouldy Tape*. Despite the traditional nature of the school, the boys were allowed their fun, and even received adjudications of their unconventional performances.

58
FRANÇOIS

It's so hard for us to really be
Really You and really Me.

Wild Eyed Boy from Freecloud – David Bowie

Eventually, François persuaded me to go to the pub with him. He was an outrageous flirt and flatterer, but it was also a bit tongue-in-cheek and he was very amusing. We set off down Marylebone High Street, coming first to the Prince Regent, but François said he didn't want to go there. We walked on past the Rising Sun, until we reached the third pub – one that I hadn't been to before – and went in. He declared it was much nicer, with no risk of bumping into anyone we knew, so he could have me all to himself. He ordered a pint of lager and a half of lager and lime for me, and by the time we had to return to the Academy, his tongue was out of his cheek and in my mouth.

So began what I remember as a delightful five months. He lived in Hendon. We came to an arrangement that he would take the Northern Line and I the Central Line into London, where we would meet at the ticket barrier at Tottenham Court Road. He was never short of cash, thanks to the large amount of pocket money he received, so he took me out frequently. His father owned a cinema in Tottenham Court Road, so we could go there for nothing and even get free ice-creams. We saw Woody Allen's *Everything You Always Wanted to Know about Sex, But Were Afraid to Ask.* I was hopeful that some enlightenment would be forthcoming, but none of my questions were answered and I didn't even find it funny. We sat through a film about a gardener working in the grounds of a convent, the whole movie showing him having it off with every nun. François' father's picture house screened erotica and the patrons were old men in raincoats. We were the only giggling, kissing couple in the back row. The films soon palled and we didn't bother to go to any more. Why watch duff movies when we could be having fun in my bedroom? We ate at the Spaghetti House in Goodge Street, sharing a carafe of house red, and often went tenpin bowling at alleys in Piccadilly with François' friends, Peter and Linda. I was terribly upset to find out that Linda had had a baby that she'd given away for adoption. I tried to talk to her about it, but she only wanted to forget. I knew she never would. Neither have I. As a foursome, we dined at Bertorelli's, drank Verdicchio and Chianti; I tried mussels for the first time and sampled Tia Maria. François paid the bills.

He visited me at Cleveland Road and met the family. I took him for a walk in Epping Forest. When we returned, everyone was out. In my bedroom we became heavily involved on the floor and one thing led to another. Perhaps we had planned it, as condoms were to hand. I had given up with the pill before Christmas, convinced it had caused me to gain weight.

"Have you done this before?" he asked.

"Yes," I admitted.

"You naughty girl! Then you'll have to teach me all about it."

"You haven't?"

"No. I've been saving myself for you."

I didn't tell him how unexciting my first experience had been. It bore no resemblance to what was happening now – a natural flow of mutual desire. This was sweet and easy, both of us laughing as we grappled with the condom. François wasn't the least bit shy, but why we had to be on the floor and not in my bed, I don't know.

"Well, how did I do?"

"Seemed fine to me."

"Marks out of ten?" Well, how was I to know?

"Nine?" I conjectured.

"Is that all? You're going to have to give me lots more supervised practice sessions then. Was it really OK?"

"François, you were lovely."

"You've never said my name before. Say it again."

"François."

"You say it beautifully, just right."

My room, to remind you, was at the back of the house. To get to it, one had to pass through Chris's bedroom. When François stayed the night, he was put up in the spare bunk bed in Chris's room, but of course he didn't stay there. Chris was most obliging and pretended to be asleep when François crept into my room, by which time I had lit candles and warmed up the bed. It was very romantic.

I went to his house in Hendon, a huge place in a road called Downage; just Downage, no Street, Road or Avenue following its name. François' room was about six times bigger than mine and he had a double bed. He was fanatical about David Bowie and played me all his records, which I had not heard before. I could understand why he liked them. He was also crazy about football, which did not interest me at all.

We were both working on the Schumann cello concerto, the set piece for the concerto prize the following term, and borrowed fingerings and bowings from each other. We were pals, playmates. François could not be serious about anything. When I tried to talk to him about deeper issues, I would catch him looking at me sentimentally, as if I were a kitten on a chocolate box.

"You haven't been listening to a word I've been saying!" I'd protest.

"It's so adorable the way you frown when you're thinking, and you have the most gorgeous green eyes."

I went to the cottage with Izzy, Chris and Mum at Easter. He wrote:

> How are you, my lovely cellist?... You have become the steadying influence which is just what I need at the moment and especially in the future when we make it a 1, 2 in the Schumann (joke!) I actually did (wait for it) 4 HOURS on Thursday. I even did some practice... I discovered an important factor as to its progress – I can't play it at all! It's such a silly work. Performed the 'Messiah' yesterday, bloody awful it was too. Have you heard the gag – "A chap dreamt he was playing the 'Messiah' and woke up to find he really was." We know how we feel about each other and we simply both want to have the

best time possible for the future.
All the love in the world, François.

I hadn't analysed what I felt about him, nor did I simply want to have the best time possible. We had good times together, but it wasn't love, and I think we both knew that. Neither of us ever said those three words, "I love you", to each other. I wish I could say that I have only spoken them when I've meant it, but there have been times when I haven't; when I've lacked honesty and courage, when I've been scared to face the truth, when evasion was easier than confrontation. Yet, spoken with false sincerity, those three syllables pollute the air like stink bombs.

The summer term began with some glorious weather. We went boating on the Regents Park canal, to the pub for lunch and lager and lime, out in the evenings to Schmidt's or San Martino's, until I was struck down with illness. I remember clearly when it began. I was sitting at a desk in the Duke's Hall with dozens of other students taking my written harmony exam. As I wrote, I noticed small red spots appearing on my arms. Fascinated, I watched as they multiplied and spread. I peered down at my legs to see that they too were covered in a rash. I began to feel hot and cold, sweaty and shivery, and knew my temperature was rising. I finished the exam, handed in my paper long before the time was up and went home. By now I was aware of a raging sore throat. When I walked through the front door, Granny took one look at me and called the doctor. Jeremy Franklin, our family GP, had recently started to have piano lessons with Mum. He called at the house, examined me, diagnosed scarlet fever, took a throat swab and sent me to Wanstead hospital to have a blood test. I went to bed. A few days later, Dr. Franklin confirmed that I had glandular fever. With Mum present, he explained that the illness is common amongst teenagers and is known as 'the kissing disease', because the virus is passed from one person to another through the mouth. He attempted to make a joke of it, but Mum was not amused.

"Who have you been kissing?" she asked accusingly, placing a smile on her face for Dr. Franklin's benefit.

"Just François, Mum. He's the only person I could have caught it from. I don't go around kissing every bloke I set eyes on, do I?"

"How do I know what you get up to?"

"Well," intervened Dr. Franklin, "you'll feel pretty bad for a week or two, after which you'll need to rest and recuperate for a while longer. You may feel tired and lethargic, so don't try to do too much. I'll pop in again in a few days."

I phoned François. He'd had glandular fever himself a few years earlier, so I couldn't have picked it up from him.

"You've been kissing other boys, you naughty girl!"

"I haven't! You know I haven't."

He teased me for flirting while I protested my innocence, smarting from the injustice.

"Hey, don't get your knickers in a twist. I'd much rather you took them off and I came straight over to see you, but I guess I'm going to be forced into celibacy until you're better."

"But how did I get it? Maybe it's you who've been kissing other girls and passed it on to me?"

"Now would I do such a thing? Eh? Come on, silly. I'm not blaming you. There are other ways of catching glandular fever, you know. I'm just feeling sorry for myself because I won't be able to see my gorgeous girl."

"But if you've already had glandular fever, surely it's OK to visit me?"

"No, my mother won't hear of it. She reckons I might catch it again. And I certainly would, because the first thing I'd do would be to kiss you, then I'd take your clothes off and kiss you some more, and... I'd better stop, it's all too frustrating – "

He couldn't see me for weeks. We spoke on the phone and he sent a card that said, "Don't try telling ME anything about SEX; show me! But get better first, thou gorgeous, naughty female."

I had a severe case of glandular fever, but surprisingly, my asthma was troubling me less. I had fewer attacks and sometimes went for weeks without even wheezing. Nevertheless, Dr. Franklin was concerned about my health and suggested I visit him at his home out of surgery hours. He lived nearby in one of the large houses on The Drive, the road that Izzy, Chris and I used to walk along on our way to the Eagle Pond. Imagine my delight when I found that it was the house I had always picked as my favourite. As I unlatched the garden gate and walked towards the front door, I realised that I would be seeing it from the inside for the first time. I rang the bell. Dr. Franklin welcomed me in. My eyes swept around the spacious hall, taking in the turned mahogany newel post, the staircase, cornices and carved woodwork. I was shown into a magnificent room at the back of the house with a superb fireplace, above which was an ornate, mirrored over-mantle. After a chat and check-up, his wife invited me to stay for tea. They had two little girls. My interest in the children and the house was so obvious that Mrs. Franklin asked if I would like to see around. She took me through to the garden via a conservatory and past some old stables. The garden was extensive, with an enormous magnolia tree, rhododendrons, camellias, japonica, laburnum, silver birch, fruit trees and many other shrubs and plants that I couldn't name. At the end of the garden on either side were two long Victorian greenhouses and between them a high brick wall espaliered with fruit trees.

It was time for the youngest daughter's afternoon nap, so I followed Mrs. Franklin upstairs, not wanting to miss an opportunity to peek at the bedrooms. As I left, I was invited to call in whenever I wanted. I felt as if I had been given a pass to wonderland. It was everything I had imagined it to be, even though the house was neglected and in need of decoration. I became a frequent visitor, with the excuse that I had come to play with the girls. Unfortunately, I did not get to see inside the turret, nor was I able to experiment leaning out of a window to call for a dashing Prince on a white horse to rescue me.

During the illness, I lost a stone without trying. Determined not to put the weight back on, I started to develop the techniques of food denial and avoidance that I had been dallying with for years. Initially, it went unnoticed. Rejecting food because I wasn't feeling well was acceptable at first; but as the weeks went by, Mum began to watch me and I watched her watching. I entered the grim game of deception and concealment, answering her anxious food questions with slippery lies. The dinner table, which had always been an uncomfortable place of hostile truce, became my silent battleground. Six o'clock was a time to be absent – one of my many methods of eat-deceit. A plate of food would be saved for me, most of which I flushed down the loo – except for a little, which I left on the plate to make it look as though I had eaten the rest. I gave up all carbohydrates, sugar and fat. I drank my coffee black. I allowed myself green vegetables, meat, eggs and fruit, measuring out what I considered to be acceptable quantities. I vowed to myself that I would never be fat again.

"Cath-er-reen. It's dinner time."

The food was served onto plates in the kitchen.

"No potatoes for me, thank you," I called.

"Just have one, dear," said Mum.

"No thank you. I'm not very hungry – and I don't want any gravy, thanks."

Mum sighed and dished me out some cabbage and meat. I took it to the table and sat down with Izzy, Chris and Dad. I cut a tiny piece of meat, speared it onto my fork and raised it to my mouth. There amongst the cabbage was a large, pale-green, boiled caterpillar.

"Eugh! There's a slug in my cabbage."

"Where? Let's see," said Chris.

A gift of an opportunity presented itself.

"I feel sick. I can't eat another thing."

"Oh Mammy!" wailed Mum. "I *told* you to wash that cabbage thoroughly. Now she won't eat."

"Eh?"

"The cabbage! There's a caterpillar in it."

"Och, it won't do her any harm."

"It's the larva of the Cabbage White butterfly – *Pieris rapae*," Chris announced. "It probably tastes just like cabbage, as that's what it's been eating."

"Well, you eat it then," I said, pushing my plate away. Eddying beneath my perfect excuse was the pitiful sound of Mum's voice – her defeat and despair as she turned her frustration towards her mother. I left the room, my stomach rumbling with the guilt of Mum's helplessness.

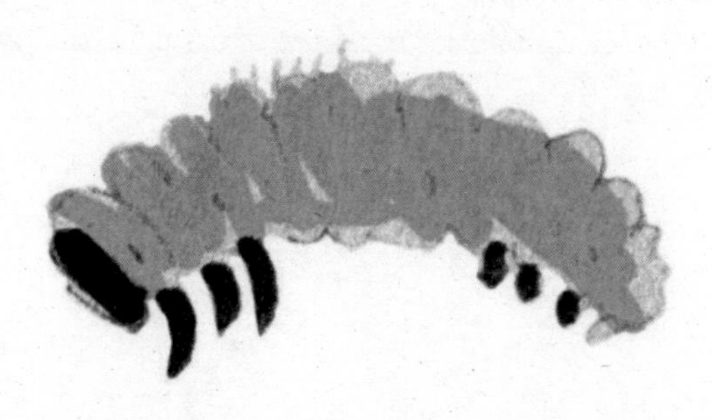

I went back to the Academy a different person. The weight loss was obvious, but I looked good on it then, and received numerous compliments. Weak and out of practice as I was, Florrie insisted I still go in for the concerto prize. François and I did not make it a 1, 2, but we did both play in the next *Concerti* concert in July – Brahms' *Academic Festival Overture* and Dvořák's 'New World' symphony. What a difference it made having Chris on first horn. Bram still remembers him "playing that hard last movement lick up to top C spectacularly well."

I was booked to play in a few concerts with the New Symphony Orchestra. It was an ad-hoc orchestra made up of mostly freelance professionals, but the rank and file seats were often filled by students. I duly turned up at Watford Town Hall for the one afternoon rehearsal followed by a concert in the evening. Imagine my surprise when I saw Florrie's daughter, Nina, in the violin section. Presumably she, like every other musician, had to earn a living and, funnily enough, orchestras provide work for the majority. The injustice of Florrie removing me from the Redbridge Music School all those years ago and her jaundiced view of orchestral playing struck me afresh. I hoped Nina would not report me, but perhaps she also kept her orchestral playing a secret from her mother. The New Symphony Orchestra engagements were known as 'bucket dates'. Eventually, I found out why. The fixer of the orchestra was a man named Peter Halling, a perfectly nice person. However, the joke goes: What's the difference between Peter Halling and a bucket of shit? Answer: The bucket.

IZZY: June 1973: *I've seen Ashley again who's very mixed up and in a terrible state emotionally. He's changed a lot – gone and dyed his hair of all the stupid things to do and become all hippy and druggy. The trouble is, I think most of it's put on and is a revolt against his parents. I do still love him in a funny sort of way, but I prefer Chris. Chris doesn't order me around as Ashley did and doesn't expect me to be a little slave who does everything for him. Also, he doesn't spend the majority of the time trying to persuade me to go to bed with him and thrusting books about contraceptives up my nose like Ashley used to. Chris says he loves me, but I don't know whether to believe him or not. The expression has been declared to me before and has not proven to be true. Blokes usually say "I love you" in the hopes that you will repeat the phrase to them and then do a quick hop into bed. Well, that's not going to happen with me. I'm not sure enough of myself or of them to take the plunge. Cathy's going out with François. They're dots about each other. It's really brilliant. I think they might even get married.*

That was Izzy being romantic. Marriage didn't cross our minds, and Mum was anxious that it shouldn't. Her one piece of advice to her daughters was: "Whatever you do, don't get married."

With François in Regents Park, spring 1973, just before I became ill with glandular fever.
We hired rowing boats when the weather permitted, taking turns with the oars.

Guardian and Independent October 27th 1972: "Boys from Buckhurst Hill County High School give concert." On the far left is Cliff Oliver and next to him is Martin Koch. Chris is holding his horn.

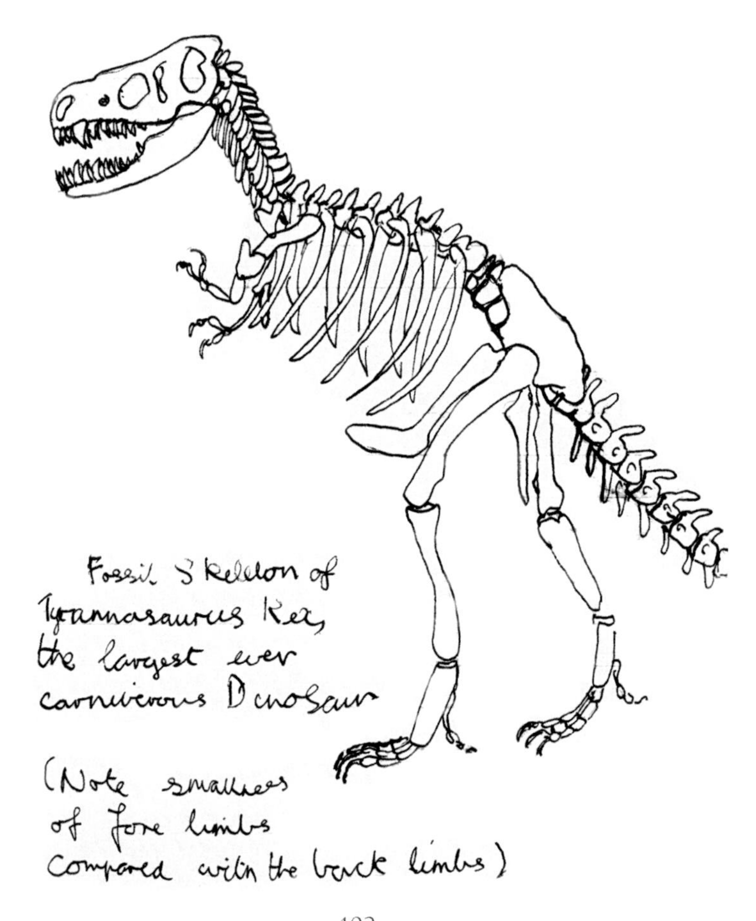

59
ELCOMBE HALL

I have made an important discovery… that alcohol, taken in sufficient quantities, produces all the effect of intoxication.

Oscar Wilde

Patricia Calnan studied the violin with David Martin, Florence Hooton's husband. She and I were friends from the NYO, both first year students at the Academy, and our respective teachers decided it would be of benefit to us to play together. The first work we tackled was the Kodály duo, which we performed at the Academy in February 1973. David and Florrie also suggested we form a string quartet, which we did, with Kathy Adams on violin and Cathy Stevens on viola. It didn't last for long, I can't remember why, but long enough to get together with Simon Rattle on piano and Sarah Mousley, soprano, to rehearse and give two performances of a lovely piece by Chausson called *Chanson Perpetuelle.*

A few weeks later, Tricia and I were asked to give a recital in Swindon. I made identical long skirts for the performance in a salmon-pink cotton print and we bought blouses to match. Tricia's parents lived in Swindon, so we went to stay with them for a few days before the recital to rehearse together. The programme included the Ravel and the Kodály duos; I was to play some unaccompanied Bach and Tricia a violin and piano sonata. She asked Simon to play the piano with her and he agreed. Tricia and I travelled to Swindon where her father met us at the station and drove us to Elcombe Hall – a beautifully proportioned, elegant stone building nestled in the Wiltshire countryside. Tricia's mother, slim, spry and upright, greeted me in the porch. I was shown to my room, which was tastefully decorated in blues, and then given a tour around the beautiful house and garden.

Tricia was impulsive, scatty, occasionally flippant, but warm-hearted, and could always be relied upon to have a good laugh. She played the fiddle effortlessly with an intensely beautiful sound that often sent shivers up my spine. We worked every day – practising by ourselves in the morning and together in the afternoon.

I noticed that Tricia was often nagged at and criticised by her mother for no apparent reasons. An uncomfortable moment presented itself one morning at breakfast. I was sipping black coffee and Tricia was tucking in to scrambled eggs on toast when her mother turned to her and said that she ought to watch her figure and should be more careful about what she ate. I was astonished. Tricia was an attractive girl of perfectly normal size: surely this was not something a mother should be saying to her daughter, especially in front of her daughter's friend? Having by now reached the dividing line between slim and thin, I shifted uneasily. Tricia, laughing it off, helped herself to another slice of toast, spread it liberally with butter and heaped a large dollop of marmalade onto her plate. "Have some toast, Cathy," she said cheerfully, seemingly unaffected by her mother's insensitive comment. I turned down the offer.

"Good girl," said her mother, glaring pointedly at Tricia's plate. "Why can't you be like Cathy? Look at her – so slim, just right."

"That's because she doesn't eat, Mummy," she responded mildly, the only sensible person at the table. I admired her for her light-hearted laughter and guessed that her glibness was the technique she had devised to deal with her own set of difficulties with her mother.

Simon arrived to rehearse with Tricia, after which we were driven to the venue to try out the acoustic before the audience arrived. The house was full, the performances well-received. Afterwards we went back to Elcombe Hall for a post-concert reception.

"What are you drinking, Cathy?" asked Tricia's mother. I hesitated, not sure what to ask for.

"Gin?" she suggested.

"Oh, yes please." She handed me what looked like a tumbler of water. It was neat gin. I nearly choked, but regained my composure and sipped it gingerly. I must have drunk half of it when my head began to float. Tricia's mother, talking rather loudly, shouted to her husband to fill my glass.

"Another gin and tonic?" he asked. Tonic! Now that's a good idea, I thought, but before I could reply, Tricia's mother cut in.

"No, darling, she has it neat." How on earth had this misunderstanding arisen? Tricia's father gave me a strange look as he refilled my glass. If only I had declined the top-up and stopped drinking, but I didn't want to appear rude.

I soon felt very peculiar. Circulating was unnecessary, as the room seemed to be doing the rounds for me. Strange sounds were coming out of my mouth when I tried to speak. I realised that I must lie down before I keeled over. I stumbled towards the door, veering into people and furniture, and managed to make it out of the room. Leaning unsteadily against the banisters, I became aware that Simon was standing beside me. He asked if I was OK. Barely able to speak, I must have managed to indicate that I was going to my room.

"Shall I help you upstairs?" he asked. I shook my head, tripped up the first step and slid down the wall. He rebalanced me and I tried again, but it was hopeless. In the morning I awoke, a little baffled to find that I was still dressed in the salmon-pink skirt, and then, horrified, remembered something of the night before.

"How did you sleep, Cath?" Simon enquired at breakfast, passing me a quizzical look.

"Fine, I think. Was I awfully drunk?"

"Staggeringly so."

"Oh, God. I hope I didn't do anything too embarrassing."

"Well if you can't remember, I'm not telling you, but it was very nice carrying you upstairs."

"Simon! What did I do?"

He laughed. "You were incapable of doing anything, but you were very sweet and funny."

Tricia, Simon and I caught the train back to London. Tricia said goodbye and Simon and I went for a coffee. He asked what I was doing over the summer.

"Going camping for a fortnight as usual."

"With François?"

"No."

"When do you get back?"

"The fourteenth of August."

"And then?"

"I'll be in London. I want to go to lots of Proms."

"I'm back around the eighteenth. Shall we get together and do some playing?"

"Yes, I'd love to."

He said he would phone as soon as he returned to London.

In 1973, Redbridge Brass Band's first record, titled *The Redbridge Phenomenon*, was released by Grosvenor Records. It had been recorded at Loxford High School the previous year. Below is the rather unclear photograph that appears on the record sleeve. John Ridgeon is sitting at the front holding a baton; Chris's face is just above John's head. The LP was reviewed in the *Gramophone* in June 1973. Here is an edited version:

> A record to be praised for its programme and performance alike. This band seems to be about 40 strong, not the conventional 26, and composed of teenagers of both sexes. It has had a very impressive career, inspiring several well-known composers to write for it. Here we have the most varied selection of martial music that I have heard for many a long day. John Ridgeon, who conducts, is obviously an excellent teacher and trainer as well as a good conductor, and secures some spirited and well-toned playing from this youthful band, many members [*thirty-four*] of which have been his pupils during the five years or so that he has been Supervising Brass Teacher at Redbridge. Strongly recommended on all counts.

60
MEETING JOHN SPENCER

It seems to me we can never give up longing and wishing while we are thoroughly alive. There are certain things we feel to be beautiful and good, and we must hunger after them.

The Mill on the Floss – George Eliot

Beneath the fun, I was beginning to feel uneasy about my relationship with François. It felt wrong that he paid for everything. I offered to chip in what I could, but he waved it away. He was the guy and I was his little girl to be treated, pampered and petted. I tried to explain my discomfort, saying I wanted to share things at a level that I could afford too. Couldn't we go for walks, to art galleries, free exhibitions, take sandwiches? The crumbs would get in the bedclothes, he protested, and don't you enjoy going out? The cost of eating at restaurants bothered me. Mum and Granny, who spent hours scouring the shops for the cheapest butter, sugar, tea and cheese, always on the lookout for special offers and reductions, could probably buy the week's groceries for the same price as a meal out for two. My protests fell on deaf ears. François refused to get into heavy discussions. "You're sounding too much like your grandmother with all her talk about feminism," he complained.

The term ended. François went off on a music course held at Roedean School for girls (which he thought rather amusing), and I went to FSC with Izzy to the Merioneth site in Wales. It was billed as an art camp and we were intrigued to see how it would be run. In fact, there was nothing unusually arty about it, but it was a great camp, our final year as Pathfinders and the last camp that we could be kids. From then on, we would be staffing. Chris decided to go on a semi-mobile camp in Swaledale, Yorkshire, with plans to walk part of the Pennine Way. A semi-mobile camp is one without a fixed base. Not quite so strenuous as a mobile that sets up camp in different spots every night, a semi-mobile stays in the same place for two or three days before moving on. Even so, the idea of pitching and striking tents, packing and unpacking rucksacks, having to shop, carry and cook food every day, not to mention the arduous, backbreaking hiking, was more than Izzy and I cared to contemplate.

FSC had become, and remains, an intrinsic part of our lives. It is unique in that it doesn't intersect with the rest of our existence. Arriving at every camp is a homecoming, a gathering of a tribe, a return to an environment that connects us to the natural elements of earth, fire, water and air. The world from which we have just travelled seems to belong in some distant galaxy. Time slows down. Keeping fed, dry, warm and protected from the weather uses up a lot of the day. It might take five minutes to walk to the dining circle from the group site. With over a hundred people to feed, meal times can be lengthy. There are lats to be dug; dry and wet pits to be constructed; fires to be stoked; washing lines, lat screens and tents to be erected;

provisions that must be carried to the kitchen; milk, meat and butter to be kept cool in the river; water fetched and wood collected. In the evenings, congregated around the main campfire, we sing our songs together. As the younger groups go off to bed, the older groups drift back to their sites to make their own fires, while the adults join up around the kitchen fire to talk, sing, pass round the whisky and beer and a joint or two, perhaps. FSC is not entirely idyllic; there may be misfits and mischief-makers – no group of people live and work in perfect harmony – and there are midges, wasps and the weather to endure, but I have only wonderful memories of my last camp as a Pathfinder. Had we not gone to that particular camp, our lives would not be as they are today, for that was where we met John Spencer.

We arrived on a drizzly evening and pitched our tents on a grassy, level spot near the river. The rest of the camp was up in the top fields, so, as Pathfinders, we felt we had a bit of privacy. Izzy and I still had the white tent, now speckled grey and black with mildew, which Mum had bought us on special offer from the *Morning Star*. It just about sufficed, but had no sewn-in groundsheet. As soon as our tents had gone up, the rain came down heavily. We saw no point sitting round a fire when it was too wet even to light one, so went to bed early. Torrential rain pelted deafeningly on the canvas. It was pitch dark when I woke to the sound of gushing water. Half asleep, I pulled an arm out of my sleeping bag to find a torch and my hand went underwater. I shook Izzy awake.

"Izzy, there's a river running through our tent. We're going to have to decamp." I shone the torch and, sure enough, we were lying in a couple of inches of water, a stream meandering gently between us. Through the canvas, torchlight flickered and we could hear the sound of sploshing footsteps. Dragging on waterproofs – though there was little point as we were soaked through – we clambered out of the tent into the rain. Yes, we were standing in the river. It had burst its banks and our field was a sheet of moving water. Most of the Pathfinders were up striking tents amidst shouts, shrieks, wobbly torchlight, hurricane lamps, laughter and excitement. We packed up our tent, rolled our groundsheets around sodden sleeping bags, shouldered our rucksacks and trudged uphill to pastures dry. Blankets were fetched from the store tent and the whole pathfinder group bedded down in the communal shelter tent. We braved it out until dawn when the rain stopped and the sun greeted us warmly.

We found a new site further uphill, still hidden from the main camp, re-pitched our tents and began to dry out. The night's adventure brought the group together instantly and we were to enjoy a fantastic two weeks. John Spencer and I were pals immediately. He had the best tent – a Blacks' 'Good Companion'. They are not made anymore, unfortunately. I don't know why, because they were an ingenious wigwam-shaped design. The tent was supported on an A frame, making it possible to almost stand in the centre. It had an extended flysheet, which created a small entrance porch. Boots, rucksacks and waterproofs could be stored between the tent and flysheet, making more space inside. I shared John's tent from night two. Izzy was happy to spread out in our tent by herself, and our group-chief, Sue Sweet, as sweet as her name, did not bat an eyelid that John and I were cohabiting.

I was with François, and John had a girlfriend back home. Both of us were feeling a little ambiguous about our partners, but it wasn't on the cards, not mine anyway, to be unfaithful; and to be honest, I didn't feel that way about John. He found a way of unzipping our sleeping bags and fastening them together to make a double-sized bag. We snuggled in contentedly, sleeping and waking in each other's arms. It was a strangely innocent closeness, even though I knew that John would happily have dispensed with the innocence. One hot day he asked whether he could give me a massage.

"I'm a very good masseur," he assured me. "I've had some training, actually."

"Really?"

"Yes. I'll show you."

Nobody had given me a massage before. I wondered what it would be like.

"OK then."

"Take your top off and lie on your front." I settled myself on the sleeping bag and he began to circulate his hands over my shoulders.

"You're going to have to take off your bra for me to do it properly," he said.

I unclasped the hooks and slipped my arms out of the straps, careful not to expose my breasts. Then the massage began, which was delicious, his warm strong hands kneading and caressing, working their way down my back, towards my waist, my buttocks. What was he doing? Pulling my knickers gently over my hips –

"John!"

"It's OK," he soothed, "I need to work on the base of your spine to loosen your muscles. I know what I'm doing. Just relax, enjoy."

He was kneeling over me now, my thighs between his legs, my body feeling supple beneath his hands, my skin silken, my knickers inching further and further down…

"John?" I asked suspiciously, "Have you really had training in massage?"

"Erm… not exactly."

"What does that mean?"

"Well actually, this is the first time I've ever given anyone a massage."

"John! You trickster!"

"Well how else was I going to see your lovely bottom?"

I turned to one side and gave him a backhanded wallop.

"Or your lovely breasts." I covered myself hastily with an arm and grabbed for my T-shirt, but he whisked it away.

"Tricked you again," he chuckled. Then we were laughing, wrestling with clothes, playing tug-of-war with my bra and finally lying semi-clad side by side.

"Honestly, John. You're incorrigible. How could I have fallen for it?"

"But was it a good massage?"

"Yes – fantastic. You should do it for a living."

"Nah. I'll do it again for you, though. You have a gorgeous body."

"I haven't."

"You have." I allowed myself to believe him. My weight loss was succeeding.

I continued to shed pounds.

François seemed a long way away, but I wrote to him. I had obviously been trying again to explain my feelings. He replied:

> Yes, I have played my Rococo and it was a minor calamity, especially the last variation as you may well imagine. We've (?) been bowling, golfing, swimming, dodgeming, penny machining, pier jaunting, drinking, swimming and – oh, of course, playing symphonies etc. Your letter was rather ghastly. Whatever made you write such dubious literature? Very confusing indeed. I'm sunbathing at the moment with a Companion and we (?) are going for a bowling session, Chinese nosh plus the daily drink. I don't fancy any more dubious discussions or arguments with you ever again, no matter whose fault it may be. Cool down and stay as sexy as usual.
>
> With love, more love and even more love?
>
> François.

I failed to absorb the obvious. François had met someone else. He wasn't even trying to conceal it, with all the question marks and many more sentences that I haven't reproduced here. Back from Roedean, he wrote again to me at camp:

> How's my gorgeous cellist. I bet she's so frustrated!?!??!!?? just like me!!!!!!!!?! I mean, camp must be a bit uncomfortable for certain activities – like conveniences and cooking – what did you think I meant, you sexy thing. As usual, the course has changed me somewhat and no doubt you'll come back rather 'changed' as well (that sounds really terrible). Heaven knows what we'll be like together when the time comes. We'll just have to wait and see. BUT I don't want any needly discussions any more and that's final. I'm not very good at those as you've probably noticed so cool down in future, otherwise I shall personally put you over my knee and give you a thorough spanking.
>
> STOP PRESS – you narrowly won "Gorgeous Female of the Month Award" AGAIN. Thanks for your letter. I was getting slightly worried with its delay because you never know. Something might have happened to you in the wilds of Wales. I must say, it sounds absolutely hideous. Whatever possesses people to go camping and experience all the harsh conditions which nature offers? It might spare expense but I'd rather spend my 'holiday' in comfort – sorry if we disagree. I went to the ECO prom yesterday and met one of your best friends – Melanie Turner! no less with 3 of her cronies. So, there you are, that was just a small note to remind you that I'm still around – are you?!! One enormous and overwhelming cuddle from lover extraordinaire.
>
> François X

John and I exchanged family histories, discussed life, ideas, society and feelings. He was the first person in my peer group with whom I talked extensively about politics. We came from the same stable – left-wing, socially conscious and eager to debate. As I talked and listened, considered and evaluated, new thoughts flowed into my mind. Ideas that hadn't occurred to me before materialised with John there to catch them and throw his ideas back. Although our philosophising and psychologising was raw and unformed, I became intoxicated with the stimulation of debate.

Apart from the first twenty-four hours, the weather was good throughout the fortnight. Our Merrymoot contribution was an FSC themed version of *Oh What a Lovely War*, directed by Izzy, who taught us all the songs.

Chris wrote to us, even-handedly addressing the envelope to Izzy and Cathy Giles then beginning the letter: "Dear Cath and Izz,

> How goes it with you? I got my tent up in blazing sunshine, and the weather has been fine (too fine?) ever since. This is a very small camp; only twenty-one people including staff and we camp in "family" (all ages) cooking groups of seven. We cook on primuses although I appear to be the only person to have brought one! There is quite a deep stream nearby and also a spring from which we get our drinking water. Today we walked four miles to the shop and four miles back to buy food for the next three days.
>
> Tomorrow we walk all day and a six or seven day hike starts on Saturday. All the 'mountains' around here are below 2,000 feet, but still supply tough walking. There is no shelter tent and no kitchen area, so the site looks different to a usual FSC one, but the scenery is good – dry stone walls everywhere, a bit like Wales. We split into two age groups (Pathfinders; the rest) for hiking, and because there are so few people we will be able to get to know each other quite well before camp is over. Although this camp is very different to a standing camp, (it's more like permanent hike) I am having a great time and this may turn out the best camp I've been to.

A few days later:

> It has rained now for two days but I have managed to keep dry. Yesterday we walked 15 miles and saw hardly anyone, and this morning we went orienteering. How are your creative efforts getting on? If you're having the weather I am having at the moment, you cannot be doing too well.

Then this:

> Dear Cath and Izz,
>
> I hope my last postcard did not sound too depressed, but that was the feeling of the moment. I got back from hike to find that my tent had fallen down. My blanket got soaked. Luckily my clothes were dry as they were in a plastic bag. Thanks for the letter, Izz, I hope the weather's good for you – you two deserve good fun, this being your last year.
>
> I got a letter from Dad – he ended "farewell, farewell my N., my L.H.L" (?) and put his thumbprint at the bottom. I might put down for an art camp next year – I have heard glowing reports from people who have been on previous years. Mum and Granny appear to have enjoyed themselves in Scotland. I have seen wild grouse and walked about eight miles on the Pennine way when on hike. The population around here speak with a softer dialect than those around Wortley. In fact, it's hardly recognisable as Yorkshire.
>
> My waterproofs are now useless – the cape and armholes leak and the over trousers have a split, so let's hope it stays dry like it did today. The camp has been a bit of a disappointment but I look on the bright side of things. You miss country dancing, and camp songs in a shelter tent, when at a semi-mobile.
>
> See Ya Soon,
> Love Chris

Camp came to an end, but John and I made plans to keep in touch. I had decided months ago to forfeit Wortley in order to spend the summer going to Proms. Having purchased a season ticket, I had already been to a number of concerts. On the evening of the day we returned from camp I went to hear Pierre Boulez and the BBCSO perform Mahler's third symphony. I sank into the music, profoundly moved after more than two weeks of aural deprivation. François and I spoke on the phone and arranged to go to our favourite Spaghetti House. It came as no great shock when he admitted that he had met someone else. I told him about John and he decided that his behaviour hadn't been too bad after all.

"But I didn't have sex with him. We're not together. I was faithful to you."

"I'm sorry. You see, she's on the pill and I just couldn't resist making love without a condom. And she's so gorgeous."

"As gorgeous as I am?"

"You're both gorgeous. I still fancy you to bits, but I suppose I can't have both of you?" he asked wistfully.

"No, you can't."

We held hands back to the tube station and parted with a huge hug, still friends, but the party was over.

Izzy, Chris, Mum and Melanie went off to Wortley on the Saturday, leaving me at home. I felt free and happy. Every day was sunny. The last three weeks of the summer holidays stretched out before me with friends to meet and concerts to enjoy. Izzy wrote to me from Wortley:

> I hope you have pushed François to the back of your mind and are concentrating on none other than John Spencer. Mel and I danced the Charleston with the jazz band at the variety concert last night – a good laugh. Got quite a few drinks out of it as well!

It had been a happy experience sharing a tent with John for two weeks and forming an affectionate friendship. I had enjoyed his stimulating conversation, the pleasure of falling asleep and waking up beside him, but it was a relationship that was encapsulated in FSC. I was not about to go out with him. Understandably, when John heard I was no longer with François, he assumed that he and I would be together. But there was somebody else who had been waiting in the wings for much longer, who had patiently witnessed my ludicrous infatuation with a person I would never go out with, who had listened to my anguish over boys I didn't want to be with, watched me hurtle off course when I first joined the Academy, and observed from a distance my relationship with François. He had heard through the grapevine that I was footloose and fancy-free. It was time for him to make a move.

61
A PRELUDE TO A KISS

Oh, how my love song gently cries
For the tenderness within your eyes,
My love is a prelude that never dies,
A prelude to a kiss.

Lyrics by Irving Gordon and Irving Mills to the Duke Ellington song

CATHY: August 1973 Journal entry:
Simon phoned me while I was out on Monday 20th August. There was a little note for me on the table saying that he'd phone me round about 10.00 the next day. I was delighted. Before term ended, he'd said he might come over round about the 18th, but I'd never expected him to follow it up – still, there it was, he'd phoned and he'd phone again.

From 10.00 I was waiting, anticipating the phone call. The first person to phone was Mel, all the way from Wortley in rather a state about goings on there. Then Clare phoned to say she'll be arriving at Paddington station at four o'clock. 10.30, nearly 11.00, still no Simon. The sudden ring of the telephone stopped me once again in my tracks – a bloke's voice – could it be? No, John Spencer, arranging to come over later. Situation desperate. Granny needs me to go out shopping, but Simon has not yet phoned. So instead, she goes out, annoyed, and I wait for the call. Ages and ages pass. Granny gets back. 11.30 now – lost all hope of ever hearing from him. Then the phone rings – this *must* be him. A call box – beep beep beep – yes, it's Simon. "Hello Cath, how are you?" – conversation easy and relaxed. First thing he asks is whether he can come over that afternoon to play through the Brahms F major. It's not ideal as John's coming over. How about the next day? Yes, great. What time? I suggest he comes over in the morning, stays for lunch and we rehearse all day. He asks whether I'm going to the Prom in the evening – Elgar symph 2.

"Yes," I reply. He says "Let's go together, then." The 2p runs out. A panic-stricken few moments before we're cut off. Just time to say he'll phone me back. A few seconds later and the phone rings again. I ask him how he's been getting on. He's been doing some Y.O. course, playing the Stravinsky piano concerto. Anyway, we say goodbye and he says he'll see me round 11.30 the next day. So looking forward to it.

I meet Clare at Paddington, John Spencer comes round as arranged and we go out for a drink with a friend and they all stay the night. The next morning, they left pretty early, Clare went shopping and I practised rather sketchily – waiting for and expecting Simon. Then the front doorbell rings. There's the lovely, happy face of Simon, greeting me on the doorstep. A quick kiss. I take him into the music room and we talk. Relaxed, friendly. I realise how happy I am to have Simon as a friend.

We played through the Brahms before dinner – God, I played like a pig – I felt v. inadequate next to Simon's marvellous playing, musicianship and understanding of the music. We had lunch and ate well and conversed well. Just me and Simon and Granny – fortunately he gets on very well with just about everyone. I made a cup of tea and we went into the garden and drank it. It was a beautiful day. Then I washed my hair, Simon standing by, talking happily all of the time. We went upstairs – supposedly to see Chris's museum, but he walked through to my room and started looking at the posters on the walls.

I changed, and he said I looked absolutely gorgeous and hugged me. Then he asked whether I was still going out with François. I said that it had ended a few days ago. "Oh, that's good," said he, "because I was going to ask for first refusal." I laughed, thinking he was being his usual joking self. Anyway, we left for the Prom. He held out his arm for me to take. I linked my arm through his and off we went. A lovely train journey – talking all the way. We got out at S. Kensington. He offered his arm again, only this time our hands met and we held hands all the way to the queue. It was lovely. I met up with Clare and we all sat down, leaning against the wall of the Albert Hall. By this time I was in a bit of a daze, and also not really looking forward to seeing John who was expected any minute. He arrived and I introduced him to Simon who went off to make a phone call, and of course John tried to hold my hand, put his arm around me etc. I couldn't respond and I didn't want to be holding his hand in front of Simon. He'd written lots of poems, which I read – all of them, I think, referred to me – I was touched and rather sad as well.

Simon arrived back – I took the easy way out by just talking to them both. However, I ended up talking to Simon most of the time. The queue moved up and we all went in. I sat on the floor between John and Simon. A marvellous concert. The music had me completely involved – I forgot both of them. At the interval, we went for a drink. John put his arm round my waist. I didn't respond but Simon quite obviously noticed. John by this time rather upset – he reckoned he had claims on me, yet could sense that he was getting no response. Back in the hall, Simon put his arms round my waist for a brief moment. He asked us all to go for a pizza afterwards but as no-one wanted one, we compromised with a coffee. Outside, Simon again offered me his arm. I took it but also took John's arm – I felt so awful about him. Clare took John's other arm. On the walk down Exhibition Road, Simon took my bag from my shoulder and carried it so he could put his arm closely round my waist. I wrapped mine around his. John gave up and broke away. It felt great – just me and Simon – somehow everything felt right. At the coffee place, Clare sat opposite me but John and Simon both sat next to me, one on either side. Simon held my hand under the table and squeezed it affectionately. John took hold of my other hand – God what an awful situation – I had no hand to drink my coffee.

The NYO Prom was the next day. Simon said he was going, so did John. Simon said if he couldn't get tickets, perhaps I could save him a place in the queue? "No problem" say I. John doesn't look so happy. We all walked to the station. Simon was going on a different train to us three. He kissed me quickly goodbye and I waved to him through the window as the train drew away. John immediately held my hand – he was obviously pretty upset. Simon's attentions had set off a thrill of possibility in me and nothing I could say would cheer John up. Clare and I left in the morning to queue so we'd be at the front of the arena – near enough to make contact with our friends in the NYO. John arrived to queue about 2.00. I was forever on the look out for Simon but he didn't turn up. I presumed he'd got a seat.

A magnificent concert. Had a right laugh shouting 'hellos' (and other things) to all our friends in NYO. However, my mind was half on Simon the whole time. The concert ended and I went charging backstage to see everyone. John couldn't be bothered, so went off with some others to have a Wimpy. I said I'd see him there. I saw everyone, congratulated all, hugged lots. Clare and I went outside. I wandered round to a great mob of NYOers, followers, fans and parents, and there, emerging from the crowd, coming towards me was Simon. He came up and kissed me and hugged me and asked me to go for a drink. I had to explain that John was expecting me at the Wimpy bar. Fortunately, Clare said she'd go to meet the others and tell them that I'd be along in 20 mins. So off we went, arms around each other to the 99 [*The Queens Arms – the nearest pub to the Albert*

Hall and Royal College of Music – called the 99 by musicians as the Royal College at that time had ninety-eight rooms]. Had one drink and chatted, then realised that I must fly. Simon said he'd see me the next day at the pub for the NYO end-of-course booze-up.

I rushed down to South Ken. John had invited himself to stay at my place again, and I didn't really want him to. So sad after a lovely two weeks at camp to be making him unhappy. But I never said I'd go out with him – only that I wanted to keep in touch after camp. He left fairly early the next day. I walked to the station with him. I really do feel awful about it, but what can I do?

Clare and I went off to the Griffin pub. I watched for Simon. He was moving flats that morning and he hadn't said what time he'd get there. I knew he'd turn up though – of that I was certain. I went back outside and there coming towards me were Simon and Johnny Martin, both carrying suitcases. I went to meet them and Simon and I walked arm in arm to the Griffin. He bought me a gin and orange and himself a half of lager and Johnny a pint of Guinness.

I was determined not to make it too obvious that I liked him a lot, far more than a lot, in case I was misreading him. So he went off and talked to old friends and I talked to my friends and if he wanted to talk to me, that was up to him. Now and then I stole a quick glance at him, although most of the time I had my back to him. Then suddenly I realised that he was beside me. He put his arm round me and held my hand, then said, "Do you mind if we go outside so that I can seduce you?" I laughed and said, "No, not at all." So we went outside and stood talking to some others and Simon held me all the time and kissed my brow occasionally. Then we sat on a step. Simon held me close and kissed me properly for the first time. He was lovely and gentle. I felt warm, protected and happy.

Time was getting on and he had to go. So did I. He had 2 suitcases to carry. He gave me one so he could cuddle me on the walk to the station. At the station he said "Well, goodbye, Cathy," and kissed me again. He said he'd send me a postcard from wherever he's going. "I wish I could take you back to Liverpool with me as a souvenir from London." I laughed – he's so gorgeous.

And now I'm waiting and thinking and wallowing in the idea that maybe Simon likes me enough to go out with me. It's a lovely thought. I wait for the postman with a postcard, perhaps for me.

Mum, Izzy and Chris arrived home from Wortley. Mum was pleased to report that she and Izzy had played in a spirited rendition of the Mendelssohn Octet.

IZZY: August 1973: *I was happy to be back with Chris. Went to the Maypole with him, then stayed at his house. The next day we went out with Mel and Bill Worrall, Chris G, Chris Freeman, Bram and others and had a good time.*
Bram is conducting the Festival Ballet at the RFH and Russell's playing in it. With a little help from Bram, Chris and I, Mel and Bill got in free to see Cinderella. Bram told us to meet him at the stage door and said none of us were to say a word. He spun a yarn to the Doorman that we were foreigners from "Up North" who were experiencing London for the first time, had never seen a live orchestra or ballet performance before and didn't have tickets. The Doorman was persuaded to let us in and sat us in a roped off section to one side where we could see the orchestra, half the stage and most of what was going on in the wings.
I went to Chris's in afternoon then on to Bram's party.
Chris S. and I went to hear LSO rehearse Mahler 2 at Ely Cathedral with Russell and Bram – Bram was depping for John Fletcher – it was really great, except that there was a bomb scare during it.

62
DUNWICH

Over rootcorpse and stone,
Whose half-buried shanks
Seem risen ghosts
From the sea-lost cliff,

I stalk into dream-deering.
Silence thumps with my heart
As if some profound thing
Is to be made visible.

...I feel the overlap of lives
And the override of time.
– This heightened life
Will plunge me down
To drown like Dunwich town.

Walking from Dunwich – Jean Lipkin

The day after Izzy had gone to hear the LSO at Ely Cathedral, Bram, Chris and Chris Freeman, a double bassist friend from Redbridge, were getting ready for their camping trip to Dunwich – for it was almost September 2nd, a significant date upon which they had planned to rendezvous.

Chris first ventured to Dunwich with Bram during the Easter Redbridge Youth Orchestra course of 1970 when he was eleven. He went again in 1972 and visited the Dunwich Museum, where he purchased a small book by Allan Jobson, which helped to fill in some of the historical details. The story of a once impressive city lost to the sea stimulated Chris's enquiring mind.

He learned that the Suffolk coastline had altered dramatically over the centuries as the North Sea pounded away at the cliffs, encroaching relentlessly inland. Talking to locals, he listened to legends of lost villages and towns submerged beneath the sea, where churches still stood intact and, it was claimed, the ghostly toll of bells could be heard emanating from the depths. There was still a superstition amongst old fishermen that when the people died they became immortalised as seagulls. By far the largest town to be claimed by the sea was Dunwich.

What initially drew Chris to Dunwich, though, was not the history of a disappearing city, or the awesome evidence of the power of the sea, but because All Saints' graveyard was falling from the crumbling cliffs and depositing human bones on the beach. When he first walked along the shore and looked up to the cliff face, he was as awestruck as a journalist from the *Daily Chronicle*, who wrote in 1904, after a massive fall:

> From the black earth and yellow sand gaunt bones protruded – not one but dozens... I counted a score of fragments of human limbs, there a thigh bone, there a part of a pelvis, and there, perched on a mound of earth and masonry, a broken, toothless skull, the sockets where the eyes had been staring out on the restless waters.

Unfortunately for Chris, the skeletons that fell to the beach did not stay there for long. Many were gathered up by parishioners and loaded into coffins to be reinterred in the newer St. James's churchyard. After each cliff fall, people from Dunwich, together with archaeologists and historians, rescued whatever artefacts they could, many of which are now on display at the Dunwich museum. Human scavengers also turned up looking for relics and carried off the skulls as souvenirs. The bones Chris found were just the few that had been overlooked.

It is thought that Dunwich was once a Roman settlement and coastal defence station. In the seventh century, the Saxon King Sigebert claimed it as the capital of the Kingdom of East Anglia and set about converting the pagan populace to Christianity. He invited Bishop Felix (for whom Felixstowe is named) over from Burgundy to establish a Christian Church and to found a school, one of England's first. After the Norman conquest of 1066, Dunwich grew rapidly. Trade boomed, due to its thriving port. In the thirteenth century, it was granted a royal charter and became a Borough. It is recorded that at this time, Dunwich had a population of around five thousand, possessed eighty large ships, boasted ten churches and as many other religious foundations; there were schools, shops, alehouses, a guildhall, hospitals, and a prison.

However, the sea was already making incursions. Nicholas Comfort writes in his excellent book, *The Lost City of Dunwich*: "...on the night of New Year's Day 1287, a fearsome storm blew up and the sea tore into the cliffs, sweeping away houses, shops, churches, orchards, livestock – and people." Defences were erected against the battering waves, but the port was doomed. A violent storm in the fourteenth century shifted so much shingle into Dunwich harbour that it was completely and irreversibly blocked. Overnight the city's source of wealth disappeared. Goods and revenues went elsewhere. Dunwich fell swiftly into decline, the town shrinking faster than the sea advanced. Merchants and artisans moved away, leaving a poor populace, many of them "holding off starvation by eating the sea peas that grew wild about the town."

By the end of the seventeenth century, of the churches and chapels, only All Saints' remained, with Greyfriars' Monastery standing beside it. A new church, St. James's, was built by subscription in 1832, but as more inhabitants abandoned the village, it became derelict. During the twentieth century, the sea began to carry off the ruins of All Saints' church. The tower fell in 1919, leaving just a single buttress, which was rescued and reset in the graveyard of St. James's in 1922. As the years went by, huge lumps of masonry fell to the beach below, to be engulfed and carried off into the sea. Dunwich had become a tiny village of some hundred and twenty souls: in centuries past it had been a prosperous city that had struck its own coins and traded with many nations.

At the Easter Aldeburgh RYO course of 1973, Chris and Bram once again made their way to Dunwich, together with their friend Chris Freeman. They walked amongst the ruins of Greyfriars' Monastery and through the archway into the disappearing graveyard of All Saints' church. Ahead of them was the edge of the cliff. They stood looking down at the fascinating array of human bones sticking out gruesomely from the stratum beneath. Nearby was a single, isolated gravestone of possibly the last person to be buried at All Saints'. A cold, biting wind blew in from the sea as they squatted to read the engraved inscription:

Sacred
TO THE MEMORY OF
JOHN BRINKLEY
EASEY
WHO DIED SEPTEMBER 2ND
1826
AGED 23 YEARS

They saw that John Brinkley Easey had died on September 2nd, which happened to be the birth date of a member of the RYO, a character by the name of John Peavot, otherwise known as 'Dog'. An idea formed in their minds. They decided that they would return on that very day later in the year to revisit the grave.

So it was that on Saturday September 1st, Bram drove to Cleveland Road, Chris loaded his rucksack and tent into Bram's car, they picked up Chris Freeman and headed off down the A12 to Dunwich. Through the vestiges of Greyfriars' Monastery they walked and pitched their tent right beside the grave of John Brinkley Easey. The evening was spent downing fine pints of Adnams at the 500-year-old public house, The Ship Inn. At closing time they staggered back to the graveyard, crawled a little drunkenly into the tent, and fell into peaceful slumber next to the bones of John Brinkley Easey. In the morning, Chris Freeman stuck his head out of the tent, quite alarmed to see that the cliff edge was but a few yards away. It occurred to him that if nature had called on any one of them in the night, they could easily have fallen, themselves ending up six feet under. He wriggled out on his stomach, peering down through the eerily projecting bones to the sea below.

Hung over and bleary-eyed, the three lads went for a walk along the beach, picking up scattered bones along the way. They spent the rest of September 2nd visiting Dunwich museum then driving into Aldeburgh, where they had a meal at the White Lion. In the evening they returned to The Ship Inn for a few more pints of Adnams. When they arrived back at their tent, a note was discovered pinned to the canvas. "Please go away", it read, "you're not welcome here". But they were leaving the next morning anyway. After another night under canvas, Bram put the bones they had collected into a plastic bag, the tent was taken down, their belongings piled into the car and they departed. However, this was not quite the end of the story.

Two severe storms in the late 1970s followed by a tide two metres above normal caused more erosion, eating five feet further inland. The sea continued to encroach during the 1980s, until by 1990 John Brinkley Easey's gravestone was perilously close to the cliff edge. The parish decided to move it to the safety of St. James's churchyard, but before they could do so, a colossal storm hit Dunwich, causing almost the worst cliff-fall of the twentieth century. Nearly everything that was left of All Saints' churchyard suddenly collapsed to the shore, including what remained of John Brinkley Easey. His tombstone and bones were ultimately carried off to their final resting place – the bed of the North Sea – along with the turf upon which Chris, Bram and Chris Freeman had slept during the two nights of September 1st to September 3rd 1973.

But what happened to the bag of human remains collected on the walk? Surprisingly, they were left in Bram's car. Perhaps Chris meant to pick them up later, but as he was no longer so fanatical about his collection, it went out of his mind. Bram took the carrier bag back to the flat he was renting at the time in Ilford, shoved it under the bed and forgot about it. A few years later, he moved. Whilst packing up, he discovered the bag of bones. He wondered what to do with them. To whom did they belong? Should he have them at all? In retrospect, he thought perhaps he ought to have handed them over to the Police, but he didn't. Instead, he went into the rear garden of his landlady's house, found a spade, dug a hole and buried them behind the garden shed. As far as he knows, they are still there.

While Chris was camping, I was hugging a delicious, anticipatory excitement. I could think of nobody else but Simon. On the day Chris returned, a postcard arrived for me, dated August 31st 1973, from Penrith, Cumberland.

Dear Cath,

Hi! Rattle now rapidly (or otherwise) recovering from the most enormous Cordon Bleu meals served in the hotel you see over. Whatever you like, it is here, enormous lakes, babbling brooks, waterfalls, old farms, stark mountains, the lot: the air is really clear and fresh and we're all sleeping like logs. No music – marvellous!! So we are now off for our après-breakfast (après ski, après Jilly Cooper) hike, 20 miles round Ullswater. Looking forward to seeing you soon, fat and happy, much love and ravishes, Simon

IZZY: September 29th: *I went out with Ashley – no, don't get worried. I'm still going out with Chris and he knows about my seeing Ashley. He's been incredibly kind, sweet and understanding about it all and hasn't taken it out on me in the least. He's threatened to bash Ashley in if he sees him though! Anyway, I met Ashley at 6.00 at Victoria. His hair is now dyed a gingery colour and he wears larger silver earrings but he still looks as yummy as ever. He took me out for a meal. It cost £4.70 – I was flabbergasted, but as Ashley was paying, I wasn't complaining. It made me so happy being with him. Actually I'm very fond of Chris. I think I take him too much for granted, always thinking he'll be around when I need him. He's too nice to me. He painted me an oil picture – really good. It's an impression of Cleveland Road on a dark, damp night and looks very professional.*

ABOVE: Chris at Dunwich, September 2nd 1973. He, Chris Freeman (top) and Bram Tovey (left) camped for two nights beside the grave of John Brinkley Easey.

RIGHT: A photograph of the tombstone of John Brinkley Easey. The tent in which the trio slept can be glimpsed on the left.

In his book *The Lost City of Dunwich*, Nicholas Comfort writes: "Late in 1990, as parishioners prepared to move the stone to safety in St. James's churchyard, a sudden and massive cliff fall swept it to the shore, leaving it buried in a pile of debris."

The Royal Academy of Music in 1970. *Photos by Robert Cooper*
ABOVE: The entrance hall. In the evenings, students queued for vacated rooms in which to practise, waiting for the porters to hand out the keys.
BELOW: The canteen rock cakes were real teeth-breakers, but strangely appealing.

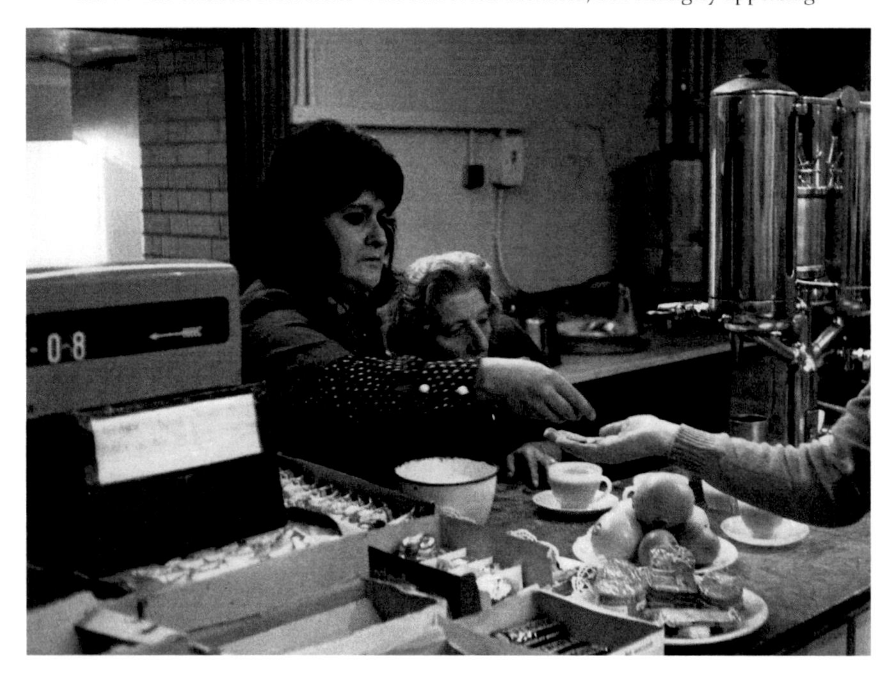

63
LET HER GO

And you have said to me
Any room we share
Will be a place for love.

I Ask You – Jean Lipkin

Simon phoned as soon as he arrived in London and invited me over to the flat in Hammersmith that he and Johnny Martin were renting. Johnny, who had played violin in the NYO, was at the Royal College of Music taking piano as his first study. They lived in Weltje Road (pronounced "Welt-jee"), a turning off King Street. Number forty-six is one of the last houses on the right before the Great West Road intersects, carrying endless streams of vehicles in and out of Central London. The flat was on the first floor of the building, not self-contained, as the stairs and landings were communal. The kitchen was at the back with a bathroom beside it, Johnny's room up a few stairs on the right, and Simon's, the largest room at the front. There was a narrow room next to it occupied by Linda, whom I don't think I ever met.

Johnny cooked roast chicken, carrots and potatoes. I ate as little as I politely could. Dessert was syllabub, Simon's speciality: calorific: problematic. I made myself eat a few spoonfuls, which I swallowed with discomfort.

"This is delicious," I enthused, which in fact it was.

Johnny made a diplomatic exit and Simon asked me to stay. I gained a night pass from Mum.

"Where are you going to sleep?" she asked suspiciously.

"In Linda's room. She's away." She was, but it was Simon's single bed I shared, sleep an afterthought.

I began my second year at the Academy in a state of euphoria, in love with the world. I met Tricia in the foyer. She looked at me searchingly.

"Have you lost more weight?"

"No, I don't think so."

"You're looking twiggier than Twiggy. I mean, are you a cellist or a model? Don't tell me – you're intending to be both."

"I was going to say neither."

An expression of concern crossed her face.

"Don't be a fool. You're a fabulous cellist," she said quietly. "I'll see you later."

Just then, Bram rushed up to me.

"Cathy! What's this I hear about you going out with Simon Rattle? Is it true?"

"Yes!"

"Wow. Well, congratulations to both of you."

"Thanks!"

"I was wondering whether you might play in *Fiddler on the Roof* for me? It's an amateur dramatic society production I've been asked to conduct. Not much money in it. I think they're offering ten quid all in. There'll be a couple of rehearsals and a week of performances. Chris Stearn and Chris Freeman are doing it too."

"Sure. I'd love to."

Chris Stearn, Chris Freeman and I waited on the steps of the Academy each evening for Bram to show up. Somehow the four of us plus double bass, cello and bass trombone squeezed into Bram's car. I sat in the front with my cello between my legs; the two Chris's sat in the back on either side of the double bass, its neck wedged between the front seats and the scroll butted up against the windscreen. I was delegated the task of passing banana sandwiches to Bram to eat as he drove. Accumulated lack of sleep from nights spent with Simon resulted in my concentration shutting down on several occasions during the shows. Bram would hiss at me and prod me with his baton to avoid my missing entries.

Simon and I contrived to see each other as much as we could and talked for hours on the phone. He came over to Cleveland Road, staying overnight, allegedly in the spare bed in Chris's room.

On October 7th, Mum invited us both to one of the Woodford Music Society concerts to hear a piano recital to be given by Murray Perahia.

"It would be great to hear him play," said Simon, "but he probably won't turn up."

"Don't be ridiculous," Mum bridled, "of course he'll turn up."

She drove us to the Sir James Hawkey Hall and parked the car. We sat in the auditorium and waited and waited. And waited. Simon and I thought it hilarious. Mum and the rest of the audience became increasingly restless and annoyed.

Mum told me to stop giggling. Then someone came on stage to make an announcement.

"Mr. Perahia has not arrived. We do not know where he is. We are very sorry about this and will of course refund the cost of your tickets at the box office."

"I don't believe it!" cried Mum indignantly. "How unprofessional. In all the years I've been coming to these concerts, this has never happened." Mum was, I think, more irritated that Simon had been right.

"Well, we might as well go home," she huffed.

I had a better idea. "Simon and I'll walk."

"Walk? But it's miles."

"Only a couple."

"Oh, alright then. Suit yourselves."

It was a warm, late summer evening. As we walked, wrapped in each other's arms, I fell in love. Every cell in my body burst into flower, from the tips of my tingling fingers to the soles of my glowing feet. A riot of dazzling colour blossomed within me. I had never felt so vibrantly, gloriously alive.

We eventually arrived back at Cleveland Road.

"Where on earth have you been?" asked Mum, "It's gone ten o'clock!"

I didn't explain that we'd had to stop every few minutes to kiss, but maybe she knew from the euphoric smile on my face. When later we made love, it was rapturous and tender. Love sealed every crack, filled all emptiness and balmed my sorrows. Snuggled close in my little bed, limbs entwined, our hearts beating together, a serene ecstasy flowed through me; the grace of love. I was happy; so happy.

"Cathy," he whispered.

"Simon."

"I love you."

"I love you too."

"I want to be with you all the time, always."

"And I want to be with you too."

"Will you come and live with me?"

"Yes."

"I've already asked Johnny and he's fine about it."

"What, before you asked me!"

"Oh, Cathy; I love your smile."

"I don't know how I'm going to tell my parents."

"Do you want me to be with you?"

"No. Yes. But no, I have to face them myself."

The next day Simon and I went with his student orchestra to York to give a concert. The programme, for a small string orchestra, included Grieg's *Holberg Suite* and Stravinsky's Concerto in D. I should have been going into the Academy that day, but had no intention of missing a concert with Simon. Knowing the Academy would not release me from a First Band rehearsal, I decided to bunk off and phone in sick, but I didn't dare admit this to Mum. Simon and I kept the concert a secret. As we were getting ready to leave, I heard the familiar, "Wheesht! – I'm listening to the forecast."

My mouth opened before my brain engaged and I was horrified to hear myself saying, "What's the weather going to be like in York?"

Simon looked at me dumbstruck as I covered my mouth with my hand, returning his look with one of deranged panic.

"York?" queried Mum, "Why on earth do you want to know about the weather in York?" Neither of us could think of a convincing explanation.

"Erm, a friend of ours lives there," I mumbled feebly.

She eyed me charily. "Hmm, seems strange to me. When are you coming back today?"

"I'm going to stay at Simon's flat tonight. Is that alright?"

"Well, I suppose so," she sighed, looking at me with hurt disapproval.

Twenty yards from the house, we both shrieked hysterically.

"What made you ask such a silly question, Cath?"

"I don't know – it just splurted out – I can't believe it!"

"You're a nutcase, Animal, but I love you. Come on, we've got a train to catch."

***IZZY: October 1973:** Ashley's going out with a girl for the first time since he met me. Would you believe I felt heartbroken at the news? This is an incredibly selfish attitude as I'm going out with someone as well. It's so hypocritical, I feel I can go out with other blokes, but I feel betrayed when he goes out with a girl. It's not until something's taken from you that you realise how much you miss it. At the time I didn't realise how much Ashley meant to me, but now I long for that happy, loving time we had together 2 years ago. I'm very fond of Chris, though. I've been going out with him for 5 months. It's a long time.*
Went with Chris (brother) to Paxmans and then went on to see Ashley at Dulwich College. Ashley's study is really tiny. It's incredibly old-fashioned, looks as though it hasn't changed since the last century. The walls are paper thin & there's no privacy from the staff as I was soon to find out. Ashley & I were sitting on his hard lumpy bed when who should walk in but Matron. Ashley says she'll report him to his master. He says the boarders are looked after really badly. The meals are atrocious. They're not allowed to smoke, drink, womanise or have long hair, all of which Ashley does. He got permission to go out but had to be in by 10.30. We went to see Sue Sweet, my Pathfinder leader from the summer, who Ashley also knows. Ashley has sewn mink furs onto his trouser legs – looks great. Sue says he looks like a rat catcher. He smoked joints which put him in an idiotic mood for the rest of the evening. Got home at 11.00. Then to bed & many thoughts to ponder over. Life at the moment is confused, uncertain, mainly happy & plenty of love.
Told Chris S. about seeing Ashley. I thought he wouldn't come round but he did, thank God. Went with his Dad to hear him play with Forest Phil at Walthamstow Assembly Hall – a great concert.

Soon after this, Ashley defied his father, ran away from boarding school and asserted his independence. He found himself somewhere to live in Brixton with friends, and made his own way.

After several more nights with Simon, I arrived at the Academy to be handed a note by the porter from Chris, which read, "Phone home. Urgent." I dialled the number.

"Chris? Is everything alright?"

"Oh Cath. Something terrible happened. Dad took a knife to Granny."

"A knife? Oh, my God."

Granny had made one of her disparaging accusations – about putting out the milk bottles of all things – and Dad had gone mad, seized a kitchen knife, pushed Granny into a corner and threatened to kill her. A torrent of abuse spewed from his mouth; shocking words he had never used in the house before – every vile obscenity he could think of. Granny shrieked and squealed; Mum shouted as loudly as she ever had. "Stop it, Derek. Stop." He hit out at her too. Izzy heard the blood-curdling cries from her bedroom and ran downstairs screaming.

"Don't be such a fucking baby, Christopher," yelled Dad, thinking it was Chris who was screaming. Chris and Mum grappled with him and the knife fell to the floor – and all of this before breakfast.

"What's happened now?"

"Dad left the house, nearly breaking the front door. Granny's crying – it's horrible. Mum's comforting her."

"Should I come over now?"

"There's nothing you could do. God knows what it's going to be like tonight."

"Where's Izzy?"

"Gone to school."

Izzy had sobbed all the way there, from the house to the station and on the train to Loughton, but couldn't tell anyone why she was so upset.

"Shouldn't you be at school, Chris?"

"I'll go in this afternoon."

"Oh, Chris."

"Yeah, I know. I guess it was bound to happen one of these days."

"I'll be home at six o'clock."

I hung up and sat on the steps by the vending machine weeping. Simon held me in his arms.

"Oh, Animal, I'm so sorry. Everything seems to happen to you."

"It didn't happen to me, I wasn't there," I sobbed. "It's just my screwed up family. Oh poor Izzy; poor Chris."

Dad came home at the usual time and nothing was said. The atmosphere inside the house was fully charged. Dad maintained a menacing silence; Granny kept to her room and knitted with a vengeance.

> ***IZZY:*** *A foul row at home. I was really scared. It was the most horrifying experience I've ever had. I haven't been able to get it out of my mind.*

I wrote to Bill Worrall at Leeds College of Music:

> There have been rather disastrous problems at home ending in civil war just about. No, it was pretty awful – Dad hitting Granny and Mum, Mum in hysterics, Izzy screaming the place down, all of which is no exaggeration. Things have far from sorted themselves out since then. In fact the tension in this household has become so unbearable that I've decided to definitely move out and move in with Simon. It's really strange, but the minute I come into this house, even if I've been quite happy during the day, I turn argumentative and hostile towards my parents, and Granny in particular. I haven't broached the subject yet with my parents, but I don't think it will come as much of a surprise.
>
> We all went to Lowri's party last night, we being Izzy, Chris Stearn, Chris Giles, Martin Koch, me and Simon, Melly, Clive Miller and various others – in fact hundreds of others but I doubt you'd have known anyone else. It was quite a laugh except that Chris Stearn got completely pissed and was puking up all the way home, which wasn't exactly pleasant. In fact, I was so revolted that my stomach wouldn't take it and I was sick in the night even though I hadn't drunk a drop – I've completely given up alcohol mainly because I much prefer Britvic orange juice. Anyway, I'm sorry, I must go and practise the Rococo Variations.
>
> Write soon (to new address, remember).

I found Mum in Granny's room with Granny. I told them I wanted to leave home and was going to move in with Simon. Mum didn't argue with me, but she was worried and looked sad.

"How do you think you're going to afford to live away from home?" she asked.

I only had my scholarship money of £100 a year and no maintenance grant, as I lived in London.

"I'll manage. I've got a bit of teaching and there are always playing jobs."

"But you're supposed to be studying."

"I will study."

"Well, I don't know. It's all rather sudden, isn't it?"

Granny carried on knitting. Clickety clack clickety clack.

"Och, let her go," she said, without looking up, "it will all be good experience."

That was Granny: blunt and to the point. Silently, I thanked her.

Mum came through with me to the living room to tell Dad. He went ballistic.

"You can't go. I won't let you. It's not right."

"Oh Derek, don't get angry," Mum implored.

I tried to stem his fury by telling him it wouldn't be permanent. I would probably be back at Christmas. I knew I was lying.

"Well, I'm not staying to say goodbye."

He stormed out of the house, slamming the front door behind him. I winced. (When he returned, after I had gone, he declared that he would never enter my room again and announced that he was going to insist that Simon and I married, to which Mum replied, "Don't be so ridiculous, Derek.")

"Cath-er-reen, come here a minute," called Granny from the hall as I was heading upstairs to pack.

"Men!" she spat, looking accusingly at the front door before turning back into her room. I followed her. She lifted her knitting from her armchair and sat down. "Before you go, I've something to say to you. Sit down there beside me." I perched on the footstool by her feet.

"I've been thinking – next year you'll be eighteen. Now listen. Always exercise your right to vote. It's been a long, hard struggle, the fight for equal franchise. Women have been imprisoned and died for it. I'm not telling you who to vote for – just make sure you vote. For it's a crime not to. And Cath-er-reen, I have two predictions. I'll not live to see them, but you maybe will. Listen now. This Queen will be the last British monarch and Socialism will come. Aye, it will one of these days. Go on, off ye go. I'll be seeing you."

I found Chris in his room. "What's going on downstairs?" he asked.

"Chris, I'm going to live with Simon. I've just told them."

"Didn't go down too well, eh?"

"Are you and Izzy going to be alright? I feel bad about leaving you."

"It's going to be horrible without you, Cath, but you have to go – and Simon's a really nice bloke."

"You can come and stay with us and I'll see you at the Academy."

"It'll be lonely without you in the next room."

"Chris, did you ever realise that I didn't always sleep alone?"

"Of course I did! The skulls in my display cases rattled when you were up to it."

"They didn't!"

"No, not really, but I'm not daft." We laughed.

"When are you off?"

"Tonight."

"I'll walk with you to the station."

Izzy understood completely. "I have to be with Simon," I told her, "I can't stay here any longer."

"You go," she said emphatically. "I can't wait to get out of this place myself. Only another year and I'll be at university."

"Have you decided which one?"

"As far away as possible."

"I'll see you at *Concerti* rehearsals and I'll be back to teach my pupils. You and Chris Stearn, and Chris can come and visit me and Simon in Hammersmith any time you want."

"But we're at school, Cath."

"In the holidays, then. Weekends."

"I hope you'll be really happy," said Izzy.

"I will, I am. We'll speak on the phone. I'll let you know when all the concerts are at the Academy."

As I was packing, Mum came into my room and sat on the bed. She seemed so unhappy and forlorn – lost somehow. I could feel it but there was no way to respond. The gulf between us was miles wide, and the abyss too deep to be bridged now. To my horror, she started talking about contraception.

"Mum," I interrupted, "I've been going to the family planning clinic since I was sixteen."

"Have you?"

"Yes."

"You didn't tell me."

"No," I replied unyieldingly, turning away from her hurt and bafflement. For some minutes she continued to sit while I carried on packing. The silence was stifling – a mother and daughter entirely unable to connect. Failure and despair defeated us both. She left without saying another word.

I took a last look around my room – the place where Izzy, Chris and I had slept together when we were small; the room I'd had to bribe Chris to let me have; the sink that I had hung over so many nights coughing and gasping; above, the mirror that had been my witness, where I had squeezed spots, tried on make-up and practised looking cool smoking; my bed; the carpet where François lost his virginity; my drawer of secret writing, now empty. I stood by the window looking out on my garden knowing that nobody would tend it after I had gone. I left the posters on the walls; my collection of knick-knacks, glass ornaments, miniature vases and brass candlesticks; my schoolbooks, asthma charts and most of my clothes, none of which fitted me any more. Goodbye, room.

I picked up my bags, went through the door to Chris's room and took a long look at his museum. It was amazing how much he had collected.

"I'll miss all of this," I said wistfully.

"Are you off, then?"

"Yes."

"I'll get Izzy."

The three of us left the house, walked along Cleveland Road, turned right into George Lane and walked down to South Woodford station.

We stopped and looked at each other.

"Bye, Izzy," I said.

"Bye, then. Have fun."

"Bye, Chris."

"See you around."

We couldn't hug, of course not, but there was a mass of love in our eyes as we waved goodbye.

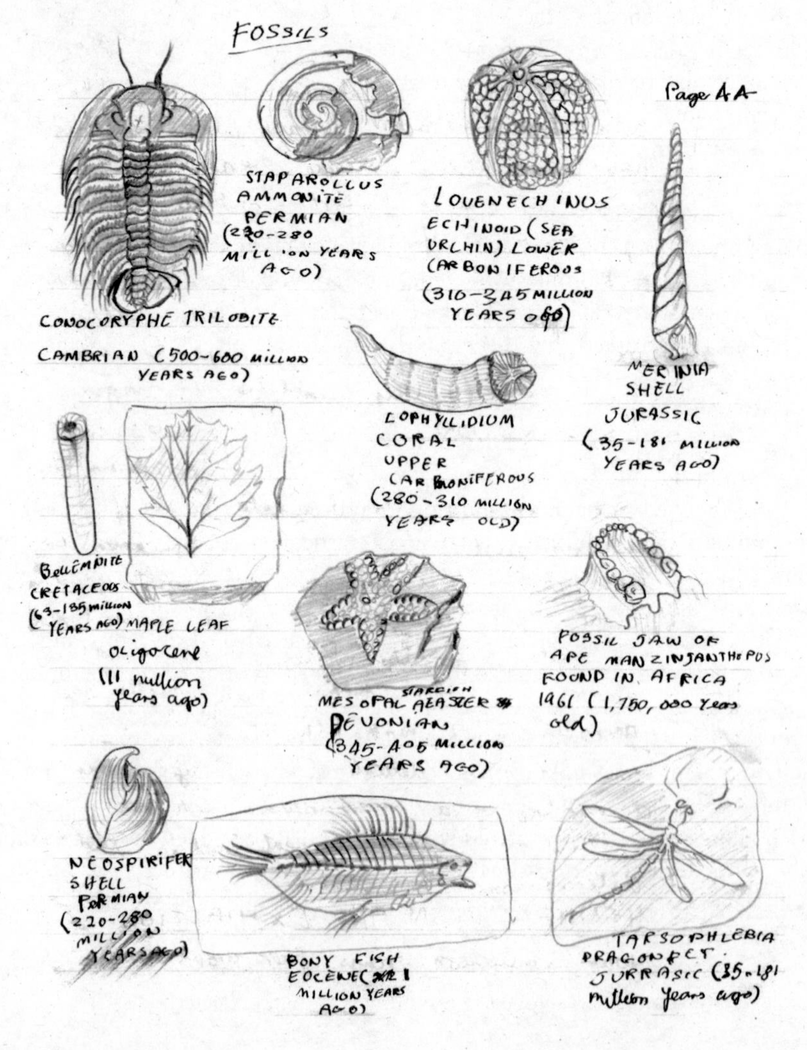

Izzy, Chris Stearn and Chris Giles in the back garden of Cleveland Road.

END OF PART TWO

PART THREE

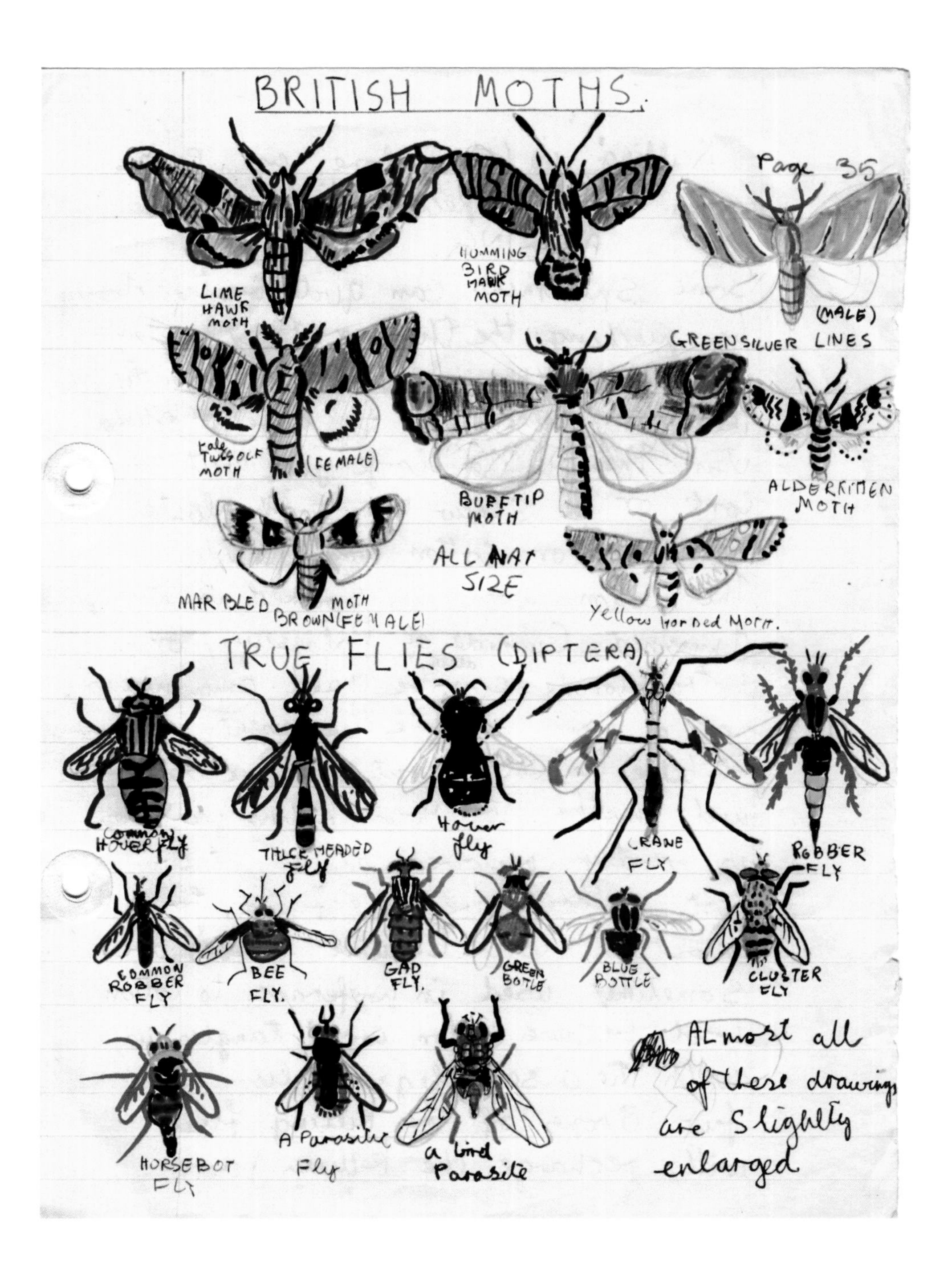

BRITISH MOTHS.
Page 35
LIME HAWK MOTH
HUMMING BIRD HAWK MOTH
(MALE)
GREENSILVER LINES
Pale Tussolf MOTH
(FEMALE)
BUFFTIP MOTH
ALDERKITTEN MOTH
ALL NAT SIZE
MARBLED BROWN (FEMALE) MOTH
Yellow horned Moth.
TRUE FLIES (DIPTERA)
COMMON HOVER FLY
THICK HEADED FLY
Hover fly
CRANE FLY
ROBBER FLY
COMMON ROBBER FLY
BEE FLY.
GAD FLY.
GREEN BOTTLE
BLUE BOTTLE
CLUSTER FLY
HORSEBOT FLY
A Parasitic Fly
a bird Parasite
ALmost all of these drawings are Slightly enlarged

A school photo of Chris taken in his lower sixth year. He admitted that he deliberately pulled a cynical, contemptuous look for the camera. Such a steely-eyed expression was not at all typical of Chris, but he was pleased with the result.

64
46, WELTJE ROAD

There's a strange frenzy in my head,
of birds flying,
each particle circulating on its own.
Is the one I love everywhere?

A Community of the Spirit – Rumi

I knew I would never go back to live at Cleveland Road. To be in charge of my own life was something I had craved for a long time. At last I had escaped from Dad's gloomy presence and Granny's timetable. Now I could eat as little as I pleased without reprimand. I would no longer have to witness Mum's suffering, or hear her strained voice when I turned down offers of food. Nor would I need to invent any more eating excuses, or cringe as I listened to my artificially cheery voice reassuring her that I was well nourished. I was so weary of lying to conceal my addiction.

Getting away from the tension at home was liberating. Living with Simon was joyous; being loved by him gave me self-belief. To fall asleep hugged together and wake flesh to flesh was a daily miracle. It wasn't a dream, though; it was real and it was forever; nobody could have convinced me otherwise.

Simon was not the most practical of people, but I was more than willing to take on the role of household organiser. I walked gladly to King Street launderette where I watched the garments of our shared life circling in the washing machine, tumbling together in the drier. As I folded sheets, shook out pillowcases and paired socks, I saw myself as a blissfully happy new bride, and indeed that is how I felt. My application to domestic tasks was my ticket to the adult world where I basked in the sensation of independence.

We both shopped, but neither of us bothered to clean. Without vacuum cleaner, mop or inclination, we didn't notice the dust and dirt. When Mum came over, she was horrified.

"Don't you ever wash the kitchen floor?"

On inspection, I had to agree that it was filthy.

"We don't have a mop."

"You don't need one. Get on your knees and scrub. At least once a week," she added.

Simon made ratatouille. That and syllabub were his two specialities. I hadn't tasted aubergines, peppers or courgettes before; even mushrooms and garlic were unfamiliar. Granny's Scottish fare did not embrace such outlandish ingredients. One day Simon bought some mangoes. I cut into the succulent, yellow-orange flesh and was surprised to find a huge flat stone inside. A delicious, exotic perfume wafted into the air. I inhaled deeply.

"Mmmm. It reminds me so much of something else. I can't think what it is."

We both put our noses to the fruit, trying to identify the smell.

"Sex," declared Simon.

"Yes! Of course."

Sex – that sweet, rampant fragrance that filled our nights with giddy waves of desire. Mango was the flavour of our lovemaking.

My obsession with food meant that I spent a lot of time in the kitchen cooking. I asked Granny for recipes. 'Beef olives' was one: get some good-quality beefsteak and bash it until flattened: next, make a dumpling mixture with flour, grated suet, finely chopped onions and parsley mixed with a little milk, salt, water and egg: shape the dough into balls, wrap with beef and roll in a mix of flour and Bisto; then arrange the beef olives in a casserole dish, cover with stock, add a dessertspoon of vinegar, two bay leaves, bring to the boil, put the lid on and simmer in the oven at a medium to low temperature for about two hours.

I placed the raw meat on the table and started to beat it vigorously with the rolling pin.

"What on earth are you doing?" called Simon.

"Just a spot of DIY on a dead cow," I called back.

He stood in the doorway looking amused.

"Well, I hope I never get on the wrong side of you!"

"You'd better not," I warned, wielding the rolling pin.

Two hours later, I took the casserole out of the oven, tasted a tiny spoonful of the rich gravy and sat down to watch Simon eat. He knew by now that I wouldn't eat anything and didn't quiz me about it.

"You don't know what you're missing, Animal – this is delicious."

"Thank you. But it's one of Granny's recipes, not mine."

"You cooked it, though."

I began to make up my own dishes, some more successful than others. Simon ate the disasters as well as the winners without complaint. My desserts usually turned out well, as I seemed to have a knack with pastry-making. I had bought some cooking apples and was going to make an apple pie when Simon decided he wanted to have a go. I said I'd show him how to make a simple crumble.

We each took a bowl and measured out the ingredients.

"Now, watch me. Put your hands in the bowl and gradually work the butter into the flour and sugar. Be careful not to squash the butter; rub it gently between your fingertips and lift your hands as you do, to keep air and lightness in the texture."

But despite Simon having such wonderful, expressive hands, he was hopeless at making crumble.

"Keep it light, Simon. Just use your fingertips. You're not making snowballs."

It was our own version of *The Generation Game*. We compared the two, and I couldn't help but laugh. Mine looked like fresh breadcrumbs, his, unevenly mixed lumps.

"What went wrong with it?" he asked.

"Stick to conducting, Simon. I'll throw this out for the birds."

That sent Simon into silly mode. Hands still covered in flour, he picked me up and carried me to the window.

"Put me down," I shrieked.

"No, it's out of the window with you." He slung me, kicking and struggling, over his left shoulder, whilst pushing the sash window up with his right hand.

"Stop, Simon, stop," I screamed as he manoeuvred me onto the windowsill. For a ghastly moment I was really frightened that Simon would lose his hold on me and I would topple out and plunge to the ground way below. I grabbed hold of the freestanding cupboard and the whole thing came crashing down. Tins, packets, pots and pans fell in an avalanche around us. We both collapsed on the kitchen floor in hysterics. Simon's silliness sometimes went a little too far.

In the flat above us lived two sisters, Claudine and Pat. Claudine was tall and waif-like with a mass of long auburn curls. She floated around elegantly and worked as a sales assistant in the trendy clothes store, 'Che Guevara', in Kensington. Pat was more down to earth with short dark hair and pretty features. Their personalities suited their names. They were both partial to a good natter, which meant that we were immediate friends.

"Anyone there?" called Pat, rapping at the door.

"Just me. Come on in."

"I'm glad I've caught you, Cathy. I must talk to you about something."

"Sure. What is it?"

"I hope you're not going to be shocked," she said, sitting down beside me on the floor. "The thing is; I'm having an affair with my boss. He's married and I suppose it's all rather sordid, but I thought you should know because he visits me here during the day for obvious reasons. He's coming over this afternoon in fact."

"I wondered why you weren't at work."

"You must think I'm an awful slut."

"No, I don't. I just hope you don't get hurt. You don't seem very happy at the moment. Are you OK?"

"Oh, it gets me down sometimes. You know, he says he's never felt this way about anyone before and his life would be meaningless without me, and in the next breath he says he'll never leave his wife."

"But if he truly loves you, don't you think in time he will leave her?"

"No," she sighed, "he's too afraid of losing everything in a divorce. Anyway, there's no such thing as true love."

"Oh, but there is!" The way she looked at me somewhat dampened my fervour. She shifted position, folded her arms around her knees and said musingly, "I sometimes wonder what would happen if his wife discovered what was going on and kicked him out. Would he want to be with me then?"

"Well of course he would."

"Hmm, I don't know. More likely to marry some other rich woman and find another secretary to screw. Anyway, now you know," she said, closing the subject. "Do you and Simon sleep in that single bed?" she asked.

I looked over at our unmade heap of sheets and blankets.

"Yes, we do. Simon sleeps on the wall side and I slot in beside him and hang on. I haven't fallen out yet."

"Well, look at you – you can't take up more than a few inches of bed space. I reckon you'd fit comfortably into a shoe box."

I saw Pat's lover arrive, climb out of his smart car, shrug himself into a well-tailored overcoat, reach across the seat for his briefcase and walk towards our house. He cast a distasteful look at the twelve-foot high privet hedge, shook his head at the gate hanging off its hinges and strode to the front door. I heard Pat hurtling downstairs to answer the bell and wondered what she saw in him; a middle-aged, married businessman with only an unwritten sexual contract to offer. Surely love must be one of the clauses?

Downstairs and spilling into the basement were the Australians. I didn't know any of them individually because they kept changing, the flat merely a stopping off place for Aussies passing through London. They were all muscular, loud and tanned, even in winter. They played music at top volume and had wild parties all too frequently. In our room, two levels up from the basement, their music arrived at a reasonable volume; music that I absorbed absent-mindedly. Later in my life, I realised I had first heard Elton John, Stevie Wonder, Led Zeppelin, Pink Floyd and The Who at Weltje Road; but good or bad, it drove us demented when it went on all night.

There was a payphone in the hall downstairs, shared by all. I wonder now how anyone managed to get hold of us. Messages were rarely passed on and there were so many scribbled notes on the wall, it was impossible to know whether they were old or recent. The telephone was still the unrivalled miracle of modern communication and expensive to use, yet we managed without difficulty to run the timetables of life efficiently. At the Academy there was a pigeonhole system – a shelved wall divided into boxes marked alphabetically – where anyone could deposit or collect a note or letter. It acted as our main switchboard and worked well.

We didn't have a television and it wouldn't have occurred to us to rent one. The radio, tuned to BBC Radio Three, was our companion. It had only to be switched on for two seconds for Simon to name the composer, piece, movement, and probably bar number if I had asked him. It never ceased to amaze me. I thought I had listened to a lot of music, but Simon seemed to be familiar with every piece ever written. No wonder he was so enthusiastic about new music, eager to lap up sounds he hadn't heard before.

Bill Worrall, the boy I had met at Wortley, was the first person to write to me at my new address:

> I've just finished a piece for cello and piano. I think I'll be awfully romantic and dedicate it to you – that is if you want it dedicated to you. If you've got any free time I'd like to try it through with you. It's quite short. If not, I'll give you the parts and you can try it with Simon. It's quite easy but you've got to play with lots of feeling, of course. Actually I'm quite pleased with it so I hope you like it. I really loved your playing on Saturday – it makes me feel my piece is a bit simple for you. By the way, don't worry about living on under £2 a week – I only spent £17 my first week.

From me to Bill:

> Hi there!
>
> Thanks a load for your letter. I could read it just about. Your piece is gorgeous. Don't ever think it's worthless or even too easy for me. As far as I'm concerned, no piece is easy – every piece has its difficulties, if not in technique, then in interpretation, and to play anything well one has to be sincere about it. Do you feel like giving the piece its first performance either at the WMA reunion or our musical evening in March? When are you next back in London? Give us a ring when you arrive and keep working hard and enjoy yourself.

One day, a small parcel arrived, addressed to Simon.

"This looks exciting. What is it? An early Christmas present?" I asked.

"Ah," he responded, "they've arrived."

I watched as he opened the package. A box of five hundred condoms!

"Simon! We'll never get through all those!"

"Want a bet?" he said, grabbing me then and there.

Afterwards we talked about children.

"I can't wait to have a baby," I said longingly.

"I know, Cath, but not now."

"No, I suppose."

"We will, though, when the time is right. I'd love to have children with you. Beautiful little golden-haired girls."

"No, little boys with mops of curly hair."

"One of each, perhaps?"

"How about two of each? I've always wanted four children."

We were quiet for a while, I contemplating future children with Simon.

"Cathy?"

"Mmm."

"I've been offered a job."

"A job?" I asked, alerted.

"Yes. Maurice Handford has asked me to be assistant conductor of his orchestra in Calgary."

"Calgary! But that's… where is it, in fact?"

"Canada."

"Oh." *Oh my God! Canada!*

"Look, this is a huge thing to ask, and you'll have to think about it, but I won't accept the job unless you'll come with me."

"I'll come with you," I said at once, relieved.

"You haven't thought about it yet," he said, tickling me.

"I have," I replied, wriggling closer to him.

"Be serious, Animal. I'm asking you to leave the Academy, leave your family, leave the country for God's sake. Without knowing what there is for you out there. And we'd also have to get married."

"Married?"

"Yes." Oh, Simon, I thought, I'd marry you whether we go to Canada or not. It wouldn't bother me at all to leave the Academy; I've already left home; Izzy and Chris would come and visit; I'd come back to see them; I just want to be with you, wherever you are. But I didn't say any of that.

He went on: "I know you're not keen on matrimony, but if we go, it would make things much easier if we were married."

"Of course I'll marry you, Simon." *And why do you think I'm not keen on matrimony?*

He hugged me. "That's all I need to know."

"Tell me about the job."

We talked. I wasn't keen on the 'assistant' conductor aspect.

"You should be the principal conductor of your own orchestra," I told him.

"It doesn't work like that, Cath."

"You could make it work. Any orchestra in the world would love you to be their conductor."

"You might love me, Animal, but I can assure you, they wouldn't. I'm just not good enough and I have far too much to learn."

"Not good enough? Simon, you're – "

"Shhh," he said, kissing me.

"Let's use another of those condoms," I suggested.

I didn't tell Simon that I hadn't had a period for three months. I'd had a test done at the chemist's and knew I wasn't pregnant. Simon asked if I would go back on the pill for safety, but I found excuses, fearful that it would cause me to gain weight. I said it used to make me feel sick, I didn't like the thought, and so on. All rubbish. Addicts' lies. I stepped out of bed, stretched my arms above my head and twirled around happily. He lay in bed watching me.

"God, my hair's like a bird's nest! I should plait it before we make love."

"No, I like it loose. Anyway, it looks more like candyfloss, soft and fluffy like you." I slipped into Simon's shirt and smiled at him. "Cup of tea?"

"You move so gracefully, Cathy. You should have been a dancer."

"A dancer? Me? You must be imagining things. Still, they say that love is blind."

"Come here you." I knelt by the bed.

He curled his fingers into my hair. "Look at me," he said, "you're beautiful, graceful and gorgeous and I love you. OK?"

"I love you too," I said softly.

Simon gave Maurice Handford's offer serious consideration, but decided not to accept it. We stayed in London and did not get married.

There was one picture in our room, which Simon had bought – a framed print of Hieronymus Bosch's triptych, *The Garden of Earthly Delights*. It is an astonishing work, wildly imaginative, meticulously detailed, nightmarish and futuristic. Packed with lurid symbolism, it is original and innovative, and appears ahead of our time even now. Astoundingly, it was painted around 1500. There were times when I found it almost too vivid to look at.

We visited the Tate Gallery where Simon introduced me to the work of Salvador

Dalí. I noticed an uncanny similarity to the imagery of Bosch, yet Dalí was born four hundred years after *The Garden of Earthly Delights* was painted. Surrealism was not such a modern concept after all, I thought. On the same day, we went to see *Paper Moon*, a touching film starring Ryan O'Neal and his young daughter, Tatum. Simon held my hand through the whole movie. I felt almost overwhelmed by the love I felt for him.

We went frequently to the ICA (Institute of Contemporary Arts) on The Mall, Simon always interested to watch the latest off-beat films, none of which came out on general release. We saw some very weird movies. In one I remember seeing some rather beautiful kaleidoscopic images that seemed to be underwater collages of sea creatures and plants, until Simon turned to me and whispered, "Good God, Cathy, we're looking at erect penises!" So we were. I watched, slightly shocked and fascinated, with Simon sitting beside me stifling giggles.

John Spencer soon recovered from his disappointment over me and we kept in touch. What neither of us, nor Izzy, realised at the time was that he had picked the wrong twin. I was simply the conduit that led him from FSC into our lives. He came to know Chris, our Redbridge and NYO friends and, of course, the Turners. He and Melanie went out together for a while, and it was Melanie who drew Izzy and John together years later, having felt intuitively that they belonged with each other; but as Lysander says in *A Midsummer Night's Dream*, "The course of true love never did run smooth".

John sent me the poems he had written in August. He dedicated the first three "To my dear, lovely and much valued friend, Cathy Giles – with much love and thought." One of them, a little rambling, ends like this:

> Tell me what disguise you wear
> How you paint yourself so white and red
> That your cheeks should be so lovely
> Your feet so small
> As to be barely visible
> Under your flowered robe.

'Feet so small'! Obviously, I thought, he couldn't be referring to me with my huge feet, but the 'flowered robe' made sense. In the early seventies, my wardrobe consisted of a couple of pairs of flared bell-bottomed cotton trousers, which were known as 'loons'; a red-and-blue-striped second-hand rugby shirt, which I wore most of the time; a multi-coloured patchwork maxi skirt, a calico midi skirt – both of which I made myself; a maroon T-shirt with long flared sleeves that tied at the wrist; a patchwork jacket (another of my creations) and the obligatory Afghan coat. We all wore those, which resulted in a whole generation of teenagers smelling of goat. My footwear consisted of a pair of black knee-length platform boots, white cork-soled extremely high sandals and a pair of plimsolls. Izzy, our girlfriends and I shopped at Kensington market – a warren of makeshift, crammed-together stalls selling cheap Indian-style kaftans, wrap-around colourfully-printed cotton skirts, loons, hot-pants,

Afghan coats and ridiculously inexpensive jewellery. I had dozens of strings of tiny glass or plastic beads, pendants of suns and Anchs, 'Smiley' and CND badges. We browsed around Biba on the way back to South Kensington tube, trying on make-up and perfume, but rarely buying anything. Laura Ashley was also fashionable at this time, but the designs were a little too twee, polite and expensive for us. Simon didn't accompany us on such expeditions. He wasn't remotely interested in clothes, only buying things when he had to, usually in 'pairple', his favourite colour.

"To Cathy – an important human being in my Life" wrote John at the top of this one, which begins:

> You whose body is in such dire want
> How can you endure?
> Doubly tormented
> By a want within and a want from without.
>
> Love and Friendship walked by
> Arm in arm and said:
> Truly
> Her life is a thin membrane
> Stretched taut like a drum-skin
> Between this and that –

He was seventeen then, just a couple of months older than Izzy and me. Adolescent the poems may be, but reading them now, his concern for me is touching. Few people have kept any of my letters, so I can only guess from the replies what I might have been writing about. In this letter, John tries to elucidate his concept of me:

> I think one of your main problems is that you are too involved with yourself and that you are constantly trying to analyse everything that you think and do, and this obviously leads you into tighter and tighter circles. When I say you're too involved with yourself I don't mean you're self-centred, vain or conceited, but that you're just too bound up with yourself and your largely imaginary problems. You say in your letter that either something's wrong with you, or that you're two people in one. Well, I don't think either of those reasons is in any way remotely connected with your problem. Your problems are that you (subconsciously) feel people only want to know you because of your very good ability to play the cello, and that the rest of you they couldn't care about. Well, I for one would like to know what goes on in your head, and wish you would pull down some of your barriers and let yourself flow out a little. It would be really nice one day to get to know you.
>
> One last thing about you and Simon – As, obviously, it is impossible to meet him – or probably anyone – on all mental planes, don't let those parts of you which aren't being contacted and communicated with be submerged and suffocated. They are so important for making one be a full human being, aware of the world in which we live. I don't think I have to stress how important it is that you don't lose sight of, (thereby letting yourself be manipulated) the various driving forces and powers behind our society and the effect they have.
>
> P.S. Write or phone soon with details of concert and your philosophy of Life.

Did John think I was slacking politically? Neither Simon nor I were slacking musically. I played Tchaikovsky's *Rococo Variations* with *Concerti Allegri*, conducted by Bram, in November 1973, which John came to. The concert also included Brahms's second symphony and Paul Hart's composition *The Light of India* (or 'The Karnapooli'), which was a rather odd work; a sort of percussion concerto and not one of his best, I have to say. However, the Indian restaurant in Gants Hill, after which the piece was named, kept the concert poster displayed in their window for years. Cleveland Road hosted the after-concert party, for which Chris had, as expected, brewed vast quantities of beer. His home-brew was becoming quite famous, in particular for its alcoholic potency.

Bram and I performed the *Rococo Variations* again at the Academy a couple of weeks later. I was also preparing for the International Tchaikovsky competition, to be held in Moscow in May. The number of pieces I had to learn was enormous: as well as the *Rococo*, Tchaikovsky's other famous cello piece, *Pezzo Capriccioso*, was included – a tricky showpiece that goes at break-neck speed. Plus there were unknown contemporary works to learn, some unaccompanied Bach, various sonatas and the fiendishly difficult Prokofieff *Sinfonia Concertante*. I was privileged to be contending. My selection was mainly due to a highly praising reference from the composer, Dr. Alan Bush, who had known me since I first went to Wortley summer school. Although neglected by the British musical establishment, he was celebrated in the USSR. His word was the open sesame to the 'Iron Curtain' and I was invited in. I had no idea of the implications; that I would be representing the Academy, Great Britain even. I just went along with Florrie's plans for my career and followed instructions.

Bram and Simon were both on the advanced conducting course at the Academy, and Simon, through me, became involved with *Concerti Allegri*, playing percussion, timpani and even violin. He sat at the back of the seconds with Izzy, who said that he made a dreadful noise but all the notes were in the right place. In one concert, when the violins were divided into three sections for *Sabre Dance*, I looked over to see Izzy in helpless hysterics. The third violins play the off beats, the tempo is very fast, and Simon's perfectly timed, enthusiastically hacked chords rendered Izzy almost incapable of keeping her bow on the strings. In the same concert we played Ravel's *Bolero*. The piece requires a saxophone, but as we didn't have a saxophonist in the orchestra, Bram gave Chris the part to play on the horn. He wrote it out for him with the message, "'Woe to him that splits' (Deuteronomy)". Chris managed to make the horn sound remarkably similar to a tenor sax by using a raspy vibrato and sultry, jazz overtones. He stuck the manuscript paper on which Bram had written the *Bolero* extract onto his bedroom door, where it remained, along with a card that read:

SEX APPEAL
GIVE GENEROUSLY

Simon was busy at the Academy with the opera group and the conducting course. He also rehearsed his student orchestra most Sundays, conducted the Merseyside Youth Orchestra, studied scores, read, went to concerts, socialised, and still had time for us. We played cello and piano sonatas together, formed a piano trio with Paul Willey and participated in umpteen groups assembled for one-off performances. Our musical life was a large part of our relationship.

The day after my performance of the *Rococo Variations*, Simon conducted Mahler's second symphony with his student orchestra and chorus. Several influential people came to hear the performance, including Martin Campbell-White from the music agency, Harold Holt. Martin was so impressed that he offered to represent Simon straight away and has been his agent ever since. The concert was a triumph for Simon and for all of us involved. It was music making of rare quality, charged with the phenomenal potency of youth. Many of us were not yet twenty.

My friend from the NYO, Louise Williams, became a student at the Academy at the start of my second year and asked me to join her string quartet. She invited Ruth Crouch, who had also been a member of the NYO, to play second violin, and Charles Pollard, viola. Charles Pollard now lived with Johnny, Simon and me at Weltje Road, the elusive Linda having moved out. He owned a car, was fanatical about practice and very serious about the quartet. He thought I should practise more, persuaded me to get up early and by half past seven we were driving to the Academy. There was almost nowhere to practise at the Academy during the day, but when the doors opened at eight o'clock, students could use the rooms until a professor turned up to teach. The porter handed over the keys, and, being first, we picked the best rooms. My preference was the largest room on the first floor. It was hung with heavy oil paintings of high-browed, grim-faced characters. On one wall was a large gilt-framed mirror. Charles told me I needed to "find my sound" and Florrie insisted I "look in the glass" to practise bow control and right arm technique. I played long open strings disconsolately, watching in the mirror to keep the bow absolutely straight. I pushed myself to keep going, working constructively on one level, restless and despondent on another. The arrival of a professor was always something of a relief.

65
CHRISTMAS APART

Narcotics cannot still the Tooth
That nibbles at the soul –

This World is not Conclusion – Emily Dickinson

Simon left for Liverpool the week before Christmas. I did not expect an invitation from Simon's parents; they assumed I would be spending Christmas with my family, as did Simon. I saw him off at Euston and made my way back to Weltje Road. The flat was empty – Charles and Johnny had gone home too. In the fridge, I found a note:

Through thick and (particularly) thin I LOVE YOU, Cathy

Tucked into the bedclothes was this:

To a little animal who has captured my heart
I love you – always
Simon

I didn't know whether to laugh or cry. I tried to practise, with little enthusiasm or motivation. In fact, practice was becoming a struggle. It exhausted me; I ran out of energy and lost my concentration. I went into Johnny's room to play the piano, but could only stare at the keys. Then I wandered abstractedly through to the kitchen. It was dark now and I could see my reflection in the window. Yes, I was thin: nearly perfectly thin, I thought; just a few more pounds for safety, to keep in reserve. I re-tuned the radio to Radio One and started dancing to pop songs, watching my movements in the window. The reflected figure didn't appear to be me; she was a stranger, a slender dancer, the shadow I had dreamt of. Was this the person Simon saw? She didn't look clumsy, disjointed or cumbersome, the ugly duckling I thought myself to be. Her arms moved gracefully, her hips swayed gently, her hair flowed around her shoulders, her waist was tiny – she seemed almost fragile. I shook myself out of my daydreaming, switched off the music and stood still, dimly aware of the traffic thundering by, the vibration of the house, a blood vessel pulsing in my neck; my cold body.

The phone rang.

"Hi, Cath. It's Chris."

"Oh, hi there. How are things?"

"Fine. Has Simon gone now?"

"Yes, unfortunately."

"I thought you might be feeling a bit lonely."

"I am. Daft really. He only went a few hours ago and I'm missing him like mad."

"What are you doing tomorrow? Shall we go Christmas shopping?"

"Oh yes, that would be great. Hey, why don't you come over here now? Stay the night. Then we'll have the whole day tomorrow."

"Yeah, OK. Why not?"

"See you soon then."

I remember the two of us sitting cross-legged in front of the electric fire with *The Prophet* by Kahlil Gibran – an insightful little book that Simon had introduced to me – and taking turns reading the words of wisdom. It was I who read the chapter that begins: "Speak to me of Children."

> And he said:
> Your children are not your children.
> They are the sons and daughters of Life's longing for itself.
> They come through you but not from you,
> And though they are with you yet they belong not to you.
>
> You may give them your love but not your thoughts,
> For they have their own thoughts.
> You may house their bodies but not their souls,
> For their souls dwell in the house of tomorrow, which you cannot visit, not even in your dreams.
> You may strive to be like them, but seek not to make them like you.
> For life goes not backwards nor tarries with yesterday.

"Wow," said Chris "that's great – and exactly how Dad isn't."

"Too right."

"It makes me cringe the way he calls me 'son'. As if he owns me. It's all so archaic. I mean, do you know of anyone else's father signing their letters 'Your venerable Papa'?"

"He's like a character out of one of his Dickens novels."

"He acts as if he *is* Dickens."

It was true. He did not relate to us. We were his imagined son and daughters.

"He never wanted us to grow up," I said. "God, the fuss he used to make about Izzy seeing Ashley."

"He makes a fuss about everything. I think he gets more deranged and peculiar by the day. The worst thing is that he keeps coming up to my room and hangs around wanting to talk about my collection. It's so irritating."

"He used to come up to my room too."

"Well, he won't go in there now – if your door's open, he asks me to close it then he stares at it with a pained expression. I keep hoping the Monty Python team are going to burst through with 'Nobody expects the Spanish Inquisition', but they don't. Then he starts going on about you."

"What does he say?"

"Oh, you know – that you had no right to leave home, that you left without his permission – that sort of crap."

"Oh Chris."

"And he keeps going on about Those Dreadful Women. It's awful. I wish he'd leave me alone."

I sighed. There was nothing I could say to help.

"You're so lucky you don't have to live there any more," said Chris, reading my thoughts.

"I know I am."

"And Granny! God, I can't stand it the way she comes through with her chamber pot in the mornings just as we're about to eat breakfast. 'Oot the way,' she says, 'I'm carrying mae potty.' It slops from side to side and smells gross – a kind of dry-baked biscuity smell – really rancid. Eugh, she's so crass. The way she leaves the toilet door open when she's taking a crap and farts and belches out loud with complete unconcern."

I laughed, remembering Granny's morning routine. Bodily functions caused her no embarrassment whatsoever. She thought other people's shame so ridiculous that she seemed to consider it her duty to be overtly unabashed and brazen. Chris, for all his easy-going acceptance of people, found both Granny and Dad difficult to tolerate. But then, he had to live with them.

"Have you added anything to your collection recently?" I asked.

"No, I don't have time to do it any more."

"Well, it's something you can go back to if you want."

"Yeah, that's true, but music's taken over and all I want is to get better and better playing the horn. It's such a great instrument. And there's so much fantastic music written for it. Plus we get the best orchestral solos. I can't tell you how amazing it is to play in a big horn section in a great orchestral piece – and you get to one of those parts when the full orchestra is blasting it out – trumpets and heavy brass, timps and percussion, woodwind pelting away, strings soaring and there you are in a row of horns, bells up, taking huge breaths, every muscle working to capacity, every cell vibrating, and you feel as if your whole body has become the horn, and the sound you're making and hearing is just mind-blowing."

Yes, I thought, playing the horn is so essentially physical, every note consciously relying on the breath, the lungs filling with musical intention.

"It's funny," he said, "I feel a complete person walking down the road carrying my horn. Do you know what I mean?"

"Mmm, I think so; the cello's a part of me, although carrying it just makes my arm ache."

But I knew I had nowhere near the same absorption in the cello as Chris had in the horn. Nor did I have the need, drive or ambition to get better and better.

"And Izzy," he continued, "I don't think she'd be who she is if she didn't play the violin, even if she's not going to do it professionally."

I knew what Chris meant by this. "Talking of Izzy, are she and Chris Stearn OK?"

"Seem fine. Hey, I'm getting my new XL soon. I can't wait."

The Paxman Studenti that Mum had bought for Chris when he first started was a good compensating double horn, but it had its limitations. At the time the LSO horn section were playing on Paxman XL instruments – hefty, wide-belled, double horns that produced a big orchestral sound. Chris greatly admired the LSO players, and after much in-depth discussion with Chris Stearn, he decided a Paxman XL would be the instrument for him. He emptied his Post Office account, sold his old Studenti and Mum, ever-supportive Mum, made up the difference.[1]

The next day we headed down Weltje Road to King Street and turned right towards the shops.

"Don't walk so fast, Chris. I can't keep up. Your legs must be at least a foot longer than mine." He slowed his pace. "I reckon you're taller than Simon now. Do you think you'll grow any more?"

"Maybe a couple more inches. The biggest growth spurt in boys is between the ages of thirteen and fifteen. I'll make it to six foot, I should think. Did you know that from the age of thirty, humans gradually start to shrink?"

"No, I didn't."

"And from twenty, the brain starts to shrink?"

"Really? So in a few years, we'll begin to shrivel up?"

"Not entirely; your nose keeps growing throughout your life."

"I wish you hadn't told me that – mine's quite big enough already."

"Why do you and Izzy always moan about your noses? They're perfectly average in my opinion. Personally, I like big noses, they give the face character."

As we were walking past a men's clothes shop, Chris stopped to admire a dark-blue corduroy jacket in the window. On impulse, I said I would get it for him for Christmas.

"But it's so much money," he exclaimed.

"I can afford it. I've been doing loads of playing jobs recently. Come on, let's go in." I saw his pleasure as he tried it on, and was thrilled to buy it for him. He left the shop wearing it, looking trendy, smart and happy.

After a walk by the Thames and a visit to The Dove, our day was over.

"Thanks for the jacket, Cath. It's the nicest piece of clothing I've ever owned."

"It really suits you. Thanks for coming over."

"See you then."

"I'll see you and Izzy the day after tomorrow, won't I? *Concerti* rehearsal?"

"Oh yeah. *Elijah*."

I watched him walk away purposefully to the station; long easy strides, straight back, head up, shoulders relaxed. He looked back once and waved, a modest raise of the hand, unlike the windscreen-wiper motions I was making with both arms above my head. With a pang I saw him as vulnerable, a kid in man's clothing, a little boy stretched out. I missed him before he was out of sight.

1. There are several types of horn of many different designs. A single horn is one that plays in one key (usually F or B flat), is simply operated and lightweight. A double horn combines the horn in F and the higher pitched horn in B flat into a composite, heavier frame, giving the player greater range and accuracy of pitch. A compensating double horn is in the main key of B flat. It does not have a separate set of slides pitched in F, which reduces its weight. To play it in F, the air is directed through the B flat slides, an F extension, and another set of smaller slides, which "compensates" for the longer length of the F slides.

From Simon: December 1973, Liverpool

Cathy! To name but a few!

O for an aardvark sandwich, he exclaimed, brandishing a rusty pair of curling tongs – yes, 95% of what my sister still indulgently calls my brain has been finally worn away by cups of tea, and I really am turning into a sheep. And I'm missing you... SHREKE (Chaucer). If I could only tell you how much I love you, but I can't afford the paper. Still, I'm coming back down to sunny, cold London on the 28th [*December*] sometime early evening, & my God, there is going to be the biggest abduction of Cathy Giles that Euston Main-Line station has seen since the Irish Potato Blight.

Last night the Rattle family went out for a Chinese meal & then on to see a play by Joe Orton called "What the Butler Saw". Meal was marvellous, a great gorge-up, financed by my sister, but the play... Well, it seemed to be going just fine for around 10 minutes, but soon enough, a new actor appeared on stage, either drunk or tired or high, who obviously could not remember any of his lines, or where he was & the show began to lurch along alarmingly, with long silences & one or two hysterical ad libs. After about 10 more minutes & a few liberal doses of embarrassment, one of the other actors shouted out "Oh my God, I can't go on; bring the curtains in; I'm sorry, I'm sorry" etc. Eventually we were all sent home, more than a little sheepishly, without being told what was going on: by the way, it was the last night of a three-week run – Baa!

We had our great reunion booze-up cum party for the gang – nobody changes any more. But I'm wrong, really – people are changing – getting older, and I never quite know how good that is. Every year you can see people gradually settling down into a kind of comfortable routine and happy though that is for them, I begin to wonder whether they're not missing out on something. Anyway, that was no worry on Friday, as we all got quickly pissed on punch, and gorged ourselves yet again. Yea, thy flesh art billowing rapturously in the breeze once again, oh sheep-herder of all Liverpudlians, and thy masses of white fat art in evidence; verily I say unto you that in New Year, thy shalt have to run round Hammersmith Pier once every morning.

So Simon sits at home, merrily tickling his sister, and looking at Cambridge Entrance Papers (interest only, he assured her) e.g. Write the following chords, which will be played once:

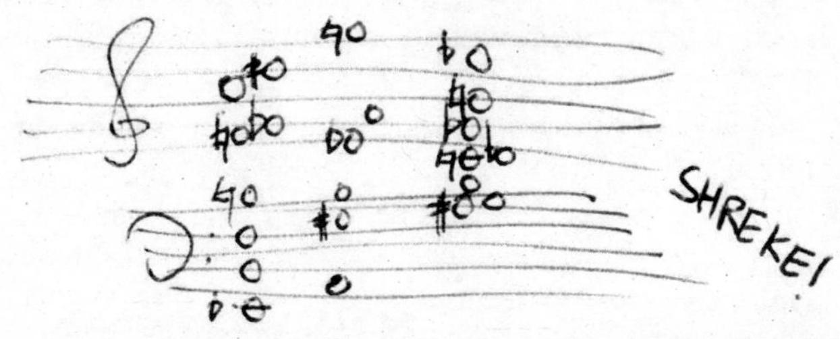

So, Cathy darling, I will be with you very soon. I cannot wait to be back in your arms, because however happy I am here at home, I just don't feel complete and at one without you. You surely must realise by now how precious you are to me, and how much I love you – it's just something I can't explain. You mean everything to me – well, nearly everything: of course I prefer Izzy, or even Chris, but they're not interested, and I can't afford Claudine, so I'm stuck with Cathy Giles.

With all my love to my Little furry animal
xxxx Simon

I did not go home for Christmas. To sit down with my family for Christmas dinner was out of the question. I went over on Christmas Eve to leave presents. I cannot remember how I evaded Dad, or what I said to Mum. She sat beside me and took hold of my hand. It was a gesture that did not come naturally.

"Your fingers are so cold and thin," she said. *My fingers? Thin? What is she talking about? I'm supposed to have big sturdy hands like hers.* I felt a surge of satisfaction. I had changed the shape of my hands!

"You'll die," she said. I almost laughed. *Die? How ludicrous.* I felt her troubled expression, the despair and compassion in her voice, but I couldn't look at her. I wished she wouldn't make me feel like this. And I wished she would stop worrying about me. I pulled my nice thin hand out of her clasp and said I had to go. She sighed and seemed to wilt. "Alright dear," she said wearily into her lap. I tried to think about other things during the journey back to Hammersmith, but I kept hearing Mum's sad voice.

Johnny had bought a Christmas tree. It stood forlornly in our room, undecorated and bare. I rushed out to buy decorations before the shops closed. As I filled my basket with tinsel, my eyes homed in on a shelf of chocolate tree-hangings. *Don't look, don't touch*, I warned; but my self-control snapped. I reached for the packets, feeling like a shoplifter. My cheeks burned with guilt as the cashier added up the total. I carried my downfall back to Weltje Road. There was nobody in the house.

A voice in my head began to speak. "There's nothing to worry about," it soothed. "Just hang them up to make the tree look pretty. No-one's asking you to eat them, of course not."

I ripped open the packets, took out the coloured foil-wrapped shapes, and tied them onto the branches by their golden threads.

"There now," crooned the voice, "doesn't that look festive?"

I seemed to have stepped into the fairytale scene where the Wicked Queen offers Snow White the poisoned apple. Before my eyes were dozens of sweetly dangling temptations. Simon, my protector, my love, was away. The witch inside my head knew he would not be back soon.

"Why don't you have a little taste? It won't do any harm, just one tiny bite."

No, no, don't listen to her.

"Come on, it's Christmas! Let me fetch one for you. The smallest, see?"

Oh no, no.

"I'll unwrap it for you."

My mouth filled with saliva, my stomach tumbled hungrily.

"There: a little treat; a delicious morsel."

Into my mouth it went; and I was gone, free falling, plummeting downwards without a parachute. There was no turning back. Manically, I stuffed and devoured, possessed by an unstoppable compulsion that severed me from sense and reason: *feed me, feed me, feed me into oblivion.* Then it was over. I had eaten every single one. There was no oblivion, just horror, hatred, shame and agony. My self-loathing was absolute. I wanted to die. I could not bear it; I had to do something.

I went to the kitchen, filled the kettle, fetched a glass, measured salt into it, poured on warm water, stirred and slugged it down in one. In the bathroom I stuck my fingers down my throat and gagged, retched and coughed. I drank another glass of warm salt-water and repeated the process. My nose was bubbling, and tears streaming down my face as I tried to empty myself of disgust. I washed my face, brushed my teeth and made a cup of black coffee. My throat was sore, my face blotched and puffy. I climbed into bed, pulled blankets and coats around me and turned to the wall. Huddled up small, icy cold and shivering, I stayed there, unsleeping, all that night and through Christmas Day, waiting for Simon to get home. At Euston station we hugged tightly, overjoyed to be with each other again. I didn't tell him how my Christmas had been.

Pat and Claudine were back. I was in the kitchen when Pat walked in.

"Well, I can see you didn't eat any Christmas dinner," she observed.

"I did," I lied.

"Hmm. How much do you actually weigh?"

"I don't know. Eight stone, maybe."

"Eight stone! Come off it. What about you, Claudine?" Pat called down the stairs.

"Me? Oh, hi, Cathy," said Claudine, dropping some bags on the landing. "Have a nice Christmas?"

"Yes, OK."

"I said, how much do you weigh, Claudine? She's another one who wouldn't eat Christmas dinner – I was there, so I know," Pat informed me.

"Oh, stop going on, Pat," Claudine complained.

"Come on, both of you upstairs. I want to see what you weigh on the bathroom scales."

"Oh, I can't, Pat. I've just washed my hair," I said, trying to back out.

"What difference does that make?" she asked, astonished.

The weight of the water in my hair will make me heavier.

"Do you want a coffee?" I enquired, changing the subject.

"No thanks, Cathy," said Claudine.

"I'm going to get my hairdryer," Pat called, as she carried her suitcase upstairs.

She plugged in the drier and shoved it into my hands.

"Or shall I do it?"

"No, I can manage. Thanks, Pat." She waited.

"Dry enough now? Come on then."

Claudine, five feet eight inches tall, stepped onto the scales. Seven stone and twelve pounds. I remember it clearly. I am five feet three inches tall, and was sure I would weigh more. I must have put on loads since the appalling chocolate binge.

"Come on. You now, Cathy."

I was much less. Six stone five. Speechless, I looked again. The scales must be wrong.

"See?" said Pat, craning to see the reading, "I knew there was no way you're eight stone. You're even less than I thought. It's crazy." Then she stepped onto the scales.

"Nine stone ten, girls. That's *normal*. I don't know what's wrong with the two of you. You're both mad..." Her voice sounded muted, far away.

"I must go," I said. "See you soon." There was a strange humming in my ears. The girls' voices drifted vaguely down the stairwell as I walked down to my room, went in and sat on the bed. I had been aiming to eat just little enough to avoid gaining weight. I thought I would weigh more than I did a month ago, the last time I had found scales to measure myself, but I was a whole lot less. Part of me was satisfied; no, elated that I was lighter than I had ever thought possible. I'd done it! And I could lose more, more, more. I had succeeded – at something I couldn't quite name. But another part of me trembled. Mum's words, "You'll die" hovered in my mind. My thinness was no longer extracting admiring or envious compliments. I had taken to wearing long skirts, layer upon layer of clothes, and bulky, baggy jumpers to disguise my protruding bones and to keep me warm. Whatever the weather I was freezing cold, except for the occasional times when my body overheated to fever pitch. I raged against the truth, but I couldn't dismiss it. This was my fifth month without a period. My body was shutting down. What if I would never be able to have those babies Simon and I had talked about? Maybe it was already too late.

I would have to put on weight. The thought was terrifying. Food is a very tricky addiction. Most addicts have to find the courage to make the decision to give up their addiction completely, to abstain; to refuse their particular poison forever. For me to nourish myself regularly and sensibly was as impossible as asking an alcoholic to drink just one moderate glass of wine a day. If I started to eat in excess of my rigid allowance, I would not be able to stop. I had fallen down the hole with the White Rabbit and didn't know whether to eat the cake or drink from the bottle, for I no longer knew what normal was. I was locked into a self-created civil war with food; a conflict that had started long ago, and one that would continue. But at that moment I was facing the horrifying possibility that I wouldn't be able to have children. I did not want to live a life without them.

It was that realisation which helped put a stop to my disappearing act. That, and living with Simon, who left me to play my tasteless game alone. Removed from the war-zone I had constructed with Mum, I was in futile combat with myself; and there was love: my huge love for Simon and the strength of his love for me made all the difference. Years later, I asked him if he had ever noticed how thin I was then. He considered my question: "I suppose it was a little like going to bed with a skeleton, but all I really remember is being crazy about you."

66
NEW YEAR 1974

And I love you for listening to me,
and my good card,
turned in at the game's end.

I Loved – Umberto Saba

Simon was booked to play percussion with the Liverpool Philharmonic at the start of the New Year and I was alone once more.

From Simon: Jan 1974, Liverpool

Dear Cath,

Here we are in beloved Liverpool Fill Hall in the middle of our tenth hour of rehearsal for Tippett 3. It is at least the most difficult orchestral piece I have ever heard – the strings all have a rare form of chromatic semiquaver diahreorra (how the hell do you spell that!). But it is all good clean fun – takes my mind conveniently off other things, & they are a friendly bunch of people.

Cut now to Sunday evening after a happy host of things have happened. On Friday night two crazy parents and self went out to the house of our good friends, one of whom is a teacher at my father's school – we talked & played etc. up til late, and finished by seeing the next day in on top of a mountain – which was great, despite Liverpool's less than moving view (old gas lamps and the odd Cathedral or two).

Then after another six hours of Glorious Tippett – during which the beginning of the start of this letter was begun, as it were, & during which we discovered that Tippett's method of development was to take the nearly impossible bit at the beginning in 2/4 crotchet = 80, & the bloody ridiculous bit 30 bars later 3/4 crotchet = 120 & put them together – making it all completely impossible and sounding like a flock of pigeons being raped by an iguana in Brixton Synagogue – fun; alas, how brief is youth, la, la, nonny nonny baa; (still the same sentence), – I went off to my friends the Dutches, who I have told you about, and had, needless to say, a fabulous time, first playing for a couple of hours with the kids (they being two girls, 2½ & 1½ & an Alsatian), then nattering & gorging & then playing baroque music until two o'clock. In many ways, they are my version of the Turners – you always know there's a warm welcome and real lively interest there. I always feel that I really have been to Liverpool once I've been with them plus the fact that David is such a marvellously off-beat guy.

So to this morning & 3 hours of Berlioz Fantastic with the [*Merseyside*] Youth Orchestra, who still all keep me as happy as ever by throwing themselves into everything – we could honestly feel the walls shaking. I have just spent an evening quietly ruminating – which always sets me thinking about you. It is a kind of empty stomach-gut feeling when you are not here that steadily gnaws away at me, the minute I stop and think, & 3000 happy families could not make up for not having you with me. Cathy darling I need you badly even when I'm with you, let alone miles away. I love you so much, furry animal, that it drives me crazy to try and express it on paper: you must know how much you mean to me & how much I need your warm heart by my side. Before we started living together I did not have the faintest idea of how strong and intense real love could be, and the more I see you & get to know you, the stronger & more marvellous it all becomes. Now at least I think we both realise what it is all about. Cathy, don't forget that I will be seeing you soon (although I have a horrible feeling that there are no trains on Sunday, leaving only a crack of dawn train on Monday morning) and that I love you more than ever – a great big hug and kiss now from Rattletrap – plenty more where that came from. All my love (+ cast of thousands)

Baaaaa xxx

When Simon returned to Weltje Road, I opened the curtains, which had been closed for days.

"Oh, look Simon. There's a huge moth on the windowsill. Come and see."

"Get it out of here," he choked. I had my back to him. The urgency in his voice didn't immediately register.

"It has interesting markings. I wonder if Chris..."

"Cath, for God's sake get it out of here."

His panic was unmistakable. I looked round in alarm.

"Simon?"

"Now. Please," he implored.

"It's OK. I'm taking it outside right now, as fast as I can." I knew the windows in our room were permanently jammed, so I cupped my hands around the poor creature, ran downstairs, opened the front door with my elbow and let the moth go when I reached the pavement. I'd been as careful as I could, but there was a trace of powder from its wings on my palms. I hoped I hadn't harmed it. I rushed back to Simon. He was sitting with his face buried in his hands and was breathing erratically. I put my arms around him. "Simon? Are you alright?"

"Yes," he said uncertainly, "I'll be fine in a minute. Oh, that was awful. How could you bear to touch it?" I held him and tried to imagine what it was like for him.

I remembered an incident that had happened a few years earlier. For a couple of days I'd heard commotions coming from the chimneybreast in my bedroom. I guessed it must be a bird that had fallen down the chimney. The fireplace was boarded up and sealed with custard-coloured paint. (Every drawer and cupboard in my room was painted turquoise, mauve or custard.) I couldn't leave it there to die, so I raided Dad's tool chest in the cellar and used a chisel and hammer to prise the board away from the wall. I made an awful mess, which landed me in trouble later as there was no more custard paint to repair the damage. When I pulled the cover away, there amongst the rubble and soot in the old grate was a bird – a thrush, I think. Suddenly it flapped its wings, frightening the life out of me. I opened the window, and then reached into the fireplace to pick it up. As soon as I put my hands around it and felt its weightlessness and terror, its papery, spiny feathers, I experienced a shuddering, flinching sensation such as one gets from the sound of fingernails on a blackboard, but I couldn't let the bird go until it was out of the window. I opened my hands and it dropped onto the kitchen roof. I thought it was injured, but it took a few hops and flew into the cherry tree. I felt quite shaky for a while afterwards. I said to Simon, "I had a very weird feeling once when I picked up a bird and felt its little heart beating incredibly fast and its wings fluttering in my hands. It gave me the heebie-jeebies."

"I don't know whether that's the same," he said. "This is a phobia. Like the phobia some people have who are terrified of spiders."

"That's arachnophobia isn't it? I wonder if there's a word for moth phobia? I'll have to ask Chris. Talking of spiders, Chris told me that when you find a spider in the bath, it hasn't crawled up the waste pipe, it's fallen from the ceiling and can't get out and it's really cruel to turn the tap on and wash it down the plughole because you're drowning it." I looked at Simon. He was calming down a bit. The panic was over.

Izzy was in her Upper Sixth year and applied to Hull, Leeds and York universities. In early January, she went for her interview at Hull, which was in the afternoon, so she was able to travel there in the morning and come back the same day. A few days later, she had her interview at York. It was scheduled for the morning, which meant that she had to go up the day before and stay the night. Chris Stearn saw her off at Kings Cross station. When she arrived, she was shown to a room in the university's residential block. Although she had been told where the common room was, she couldn't face meeting anyone. Feeling lost and lonely, she stayed in her room and spent the whole night crying. She didn't tell anyone what an ordeal it had been for her. A couple of weeks later, she went to Leeds, which was a much happier experience. She travelled up in the morning and was met at the station by Bill Worrall, who accompanied her to the university campus. Her interview in the afternoon went well and she was home in the evening. Within a few days, Leeds wrote offering her a place on the BMus degree course, conditional on a 'B' grade in music A level and one other 'C'. Leeds University obviously wanted her, and Izzy decided to accept their offer. Chris Stearn would remain in London, having gained himself a place at the Guildhall School of Music.

I started to put on weight, although I hated every pound and loathed myself for every mouthful. I decided to make another appointment at the Margaret Pyke Centre and go back on the Pill. I think there were still a few condoms left in Simon's wholesale box, but I knew it would be safer to be on the Pill. If it gained me a few pounds, I would just have to put up with it. Reluctantly, I had to agree that now was not the time to have a baby and I didn't want to get pregnant accidentally. At the clinic my blood pressure was taken and I was weighed.

"You've lost quite a lot of weight since you were last here. Have you been ill?"

"No, I'm fine."

"Hmm. Date of last period?"

"Two weeks ago," I lied.

"OK. You know the procedure. Make another appointment before you go."

A few weeks later, to my enormous relief, a period arrived, the first for many months. I had not destroyed my potential to generate new life, but my body was far from back to normal.

Simon decided to put on a performance of Richard Strauss's *Metamorphosen* for twenty-three solo strings at the Academy. As I was now leading the cellos in his student orchestra, I had the privilege of playing the first cello part. *Metamorphosen* was completed in 1945 when Strauss was over eighty years old. He wrote the first sketches for it in 1943 on the day that the Allied Forces bombed Munich, destroying the city in which he was born, including its magnificent opera house. When the cities of Vienna and Dresden were also bombed, and their opera houses and other wonderful buildings reduced to rubble, he was heartbroken. *Metamorphosen* is a work of unimpeachable beauty, saturated with melancholy and mourning, encapsulating the grief of an era of loss and destruction.

The performance was overwhelmingly moving. From restrained lamentation to ferocious passion, we played our hearts out. To rapturous applause, the ensemble made their way backstage. Members of the audience rushed after Simon to congratulate him, but he wouldn't stop for them. He manoeuvred his way through performers and instruments and came towards me with outstretched arms. I leaned into his body and clasped my hands tightly around his back. He hugged me as if he would never let go. The demands of the crowd forced him to loosen his embrace. For a moment we looked deeply into each other's eyes, acknowledging an intensely shared experience.

A few days later, I turned up for a cello lesson and Florrie did not greet me with her usual exuberance. "I have to talk to you, Cathy. The Principal, Sir Anthony Lewis, spoke to me yesterday. He insists that you withdraw from the Tchaikovsky competition."

"Withdraw?"

"Yes. He says the Academy will not consider you going to Moscow or any other International Competition until you have put on at least a stone in weight."

"A stone! But I've put on loads of weight since Christmas. I can't put on another stone."

"Cathy, let me tell you something. I was very slight when I was a student – naturally so. It doesn't matter to me how much you weigh (Florrie was one of the few people who had never referred to my weight loss – or gain) as long as you're practising and looking after yourself. I've always been thrilled with your playing and progress, but if Sir Anthony says you cannot go, I'm afraid that's final. You're a student of the Academy and can only compete with his consent."

Florrie was more disappointed than I was. It would have been interesting to go to Moscow, but it was a relief to be released from having to work all those difficult pieces up to concert performance standard. The sting was the Principal's dictate that I must gain a stone. I stared uncomprehendingly at the floor. Florrie uncharacteristically gave me a big hug and I burst into tears.

"Come on, Cathy!" she said, mustering her boundless energy. "Let's get to work. There will be other competitions. How old are you now?"

"Seventeen, nearly eighteen," I managed, between sobs.

"Seventeen – I'd forgotten you were that young. Plenty of time for everything. Right. Two octave shifts, loads of vib, near the bridge and a *ping* on every note!"

Izzy and Chris Stearn came over and stayed the night. Johnny was away, so they slept in his room. We went out to the Indian restaurant in King Street. Chris and Simon tucked in to their curries, Izzy picked at her korma, not keen on even mildly spicy food, and I made half a popadom last for the duration of the meal. Eating was difficult in front of people, but by myself I binged. Most food passed my lips covertly, every mouthful marinated in guilt. Afterwards, we walked under the Great West Road to the Thames and went for a drink in The Dove. I asked Izzy how things were at home.

"Same as usual. You know how it is. Dad's so crotchety and disapproving of everything. Drives me round the bend."

"He's not so bad," said Chris, "just a bit eccentric."

"You don't have to live with him," commented Izzy sourly.

"He puts on a show for visitors," I added, backing Izzy up, "you don't see him as he really is." I thought how impossible it was to explain to outsiders how bad the atmosphere was at home.

"Another drink, anyone?" asked Simon. "Izzy?"

"Gin and orange, please."

"Nothing for me," I replied.

"Chris?"

"I wouldn't say no to a pint. Thanks, Simon."

Simon made his way to the bar.

"Talking of beer," chuckled Chris, "have there been any more explosions recently, Izzy?"

"Oh yes, did you hear about that, Cath? Chris put too much sugar in the beer he was making and the bottles started to explode. Mum wouldn't let him into the cellar in case he was injured by flying glass and she called the fire brigade to come and remove them to make them safe! Dad was furious because they blew up all over some chair he was French polishing, and Chris was devastated to lose forty bottles of beer."

"Yeah, Chris is almost as fanatical about his beer as he is about the horn," mused Chris Stearn, who told us how each time Chris made beer, he experimented by adding a little more sugar to increase the alcohol content. "He simply won't give up until he's found the perfect balance. He's incredible – he latches onto everything with such enthusiasm and doesn't do anything by halves. Whatever he's interested in gets his full attention."

"Yes, you're right," I said, "look at his Natural History Collection – it's amazing. I can't imagine many other boys asking for a human skull for their ninth birthday."

Chris laughed, "Even more amazing for him to actually *get* one. The thing about Cleveland Road is you never know what's going to happen next. There's your Granny stirring her cauldrons of jam, Chris taking you upstairs to show you his newly-bottled guinea pig, or sitting you down to listen to some outlandish piece of horn music, your Dad coming through the door pretending to be a Japanese warrior or something – oh, and fishing those grubby hankies he collects out of his pockets. And now there's self-detonating beer. Never a dull moment!"

Funny – it hadn't occurred to me to look at Cleveland Road in that way. I was oddly chuffed that Chris saw it as a quirky, amusing place.

"It's only because his home life is even worse," Izzy told me wryly.

> ***IZZY: February 1974:*** *Believe it or not, I'm still going out with Chris Stearn – 9 months and one week! I find it absolutely impossible not to compare my time with Chris with my time with Ashley. Although I only went out with Ashley for seven months, we just seemed to know each other from the very first moment. He was so uninhibited and self-assured that he made me feel at ease and I could talk to him about absolutely everything. Don't think I'm running Chris down – I'm not, but it's taking longer to get to know him. I've seen Ashley again and he keeps in touch. I still adore him. He says he'll be a friend for life. I'd really like to see him more often, but I have to consider Chris. I'd like to explain my relationship with Ashley to him, but he doesn't ask and never reprimands me. Chris keeps hinting that maybe one day we'll get married and his Mum calls me his "future intended". Oh dear, although I love him, I can't really see myself married to him, yet when I'm feeling sad I think it would be the best thing to be with him all the time. I'm mixed up. You'd never believe I was nearly eighteen & could have at least ten more years before I need to decide about choosing a partner for life!*

Simon turned nineteen on January 19th, and Izzy and I were eighteen on February 26th. Conveniently, there was a *Concerti* rehearsal on the afternoon of Saturday the 23rd, so we had our eighteenth birthday party at Cleveland Road that evening. Paul Hart and Bram played a hilarious improvised version of *Happy Birthday* on Mum's upright piano in the living room. Mum looked more and more alarmed as their performance increased in volume, the piano visibly lurching under their four-handed, excessively loud attack, but she was so fond of Bram and Paul that when two piano strings snapped she took it with remarkably good humour.

Pat and Claudine were going away for a short break. "Have a good time," I said as they were leaving. "You'll be glad not to be here, as the Aussies are planning to party all weekend, again."

"We don't hear them upstairs. Hey, why don't you and Simon stay in our flat while we're away?"

"Really? That would be fantastic if you're sure it's OK."

"You're more than welcome – make yourselves at home."

We moved to the top of the house and slept in Pat's double bed, which was a luxury compared to our narrow bed. When Simon wasn't looking, I stepped onto Pat's scales. I was nine pounds heavier. I could have wept.

All too soon the weekend was over and we were back in our single bed, until one day I saw a double mattress propped up in the hall, which the Australians were chucking out. I dragged it up to our room. When I had covered it with several blankets to hide the stains and borrowed double sheets and bedding from Mum, it looked fine, it felt comfortable, and we could finally spread ourselves out at night.

For the last two months, the onslaught of food to my shrunken stomach and emaciated organs had been causing some physical malfunctions. To be frank, I felt awful. More weight had gone on. My belly was bloated, my bowels had seized up, my heart raced, I became out of breath and was beset by headaches. Every so often I was gripped by unspecific abdominal pain; my limbs ached; I felt lumbering and gross. One day I had to leave a First Band rehearsal doubled up with pain. Mum was called. She drove me back to Cleveland Road and made me go to see Doctor Franklin. When he felt my abdomen, every prod made me wince. He referred me to Charing Cross Hospital, where I underwent a ghastly kidney test, and had blood taken for liver function tests, to check for anaemia, and other things. My kidneys were not working too well and I was told I had hepatitis – not the infectious type, just hepatitis, which literally means liver illness. The consultant couldn't work out what might be wrong with me. Nobody guessed that it was the result of drastic weight loss and unmonitored gain. But despite my weight problems, I couldn't believe how lucky I was. I had left home, I was living with the man I would be with forever; there were only a few more steps to go to reach my conception of complete happiness: learn to drive, buy a car, get our own place to live and become a mother. I obtained my provisional license and booked some driving lessons, which I funded from playing jobs and teaching. Already able to drive, thanks to Des, all I needed was practice on the roads. One regular job I had at this time was coaching the cellos in an orchestra affiliated to London University. It met one evening a week at the London Collegiate Theatre, for which I was paid £4 per rehearsal.

Simon was selected to compete in the newly established John Player International Conductor's Award. Out of two hundred applicants, he was one of ten to be chosen. The competition was part of a scheme implemented by the Bournemouth Symphony Orchestra to provide substantial opportunities for young conductors. Unlike other conducting competitions, which offered only a few future engagements, the winner of the John Player Award would be contracted to work for two years with the Bournemouth Symphony Orchestra and its smaller Sinfonietta, alongside their regular conductors Paavo Berglund and Kenneth Montgomery. Simon joked about it, saying there wasn't a chance of him getting anywhere.

"I'm sure you'll win it," I said, "you're so brilliant, you're bound to."

"No, Animal. No way. I'm very surprised I've even been selected."

"There you are then. I knew you'd be selected and I'm convinced you'll win. I'm just shocked that you've entered a competition funded by cigarette manufacturers. If you think about it, that makes me one of your sponsors! You should be grateful to me for smoking," I jested. I didn't smoke much any more, certainly not when I was with Simon: he hated it.

At Euston station we said goodbye yet again as Simon went back to Liverpool to see his family and rehearse with the Merseyside Youth Orchestra. On my pillow was one of his little notes. He left them for me in all sorts of places – in my coat pockets, tucked into music, hidden amongst my clothes.

Cathy darling,
You mean everything to me – you are my life. I miss you even now,
Love,
Dracula

A few days later, a bouquet arrived for me, with Simon's writing squeezed onto a tiny florist's card:

"And ever has it been that love knows not its own depth until the hour of separation." The Prophet [*Kahlil Gibran*] With love from Simon

From Simon: April 10th 1974, Liverpool

My dearest, dearest Cathy,

You must excuse this letter well in advance, because I am sure that I am going to ramble on into incoherence. Let me explain – in the early hours of this morning I was taken with the most violent sickness, which recurred again and again every half-hour – food poisoning from something or other. Thank goodness the vomiting stopped after about four or five hours, but has left me lying in bed being all weak and wan and protesting that I am dying – at the very least!! So it is only now, accompanied by the odd entertaining fit of diahreorra (how do you spell it?) that I have finally summoned up the strength to write to you – Yes, love, I know I make a hell of a fuss, it's more fun that way.

Now, after all that rubbish, I can try to tell you what I am thinking. Perhaps it is just a trick of the moment, but I am now desperately missing you. Little animal, I need your affectionate and loving arms around me, you are the only person who gives me security and happiness so uncomplainingly. All I want now is to kiss your precious lips again and again & tell you how much I love you. I need you so much, Cathy, that I could cry out: it seems that in the last couple of months we have moved so much closer. Never before have I experienced a love so deep and passionate as ours. Oh, if only you were here, I would kiss you as you have never been kissed before, and caress your body and love you and love you and love you more than ever.

I am realizing now, furry little animal, how dependent I am on having your presence to guide and love me always, all the time. I cannot live without you – my whole self rebels against it. Without you I am becoming nervy & dissatisfied & unable to concentrate, and all I need is to hold you in my arms and be held tightly by you. Sleeping alone is a barren experience – no you to cuddle up close to or to welcome in the day. You are my heart's delight, Cathy, my darling little furry animal.

I cannot now write anything more that will make any sense at all, except that I love you, I love you, I love you, and I need you so much.

Think of me darling, & you know that I am always thinking of you,

With all my love and more

Simon

67
TRUE LEGATO

True legato depends on integrity,
not breath control.
When you no longer strive to impress,
when you are no longer riddled
with the ego's false humility,
a line will pour unbroken from your lips
like liquid from the lip of a vessel.
A blood vessel; a chalice.

Your ears, your lungs, will recognise
the flux of emptiness
only when it ceases; then
you'll tilt your head and close your eyes
as if in prayer, and long for more.

But truth, like legato, is not more
or less.
It is constancy. And selflessness.
And breath.

A Correspondence Course in Singing – Gregory Warren Wilson

Chris was invited back to the NYO for the 1974 Easter course, held at Holbrook, which finished with a concert at the Festival Hall. The NYO had moved on since Chris had been chucked out nearly three years earlier. The official attitude was a little more flexible, the rules slightly less ridiculous, and Chris enjoyed himself. Clive Miller and Martin Koch, friends from Redbridge, were still in the orchestra. They were delighted to have Chris back. Clive, who had been promoted to principal trumpet, told me: "For Martin and me, who'd known Chris for years, he was like our mascot. We were proud of him, almost feeling as though a bit of him belonged to us, which put us in a privileged position."

In the NYO horn section Chris met Gareth Mollison and Phillip Eastop. Gareth was fifteen, Phillip would be fifteen in May and Chris, the youngest, would be fifteen in June. The three became instant friends. They were very different in looks and in character – as if they had been deliberately picked by a casting director for contrast: Gareth, slight in build, with red curly hair and glasses; a modest, easy-going, observant person whose horn playing reflected his musicality and intelligence: Phillip, the tallest, with thick blond hair and glasses – he was the showman, a dominant character who liked to produce louder and higher notes than anyone else and was able to make his horn emulate the sound of an alto flute, for example, or a motorbike revving up, or a car screeching to a halt: and then there was Chris, whom

I don't need to describe. As Gareth said, Chris could do all the tricks Phillip could do, and more if he had wanted, but it wasn't in his nature to show off.

Gareth had been in awe of Chris's horn playing for a year before he actually met him. The previous May, Redbridge Orchestra One had played at Alexandra Palace. Gareth happened to be there and walked in during the rehearsal as they were playing Weber's overture from the opera *Oberon*. His ears lit up at the sound of the first horn; he had never heard anything like it. He asked someone if they knew the name of the boy playing first horn. Chris Giles, he was told. Gareth stayed to listen to more. Rimsky-Korsakov's *Scheherezade* was next. The first horn has to begin an exposed phrase on a high G. It is a notoriously hazardous entry and Gareth was anticipating a 'split' – a term used to describe an unfortunate miss-hit. Instead he heard a flawless opening note with a sound so divine and effortless that Gareth still retains the memory of that high G to this day. As he began to know Chris, he felt the same high regard for him as a person. He admired Chris's humility and found him wise and sensitive beyond his years. Of his horn playing he wrote: "Chris was the guardian of that elusive grail; a golden horn sound. With a smooth burnished quality he could cover a four-octave range yet retain a resonant, 'full' tone. The kiss of perfect production from a textbook, symmetrical embouchure, gave his sound an heroic quality that could rip open a chest and wrench at the heart. Incursion upon the emotions is the mark of a master horn player."

Martin Koch, now a successful composer and musical supervisor of many West End and Broadway shows, told me recently: "I spent so many years sitting next to Chris in the school orchestra and hearing him play in the Redbridge Band and so on. Of course I knew he was good, and a great musician, but I assumed that the way Chris played was what good horn playing sounded like. It was only when I started working in the profession that it hit me just how amazing he was. In all these years I have never heard another horn player make the sound that Chris could make; or anyone with the technical ability to do some of the things he could do."

Chris's sound was clear and expansive, with subtleties of colour and tone that were astonishing. He found rich timbres in the lowest part of the instrument's range, yet he could also play the highest notes with accuracy and sweetness. Technical ability, though, is merely a tool. It was Chris's musicianship that moved those who heard him. An artist convinces not by drawing attention to his or her skills, but by detaching from and transcending the ego. A phenomenal technique may produce gasps of admiration, but it takes more to touch our hearts. Olga Korbut, the little Soviet gymnast, is remembered not so much for her extraordinary physical ability, but for her endearing performances that turned gymnastics into pure dance. She went way beyond the display of her routine tricks, not because she was trained to do so, but because her spirit compelled her to risk revealing emotion. She captivated millions, as did the ice skater John Curry, whose artistry was so deeply emotive that one barely noticed the skates on his feet. There was something of this with Chris's playing – breathtaking depth and pathos; generosity and openness.

At the NYO Chris became friendly with three girls from Glasgow – Aileen Morrison and Paula Midgley, both viola players, and Gillian Taylor, an oboist. The girls had known one another for years, having attended the same schools and played in the Glasgow orchestras. They were a lively, confident team. Not as extrovert was Helen Chapman, a striking, pale, dark-haired girl from Dinas Powys who also played the oboe. She may have thought that she was too timid and subdued for Chris to notice her, but that wasn't quite true. It seems clear that he was taken by her gentle manner and thought her very pretty. However, it wouldn't be until the next course that Chris would get to know her better.

Helen was drawn to Chris as soon as she met him. "He was so entertaining," she told me, "and friendly, cheerful and happy." At the beginning of full orchestra rehearsals, before the tuning-up process began, the horn section often showed off their virtuosity by playing extracts from Richard Strauss's tone poems and other symphonic works – or making up arrangements of well-known film and TV themes. Helen, from her seat in the oboe section, used to look over her shoulder to watch them, paying particular attention to Chris.

To Chris's delight, the Philip Jones Brass Ensemble was to give a concert during the course. The PJBE was world renowned – a group of fine musicians whom Chris admired tremendously. Not long before the performance was due to start, Chris, Phillip and Gareth were larking about together in their dormitory. In a mood of collective silliness, they decided to hide all the dormitory's pillows in a large wardrobe at the end of the room. Gareth opened the wardrobe doors and swiftly shut them again, pretending that there were a couple of girls hiding inside. Chris took the joke further, climbed into the wardrobe and pulled the doors shut behind him. As Phillip and Gareth listened to Chris's wildly creative character acting emanating from within, they noticed a broom propped against the side of the wardrobe. Thinking as one, they grabbed the broom and jammed it between the door handles.

Phillip suggested they leave him there for a laugh. They called to Chris that they were going and made their way to the concert. Phillip took a seat in the hall, apparently unperturbed, but Gareth was worried that Chris would not be able to get out and went back. He told me he wouldn't have dreamed of denying Chris the opportunity to hear the Philip Jones Brass Ensemble. Chris was still trapped and none too pleased with Gareth when he let him out, but they got to the concert just in time and sat together at the back of the hall. During the applause between pieces, they hatched a plan. At the end of the concert, as soon as the last note had been played, they rushed back to the dormitory, Chris climbed into the wardrobe, Gareth wedged him in, and then he returned to the hall to look for Phillip.

"I hope Chris is alright," said Gareth to Phillip, in a voice of concern. "He's been stuck in a small space for a long time. He might have suffocated." The two boys ran swiftly up the stairs to their room and Phillip pulled the broom out of the wardrobe handles. The doors swung open and Chris fell to the floor, limp and seemingly unconscious, performing his part to perfection.

"Oh, God," gasped Gareth, shaking the inert body. "Chris, Chris – speak to me," he pleaded. Phillip turned pale. Gareth and Chris played out the drama until they could no longer contain themselves and exploded with laughter.

68
EASTER IN NORFOLK

The long line of woods and rounded hills behind – the pewter-grey sea before – this corner of England which once it holds your heart is more lovely than any place on earth. Beautiful with a hint of secrecy which haunts it, as the memory of a dark and tender sadness clouds the brilliance of a summer day.

Norfolk Notebook – Lilias Rider Haggard

Since Christmas my eating addiction had gone off the rails. I had lost control. Being thin had given me confidence. Now I was frightened by the weight I was gaining. It seemed to me that eating sabotaged happiness. I shopped and cooked endlessly: I threw up, trying desperately to exorcise my gluttony, but as I knelt on the bathroom floor staring into the toilet bowl, perspiring with fear and disgust, I often couldn't bring myself to do it. I longed to retrieve my governing power of denial, to return to the ethereal liberty of emptiness, but I couldn't find my way back to that imagined place of safety.

I prepared meals for Simon, wolfing stolen mouthfuls as I cooked, and laid my offerings in front of him. Never once did he ask why I was not having some too. He didn't question or challenge me, because that was not where his relationship with me was centred. As my flesh plumped up and started to cover my bones, I loathed myself more and more. The body I had forcibly starved was growing into something I could no longer contain. I felt ashamed and embarrassed by my size and shape. I couldn't let Simon feel or see how heavy I was. I wouldn't let him lift me up any more; I refused to sit on his lap; I undressed with my back to him; I doubted his love for me. It was all in my imagination, my distorted, food-addicted mind. He loved me whether I ate or not, whether I was thin or fat. I didn't understand that self-hate annihilates happiness; and love cannot flourish without joy.

I asked Mum if Simon and I could go to the cottage for a holiday when he returned from Liverpool. We invited Louise to come with us. Her father had died suddenly and we hoped that a break would give her an opportunity to relax and offer her some distraction. To our delight, she accepted. I was stressed before we even arrived. Concerned that everyone should be comfortable, I started worrying about sleeping arrangements, what we should do, where best to visit, and the big one – what were we going to eat? Having not been to the cottage for several years, I found myself back in a childhood place filled with mixed memories. I wrote to Bill Worrall:

> Hi there fella! We've actually arrived at the cottage and have been here for almost a day. Simon's train, due in at 5.49 didn't arrive until 7.20 – I was beginning to think I'd never see him again. Mum drove me and Louise here last night. She had to get up at 6.45am to get back to London to teach – mind you, I got up at 6.45 to see her off but promptly went back to bed again. The three of us are sitting around the fire toasting our toes – Simon studying Mahler 6, Louise reading comics and me writing letters.

But my attempts to create a happy holiday were failing. I felt myself sliding into an impossible place. I started to wheeze. We went by bus to Fakenham to shop. I kept asking what we should eat, who was going to cook, what ingredients were required, and made unnecessary lists of groceries. In the supermarket Louise said to me, "Cathy, will you stop fussing about what and when we're going to eat." Simon, well used to my strangeness around food, joked about it, but even he was finding it difficult to relate to me. My asthma got worse. I felt isolated, distant and tense, and awful that I was not being of any help to Louise.

The next day, there was a tap at the window. To our surprise we saw Bram peering in, his crooked nose pressed to the glass. We shrieked with delight and leapt up to open the door. He was besotted with Louise at the time, and had somehow managed to find his way to Great Ryburgh. He remembers *Don Juan* coming on the radio and Simon getting out his score to follow, as it was one of the pieces he had to learn for the John Player Competition. Bram brought some cheer to the cottage, but I trumped it with gloom. I could not find a way out of the dark, awkward, miserable mood that had taken hold of me. Simon tried everything he could to cheer me up, but I was too far away for him to reach me. I didn't know where I was myself. Back from Norfolk, I wrote again to Bill:

> Hi there you there! Yes, wonder of wonders it's me again. Norfolk was OK but not half as wonderful as I'd hoped. Things didn't go too well and I was in a bad mood most of the time, which must have spoilt it for everyone else. The worst thing was that I had asthma nearly all the time – I haven't had it so badly for 2 years and I hadn't taken all my drugs with me so it got worse and worse. And I ended up getting a cold, which I've still got and I'm feeling even worse (aren't I cheerful?)
>
> Bram, believe it or not, did in fact arrive and stayed for a day and a half. It was lovely having him – he really makes me laugh. Also we had a visit from a friend of Simon's – a lorry driver called Don who drove us in his lorry to some jazz club in Norwich. It was supposed to be Ronnie Scott playing but turned out to be someone else – but they were very good. We got back at 1.15am and Don had to get up at 5.00 to get back to Liverpool to pick up a load.
>
> Then the day after Bram left, another of Louise's friends turned up and stayed for the rest of the holiday, all of which I wasn't really bargaining for. The result was that Simon and I had hardly any time to ourselves and I seemed to spend the entire time in the kitchen. Simon's back to Liverpool again today and I won't see him for another week. I feel somewhat depressed and not quite sure about what's happening. Things between us were definitely worse than they've ever been before.
>
> I've got a cello lesson tomorrow then I'm trotting off to Newbury to stay with Louise and practise 4tets for 3 days (with Ruth and Charles). I'll be back on Tuesday then off to the hospital on Wednesday. Term starts the next week.

From Simon to me at Newbury, Berkshire: April 28th 1974

> What do I say to you now, is the question that I am asking myself. All that I know is how much I love you and how much you mean to me – I could go on repeating that all night, and in fact I will if I get half the chance. That week was probably the strangest we have had yet in the course of our relationship. There we were in idyllic surroundings,

with every possible aid to moving closer together, and we spent the time peering over an enormous brick wall, hardly recognising each other. For some reason I found it impossible to be either really happy or communicative, so don't blame yourself that we hardly got through. What happened to us? I suppose that this is the first test of fire: I hope that we can come through it intact. Cathy, you know how I feel about us, that we must both have maximum freedom to move and breathe: if you want to go you must & we can try to reconcile ourselves to it. BUT, I pray inside my being that you want to make this work as much as I do, because life would be so empty without it, without your love and mine for you. I need you, Cathy, you do not know how much you give me in every way, and I need our contact desperately. Oh, how can I show you what I feel?

You see, and I'm sure you know by now, I am very susceptible to people's moods and feelings, and have never been a person who has been able to 'cheer' other people up, only to try and console and understand – as usual nothing positive! The same goes for you – when you erect a barrier, intentionally or not, I am hopeless at breaking it – every minute it just seems more and more impossible and insurmountable. I am left really helpless in your hands, without the power to help either of us. Somehow I have to get good vibrations from you to penetrate the wall – then we can do something. But we have got to do something together. Little animal, I want to know you, I want you to be able to lean on me as much as I lean on you, so that we can restore our relationship back into the marvellous experience it was. I wish I could be more help towards you, then we might get to the bottom of it.

Do remember, Cathy, that I am always here as long as you still want me – I cannot waver, as you have caught me completely. I adore you to the depths that I can hardly fathom. I feel so empty without you.

Finally Cathy, please write if you can, reassure me or something that I am not being over possessive or stifling, because at the moment I feel like a nutty romantic poet, who pines away for the favour of his lady-love. Cathy, I love you. Forgive me for this morbid and totally selfish letter to the very end, take care of yourself and Louise, in that order, and remember...

All my love, S.

From Simon: April 29th 1974, Liverpool

Cathy darling,

I am lovesick again, and so I hope that this will not irritate you on your return home. Dearest sweet girl, I adore you. Here is an American Indian love-song, which I write solely for you, and because it depicts my feelings for you.

Cathy, believe me that I love you for Ever
Simon

Here is one of the three stanzas that Simon wrote out for me:

That was no beast that stirred
That was my heart you heard
Pacing to and fro
In the ambush of my desire,
To the music my flute let fall.
That was my heart you heard
Leaping under the willows.

Simon managed to retrieve me from my sad place that time; we weathered the storm I had brewed in Norfolk and the summer term began.

From me to Bill: May 6th 1974

> Dear Bill,
>
> Everything seems to have settled back to normal with Simon – in fact it's better than ever before, so I'm very much happier. I'm going out to dinner tomorrow with one of Simon's posh friends (and Simon, of course). Academy is much the same as usual. I started off the term well by getting into trouble on the first day for not having turned up to enough lessons last term. Actually, I spent most of last term being ill, so it wasn't entirely due to laziness. Anyway, it's been sorted out and after a fairly successful lunchtime concert on Wednesday (I played in a Haydn trio) they're not so annoyed with me. That same day I went charging off to Oxford for a 4tet concert that night (Beethoven op 18 no. 4 and Vaughan Williams' 'On Wenlock Edge' for string 4tet piano & tenor), which also went well. A few days later we gave another 4tet concert, this time Haydn op 2 no. 5 and Shostakovich no. 10 – also good! (aren't I modest!)
>
> But by far the best was last night. I led the cello section in a most incredible concert at the Academy. Simon conducted Wagner's Prelude and Liebestod from 'Tristan and Isolde', Vaughan Williams' 'Serenade to Music' for 16 soloists and concluded with Mahler's 6th symphony, which went amazingly well – Simon received a standing ovation at the end.
>
> Tomorrow I'm playing the Beethoven D major cello sonata in yet another concert – busy life these days. Must go now, love Cathy.
>
> P.S. Pat Turner's got on to the Council at the local elections – good isn't it?

Chris came to one of our quartet concerts in May, in which we played Shostakovich's tenth quartet. During the performance, Louise's music fell off the stand. Unperturbed, she played the rest of the movement from memory without a single slip. Such was her quiet authority and confidence, that after a sudden shot of panic from Ruth, Charles and me, the music continued with increased concentration; Louise fixed her eyes on us and we played as one. Chris had never heard a Shostakovich string quartet before or indeed much quartet music at all. Always generously complimentary about my performances, he was completely knocked-out by the quartet and riveted by the Shostakovich.

"It was the most amazing playing I've ever heard," he said on the way home. "You performed so brilliantly together and that Shostakovich is incredible."

"Hey thanks. Louise is an amazing player."

"You all are. It was great."

Chris went straight off to music libraries to borrow recordings and scores of all the Shostakovich quartets. To my shame, he soon knew them all a lot better than I did.

69
PRIZES AND PROBLEMS

So always look for the silver lining
And try to find the sunny side of life.

Lyrics by Buddy DeSylva to the song by Jerome Kern

On Sunday afternoon, May 26th, Simon left for Portsmouth to compete in the John Player conducting competition. The first round would last two days, at the end of which four of the ten contestants would be selected to go through to the finals.

I gave him a hug goodbye. "Good luck, gorgeous. I'm going to miss you terribly."

"I'll be back on Tuesday night, silly." He picked up his music case and a small bag.

"Where's your suitcase?" He held up the bag and said, "I'm taking a clean shirt and underwear, that's all I'll need."

"Simon, I keep telling you, you're going to win. You'll be away for the whole week. You need more than that, and you *must* take your tails," I said firmly.

"Animal – can't you understand? I'm not going to get past the first round."

I looked at him sternly.

"Oh, OK, if it makes you happy." He fished his tails suit out of the cupboard, dropped it on the mattress and gave me another bear hug. I heard him going down the stairs and then spotted his tails bag still lying on the bed.

"Simon! Your TAILS!" I called, running after him. He took the bag and gave me another kiss. "See you on Tuesday."

"See you next week. Phone me every day. I love you!"

I walked back upstairs to the kitchen and found a package on the table:

One cigar for my little furry animal, with all my love and affection from Simon.
I ADORE YOU CATHY
P.S. Remember to put it in your mouth

in the fridge:

Little animal,
I love you
See you soon for a violent ravish!

and in my cello case:

Cathy Darling,

You would burst if I could only tell you how much I love you. You are the most gorgeous person ever to have come into my life, and all I am thinking about now is when I shall see you again. I can't tell you how much you mean to me & how much you have done for me. I love you so much, Cathy.

With all my love, and more
Simon

He gave me regular progress reports. Everything was going well, but he was still sure he would be home on Tuesday. He phoned that evening.

"Animal?" I could tell from the tone of his voice.

"You're through to the finals!" I shrieked. "Oh, Simon, that's fantastic. Bet you're glad you took your tails with you now! You're going to win!"

"Now Animal, don't be daft."

"I'm not. Look, have a great time. I wish I could be there with you."

"I wish you could too."

On Wednesday and Thursday the four finalists were interviewed and also critically observed as they rehearsed with the orchestra. On Friday they each conducted *Don Juan* in concert in front of a panel of judges. I sat in the kitchen waiting for the phone to ring. When it did, I flew down the stairs and grabbed the receiver.

"Simon?"

"You're not going to believe this."

"You've won?"

"Yes!"

"Oh, wow – well done! What did I tell you, eh? You're an absolute star. How do you feel?" I asked, leaping about in the hallway.

"Well, I want to come back right now and give you an enormous ravish, but – well, you already know, I should have been with the Merseyside Youth Orchestra this week – I have to get to Birmingham to conduct the Rite."

"I know. Never mind. You're so brilliant – I'm over the moon. I'm giving you a huge hug right now – can you feel it?"

"Cathy? Thank you for your incredible love and support. Let's try to have some time to ourselves when I get back. I miss you."

"I miss you too."

It was about two in the morning. I was sitting with Johnny in his room talking about Simon, his success and how his life was going to change, when we heard someone coming up the stairs. The door opened. I gasped.

"Simon! What are you doing here?"

"I had to see you before I go to Birmingham." He was still in his tails. He had cadged a lift with someone driving back to London. At least he went off the next morning in clean clothes.

When he returned, we had several days to ourselves. We went for walks and talked about the future. He would have to find somewhere to stay in Bournemouth, but he wanted to remain based in London. We decided to leave Weltje Road and find ourselves a flat. The situation had been getting a little touchy with Johnny. He had taken to locking his room when he went out, which I suppose was fair enough, as anyone in the house could walk into it, but he would not give us a spare key, which meant that we no longer had access to his piano. To begin with, he had been happy for us to use it. He had also let me have some drawer space to store my belongings. Now when he was out, I was unable to get to them.

"Let's pick the lock," Simon suggested.

"Simon!"

"Come on, let's try."

With patience and a bent coat hanger, we succeeded. I felt rather bad about it, but took the opportunity to move my stuff out of Johnny's room. The piano itself was locked, which Simon thought very mean-spirited. Before we left and re-locked the room, Simon made some small adjustments; turned a few things upside down, rearranged some books, moved a chair and faced a picture to the wall.

"He's going to be mad at us," I said.

"Don't worry; he'll see the funny side."

Johnny didn't say a word. It was time to move on.

Mum had a friend who let various properties in north London. The upstairs flat of a house in Highgate would become vacant in July. We went to have a look at it and decided it was perfect for us. The rent was a very reasonable £11 per week.

The academic year was coming to a close. My second year was nearly over and Simon was finishing his third.

"Don't laugh," I said to Simon, "I've enrolled for the conducting course at Wortley this year." I had no aspirations to be a conductor whatsoever, but I thought it would be interesting to try.

"Good for you," said Simon. "What are you studying?"

"Britten's Simple Symphony." Not so simple to conduct, as I was to discover. "Do you think I could borrow a baton?"

"Of course you can," he said, finding one for me.

"Thanks – and would you give me a conducting lesson?"

"OK. Beat three in the bar and I'll clap on your beats."

Easy enough, I thought. He failed to clap on my first beat.

"Simon! You're not keeping time."

"That's because you're not giving me any time to follow."

"Oh."

"Think about your tempo; then be very clear that your upbeat directs the speed of your down beat."

"OK, here goes," I said. He stopped clapping after two beats.

"Now what's wrong?" I demanded.

"You're stirring porridge. Every beat has to have a 'click' to it. Relax your wrist and give a down beat that arrives." He stood behind me and took my arm.

"Keep loose. I'll show you."

"Oh! It's like shaking down a thermometer."

"That's exactly it. Now, don't grip the baton. Let it balance in your hand. Well done. Now try again." He stood in front of me once more.

"How do I shake a thermometer sideways?"

"Keep your wrist flexible – and your arm and shoulders relaxed, and click on the beat. Better, but more energy! Your orchestra would sound limp following a beat like that." I persevered, but began to laugh at Simon's erratic clapping.

"I'm only doing what you're telling me to," he said.

"I can't be that bad!"

Then he stood behind me, took my arm and conducted the beginning of the pizzicato movement, singing the string parts and bringing in sections of an imaginary orchestra. It was amazing to feel Simon's energy through my arm, but after a few bars I was laughing so much I could barely stand. He carried on, *con spirito* turning into *con fuoco* until we both overbalanced in a heap on the mattress. He should have said, "Stick to pastry-making, Cath," but he didn't.

As usual there was Prize Giving day. I couldn't get into Nina's white satin dress any more. I wasn't going to waste money buying a white dress and nobody had one I could borrow. The day before the event, I was in a panic. I would just have to phone in sick. Looking at our dishevelled bedclothes, I had an idea – a sheet would do! I found one of the single sheets we no longer used. It was clean, if a little worn in places. I folded it in half, cut out a hole to put my head through, sewed up the sides, left a gap for the arms, trimmed the bottom and gathered the waist. With any luck the red sash would disguise the fact that it was a sheet. Our quartet had to collect the quartet prize. At the Academy, Louise, Ruth and I changed into our dresses.

"What on earth are you wearing?" asked Louise.

"It looks like a sheet," said Ruth.

"Is it that obvious?" I asked.

"Yes," they replied in unison.

"Oh, never mind. Could you help me pin my sash? Do you know; this is the same sash my Mum wore when she was a student here?"

The prize-winners sat in rows on the Duke's Hall stage waiting to be called. We duly collected our quartet prize, but I had to line up twice more to collect other cello prizes, my nouveau designer-wear on show rather too often. Mrs. Deller hurried backstage afterwards, probably to tell me off. Fortunately, she didn't see my sheet-dress close up, as I was already changed back into my loons and rugby shirt.

Our quartet gave a few more concerts in London. I enjoyed the repertoire and performances, adored Louise, loved the hyperactive Ruth, and took great pleasure in Charles's company, but I found the rehearsals increasingly irksome. I was not cut out to be a serious quartet player. It is an occupation that requires phenomenal commitment and dedication. We stayed together for about two years then amicably agreed to disband the group.

On July 6th 1974, *Concerti* gave another concert in which we played Holst's *The Planets* – a challenging piece for Bram to choose, as it is scored for full symphony orchestra with a quadruple woodwind section (including bass oboe and bass flute), two three-part female choruses, two harps, an extended brass section (including tenor tuba) and a large percussion section (including tubular bells and celesta). Rod Elms rehearsed and directed the *Concerti Allegri* chorus; the extra woodwind, brass and percussion players were found, but the celesta was a problem – we didn't have one. However, all was well, as Simon came to the rescue: he played the part on glockenspiel for every movement except 'Neptune', which he played on the piano with a remarkably celesta-like tone.

For Chris, though, it was during rehearsals of *The Planets* that a problem with his embouchure became apparent. For some weeks he had been noticing a strange phenomenon. When he played he could discern a high note sounding an octave above the one he was making. He didn't know what was causing it and was very worried. He tried to disguise it by manipulating his muscles to eradicate the echo, but when he played the opening phrases of 'Venus', the phantom octave was so obvious that Bram thought Chris was doing it deliberately and stopped the rehearsal.

"Come on, whoever's playing that high octave, stop doing it. It's not funny and it's wasting time."

"I'm sorry, Bram. I can't help it. I don't know what's happening."

Bram could see the anguish in his face and hear the distress in his voice and smoothed things over at once. "Hey, don't worry about it. It'll be fine. Let's rehearse the next movement."

It wasn't fine. Chris was devastated. Back home, he scrutinised his mouth in the mirror and saw a small lump on the inside of his upper lip. It was soft, painless when squeezed, not a blister or an ulcer, but he was sure it was causing the problem. During the final rehearsal at Ilford Town Hall, he exerted himself to produce his own pure sound. In the different acoustic from the resonant school hall in which we had rehearsed, the parallel octave was unnoticeable. Bram reassured him that he didn't hear it, but Chris knew it was there. His terror about the 'octave buzz' and his efforts to disguise it affected his playing in that particular concert. There was some insecurity, an occasional split note, some tentative entries – quite unlike him. He became convinced that the lump was growing and took to carrying a hand-mirror around with him, checking his lip umpteen times a day.

The BHCHS Music Festival took place a few days later. Chris performed the second movement from Mozart's third concerto and also played in a version of Jerome Kern's song, *Look for the Silver Lining*. Martin Koch had arranged it for the unusual combination of trombone, horn, viola and oboe – for himself, Chris, Cliff Oliver and Nitram.

The octave buzz persisted, scarcely audible to anyone else, but sickeningly obvious to Chris. John Ridgeon told him to try and put it out of his mind. The summer holidays were about to begin: two weeks camping and a rest from playing would probably cure the problem. Chris, usually one to find the funny and sunny side of life, was not persuaded. He carried his deep anxiety and his mirror to camp with him. He tried to be laid-back about it, but he had already concluded that if his octave buzz could not be eradicated, he would have to give up the horn, and for him that would be the end of the world. It occurred to me that if some physical problem were to crop up to thwart my cello playing, I wouldn't be too bothered. It would give me a chance to do something else. Chris was different. His horn playing mattered intensely to him. Although all sorts of things fascinated him, the horn was his passion, his voice, the instrument that enabled him to live and breathe, create and consume music.

46, Weltje Road, taken in 2008. Simon and I lived here from 1973 to 1974. The privet hedge has gone, the front door has had a coat of paint, but otherwise it looks much the same. Our room was on the first floor; the bay window seen here with torn curtains.

Photos by Martha Giles

ABOVE: With Simon in Great Ryburgh, Easter 1974
BELOW: At Weltje Road

WEST LONDON OBSERVER Friday, June 7, 1974

Hammersmith superstar, Simon Rattle, at work.

Youngest finalist wins prize

A 19-year-old Hammersmith boy, the youngest of ten finalists, has won the first John Player International Conductors' Award.

Simon Rattle, of Weltje Road, Hammersmith, won the award which is considered to be the most valuable prize available to a young musician.

He wins a two year contract to conduct the Bournemouth Symphony Orchestra and Sinfonietta involving a minimum of forty concert appearances and accompanying fees of £6,500.

The runner-up was Australian, Geoffrey Simon, and the "Most Promising" Award went to Hikotaro Yazaki of Japan.

Another West Londoner, Colin Metters, of Grosvenor Road, Chiswick, took fourth place.

Such was the standard of the semi-finalists that the jury, including two international conductors, Paavo Berglund and George Hurst plus pianist, Peter Katin, created a previously unspecified award for Colin — one conducting engagement with the Bournemouth Symphony Orchestra.

Simon Rattle, a prodigy of Sir Charles Groves, has worked principally with the Merseyside Youth Orchestra, starting his musical career at eight years old as a percussionist.

In the final concert of the competition he conducted pieces by Handel and Strauss. Over 200 applications for the award were received from all over the world.

Soon after Simon won the John Player competition, George Hurst's wife, Tiggy, invited us to their home in Bournemouth for a weekend. It didn't go unnoticed that Simon and their dog, Spider, shared remarkably similar hairstyles.

Photos by Tiggy Hurst

70
28, ORCHARD ROAD

Listen! The music has become
Invisible. Between breakers
There is silence. Fine as sand.

Recycling the Dream – Jean Lipkin

Simon had to go back to Liverpool, so I spent the last few days at Weltje Road on my own packing up our stuff. Mum told me to make sure I left the place clean, so I borrowed Pat's vacuum cleaner. To my surprise, the dark and dirty carpet in our room turned out to be plum red. I gave the kitchen floor a cursory wash then carried everything down to the hall. Mum arrived, ready to transport me to Orchard Road. I had said goodbye to Pat and Claudine the night before. We promised to keep in touch, but apart from once paying Claudine a surprise visit at Che Guevara's, we haven't seen or spoken to each other again. Mum and I loaded the car and we drove away. I looked up wistfully at the window of the room that Simon and I had shared for ten months and imprinted the picture in my mind. It was strange to think that I would probably never set foot inside that house again. Mum, ever willing, helped me carry our boxes into the new flat and then left. I looked around with pleasure. My only sadness was that I had moved in alone. Simon would not spend his first night here for several weeks.

From Simon: July 29th 1974, Liverpool

Hello there, little animal. Yes – it is perfumed!!

How fares your life? I got your lovely letter through the post this morning, and it cheered me up no end – I'm afraid that my pangs began the minute that a little rugby-shirted object disappeared from view on Euston Station. And as for sleeping in a single bed, I don't see what all the fuss about an uninterrupted full night's sleep is; I would much rather be able to turn over into receptive arms and love, regardless of exhaustion. But wait until I get hold of you on that Friday – I'll hug you to death – molto abductzione. Look you, I love you, and you're mine, and you're gorgeous… and so on. I will leave you to imagine the rest…

At nearly 1 o'clock A.M., Denby Richards, the critic, phoned from Germany, asking if I would like to conduct the Munich Phil, no less, on Thursday, no less, in a Mozart concert, no less. Thank God I'm in Aberdeen, no more – too much temptation is not a good thing. My mother is not too well even now, and has been to the doctor again, but he cannot diagnose anything except possibly a thyroid condition – I didn't bother to suggest hepatitis!!

Nothing else has happened, except that I have decided that my father's brusqueness and grumpiness, which have been appearing, is due to school-teaching – sometimes he falls into the trap of treating us all as 11-plus or minus candidates… Which does not alter the fact that I am dying to have you in my arms again, little one.

With all my love, Simon

Izzy and I set off to camp on the Isle of Arran; Chris went to Radnor, Wales, for another semi-mobile. Izzy and I were staffing for the first time and were delegated to the Woodling group. Also staffing Woodlings was another eighteen-year-old, Matthew Rea. He had a car, which he brought to camp. That was about all he did bring. He didn't have any eating things, so took items from the kitchen at every mealtime. He put up an FSC bivvy and borrowed a groundsheet, sleeping bag, blankets and waterproofs from the store tent, saying he hadn't had time to pack, and why bother when FSC had everything anyway? It was a novel approach, which illustrated Matthew very well. The site was in fields next to the sea. I filled my lungs with fresh sea-air and thought it was perfect. Matthew's easy-going personality appealed to me. He was quick and energetic; he rounded up children for walks and set off at a brisk pace. With his designer's mind, he got teams involved making steam baths, clay ovens and beach barbecues. I often saw him striding purposefully off on a mission – massive, dark-green raincoat flapping in the wind, with a few stray Woodlings running along behind, trying to keep up.

We arrived on Arran when the moon was half-full and waxing. Perhaps it is the geographical position of the island, but I have never known such bright moonlight. After the Woodlings were in bed, Matthew and I often walked along the beach by the light of the moon and sat on boulders looking out to sea. We wrapped ourselves in an FSC blanket and talked while Matthew rolled a joint. There was a tranquillity and intimacy in those moments. Over the next week, the moon reached fullness and became so startlingly bright that one could easily read a book by its light.

When it came to hike, Matthew, Izzy and I took half the Woodlings with us and the rest went off with the other three staff. Matthew piled the rucksacks and tents into and on top of his car and drove them to our destination, while Izzy and I set off with the children. He met us for a packed lunch and then we walked on to our hike site, pitched our tents and settled in. We decided to stay in the same spot for the three nights and would walk to different places each day. On day three, several Woodlings came down with diarrhoea. When we packed up, we thought it would be best to take the children who were unwell back to base camp by car.

"We'll have to do two trips," I said.

"No we won't. We'll get everyone in," said Matthew confidently.

"What about all the rucksacks?" I asked dubiously.

"They'll go on the roof."

Izzy went on ahead with the able Woodlings while Matthew and I cleared up, damped down the fire, re-laid the turf and rolled up the tents. We helped the children pack their belongings and loaded the car. Four Woodlings sat in the back with luggage across their laps. Matthew made a mountain of tents and rucksacks on the roof-rack. I sat in the front with another Woodling on my lap, Matthew climbed behind the wheel and off we went. This was long before compulsory seat-belts or the safety precautions we are used to today.

There are two roads on Arran – one that goes across the island and the main one that zig-zags all the way around the coastline. That was the road we had to take. There are places where it is just a few feet away from a sheer rocky drop down to the sea. In moments, I was telling Matthew not to drive so fast. He laughed, accelerated and swerved recklessly around the hairpin bends. I was scared: the kids were screaming.

"Slow down," I pleaded with him, "please slow down. This isn't funny." We careered right, the road veered left, and then another sharp right turn loomed up. The brakes screeched as he tried to control the car. He was going far too fast to make it. We ploughed straight through the hedge and hurtled towards the sea. For a split second we were suspended in mid-air: then the car overturned and we fell upside down from the sky. In that moment, time seemed to stop: there was silence. With detached resignation, I thought, "Oh well, this is it."

Wind rushed through the open windows. There was a shuddering impact: then – nothing. I was still alive. *The car's about to blow up*, was the next thought that registered in my mind; then I heard Matthew shouting: "Cathy! Come on. Move. Help get the kids out."

The car was slowly sinking. Extraordinarily, it had landed belly-up on a stretch of boggy marshland. The front windscreen had shattered. Matthew had already climbed out and pulled the child who had been on my lap after him. The children in the back were whimpering. I manoeuvred myself around and held out my arms for them, telling them everything was going to be alright, even though I was expecting the car to explode at any moment. I handed each one out to Matthew, who carried them to the bank beneath the road, where they sat, dazed and crying.

He came back for me. "What are you doing?" he said, annoyed. "Get out of the car." I crawled through the window and reached for his hand. He pulled my arm, none too gently, and my feet squelched into the cold marsh. I saw the hole that had been ripped through the hedge and the row of forlorn children waiting pitifully beneath the gash.

We helped them to clamber up to the road; I pushed the last child up, and then struggled up myself. Matthew had cut his hand slightly, but apart from that, none of us were injured – not even a scratch. I tried to comfort the children while Matthew considered what to do next. There were no houses or buildings to be seen and not a single vehicle had passed in either direction. Just as Matthew had decided to walk back in the direction of the main camp, a car pulled up and a man got out.

"Is everyone alright?" he asked. "I hear there's been an accident."

"We're all OK. Nobody's hurt," said Matthew.

"How did you know there'd been an accident?" I asked

"A girl with some kids stopped me a few miles back and asked me to come and help."

Izzy had been walking along the road with the rest of the Woodlings when she suddenly had a feeling that there had been a terrible accident. She was so sure of it that she flagged down the first car coming towards her and sent the driver to find us. She cannot explain the feeling that overcame her, or why she responded to it without question. Neither can I, but maybe her apprehensions about Matthew's driving and her concern that his car had not yet caught up with her were factors that led to her extraordinary and uncharacteristic impulse.

The motorist drove the children to the campsite. Matthew's car lay with its wheels in the air. Scattered nearby were a few partly submerged rucksacks. The rest of the luggage was trapped underneath, sinking into the bog. Matthew waited by the scene of the accident and I walked back alone. Eventually, the car was hauled by tractor back up to the road. The rucksacks and tents were retrieved. Apart from the broken windscreen and a few dents and scratches, the car was fine and still drivable. When I looked at a map of Arran, I saw that we had left the road at the one place on the coastline where a shelf of marshland lies between the rocks and sea. That we were all alive and unhurt was extremely lucky. I didn't know until years later, when I was on the FSC children's committee, that Matthew's irresponsible driving had shaken FSC into drawing up much stricter rules about safety.

From Simon to me at camp: August 4th 1974, Aberdeen

My Dear darling ravishing Cathy,

An enormous hug to start this letter off in style. Does that cheer you up, you poor wet, starved, lonely gorgeous creature? Well, here I am in Aberdeen, in bed at dead midnight, half-dead myself. It's Friday, & I suddenly realise that I have only been here one full day, and exhausted already! My journey, although it was not as long as yours, was a bit much – starting at 9 from Liverpool and finally reaching Aberdeen at 7, via Glasgow Central.

On arriving here I was besieged (really!) by old Japanese friends from both last year & the year before in Lausanne. As you might have guessed, I had a jolly time. Look, Cathy darling, I am wilting, and must go to sleep now, otherwise this will degenerate. Just know how much I love you, how much I need you right now, just to fold into my arms, & to stroke your beautiful hair; I want to kiss you, hug you, hold you for ever & ever, my lovely little animal. I keep on thinking about you, believe it or not – you're marvellous, you are everything I could ever want.

I LOVE YOU...........goodnight!

Well, here I am, the next morning, no less, in Aberdeen's famous Music Hall and I am here to conduct my second rehearsal of the Tokyo Youth Symphony Orch. They are attacking the Zdeněk Lukáš piece (you remember that ridiculous black score?) with enormous enthusiasm. It has proved to be fiendishly difficult, extremely dissonant and really very effective. The standard of the orchestra is quite unbelievable – many times better than 1st band, and rather more like the LSO than anything else. They all play so intensely – sometimes I think they could bairst! It's also going to be bloody deafening – so if you hear an earthquake in Arran, it's from sunny Aberdeen.

It's going to be hard work here, but, as always, just the most fantastic experience – there is an unbelievable feeling of warmth between everybody.

I wish I didn't miss you so much – it becomes really painful sometimes – You mean so much to me I could just scream. How stupid that you could not have come (as the actress etc.), you would have had the time of your aardvark. And talking of aardvarks, there's one loose right now. It's coming to give you a great hug, kiss & ravish. Cathy, I cannot wait to be back in your arms, making love to you.

I love you so much!!!

Enjoy your camping, and don't strain yourself, for goodness' sake.

Love to Izzy, if you can wake her up, and even more love to you, furry animal.

Simon

From Simon to me at camp: August 8th 1974, Aberdeen

Hello, little one,

Well, here I am again, dying of frustration, surrounded by hundreds of nubile maidens, and being (so far!) a very good boy in every sense. If only you were here, everything would be just perfect. As it is, it has been marvellous, an experience never to be forgotten. If I ever come again, you will come with me, & I'll pay for you to stay in the guest rooms; then perhaps you will see what I am raving about. On Monday the opening ceremony went like hell – great for me with at least 200 instrumentalists for my piece (not peace), & the Japanese playing like the LSO. As a result of this & also a rehearsal of Dvořák New World with another Jap orchestra, I have been invited to Japan to do all types of weird & vunderval zings. It's going to be hard to refuse.

Life here is so full, there is hardly time to breathe. All the time, we try to make more time by staying up to all hours – 4.30 this morning for instance! It is the Japanese who I am coming most close to – they are such an astonishing race. But I will tell you all this when I see you next.

God, if I don't see you soon, I will go crazy. I love you, little animal, even tho' I have almost forgotten what you look and feel like. Thank you for all your fabulous letters, which tell me a hell of a lot more than mine tell you – it is so good always to hear from you. I can nearly touch you in your letters. I wish I could write more, but there is so little time – now I must fly or I'll miss the post.

I love you, Simon

I hadn't seen Simon for three weeks and we had still not spent a moment in the flat together; but he would be in London for one day before I went to Wortley. It would be wonderful: I anticipated a passionate reunion; a joyful first homecoming; a celebration of the promise of our future happiness. I was longing to be with him again, and from everything he had written in his letters, he felt the same way. I leapt up in excitement when I heard the door opening and rushed to the stairs to meet him. That was the only part of my beautifully conceived screenplay that ran as I had dreamed. Simon seemed different. My elation collapsed instantly. We felt strange with each other; conversation was stilted and awkward: all that was familiar seemed to slip away like a mirage. I kept my smile in place while dread jittered inside me. After a while, there was a subtle reassembly that shifted us into a weirdly parallel place where everything appeared to be fine. I loved Simon; he loved me. Nothing had changed. I was imagining differences where there weren't any. But, as I have so often found to be the case, my instinct was right. Something indefinable had changed. The heart of our love, filled with the unique, delicious essence of the mixture that was Simon and me, had somehow perforated, and it began to leak away, exposing pores for the world to seep in. I left for Wortley perturbed. I had to get through another week before I would see him again, and that would be in Liverpool, with his family.

From Simon to me at Wortley: August 21st 1974, Penrhyndeudraeth

Dear Cath,

I want you! Now, for God's sake, try to forget last Friday – that I am sure is just one of those strange things that tends to happen to us now and then. It is as though two new beings just happen to come together, with full understanding, but in a different light. Please do not worry that things have suddenly altered in either of our feelings – I know that we still need each other and need to love each other. Now, obviously there are many sides to a human being, and while we are together we will always explore the most compatible sides. However, when we are forced apart by circumstances, as in the last few weeks, we are equally forced to rely on the other part of our natures, otherwise, separation would be an endless torture – I suppose, unconsciously we have to discover ways to overcome it, and we must not be anguished to find that there are parts of each other which need to be completely independent. Perhaps this may leave us sadder as well as wiser, but we should be happy now that we know more of each other. Just please do not think that it affects our love or togetherness. Even now, I still feel detached from the situation – perhaps a good thing as it enables me to analyse it calmly, & I know in my heart that everything will work out, just as long as we allow it to. So take heart, little animal, & try not to be upset. We can come through everything, and just look forward to Saturday when we can start to work everything out once more. Remember all we have been through, and think how ridiculous it is for everything to finish now!

I hope this will reassure you, as you must be worried sick. Thank you for your letter – it was good to hear from you at this time. I am sorry that you will get this letter one day later than you should; it is now Monday evening, and I have slept about 20 hours non-stop since early yesterday evening! You must of course realise just how exhausted I was by Friday. Now add to that 2 days of solid work (including playing piano in Albert Hall!) & also the fact that I did not get to bed at all on Sunday night – this added up to quite a staying-awake marathon! Now, as you might imagine, I still feel like a zombie, but many times better for having written to you. Just one thing, please don't come to Liverpool too early, as we have a tenant in the downstairs flat, and he is going on a weekend stay away, so that you can come – he may not want to share his bed with you!

But I do... All my love, furry one,
Simon

Simon's letter did not reassure me; it caused further apprehension. I wasn't ready to move into a different light; to redefine our relationship; for it to become nothing more than ordinary, like all those other couples who had fallen out of love and accepted it as a natural progression. I railed against such complacency. There was no part of me that wanted to be completely independent. Yes, I could rely on myself, but I couldn't do without the continued assurance of our togetherness, the constant affirmation of our love, the urgency and breathlessness. Simon's sensible, realistic, positive words did not go with my deep desire for passionate, rapturous, exclusive love – my happily ever after.

I conducted an orchestra for the first time, which was nerve-racking. The first attempt at a run through of the Simple Symphony was pathetic. My hands were shaking so much I could hardly hold the baton. During the week, things improved. I found it relatively easy to rehearse, and was able to offer helpful suggestions about bowing. Gradually, the piece came together. In one rehearsal, feeling a little more relaxed, I looked at the cellos to indicate an entry and, more by luck than judgement, made eye-contact with the leader. It was a moment of illumination. She held my eyes, following my instructions intently. I was surprised by the thrill it gave me, the empathy that passed between us. Here was the connection I needed between the silly waving of my arms and the notes on the score. I had to look at the players, find the courage to lift my eyes from the printed music and visually give directions. Only then could it work. When I walked out to conduct in the final night's concert with just Simon's little baton to hold onto, I was a jumble of nerves. I tried to maintain eye-contact with the orchestra, but in truth, they played the piece for themselves. It was an educational experience, but I have not had the slightest inclination to wave a baton again.

Bruce Fox, the horn player we had met in 1969, and his friend Alistair, drove to Wortley for the final night. Bruce had not been to the summer school for two years, but he and Chris kept in touch regularly. Bruce had stayed at Cleveland Road from time to time, and Chris had visited him in Southport. Bruce was now a music student at Leeds University where Izzy would be going in September. He and Alistair offered to give me a lift to Simon's parents' home in Crosby, Liverpool, the next day. It transpired that Bruce knew Simon from years ago. "Not that he would remember me," said Bruce. "It was when I played in the Southport Youth Orchestra. Simon used to come along occasionally and play timpani."

I arrived in the afternoon, not too early, as Simon had requested – which had been bothering me. Why would it have mattered if I had arrived before the tenant departed? Didn't Simon want to see me as soon as possible? He met me on the doorstep and gave me a generous but not ecstatic hug. He showed me into the bedroom of the vacated downstairs flat. It was clear that I would be sleeping there alone. Since we had been living together for nearly a year, I couldn't understand why we were not allowed to sleep in the same bed under his parents' roof. I suppose it was because they barely knew me. They did what they thought best, but at the time I felt that my relationship with Simon was disregarded. Denis, Simon's father, alarmed me by being overly charming, almost flirtatious. He could also be rather brusque and cavalier. Susan, Simon's older sister by eight years, mostly ignored me. Simon had told me that she was partially disabled – although cognitively bright, she remained emotionally immature (nowadays the terms 'special needs' or 'learning difficulties' would be used). She was fiercely attached to Simon and so adored him (and he her), that when her brother was home, she wanted him to herself. I was more comfortable with Pauline, Simon's mother. Even so, I worried that she was appraising whether I was good enough for her son, and found me wanting – and to be fair, her misgivings were not unfounded. My difficulties with eating did not make me an easy houseguest. I turned mealtimes into uncomfortable occasions, embarrassing myself and everyone else. My shame and self-consciousness choked me. Pauline was clearly perplexed by my behaviour, but she was perceptive enough to give up with meals around the table. She suggested we took what we wanted and ate from trays on our laps. I was so hoping that Simon's family would like me – love me, even, and I would feel a sense of belonging. It didn't happen. I don't think Pauline or Denis ever took our relationship seriously – as if we were too young to love and were only playing nursery games. We were young, it's true, but our love was not childish.

At the end of the evening Simon accompanied me downstairs. We made love quickly on top of the bed, and then he left. I slipped between the sheets alone, sad, dissatisfied and deprived of his comfort. In the morning, he brought me a cup of black coffee. I complained about our separation. Couldn't he stay downstairs with me if I wasn't allowed in his room? He refused to be drawn into an emotional wrangle. Don't make a fuss, he said. It's my parents' home and we have to respect that. They've gone to a lot of trouble planning this. After all, it's just a few days and we have our very own flat to return to where we can do as we please.

Yes, I was being unreasonable, behaving selfishly. Yet – was it again my imagination, or did Simon seem even further away? We had moved into Orchard Road a month ago, but had spent only one uncomfortable day there together. He had been in Liverpool, then Aberdeen. I had been camping for two weeks, and then gone almost straight on to Wortley. We hadn't been in the same place at the same time for ages and I was beginning to flounder. It didn't occur to either of us that we could or even should change plans that had been established six or more months ago in order to be with each other – but what if we needed time together now? When phone calls and letters were not sufficient to sustain our connection? When our entirely different existences and recent experiences had created a distance that needed to be closed? The accident on Arran had shaken me. I was no longer complacent about life or patient with time.

I wondered how much time we would actually have when we returned to London. Simon would be working and living in Bournemouth. He would only be home when his schedule permitted. I fantasised about not returning to the Academy for my third year – chucking it all in and following Simon. But I knew I wouldn't be allowed to do that. Simon himself would have insisted I stay to finish my studies. To go with him to Canada was one thing, but Bournemouth wasn't thousands of miles away. He would be back in London as often as possible, he reassured me. We had all the time in the world ahead of us; when I had finished at the Academy; when his contract with Bournemouth was over; the rest of our lives to be together; children to be born one day. How I yearned for children! Now we must be patient, we must study and work. It is expected of us; we expect it of ourselves. Do we? Or do 'they'? Do you, Simon? A pool of fear began to accumulate, each new droplet carrying ever-widening circles of trepidation across the surface tension of my life. What if I were to lose him? The thought sent icy shivers of alarm through my increasingly edgy nervous system.

The next evening, Simon's parents took us to the theatre. Denis drove fast and impatiently, cursing other drivers and overtaking dangerously – the complete opposite to Dad's driving, but just as awful. I have no idea what we saw. Whatever it was, I couldn't grasp what was going on and felt out of my depth. Nothing was going as I had hoped. I had made a bad impression on Simon's parents and knew I was creating an uncomfortable atmosphere. I decided to visit Bruce to give everyone a break.

I managed to get to Southport by rail on a shabby train that chugged across rather dull countryside. The day was grey and overcast, which matched my mood. Bruce was pleased to see me. He took me through to a small, cluttered kitchen at the back of the house, where we sat at the table drinking tea. I don't remember our conversation, but he cheered me up. Laughter is the greatest balm. The weather didn't seem so bleak on the return journey.

The visit described above was the last contact I had with Bruce until I started writing this book. At the same time as I was assembling my memories of Bruce's connection with the past, I received a letter from him. It was a curious moment of synchronicity. We had not been in contact for thirty years. I phoned him straight away. Over the course of several more letters and emails, he told me this: "I certainly loved your family in a way that is probably unique in my life. Chris was without a shadow of a doubt the best friend I had in those few years after my first Wortley week. We used to exchange letters. Mine were inevitably a long and tortuous rigmarole, getting nowhere in particular; but I enjoyed writing them, just as I enjoyed reading Chris's more succinct but equally outrageous replies. I once received a letter in which he told me he'd joined the Young Conservationists. I was quite disgruntled for a while, having misread his handwriting: I thought he had said he'd joined the Young Conservatives. I kept all those letters until I moved to France in 1984. I must have left them in my parents' home in Southport, where they presumably got destroyed when the house was sold. I remember coming down to London in 1971 to hear you and Chris play in Bruckner 7 with the NYO, then to Aldeburgh to hear Izzy play with the RYO. I don't think your Dad came to either concert, but I remember your Granny coming to The Maltings and Chris, Izzy and myself howling with laughter in the back of the car on the return trip, mostly recalling Monty Python sketches."

Back in London, Simon and I had about a week together. 28, Orchard Road was (and still is) in the middle of a long row of identical terraced houses. The front door led into a narrow hall where our gas and electricity meters were mounted on the wall. At the top of the staircase was the door to our flat. The flat was tiny, but seemed spacious after our one room in Weltje Road. We could wander from kitchen to bathroom, from bedroom to living room without bumping into anyone but each other. It was also blissfully quiet. The kitchen window looked out onto the back garden. Beyond the garden was a disused railway cutting along which one could walk from Highgate to Hornsey. The bathroom was the smallest I have ever seen. The door only opened a third of the way before hitting the edge of a narrow hipbath. Beside the bath was the lavatory, opposite which was a miniscule sink, so close that it was possible to wash one's hands whilst seated on the loo. The bedroom had just enough space for a double bed, a little wardrobe and chest of drawers. The living room was large in comparison – the full twelve-foot width of the house – with two sash windows looking down to the road. We had a telephone installed – a red one; what a treat that was, having our own phone line.

We explored the immediate area, discovered Waterlow Park and Highgate Woods and walked the length of the disused railway. The local shops provided every amenity; a Post Office, launderette, chemist, butcher, newsagent, ironmonger, a general store and a shop called the 'Highgate Dairy', which was open every day. Highgate station, on the Northern line, was a two-minute walk away. A Doctors' surgery, some interesting junk shops and a pub were nearby on the Archway Road. We settled in and my worries almost evaporated. Our relationship seemed to be as strong, passionate and loving as ever. Then Simon went to Bournemouth, found himself somewhere to stay, and started rehearsals.

71
CHRIS'S SUMMER OF 1974

How silver-sweet sound lovers' tongues by night,
Like softest music to attending ears!

Romeo and Juliet – Shakespeare

The summer NYO course began at St. Lawrence College in Ramsgate. Mum drove Chris there the day after he returned from camp. Chris was happy to be back with Gareth Mollison and Phillip Eastop, Clive Miller and Martin Koch. Also in his 'gang' was flautist Andy Findon. Girls included Aileen Morrison and Paula Midgley, the Glaswegian viola players; flautist Sigi Turnlund; and the oboist Helen Chapman – the girl whose quiet demeanour had already caught Chris's attention the previous Easter. Gillian Taylor, to her everlasting disappointment, did not attend that particular course, as she had been offered the position of first oboe with another youth orchestra; but the prestige of playing principal went nowhere towards compensating the missing of an NYO course.

Perhaps it was Chris who started to say "Watcha Doll" or "Hiya Chick" whenever he saw one of the girls. Within hours, all the boys had adopted the same phrases.

Sigi remembers sitting at breakfast when Chris suddenly decided to tell the assembled company about the cyst he had above his eye. She told me: "He made us all feel it (a little lump on his eyebrow), and then he and Phillip started to joke about why he was offering to let everyone feel his (cyst) sister – you were well known in the NYO of course. It was funny and charming and typically irreverent and inclusive. He was so alive and vivacious and crazy and happy."

On free afternoons the group walked down to the sea. They would usually stop on the way for a drink at the Honeysuckle Inn and then visit the Ramsgate funfair. Helen remembers going on the dodgems and sharing a car with Chris.

The orchestra gave a Prom concert at the Albert Hall on August 23rd, but the next day, instead of going home, they travelled to Belgium to give three concerts at the Flanders Festival. Those who played viola, horn, oboe, trumpet and flute were assigned to one of the three coaches. To their delight, this meant that most of the friends would be travelling together.

When they boarded the coach, the group secured a block of seats so that they could all be nearby. Chris must have seen his chance, for he neatly manoeuvred himself into a seat beside Helen Chapman. I remember my own scheming ways of planning 'chance' ways to sit next to boys I fancied on NYO journeys, but Helen was not a bold or devious type. The fact that she and Chris sat together was, I would think, by Chris's design.

The NYO had not been abroad for nine years. Society had subtly shifted over the last decade. Adults no longer held unquestionable authority. It was a more liberated, independent group of youngsters who set off by coach to board the ferry to Calais.

The NYO staff had maybe not thought through what might happen when 150 youngsters were let loose on a public ferry for nearly two hours. It was impossible to keep the group together, useless to try to police them. There were duty-free shops and bars. The older members were eighteen, nineteen, twenty – university students, not children; the thirteen- to seventeen-year-olds were hardly children either. The orchestra was no longer insulated and enclosed within the grounds of a boarding school. As Andy Findon put it, "the lid came off". It was a cheerful bunch that stepped off the ferry and continued by coach to Flanders.

Having established the seating arrangement, Chris again sat with Helen. Their relationship had begun to deepen into something more than friendship. Upon arrival in Ghent, the orchestra was invited to a reception and welcoming meal hosted by the Mayor and local dignitaries. Andy Findon told me: "It was a posh do – wine on the tables and waiter service. Of course we all drank and the waiters kept refilling our glasses. But the most extraordinary thing was that when the dessert plates had been cleared away, packs of cigarettes were distributed for an after-dinner smoke with the coffee. They were those continental-type soft packs, and the waiters literally threw them on the tables, as if they were sweets at a children's party. And yes, many of us lit up and smoked openly in front of the staff. There was nothing they could do to stop us." The un-smoked cigarettes were pocketed when the meal came to a close. As the orchestra filed out, every member was presented with a large poster of the forthcoming concert and a gladiolus. The photo of Andy, Helen and Chris on page 483 was taken just after the reception. To me it seems clear from the picture that Helen and Chris had become a couple: their body language says it all. Having recently come to know Helen, I have a sense of the girl she was then from the woman she is today. I can understand why Chris was attracted to her. Apart from being so very pretty, he would have loved her laugh, her thoughtfulness and quiet sensitivity; her intelligence and slight shyness; and possibly the fact that she wasn't as boisterous as the other girls.

The orchestra were put up at Ghent University in the student residential housing. The buildings were modern, almost luxurious, each person having a single room. Although girls and boys were assigned to different floors, lifts connected them. Abroad and in hotel-style accommodation, the battle to keep girls and boys segregated was about to be decisively lost.

Helen kept her gladiolus and put it in water in her room, but others used their sinks for a different purpose. Clive Miller, Martin Koch and Chris decided to throw a pyjama party. Surprisingly, Mr. Murray, the NYO housemaster, gave his consent. Perhaps he felt that after the ferry crossing and reception there was little sense in banning something that would happen anyway. At least the boys had been open and asked first. He made the proviso that they had to be discreet and the party must not get out of hand. Secretly, people went out to buy beer and kept the bottles chilling in cold water in their washbasins. Clive's bedroom started to fill with people – girls as well as boys. Chris and Helen spent the party in each other's arms kissing.

Helen, it has to be said, was not the first girl had Chris kissed. There were two others that I know about; one at a local party and another at a Redbridge Youth

Orchestra course, and there may have been more. But this was different. There is no way of knowing if Chris fell in love with Helen, but there is no doubt that she fell in love with him.

Mr. Murray kept out of the way, but at two o'clock in the morning he knocked on the door to ask them to go back to their own rooms. His face was a picture of disbelief as person after person tumbled from Clive's room. However, members of staff were not so lenient when a girl and boy were caught in bed together in another room. The girl was leaving the NYO anyway, but the boy, who was set to become a principal player the next year, was not invited back.

The orchestra gave their first concert at the Royal Opera House in Ghent and the following day they went by coach to Lokeren to perform at St. Laurentius Church. Their final concert was in Aalst, in St. Martin's Church, an impressive Gothic styled building dating back to 1480. High up in the roof space were bats, which flew about during the concert.

On every coach journey, Chris sat with Helen. Her clearest memories are the return trips. Aglow with post-performance excitement, having just played Tchaikovsky's passionate *Romeo and Juliet* overture and Brahms's magnificent first symphony, they embraced. Chris told Helen that she had the most beautiful eyes; and they are still beautiful – light crystal-clear green. What he loved about them, he said, was that he could see the whites of her eyes below the iris. He was also taken with the fact that one pupil was slightly larger than the other. Chris, the observer, spotted little details about Helen that nobody else saw – and appreciated them all.

The next morning the orchestra returned to London; that is, everyone but Helen. Her parents and brother were in France on a family holiday and it had already been arranged that Helen would join them when the NYO course ended. She was in floods of tears as she said goodbye to Chris. To be deprived of the journey back with him was very upsetting. The coaches departed and Ivey Dickson, the director of the NYO, drove Helen to the train station. In her arms she carried her gladiolus. She only just managed to get her suitcase, bags, oboe and self onto the train before the doors closed, squashing the gladiolus between them.

The trip to Flanders was the last time that Gareth Mollison and Phillip Eastop would play with the NYO, as they were both going to the Academy in September. Gareth was at this time going out with another horn player, Alison Jenkins. It seemed obvious that Phillip, Chris, Gareth and Alison should play the *Concertstück* – Schumann's concerto for four horns. Bram scheduled it for a *Concerti Allegri* concert the following March.

NYO course August 1974

Andy Findon, Helen Chapman and Chris in the grounds of Ghent University, Flanders.

BELOW LEFT:
Helen aged about seventeen

BELOW RIGHT:
Chris's passport photo taken for his trip to Flanders.

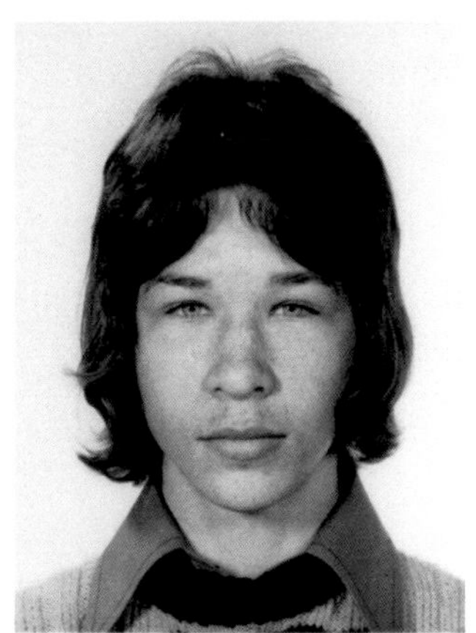

Early summer of 1974

ABOVE: Chris Stearn and Chris Giles

LEFT: Chris, Izzy and Simon

BELOW: A school photo of Izzy in her lower sixth year.

72
A DEATH

All that we are not stares back at what we are.

W. H. Auden

Grandad died on September 2nd 1974. I hadn't seen him since leaving home and was surprised how unmoved I was by his death. Auntie Lilian insisted that he be laid out and summoned Dad to assist. Izzy heard Mum and Granny muttering about this being "a ridiculous, unnecessary palaver." I had little idea what laying out a body entailed, but gathered that the corpse had to be washed, dressed in a best suit, shirt and starched collar, and the eyelids had to be closed and held shut by weighing them down with pennies. I wasn't surprised to hear that Dad found the procedure disturbing. He came home with a bottle of whisky and slumped in a chair in the living room, drinking it openly for once. I wasn't there, but Izzy remembers him saying, by way of explanation, "A man needs a glass of whisky when his father dies. It's the worst day of his life when there's not a soul left in the world to call him son."

I don't remember anything being said about a funeral, and anyway we knew that we would not be asked to attend. Funerals were considered to be as nonsensical as weddings – irrelevant religious ceremonies that were a complete waste of time and money. I assume Dad attended, but I don't actually know. Auntie Lilian would, in all sincerity, have wanted the correct rituals to be observed. Having nursed Grandad for a long time, she was not well herself and soon after the funeral moved to Torquay, where her children lived. I kept up a regular correspondence with her, but later realised that I was the only one of the family to do so. Mum didn't bother to keep in touch and Dad would have nothing more to do with her. He never saw her again. Sadly, neither did I. Her letters, written in a tremulous hand in one long sentence with no punctuation marks or paragraphs, were not easy to decipher, but it was touching that she managed to write at all.

> My Dear Cathy,
>
> I am so delighted to get your letter… now dear I found the other Table Cloth I hope you will like it took me a long time to do now dear will you ask Dad to give you the table the Pale Green and Pale Pink tiled top Just right for a Coffee Table you have it with my Love it was mine… will you tell Dad to give you the Tea Caddy and Tea Pot it only wants a little Soda and Hot Water left for a day it was given to me by Gordon's mother… Cathy I am very pleased to hear of your Wonderful Concerts I am very delighted to hear of your success at the Academy, you know my dear I am not surprised to hear you have won Prizes, yes Cathy I am very proud of you How I miss my trips to Ilford to hear you it was a joy to be there. I hope you find the Little Table useful for Coffee when your friends visit you I watch the papers for you and Simon. Give my love to all and a big kiss for Simon good luck for all you do.
>
> All my Love Auntie Lilian XXX

She had finally given up with the name 'Nana', signing off her letters to me as Auntie Lilian. I did not receive the coffee table, tea caddy or teapot, needless to say, but each time she wrote, she sent me something, and often included cuttings she found of Simon in newspapers.

Dad wallowed in grief. I had never seen any evidence of fondness between Grandad and Dad. Dad always complained bitterly about his father's meanness, bad-temper and narrow-mindedness. He loathed having to pay visits, resented being duty-bound and couldn't stand listening to his father's bigoted, reactionary opinions. Now that his father had died and there was nobody left to call him "son", I believe Dad was grieving for himself; his imperfect past; his aloneness. It seemed as though he used his bereavement as an excuse to flip into melodrama. He went to 82, Dumbarton Road, the place where he was born, and paced back and forth outside the house, staring at it. For a while, he sat crumpled on the doorstep – the same step where he'd seen his little sister, Betty, fall and crack her head. Then he wandered around the streets of Brixton. When the pubs opened, he shuffled to the bars, ordered large whiskies and sat alone, a picture of decrepitude. Late at night, he turned up again at Dumbarton Road, drunk, dishevelled and peculiar. An alarmed resident called the Police. Des Turner went to pick him up, after a call from the Brixton constabulary. The GP gave Dad time off work, prescribed anti-depressants and referred him to a psychiatrist. Mum, well practised at masking her despair, was at her wits' end, dragged down by the debilitating effects of Dad's depression.

A week after Grandad's death, Chris, now sixteen, began his Lower Sixth year at BHCHS, having passed eight O levels with high grades the previous term. As predicted, he had failed Maths. For his A levels, he chose English and Music and decided to take Sociology as his third subject. Sociology had not been an option at O level, so the idea was to sit the O level exam at the end of the Lower Sixth year and take the A level the following summer. Martin Wheatley (Nitram) had decided upon the same three subjects, so Chris and he spent most of their Lower Sixth together.

Only four boys opted for Music A level (Martin Koch and Cliff Oliver being the other two), and just six chose Sociology. The Sociology teacher, Mr. Stubbs, was an odd character who, until recently, had been a farmer in Lincolnshire. With little experience of teaching, his students automatically took up the slack, causing him to declare on more than one occasion that he had left farming in order to get *away* from animals. He arranged a Sociology trip to the Old Bailey, escorting his half-dozen pupils on the tube to St. Paul's station. There were no cases of interest going on that day, so after traipsing around the building, Mr. Stubbs was persuaded to spend the afternoon in a nearby hostelry. Whilst contentedly supping his pint, he complained that he didn't know how he had allowed himself to be talked into such a thing and the boys had better not be letting on to the school or their parents. Suppressing amusement, his pupils reassured him that they wouldn't breathe a word. As Martin Wheatley told me, the same boys were well-used to drinking during school hours: they slipped out frequently at lunchtimes to the Three Colts to have a pint or two and play bar billiards.

The summer break had not improved Chris's embouchure problem. The lump on his lip and the octave buzz were still there. However philosophical and positive he tried to be, part of him was going insane. John Ridgeon worked with Chris to find ways to reduce the buzz, so that it was inaudible to most listeners, but Chris heard it constantly – a tormenting noise that shadowed his every note. With all John's experience of embouchure difficulties, this was something he couldn't cure. However, he refused to be beaten – there had to be a solution. He decided to send Chris to see Maurice M. Porter, a consultant dentist who had devoted many years of research and study into the specific dental problems that affect the embouchures of wind and brass players. It was an inspired decision, as Maurice Porter identified the problem straight away. Chris had a narrow gap between his two front upper teeth. As he blew, a powerful jet of air was directed through the gap, which caused the swelling in his lip and, in turn, the octave buzz. The solution would be to fit a bridge between the teeth to fill the gap permanently. This would have to be done expertly so as not to change the shape of Chris's teeth, which might affect the embouchure in other ways. John suggested that Chris stick chewing gum between his teeth until the dental work could be arranged.

Chris went to Mr. Roger in Wimpole Street, the orthodontist whom Izzy saw, to have the work done, but once the bridge had been fitted there was still the problem of the lump. Maurice Porter thought it would disappear over time, but Mr. Roger suggested that it might be an enlarged salivary gland, which caused more worries. Chris fretted about it and discussed the possibility of plastic surgery.

From Chris to Paula Midgley, Glaswegian viola player in NYO: September 6th 1974:

Dear Paula,

It seems our letters crossed in the post. Let's hope that the same thing doesn't happen with the next two. Strangely enough you did sound like yourself in the letter – well done!

The Prom was a great success yesterday – I spent most of the afternoon not in the queue but in Paul Davis's flat with Dave Lockington, Paul, Vicky, Clive and Anne Baker.

The performance – the Rite of Spring, Covent Garden Orchestra under Colin Davis – was good but not exceptional. The horns were good, which is a shame because I prefer coming out of a concert thinking the horns were duff – it cheers me up. After the concert we all bombed down to the "99" for a drink.

Got a parcel from Liverpool yesterday morning containing my long lost pair of swimming trunks that John Kerrigan borrowed on the NYO course – isn't that interesting. I hope I sound like myself – all I do is write what first comes into my mind. But that's enough of the "Analysis of Human Psychology".

Love from Chris

73
THE FAIRY-GOD-CLARINETTIST

You give but little when you give of your possessions.
It is when you give of yourself that you truly give.

The Prophet – Kahlil Gibran

At the beginning of September, Izzy split up with Chris Stearn. Chris had been devoted to Izzy, with an anticipated future mapped out, but Izzy had not seen herself making the journey with him. Now she was feeling sad and wasn't sure if she had done the right thing. She prepared to leave for Leeds University with mixed feelings. Part of her was relieved to be leaving home, but she was also apprehensive about living in an unfamiliar place with people she didn't know: and she was worried about our brother, as was I. He was dreading being left on his own.

Rory Allam had arrived in London from Scotland the previous September. He played the clarinet and I met him on his first day at the Academy. Softly spoken, sweet and tender, hopelessly disorganised and utterly lovable, Rory and I became close friends. I think it was I who named him 'The fairy-god-clarinettist', because he wanted everyone to be happy and couldn't help but sprinkle his delightful blend of happy-dust amongst us all, and because one never knew when he was going to materialise. There was something innocent and elfin about him. If he wasn't always at the right place at the right time, it didn't seem to matter. I met him at the Queen Elizabeth Hall a week or so after the beginning of the new Academy year and asked how he was doing. I discovered that he had nowhere to live, having failed to arrange anything before coming back to London. He had been of irregular fixed abode the previous year, but now he was sleeping on people's floors, moving from place to place, never sure where he would be spending the next night. The nomadic lifestyle didn't bother him particularly, but having to cart around his belongings wherever he went had become a burden; it was also a problem that he was unreachable by telephone. I had an inspiration.

"My room at home's going spare since I left, and my sister's about to go to university. I'll ask Mum whether you could stay there." I phoned Mum, excited by my plan. Somehow, I had to persuade her. She sounded a little doubtful.

"But Mum, you always said you'd take in students when we left home."

"Did I?"

"I'm sure you did. Anyway, he's Scottish." That clinched it.

"Well OK, Cathy. I'll give it a trial period, see how it works out."

I told Izzy and Chris about Rory. "You'll adore him. He's the sweetest person – a lovely sense of humour, crazy about music... honestly Chris, I know you'll be friends."

"I'll let you know when I've met him."

"At least you won't be on your own, Chris," said Izzy.

From Chris to Paula Midgley: September 29th 1974

Paula Doll,

Thanks for the letter – why do you always knock yourself when you write? Rory, a 2nd year Academy Clarinet Student (he's Scottish) is coming as a lodger as from next weekend when Isabel leaves home for Leeds University. He'd better be a nice bloke!

On Saturday there's a horn quartet rehearsal in Reading, so I'll see Phillip, Gareth and Alison again – I'll give them the address of the International Horn Society – a 'World Horn Club' that Barry Tuckwell runs from America that I want to join.

Saturday: – the rehearsal went well and I was only slightly troubled by my '8ve buzz'. This (I think I told you) is caused by a lump of flesh in the top lip closing the aperture & vibrating at half the frequency of the rest of the lip. I thought this lump was being caused by being pressed between the gap between the 2 front teeth, but according to the Wimpole St. dentist it is more likely to be an unnecessary salivary or lymphatic gland within the lip – it might need surgery to remove it, so I'll just try to ignore it.

Thanks for Helen's address. Phillip's new horn is brilliant. Better than mine, but for £150 more that's what you expect. Andy Findon did not get his Midland Light Orchestra first flute job – the guy who retired came back. So he's going to the College.

I am reading a really "supeerrb" book by Ken Kesey (some unheard of Yank) called 'One Flew over the Cuckoo's Nest'. It is a book with sort of Clockwork Orange overtones written in the sixties. It's taken me nearly a week to write this letter – ridiculous. I'll post it now or you'll never get it.

Lots of love from Chris.

Chris called me up to his room when I was home one day.

"Cath, would you listen to me playing?"

"Sure."

"How does it sound? Can you hear the octave buzz?"

"No. Not at all. It sounds pure and clear to me."

"Come and stand next to me. There. Can you hear it now?"

"No."

"You must be able to. Put your ear as near to my mouth as you can. See? You must have heard it then."

"Well, I can hear a buzz – "

"Oh, God, I knew it."

"– but I'm sure it's just your lips vibrating as they should. Obviously they're going to vibrate. Look, play something else," I said, stepping a few feet away. He put the horn to his lips and out poured the opening phrases of Bruckner's fourth symphony.

"I can only hear your beautiful sound. Even playing that quietly, I don't hear any extraneous notes."

"It's definitely there."

"But Chris, nobody else can hear it. Maybe you've been so anxious about it that now you're imagining it?"

"I don't think so."

"Well, try not to worry too much. You don't need to. You're making a great sound. Go on – play me the opening of *Till Eulenspiegel* – I love that."

I had been aware of anxiousness in Chris's nature since we were very young. If something went wrong, he tended to go into a panic. If he couldn't find something, for example, he at once assumed it was irretrievably lost and quickly became too alarmed to look for it in a calm, logical way. He tried to be rational about his octave buzz, but he suffered the most awful anxiety about it.

Chris spoke to me about his worries, was always ready to have a laugh, tell a joke or converse at length about music, but he never talked to me, or Izzy, about girls. It seemed odd that our gorgeous brother, now sixteen, didn't appear to have a significant girlfriend, even though there were plenty of girls who fancied him. At the time, we knew nothing about Helen Chapman. Indeed, Chris does not appear to have confided in anyone about his relationship with her. There was a private part of Chris – something that his teacher, John Ridgeon, knew – a place of deep sensitivity, fragility and vulnerability; a part that, instinctively, he protected.

Chris had written to Paula for Helen's address – I think he must have forgotten to ask for her new address before they said goodbye in Flanders. Helen's family had moved from Dinas Powys to Reading after their holiday in France. Helen, though, decided to remain at her school in Wales and was now boarding at Howell's School for Girls. It was to her school address that Chris wrote. Helen recalls that they corresponded regularly, but unfortunately she cannot find any of his letters, or indeed the diaries she kept at the time. She suspects that they no longer exist.

The day before Izzy left for Leeds, she, Chris, Melanie and Jon Turner came over to Orchard Road. I must have cooked for us all, as Izzy comments in her diary: "A great meal." Mum drove Izzy to Leeds and she moved into Ellerslie Hall, one of the university's halls of residence. I arranged for Mum to meet her new lodger, Rory, at South Woodford station the next day.

Mum told me that she saw Rory at the end of the platform, long after all the other passengers had passed through the ticket barrier, struggling with rucksacks, bags, boxes, clarinets and bass clarinet. Rory had arrived, and there he was to stay for years, becoming an integral part of our disintegrated family and somehow gluing bits of it back together. He was a sparkling gem of a person who brought sunshine into the lives of everyone he met. Mum loved him to bits; Granny spoiled him; even Dad warmed to him. Rory was thrilled to find porridge and bramble jelly on the table and I dare say pleased to have a bed to sleep in, although the basics of life were never of any great importance to him. For Chris, Rory was much more than a companion: he was also music mad and madly silly.

"Well? How are you getting on with Rory?" I asked Chris at the next *Concerti* rehearsal.

"You were so right. He's a real laugh. We have some great conversations. You wouldn't recognise your room now. It's a complete mess – music that he's copying all over the floor, wires and cables running everywhere. And he can't wake up in the mornings. He sets four alarm clocks and puts one with bells on the top into the sink, so when it goes off it clatters around in the washbasin. Everyone but Rory is woken up. I go into his room, the noise from the alarm clocks is deafening – and there he is, sitting up in bed, fast asleep with his headphones on, the record player still revolving, clicking endlessly on the last groove. On his lap is a pad of paper, a pencil still in his hand, a line trailing from the last word he wrote – he never goes to sleep; sleep has to come and get him."

"I knew you'd like him."

"I can't imagine anyone who wouldn't. Even Dad seems more cheerful since his arrival."

From Chris to Aileen Morrison, another of his Glaswegian friends from NYO: September 1974

Dear Aileen,

Wednesday pm.

I am writing this just before departing for a festival hall concert – The Planets with the New Philharmonia. Concerti Allegri have started rehearsing and last Sunday I rehearsed with Gareth, Phillip and Alison and the Berkshire Wind Ensemble for a concert on Oct 20th doing the Richard Strauss Wind 'Symphonie' – you heard part of it at the NYO Brass concert.

Rory, our lodger, has arrived. I will probably have a lesson off Ifor James soon. I split my trousers right the way down the bum at school today – really funny for everyone but me. Getting off the bus was quite embarrassing.

Thursday pm.

Hi again – have just broken off from 1½ hours horn practice – I had a really good lip. Horn playing tends to be either very satisfying or very frustrating depending on the lip. I have just joined Barry Tuckwell's International Horn Society – a world horn club run from America. Oh yeah – the Planets last night was very good. Adrian Leaper (another of these lucky ex-NYO horns) was 'bumping'.[1]

We got a circular at school today saying that the VI form is a "full-time non-paid occupation" & that we ought to be doing 3 hours a night homework & 5 hours at weekends (Ha! Ha! Well, the headmaster must have his little joke)

Sunday.

Martin Wheatley came round last night (a school friend) & we played records & had a jam. One record with Frank Zappa & the "Mothers of Invention" was called "Weasels ripped my flesh"! Martin is a real weirdo and looks like a flat slug with pleurisy.

Anyway, I'll go now, so write soon & keep up the practice.

Lots of love Chris

I went to Simon's debut concert with the Bournemouth Symphony Orchestra in Aldershot. The programme was Schubert's 'Unfinished' symphony, Strauss's *Four Last Songs* with Linda Esther Gray and Dvořák's seventh symphony. I found my own way there and sat in the auditorium by myself, feeling lost and disconnected. There was no post-concert glow afterwards. Simon's agent drove us back to London. I listened to them talking, feeling as if I had been left behind – that they were on a

1. Many big orchestral works demand enormous stamina from the first horn player. When possible, the first horn has a 'bumper' sitting beside him or her – an extra player who will play in the tutti sections, bumping up the volume, in order to allow the first horn to preserve his or her embouchure and stamina for the solos.

train I had missed. Simon pushed his arm through the gap between the front seats and reached for my hand. I held onto the connection, perched sideways in the back. He gave a reassuring squeeze every now and then, as if to apologise for my being left out. It seemed he was saying: "Sorry Animal, this can't be much fun for you, but Martin and I have to talk about these things. Just hang on; I'll be with you soon." But I felt gauche and inhibited with the new people who were beginning to appear in Simon's life.

Our landlady contacted me to say that the downstairs flat would shortly be vacant, and asked if we would like to find some musician friends to rent it. I knew exactly whom I could ask – Corinne-Ann Frost and Trevor Snoad, fellow students at the Academy, who were looking for somewhere to live. Corinne was the girl who had won an Associated Board Scholarship at the same time as I, and Trevor played the viola. They moved in. The flats were self-contained, but Corinne and I phoned each other and met upstairs or downstairs for a coffee, cigarette and chat. Corinne enjoyed feminine pursuits such as buying clothes from catalogues, browsing through glossy women's magazines, taking care of skin, hair and nails and trying out cosmetics. I didn't spend time on any of these activities, but Corinne nagged me gently to try using hair-conditioner, allow her to deal with my split-ends and wear a bit of make-up. Soon after they moved in they acquired a kitten and named her Sugar. Simon, however, called her Fred.

Izzy returned home to attend the *Concerti* concert on October 5th. For once she sat in the audience, not the orchestra. I was performing the Elgar cello concerto, in which there are some exposed moments for the horn. Chris played them beautifully. Nobody would have believed that he was still agonising about his embouchure. Simon, back for the weekend from Bournemouth, played timpani. Bram conducted with flair and authority and the orchestra played very well. Izzy met Rory and found him as delightful as I had promised. Without a doubt, Rory had brought his magic wand to Cleveland Road.

From me to Izzy: October 9th 1974

Dear Izzy,

Thought I'd drop a line to my little sister in Leeds. How's everything going then? I didn't even have time to ask you on Saturday. Thanks everso much for coming to the concert by the way – I think you take all the nerves for me. Actually I was much more nervous for that than the Rococo. I had a really bad cello lesson today – a post mortem on the Elgar basically – Florrie is never satisfied with anything.

I've seen Matthew quite a few times since camp – he only lives a couple of roads away from us in Highgate. He's found us a kitten by the way – a silver tabby, ready in 4 weeks. One evening he turned up at about a quarter to 10 and took me off to someone's house to watch a film on TV called 'Ottley' – twas really good actually (so much for my early night). There were a couple of little kids there – only about 5 and 4, but they stayed up and watched the film also – a really disorganised household – not a bad thing in many ways – I'm sure the whole family feels much freer and more relaxed when they can do what they like when they like and know that it won't be frowned upon as odd or irresponsible.

Matthew & I might hitch to Leeds to see you by the way – let us know a good time to come (coinciding with a party or something). I've been having a very active social life during the weeks when Simon's been away – I have to see lots of people to stop me from getting depressed. It really can be very lonely living on your own. It's the mornings that are worse – waking up to nobody and not saying anything at all – only having the radio to scream at.

Anyway, if you have time, do write and tell me what you're doing – it must be very different from anything else you've experienced. Simon sends you an enormous ravish and says to look after your "ace bum"!!

Lots and lots of love, Cathy

From Izzy: October 10th 74

Dear Cathy,

University is great fun. I spend most of my time with the music people. There are some ex-NYO people here who know you. Bruce Fox is here and another horn player called Duncan Hollowood. I'm in a clarinet quintet and the University orchestra, and I hope to be getting lessons from Eta Cohen.

On Nov 3rd, the BBC Symphony Orchestra and Pierre Boulez is coming up here to play at the University. In one of the pieces, they need music students to sing, so I might even get around to being conducted by Boulez!

Give Simon a big hug from me.

See you soon, loads of love, Izzy XXX

My reply: October 13th 1974

Dear Izzy,

Ta for the letter. Glad to hear you're enjoying yourself.

Simon and I went to Windsor Castle yesterday night (mixing with Royalty now, yer know!), with Simon's agent, Martin Campbell-White – went to his house for tea first and met his little son, Benedict. Anyway, Andrew Davis conducted the Verdi Requiem – Andrew Davis is under the same agent as Simon – another budding young conductor (actually he's 30, but that's young amongst conductors – incredible when Simon's still only 19!) We were in the best seats and afterwards were taken to a select coffee party in another part of the Castle – it's an enormous place.

I don't know that I like the atmosphere of the backstage music world – with so many people, you have the feeling that they're false and insincere, only being nice to push themselves forward. However, Martin, (Simon's agent) is very nice.

I received a letter from Mel – have you heard about Paul Hart? – playing with Cleo Laine, John Dankworth and Stephane Grappelli!! – in the Carnegie Hall! It's incredible.

Simon sends you an enormous ravish by the way.

Lots of love, Cathy

Izzy started going out with Duncan Hollowood, who happened to be a friend of Gareth Mollison's. Chris was pleased to hear that his sister's boyfriend was a horn player – another person with whom he could converse about horns.

From Chris to Izzy: October 27th 1974

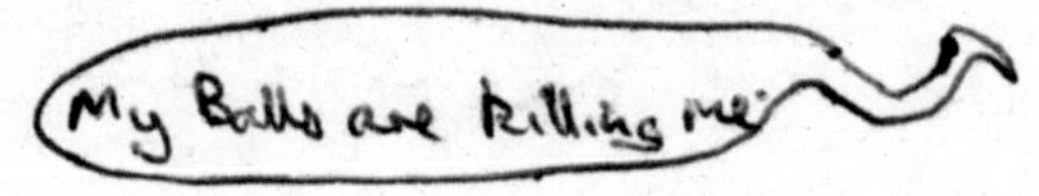

Dear Izzy,

I did give Gareth Duncan's message and Gareth sends his best wishes. I will be seeing Alison, Phillip and Gareth for a horn 4tet rehearsal tomorrow afternoon on the Schumann. Yes, I agree, the Brahms horn trio is hard. At the Reading concert (which went excellently except that I haven't got my money yet!), Marios Papadopoulos (the brilliant pianist who did a Hawkey Hall recital), Phillip and Haroutune Bedelian (the violinist who won the BBC fiddle competition 8 years ago) played it. (what a sentence).

I "did" the Musici day series yesterday. Redbridge has a new horn teacher who is a really nice bloke and (unfortunately) a very good player too – he was an engineer but was made redundant so he applied to all the music colleges. Mid-term, he could only get into the London College where he stayed for 3 years. He gets all the 8th horn jobs for the BBC Symphony Orchestra, but he plans just to teach for the next few years – he was on the short list, (but didn't get the job), for the BBC Scottish Orch., out of 60 applicants!!! Just for the record, he plays an Alexander B*b* and A single horn with an H/P/C Paxman mouthpiece. BUT ENOUGH OF THIS SHOP TALK. Musici are doing a QEHall concert in Jan. – Berlioz Fantastic Symphony.

Monty Python's Flying Circus is coming back this Thursday (minus John Cleese) so try not to miss it. I am writing on large paper because ordinary notepaper gives me literary claustrophobia.

Lots of love, Chris

28, Orchard Road, Highgate, photographed in 2008. Simon and I moved into the upstairs flat in July 1974. Trevor and Corinne moved in downstairs a few months later. The house looks almost exactly the same as it did then.

Photos by Martha Giles

BUCKHURST HILL COUNTY HIGH SCHOOL FOR BOYS, OCTOBER 1974
Back row, left to right: Cliff Oliver, Simon Mansfield, Martin Koch, Martin Wheatley, Chris Giles, Michael Maxwell (staff), Brian Harper, Ian Theodoreson
Front four, left to right: Andrew Williams, Neill Cotton, Jeremy Dibble, Ian Brown

74
LOST AND FOUND

It's in the seeing,
the half full/half empty
moment by moment
way of being.

It's in the not saying,
not lifting the lid
of the can; the choice
between smiling and crying.

It's in the winging, singing
C major, when what's
in her mind is D minor;
it's in not clinging.

Brave Face from *The Other Woman* – Carole Satyamurti

Simon was finding it tough going with the Bournemouth orchestras. I knew he was struggling, but there was nothing I could do to help. He was used to working with his student band and being greeted by warm, supportive friends. The Merseyside and International Festival Youth Orchestras adored working with him and he with them. He had never before been in a situation where musicians resented him. The hostility that was shown towards him by some members of the Bournemouth Symphony Orchestra and the Sinfonietta, their resistance and unwillingness to co-operate, was shameful. They seemed intent on doing their best to destroy him. For the first time in his life, he was unwelcome and unpopular. Typically, he underplayed his distress, insisting that his inexperience was the cause of the problems; but I wasn't persuaded. I thought they were a bunch of bitter, musically-anaesthetised old pros. Perhaps it was his youth and energy, his precocious talent and passion that antagonised them. They had no time for an enthusiastic teenager looking to bring freshness and vitality to the orchestral repertoire – music that they had been playing in their own entrenched way for years. They also took exception to Simon introducing 'modern' works into their programmes – Stravinsky, Janáček and Bartók did not go down well. However hard Simon tried, he did not get the emotional response to the music that he wanted from the orchestras. He found rehearsing with them very difficult, and most of the concerts were, for Simon, unrewarding and musically stymied.

Simon was troubled and I was unhappy with Simon away. We spoke on the phone every day and he returned to London as much as possible – sometimes just to come back for a night and leave again the next day – but I started to become clingy. He didn't talk much about the opposition and unpleasantness he had to contend with in Bournemouth. Most of it he kept to himself. Instead he told me the nice things that happened, but when he spoke about going out for dinner with people I didn't know, I felt jumpy and jealous. On several occasions he mentioned a Finnish girl he had met at the IFYO in Aberdeen and told me she was also a twin. He described her as having long, white-blonde hair and said they'd had enjoyable conversations. Did he fancy her? Did he compare us and find me wanting? She had written to him and he had written to her. How frequently were they in communication? Had something gone on between them over the summer? Every word he spoke of her stabbed me with panic. Insecurity alerted me when any woman's name came into our conversation. If I answered the phone to a female voice, I would ask who was speaking then quiz Simon about the caller, unable to leave it alone. The suspicious response he received from me inhibited his desire to share his experiences: his silence increased my qualms. Simon loved as he always had: I faltered.

I was also unmotivated and under-occupied. The Performer's Course I was taking required me, in my third year, to be at the Academy for just four-and-a-half hours a week – a three-hour Chamber Orchestra rehearsal and a ninety-minute cello lesson. I had dropped second-study piano and no longer attended aural and harmony classes, having passed the exams needed to gain the RAM Professional Certificate. I was still supposed to have a thirty-minute lesson on a second instrument, but couldn't make up my mind what to play. Then, on one of my infrequent appearances at the Academy, I happened to meet the charming, corpulent Norman Knight, who suggested I take up the flute. Norman coached the NYO's flute section and was an Academy professor. My lessons took place in a pub down the Marylebone High Street, where he bought me drinks and we would spend a pleasant while chatting. During the two years I studied the flute I became knowledgeable about cocktails, but failed to learn how to produce a sound. Indeed, I didn't even have a flute for the first two terms. I could have practised the cello for hours and hours a day – it was what I should have been doing – but practice had become unstimulating; a repetitive chore that gave little pleasure. I hadn't lost my passion for music, but with the cello I felt as if I were on a treadmill. I had no enthusiasm or ambition for a solo career. The only escape route, it seemed, was relationship: there I would find fulfilment and happiness. I wanted to collapse into a place of safety where I could abandon the cello and share every moment of my life with Simon.

Then something happened to brighten our lives. The Nash Ensemble invited Simon to conduct Schoenberg's *Pierrot Lunaire* in some concerts in Spain. As I knew a couple of the members of the Nash Ensemble, Simon asked me if I would like to come along to the London rehearsals. I sat in the Craxton Studios feeling great love for Simon and listening in awe to the musicians. In the breaks they chatted to me and treated me with the same respect they showed to Simon.

Simon was in his element, working with intelligent, dedicated, sincere people whose objective was to create music of the highest quality. It was exactly what he needed. After rehearsals, we all went out for meals, with musical debate on the menu along with fun, friendship and wine. Love was not far away, but neither were the destructive forces within me.

Postcard from Simon showing a banana tree, October 30th 1974, Las Palmas

Dear Cath,

I thought bananas would probably suit you just now. Las Palmas itself is very commercial & touristy, but in a good hotel tonight. Loads of bureaucratic mishaps, worries of plane seats for cellos etc. A marvellous concert tonight – I have saved you a programme & we had a standing ovation for Pierrot, which went very well. As you would imagine, wonderful people to travel about with. It is now past midnight – we leave hotel at 5.45 a.m.!! Be thinking of me, not forgetting how much I love you from Simon.

Postcard of the Prado Museum from Simon, October 31st 1974, Bilbao

Dear Cathy,

As it now seems a little probable that we will have time to visit the Prado, I thought you should have a souvenir. Last night after the concert, we had our first real Spanish meal in Bilbao. Fish soup, artichokes etc and delicious molto vino. Most of the evening spent in hysterics! Now at Bilbao airport, we set off for Madrid soon. We will have 3 or 4 hours to look round – still looking for a suitable present for you: we shall see. Try to keep the bed warm. I'm looking forward to seeing you yesterday (probably) Great love Simon

Back from Spain, Simon began rehearsing Ravel's *L'Enfant et les Sortilèges* and Stravinsky's *Pulcinella* for three performances at the RAM with the Opera Group and the Chamber Orchestra at the end of November. By coincidence, I found a complete set of 78rpm records of *L'Enfant* in a Highgate junk shop and bought the lot for very little. The discs were warped and scratchy, plus there were so many sides to listen to that the order of play became a little muddled. Still, I heard it in four-minute bursts on our ancient record player and became familiar with it before rehearsals started. Working again with Simon, sitting almost directly under his baton, my spirits lifted. It was wonderful to be absorbed into the enchantingly atmospheric musical interpretation he brought to the production.

A particularly memorable moment was when Simon and I went to the Festival Hall to hear *The Firebird.* I was astounded when Marnie's theme re-materialised. The music I hadn't heard since I was ten poured into me and tears streamed out. Simon squeezed my hand. "What's wrong?" he mouthed. I turned to him with watery eyes and a smile of relief on my face. In the interval I told him about my lost melody. He explained the puzzle. *The Firebird* that Chris and I had listened to was the 1910 version of the entire ballet music. Later, Stravinsky arranged the score into *The Firebird Suite*, which does not include Marnie's theme. This was the record I had been given as a present and also the version used in our Junior School *Cinderella* play. At long last the mystery was explained. Simon hugged me tightly, but was quite bemused by my emotional upheaval. Chris was also at the concert, but he had known about the different versions of *The Firebird* for ages and only vaguely remembered the story I had read to him all those years ago. He was already way ahead of me in musical knowledge. In the programme notes, I discovered that the tune Chris and I had thought of as Marnie's is the one used to portray the 'Appearance of Thirteen Enchanted Princesses'. So you see; there *is* magic in it.

Another series of concerts was scheduled for *Concerti Allegri* and an AGM was held. Since its inception, *Concerti* had been organised by a committee. Bram was the conductor, but others booked rehearsal venues, concert halls, hired music and stands, printed programmes and tickets, sent out schedules and organised fundraising events. It was a collective endeavour. Bram and the committee put in a lot of effort and it was hoped that every member of the orchestra would contribute in more than just a playing capacity. At the AGM, there was the usual business of persuading people to volunteer for various jobs, but there were two other major items on the agenda. One was that of programme planning. Everyone had different ideas as to what we should play. Some thought that more opportunity should be given to young Redbridge composers to have their works performed; others felt strongly that we should stick to the standard repertoire. Some held out for Mahler and Schoenberg, others for Mozart and Schubert. The second issue was that of personnel. Why was so-and-so not invited to play in the last concert? Should we hold auditions? Who would choose the players? Wouldn't it be fairer to rotate the leaders' chairs? Why shouldn't the wind players all get a chance to play principal if they wanted?

Bram sat at the table with the committee saying not a word while lively debate zapped between the floor and the chair. Separate conversations sprouted from other parts of the hall until the chairman had to call for order. He rounded up the meeting, suggesting a working party be formed to democratically agree upon programmes, personnel and possible rotation of principals.

"Does anyone have anything else they wish to say?"

There was silence, then – "Yes," said Chris, getting to his feet, the only person so far to do so. He had, as yet, not contributed to the debate at all. "I've been listening to everything people have been saying and I think you're all missing the point. An orchestra by its very nature is a dictatorship. It is not possible to run an orchestra democratically. How can you swap around players without losing the integrity of the sound of the orchestra? The principals who are in place at the moment are there because we all know they're the best players. If better players come along, they should assume those positions. We want the orchestra to sound as good as possible, don't we? If Bram feels that someone isn't up to scratch, they must be excluded. It shouldn't be open for negotiation. And as far as programming is concerned, we can make suggestions, but it has to be Bram who makes the decisions. It's up to him what he wants to conduct – he's the conductor. Politically, a dictatorship works perfectly as long as the dictator is a nice and reasonable man. I think we all have complete respect for Bram as a person and a musician, so, in my opinion, I think it's a waste of time to debate programmes or personnel – we should leave Bram to make his own decisions and support him to implement them." He sat down.

I had been listening with stupefied admiration whilst watching Bram, who had been staring at Chris with a look of astonishment mingled with pride. He dropped his head to his chest, but I could see he was grinning. A little ripple of applause lapped around the hall.

"Well," responded the chairman, slightly ruffled, "I wish you'd spoken sooner, Chris, rather than leaving your observations to the very end. Does anyone else have anything more to say?"

"Yeah, I think Chris is right," said Chris Stearn.

"So do I," chorused more voices.

Afterwards I told Chris I thought he had spoken absolutely brilliantly. He shrugged his shoulders and said, "I was only stating the obvious."

From Izzy: Leeds, November 8th 1974

Dear Cath,

We were conducted by Boulez. Actually, I thought it was a pretty chronic concert. We only had one rehearsal and none of us are particularly fantastic singers – not that we did anything wrong but we just didn't sound that good. The orchestra was very diminished – none of the great names in the brass world were there. The 1st trumpet was grotty. We were sitting right behind him and following his part. In the Bach/Stravinsky thing he counted all his bars wrong and completely missed all his entries & didn't know where he was – you should have seen Boulez' face!

I'm having fortnightly lessons with Eta Cohen. At least she'll make me practise! Parties are in abundance up here, which is rather good, except it means forking out a lot on booze. I'm going to two this weekend and a football match with Duncan in Manchester. How's Simon? I hope Bournemouth's going OK. Manoug Parikian came up on Monday and coached us in Brandenburg III for concert on Nov 30th and I'm playing in the orchestra for the Light Opera's production of 'Orpheus in the Underworld' – should be good fun.

Love to Simon, loads of love,

Izzy

From Chris to Izzy: November 11th 1974

Hija. I met Penny, Sigi, Phil & Gareth at the Academy over half-term – we spent most of the time in The Rising Sun, Prince Regent, and boating on the Regents Park Canal! I saw yours and Duncan's letter to Gareth – we will take you up on the offer to go to Leeds some time. Anyway, I must tell you about the exciting events of yesterday.

I was doing a job with Gareth and Alison for the Heston and Isleworth Symphony Orchestra in Ealing, bumping in Brahms One, and I fear a few other things (for a fee of £3). On the way back from the afternoon rehearsal, in Gareth's car, we had a juicy crash. We were coming down the right hand lane of a dual carriageway quite fast, as a white van pulled out from an intersection. It did not see us (driver drunk??) so we changed to the left lane and braked. It still did not stop, and Gareth couldn't go onto the pavement, as there was a lamppost, so we crashed. Both cars were spun right round, and G and A would have been thrown out of the windscreen but they were wearing safety belts. Alison's horn got dented, I got a bruised leg and Gareth was taken to hospital with his hand cut open (Alison screamed, but Gareth and I were cool and calm, having nerves of steel). Now here comes the good bit. After the crash, the driver of the white van got out and ran away as fast as poss (had he stolen the car?) up a driveway. The house he appeared to be going towards was totally empty, but with all the lights on, both back and front doors open and an apple pie baking in the oven! The police are investigating, but unless the other driver is found, Gareth will get no insurance paid as he only has 3rd party. After all that, the concert went very well.

Went to BBCSO Firebird concert at Festival Hall on Wednesday – the Complete Firebird with two offstage Tubas and 2 offstage Trumpets. Forest Phil have started rehearsing again – 'Till Eulenspiegel' and 'Mathis der Maler' by Hindemith (do you know it? – it's really good). Concerti starts this Thursday for the Nov 23rd concert, Musici starts next Friday (I think I've told you this before). 40 pints of lager has just been bottled, £10 job money is owed to me and Forest Phil are doing MAHLER 3 next June – (Gareth wants to play in it). It starts with 8 unison horns – knowing Frank,[1] he'll have 16. Went to B & H's[2] after Siegrid's party (James Brown and half the LSO were there – at Sigi's I mean) and I played a shop sign – an imitation quadruple 'C' tuba where any note can be bluffed because harmonics are ¼ tone apart. B & H's are also starting to make Imperial French horns again (tell Duncan).

While I'm here I might as well tell you about Sigi's party. It started off with fireworks and a barbeque for the kiddies. Me, Phil and Gareth were going "Wheeeeeee" at the rockets – it was a real joke and all the kiddies thought we were really awed, and not just having a joke. At about 10.00 it became a hard drinking session in one room, a master class cello lesson in the other, and 'session men' and ex LSO people reminiscing about the old NYO days in another. We felt a little out of our depth, especially when James Brown (Academy horn teacher) came in as Phillip was running through the Brahms horn trio! James Brown drank half a bottle of wine when we were there and apparently got through another whole one after we left. Rutledge Turnlund (Sigi's brother) who is about 5, looked at me just after I had come through the door, and the very 1st thing he said was "Coo you n' half got funny eyes". I was very flattered.

Lots of love from Chris

P.S. try and be home for an NYO/Academy/Locals party on Dec 14th

P.P.S. Don't forget December 14th

In late autumn, I went for a walk along the disused railway as far as the tunnel near Archway. As I turned around to make my way back, I noticed a sodden wad of paper on the ground. Then I saw that it was actually a large number of folded £5 and £10 bank notes. It seemed to be a lot of money and looked as though it had been there for some time. I couldn't leave it – someone else might pick it up and keep it.

1. Frank Shipway, conductor of Forest Philharmonic and Hatfield Philharmonic Orchestras.
2. Boosey and Hawkes.

No, the best thing to do would be to take it to the Police Station. I walked straight there. Having not been in a Police Station before, I entered with a curious feeling of trepidation. There was nobody around, but a notice on the desk said to ring for attention. As I lifted my hand to hit the bell, a Policeman materialised, which made me jump.

"What can I do for you, young lady?"

"Well, I've just found this money," I said nervously, depositing the damp bundle on the desk, "and thought I should hand it in so whoever has lost it can claim it back."

His look of disbelief scared me – perhaps he thought I had stolen it myself, or that it was wrong to have picked it up.

"And where exactly did you find it?"

"Along the disused railway, outside that tunnel, the one by Archway," I explained, speaking at twice my normal speed. "It was just lying there on the ground, wet and dirty – in fact it may have been there for some time…"

"OK, OK," he interrupted. Yes, he had me down as a criminal; it was obvious.

"How much money is here?"

"I don't know exactly. I haven't counted it, but it seems a lot."

"You haven't counted it? Then I suggest we count it together."

It was £120 – a fortune.

"I'll be back in a moment," he said, disappearing behind a door. I waited, feeling foolish and vaguely guilty.

"Right, young lady, you need to fill in this form. Name, address, contact telephone number if you have one, where and when you found the money, its value, today's date and sign."

I did as I was told. He checked it over, signed and dated it himself and put the document and the money into an envelope. Then he explained that they would keep it for four months, but if it hadn't been claimed by that time, they would contact me, and the money would be mine.

"Really?"

"Yes, that's the procedure. You found it and if nobody claims it, it's yours. To be frank, I very much doubt that anyone will come forward. Nobody expects lost cash to be handed in. You're a very honest person."

"Well, thank you." So I wasn't a suspect after all. I left the station with a cheery goodbye, excited by the thought that I might be getting £120!

True to his word, the Police Officer phoned four months later to say the money had not been claimed and I could come and pick it up at my convenience.

From me to Izzy: November 25th 1974

Dearest Izzy,

Concerti Allegri was pretty chronic this time. Bram wasn't conducting and the first 'rehearsal' I was able to go to was the concert. I found myself landed with several big cello solos, which I had to sight-read. One of the pieces started off with a cello solo – no one else playing at all. Simon came to the concert and we stayed the night at Cleveland Road.

There wasn't even a party this time as no-one offered.

Chris has got some stuff to put on his lip to cure his embouchure problem and it seems to be working. I hope it'll be OK. I have to perform the Elgar at the RAM on Dec 9th with 2nd Band, Bram conducting – they told me today, which gives me 2 weeks to relearn it. I performed the Bach C minor unaccompanied suite at the RAM last Wednesday, which went very well – I was very pleased.

We did a ridiculous string 4tet concert last Friday. It was after a banquet at the International Press Centre. Well, all the speeches went on so long that at 10.30pm we were told that we weren't required to play. They're still going to pay us £10 each for not playing a note.

Mum took Simon & me back to Highgate on Sunday afternoon and I drove – we're still in one piece believe it or not! Write soon if you can,

Lots & lots of love & a big hug from Simon,

Cathy

From Izzy: December 8th 1974

Cathy love,

Ta muchly for the letter – glad to hear everything's OK. Everything with me is just great, mainly, in fact wholly, because of Duncan. We want to live together after Christmas; the trouble is finding someone to fill my place at Ellerslie Hall. Everything's happened so quickly – I feel I'm in a whirl the whole time – rather a gorgeous feeling though. Would you believe, I've taken the plunge and am about to go on the Pill – so if I begin to bust out, (literally) don't be surprised. Knowing my luck I'll probably put all the weight on my bum, and my top half will remain sadly flat as ever. Cathy, this letter is not meant to be frivolous – I haven't told anyone else all that is happening to me – don't be worried for me – I know everything's going to be great – it is already! I'm dreading telling mum & dad about living with Duncan – Mum will be really surprised and probably quite worried. She won't think I'm mature enough and'll think I'm diving in at the deep end with my eyes shut. I don't think I am, though. Duncan & I have reasoned things out together and have come to the conclusion that we can't bear it if we're not together the whole time. At the moment I spend most of my time at 4, Autumn Street, but I still have to drag myself back to Ellerslie – it hurts.

I'm going to a music course with Duncan over Christmas from 27th – 29th at Abingdon and sometime in January we're going to Brighton to stay with his sister. Last time I came home, we went to Highgate to see his other sister – she lives very near you & Simon. We came round to Orchard Road to see you but you were out!

Tonight Duncan and I are going to a Ball – £2.75 double ticket. I splashed out and bought a new dress – £11, don't faint! I'm cooking supper for 4 round at Duncan's – yes, I'm actually cooking – all instructions from Duncan! Going to a party on Saturday – the biochemists are making punch – guaranteed really potent.

I saw Chris Stearn last time I came home, the first time I've spoken to him since we split up – he was really sweet. Chris (Giles) never stops talking about Aileen, viola player in NYO. I don't know if he's still mad on her, but he was then.

Anyway, I'm glad I've told you everything – I feel better!

Loads of love, Izzy XXXX

Even though I had been living with Simon for more than a year, Izzy was worried about Mum and Dad's reaction to her living with Duncan. As I had done, she went to a family planning clinic and started taking the pill before getting sexually involved. I had always thought that Izzy had parted with her virginity before I had. I was wrong.

My reply:

Dearest Izzy,

Ta lots for your letter. I'm so happy for you – tell Duncan he's a very lucky bloke! Don't worry at all what Mum says. You're doing the right thing & you're obviously very sure of everything. I've never told you, but I had a hell of a time with Mum when I moved in with Simon. I'll tell you more about all that when I see you at Christmas. Basically, she thought that the only reason I wanted to live with Simon was because I couldn't bear to live at home. Also, if you remember I was something like six stone at that time & I'm sure she thought I was going to starve to death. But as none of these things apply to you i.e. you're already away from home anyway – I shouldn't think she'll create too much. Dad'll probably be your problem, but don't take any notice of him either. He's getting more and more impossible. You really can't have a rational conversation with him any more.

I'm afraid I haven't time to write any more – I'll see you at Christmas and we can talk then. Meanwhile, don't worry about anything! I'm so glad you're so happy – look after yourself – and – CONGRATULATIONS!!

Lots of love to Duncan – we'll meet on 19th or 20th no doubt.

And lots of love to you,

Siya, Cathy XXXXX

75
FALLING APART

There are times you know nothing of –
the insistent now, and now, and now…
It's not as if I've anything momentous to say
but in not saying it, in leaving it unsaid
there is a small influx of anguish –
the death of something ungiven.

Ungiven – Gregory Warren Wilson

I was missing Simon unbearably and decided to go to Bournemouth to see him. On arrival, I called him from a telephone box. "Guess where I am?"

"You're in Bournemouth."

I hadn't surprised him at all. He sounded weary and deflated. My heart sank. I found my way to his address and he let me in. The building smelt of cheap air freshener and toilet cleaner. I followed him up several flights of stairs and entered his flat, which was nothing more than a partitioned-off section of what had once been a large room. At the far end was a tall, narrow window, which looked out onto the wall of another building. At the other end was a mean cubbyhole of a kitchen with no window at all. He had to share a shower and loo with the other tenants. What a miserable, claustrophobic place, I thought. I asked him why he couldn't find somewhere nicer to live. Everywhere was expensive, he said, and anyway he didn't have time to look. I was shocked when he told me he was paying £15 a week for it: our whole flat was only £11 a week. He said it wasn't his home – just somewhere to sleep: home was Orchard Road, with me. I had never seen Simon so low and cheerless. Even making love didn't lift the gloom. He was tired and depressed, worried about the next day's rehearsals and needing sleep. I tucked him into the single bed, settled myself on the floor and listened to him breathing. I realised that my unplanned visit had been a mistake. Back at Orchard Road, another letter arrived for him with a Finnish postmark: my stomach did a full somersault.

A few days later, the principals of the Chamber Orchestra were sent to Guernsey to play in Handel's *Messiah*. It was something the Academy did every year: I had no choice but to go. The journey, in a twelve-seater plane from Southampton, was terrifying. It was the first time I had flown. We were met at the airport and farmed out to various hosts. I was placed with a woman whose husband had recently died. She spoke openly with me about her late husband, not trying to hide her grief. Charles Pollard was also on the trip. He met up with me every day and took me out in a car he hired. We went to the fish market where I was horrified to see live crabs tossed into cauldrons of boiling water and even more horrified when I heard their high-pitched screams. It might have been the noise of air escaping from the shells, but it sounded like torture to me and put me off crabmeat for a long time.

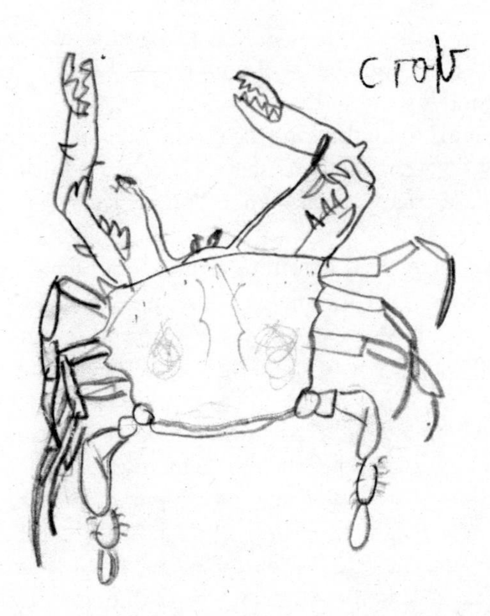

I was restless and lonely, worried about Simon, our relationship and my uncontrollable eating. My hostess cooked meals, which we both nibbled at – her lack of interest in food equal to my obsession with it. At night, I raided her kitchen, stealing things from the fridge and cupboards. She was too heartbroken to notice or care. She just wanted to talk, and seemed to find my company comforting.

One day a trip was organised for us to Sark, the tiniest of the islands. We were rowed over in a boat and led up a winding track to a quaint church. The roof had holes in it and some of the stained-glass windows were missing or broken. Ivy was growing freely through the gaps, its tendrils creeping along the walls. We sat through a service, sang carols, and soaked up the tranquillity of the setting. Afterwards, we assembled in a large house by the sea where we were served mince pies and mulled wine. I refused the mince pies and drank far too many glasses of wine on an empty stomach. I felt horribly queasy on the boat trip back. Charles looked at my green complexion and said, "If you're going to be sick, make sure you throw up over the side." I can't remember whether I disgraced myself or not.

We rehearsed the *Messiah* with the amateur orchestra, who were delighted to have us there and made us feel most welcome. My hostess was singing in the chorus, so she and I made our way to the venue together for the concert. The performance began and was going along fine, when suddenly one of the male choir members crashed to the floor right by my feet. The *Messiah* ground to a halt. A plea was made to the audience for a doctor, but nobody came forward. An ambulance arrived to carry the singer away, after which the performance resumed. At the end it was announced that the man had died. I was in tears as we left the concert hall. Charles was concerned. My hostess, a frail little woman, wrapped a surprisingly strong arm around me. "She's shaken up, aren't you, dear? Don't fuss, Charles, I'll look after her. Come on, Cathy. Let's go home."

She took my arm, linked it through hers and led me away, saying, "When we get back, I'm going to pour you a glass of brandy – in fact, I'm going to pour us *both* large glasses of brandy."

We sat in her living room drinking the promised brandy, and I cried my eyes out.

"There, there, dear," she said. "You have a good cry. I know how you're feeling."

Perhaps she did. Perhaps she also knew that my tears were about everything.

I tried not to be gloomy, yet the unsettling feeling of distance between Simon and me that had been niggling over the summer appeared to be getting wider. I started to complicate, then distort. My imagination was wild and self-injurious. I was not just fearful of abandonment; I was tortured by jealousy; overcome with possessiveness. An ugly voice contaminated my words. With helpless horror, I watched as I destroyed our love. We were both fearful of the monster Simon's little animal had become.

I had been writing in the kitchen while Simon was studying scores in the living room. I called to him that I was going out shopping. He asked if I could post his letters. I walked up Orchard Road to the post box at the top of the hill. As I was pushing the letters into the box, I stopped, chilled, when I saw one addressed to the Finnish girl. I stared at Simon's writing, my heart thumping furiously.

Instead of posting the letter, I walked along the disused railway cutting. Out of sight from the road, I sat down on the verge and turned the envelope over. It was not very securely sealed. It would be easy to open, then carefully reseal and put in the post box. Nobody would know; except me.

I struggled with myself. How could I think of doing something so deceitful and sneaky? I'd be breaking every last shred of trust. Simon would never forgive me. Did I even want to see what he had written? And what about the consequences? The guilt? The secret I would have to keep? I must get up and post the letter now. It was bad enough to have even thought of opening it.

But I was gripped by jealousy and the fearful, terrible need to know the worst. My fingers slipped beneath the flap and prised open the seal. I withdrew two flimsy sheets of airmail paper. I looked at Simon's familiar writing and scanned the pages, but I was unable to take in a word. It was meaningless to me. All I remember was the final sentence, which read something like this: "You have your whole life ahead of you – embrace it with open arms, lots of love, Simon." I do not even remember the girl's name. It was obvious that this was not a love letter. If there had ever been anything between them, it was either over or hadn't happened as I had imagined. I couldn't bear to try and read it again. Burning with shame and sickened with myself, I folded it back into the envelope, licked and pressed down the flap, holding it firmly to make it stick. I walked back to the pillar-box, dropped the letter inside, and then wandered up towards Highgate Village, hands thrust deep into my jacket pockets, feeling wretched. How could I have stooped to such a base level; what did I think I would achieve by opening it anyway? "I have ruined everything," I whispered.

76
CHRISTMAS 1974

There's a place for us,
A time and place for us.
Hold my hand and we're halfway there.
Hold my hand and I'll take you there
Somehow, Some day, Somewhere.

Somewhere from *West Side Story* – Stephen Sondheim

Meanwhile, Chris was preparing for his party. His 1974 pocket diary reveals that he began to make beer on October 29th. On November 1st he reminds himself to "make finings" and the next day "add finings". He bottled it on November 8th. At the front of his diary, he filled in his personal details. After the printed line 'In case of accident please contact…' I was amused to find that Chris had written "Heaven". There were problems with the date of his party. He had planned it for December 14th, but in the end, it took place on December 20th, after a great deal of arranging, rearranging, letters and phone calls.

From Chris to Paula:

November 4th 1974

Dear Paula,

I too have been too busy to write before. Tomorrow I go back to school, half-term is over (sob, sob). Anyway, I am throwing an NYO reunion party on the 14th or 20th Dec (40 pints of home brewed lager are fermenting in my bedroom) so if you are down in London at the time, you know where to come.

Sorry, but I've given all my photographs to other fans already.

Oh yeh, Phillip wears flared trousers and has a really trendy great coat!

Love from Chris

November 11th

Paula Doll,

What can I say? I'd love you all to come of course, but there are problems.

1. There is a Concerti Allegri party on Dec 19th – maybe Martin, Clive etc. would not want to go to 2 parties in a row –

2. Being so near Christmas, some people may be put off.

3. Some people who I phoned said that they were working on the 20th, so I definitely told them the 14th.

BUT I am open to reconsideration of course. Please try to see if it is at all possible to come on the 14th because I think some people can't come on the 20th, and all people must be treated equally. Anyway I'll phone everyone up again after your phone call. I just hope everything works out OK & au revoir till then.

Lots of love from Chris

P.S. I'm sorry this letter was so untidy but I was trying to copy your writing.

December 13th

Dear Paula,

Please come next Friday. I sent a map to Aileen but you can phone from S. Woodford station to be picked up if the map has been lost. You must come.

There's nothing more to say really so I will see you next Friday.

Lots of love,

Chris

But despite all the letters and Chris's best attempts at persuasion, Paula and Aileen did not make it to Chris's party. He of course invited Helen. She says now that she has no idea how she managed to persuade her parents to allow her to travel alone from Reading to London and to stay overnight. She was desperately excited about seeing Chris again, and painted her fingernails dark blue for the occasion. Izzy and Duncan, and Simon and I were at the party, but neither Izzy nor I can remember meeting Helen. Perhaps that was because, according to Chris's friend, Sigi Turnlund, the two of them spent much of the night in the music room with the lights off.

After Chris's party, Simon went back to Liverpool for Christmas. I managed to sit around the table with my family and escaped to the Turners in the afternoon. A few days earlier, Melvyn Gale, my original desk partner in the Academy First Band, had phoned to ask if I would deputise for him in *West Side Story* at the Shaftesbury theatre for two shows on Boxing Day and one the day after. His regular deputies were unavailable, and he had to find someone to do it for him.

"Well, I'm free, but I've never played *West Side Story* before. Is it hard?"

"It is, but I wouldn't be asking you if I didn't know you could do it. You're a great sight-reader; you won't find it a problem. Are you a member of the Union?"

"No."

"So, you must join. Phone now and you'll be a member before Boxing Day."

"I will, and thank you for asking me."

"Thanks for doing it. It's £4 a show, but Boxing Day's double, so I'll leave a cheque for £20 for you in the pad. Is that OK?"

"Twenty pounds! Are you kidding? That'll pay my rent for nearly a month."

I phoned the Musicians' Union and joined up then and there. On Boxing Day, I travelled by tube to Tottenham Court Road and walked down to the theatre for my West End début. In those days, there were few, if any, women working in the pit orchestras. The band of *West Side Story* was no exception – all men, seasoned professionals and heavy drinkers. The first person I met was Bob Burns – big, hearty, grey-haired, red-faced and older than my father. He took one look at me – a little, naive, eighteen-year-old girl who had just walked through the stage door carrying a cello case – and laughed. "You must be Cathy. I'm Bob."

"Hi."

"Follow me – I'll take you down to the pit."

We descended about four flights of stairs to the very bottom of the building and entered a dimly lit basement – the pit area.

"Mind the river," he said. Water was running along a four-inch-wide channel in the floor. Bob told me that this wasn't the only West End theatre with a river – there were lots of underground streams in London that flowed through the foundations of old theatres.

"You can leave your case here somewhere."

"Where do we play?"

He opened a dwarf-sized door into the pit. I peered in to see chairs and illuminated music stands holding dense pads of music; a drum kit, guitar amps and various instruments. There didn't seem to be much room.

"Would it be OK to have a look at the music?"

"Nah, don't worry about that. Come up to the band room and I'll introduce you to the lads."

We climbed back to stage-door level and went on up.

"It's right at the top. Are you fit? If you're not, you soon will be."

We walked into the band room where I was met with wolf whistles and catcalls. I peered through the smoke to see a group of men, some slouched in chairs, others standing, all watching me curiously. At one end of the room was an extended table, above which was a long line of upturned bottles fitted with optics: on the table were crates of beer, glasses and brimming ashtrays. Everyone was drinking and smoking.

"Cathy, this is Mike, Lance, Derek, Dick, Roy, Bob, Dezzy, Alan – oh and this is Ed, the MD." *MD? What does that mean?*

"Hi, Cathy," said Ed in his American drawl.

"What can I get you to drink?" asked Bob.

"Erm, do you have some orange juice?"

"Don't serve soft drinks here. How about a gin and tonic?"

"OK, thanks."

I was a lamb to the slaughter. I wasn't sure whether they were amused by me or pissed off that a girl had entered their ranks. Someone started to tell a dirty joke and another said, "Watch it, there's a lady present."

"It's alright – don't mind me," I said, drinking the incredibly large gin and tonic that Bob handed me. I had never been anywhere like it, and felt a little tongue-tied, but not intimidated.

"Another drink, Cathy?" asked Bob.

"I should be buying you one."

"That's alright. You can get me one in the interval."

Before I had time to refuse, he pushed another tumbler of gin into my hand.

"Drink up lads. That's the five-minute call." Just as well, I thought, leaving my second drink on the table.

"Bob? Where's the ladies?"

"You've got me there. Anyone know where the ladies is?" he shouted.

"Next landing down, I think," someone replied. I stumbled into the loo, came out and everyone had gone. I raced downstairs, stepped straight into the river and fumbled to get my cello out of its case.

Behind me I heard a mellifluous voice say, "Don't panic. There's plenty of time." I turned around to see who was speaking. "I'm Nigel," he said, "pleased to meet you."

Nigel was one of the other two cellists. Unlike the majority of the men in the band, he was only a year older than I was. He held the door open for me and I climbed up the step to take my seat in the pit. The orchestration for that production of *West Side Story* was drums, bass, electric guitar, four saxes doubling on other wind instruments, five brass, percussion and three cellos. I was playing third cello, but every cello part was different, each with some exposed solos. Almost as soon as I had sat down, with one foot soaked, Ed walked on and the show began. *West Side Story* is not easy. It has complex rhythms, key signatures of five or six flats or sharps, and some very tricky moments. There were no second chances: this was it. Nigel leaned over, whispering some instructions to me during bars' rests and Ed, the MD (Musical Director, I'd worked out) was very helpful, cueing me when he could. Something happened: adrenalin sobered me up; I focused all my concentration on the notes in front of me, watched Ed like a hawk, listened intently, and counted, counted, counted. My cello playing looked after itself while my brain went into sight-reading overdrive. Before I knew it, we had reached the interval.

"Well done," said Nigel. The players pushed out of the pit. Twelve flights later and we were back in the band room.

"Could I buy you a drink now, Bob?" I asked.

"It's my round," interrupted Nigel. "What are you drinking?" I was sipping the remains of my pre-show drink.

"I'm fine, thanks."

"I know you're fine. I asked what you were drinking."

"G and T," said Bob, supplying the answer. "Come on Cath – drink up!"

"You're playing well," said Roy, one of the trombonists.

"Thank you."

I mustered my concentration for the second half and immersed myself in the music – one of the best show scores ever – it was a joy to play. At the end, the combination of the closing music, the tragedy of the story, and possibly the gin, brought tears to my eyes which rolled down my face while I was playing.

"What's up with you?" asked Nigel as we waited to start the bows and play-out.

"It's so sad, Tony getting shot... Maria – I can't help it," I blubbered, wiping my cheeks with the back of my hand. He looked at me nonplussed. Ed leant over and congratulated me.

"Great playing, Cathy."

Everyone said something complimentary. It had taken all my skills, but I knew I had played well. The second show didn't go quite as well as the first, but it was still fine. I tried to contain my emotions during the last scene, but it was no good: tears welled up and spilled over.

"Not again!" said Nigel incredulously.

I went back to Orchard Road that night on a bit of a high, with all the songs going round in my head.

The following evening I returned to the theatre and went straight up to the top floor. Later I discovered that the Shaftesbury theatre band bar was renowned within the London theatre circle: musicians and actors from other shows arrived after their curtains had come down and stayed there drinking for as long as they wanted.

"Hey, Cathy," said Ed, "come here." He gave me a bear hug and kissed my cheek.

"Oi, put her down," said Derek.

"Can I have one too?" asked Bob, hugging me.

"My turn next," said Dick.

That was it. They decided they liked me and I was accepted as one of the lads. Melvyn Gale booked me for some more shows, then Nigel and the other cellist started asking me to deputise for them too. I soon knew all three cello parts so well that I risked leaving the pit during the ten-minute dialogue section in the first half with some of the others. I thought they only stepped out to smoke, but no, they also relieved themselves into the river. I declined their encouraging invitations to make use of the facility myself.

Lance, the guitarist, was apt to get completely legless. On a matinée day, he often fell unconscious over his guitar during the evening show. Sometimes Nigel would prod him awake; other times it was better not to. One evening Ed had some important producers from the States in the audience. Lance had drunk himself into a particularly paralytic state, so much so that at the end of the show nobody could rouse him. Ed's American guests came down to the front of the theatre at the same time as three members of the band, not altogether sober themselves, were endeavouring to carry the comatose body of Lance out of the pit. The Americans stared in horrified fascination, while Ed buried his head in his hands. It was another world, and I liked it – not just because of Bernstein's music, but also because of the people. This was not the world of Florrie, International Competitions, backstage insincerity or the 'musical establishment'. I am most grateful to the band of *West Side Story* for my introduction to the West End.

The NYO held its Christmas/New Year course in Ramsgate. Clive Miller was still principal trumpet and Martin Koch had now been made principal trombone. Sections of the orchestra had to produce musical items for the New Year's Eve party. String groups and wind ensembles played chamber music; composers aired new works – all very correct and excellent. Then the brass and percussion made their contribution. Martin had written an arrangement of *Rudolph the Red-nosed Reindeer* as a Cha Cha Cha. He and Chris raised the roof with their improvised solos; the party leapt into life, *Rudolph* was repeated, and most of the orchestra got to their feet to Cha Cha Cha along. Martin told me that the house staff wore looks of disapproval, but that later, several sought him out to tell him how jolly good they thought his arrangement was and one even asked for a copy.

Aileen and Paula were still in the orchestra and Gillian Taylor was back along with another Glaswegian oboist who had just joined – Vyvian Howat. Vyvian had heard all about the NYO and Chris long before she became a member. Straight away, she was part of the gang. She remembers the first thing that Chris said to her was "Watcha Doll". As well as playing the oboe, Vyvian was a pianist. When Chris heard this, he fell about laughing, not because he doubted Vyvian's pianistic ability, but because the Glaswegian pronunciation of 'pianist' sounded to him just like 'penis'. It became another joke between them – "Watcha Doll" or "Hiya Chick", followed by "go on, say 'pianist'." Vyvian told me: "Chris was not one to dominate a conversation. His genuine interest in people made those who talked to him feel special; his openness inspired confidence; his gentle, empathetic nature encouraged intimacy and trust." It wasn't only Gareth who found him wise and sensitive beyond his years.

Helen and Chris's relationship continued, but Helen told me that they were discreet about it. She says that she was too reserved to be overtly flirtatious with Chris and anyway, she didn't need to be. She remembers feeling that she and Chris had a mutual understanding: what they felt for each other did not need to be publicly stated or demonstrated. Nevertheless, it does surprise me that their closeness went unnoticed. Perhaps it was because Chris was attentive to all the girls. He bantered with them, cracked jokes, and always had a pun or clever rejoinder to throw back. He complimented and charmed them – but genuinely. He wasn't smarmy or falsely flattering – he meant what he said. He gently reprimanded the girls if they were self-deprecating; he soothed insecurities and bolstered self-esteem. They all adored him. One wrote to me recently: "I was on the fringe of his friends really, but I loved him. I think he was the first person I fell in love with."

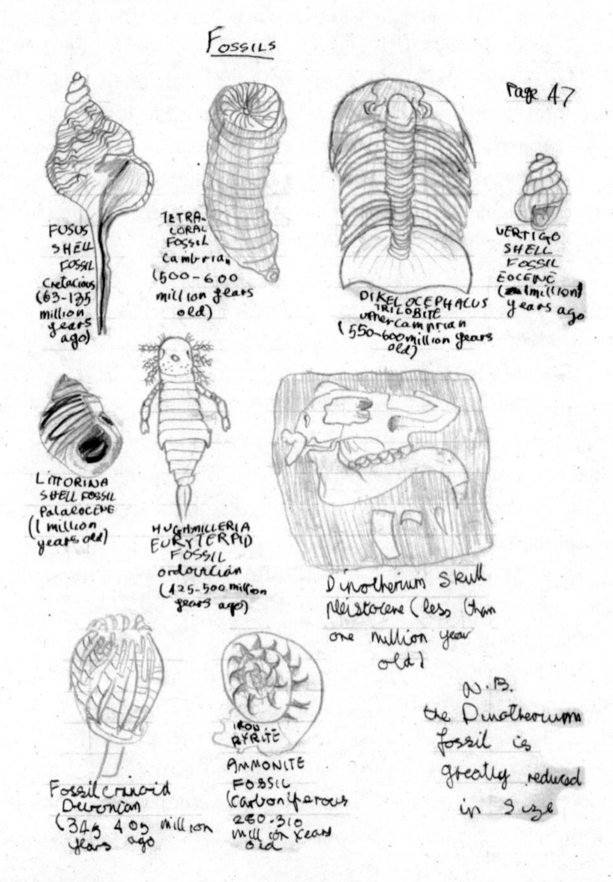

77
GODNOSE

"Hope" is the thing with feathers –
That perches in the soul –
And sings the tune without the words –
And never stops – at all –

"Hope" is the Thing with Feathers – Emily Dickinson

Rory Allam, the fairy-god-clarinettist, had gone back to Scotland for Christmas and wrote to me from West Smailholm, Kelso.

Thank you for your Christmas card – I'm afraid my family didn't send any. I was going to buy some but they were all horrible and I could never have made one as nice as yours. Simon introduced me to Tony Pay[1] after the London Sinfonietta concert and he gave me his address and phone number!!! Very kind of Simon.

I've decided that one of the worst things about my playing is intonation. I was listening to some tapes and it hit me more than anything else – basically I was never in tune. I'll have to get something done to the clarinet for a start because the high notes aren't in tune with the low notes. Why is Simon always right?

I'm coming back on Sunday and should be in London between 4 and 6 o'clock. I don't suppose you'll be at Cleveland Road, but I'll be looking out for you next week at the factory [*RAM*] and you can tell me all about flying. Not only do I have to hug you for Christmas but even more important New Year, then another hug for seeing you again – at last I've found something to look forward to. I hope you have been taking care of yourself – remember you're irreplaceable.

All my love,
Rory.

From Izzy to me: January 1975

When I came home at Christmas, I was really unhappy to see how much Dad has gone downhill, both physically & in his general attitude. He's practically on a starvation diet. Des said Dad was talking about committing suicide/chucking in his job (in which order, I wonder?) Des thinks Dad should take a long holiday (e.g. go to Egypt – he's always wanted to go there) and come back able to look at things a bit more in perspective. Dad feels that nobody wants him and that he is no use to anybody – his life can't be very happy with us 2 gone & Chris out most of the time – but then he doesn't help himself very much. It's very difficult & it's going to have to end somewhere. If anything drastic happens – please write & tell me.

Duncan sends his love,
lots of love from Izzy XXX

1. At this time, Antony Pay was principal clarinet of the RPO, a founder member of the London Sinfonetta and a key player in the Nash Ensemble.

My reply:

Dear Izzy (and Dunc if around),

Ta for your letter. Yes I know all about Dad, but I see him every week, when I go to do my teaching, so the change to me hasn't been so drastic. But really, Izzy, there's nothing any of us can do. I find it impossible to talk to him any more – always on edge and tense. And all he ever talks about is "That Awful Woman". In the end one's patience goes completely. I try to be tolerant with him but sometimes it's impossible. I won't bother to go into details but we had a bit of a clash the other weekend. In a way, I think it did him good. Try not to worry about him, Izzy.

Now for the good news! We've acquired a kitten! Matthew phoned up so we went round that very night and got him then and there! He's 9 weeks old, fully housetrained, tabby with white paws, big ears and greeny/browny eyes, full of mischief, exceptionally energetic and one bundle of gorgeousness. The problem is his name – have you any suggestions? At the moment he's known as Godnose as a result of the following conversation: "Simon, what shall we call him?" "Oh, God knows."

So Godnose it was – although it's a little embarrassing calling for him in the garden. He's got an exceptionally loud purr as well, but he's very clean and lovely company. More good news – I went to hear Fournier (you know, Pierre!) at the QEH last night and Florrie took me to see him afterwards and he says he'll hear me play and give me some lessons! So I'm to go over to Geneva in February (on £20 in the red??) and hope that everything goes well from there.

Simon conducted the RPO last Tuesday at the ICA in the Mall. Both first London performances of Czech and Polish pieces. The Polish piece was one of these ultra-mod things, where the conductor puts down a beat, waits 30 seconds, puts down another, waits another minute and 7 seconds etc. while weird and not-so-wonderful unbarred things go on in the process. Unfortunately Simon mistimed, and the piece that should have lasted 11 minutes lasted only 4½!! (I'll enclose newspaper cutting for you to see). There were heated discussions following this, led by Bernard Keefe. The main argument was that if the piece had lasted 11 minutes, as the composer intended, rather than 4½, it would have had greater effect. Poor old Simon had to do it again with a stopwatch in his hand! I felt awful for him but he wasn't at all perturbed. At the end of the second performance, someone said, "Yes, the effect was greater – it was even more boring".

Simon's off on a West Country tour now and won't be back til February – still, I have my kitten to keep me company. Actually, I must work like hell now if I'm to play to Fournier. Nothing much more to say, except look after yourself & keep smiling.

Lots & lots of love, Cathy

From Izzy to me: January 15th 1975

I got a letter from Mum and she's had a long talk with Dad – he's now eating breakfast and an evening meal, and has also bought some new clothes, so maybe things are improving.

Your kitten sounds really gorgeous – when I'm next in London I must come over and see it – Godnose – I think that's a perfectly good name.

Going to a concert tonight – Strasbourg percussion Ensemble, which was formed by Pierre Boulez. They're playing Cage and Birtwistle – it should be interesting if nothing else. I hope you're working hard for Fournier, but I bet you are.

Love to Simon.

Lots of love, Izzy

From Chris to Izzy: January 17th 1975

Dear Izzy (and Duncan),

Have just come home from a crappy job at Chigwell School, but I got £7.50 so I can't complain. My playing is going OK at the moment – Mr. Roger replaced my tooth thing last week & Mr. Porter is giving me a skull X-ray while I play the horn next week.

Duncan – Good luck with the Brahms. There is quite a good chance of you being asked to play in the final Concerti rehearsal and concert on March 8th – the rest of the programme is William Tell, Peter & the Wolf and Tchaik 4 which is quite a blow for the 4tet as Ian Grainger is the only extra horn, so bring your instrument. Ifor (James) is doing the Brahms at the Purcell Room in a fortnight. I'm having a lesson with James Brown on Feb 5th.

Yes, Musici did do Haydn Creation at the QEH last week. Ivor Evans was conducting off a vocal score with piano reduction hidden in the middle pages of a full score (he's a bungling incompetent). They fixed Pete Goodwin (New Phil 2nd trombone) to play the alto trombone part – he was really good. The concert was good except for the Bass bits – Eric was pissed out of his tree so even the audience was laughing at the Bass/Continuo/Recit bits. The Discipline is better on NYO now but Ivey has banned girls' trousers again (Aileen in trousers: OOAWRRR!!!)

There's a new Scottish oboist called Vyvian Howat. Gareth is half-right about the playing – it is worse than last year (I'm second horn) but Gareth only heard the 2nd run thro' of the New World and half the Orchestra is new & it was the 1st course of the year and a rehearsal course too – but the playing is potentially as good as last year. The rest of the programme is Elgar 1, Will Tell, Mendelssohn fiddle conc., Mars from Planets, Thieving Magpie – the reason there's so much is that we are doing 3 concerts at Easter (Lancaster, Liverpool, Coventry). The course is at Lancaster University (single rooms and all that).

4tet rehearsals are going fine (Bram was 2 hours late for the last one). Did you hear Mick Thompson's Strauss 1 on the radio on Tuesday? If not, make sure you hear Alan Civil's Strauss 2 on Friday,

Till March 8th

Lots of love, Chris

The lump had gone, the gap between his front teeth was filled, but Chris still imagined that he could hear a faint octave echo. Maurice Porter suggested that the sound Chris was hearing might be the vibration of the bones in his head and decided to X-ray Chris's skull while he was playing the horn. Nothing odd was discovered and at last Chris's anxiety began to abate. I have often wondered whether the purpose of the X-rays was simply to put Chris's mind at rest.

From me to Izzy: January 20th 1975

At the moment I'm sitting on a train on the way to Plymouth for one of Simon's concerts. I must be mad – it cost me £6.04p single! Still, I suppose this is why I play in West Side Story. I've done lots more shows since Boxing Day – about 10 I suppose and three more to do next week. Matthew came to one show and Dad and Chris to another. I've also been asked to dep in Jesus Christ Superstar. I haven't decided whether I will or not yet.

Also, I've passed my driving test, much to everyone's surprise. Mum lent me the car for the weekend so after I'd finished teaching, I drove myself back to Highgate. Then, just to be mad (although I didn't tell Mum this) I decided to drive to Mel Gale's party in Morden – miles away. I left at midnight and arrived at 20 to 2! I had great difficulty in getting across the Thames and got lost in various one-way systems. In fact it took me longer to get from Highgate to Vauxhall Bridge than from there to Morden. I gave someone a lift home (we left at 3.00am) to Hampstead and then got lost between there and Highgate. I was also stopped by the police at 4.45am as they thought I'd stolen the car. Altogether I must have done about 7 hours driving the day after my test.

Dad really does seem a lot better. He's bought himself 2 new suits, several new shirts, new shoes etc & generally seems fairly healthy. He's even been over to see our flat, which he swore he never would.

Mum's decided to call Godnose, 'Spice' because downstairs' kitten is called Sugar. But Simon still prefers Godnose. I took him home last weekend. He met Tinker and Rusty. They weren't exactly friendly towards him although neither of them attacked him. Anyway, everyone thinks he's very lovely. I've given him to Matthew to look after for a few days while I'm in Plymouth. Matthew's in the process of building himself a 5ft long, radio-controlled aeroplane!

One good thing about having passed my test is that I can do all the driving of Chris and me to and from Concerti rehearsals. We're doing William Tell overture (God knows what the opening is going to sound like – 5 cello solos) and of course Chris, Phillip, Gareth and Alison are playing the 4 horn Schumann Concertstück with a party at 32 Cleveland Road afterwards.

I've been managing surprisingly well without Simon – he's been away since the beginning of January, but I'm seeing him for a few days now, then he's back on Feb 5th. All I need now is a car of my own. I'm going to Geneva to play to Fournier on Feb 14th (Valentine's day). I'm getting nervous about it already. It's going to cost a hell of a lot more than I thought as well – £80 return air fare, £25 for the lesson itself, not to mention hotel accommodation and food while I'm there. Oh well, I'll manage somehow.

Hope you're both well. Siya soon,

lots of love, Cathy

In Plymouth, Simon conducted Ravel's *Mother Goose Suite* and Rodrigo's *Concierto de Aranjuez* for guitar. It became apparent during the rehearsal that the guitarist was completely incompetent. Simon and I knew him from the RAM. He was super-confident, ambitious, and laid claim to an already established reputation as a top-class soloist. Unfortunately, Simon was taken in by the guitarist's illusions and was persuaded to suggest that the orchestra book him. The rehearsal was a nightmare. In the break Simon came to find me, his face a picture of horror and panic.

"Cath, the guy can't play!"

"I know. What are you going to do?"

"Perhaps we could organise a bomb scare. Or maybe I should take all my clothes off and run through the hall screaming 'Aardvark'. Better still, you could take your clothes off – that would be more distracting and much prettier."

"Couldn't you say he's been taken suddenly ill?" He sighed in defeated resignation. "No, we'll just have to get through it. I'm going to work on it with him now in the hopes that I might at least teach him when to come in. Pray for me."

It was a monumental embarrassment. Somehow, Simon managed to return to the rostrum and conduct a good performance of the *Mother Goose Suite*, encouraging the truculent band to bring some flavour to Ravel's piquant, alluring score. Afterwards, he filed the experience away as a mistake not to be repeated, but it can't have improved already strained relations between him and the orchestra. I wished I could have helped him, but there was nothing I could do. He had to build his own survival raft.

Simon and I were invited to Guildford to visit one of Simon's friends. Mum agreed to my borrowing her car to drive us there. I was managing quite well until we reached Hyde Park Corner. There were no traffic lights at that time to direct the endless streams of traffic around the largest and busiest roundabout in London. The Highway Code was of no help at all – there was simply no gap in the fast flow of vehicles through which to filter into the roundabout. Cars behind honked furiously as I hesitated and halted, unable to move forwards. "We're just going to have to go for it," I said. "Tell me when you see a slight space and I'll put my foot down."

"Are you sure about this, animal?"

"What else can we do? We'll be stuck here forever otherwise."

"OK, NOW." I shot forwards, horns blaring from all sides. We both screamed our way around Hyde Park Corner, apoplectic with fright. Simon hadn't shown any interest in learning to drive, but I think that experience must have decided him – he was never going to get behind the wheel.

From Izzy to me: February 10th 1975

Really good about passing your driving test! I'd have thought Dad would have been worried about you using the car, but I got a letter from him on Saturday and he seemed really happy and pleased. I hear Simon's got backache through overwork – I hope he's OK now and his tour went well.

Lots of love, Izzy

From Chris to Izzy: February 12th 1975

Dear Izzy and Duncan,

Really sorry, but Arran 1 is on during NYO and Arran 2 is only for 11-14's, so I'll probably go to Lake District 2 Art Camp (it's supposed to be in a tourist free area) which is on at the same time as Wortley!! My lesson with James Brown went well last week & tomorrow he's giving a free Concertstück lesson to the 4tet (my lump is getting smaller every day). Gareth has been conned into doing Hatfield Phil next week.

Limerick:

An outstanding young pupil of mine,
Produced a note that was so divine,
That with one rip,
I pulled off his lip,
So he could never do it agine.

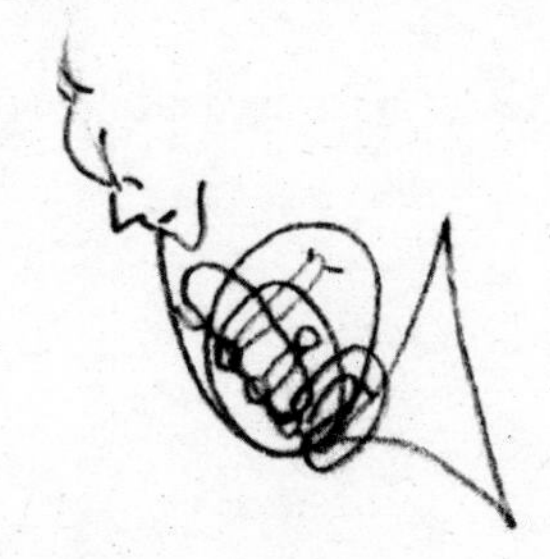

Did a Woodford orch. job on Sunday, dented my horn and didn't even get expenses – (Duncan – I was doing Karelia suite – I got my top B*b*'s but I split the top G before it). Met a 12 year old genius girl horn player who warmed up on Strauss 2 and C lip trills, but cried because she couldn't play her orchestral part (ha! ha! arrogant, precocious, whiz-kid, bitchy, stuck… no, she was quite sweet really).

Frank had a go at me at last night's Forest rehearsal. He said "That sounds effeminate… no balls." Apparently (as he likes a pornographic approach to music and wants each note to have sexual overtones) he once said to Ed Garner "It sounds as though you don't even know how to wank."

Met Gareth's brother in George Lane on Sunday going back to his Halls of Residence up by the library which is really flash (the library). Brynly Clarke is playing in Forest Phil now. He's at Cambridge and wears nail varnish but only on his left hand.

Lots of love from Chris.

P.S. I'm feeling quite horny at the moment

78
DEPARTURE

Dread has followed longing,
And our hearts are torn.

Love's Loneliness – W.B. Yeats

I had become withdrawn since the letter-spying incident. It preyed on my mind, an ugly secret that festered inside me. Simon knew something was wrong – we both did. It wasn't just the crime I had committed; it was the sadness that engulfed us, the speed with which merriment turned to misery. One afternoon, Simon lay down on the divan in the living room.

"Come here, Cath. We need to talk." My heart sank. This is it, I thought. I lay beside him; he put his arm around me and held my hand. He said he hated to see me so unhappy and was there anything he could do to help? Had he upset me more than he realised?

"What do you mean?"

"Well, it's been difficult for us both with me in Bournemouth and you've had to put up with me feeling lost. I've probably been leaning on you too much and haven't been attentive enough to your needs. You seem so far away, Animal, and I don't like this distance. I want us to be close again."

"So do I. It's all that matters to me. And you haven't upset me. I'm the one who's been making things difficult."

"No, Cath. I'm to blame. I've been too preoccupied. It's true that we don't see enough of each other, but we mustn't let the geographical distance between us create an emotional one. We must close the gap, be open with each other. Please tell me how I can make you happy. I love you, Animal. I hope you still love me."

"Of course I do. I always will." Then, in the quiet moment that followed, I decided I must tell him. He had given me the opportunity and it might never happen again. I almost felt as if he already knew and was waiting, holding out a lifeline, prepared to rescue me and to understand.

"Simon, a few weeks ago I did a terrible thing. I read one of your letters. I know it was wrong, but I was so afraid you didn't love me any more, that you'd fallen in love with another girl. I'm sorry; so, so sorry." He sighed. I bit my lip and held onto him.

"You shouldn't have done that, Cath."

"I know, I know."

Writing this, it has dawned on me that maybe he thought I had rifled through his music case and read one of her letters to him. Would that have been any worse? Would it have made any difference? No. Either way I would have been guilty. I felt oddly calm after I had told him. Was it the confession of my furtive espionage that marked the end – was there nowhere to go after that, or had we already passed the finishing post?

We rallied for a little while. Simon was enthusiastically supportive when I went off to Geneva to play to Pierre Fournier. I rather dreaded it myself. It was my first trip abroad and after the scary flights to Guernsey and back, I wasn't looking forward to more air travel. I needn't have worried – the plane to Geneva was huge by comparison and also half-empty. I took my cello onto the plane with me – none of the airline officials made any objections. It was daunting arriving in Geneva to find that my schoolgirl French was hopelessly inadequate. Still, I succeeded in finding the correct hotel, slept badly, covered by a duvet for the first time, ordered breakfast self-consciously the next morning and set off to find Fournier's house. I should have gone by taxi, but it didn't look too far away on the map. It was miles; I was soon lost, had to ask for directions in my incompetent French and couldn't understand the answers I received. I arrived a bit late and exhausted from carrying my cello so far. I felt inhibited and nervous with Fournier. I played him some unaccompanied Bach. He stopped me and said it was all wrong. He told me to buy a copy of his edition of the Bach suites and come back when I had learnt it correctly – his way. He seemed a little happier with the Beethoven A major sonata, but changed lots of bowings and fingerings. Then he asked me what I wanted to learn from him. I said I was interested in studying technique and hoped I would learn from him musically.

"What do you want to know about technique?" he asked. I was now a little flummoxed.

"Well, my bowing. Do you have any advice for spiccato, or bow changes?"

"Spiccato – it is all from the wrist. And bow changes? What nonsense people talk about bow changes! It is so simple. You just bow in one direction then the other. There is no big mystery."

That was it, in a nutshell. I didn't know what to make of him. His wife gave me a cup of tea in the kitchen and then he came in and asked when I would like another lesson.

"Whenever is convenient for you," I replied respectfully.

"Next month, then: I will write to suggest a time."

I thanked him very much and left.

Mum and Simon were at the airport to meet me. I felt shattered and deflated. Simon gave me a huge hug; Mum didn't.

"How did it go, Animal?"

"I can't really tell."

"What did he say?"

"Well, he's giving me another lesson next month."

"Then he's accepted you as a pupil! That's great. Well done." I wasn't so sure.

In all, I had about a dozen lessons from Fournier, but I never felt comfortable with him. Every fingering and bowing, every nuance, dynamic, tempo and rubato had to be executed in his way. There was no allowance for personal interpretation, and although I did pick up a few tips on technique, I did not get as much as I had hoped from the lessons. Florence Hooton was without doubt a far superior teacher. I hasten to add that Fournier was a great cellist, but he was not a great teacher, and to study with him cost a lot of money. To save a bit, I made subsequent trips in one day, flying out in the morning, having a lesson in the afternoon and back in the evening. I also won some scholarships and was given money from various trusts, which paid a good way towards the lessons.

Travelling on my own to Geneva with my cello was a sinking, lonely experience. Time limped by as I dragged my feet along foreign streets, alienated from my surroundings and myself. I wondered how international soloists could endure such a solitary existence, and deep down I knew I could never do it. I battled with myself: I was very privileged to be studying with Fournier; I must commit myself to it, practise and learn; this opportunity would not come along again. Every shadow of doubt that flickered into my thoughts had to be banished. But I felt sluggish and miserable; depression sometimes overwhelmed me. I was half dead in that world but too well programmed to deviate.

Then, on February 26th, which happened to be my birthday, the moment I so feared arrived. Simon reached the point where he knew it was impossible to go on as we were. Such moments cannot be planned or timed. They occur when a relationship has passed beyond retrieval, when despair overwhelms hope, when resistance, denial and pretence can no longer suppress the truth. I heard Simon leave the flat and found a note from him on the kitchen table.

Dear Cath,

I must be alone for half an hour or so – I am going to walk in the park and think for a while. I know that you need to know what I am thinking – before I can tell you, I must find out for myself. Don't worry – I will be back soon. Somewhere is that enormous love we had such a short time ago. I must find it again.

Please believe me, I want this to work if it can. Give me the chance – please do not suffocate it!

I know I love you – please help me.

I am not sure what happened next, except that he left for Bournemouth, saying that he couldn't make things work between us. Trevor, our downstairs housemate, and I had planned a joint birthday party that night. We were going to open up both flats so that our guests could fill the house. I phoned Corinne to tell her that Simon had left me. I couldn't face a party. I locked the flat and hid upstairs on my own while the party raged downstairs. Several times there were knocks at the door, but I ignored them and took the phone off the hook. It wasn't a great birthday. I was nineteen. The following day I sent a card to Izzy:

Darling Izzy,

I haven't forgotten about you on our birthday. I apologise for this being late but Simon & I have just split up & as you can imagine, birthday cards are not the first thing one thinks about. Don't worry about me. I'll be OK. I hope that life will always be wonderful for my little sister. Thank you for the present and card. Love to Duncan. Look after yourself, my love.

See you soon.

All my love forever, Cathy.

In the evening, I travelled over to Ilford for a *Concerti* rehearsal. Two days later, Simon was back from Bournemouth. It was surreal. There he was, standing in the living room.

"Cathy. I'm so glad you're here. How are you, little one?" I was overjoyed to see him. We hugged tightly, he kissed me, we kissed some more. Neither of us made any attempt to stop. In the morning, I woke with Simon beside me, thinking I must have misunderstood what he had said – or maybe he had changed his mind and realised he did want to be with me after all. Making love had brought us back together. I cuddled up to him, so glad that everything was OK.

"No, Cath," he said gently, "I meant what I said. I still love you, but this isn't going to work."

"Please, Simon, please. I'll make it work."

"I'm sorry."

The next weekend, something similar happened. It was so natural to make love, so easy to be close in that way, yet in my head I was desperate, pleading for him to love me, to come back to me. When I woke, I experienced a moment of dreamy euphoria, followed by a hollow, stomach-lurching pain – as if suddenly realising that today was the day you have been dreading and here it is.

On March 8th, Phillip, Chris, Gareth and Alison gave their performance of the *Concertstück* with *Concerti* and I held myself together enough to play the solo introduction to *William Tell*. The horn soloists excelled themselves, Bram pulled a splendid performance out of the orchestra and Mum once again opened her doors for the party. The unstoppable journey of our musical lives flowed onwards. I was working for my Recital Diploma; Florrie had entered me for two international competitions – one to be held in Geneva in September and the other, the 'Tortelier' competition, taking place in Bristol in October; plus I had another lesson with Fournier lined up. I had no choice but to get on and practise.

Also, I was no longer on my own. Lesley Garrett, a singing student at the RAM, had moved in with me. I had found her in tears one day in the Academy bar, about to be chucked out of her bed-sit with nowhere to go. Always looking for solutions to other people's problems and thinking that some warm and buoyant company wouldn't do me any harm, I said she could stay with me, sleep in the divan bed in the living room and I would find some cupboard space for her.

I borrowed Mum's car, the Hillman Minx Estate, and drove over to Childs Hill to pick her up. Back and forth we went, from bed-sit to car, piling more and more bags, cases and boxes into the back.

"I thought you said you didn't have much stuff?"

"Just a few more things love. Nearly done."

The hatchback door would hardly close. I didn't know how it was all going to fit into the flat.

"Oh – I've forgotten something. Back in a mo," said Lesley, climbing out of the car. She returned with a guitar. I smiled at her faintly.

"Don't worry, love, it looks more than it is. Soon get it sorted. Oh, I'm so grateful to you, Cathy. I'll never forget your kindness. You're my knight in shining armour come to rescue me!"

"And we're galloping off in a Hillman," I said, sounding more cheerful than I felt.

We spent the rest of the day revamping the flat. Every square inch of space was utilised. She was right – we found a place for all her belongings and the flat did look quite nice when we had finished. Lesley chatted non-stop while we worked. I couldn't be too miserable around someone with such a lively personality. She also decided I should make more of myself. A decent bra that fits properly would be a start, she said, and don't you have anything other than that awful, dog-eared, red-and-blue rugby shirt to wear?

Simon was back and forth between Bournemouth and Highgate. Separating is never simple. No doubt there were times when he felt isolated and lonely and missed me. We talked on the phone every day and made love urgently when he returned. This became a bizarre pattern for a while that neither of us attempted to talk about. For me, lovemaking felt like passionate despair, yet I still fooled myself that our relationship could be retrieved. Perhaps if I were cheerful, chirpy and good fun to be with, the dark clouds would blow over and we would simply carry on. Deep down, though, I knew that Simon had flown away. He had a soaring spirit and expansive, strong and beautiful wings. He fell in love with my humour and resilience; my passion, sexuality, creativity and intelligence; not the angst, insecurity, inhibition and misery that burdened me, that hindered the freedom of us both. He acknowledged my difficulties, but understood that he could not heal my emotional wounds. He saw that I too had a pair of beautiful wings, but could not teach me to fly. I think it had become increasingly alarming for him to see me hectically building a nest and longing to lay eggs, when I had hardly hatched from my own. He had asked me to be patient; he wanted to see me stretch out and embrace life – he would have loved that: I believe it was what he was hoping for, for me.

> But if in your fear you would seek only love's peace and love's pleasure,
> Then it is better for you that you cover your nakedness and pass out of love's threshing-floor
> Into the seasonless world where you shall laugh, but not all of your laughter, and weep, but not all of your tears.
>
> Love one another but make not a bond of love:
> Let it rather be a moving sea between the shores of your souls.
> Fill each other's cup but drink not from one cup.
> Give one another of your bread but eat not from the same loaf.
> Sing and dance together and be joyous, but let each one of you be alone,
> Even as the strings of the lute are alone though they quiver with the same music.
>
> *The Prophet* – Kahlil Gibran

But my sea was tideless: I drank thirstily from Simon's cup and stole his bread; my voice was tuneless, my feet leaden; I could only hear his music, not my own; I clung to him for fear of being alone. His world beckoned him and he reached out to it with open arms. And he was right to do so – besides, he would have had to wait a very long time to see me take wing. It is only now, writing this book, that I have leapt from the nest and am flying my maiden voyage. My wings are broad and secure: I am turning cartwheels in the air.

I had a few free days and arranged to go to Leeds with Gareth Mollison to see Izzy and Duncan. We went in Gareth's car and took turns with the driving. Izzy and Duncan lived at 4, Autumn Street in Leeds 6, a slum area with street after street of back-to-back housing. Landlords looking to make a quick buck bought up cheap property in the district and let it to students. There were no trees and no parked cars – the people who lived there could not afford cars. Nor were there any gardens. Washing was hung across the cobbled streets, and the front doors opened directly onto the narrow pavements. I wondered how Izzy managed to sunbathe. She told me that whenever the sun shone and it was warm enough, she carried a chair outside and sunbathed in the road. Nothing was going to prevent her from getting a tan. It was good to spend some time with Izzy, to see where she lived and to get away from London for a short while.

On March 23rd 1975, Chris played the Edward Gregson horn concerto with Redbridge Band at the Kenneth More Theatre. Rory, back in Scotland for Easter, wrote to me:

> Thank you for your letter, which arrived at breakfast and brightened up my bowl of cornflakes and thank you for helping me down to the platform with all my luggage. Chris phoned yesterday and told me about the Gregson, and Gareth wrote and said it went really well "What a player" (quote). I am playing in 'Oklahoma' which is very long and very tiring. My mouth is bruised and sore – in fact it really hurts. There is a girl playing violin who knows Chris. She described him as the boy who is always surrounded by Scots girls – she also knows Phillip and Gareth – you can't escape from them! Your Bach was advertised in the Sunday papers. Your rehearsal will be this afternoon. Good luck with continuo and camping, I very much hope that you are a happy-fairy-god-kitten-cellist. Thinking of you, take care, big kiss for Godnose
>
> All my love, Rory

FSC phoned at the last minute, short-staffed for an Easter camp. I decided to go. Maybe a little time away would be of benefit, and Simon would be around to look after Godnose. It was a small camp of eighteen Trailseekers and four staff. I was arm-twisted into being the caterer and spent hours planning menus and ordering food supplies. We met somewhere in Shropshire, picked up a seventy-foot long boat and set off along the Llangollen canal into the Welsh mountains. With a few people on board to steer and cook, the rest of us walked along the towpath. Each evening, when we had found a convenient mooring place, we pitched our tents, gathered wood and lit a fire to keep warm. There were four berths on board, so we took it in turns to sleep on the boat. It was an unusual camp that involved a lot of walking, with some big mess-ups at locks until we learnt the procedure. On the way back, we prided ourselves with our lock efficiency. It was also freezing cold: the ice had to be broken on the water tank every morning before we could make tea. It snowed, making it difficult to collect wood and light fires. The weight of snow that fell on the tents during the night caused one or two to collapse – not a pleasant way to be woken up. I wheezed through the week with asthma, puffing my inhaler far too frequently. It was too cold to undress, so most of us stayed in the same clothes, clad with every garment we had brought with us. It was so good to be warm that nobody complained of the pace we set ourselves, preferring to walk rather than to travel inactively on the boat. The leader spared no expense on extras: paraffin was bought to light the fires; a dozen hot-water-bottles were purchased: if anyone felt the slightest bit hungry, they ate. Jam sandwiches and Mars bars were thrown to the walkers from those on the boat to keep energy levels up. My menus were largely ignored – we needed to keep warm and eat quickly – no time to braise chickens or steam puddings.

I remember two children distinctly – a tall, cheerful girl who never flagged and led us all in loud songs as we travelled along. She became chief lock-organiser, running ahead to get to the next lock, fetch the key from the lockkeeper's house and round everyone up to push the lock gates open. The other was a small, wiry boy who trotted beside me chatting about astronomy and asking complicated questions that I couldn't answer. He talked about light-years, stars, planets, moons and orbits. Disappointed that my response was invariably "I don't know", he suggested that I ask him questions instead – he knew all the answers. So absorbed was he in his scientific pontificating, he didn't look where he was going. Several times he nearly fell into the canal, and then, inevitably, he did. He only went in up to his waist and we fished him out quickly, but he had caught his leg on some metal shoring and gashed it open. He seemed unaware of his injury, carrying on from where his theoretical debate had been interrupted. I helped him clamber up the bank to a road, where we hitched a lift to the nearest hospital. While we waited in the overheated casualty department, we started pulling off layers of clothing. We must have both stank. The nurse who stitched him up was obviously appalled at the state of his underwear and spoke very disapprovingly to me. He chatted away regardless, generously sharing his vision of the universe with her. He was limping a little, but not complaining, as we left the hospital. I persuaded a taxi driver to take us to where we had arranged to meet up with the rest of the group.

On the last day we steered the longboat back to our starting point and the children were returned to their parents. They all declared it was the best FSC they had ever been on. If the parents were shocked at their children's appearance, none said so. Even the little boy's mother took his accident calmly, saying that he always did have his head in the stars. For me, the blank space inside had been echoing less hollowly for a while. I had written a few times to Simon during the week and this was waiting for me when I let myself into our flat:

Hello Little Animal,

I hope that you have thawed out by now – I have thort of you often shivering by locks etc. (what I want to know is what "etc" means)! I'm sure you had a fabulous time. I'm sorry I can't stay, but I will ring tomorrow sometime for one of our short 2-hour natters. It is quite possible that someone may ring up from the ECO – they want me to do a tour of Spain with them in a fortnight – gasp, groan, spurt, faint, fart, explode! We are having a nice aggro over programmes at present, as I am insisting on doing pieces I know, and vice versa for them. So, we'll see!

It's been a pretty good week, despite Godnose going slightly mad (e.g. upsetting bins, scratching Fred, pissing on the kitchen floor – yes in the 30 secs while I emptied his litter!!)

I've bought a few bits & bobs for you, just in case you are here, some soup, cheese & eggs to feed your little sexy body on (give us a kiss, gorgeous). Anyway, must now dash quite presto for my train back to the 'Pool. A great hug & kiss for you, little animal & may you always be happy.

All my ravishes & love
Simon de Montfort
(History)

P.S. If you are not getting rid of Godnose today, Corinne is interested in having him – nice thort!

Yes, Godnose was going to a new home. A first floor flat with limited access to a garden was not a good place for a cat. Also, I was going to be away from time to time, so making arrangements for Godnose would be difficult. Mum's cleaner was happy to take him, so I knew he was going to a good home. He was renamed and lived a long cat life.

One night Simon came back from Bournemouth very late. I was already asleep, but woke up when he came into the bedroom. He climbed into bed with me.

"Don't touch me."

"Animal? What's wrong?"

"I said, don't touch me!"

"Alright. It's alright, Cath. I'll sleep on the floor."

He found a sleeping bag; I threw him a pillow; he lay beside me on the carpet and was soon asleep. I turned to the wall, soaking my pillow with silent tears, wanting so badly to be held, but unable to endure waking up once more to nothing. We never made love again.

Chris taking his bow after performing Edward Gregson's horn concerto with Redbridge Brass at the Kenneth More Theatre in March 1975. Clive Miller is seated second from the left. *Photo by K. E. Larnder, L.R.P.S.*

Redbridge Brass Band at the Kenneth More Theatre, March 1975. Conductor: John Ridgeon.
Chris is on the far right holding a tenor horn, which he played with a French horn mouthpiece.

Photo by K. E. Larnder, L.R.P.S.

79
LIFE GOES ON

It was a very slow snail
Crossed through my head
When you said "It's over."

Yet Further Fragments – Jean Lipkin

I had put on all the weight I had lost and more. People commented that I looked well, but I felt disgusting and was sure they meant that I looked fat. My bulging, uncomfortable body was a torment to me. I couldn't leave food alone. I picked, nibbled, stole and binged: my furtive, rampant addiction consumed me in a far more aggressive, emotionally destructive way than when I had been in anorexic control. Losing weight had been empowering; now I felt beaten. And I was the ruthless mastermind of my own defeat. I have no doubt that my pathological eating disorder played a major part in the breakdown of my relationship with Simon.

I wanted to see Izzy and went back to Leeds by train. Whilst there, Izzy and I got together with Paul de Keyser and Marshall Marcus, fellow NYO members, to play string quartets at Paul's home. In the evening, Paul's mother, the piano teacher Fanny Waterman, took us out to a cheap and cheerful Chinese restaurant. Open-hearted and unpretentious, she encouraged us all to tuck in, making more of a mess with the spare ribs than the rest of us. A letter arrived from Chris, who was with the NYO at Lancaster University:

> Food and accommodation here is fine, the hall is good & Ivey's got Laryngitis. There are 7 bars on the campus so Ivey will be occupied full time if she wants a teetotal brass section. Chris Blake (1st horn) and Cynthia Mitchell (5th horn) are going down to London on Monday to do RAM auditions, so I might get a chance to play 1st horn. We had to go to bed at 10 p.m. As a special concession we can keep our lights on til 11.30, but as we cannot visit each other's rooms, there's no point really. Tons of people are madly revising for Highers and A levels which is what I might be doing this time next year. Must go.
>
> Love from Chris

Izzy and I went to Lancaster to hear Chris play in the NYO concert. We met up with him before it started.

"Which one's Aileen, then, Chris?" asked Izzy.

"I can't see her at the moment – but check out the viola section. You can't miss her, she's stunning; long silky straight hair. Must go and warm up. See you later."

We scrutinised the female viola players as they walked on stage, but couldn't decide which girl it was who mustered Chris's extravagant praises. His relationship with Helen Chapman continued. I asked Helen what they talked about. She finds it very difficult to remember, but she did tell me that they talked about God.

"Chris was an atheist, wasn't he?"

"He was."

"Well, I wasn't. But Chris and I talked a lot about God. He didn't try to alter my views. He always listened to me respectfully, but he quizzed me about my faith and challenged my thinking. I enjoyed those discussions."

I had a clear vision of Chris at that moment: his tolerance, his kindness. He was never confrontational or remotely aggressive. He accepted people the way they were. Debate was always fun with Chris. He liked to find common ground, the peaceful solution. It didn't matter if his friends didn't see the world in the same way as he did. It was always the friendship that was important. Difference was interesting. Helen might have been reading my thoughts, for the next thing she said was, "Chris liked the unusual, the obscure; the oddities of life. I remember being self-conscious about my hairy arms. They weren't abnormally hairy, but with my pale skin and dark hair, they were, to my mind, embarrassingly obvious. Chris told me I shouldn't hide them under sleeves – couldn't I see how beautiful they were."

But Helen was aware that she had competition. One girl who really liked him, and whom Chris liked too, was Gillian Taylor. Gillian had applied to the College and Academy, the dates of her entrance auditions falling during the week after the NYO course. Chris at once arranged for Gillian to return to London with him and stay at Cleveland Road – which is something he would have done for any friend in a similar situation – but Helen, understandably, felt some uncomfortable pangs of jealousy and a little resentment that Gillian would have several days of Chris's treasured company. However, Gillian was not alone with Chris. Phillip Eastop came over to stay as well and the three of them went out to Epping Forest, the boys taking their horns and Gillian her camera. That Chris and Gillian were friends was obvious, but was it more than that? When I talked to Gillian she said that there might have been something in the air. She felt a shy attraction to Chris, but there was no physical contact between them. "Most of our friendships in NYO revolved around a 'gang' of us so that even admitting to *liking* someone was a no go area."

When Mum discovered that Gillian did not have an accompanist, she offered to play for her. Mum rehearsed with Gillian and accompanied her at both auditions. She also played for Chris, who auditioned for the Intermediate School of the Academy.

Back in Highgate, I resolved to get on with life. I depped frequently in *West Side Story*, which I loved, and *Jesus Christ Superstar*, which I loathed, but at least it was an early finish and paid the rent. Izzy and Duncan appeared to be happy together, although I had noticed Duncan making the mistake of ordering Izzy around once or twice, had heard hints of condescension in his voice, and felt Izzy's irritation and stubborn refusal to comply; but I hadn't picked up on her underlying misgivings.

IZZY Journal: *I'm with Duncan at University but I miss Chris Stearn. I love him still. God knows why I ever chucked him. Duncan wants me all to himself the whole time, even in the holidays, but I want to be at home with my family and friends. Sometimes I wish I could put the clocks back and re-live my time with Chris. I felt secure then, I don't now. Sometimes I feel so young, not at all ready to go out in the world. I don't really know where I belong. I wish I was still with Chris – he gave me the kind of love I wanted.*

Rory wrote to me again from West Smailholm: April 10th 1975

It's good that you're immersed in work – it's definitely the best thing to occupy your mind. I saw Simon the day before I left. It was the first time I'd talked to him since December. He seemed quite tired. He was talking about the Northern Sinfonia concerts, the Academy and people. I hope things work out from your point of view with the flat. I don't think I could do it if I were you. I guess it really depends how much Simon is in London. Anyway, I'm v.v.v.v. glad to hear that you're OK. I can't tell if you're happy or not – I hope so. Tonight's the night you'll be in Lancaster – I hope that's good as well – Chris the lad with all his Glaswegian girlfriends.

I often wonder what things will be like in a year's time or six months or six weeks, things change so fast. I'll see you in about 9 days. You'll have to get a big hug for your recital and one for your bronchitis and one for the beginning of the new term! See you soon, take care, I'll be thinking of you (I've been thinking so hard I've been losing weight). All my love, Rory

From Chris to Izzy: April 21st 1975

I've got into the Intermediate school at RAM even although the sod gave me sight-reading for horn in A and B*b* alto, which I cocked up. After I last saw you, the NYO Liverpool concert went very well, but the Coventry concert due to echo and time lag was a bit duff. Phillip came after the course and I took 3 days off school. Gillian took photos of me and Phil playing Eroica in Epping Forest in the pouring rain with our trousers rolled up.

Marshall Marcus wants me to play Wagner tuba in Bruckner 7 in Oxford but you probably know about that already. Sight-read Fauré Requiem in a concert on Saturday and at the party it ended up with everyone watching 'That's Life' on the telly, which shows how the art of conversation is being destroyed. I'm going to the next rehearsal of the National Youth Jazz Orchestra and might join it permanently. I got a letter from Vyvian this morning (NYO oboist) – no stamp, just a GPO paid thing. Her father owns a chain of booze shops & is a whisky broker. She lives in a 3 storey house by the side of a lake in the poshest part of Glasgow and her Dad's got a bronze Rolls Royce.

Oh yeh, Dad came to this Fauré Requiem concert (at the Woodford Parish Church – the orchestra is 'Pro-Musica' – a watered down Concerti with a loony conductor) and asked at the door whether he was allowed to clap. When they said no, he said "Stuff you, then," got his money back and walked out!

How's Duncan's Villanelle and Mozart 2 going? What were your Lower 6th exams like?

I split my lip so can't practice today (un)fortunately. I expect your heart bleeds for this picture of abject misery. Ha! Ha!

Love from Chris.

From Chris to Paula Midgley: April 21st 1975

I am listening to DENNIS'S [*Dennis Brain*] recording of the Brahms horn trio, which must be the best horn piece ever. Rory is coming back next week. Gareth, Phil & I are the horn section in the MAYC show orchestra at the Albert Hall next month. Come and hear us. How are the Highers going? If they are going then soon they will be gone, which is a consolation.

"The trouble with having an open mind is that people come and put things in it."

Lots of love from Chris

In May, Chris took part in a master class at Craxton Studios given by the distinguished horn player and teacher, Ifor James. One of the other five students invited to participate was thirteen-year-old Richard Watkins.[1] Richard had never met Chris Giles before and felt slightly overwhelmed by the whole occasion. He told me: "Chris was already known in the horn world as one of the leading players of his generation and as such had an enviable reputation. On nervously arriving at Craxtons, Chris seemed to go out of his way to welcome me and put me at my ease – I was so grateful to him for his kindness and friendship. When he played in the class however, normal service resumed and he regained his God-like status!"

At around the same time, Chris became a regular player in the National Youth Jazz Orchestra. In chapter eight of *The Story of NYJO*, a history of the band that was published in 1992, Bill Ashton, NYJO's director, writes: "Chris Giles was probably the finest horn player ever to play with NYJO. He had a phenomenal technique, a perfect embouchure, could sight-read anything and could even improvise on the horn, a very rare gift." On July 6th, Chris spent a day with NYJO in the BBC Maida Vale studios where the band recorded eleven tracks. Chris was sitting directly in front of trumpeter Guy Barker, now an eminent and highly acclaimed jazz musician and composer. Guy remembers that one of the tracks had a particularly demanding and exposed horn solo. He told me, "Chris nailed it on every take." Five of the tracks recorded that day were later included in the NYJO double album, *Return Trip*.

Redbridge Brass Band also recorded at Maida Vale studios on several occasions for BBC Radio Three broadcasts. Chris had been there with John Ridgeon and the band just a few days earlier on July 2nd. As mentioned on page 201 in the chapter *The Horn*, John Ridgeon had acquired an in-depth knowledge of the physical aspects of brass technique from having to solve his own embouchure problems when a student. His knowledge, combined with his gift for teaching, turned the Redbridge Brass Band into champions and his pupils into fine players. Nine gained places in the NYO and of the hundred-strong National Youth Brass Band, twenty-five were John's students. His work as a player, teacher and researcher led to the publication of a series of books, which he began writing in 1975. To demonstrate his methods of establishing the correct physical approach to brass playing, he used his Redbridge pupils as models. In his book, *Brass for Beginners*, Chris was photographed to illustrate a correct embouchure.

Although Rory's amiable character helped to diffuse some of the daily tension, the dynamic between Mum, Dad and Granny had long been set in stone. Like Izzy and me, Chris had had enough: it ground him down; he desperately wanted to leave home. Gareth Mollison, Chris's friend from the NYO, was already at the Academy and Chris would be going at least one day a week to the Intermediate School in September. They talked about sharing a flat together. Chris would still be at BHCHS in his Upper Sixth A level year, but if they could find somewhere towards the east of London near the Central line, it would be possible. They decided to go flat-hunting over the summer.

1. Richard Watkins has an enviable reputation himself now as one of the UK's finest horn players.

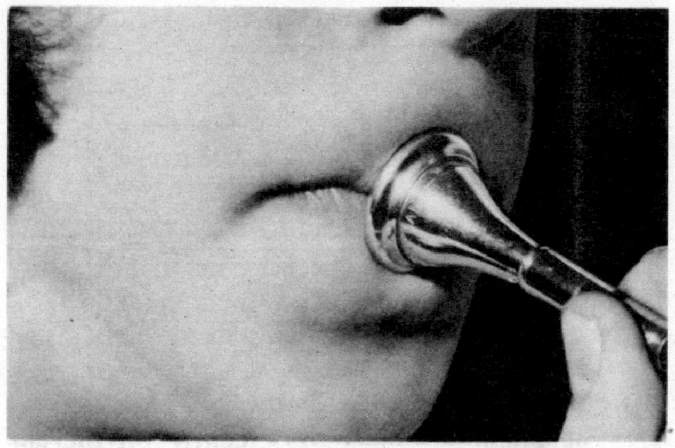

Fig. 15
Correct embouchure

Simon continued to stay at Orchard Road when he was in London. We couldn't help but be friends; we liked each other too much. But the rush of desire, the urgency and breathlessness had gone. The love that I was convinced would never end had ceased to be. Some little fragments of me disappeared with it and I had to reluctantly acknowledge that things do change. We don't live our whole lives in the same skin; cells die and fall away to be replaced with new ones, some of which retain the memories of the old – that is all. In May I wrote to Izzy:

> I got my LRAM (Catherine Giles LRAM now if you please!) Also won £650 from the Boise Foundation Scholarship – I can buy you all drinks now, a new amp for Dunc – oh and some more cello lessons with Fournier. I've at long last bought a flute (well, Mum has – £75!). Chris, Rory, Simon & I are going to hear Giulini conduct Mahler 9 at the RFH tomorrow (May 11th) – splashed out on £1.45 tickets! Well, it's worth it for Giulini (and Mahler for that matter).
>
> Simon sends his love,
> lots of love, Cathy.

Izzy and Duncan came down to London for a *Concerti* rehearsal with a concert the next day in which we all played. Unfortunately, they couldn't remain until the following week when I threw a party at Orchard Road. It was Whitsun half-term for Chris. He and Rory came to stay with me. I launched myself back into extrovert mode for the party. The flat was crammed with people – including Pat, Des, Mel and Jon. On the surface it was such fun, yet I disliked my party-animal behaviour, my loud voice, the way I drew attention to myself. Chris once said to me with distant amusement, "You're such an exhibitionist, Cath." I took it as a valid criticism, and felt ashamed. For not far beneath the surface was a shy, lonely person without a voice; the self I kept hidden; the unhappy clown without a red nose or greasepaint.

I found one letter from Helen Chapman, written in May 1975 from her boarding school in Cardiff. It begins: "Dear Chris, Thanks very much for your letter." The rest contains innocent descriptions of events at school. She tells Chris that during half-term "Dad and I will be able to go messing about happily down at the sailing club." Apart from signing off "Lots of love from Helen xxxx", there is nothing to give any indication of the depth of her feelings for him. However, Helen told me that the simple words, "lots of love", were actually most significant: for her to write them meant a great deal.

From Chris to Izzy: June 12th 1975

Dear Izzy,

Thanks for the letter & camp info. Forest is over – the concert was on Sunday. We had 10 horns, 8 clarinets, 4 troms, 4 trumpets, 8 perc. etc. It was the best concert we've done so far – the 1st trumpet really excelled himself. Mahler 3 is a terrific piece – you must get to know it. My exams start on Monday and I have done no work for them yet. I have a sociology O level next Wednesday for which I have written one essay since September (pride). I was totally exhausted doing nothing today at school. Still, my playing is going alright, which reminds me – when I got my observers ticket for the Neill Sanders masterclass, it said on the back "please bring your horn. Mr Sanders wishes to conduct a horn choir rehearsal". Phillip is doing the Britten Serenade on Saturday. Gareth, Alison, Chris Stearn & Cathy are all coming to it.

Gareth's car crash court case is on July 3rd. He, Alison and I will be there to give evidence. Anyway, I'm looking forward to camp and I'll seeya on July 6th when you get back from Leeds.

Lots of love, Chris

ABOVE LEFT: One of Chris's cartoons of Gareth Mollison

ABOVE: Rory Allam, the fairy-god-clarinettist, and Izzy at Cleveland Road.

BELOW: Izzy and Duncan Hollowood in Autumn Street, the student house they shared in Leeds.

BELOW: Rory

ABOVE: Chris and Phillip Eastop in Epping Forest, April 1975

BELOW: Chris, March 1975

BELOW: Chris and Gillian Taylor

80
PAUL

Into the street the Piper stept,
Smiling first a little smile,
As if he knew what magic slept
In his quiet pipe the while.

The Pied Piper of Hamelin – Robert Browning

A few months earlier, Paul Hart had phoned me to ask if I would play and record a suite of cello pieces he had written. The work begins with an Intro followed by six short movements and a coda. The titles Paul gave the sections were as follows: 'Empty Your Brain', 'Packet of Smarties', 'Honey-Child', 'Right-On Mrs. Warthog-Smythe' and 'Now Empty It Again'. Two movements were untitled and have remained so. I must have practised it, as some passages look quite tricky. He said he would phone when he returned from a tour of the USA with Cleo Laine and John Dankworth, to arrange a recording date.

Paul won an exhibitioner scholarship to the Royal College of Music when he was eleven and became a full-time student at sixteen. However, he only completed a year of the degree course, partly because it didn't inspire him, but also because he was getting too busy to attend. His early work in the music profession was as a bass guitarist. At eighteen, he joined the Johnny Dankworth big band. John was so impressed with Paul that he asked him to play bass with his wife, Cleo Laine, on their next trip to the USA. John and Cleo toured with just three musicians: Paul would be working with pianist Tony Hymas and drummer Kenny Clare. However, a few weeks before they were due to leave, Tony Hymas said he would rather not go as his wife was expecting a baby. There were very few pianists John could think of to replace Tony at such short notice, until somebody suggested Paul Hart. "But Paul's a bass player," protested John. It hadn't occurred to either that he could be both. John knew it would be less difficult to find another bass player – but would Paul be a good enough pianist to accompany Cleo? The Dankworths were holidaying in Malta at the time, so Paul was flown over. When he arrived, John and Cleo showed him round the island, took him out for a meal, and said they would do an audition in the morning. Paul writes: "When we got up, there was some pandemonium as John suddenly realised that one of the basic ingredients he required to conduct this audition was a piano, and he hadn't got one." A friend living at the other end of the island said they could use his. They drove there but "there was only about a quarter of an hour before I had to catch the plane back to England. So we played a few tunes with Cleo, John dispatched me back onto the plane and said that I had the job!" John must have known that he had struck gold. Two weeks later, in September 1974, Paul gave his first concert with Cleo at the Carnegie Hall. An American, Brian Q. Torff, was booked to play bass.

John was in for more surprises when he discovered Paul's skill, and speed, as an arranger. "Is there anything else you can do?" he asked, half joking.

"I play a bit of jazz violin," Paul admitted. In a later interview, John Dankworth said of Paul, "If he's not a genius, he's the nearest thing to it that I've come across."

Paul phoned as promised when he was back in the country and we fixed a date in May to record his cello pieces. We set up in the front room of his parents' house in Seven Kings, more than half of which was taken up with a Steinway grand piano, the rest with Paul's instruments and recording equipment. For several hours we rehearsed and recorded. Paul seemed happy with the result when we listened back. He asked whether he could take me out for dinner to thank me.

"Not next week. I'm working every evening."

"Well, the following week, then."

"No, I don't think so. I'm busy non-stop."

"What are you so busy non-stop doing?"

"Playing in *West Side Story* mainly."

"What time does the show finish?" asked Paul.

"About ten-thirty."

"Could I come and pick you up after a show and take you out then?"

"I guess so, but where would we go at that time of night?"

"We could go to Ronnie's."

"Where?"

"Ronnie Scott's Jazz club – it's open till three in the morning."

Paul met me after a show and drove me in his dirty-white Mini van to Ronnie Scott's. Linda Lewis was the supporting artist, and she was excellent. I don't remember the featured group, but I shall never forget the evening. I had first met Paul when I was seven and he was nine. Even though I couldn't recall that precise occasion, we had played in umpteen concerts together: we were long-standing friends with a shared history. I had huge admiration for Paul and liked him enormously. We had both been to Wortley, spent many evenings in the library playing chamber music together, or sat in the bar, Paul getting up to play jazz. He was now Cleo Laine's pianist. I asked him to tell me all about it. Never boastful, he simply said that Cleo was fantastic, and if I'd never heard her live, I should come to one of her concerts.

He produced a pack of duty-free cigarettes – an American variety called 'Larks' – tore the corner from the soft wrapping, tapped the bottom of the pack deftly and offered me one with a flourish. He performed the routine as dextrously as a magician. Paul smoked a lot, and that evening I probably smoked more than I had in the previous month. It hadn't occurred to me that he might be interested in me in a romantic way, but as the evening progressed, I began to think it would be rather nice if he did. During the third set, he reached for my hand. It felt as if an electric current shot straight through me; my heart began to hum; the whole of me melted into one huge smile as I looked at him and beamed. In his eyes I could see that what he was returning to me was his love; all of it. That was the moment. He drove me home to Orchard Road, I invited him up, he stayed the night and the following day he moved in. It wasn't something that needed discussion. He went home to pick up a few things, namely his manuscript paper, black felt-tip Tempo pens (he does not use pencils to write scores), musical instruments, tape recorder and, abracadabra, we were living together.

Is it possible to fall in love so instantly? The answer is yes – and no, it wasn't the same as the first time, but it was still spiced with wonderful sensations. The first time it will last forever: the next time carries the possibility that it might not. Even so, I sometimes find myself catching my breath recalling the feel of Paul's hand squeezing mine in Ronnie Scott's. Is it possible to switch off the circuit of love that has connected one deeply to another for a long time? No, I don't think it is. To this day, I have an enduring memory of the love I shared with Simon and recall our time together with immense fondness. I consider myself fortunate to have experienced the relationship, not just the happiest moments but also the sad: I am grateful for all of it. But at the end of May 1975, Paul took my hand and I flew with him into a new world. I didn't give much of a backward glance to the landscape I left behind. Flushed with love, I told Simon about Paul. He and Paul had met in *Concerti* and on other occasions. Both of them admired and respected each other as musicians and people. Simon was happy for me and very complimentary about Paul. It seemed that he didn't mind at all, but that wasn't entirely true. I heard from others that he was quite cut up about it, but he didn't dampen my spirits by off-loading his sadness of loss onto me.

Paul was my heartsease; uncomplicated, humble, generous and tender. His musical accomplishment was staggering, but he was completely unassuming about his ability. His character and his talent utterly captivated me. Paul had a quirky style of clothing, as can be seen in the photograph of the two of us [*on page 555*] where he is wearing his half-red/half-yellow tartan jacket. He never put on matching socks and liked to wear odd shoes – he would buy the same styles in different colours, and then pair them oddly. He once bought three plain track suit tops in red, blue and white and asked me to cut them in half and sew them, mismatched, back together.

Bram spotted me at the Academy and bounded over.

"Cathy? What's this I hear about you and Paul Hart? Is it true?"

"Yes! We're going out together. In fact, he's moved in with me."

"My goodness. Well, do send Paul my very best regards."

"I will."

Paul and I only had a month with each other before he went off on tour again with John and Cleo. He would be back in the middle of August, in time for us to go to Wortley. I decided to go on Leslie Holden's camp in Montgomeryshire. For the first time since we were nine, Izzy and I would not be going to the same summer camp. However, I was competing in the *Concours International d'Execution Musicale* in Geneva in September, and I had been selected as one of fifteen to take part in the Tortelier International Competition in Bristol in October. There were four British entrants, the others being Steven Isserlis, then aged sixteen, Robert Glenton and David Waterman. I had a great deal of preparation to do and could not afford two weeks away from the cello. I spoke to Leslie about my predicament. He contacted the farmer, who said it would be fine for me to bring my cello, and offered me the use of a cottage at the top of the field where I could practise.

Chris would not be camping with either of us as the NYO course clashed with the first fortnight camp. He was making plans with his Scottish NYO friends to spend a week in Glasgow with them after the course finished, and then go to a later summer camp.

From Paula Midgley: June 1st 1975, Glasgow

Dear Chris,

Please write and tell me more about when you're coming up and what you want to do. I think it's absolutely brilliant! Do you want to go out to lochs and things?

Lots of love, Paula

From Vyvian Howat: June 19th 1975, Glasgow

Dear Chris,

You can expect this to be a short letter – just to make you die of curiosity, I'll tell you why. Gillian was staying with me and we wrote you a joint letter. She wrote the first page (and what a page it was, I can tell you!) and I composed another seven. Just as I was about to post it, there was an urgent phone call from Gillian: "Stop! Forget it! Don't post that letter!" So I tore up all eight pages and threw them in the bin. And you'll never know what was in them. Having used up so much valuable writing paper already, I can only afford a few more precious sheets.

Talking of affording – this Trip To Scotland plan – It sounds a great idea, but I'm afraid I'm going to France with my family on the Monday after the course and won't, of course (Ha, Ha) be coming back here. What I could do, though, is buy an NYO half-fare return ticket and give you the return half. This should save you a good few pretty pennies and will also allow you the privilege of using my very distinguished name. You must write back quickly and tell me whether you want me to buy a return ticket and on what date you'll be coming up north. Also, can you put me up on the Sunday night after the course?

Love Vyvian.

From Chris to Paula: June 1975

Dear Paula,

Me & Phil are coming up from the 4th to the 12th (or longer for Phil) so why don't you all stay at my place after the course for a couple of days? I'll have to get clothes washed etc, but we can play duets etc. It's going to be really A1, and there are plenty of beds, as both sisters & Rory will be away. Gillian wants us to go canoeing on Loch Lomond, a prom would be a laugh, and we could sleep around at yours & Gillian's & Aileen's (if that's all right) rather than stay in 1 place. REALLY ACE. Must be in, however, on the night that the LPO does a prom tele broadcast – Tchaik 5!

The concerto Mick Thompson played is the same one I am playing with Redbridge Brass at St. Johns Smith Square on Sunday (wish me luck). Martin Koch is also doing a concerto, Buxton Orr's (BO to you) & also brass 5tets & tons of ultra-modern brass band works. Coming?

I might soon be able to try out a 2 years old Alex F/B*b* full double horn, just like Phil's.

Do stay here after NYO Prom. Sort out tons of Chamber Music for oboe, 2 violas, 2 horns. I'll see you at Holbrook,

Love Chris

Ever since Chris had tried Phillip Eastop's Alexander, he had realised that it was far more suitable for his style of playing. Although he appreciated his Paxman XL, compared to the Alexander it was brassy, brash and heavy. Chris Stearn, who remained Chris's horn-talking partner, heard that a student at the Guildhall was selling a second-hand Alexander double horn and arranged for Chris to try it out. He played a few notes and knew at once that it was exactly what he wanted. Having agreed to buy, the seller allowed him to keep it to play immediately. Chris went straight from the Guildhall to the Academy to show the horn to Gareth Mollison. They were lucky enough to find a free room. Gareth remembers Chris demonstrating the whole range of the instrument, and his delight as he found how easily the horn responded. It didn't take long to sell the XL. Mum, as usual, made up the difference. The Alexander took Chris's playing into new dimensions.

On June 24th 1975, Chris turned seventeen. Helen sent him a birthday card – that and the one earlier letter are all that survive of their correspondence. In it she again wrote "lots of love from Helen xxxxx". Five days later, he played the Gregson horn concerto with Redbridge Brass Band at St. John's Smith Square. It was a marvellous performance – even Chris was pleased with it. He received a tremendous ovation at the end. Edward Gregson shook hands with him and Chris nodded his head modestly to acknowledge his respect to the composer. I was overcome with admiration. I felt so proud to be his sister. He repeated the concerto on July 10th at Gipsy Hill, which unfortunately I was not able to attend. He was ridiculously busy – I don't know how he managed to do everything. His engagement diary shows him working with *Concerti Allegri*, *Musici*, Wind Band, Forest Philharmonic, NYJO, GYO, NYO, Redbridge Band, having weekly lessons with John Ridgeon, consultation horn lessons with James Brown, piano lessons and daily practice – and he was also going to school. In amongst the rehearsals and concerts are entries that read: 'English Modern exam paper I; Sociology O level; Chaucer and Shakespeare paper II; A level music.' Plus he continued to make his brews of beer and go to concerts and parties.

Lesley Garrett was still living at Orchard Road, but it was obvious that Paul and I needed the space of the whole flat. She found herself somewhere else to live and moved out. We parted the best of friends and she continued to be peripherally involved with our lives: when Paul established his jingle-writing company, if he needed a soprano to sing on one of his jingles, it was Lesley he asked.

Before Paul left for the USA, he insured me to drive his car, gave me the keys and made me a second signatory on his credit card in case I needed money while he was away. I didn't ask him, he just did it. We agreed that it would be fine for Simon to continue to stay at Orchard Road until he was able to find himself his own flat. I drove Paul's Mini van, over the moon to have a set of wheels, but didn't use his credit card. I motored around listening to his tapes – Maynard Ferguson, Stevie Wonder and Paul's own music, including *Seven of Harts*, a gem of a piece that he had recorded with John Dankworth, Daryl Runswick (bass) and Kenny Clare (drums), with himself on Fender Rhodes. I wrote to him daily, he wrote every other day and phoned quite often, nearly always getting the time-lag wrong and waking me in the middle of the night – not that I minded.

From Paul to me:

July 5th 1975

Dear Cathy,

It's four o'clock a.m. Strange to think that you're just getting up as I'm going to bed. We've just done the first concert. It was a great success. The American audience is so different. Cleo got an amazing ovation just for walking onto the stage, and a standing ovation at the end of the show and after each encore. It makes playing so much more fun when you get such a strong feedback from the audience.

Good luck with your various exams and things. I'm thinking of you all the time,
Molto love, Paul

July 7th 1975

Dear Cathy,

As you will probably notice the last letter I wrote was in New York but it was posted in Cleveland, Ohio. I always seem to have this problem. Basically because post offices are very rare and cunningly concealed. So you have to rely on stamp machines, which issue stamps that don't stick properly and taste horrible. If you do manage to stick all the stamps on, you then have to locate and identify a mailbox, which all look like litterbins to me. I found a mailbox this morning, which was just a hole in the wall of the hotel with a little motto written above it, 'Keep Ohio tidy – drop your mail here'. The other sort of mailbox is literally a mail 'drop'. In the multi-storey hotels, to save you going downstairs to hunt for litterbins, they put litterbins and ashtrays in the corridors on each floor. If you look above the ashtray near the lift you see a mail drop, which allows the letters to fall into the main mailbox fifty-six floors below... We're back in New York now, to Philadelphia tomorrow to do a TV show, then the next day we do the 'Today' show in NY. This comes on air at 7.00 in the morning and is transmitted live. We've got a rehearsal called at 5.30 am!!

I'm going through a 'dry' period. My powers of invention have dried up. I haven't written anything since the album, which you played on, and have been struggling with this problem for the last eight months or so. It makes me so frustrated. Maybe I should just sit back and accept it but I can't. I get obsessed and seem to be squeezing very hard trying to force something out that's withered. Sometimes I manage a few bars, which look quite promising but they never lead anywhere.

We haven't even been away a week yet. August can't come too soon. I can't wait to see you again and in case no-one's told you recently, you're beautiful, and unreal, and I love you very much. Paul

July 10th 1975

I've just read your first four letters (I fell about at some of them) and it's about three hours since you phoned. What with the letters and phone call, I feel incredibly uplifted, in fact sort of floating. I had a terrible hangover the other morning, the first I've had for years. I must be getting old. It didn't help matters having to travel for two hours without being able to smoke on account of Cleo sitting in the back. Then the chauffeur, noticing me fidgeting put up a partition and Kenny and I filled the cab with lethal fumes within two seconds. It was quite funny at the time. It was even funnier on the way back. Fred Harris, Cleo's representative, came with us. He wears a glass eye and makes jokes about it. He says, "if I go out in a rush in the morning and put it in without having time to look in the mirror, I don't know which direction I'm looking in for the rest of the day." As we were driving, the chauffeur suddenly let out a scream, "Aarghh!!! The agent guy in the back is dead!!" I turned round to see for myself what a deceased agent looked like. Fred had fallen asleep. His mouth was wide open, one eye was closed and the other (his false eye) was staring grotesquely at the roof of the limousine. I then had to pacify the driver by explaining that Fred never knew what his right eye was doing.

I went to see 'Tommy' the other night – stunning, moving and vivid most of the time. That's what I like about Ken Russell films – they're really enveloping. Then last night I went to see 'Monty Python and the Holy Grail'. The American audience is just beginning to wake up to Monty Python, but I was a bit disappointed in this film. Brian, the bass player, is very into Monty Python so every time we go into a restaurant we both ask for "spam, spam, egg, spam, spam, egg, beans, spam, spam, egg and SPAM." And we normally end up with a medium cheeseburger. We're thinking of opening a 'Spamine Relief Appeal'. How can I say what I feel about you? (changing the subject). I long to be with you yet I've got another 15,000 miles to go before I get to see you. You're the most beautiful person ever, and I'm the luckiest person I've ever been.

I love you so much, Paul

I took my Recital Diploma, which involved giving a public performance in the Duke's Hall to an audience and the adjudicators. Mum wasn't there because of her teaching timetable; nor was Dad. But Granny and Chris came along and I gave them a lift home to Cleveland Road. Chris had to sit with the cello in the back of Paul's van. At a roundabout I stupidly bumped into a Volvo. The driver didn't appear to notice and drove on. I couldn't see any sign of damage on the car I'd hit and thought all was well, until I turned left at the next lights and heard an awful grinding noise. Nearly back, I drove on, parked outside the house and inspected the damage. The offside front wheel arch of Paul's Mini was crumpled inwards. I drove it to the local garage to be told it could be fixed for the sum of £26 – I would have to do a lot of shows to pay for it. I left the van there and travelled back to the Academy to check the notice board to find out whether I had passed my Recital Diploma. To my relief, I had. To my complete surprise, I had also won the Moir Carnegie prize, awarded for the best cello recital; but the thought of having damaged Paul's van mattered more.

When I picked it up, the newly sprayed wing was a brilliant white. I washed the rest of the van, hoping it would tone in, but the shiny new paint still looked glaringly obvious. However, when Paul returned, he failed to notice anything different about his van and I neglected to tell him. It was years before he found out.

July 12th 1975

Dear Cathy,

That's fantastic news about your recital diploma. Out of all the people who've been to the Academy since its foundation you must be one of the few to be given such unreserved recognition. That makes you a very special musician. How lucky you are to be a very special person as well; there are not many people who manage both.

We've just done a concert at the Wolf Trap Festival (not too far from Washington D.C.) Today we do a concert in Atlantic City and tomorrow we play at another big outdoor festival – the Temple Festival near Philadelphia with the Pittsburg Symphony Orchestra. The end of this tour will be rather berserk. In the space of eight days I will travel to Minneapolis, Chicago, New York, London, Monte Carlo, London and Wortley. I can't wait to get back and be with you again. The time that must elapse before that happens seems like a race between two tortoises across the Alps filmed in slow motion.

I tried to go to the museum of Prehistoric Art in NY the other day but found it closed – for two years! I wondered if perhaps they had some exhibits that were as yet only 'Historic' and are allowing some time to elapse until they become 'Prehistoric'.

I love you like crazy and I'm missing you very much,
moltissimo love, Paul

Things were not going so well for Izzy. She had passed her end-of-year exams but she wanted out of her relationship with Duncan. Months ago, they had both agreed to staff with FSC in the summer and were committed to a fortnight camping on the Isle of Arran. She felt that she couldn't let FSC down, so thought it best they go camping anyway. She had already suggested to Duncan that they live separately the following academic year, a suggestion he did not want to accept, so the prospect of having to camp with him for two weeks was daunting.

The examination period was over at Buckhurst Hill County High. It was, as usual, time for the school's music festival. Izzy, back from Leeds, went along to listen. As well as performing in the instrumental classes, Chris, Nitram, Martin Koch and Cliff Oliver sang *By the Light of the Silvery Moon* in a barbershop-style vocal ensemble, which Izzy remembers as being very well done. In the same vocal class, Nitram and Chris, and a boy called Trevor Poole, entered a piece entitled *Macbeth Rocks (but Gently)*, composed by Nitram, 'lyrics' by Shakespeare. The title was a spoof on a recently released Val Doonican album called *Val Rocks (but Gently)*, which pictured Val seated in a rocking chair on the cover. The three lads appeared as witches wearing black cloaks not dissimilar to their masters' academic gowns. With Nitram at the piano, he, Chris and Trevor sang these words to a tuneful little ditty:

When shall we three meet again,
In thunder, lightning, or in rain?
When the hurlyburly's done,
When the battle's lost and won,
There upon the heath to meet Macbeth.
Eye of newt and toe of frog,
Wool of bat and tongue of dog,
Liver of blaspheming Jew;
Gall of goat and slips of yew.
Finger of birth-strangled babe,
Ditch-delivered by a drab.

At this point, Chris and Trevor provided a background riff while Nitram launched into a recitation of Macbeth's soliloquy:

Tomorrow and tomorrow and tomorrow,
Creeps in this petty pace from day to day,
To the last syllable of recorded time;
And all our yesterdays have lighted fools
The way to dusty death. Out, out, brief candle!
Life's but a walking shadow; a poor player,
That struts and frets his hour upon the stage,
And then is heard no more: it is a tale
Told by an idiot, full of sound and fury,
Signifying nothing.

The festival adjudicator wrote two words on their report sheet:
"Totally convincing".

81
THE SILENT-FOOTED BUTLER

Life is bottled sunshine and Death the silent-footed butler who draws out the cork.

The Martyrdom of Man – Winwood Reade

On July 17th there was a *Concerti* Disco – an attempt to raise some money for the orchestra. Izzy, Chris and I went together. The disco was an ill-conceived event. Flashing coloured lights did little to improve the drab school hall. People were slow to arrive and awkward about dancing. The DJ whacked up the volume in the erroneous notion that it would get things going. We stood around in small groups, shouting over the din, sweating and shifting uncomfortably in toe-pinching shoes. I stepped out to the foyer to escape the racket and get some fresh air. Chris was standing there looking amused.

"OK Chris?"

"Yeah, fine. I've just been talking to Bram."

"Where is he?"

"Gone to the pub, I think. God, isn't this stupid?"

"How do you mean?"

"Well, look at everyone. Too embarrassed to dance. The music's crap and it's deafening. Why a disco?"

"I suppose they thought it would attract a crowd. Bring in more money."

"Yeah, but we could have done our own thing – put a jazz band together like the last nights at Wortley, played folk music for country dancing – or done a Jubilee-Hall-style concert – lots of things come to mind."

"Mmm, you're right, it would have been much more fun. You should suggest it for next time. Do you want to go to the pub?"

"Nah. Maybe later. I'm happy talking to people as they come out. When are you off to camp?"

"I think I'll go next Saturday for prep-camp. Paul says I can take his van – just as well, as I have to take my cello, worst luck. It's going to be a real drag having to practise at camp."

"It'll be worth it when you win the competition."

"Oh Chris, I'm not going to win. I'm rather dreading it, really."

"Don't say that. You'll enjoy it."

"Perhaps. Anyway, are you looking forward to NYO?"

"I can't wait. I think it's going to be a brilliant course, and as soon as it's over there's the trip to Glasgow, then two weeks camping. An action-packed summer."

"We're not going to see each other for ages. Make sure you give me your addresses so I can write."

"Will do. Well, I think I'll go in there and throw myself around a bit. Got to show willing, eh?"

Izzy spent the entire evening talking to Chris Stearn. In her diary she wrote: "I still adore him." I gave Izzy and Chris a lift back to Cleveland Road. It was the last time the three of us would be together.

The next day, Izzy went to Somerset to play in the Minehead and Exmoor Festival Orchestra, pleased to have a break from Duncan. Chris went to the cottage with Mum and Dad for a few days before going to the NYO course. I drove to Montgomeryshire with camping equipment and cello, pitched my tent and forced myself into a routine of practising for a couple of hours every morning. The day after Izzy returned from Minehead, she set off with Duncan and the FSC escort party to the Isle of Arran.

From Paul to me at camp: August 1st 1975

Greetings, fair maiden, who cooks over a spit and doesn't wash. We're in San Francisco presently, a fairy tale city of people who pretend. It has been named the prettiest city in America. I suppose in a lot of ways it is. Ever since gold rush days it has been a city where people escape to and search for dreams. All the postmen and garbage men are University dropouts who come here to slow down and mellow out. It's a happy city, despite the high crime rate! It has the largest Chinese settlement outside of China. Consequently half the taxi-drivers are Chinese. The other half are, for some unknown reason, all struggling bass-guitarists. Every time we get in a cab the driver starts quizzing Brian about guitar technique and bass tutors. Another funny thing about them is that the cab companies don't allow them to wear long hair. They get round this by wearing the most grotesque wigs you've ever seen, absolutely bulging in every direction and you can often see a pigtail poking out of the back of their Irish's and shoved inside their collars.

We're back in LA again. In a way it's similar to San Francisco and yet completely different. It's not pretty like SF and on the whole, the people who live here moved from the East coast as a means of escape to a sort of glamorous Hollywood dream. But they don't escape as successfully as the people in San Francisco. LA went through astonishing growth just after the last war and it is really no more than a megopolis (as they call it) of suburbs, which are sprawled out over an area of eighty square miles or more. Everywhere is miles away from everywhere else and there's not any efficient transportation system – every family has three or four cars and a freeway is built in every space possible. Pollution, due to cars and geographical conditions is heavy. Orange smog of varying density hangs over the city all year round. Sometimes it gets really thick. Do you remember a Bacharach/ David song 'Do you know the way to San Jose?' It really sums it up:

LA is a great big freeway
Put a hundred down and buy a car,
In a week or two they'll make you a star.
Weeks turn into years how quick they pass,
And all the stars that never were
Are parking cars and pumping gas.

I hired a car for the first time today. It's really weird having a left-hand drive – everything's backwards. The hardest thing is trying to find the traffic in the mirrors and making any sense of it.

All my love, you're a very special and rare person, Paul.

The NYO course was held at Holbrook again. I asked Helen what she could remember about it. She finds it hard to recall details, but she is clear that she and Chris were still together. I have two rather blurred photos that were taken on that last course, which show Chris with a group of friends gathered around a road sign. I have included them [*on page 556*], as they are the last known photos of Chris. The girls in the group are Vyvian, Helen and Gillian.

On July 30th there was a concert at Holbrook. The programme included Kodály's *Peacock Variations* and Tchaikovsky's fourth symphony, conducted by Christopher Seaman. The concert was repeated at St Andrew's Hall, Norwich, and the final performance was a Prom on Saturday, August 2nd 1975. After the Prom, most of the orchestra returned to Furzedown College in Croydon, where the NYO was staying, as usual. The next morning, Helen was whisked straight off by her parents to France. She cannot even remember saying goodbye to her beloved Chris.

Chris had been romantically involved with Helen since April 1974. It was innocent in the sense that they never went as far as actual sex, but nevertheless, their relationship had evolved into one of desire, intimacy and love. The time they had spent together only amounted to about seven weeks in total – four NYO courses and Chris's Christmas party – but those days and weeks had been periods of intense connection. Chris may well have kissed other girls outside of the NYO during the time he was with Helen; I do not know: plenty of flirtation went on at the numerous parties we went to, and I do not wish to portray Chris as a model of virtue. All I know is that during the fifteen months that he knew Helen, he did not go out with anyone else. But he was a boy of seventeen: he would surely have been as attracted to girls as they were to him.

As usual, there was an end-of-course booze-up at The Griffin on Charing Cross Road. Chris, Gillian, Aileen, Paula and Vyvian made their way there and met up with Phillip Eastop. As the day progressed, Gillian began to sense a frisson between Chris and herself. The six of them travelled back to Cleveland Road, where they were all going to stay that night. It was a gorgeous sunny afternoon. Chris suggested they walk to Epping Forest. Vyvian remembers that they lay on some grass in a circle and each person placed his or her head on another's stomach. They laughed so much that their abdominal contractions caused everyone's heads to bob up and down. In the evening they stayed up gossiping. Perhaps they played our old childhood game of What do you prefer? Custard or gravy? Blindness or deafness? To freeze to death or burn to death? However it transpired, the conversation led to Chris commenting that if one had to die, drowning wasn't a bad way to go. He explained that after a minute or two, once the person has stopped struggling and water has been inhaled, the brain releases endorphins, which cause an overwhelming euphoria and calmness, making death serene and peaceful. We know this to be the experience, he said, because those who have been resuscitated from drowning have been able to testify what it felt like, and have described a sense of release and pleasure.

Aileen and Paula went to bed in Rory's room – the room that had once been mine. Gillian, Chris, Phillip and Vyvian stayed up longer, until the girls decided they should turn in. Gillian and Vyvian were sharing Izzy's double bed in the front bedroom. The boys followed them upstairs. All four of them lay down on the bed together. Phillip and Vyvian started to kiss; then Chris and Gillian began to do the same. Using the terminology of the day, they 'got off' with each other. It did not go far or last for long – clothes stayed on; nobody got under the sheets. For Gillian, though, such closeness with Chris was something she had barely dared to dream about.

On Monday, August 4th, Granny and Mum left by car for Scotland. They were looking forward to a leisurely tour of their homeland and planned to reach Oban by the following day. Vyvian met up with her parents and departed for France. Chris, Phillip, Gillian, Paula and Aileen set off to Euston station. Dad was the only one left at home.

The five friends boarded the train for Glasgow. Gillian wondered if she had read too much into what had happened the previous night. After a while, she left the compartment to stretch her legs. She stood in the corridor looking out of the window, when she felt Chris's arms slip around her waist. "Watcha doll," he whispered. She turned towards him and he kissed her. There were no more doubts. And now they would have over a week in Glasgow to enjoy together. After that, it would only be a short while before she would be moving to London. The auditions she had taken in April, when Mum had accompanied her, had been successful. She had gained herself a place at the Royal College of Music. Chris spoke enthusiastically about her coming to London in September.

Gillian's father was waiting for them when they arrived at Glasgow Central station. Aileen and Paula waved goodbye. Mr. Taylor drove Chris, Phillip and his daughter back to the house. Gillian had not brought friends home to stay before. Her parents were anxious to make the boys feel welcome. Her mother showed them to their room and then served a thoughtfully-prepared dinner. Her father was looking forward to introducing Chris and Phillip to the beauty of Glasgow's surrounding countryside. Loch Lomond was surely the first place they should see: it is one of Scotland's most idyllic stretches of water and the largest freshwater loch in Britain. From as young as he could remember, Chris had heard Granny singing to him of the 'Bonnie, bonnie banks of Loch Lomond', but he had never seen them.

The following day dawned bright and sunny with a clear blue sky and a high summer temperature. Mrs. Taylor prepared a picnic and Mr. Taylor roped two canoes onto the roof-rack of his car. Paula arrived to go with them, as had been arranged. There wasn't room for more than five people in the car, so Mrs. Taylor stayed behind. She waved goodbye as Paula, Phillip, Chris and Gillian drove off with Mr. Taylor towards Rowardennan Point, a beauty spot situated on the rugged east side of the loch that the Taylor family had visited for years. With its small sandy beaches, surrounding woods and breathtaking views of Ben Lomond, it was the perfect place to launch the canoes.

Mr. Taylor parked the car. The loch stretched out spectacularly before them, the sun glittering like crystal confetti on its gently rippling surface. Gillian and Paula went to the changing hut to get into their swimming costumes while Mr. Taylor unroped one of the canoes from the roof-rack. The boys pulled off their clothes. They were already wearing their swimming trunks underneath their trousers. The canoe was carried down to the water's edge and launched. Phillip jumped into it. In seconds, he was paddling out into the loch. He had not gone far, when, with a show of bravado, he deliberately capsized the canoe and executed a 'roll'. Rolling is the technique used by canoeists to right themselves and their canoe after they have capsized. It is a tricky manoeuvre, but Phillip knew what he was doing as he had tried it before. The girls didn't see his roll; they were still getting changed. But Chris saw it. Phillip rowed back to the shore and stepped out. I imagine there was some friendly banter between the two boys. They were having fun. Then Chris climbed into the canoe. As Phillip watched him paddling out into the loch, it occurred to him that Chris might try to do a roll too. He was pretty sure that Chris had never been in a canoe before. He also knew that Chris was not a strong swimmer: surely Chris would not try anything so risky. But he wasn't certain, and decided it would be wise to swim after him.

Chris rowed out to about the same distance that Phillip had gone. Then, whether by accident or intention, the canoe capsized. Chris plunged into dark, icy water. Immediately, he was in trouble. The canoe was on top of him and he was not able to right it. He must have been terrified, but somehow he managed to get out and back up to the surface. The canoe was floating upside down, and could perhaps have been a life raft. Phillip, still some way away, shouted to Chris to hang onto it. But Chris, a boy who had always been quick to panic, didn't hear, or didn't understand, for instead of hanging on, he started to turn the canoe over. Inevitably, it began to sink. Chris fought to keep his head above water. Paralysed with fear, he shouted to Phillip, "I've forgotten how to swim."

Gillian and Paula had just changed and were on their way back to the loch when they heard shouts from the water. At first they thought the boys were larking about. It took a few moments to realise that the cries for help were real. Gillian, a strong swimmer, dived off the pier. Paula did the same. Then Chris disappeared from sight. Phillip, having been swimming as fast as he could, reached the sinking canoe. Before he had a moment to think what to do next, Chris grabbed hold of Phillip's legs from beneath the water and pulled him down. There was a desperate underwater struggle. With all his effort, Phillip tried to get them both to the surface, but it was impossible. He had to push Chris from him and pull himself away to save his own life.

Gillian and Paula dived down again and again, frantically searching. The water was dark brown – they couldn't see through it at all. Phillip could do no more. He swam back to the shore and sat on a boulder, utterly exhausted. He knew by then that it was too late. Chris had gone. Then Gillian heard her father screaming at them to get out of the water. He was a man who never shouted or spoke angrily, but at that moment he completely lost it.

There were other bathers and picnickers around. Gillian remembers sitting on a log and a woman sat beside her. Paula was some distance from Gillian, on her own. Phillip was still sitting on a boulder. Then they all had to wait. Paula said it seemed like hours. The police and coastguards arrived. A team of divers went out in a motorboat and eventually found Chris's body. Gillian told me that when she saw his body being carried past her, she knew he was dead by the unnatural way his head was hanging. The canoe was brought out of the loch. On the way back home, Mr. Taylor drove to a council rubbish site and threw both canoes onto the dump.

It was Tuesday, August 5th, 1975. I set off on hike that morning with another member of staff and a small group of Woodlings. We stopped to eat our lunch near a shop and bought food for our evening meal and the next day's breakfast. With the provisions packed into our rucksacks, we headed down to the river and followed it along the valley to a pre-located site. Tents were pitched, sleeping bags unrolled, a fireplace turfed and wood gathered. We lit the fire, fetched water from the stream and prepared our meal. Sausages began to sizzle in mess-tins. The weather was perfect. The sun had dipped behind the mountains, cooling the air, but it was a dry, calm and peaceful evening.

On the Isle of Arran that same morning, Izzy and Duncan had set off hiking with their group of Elves. She had put her collapsing relationship on hold whilst dealing with group-chief responsibilities and showing Duncan the ropes of FSC. They walked along the beach, stopping when they were hungry to eat their packed lunch. The Elves paddled in the sea, made sandcastles, collected shells and left their footprints in the sand. When they reached their prearranged destination, the large communal Elf tent was already pitched on the grassland above the beach and provisions had been delivered. Duncan lit a fire while Izzy and the Elves collected driftwood. She gazed out at the sea, watching the waves lap at the shoreline. It was a warm, dry evening with hardly any breeze.

At about half past six, I glanced up from the fire to see two figures moving purposefully down the valley towards us. One was Leslie. It was not unusual for him to visit a hike site to see how the groups were settling in, but even at a distance I could see from the way he was walking that something was wrong. As he approached, it became obvious that I was the one he had come to find. He took my arm and led me away while his companion went to talk to the other Woodling leader. In a quiet voice, he told me that the police had contacted the farmer and given him a message that I must phone home. I asked whether anything awful had happened. He said he didn't know. We started walking up the hill, Leslie setting an urgent pace beside me. My heart was thudding with dread. What had happened? Was someone in hospital? Had Mum and Granny been involved in a car accident? Had Dad committed suicide? Was Izzy OK?

It was also at about half past six when Izzy turned away from the sea. She looked at the Elf tent, its white canvas framed by a blue sky, and had a strange feeling that she would never sleep in it. Glancing along the beach, she saw a distant figure running swiftly across the sand from the direction of the main camp. She could tell it was one of the Trackers and could see that the girl was heading straight for her. It was obviously an emergency. Izzy ran towards the girl, who told her to go quickly to the main campsite; something had happened: the police were waiting to see her.

Adrenalin shot through Izzy's bloodstream. Tearing back, feet pounding across the sand, her heart thundering, she mentally flicked through the family. Something must have happened to Mum or Granny. Had Dad finally flipped? Could Cathy have had an accident at camp?

At the farmhouse, I picked up the phone and dialled the number. Des answered.

"Kate?" What a relief to hear his voice.

"Des? Is everything OK?" I asked anxiously.

Before he could answer there was a clatter. Dad cut in on the other extension.

"It's Chris." His voice sounded high and manic.

"Derek!" Des warned, trying to stop him.

"He's drowned," howled Dad.

But of course they gave him the kiss of life, my brain screeched.

"He's alright, though?"

"No. No." Dad wailed, "he's dead… dead… dead."

My knees buckled. There was a crash as the phone fell to the floor.

The police met Izzy. One of them spoke:

"I'm terribly sorry, Isabel. I have some very bad news. I'm afraid there's been an accident. Your brother, Christopher, drowned earlier today in Loch Lomond."

No, not Chris, not Chris.

With Paul Hart in a pub somewhere in Ilford soon after we started living together.

A cutting from the local *Guardian and Independent*, which reads: "Mahler has plenty of work for the horns to perform, and they will be in evidence on June 8th at Walthamstow Assembly Hall when Forest Philharmonic perform the composer's third symphony." Chris is in the foreground. Notice his physical poise, the effortlessness of his embouchure, all the more apparent when compared to his colleagues.

These are the last known photos of Chris (wearing orange trousers) taken at the NYO course in Holbrook, August 1975. The girls with him above, left to right, are Helen Chapman, Vyvian Howat and Gillian Taylor, who can also be seen below. I shall not identify the other boys in the photos as they are not mentioned elsewhere.

82
AFTERMATH

Late, by myself, in the boat of myself,
No light and no land anywhere,
Cloudover thick. I try to stay
just above the surface, yet I'm already under
and living within the ocean.

Acts of Helplessness – Rumi

At the farmhouse, Leslie helped me up from the floor and guided me into a living room. He went back to the phone to talk to Des, while I sat in an armchair and was handed a cup of sweet tea. I said I didn't take sugar, but was told it would be good for the shock. I sipped it reluctantly. The room was hot, the lights too bright; people were talking; I could make no sense of what they were saying. Then Leslie said we were leaving. He led me outside to the cool darkness and into a car. We were soon driving along the narrow roads, headlights illuminating the high hedges.

Back at the campsite, Leslie decided I should sleep in the medical tent and arranged for a female member of staff to stay with me for the night. I lay awake, thinking that I would never fall asleep. I did, but not for long. It was still dark when I woke. For a moment I couldn't work out where I was; then I remembered and groaned. The woman beside me asked if I was OK. I said yes, and then thought: what a mad question, what a mad reply. I turned on my side and buried my face into the sleeping bag. I cried a little; silently, painfully. It was a kind of weeping I had never experienced before. My throat felt swollen, my breathing laboured, but I was breathing air into my lungs and out; in and out. Chris had breathed in water. How must that have been? I tried not to think or imagine, but I could not stop thinking or imagining. And then I said to myself: if I can get through this, I can get through anything; nothing could ever be worse than this.

Izzy did not remain at camp. The policeman who had broken the news to her took her back to his house. His wife made her supper, a doctor prescribed a sleeping pill, and she stayed there that night. In the morning, the policeman drove her to Brodick and put her on the ferry to Ardrossan. She sat by herself crying quietly. A woman tried to comfort her. When the ferry arrived at Ardrossan, the woman and her husband gave Izzy a lift to the station and waited with her until the train left for Glasgow.

Des had told Leslie on the phone that I must go back to Cleveland Road. Izzy was going straight to Glasgow from Arran. Rory was on his way to Glasgow too. Mum and Granny were somewhere in Scotland, but had not yet been found; which left me to deal with Dad. It meant I would have to travel to London before I could get to Scotland – and I was anxious to get to Scotland fast, because I desperately wanted to see Chris, to see his body, to touch him. I could not persuade Leslie to let me drive home by myself, although I was quite sure I was fit to drive. Instead, I was taken back to London, with my cello, in Paul's Mini van by Leslie's father-in-law, a person I didn't know. For six long hours we had to endure awkward conversation or uncomfortable silence. As soon as he had parked outside 32, Cleveland Road, he left for the station, refusing to stop even for a cup of tea. I felt awful that it had been such a terrible journey for him.

Des was with Dad. Dad looked a wreck. He stared at me as if he had never seen me before; he seemed deranged. I knew I ought to try and comfort him, but his helplessness and hopelessness scared me. I didn't know what I should do, or how I was going to manage, but it was clear that I would have to take charge. Dad was incapable of doing anything.

I asked Des if Mum and Granny knew yet. He told me that they had still not been found. Then I said, "Des, I want to see Chris."

"No, Kate. Not a good idea. It would be far too distressing."

"Just one last time. I have to see him one last time."

"His body was in the water for hours. You wouldn't want to see him like that."

"I don't mind. I just want to see him."

"No, don't put yourself through that. It's best to remember him as he was."

I couldn't ask again. I was not going to be allowed to see him.

"Your Dad needs you, Kate."

"I know."

"It's the worst thing for a father to lose his son."

"I'll do my best to look after him," I replied, but I was taken aback by Des's statement. It was such an odd, misogynistic thing for him to say. Was he telling me that it was more of a blow for a father to lose a son than to lose a daughter? Did he think Chris's death was worse for Dad than it was for Mum; worse for Dad than for Izzy or Granny or me? If that was what he meant, he was wrong; but I also understood what he was telling me: I had to take responsibility for Dad. It was my duty. And that did not make sense either, because some years ago, Des had told me that children were not responsible for their parents. Now, though, he was telling me I was. There was no need: I would have taken care of my father whether he had asked me to or not.

When the police informed Dad of Chris's death, they had asked him whom they should contact. Dad gave them Des's number. Pat took the call and the police phoned Des at work. He had gone straight to Cleveland Road. It was he who had helped the police to locate Izzy and me. Having been with Dad for more than twenty-four hours, he had to get home. He departed with a bayonet he had removed from Dad, who, in typical irrational fashion, was threatening to kill Phillip, blaming him for Chris's death.

I was alone with Dad. I tried to be kind and helpful; I was positive and practical. I did what I could for him, picking up the role of nurse without the safety net of professional distance. He shuffled about in his dressing gown, making moaning sounds and shuddering. He seemed not to understand anything I said. It was draining, distressing and dreadful.

I tracked Paul down on tour. He said he wished he could come back right away and be with me, but we both knew he couldn't. I phoned Florrie. I had to tell her I wanted to withdraw from the Geneva competition. I thought she would be angry, would say I must go. She didn't, but said I should still compete in the Tortelier competition in Bristol in October. I phoned John Ridgeon and spoke to his wife. I contacted FSC to let them know Chris would not be camping. I made a dozen more calls then had to stop. I could not say it again.

Chris, my darling Chris. Oh Chrissie.

The doorbell rang. It was Jon Turner. "Come on, Kate," he said, "I'm taking you out for a drink."

Dad seemed to be asleep in a chair. I left a note: 'Dad, Jon has taken me out for a quick drink. I'll be back soon. Love Cathy.' Jon gave me some cash for train fares and expenses – the banks would not be open before leaving for Glasgow in the morning. Dear, thoughtful Jon.

The journey was gruelling. I had to administer to Dad every second of the way. Mr. Taylor met us at the station and drove us back to his house. Izzy and Rory were already there. The Taylors did everything they possibly could to make us comfortable. It was painful to watch how carefully Mrs. Taylor laid the table. My bed was turned down; there were neatly folded towels on the counterpane.

Mum and Granny had still not been found. The police were given the car registration number, but did not look very hard – Mum's car was parked opposite a police station for the whole time that we were trying to locate them. I was kept away from the mortuary. Chris, dearest Chris, I wanted to see your body, however it may have looked, just one last time.

Death requires immediate decisions. Arrangements had to be made. I knew that Chris would have wanted his body donated. When he was born in 1958, organ transplants were in their infancy. He followed the medical advances in that area keenly, applauding the increase in success rates, impressed by the skills and innovations of the surgeons and medical scientists. The fact that vital organs from the dead might be transplanted to extend another life was something he wholeheartedly supported. It satisfied him to think that a blind person might see again, that someone whose kidneys or heart were failing might be saved by a donated replacement. That death can and does promote life was a concept that Chris found inspiring.

I put the idea to Izzy and Dad. Izzy fully agreed; Dad responded with a blank stare, which I had to take as approval. In the morning, I phoned the Stirling Royal Infirmary where Chris's chilled body lay in the mortuary, thinking they would deal with the necessary arrangements. They couldn't help. They had no suggestions. Mr. Taylor handed me the telephone directory. "Try the universities," he said.

I phoned Glasgow University. I had to go through the facts several times before I was put through to someone who could help. When I said that Chris had died three days ago, I was told that it would be too late for his organs to be of any use.

"His body, then? Could you use it for research?" I asked

"How did he die?"

"He drowned."

"How long was the body in the water?"

"I don't know. Divers had to search for him."

"We don't usually take bodies that have been underwater for a prolonged time."

"He was young," I pleaded, "Seventeen. Fit and healthy. He didn't smoke."

"I'm sorry. We can't help. Have you tried Edinburgh University?"

I phoned Edinburgh, Newcastle and Aberdeen Universities. I had conversations about the merits of a dead body. But I couldn't persuade any University to take it. My darling brother. Beautiful Chris. What was I going to do?

Then a man from Glasgow University phoned back and spoke to me in a gentle, kind voice. He said he had been informed of my call, and, contrary to what I had been told, the anatomy department would be pleased to take Chris's body. It would be of invaluable educational help to the medical students. I wept with relief.

"We'll need the written consent of your parents," he said, "then we can work things out directly with Stirling Royal Infirmary." My heart sank.

"My mother doesn't know yet, we still haven't found her."

There was a silence. Then he said, "Phone me straight back when you have. Meanwhile, you could write the letter ready for your mother and father to sign."

Mr. Taylor gave me some paper and I composed the letter. While I was writing it, the phone rang. Mrs. Taylor answered it in the hall. A few minutes later she came into the living room. She looked at her husband and then me. "That was Mrs. Giles," she said quietly. "She phoned to speak to Chris. I had to break the news to her."

Gillian wrote to Vyvian, who was still in France and would not receive the letter until she returned.

August 8th 1975

Dear Vyv,

I hope you had a wonderful holiday in France. But now I must break to you the tragic news. Vyv, last Tuesday, Chris drowned in Loch Lomond. I know you won't be able to believe this. Neither could any of us. It was so sudden. Phil nearly went as well, but he is fine. It happened only yards from the shore. Chris fell out of the canoe. Phil tried to save him but got completely exhausted. Anyway these details are unimportant aren't they? Phil has been wonderful. I couldn't have managed without him here.

All the Giles family is gradually arriving here and will all be here by this afternoon. I just don't know what else to say to you. I wanted you to know before I spoke to you. Rory is here as well, and is a great help to Phil, as I don't know how long Phil can keep going like this.

Little did we know that the holiday Chris looked forward to so much would end in such tragedy. I can only say that he was as happy as I have ever seen him. He kept saying it was just like camp and how much of a compliment that was! There is little more I can say except how sorry I am to have to break this to you like this.

All my love,
Gillian.

Paula wrote to Helen. Helen was also in France and would not get the letter for some weeks.

Rory went with Paula's mother to pick up Mum and Granny from Oban. Granny sat in the front. Rory sat beside Mum in the back holding her hand while she wept. By the time they arrived, Mum had dried her tears. Izzy and I were relieved to see her, but of course we didn't hug. Mum was quiet, dignified, spiritless, broken.

"At least I still have my two lovely girls," she said. She did not want to know how it had happened. "He's gone," she said, "my beautiful son has gone."

Mum looked at Dad. Their eyes met. Hers fell. There were no words. They had been communicating artificially for years. Mum had not a shred of pretence left in her. They barely uttered another word to each other.

And Granny – I had thought the shock of losing her bonny boy might have killed her. Instead, her inner strength surfaced. She stayed by her daughter's side. For the first time I understood the depth and integrity of Granny's loyalty, dependability and anchorage. It was she who talked with the Taylors – about Glasgow, living in the tenements, the marvellous countryside, the open-heartedness of the Scots. She alleviated some of the clogged atmosphere. Mum agreed that donation would have been Chris's wish. I finalised the arrangements. There was no funeral.

I returned to London alone. Mum, Dad, Granny and Izzy would be making their way home later. I picked up Paul's van from where it had been parked in Cleveland Road, drove myself to Orchard Road and let myself into my home. On the divan bed in the living room I keened and wept a sea of grief. It was Sunday August 10th; five days since Chris had died. I fell asleep.

Sounds in the flat awakened me. It was dark. I sat up. The door opened. I yelped.

"Cathy! What are you doing here? I didn't think you'd be back from camp until Tuesday."

"Simon! You startled me."

"What's wrong, Cath?" He sat on the bed. I told him.

"Oh, my love." He held me tightly. What a relief it was to rest my head on his shoulder and sink into his compassionate arms.

"Cath, I'll be straight back. My parents are waiting outside. I must go and explain to them."

"Simon – don't leave them out there. Please, ask them in. They can sleep in the double bed and you can sleep on the couch."

"They wouldn't dream of it. We can find somewhere else to stay."

"Wait, Simon." But he was already running down the stairs. A few minutes later he was back. "Cathy, is there anything at all I can do to help?" As soon as he asked, I knew what we should do.

"Yes," I replied, "would you conduct a concert in memory of him?"

"Of course I will."

"We can ask everyone who knew him to come and play. We'll get a great orchestra together."

"I'll look in my diary. We'll fix a date."

"What do you think we should play? A requiem maybe? "

"No; not right for Chris." He thought for a moment and said, "Bruckner four."

And in my head, I heard the opening horn solo from Bruckner's fourth symphony, which Chris had played so many times.

"Yes. That would be perfect. He loved that piece."

"He was an incredible musician. Oh, Cath."

We hugged each other again. Then he said, "I should go." He stood up. "Animal? Are you sure you're OK here on your own?"

"I'm fine. Don't worry about me."

"I'll phone you tomorrow."

To this day I do not know where he and his parents slept that night.

Mr. Taylor drove Mum's car to Carlisle to put on the Motorail, British Rail's long-distance service that carried passengers and their cars, now discontinued. Mum, Dad and Granny travelled home together by train. It does not bear thinking about. There were hundreds of letters of sympathy lying on the hall floor. Dad went upstairs and shut himself in the front bedroom – Izzy's room, which she vacated during university terms. There he stayed, never again appearing downstairs during the day.

From Len Davis, orchestral tutor at Wortley:

Dear Elizabeth, Derek, Isabel, Cath and Mrs. Fraser,

There just aren't words to express my sorrow or sympathy. I mourn with you all as though Chris were my own son. In fact, not since my own younger brother was drowned in action during the war have I suffered such a searing personal loss.

I can only hope that the love and high regard which so many people have for Chris will help to sustain you.

From Dr. Alan Bush to Mum: August 9th 1975

Dear Elizabeth,

The news of the fearful disaster which has befallen you and your family was conveyed to us some days ago. There can be no consolation for death except in those cases where it has come as a release from irremediable bodily conditions of pain or frustration.

You may or may not know that Nancy and I lost one of our three daughters when a child of eight in a street accident; a senseless occurrence which happened here in Radlett a few hundred yards from where I am sitting now. It was a terrible time.

For many months after it happened I wondered whether Nancy would ever face life again. I knew her life would never be the same again. Nor will yours. And it seemed as though the fact that she was needed by her two remaining children and her husband was not weighing with her at all. Her loss occupied her whole mind continually.

When I hear of something similar happening to someone I know, it brings the sensations of that terrible time vividly back to me. And I suppose that this may well occur with Nancy also. I asked her, when we heard the news of Christopher, did she think about our Alice all the time? She replied; no, not all the time any more.

And she has found a way of facing life again through the existence of us whom she loves and who love her, and through her work as a writer, especially as the librettist of three of my operas. You will find a way again.

I have only quite recently arrived at an understanding of how we should regard death: it is the price we all must pay for the wonder of having been alive, and we should pay it without rancour, if without enthusiasm. But this only applies to each of us in relation to our own life and death. The death of anyone near to us is quite another matter. Yet it does help to know that there are people around who understand what we are going through.

Yours, Alan

I collected Mum's car from the Motorail terminus at Paddington. In the glove compartment was an envelope. I opened it and found a Death Certificate. All the wind was knocked out of me: the name – Christopher Colin Giles. Death by drowning. There was also a letter from Mr. Taylor, written in Carlisle just before he put Mum's car on the train.

Dear Cathy,

There is a letter of sympathy and of appreciation on its way from the University Anatomy dept – and yet another form to be filled in. It is addressed to your father, so intercept it if it will upset him too much – the envelope will have the University crest on it, as the large envelope herewith. I have had the pink ticket herewith counter stamped to show that no-one is travelling with the car – reclaim is thereby expiated.

I hope we can meet again under happier circumstances when we have returned to a new normality.

Yours, Lawrie T.

His letter reads as from one executive to another. For those few days, Lawrie Taylor and I were a team. We just got on with it.

Izzy stayed with the Taylors for a few more days. On August 12th, she met up with the FSC escort party at Glasgow Central station and travelled back with them to London. Her relationship with Duncan had ended. He handed over her tent and rucksack, and watched her disappear into her own tunnel of grief.

Rory arrived back at Cleveland Road. So did Phillip, who moved into Chris's room. Mum found it a comfort to have Rory and Phillip living in the house. She gave them Chris's clothes. She gave Phillip his music and his horn.[1]

I picked Paul up from Heathrow, overjoyed to see him again. He said I didn't seem very cut up. He had no idea. I didn't know myself that I was only at the tip of the iceberg of grief. Shock paralyses the magnitude of it. It was disconcerting to find that laughter, love, and even desire, were still manifest.

Eleven days after Chris's death, Paul and I drove to Wortley in the Mini van, which was packed to capacity with instruments and equipment. Mum drove herself and Izzy there. Izzy saw Mum crying at Wortley, but when Mum saw that Izzy had noticed, she stopped at once.

1. I purchased Chris's Alexander double eleven years later when I heard that Phillip was about to sell it. Mum was extremely relieved to hear that I had intervened and rescued it. I have now had it completely overhauled and restored by master craftsman, Gale Lawson. When I went to pick it up, Gale phoned Gareth Mollison – he knew that Gareth and Chris had been close friends – to ask if he was free to come over and give the horn a blow. Gareth, who lived nearby, arrived twenty minutes later. He had been the first person to hear Chris play the Alexander horn – and now he was the first person to play it after its restoration.

At the end of August, Paula tried to reply to a letter from Sigi:

> Dear Sigi,
>
> I really feel it's so much easier to write now I've had a letter from you. I'll try to explain the way this has taken me, but I'm not sure you'll understand. I envy you for being able to realise what has happened, and cry over it. My mind just seems incapable of accepting it. When I cry, it just seems to be in utter despair – it doesn't bring me any relief. I think of what happened that day – and that makes me cry and want to scream, and feel everything's hopeless. And yet I can't believe that Chris really died that day. I still think I'm going to see him again,
>
> After the accident I was stunned and shocked and numb. I just felt a complete emptiness inside me. I didn't seem to have enough left in me to cry. On the way back in the car after it happened I felt as if all the life had gone out of me, and Gillian cried and cried, which made me feel worse, because I felt I should cry too – but there was just nothing left there. It was almost as if it lay too deep inside me to come out like that. Even now it feels as though it's just eating away inside me. I feel that it hasn't come to the surface yet.
>
> I wrote that about 2 weeks ago. I had to tear up the rest of it because it was so awful. I was trying to tell you how it happened, but I had to stop, because I knew I couldn't send it. You probably can't understand any of what I've written, anyway.
>
> I went lifesaving last Wednesday – I decided I had to have lessons. I had to borrow a swimming costume from Aileen because I couldn't bring myself to wear my bikini again. It is still lying wet in a plastic bag from that day. I tried to tell myself not to be stupid, and to take it out and wash it, but I couldn't.
>
> Sigi, please don't think about Chris drowning and feel you might have been able to help him. I know how you must feel, because before, I couldn't really understand how people could drown, but it was so frightening, because it happened in seconds. And also, as I found out last week, there is only one correct way to lifesave, and unless you have been taught it, it is just impossible to do anything.

Paula's letter stops there. She never posted it. At this point, I would like to remind you (for I have had to remind myself), that at the time of Chris's death, Gillian, Paula, Aileen, Vyvian, Sigi, Helen, Phillip, Gareth and most of Chris's NYO and school friends were only sixteen or seventeen.

As soon as the school holidays were over, Mum resumed her teaching. Dad did not go back to work. The Academy term began. I didn't know how to respond to the few brave people who approached me to offer condolences. One day, when I was sitting in the Academy canteen, I saw Chris walk through the door – for a wonderful split second I believed it. But it was Phillip wearing one of the pullovers that Granny had knitted for Chris.

Izzy returned to Leeds. Mum drove her to Kings Cross station and unexpectedly gave her an awkward kiss goodbye – a bump on the cheek, a grazed touch of dry lips. Mum never kissed us – Izzy remembers the moment with clarity.

Dad roamed the house at night, taking things that were 'his'. He left notes for Mum. She left notes for him. They were spine-chillingly polite. I visited him. I was the only one who could. I would knock on the door of Izzy's room.

"Who is it?" he would ask in a quivery voice.

"Dad? It's Cathy. May I come in?" I was careful not to say, "can".

"How are you, Dad? I've brought you some bread and cheese. Pickled onions. Rollmops. Shall I make a pot of tea?" He would shudder and stare whilst I circled nervously, hoping to steer clear of his bitter fixation – those evil, wicked witches. His savage words erupted anyway. I closed my eyes and ears. It was bleak.

Then Dad was admitted to Claybury Mental Hospital. The police had picked him up on London Bridge behaving strangely. They were concerned by his apparently suicidal state and thought he might be about to jump into the Thames. He may well have been staring into the river and flirting with the idea of suicide, but I am absolutely sure he had no real intention of throwing himself off the bridge.

I received a phone call from his psychiatrist. She asked if I would meet her. I did not think it would serve any purpose, but I went. She shook hands with me, smiled without warmth, indicated a chair for me to sit in, and sat opposite.

"Your father, Derek – do you mind if I call him Derek? – has spoken a great deal to me. There are some issues he needs to talk to you about. Things he feels you are unaware of that you ought to know."

"Let me guess. Would this be about my mother and grandmother?"

"Well, yes, partly. But also, it would be of great benefit to both of you to work through your grief together. He needs you to put your arms around him, he needs to mourn with you. It is the most terrible thing for a father to lose his son, but particularly for Derek, as he and Chris were so very close."

I could not believe what I was hearing. She had swallowed everything Dad had told her without question. "Close? They were not. He didn't relate to Chris at all. Chris couldn't wait to leave home to get away from him." There was a pause before she spoke again.

"Well, Derek tells me they had a very special bond. And what he believes is what we must work with, to help him get better. Now, I know you love your father, as he loves you..."

"Love?"

"You're his daughter; you must love your father."

How could she toss the word so flippantly into the air? A word I had never heard Dad utter? What authority did she have to assume love?

"I don't love him. Not how you mean. And he doesn't love me; he needs me. I don't know what I feel for him. It's all wrong. It's not love. As for putting my arms around him, no, the thought is unbearable. I don't want him to touch me."

She looked shocked. "If you don't mind, I won't tell Derek what you've just said."

I had thought that our discussion was confidential. She hadn't told me that she would be repeating it to Dad. Not that it mattered anyway. Obviously, she had been expecting an entirely different conversation.

I sighed. She cleared her throat. "May I make a suggestion? If you find it difficult to embrace him, might you at least be able to shake his hand?"

I looked at my hands; I remembered having to squeeze a drop of blood from my thumb. They were only hands after all. I sighed again.

"Yes, I could do that."

"Good. That will be a positive start. I will tell Derek you are happy to shake his hand."

I looked at her through leaden eyes. "Could you also tell him to stop slagging off my mother? She is a good and decent person. She doesn't go around saying revolting things about him. How does he think it makes me feel when he says my mother is a wicked, evil woman? And he says even more revolting things about my granny. I can't stand it, but I still visit him every time I go home. Has he told you that? I try to help, but however much I give is never enough. It's exhausting. Impossible. And it's been like this for as long as I can remember. I'm sorry, but whatever he's told you, it's not the truth. You don't understand. Nobody does."

She was silent. I could tell she did not like me. I did not like her much either. I was nineteen years old. My brother had just died. She was not much of a psychiatrist.

Her professional mask blinked into place, offering nothing.

"Well, so, thank you for coming today."

I rose to leave. She did not hold out her hand.

Dad was back in Izzy's room a week later.

Mum wrote to the Headmaster of Buckhurst Hill County High School, Mr. Colgate, to ask if the Science department would like to have Chris's Natural History Collection. He replied:

> Thank you for your letter. We should like your views on the matter of a memorial concert later this term. Any money raised could be put to a memorial prize or fund. We would not want to do anything against your wishes, however. Mr. Price would be interested in viewing Christopher's "museum".

Mr. Price, the school's biology teacher, came over. Mum showed him into Chris's bedroom. He stood transfixed, his eyes travelling around the room. He was completely overwhelmed. In a shaky voice he said that he had taught Christopher for four years, and in all that time, Christopher had never told him about his collection. Mum saw that Mr. Price's eyes had filled with tears. "Forgive me," he said, "I had no idea, no idea at all. Of course I knew he was interested in natural history; but this… you surely don't want to part with it?"

"I'm quite sure I do. I'd like others to benefit from it. It's of no use to me."

But she did keep a case of stuffed birds, the stuffed fox, the Giant Atlas Moth and the most beautiful of the butterfly displays. Chris Stearn rescued a shell; Phillip took Pierre, the human skull that Chris had been given for his ninth birthday; I kept a couple of fossils and shells, and then it was all boxed up and carried away.

> **Buckhurst Hill County High School, October 9th**
>
> May I thank you very much for Christopher's splendid collection of specimens. They are so good and so useful, that we would like to arrange them in a special display case with a small memorial tablet. This would be in addition to the memorial scholarship or whatever is decided after we have had the memorial concert.
>
> Kind regards, Hugh Colgate

I went to Bristol. I did not get anywhere in the competition. Tortelier's pupils came first, second and third. Even Steven Isserlis was not placed. In the final gala concert, Tortelier's pupils played their competition pieces; Tortelier and his wife gave a first performance of Tortelier's concerto for two cellos and orchestra, conducted by his son, Yan Pascal Tortelier. It was a family show. I visited Clare Ziman, my NYO friend, while I was there. She had not heard about Chris and I did not tell her, even though he filled my mind every moment of every day. It was more than I could bear to speak the words again.

At the end of October, Buckhurst Hill County High School hosted a memorial concert. Nitram, Martin Koch and Cliff Oliver were amongst the performers. Mr. Rippin conducted the school orchestra augmented by others including Phillip Eastop, Gillian Taylor, Gareth Mollison, Alison Jenkins, Chris Stearn and Melanie Turner. Paul and I also played. Oddly, I haven't a single memory of the occasion. Were it not for the concert programme, I would not have known I had been there.

I had been writing to Auntie Lilian regularly since Grandad had died the previous year, and continued to do so after Chris's death. I have letters from her in reply to mine during the months of August, September and October. It didn't occur to me as odd that neither of us wrote about Chris. I assumed it was as awful for her as it was for me to write about it. However, I must have told her that Dad was not doing well, for in a letter dated September 25th, in amongst pages of her spidery, almost indecipherable scrawl she writes:

> I am very sorry to hear he is not what he should be… I am sure Mother has a great problem on her hands, she works very hard long hours with her music teaching… he should be very thankful for having a very Good Family and very Brilliant Children… I spoke to him on the phone last week to ask him if he had an address of Mr. Ghooch as Grandad always sent him a birthday card but I have not heard from him so I will let it go… I also said, Colin why not write me sometimes we are not bad friends are we He said No he wouldn't. Never mind, we will let well alone, but I do understand how you must worry about him, can Mother or someone get him to see a Doctor… would you let me have Isabels address I would like to send her a card for passing her exams… give my love to Mother she has all my sympathy also Granny and yourself… Cathy I am so very delighted to get your letters All my love Auntie Lilian XXX

Of course, I thought she knew about Chris – it sounded from her use of the word 'sympathy' in the letter that she did. She had spoken to Dad on the phone – he must have told her; but at the end of November, I received this:

> My Dear Cathy
>
> I must say what a dreadful shock I had when the news was sent to me by an old friend about my Chris. Cathy, I saw him a few hours after he was born. He was a most beautiful baby. I feel very sad that Dad did not write me or phone me. You could not expect Mother to write she must be so grieved more than anyone will ever know. I could not write her I asked a nurse to write me a short letter I was too ill to write myself as I have had a Cerebral Haemorrhage the shock was so dreadful… the Doctor sent me to

hospital... Please excuse writing I am in bed. Cathy, will you write me all the news... Cathy if I have said or done anything wrong please tell me. I could not bear it because you were so kind to me.

Bless you dear, love Auntie Lilian.

How remiss of me to have assumed that she knew. Surely Dad would have taken responsibility for breaking the news to Auntie Lilian? Appalled, I wrote straight back. Our correspondence continued. She recovered sufficiently to go to Australia the following summer of 1976 to attend her granddaughter's wedding. Her post card from Australia describing the event was the last communication I received from her. I wrote several more times, but my letters were unanswered. I could only assume that she must have died. I still think of her; she was a sweet and lovely person.

I started to organise Chris's concert. Simon wanted two rehearsals – one the day before and one on the day. I booked a school hall for the rehearsal and Ilford Town Hall for the day. Everyone I contacted wanted to play. I asked Louise Williams to lead the orchestra and Rod McGrath to play principal cello. Chris's friends phoned, almost begging to be included. I found it difficult to say no, but we had to keep the orchestra to a normal size. The support was overwhelming. Redbridge Music School generously provided the orchestral parts and music stands. The father of one of Margaret Sprakes's pupils designed the programme and organised printing of posters and tickets. In consultation with Mum, Izzy and the headmaster of Buckhurst Hill County High School, it was agreed that money from ticket sales would be added to the Christopher Giles Memorial Fund. The school would invest the capital and award the interest it produced as a music prize to a deserving pupil each year.

On Saturday, January 10th 1976, the orchestra assembled for the first rehearsal.

"Let's play," said Simon. My body erupted in goose bumps as the strings began the pianissimo, ethereal, shimmering tremolando and Phillip played the sublime opening horn solo, perfectly. I looked up at Simon, his every musical nerve alert and flowing. I scanned the orchestra. My heart swelled with deep gratitude, with love for these wonderful friends giving their fully absorbed concentration. For a moment I was an onlooker. Then my eyes went back to the music; I sank into it and became a part of the whole.

The concert was unforgettable. It was everything for everyone. Within the padded womb of music, our private memories of Chris pleated into the emotive tapestry of Bruckner's symphony. Those whom I hadn't been able to include in the orchestra were in the audience along with dozens of Chris's non-playing friends. Simon was incredible; the playing was extraordinary. There was no doubt that the most conspicuous chairs in the orchestra were those of the horn section. One's eyes could not help but travel along the row and be struck by an absence. Sadly, there was another absence. Helen Chapman was not there, because at the time I had no idea that she had been Chris's girlfriend. Unfortunately, Paul was not there either – he had left on another tour the day before.

Simon's words in the programme were:

We chose this symphony because it was one of Chris's favourite pieces – probably owing to the fact that the horns play a dominant part throughout the work. Indeed, one would often hear Chris practising the many glorious horn solos. Also it is a work of enormous emotional commitment, without sentimentality, and seemed a fitting memorial tribute to a fine musician and treasured friend.

Simon Rattle

Leeds, January 16th

Dear Cathy,

How are you? I thought the concert went really fantastically on Sunday – all your fantastic organisation. I could never do anything like that! Russell and Ian Grainger said they'd never heard a string section like it. Write soon, Loads of love, Izzy

On February 26th 1976, Izzy and I turned twenty. We were six months and three weeks into our second life: life without Chris.

The NYJO album, *Return Trip*, with Chris playing on five of the tracks, was released by RCA. Bill Ashton's sleeve notes for track two, *Velvet Lady*, by Dave Firman, include the following words: "Listen to the immaculate playing of the difficult and exposed French horn line. This was sight-read in the studio by a brilliant young horn player called Chris Giles, who died tragically in a canoeing accident in Scotland just over a month later."

Mr. Colgate sent home Chris's BHCHS report book. The Upper Sixth form pages were empty. At the end of the book, in the space reserved for the Headmaster's final comments, he had written: "An excellent record of service and achievement." Chris's Sociology O level certificate was enclosed; he had passed with a 'B'.

Divorce proceedings began. Dad instructed his solicitor to send copies to Izzy. She opened the package. Baffled, she scanned the pages and came to the following words: "...the Petitioner blames the breakdown of his marriage on his wife who has for years denied him his conjugal rights. Her sexual frigidity has led him to..." She read no further. Disgusted, she posted the documents back with a curt note: "I do not wish to read about my father's sex life. I am sickened that you consider it appropriate material to send to me."

I embarked upon a year of careful diplomatic negotiation with Dad. I had to persuade him to leave the house. Mum, I could tell, was at breaking point.

"Dad, you know you can't stay shut away like this forever."

"I'm not leaving the house where Chris lived."

"Wouldn't you be happier to leave the house where Mum and Granny live?"

I searched the newspapers for places to rent, and read them to him to consider. The cajoling continued – careful not to push too far, but tactfully trying to persuade him little by little that moving would be a good idea.

Mum did not speak of Chris at all. A year after his death, I asked her how long she thought Glasgow University might use Chris's body. She told me that they had written to her to say they had finished with it; there had been a cremation a few months ago.

"A few months ago? Why didn't you tell me?"

"I didn't think you'd be interested."

"Not interested? Mum, I'd have liked to be there. So might Izzy."

"Well, I'm sorry dear. It didn't occur to me that you'd want to go. I thought we all felt the same. It was just a body. It wasn't Chris. I honestly didn't mean to upset you."

"I know, Mum. I just wanted to say goodbye."

More than thirty years later, Izzy and I found a bundle of old newspapers. Pressed between the pages were not one, but six copies of Chris's death certificate. Lawrie Taylor is registered as the informant. The newspapers carried articles titled: "Memorial Concert for drowned music boy"; "Concert recalls talents of young musician"; and so on. In the Classified section of the *Morning Star* of August 12th 1975, the only entry under Deaths read: "GILES, Christopher. Seventeen-year-old son of Elizabeth and Derek, brother of Catherine and Isabel, grandson of Mrs. Fraser. Drowned on holiday, Aug 5." I remembered that I had placed the announcement in the *Morning Star* at Mum's request. In the same newspaper two days later was this: "The Wanstead and Woodford branch of the Communist Party offer their deepest sympathy to Elizabeth and Derek on the tragic loss of their son Christopher and extend condolences to his sisters and grandmother."

We also found a letter from the University of Glasgow Anatomy Department, dated January 8th 1976, which Izzy and I read for the first time:

> I am writing to let you know that the body of your late son is now being released by Glasgow University, and I have arranged for cremation to take place at Linn Crematorium, Lainshaw Drive, Glasgow, G45, at 10.15 a.m. on Wednesday, 14th January 1976. I note that you do not wish a service to be carried out at that time, but I would be grateful if you could confirm this and also let me know, by return, if any relatives or friends will be attending.

Mum replied with the words:

> As already indicated, we do not wish a service to be carried out at the time of the cremation on 14th January nor will there be any relatives or friends attending.

So, Chris was cremated on January 14th, much sooner than we had thought. In the same envelope was a programme of the memorial concert we gave on January 11th 1976, which Mum had sat through knowing that Chris's body was to be cremated three days later. It still upsets me that there was nobody at the cremation who had known him. His body turned to ash without witness or ceremony.

At last Dad said he would move out if I promised to visit him every week. I promised. It was the price I had to pay to preserve Mum's sanity, to rescue her from Dad's oppressive occupation and, furthermore, to release him from his self-imposed incarceration. He made me shake hands on it.

In January 1977 I helped him pack and transported him and his belongings into a large room in a house of a woman he knew in Woodford. Izzy's room was restored to her. I visited him every week; Izzy avoided him.

In April, Mum and Dad were legally divorced. Mum had to buy him out – anything to get it over with. It was a great deal of money – the equivalent of half the value of the house – Granny's house. She had to borrow. People lent.

Dad bought himself a caravan on a fixed site in Waltham Cross. I again helped him move. He met Jean, a woman who lived in another caravan. In October 1977, just over two years after Chris's death, he married her. I talked Izzy into coming with me to attend their wedding. They moved to Derbyshire. I was released from my weekly contract, but I was not set free. I could not escape from the emotional bondage. He was my father and there was something in him that I recognised in myself, a part I could not deny; a part of him that I wanted to love. I didn't want to hurt him, I didn't want to be the cause of his unhappiness – but I couldn't love him enough. What he needed from me, what he made me feel that I owed him, was too much. I couldn't meet his needs: to meet them I would have had to go all the way; leave myself behind to become the daughter he wanted. So I had to compromise; give what I could and suffer his disappointment, his bitterness, his cynicism. He knew I kept my distance; he sensed when I pulled back, but he made out that I did so with cold calculation, cruelly withholding the love that, as my father, was his right. Crippled by guilt, burdened by responsibility, hurting with compassion, I was compelled to maintain contact, to keep trying to relate to him for the rest of his life. For somewhere, out of reach, I believed that he loved me. In our letters, it seemed that we did find a medium in which we could fruitfully communicate; or so I deluded myself into believing. Nevertheless, when a letter arrived from him, I opened it with apprehension, not joy, afraid of what it might contain. It was often several days before I found the courage to read it. Speaking to him was another ordeal, which I put off until the guilt at not having contacted him made me feel so sick that I had to phone to relieve my nausea. If Jean was there, he sounded nervous and agitated. If she was out, he was pleased I had rung at an opportune time. "Jean," he told me, "says that when I receive a letter or phone call from you, it sends me into depression. I'm not sure if that is really the case, but she's convinced of it. No matter, my dear, I don't have to tell her you phoned, do I?" But even if I caught Dad alone, our conversations were minefields: there was so much to be avoided. The tension and trepidation was still there. I never felt on safe ground with him.

He and Izzy became completely estranged. She too became a target of his malicious resentment. Ultimately, I now know, my efforts to sustain a relationship with him were all in vain. He threw me into the same bitter place, and even contrived to wreak cruel revenge from beyond the grave.

Before I end this chapter, I would like to return to the girls who came into the last part of Chris's life and to thank them for sharing their memories with me – memories that carry immeasurable grief for all of them. I am indebted to Aileen, the girl Chris refers to with such admiration in his letters, who has been most helpful in giving me details from her diaries of the time that she and Chris were in the NYO, and in answering my questions. I am deeply grateful to Paula for her bravery in telling me what she could remember of the day of the tragedy. I owe Vyvian my thanks for her candidness and perception, and for going to a huge amount of trouble to find the letter that Gillian wrote to her three days after Chris's death.

To Gillian I acknowledge my profound thanks for her openness and courage in talking to me when I first phoned her in November 2004. We had never spoken about Chris and hadn't seen each other since 1976. There were two particularly probing questions I asked: where in Loch Lomond did Chris drown and would you feel able to tell me what happened? – I had never known exactly where Chris had died. In writing earlier about how Chris's life ended, I combined Gillian's memories and Paula's, together with what I recall of an account that Phillip gave me, and wove them together. It is not a definitive version – I was not there: and those who were carry memories overlaid with the passage of time and its adjustments.

When I asked Gillian about her relationship with Chris, she told me everything she could remember, but was concerned that I should not make too much of her being Chris's girlfriend. She wrote, "I know that at the time, I felt acutely aware that the extremely shy (on both sides) beginnings of teenage flirting and getting together were, and should be, irrelevant in the scheme of things, and that I kept much to myself." I hope Gillian will forgive me for taking a different view. Her getting together with Chris was not irrelevant in my opinion. In a life that was so very short, every moment of it matters. She added, "I don't presume to lay any claim to Chris's affections but I do know that what few memories I have recalled with you are how I remember them. It would definitely have all been in my five year diary, with every last detail and a lot more besides, which sadly I must have found too excruciating (and sad) to keep."

I have not seen or communicated with Mr. or Mrs. Taylor since. Gillian told me that her parents, now in their eighties, have never spoken about Chris. She knows, as do I, that they still carry the horror of what happened, and will do so to the end of their lives: their daughter's friend, the boy for whom they felt responsible, died whilst in their care. What an appalling, merciless burden to bear. I have always felt deep sorrow and pity for the suffering they endlessly endure. I did not contact them during the writing of this book. I felt it would be cruel to do so – a supposition that Gillian confirmed.

And now I come to Helen, a girl in Chris's life who would have remained hidden had it not been for an email that I received in February 2009 from Alan Torrance:

> I had been chatting on the phone with Helen Chapman and Chris came into conversation. Chris was dating her around the time that he died. I came to know Chris when I led the second violins in the NYO. Indeed, I travelled with him by train to London before our final concert and just before he headed north to Glasgow. We chatted away – he talked about the forthcoming holiday in Glasgow and he also showed me tricks on his horn mouthpiece. He was a delightful guy with incredibly musical flair. Anyway, I spoke to Helen before sending this email to see if she would like to contact you given that you are writing about Chris's life. She says that she only has a few personal memories of Chris and nothing would be gained from her being in touch. I am not sure she has yet got over the shock.

My reply:

> Thank you very much for contacting me. What has almost floored me is that you say Chris was dating Helen Chapman at the time of his death. This is completely new to me. I am very concerned that I get this sort of information correctly in the book, and would really like to chat to Helen. Do you think she might be persuaded?

Alan's response:

> Helen definitely dated Chris for over a year. She even went to a party at Chris's home once. Moreover, I vividly remember seeing them (just before we were to return from Flanders) kissing passionately and for a sustained time outside the residence where we were all staying. It was very public – half the NYO must have seen! Indeed, one of my first thoughts when I heard of Chris's death was how Helen would be coping with the news. I immediately assumed that she would have been with the rest of them in Glasgow.

Via Alan, I wrote to Helen. A few days later, she phoned. We had a long, emotional conversation. She agreed to meet me. As I mentioned earlier, Helen went directly from Chris's final NYO course on a holiday to France with her parents. Consequently, she did not receive the news until she returned home and read the letter from Paula (which no longer exists). Helen's parents knew nothing about Chris – she had never been able to tell them that she had a boyfriend. They could see that their daughter was upset after reading the letter, but they had no idea, and never would, that the NYO boy who drowned was the love of Helen's life. To Helen I humbly extend my respect and gratitude for agreeing to unlock those heavily sealed doors and talk about the boy she loved so much. For me the most poignant thing she told me was this: "What I remember most of all about Chris is how he felt. I loved kissing him. I shall never forget his kisses."

Alison Jenkins, Chris Giles, Gareth Mollison and Phillip Eastop (standing at the front, left to right) taking a bow after their performance of Schumann's *Concertstück* at Ilford Town Hall on March 8th 1975 with *Concerti Allegri* conducted by Bram Tovey. I apologise for the very poor quality of the photo, but I decided to include it as it is just about possible to identify some faces. Playing in the orchestra are Russell Jordan on timpani, Duncan Hollowood and Ian Grainger playing horn, Martin Koch, Chris Stearn and Clive Miller in the brass section, Chris Freeman on double bass, Melanie Turner in the cello section. Bram, in white tuxedo, is standing on the right applauding. I am just behind him, partly obscured.

END OF PART THREE

EPILOGUE

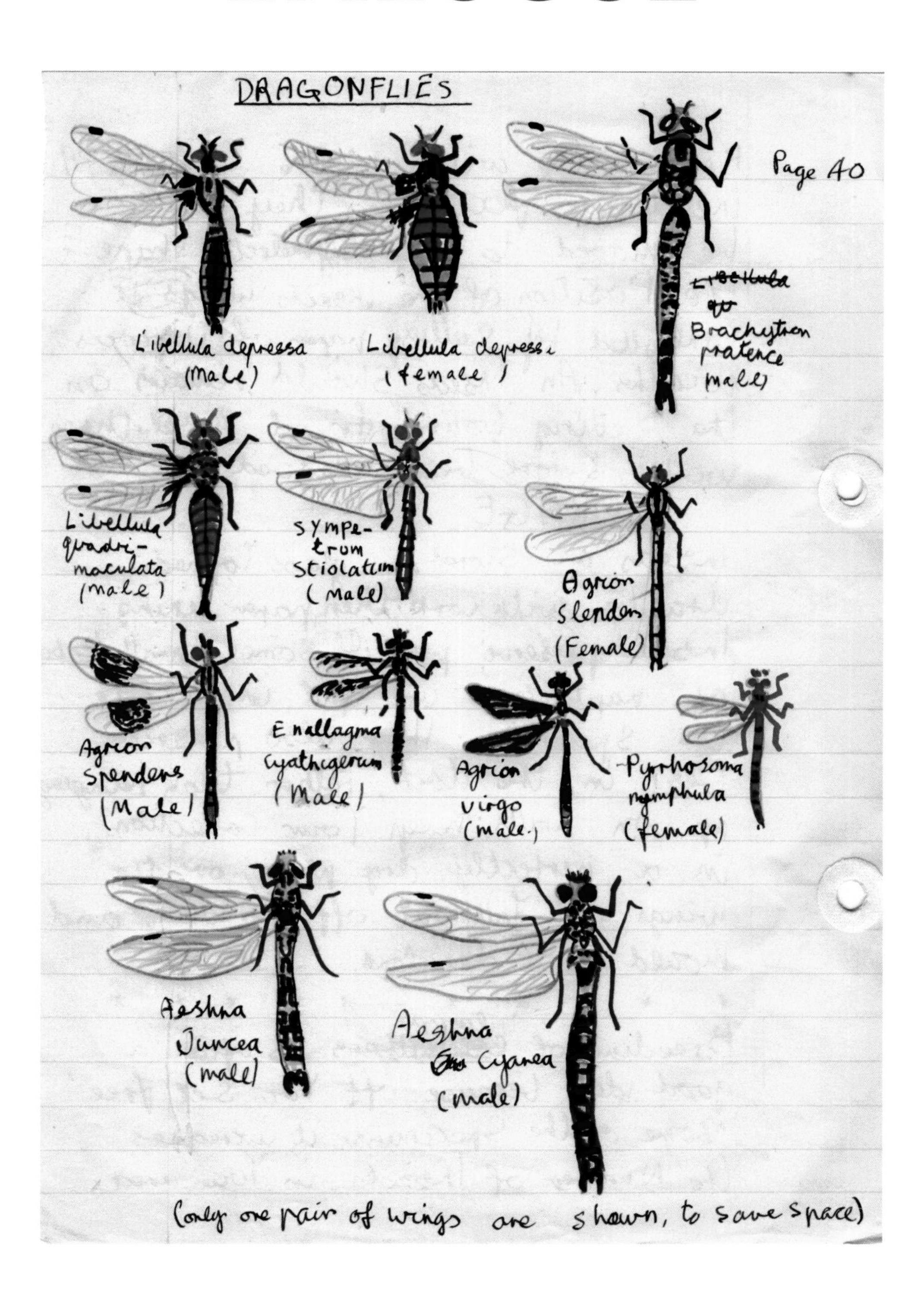
DRAGONFLIES
Page 40
Libellula depressa (male)
Libellula depressa (female)
Brachytron pratence (male)
Libellula quadrimaculata (male)
Sympetrum Stiolatum (Male)
Agrion Slenders (Female)
Agrion Spenders (Male)
Enallagma Cyathigerum (Male)
Agrion virgo (male)
Pyrhosoma nymphula (female)
Aeshna Juncea (male)
Aeshna Cyanea (male)
(only one pair of wings are shown, to save space)

Chris playing his Paxman XL horn in the back garden of Cleveland Road, Autumn 1974.

83
ENDINGS

Without balm of memory
We'd be too wounded
To accept our scars.

The Necessary Period of Mourning – Jean Lipkin

More than a year had passed since Simon and I separated, but he still had not collected his belongings. I had packed everything into boxes, which remained stacked floor to ceiling in a corner of the kitchen. Paul discovered Simon's violin.

"Do you think he wants this?"

"I doubt it. He doesn't seem to want any of his stuff and I shouldn't think he'll ever want to play the violin again."

I phoned Simon to ask if he would like me to put his boxes in Paul's van and bring them over to his flat.

"Would you?" he asked sheepishly. "I'm sorry I've done nothing about it, but you know what I'm like – baaa, baaa."

"And Simon – do you want your violin? Only, if you don't, could Paul have it?"

"He's welcome to it, although I can't think what a fantastic jazz violinist would want with such a ropey instrument."

"He wants to lacquer it half-yellow and half-blue to match his yellow and blue patchwork leather jacket. Then he'll put a pick-up on it and turn it into an electric violin." And that is exactly what he did.

Paul and I bought a house in Leytonstone, about a ten-minute drive from South Woodford, and left the flat in Orchard Road. That was when I packed away all the letters I had received into cardboard boxes – boxes that would remain sealed for the next twenty-seven years. Izzy finished at university and Mum went to Leeds for her graduation. Izzy was dressed in a rented gown and mortarboard – the smallest sizes that could be found – to receive her degree. A photographer was on hand to take pictures of the students on their graduation day.

"What nonsense," Mum scoffed. "You don't want a photograph, do you?"

"Er, I suppose not," said Izzy in a small, disappointed voice.

"A complete waste of money."

Izzy moved in with Paul and me – she could not contemplate going back to live at Cleveland Road.

In the summer of 1978, Paul and I went to visit Mum and Granny. We had some exciting news to tell them: I was pregnant.

"Och well, the die is cast," said Granny forebodingly, without looking up from her knitting.

"I hope you've given up smoking," said Mum.

In January 1979, Paul and I married. I was apprehensive about Mum's possible reaction, so didn't tell her, or anyone else but Izzy. We left a note on the kitchen table: "Dear Izzy, we've just gone to get married – back soon. P.S. Don't tell anyone." Toby was born a month later. Rory was naturally appointed his fairy-god-clarinettist-father, and Izzy became co-principal mother. Our second son, George, was born in August 1980. Grandchildren brought Mum some way back into the world.

The chronic asthma I had suffered from for so long was much improved. I used the Ventolin inhaler to ease occasional wheeziness, but I rarely had full-scale attacks. After George's birth, it came back severely for a few months, and then miraculously disappeared. From the age of twenty-five, I have been asthma-free. I carried my inhaler around with me for another ten years though, just in case.

In 1981, Paul and I started looking for a larger house in the South Woodford area. I particularly wanted our sons to go to Oakdale Infant School, where Margaret Sprakes was still the Head. There was a property for sale in The Drive. I held my breath: could it be the very one that I had always chosen as a child? It was. My fairytale house with the turret was on the market. Dr. Franklin was selling it. The only disappointment was that he was dividing the plot and would keep half the land. The coach-house had already been demolished and a new building was in the process of construction. Paul fell for the house too. It was beyond our ceiling price and in need of a lot of work, but we bought it. I adored that house and its garden. It was amazing to find myself actually dwelling in the place of my imagination. Izzy moved with us.

As George grew older we began to notice in him an uncanny resemblance to Chris, partly in looks, but more so in personality. There was a strange familiarity, a feeling that some essence of Chris had been born with him. By the time he was eleven or twelve, Mum sometimes called him Chris without realising it. She began to talk occasionally about her son, having been silent for so long. During the last decade of her life, as Alzheimer's destroyed her brain, Mum called George Chris more often than she called him George. We didn't bother to correct her. We knew what she meant. George's resemblance to Chris has lessened as he has grown into a young man; Chris will always be a boy of seventeen.

In 1989, Buckhurst Hill County High School closed along with many other grammar schools when the Comprehensive education system took over. I wondered what ever became of Chris's collection and the memorial scholarship fund. The school conventionally addressed letters to Mr. and Mrs. Giles. I suspect that after the divorce, communications were sent solely to Mr. Giles. When the school closed, was the capital from the memorial fund sent to him? I do not know. What about Chris's collection? What happened to that? I was not informed.

When George was ten, I had to go through the process of finding a secondary school for him. Toby was already at Forest School for Boys, but George turned his place down. "I don't want to go to a school where I have to have my hair cut and there aren't any girls." This seemed fair enough to me. George was fully engaged with music by this time and I heard that Roding Valley High School had a good music department. In fact, he didn't go there, but George and I went to the open day. Roding Valley High is an amalgamation of BHCHS and Loughton County High, the schools that Chris and Izzy attended. It is on the site of Loughton County High. The old school is still standing, but with almost twice the area of new buildings annexed on. We took the guided tour, which included a visit to the science department. I stopped in my tracks, transfixed. Along one wall were display cases and behind the glass doors were objects so familiar to me that the blood drained from my face.

"Mum, are you OK? You look as though you've seen a ghost."

"Oh George, this is Chris's collection! I haven't seen it for fifteen years."

There they all were – the skulls, skeletons, birds' eggs, fossils, moths and butterflies.

"Look George – the cards! These are the very cards that Izzy and I typed out for Chris all those years ago."

Fox: *Vulpes Vulpes*
Sheep: *Ovis Aries*
Hare: *Lepus*
Badger: *Meles Meles*
Weasel: *Mustela nivalis*
Rabbit: *Oryctolagus cuniculus*
Stoat: *Mustela erminea*
Swan: *Cygnus*

There were quite a few things missing – some of the tiny skulls and skeletons of voles, mice and birds had, I supposed, been lost. I couldn't see the bottles of preserved animals or the insects. Perhaps they had gone off. There didn't seem to be any shells and not so many stuffed animals. Nor could I see a memorial tablet.

"May I help you?"

"Are you the science teacher?"

"Yes."

"These cases…"

"They're amazing aren't they?"

"Do you know where they came from?"

"No. They were inherited, I believe. We're so lucky to have them. I can't imagine there's any school that has such an extensive collection of natural history. This isn't all of it, by the way. The Art department has borrowed some antlers and skulls and other things for their still-life classes. It's fantastic for the students to see and hold the real things. At the last school I taught, we had a couple of skulls, but mostly we had to rely on photographs and diagrams, which just isn't the same."

I smiled, warmed by his enthusiasm.

"Well, I can tell you all about them. They were collected by my brother, Christopher Giles."

84
CHRIS

They say that "Time assuages" –
Time never did assuage –
An actual suffering strengthens
As sinews do, with age –

Emily Dickinson

As weeks turn to months and then years, grief deepens, evolves and matures within the life one must continue to live. Gradually I slipped down my iceberg of grief, became familiar with its contours, the numbing cold of loss and the tricks it could play. It is said that if one falls asleep in snow, its soft blanket fools the sleeper into comfort even as the body freezes to death. Similarly, in dreams so convincing, I am deceived into finding Chris alive. To begin with, it was incredible to see him again. In my dream I would maybe walk into his room and there he would be, standing by the window examining a skull.

"Hi, Cath."

"Chris! You're alive!" I'd bubble over with wild relief. Of course he's alive! How ridiculous to have ever thought he was dead. I would laugh deliriously; he'd give me one of his sweet head-shaking smiles, looking at me as if I were daft.

"Would you have time to type out a few more cards for me?" he'd ask.

"Yes, yes. Oh Chris, I'm so happy!" Then I would wake. It would be like a Tom and Jerry cartoon – one where Tom finds himself suspended in mid-air, floating happily, until a bird flies past, followed by a Jumbo Jet. Suddenly, he realises the impossibility of his position. Like Tom, awakening from my Chris dreams sent me plummeting down, down, down, to crash into shattering reality. As the years went by, my dreams became more convoluted – harrowing nightmares, which replayed in slightly different formats, following changeable paths. But the shocking message in the dreams is always the same; his drowning was an illusion, a hoax. I learn that he staged his death to escape from the life he was living in order to begin a new life where nobody could find him.

"Why, Chris? Why? I know you couldn't stand living at home; I understand your need to go, but surely you could have sent word to us that you were OK? Chris, we've all thought you were dead! It's been absolutely awful. You have no idea. Oh, it's so wonderful to find you. Where do you live? I'll come and visit you! It'll be so fantastic! And Mum – she won't believe it when I tell her you're alive – oh, Chris, she'll be so happy!" But even as I am talking excitedly, I know something is wrong. Chris is not responding. A cold stone of fear fills my stomach.

"Cath," he says with infinite regret, "you can't visit me."

"Please Chris, please," I implore, "I won't tell anyone you're alive if you don't want me to. I won't betray you, but please let me see you again." He turns away, shaking his head. "Or if you won't let me see you," I go on desperately, "then at least we can speak!"

"Cath, listen. It has always worried me that we might accidentally meet and I wish this could have been avoided." He looks perplexed, anxious – an expression I know so well that arouses my empathy and compassion. I want to hold him and tell him not to worry. He doesn't respond to my smile of assurance. He sighs. "There are no explanations I can give that you will understand, but you can't come into my life."

"But I'm your sister!" I cry.

"You'll always be my sister, always, but you have to let me go."

"No, Chris, no."

He looks at me with utter sadness. It is unbearable to see such sorrow in his face.

"I have to go now," he says quietly.

"Chris, come back. Please. I can't bear not to see you again."

"Cath, I'm not coming back." He turns and walks away.

My wracking sobs wake me and yet again I have to go through those agonising minutes of emerging consciousness as I reassemble reality. Chris is dead. He really, truly is.

Recently, I had a different dream: I check into an old hotel – one where actors and musicians often stay, somewhere in a slightly run-down area of London. It is late. I am tired. The receptionist shows me to a room on the top floor, which has not been cleaned – unmade bed, towels on the floor. She apologises and says she will get the room made up straight away. I tell her not to bother, but would she please bring some fresh towels? I know why I am here. Chris has died in this hotel. The manager shows me the room where his body is lying and says I may take him home… I sit Chris's body in a chair beside a grave I have prepared for him. It occupies the parking bay outside my house and I have marked the outline with chalk. All around the grave I have placed flowers, fruit, berries and dried grasses. I leave Chris sitting in the chair for the night. In the morning, I go to him, kneel in front of him and hold his left hand; his strong, shapely hand, utterly cold, but not stiff. I squeeze and stroke it and love the broad feel of it. I kiss his hand and stand to kiss his face. Then I put my arms under his, around his back and pull him up to standing position. I wonder if I can manage, as he is heavier and taller than me. It is easier than I thought. Chris's head rests over my shoulder and I carry him, his feet dragging on the ground and lie him down gently in the grave. His blue eyes are open and lovely, but unseeing. The grave is as big, if not bigger, than a double bed. I lie beside him for a while, settling his limbs and head… Then I am standing beside the grave. I move the flowers, grasses, fruits, nuts and berries around him to cover the chalk marks and enclose him, so that he is surrounded by the harvest of all seasons. The sound of deep sobbing – my own – wakes me. My face is wet with tears.

If I continue with my metaphorical iceberg of grief, I reckon I have reached sea level and am waist deep in water now. Occasionally, I plunge beneath the surface to fathomless depths, but I return to breathe and must leave Chris in the fascinating underwater world he dreamed of, swimming and conversing with his school of dolphins and, of course, playing his horn.

85
GRANNY

When day, expiring in the west,
The curtain draws o' Nature's rest,
I flee to his arms I lo'e the best,
And that's my ain dear Davie.

Dainty Davie – Robert Burns

Granny died on July 9th 1991, two weeks before her ninety-ninth birthday. She lived at 32, Cleveland Road until a year before her death, when Mum had to reluctantly acknowledge that caring for Granny was more than she could manage. Luckily, there was a pleasant nursing home at the end of Cleveland Road, a minute's walk away. Mum went there every single morning to comb and pin her mother's hair and again at three o'clock each afternoon to partake of their ritual cup of tea. When death came, Mum phoned her brother Robert, Izzy and me. She imparted the news in a tired but calm, matter-of-fact way, telling us all that there was no need to attend the funeral. Robert decided he should be there. The reason he gave to Mum was that his neighbours in Abergavenny would think it very odd if he did not go to his mother's funeral. Mum found it odd that I wanted to be there. She persuaded Izzy not to go, saying it would be ridiculous for her to take a day off school and abandon her class of Infants. So it was that there were just three people at Annie Fraser's funeral. The hearse arrived. Robert, Mum and I entered a silent chapel at the City of London Crematorium. The coffin was carried in. The funeral director approached us to ask what the order of service would be.

"We're not having a service," said Mum.

"Some music?"

Mum shook her head.

"Are any of you going to speak?"

"No."

"Would you like a few minutes of silence then?"

"No, I don't think so." At this point I intervened

"Let's have a couple of minutes, Mum." I nodded to the baffled funeral director, who walked softly away with practised, reverential tread. Mum sat with her head slightly bowed, her brother on her left, I on her right. I wondered what she was thinking as I said goodbye to Granny in my head. Then she pushed back her sleeve to look at her watch. She broke the silence.

"Surely we've had two minutes by now, Cathy?"

"Do you want to go, Mum?"

"Well, there's no point in just sitting here, is there? What about you, Robert?"

"Aye, that's fine by me."

We walked out, receiving quizzical looks from the sombre-suited pallbearers.

Granny's body was cremated without any 'stuff and nonsense', which is, I suppose, exactly how she would have wanted it. Yet when Izzy and I were clearing Cleveland Road, we found the Title Deeds to a Lair in the Cathcart Cemetery, which Granny had purchased in 1935, for her body to be buried next to her husband, Davie.

During the last years of Granny's life, I 'Granny-sat' when Mum had to go out. There were times when we talked about Chris.

"I'm glad to speak of him, Cath-er-reen, for your Mammy doesn't like me to. You don't mind do you?"

"No, I like to share memories."

"It's good to remember. Och aye, it is. Chris is always in my mind. And I tell you this, there is never a day goes by that I don't think of my Davie. He was a good man, he surely was. It's a shame you never knew him."

On one occasion, I was keeping her company with my two young sons.

"Cath-er-reen," she called.

"Yes?"

"Come here." I walked over to her chair. Rheumatism had robbed her of mobility.

"What is it?"

"Come closer." I leaned towards her. She lifted an arthritic arm to my shoulder and pulled me nearer. It seemed as though she wanted to whisper something in my ear. To my astonishment, she kissed me firmly on the cheek.

"There," she said, satisfied, pushing me away. "Now you'd best be getting those wee boys home. It's way past their bedtime and your Mammy will be back soon." I reached for her hand, wanting to give her a kiss back, but she wouldn't let me.

"Go on, away with ye."

The one kiss Granny gave me told me everything I needed to know.

Mum's brother, Robert, died suddenly from a heart attack in 1993 aged seventy.

Rory, the charming, sweet-hearted, fairy-god-clarinettist was tragically struck down with multiple sclerosis in his late twenties and died in April 1995.

Des Turner died in February 2010: the man who guided Izzy, Chris and me through our teenage years with uncommon sensitivity, perception, care and love. He was an exceptional person.

86
DAD

Why should he think me cruel
Or that he is betrayed?
I'd have him love the thing that was
Before the world was made.

A Woman Young and Old – W. B. Yeats

My father died on November 5th 1999, but it was not until November 16th, a week after his funeral, that I received a letter from his wife, Jean, informing me. I phoned her, shattered by the news and bewildered that she had not contacted me. She sounded wary, perhaps alarmed, to hear from me. All she could say was that she had been too grief-stricken to let me know and had written as soon as she felt she could. Although the funeral was over, I explained that I needed to come to Derbyshire to mourn my father. Was there anywhere special to him where I could go – a favourite park perhaps? She said that the only place where Derek had felt safe was here in his home. Then that is where I will come, I replied. I arranged to pay a visit a few days later, assuring her that I would not stay long – I just needed a little time by myself in his room.

Accompanied by my close friend, Maggie Baron, I drove to Derbyshire in an emotional turmoil, fearful that Jean might not even let me in. We arrived at the house Dad had shared with her in Milford. I asked Maggie to wait in the car. Jean answered the door. I gave her a bouquet of flowers – white, cream, blue and purple blooms. She greeted me coldly. Over a cup of tea, she told me of "the most terrible time of her life"; the last three weeks of "her Derek's" life, spent in the Derbyshire General Hospital. I said I wished I had been told that he was ill and been given the opportunity to see him before he died, but she did not respond. I offered to pay towards the cost of the funeral, but she declined. She was not keen on the idea of my going up to Derek's room alone, but I managed to insist. I had been in his room before when I had visited with my children. It was unchanged. Many things were familiar from childhood – the Renoir prints of *La Petite Irène*, and the nude that used to hang above the upright piano in the living room; his collection of rocks, crystals, fossils and semi-precious stones. Other items, though perhaps not the very same ones, were simply Dad's style – walking sticks, well-worn boots, a row of cravats, ties, waistcoats, old jackets – typically Oxfam shop purchases. I looked at it all carefully before reading in a quiet voice a memoriam that I had spent the previous days writing. I did not weep, but I said goodbye, leaving hand-drawn cards from my daughters on his patchwork-quilted bed.

Before I left, I asked Jean if she would kindly send me all the letters I had written to Dad, so that I would have both sides of our correspondence. She did not return them. When I phoned some months later, she told me she had not yet felt able to go through his papers. In January 2001, more than a year after my father's death, I applied to the Probate Registry to obtain a copy of his will. It was dated September 1996. He had left everything to Jean, as I expected; I had simply wanted to know. But what cut me to the quick was a specific clause that read:

"I MAKE NO PROVISION for my daughters as they and I have long been estranged."

This was true of Izzy, but certainly not true of myself. I wrote again to Jean, begging her to return my letters. Eight months later, she replied: "I have now had the strength to go through all Derek's papers. There are no letters from you among them. I trust that this will be the final correspondence between us." It was.

It is also the reason why I have not been able to find out more about my father's years in the Royal Navy. When I made enquiries, I was told that information from the personal record of a deceased ex-serviceman could only be released with the consent of the official next of kin.

Here are a few extracts from some of my father's letters to me from 1986 to 1998. When I moved house in 1986, his earlier letters to me from 1977 were lost:

My Dear Cathy,

I have carefully kept all your letters since we first came to live here, yet just when about to reply to your last one I can't find it!

I'd like also to say that I regard a letter from you as something of immense importance. When I get one I'm very conscious of an enlargement to the day, a keener appreciation of being here, free forever to enjoy amiable peacefulness, yet more aware that somewhere may yet be found yet another dimension to life in a daughter and grandchildren.

Here's hoping that all will be just right for both of us until we meet again.

Lots of love, Dad xxx

It was lovely to talk to you last week. I think it was a very useful exchange, don't you?

Thank you for your letter and your story. The letter I read immediately, but the story much later. I saved it until the 'Right time'. I don't know how one may define the right time – but one knows when it has arrived. I expect you know too. Your sending one of your stories was a great idea – I was 'in Whoops' to receive it. We're two of a kind.

With much love, Dad xx

Thank you for your letter, to be studied several times in endeavour to respond in a useful way as soon as the right moment comes. Meanwhile, please know how gratified I feel in your wishing to share some of your deeper thoughts. It will be a little while before I write more fully, so this quickie must do for the moment.

Another quickie to keep the pot a-boilin' (one day there really will be a considered reply to yours of 2nd May). But I'm not forgetting your needs. You'll know, though, that I like to devote much care in the writing of important letters – but I'm forgetting that which I intended to say: it is simply that I can't adequately reply to your letter until that necessary smoothness and clarity of thought and the opportunity to use it be present. It will be fun to jointly examine that which I suspect to be a mutual problem, and, (possibly) an all but universal one. Meanwhile (I mean this): Don't go overboard for anything! – keep all options open! (and any other platitudes of like nature).

Lots of love, Dad

My Dear Cathy,

To let you know that I am not forgetting the matter of dreams, herewith some comments. The whole theme, so intangible and subjective, does not readily lend itself to close scrutiny, least of all my own. Nevertheless, your raising the subject in your letter and in your story has, over the weeks, slowly brought about a rough arrangement of thoughts on the matter. Doubtless you already know that I too experience (far too often) those unbidden visitors of the night. It may truly be said that here we stand on common, if uncertain ground. The dream experience seems to have engaged the attention of humanity since the year dot; which suggests that to dream is to be a normal person, that to dream is to undergo normal, necessary sleep process.

One wonders about those who set forth to interpret other people's nocturnal fantasies. Surely they take monumental tasks upon themselves – of the same order as attempting to balance four slippery snooker-balls on the point of a finger? You'll probably agree that the best interpreter is oneself? Sometimes when fragments of my dreams survive into waking consciousness, I am able to trace a few distorted details thereof to fragments of recent or distant past; never have I found reason to assume any influences at work from beyond the confines of my own body.

Although I've said nothing new, I am, like yourself, finding that to set it down in writing is a sound exercise and a valuable addition to one's personal notes. I'm enclosing fresh copies of pages from my diary written about ten years ago; a useful reminder of our total unimportance vis-à-vis universal forces. Dum vivimus vivamus!

I've much appreciated receiving your communications during recent years. Let the good work prosper – I hope to receive others in due course. Yet as I well understand the time/energy situation I don't look for an automatic speedy reply to anything you may receive from this end of the line. Feel free, my dear!

Lots of love, Dad

My Dear Daughter,

Just the briefest of notes to let you know how much I enjoyed our telephone contact last week. I've temporarily mislaid your last letter, on which, after further study, I had intended to base a much longer letter to yourself; something involving a deal more thought and patience than this one! Hope to be able to write to you more often during 96 than I have in 95.

With lots of love, Dad xxx

Every three months or so I receive a letter from my cousin, Sallie Anstruther, who enjoys researching family history. Because of our many mutual relatives, both living and dead, we have been able to act as each other's clearinghouse in sorting out some aspects of the puzzling and sometimes stressful past.

My Dear Cathy,

I'm glad to have written to you again for there's real pleasure in communicating with my 'Daughter of Earth and Water'.

With lots of love, Dad xxx

To Emily [*my daughter*]: February 1998 [*when she was nine*] Extracts

Dear Emily,

I was very pleased to receive your extra-special letter written upon extra-special notepaper. Have you been supposing that I'd forgotten? Alas, I'm always well in arrears in matters of correspondence, which must be most disappointing, annoying even, to those who have taken all the trouble to write to me. There are cogent reasons for such delays, which would take far too long to explain to you now. When we all meet again I'll tell you all about it.

I am sure that you have been enjoying all manner of adventure since we met in Milford all those months ago. Please thank your mother, on our behalf, for the beautiful photos of us all during the visit.

With Lots of Love to yourself, your dear Sister, your dear Mother,

Grandad

To Martha [*my daughter*]: March 1998 [*when she was eight*] Extracts

Dear Martha,

How are you? We've been thinking of you (and also of your Mother and Sister), and look forward to seeing you again some time during the merry months of April or May. I hope you are happy and well – enjoying yourself, observing all manner of interesting events, people and things; for to exercise ones sense of curiosity is surely a great satisfaction to every intelligent young person.

With lots of love, Grandpa

But while my father was writing the above, his letters to others were somewhat different. As a result of my research for this book, I contacted Sallie Anstruther, Dad's cousin, and also Amanda Heath, Florrie Lupino's granddaughter. Florrie Lupino, to remind you, was my father's half-sister. To my amazement, Dad's wife, Jean, had not been too overcome to telephone both of them to impart the news of Dad's death. They attended his funeral, assuming that Izzy and I were absent because we were indeed totally estranged from him. And this was precisely the message that Jean intended to give. We were not there by her design. It was crucial to her that we, particularly I, should not be seen at the funeral by anyone. Sallie and Amanda were stunned that Jean had withheld notification of Dad's death from me and appalled by her behaviour. After initial surprise at my contacting them, we soon became friends and found much to talk about and share. (Sadly, Sallie Anstruther died in September 2009 after a long struggle with leukaemia.) Both independently decided to give me the letters that my father had written to them; letters composed at the same time, sometimes within a day or so, as the letters he wrote to me. They knew his words would hurt, but they felt that I should see them. Here are some extracts:

To Aunt Violet, Sallie's mother: 1982

You know, I think we might well benefit from this re-establishment of communication. As Terry [*Dominick Anstruther's eldest son*] would say 'Blood is thicker than water', something I had forgotten for a long time. I guess I wasted a lot of my youth, but now, after much suffering have learned the hard lesson, which leads, or should lead, to humility. My own dear natural daughters of my first marriage completely withdrew from me after the divorce and there is no way to their Hearts any more. It is dreadful that there was never once one single occasion that we could share our grief over the loss of my Son. My ex-wife was a very wicked woman.

I think it would be a relief for me to tell you that the news of the loss of my Son came when the entire family had gone off on holiday. I was alone when the Police called. Unfortunately I collapsed on receipt of the tidings and spent ten days in a mental hospital. That is one of the things for which my daughters will not forgive me. It did not improve matters by divorcing their mother!

To Amanda: 1983

How very pleasing to hear from you; I am most happy to make the acquaintance of another member of the family. As you know, Jean and I were married in 1978 [*sic: actually 1977*], having previously suffered long years of misery in previous marriages. Since then we have both tried to find some kind of family roots dating back to the time before those marriages. Needless to say, my first thoughts were for my half-sister, Florence, and later on, the Anstruthers. My very own nearest and dearest, my own daughters, decided some years ago to cut themselves off from their father, and now I know them not. Such a calamity, but such was THEIR decision. You will perhaps know that I have two grandsons whose company might have sometimes made great recompense for the loss of my own dear son, but this too was crushed by their mother.

I wish so much that I had known a little of the family background when I was a younger man; for then I might have understood some of the reasons for the mysterious undercurrents of secrecy, of which I was very conscious even as a small schoolboy. As a schoolboy I had no way of knowing why certain matters should not be discussed; and why my parents insisted that I should "Never let other people know your business". It has always been my nature to avoid secrets (as you see by this letter) for Family Secrets are bad burdens to carry around. Just think of the ever present dread which must have oppressed my parents during the course of their thirty year struggle to keep from me the knowledge that they had never been married. Yet it was bound to come out eventually, and in a very nasty way indeed. Complete frankness right at the beginning would have been the best policy.

To Sallie: 1983-1993

As for family history it may be a little while before I send you my remarks, as I feel I should compile some notes first, and that will require a bit of organising. However, this seems to be the occasion to tell you that it is useless to make enquiries of Florrie, for she is one of the prime parties to the 'cover-up' to which you referred.

The 'secret' [*that of his parents' not being married*] was known to my ex-mother-in-law and my ex-wife and used by them as a further weapon in their campaign to estrange my children. My children knew before I did! Whom do you suppose TOLD my wicked ex-mother-in-law? It was Florrie who kindly gave them that useful information! [*In fact, Dad knew of his parents' unwed state in 1951, years before he met Mum.*] Thank Heavens I am no longer so foolish as to suppose that the world owes me a living; but the Family certainly do! (not you of course).

Does one not shudder to think of all the careful obscurantism, lies and destruction of personality which must have gone on in the fashioning of the false 'official' version of our family history? All in vain, of course, for we, the obscure third generation have found 'em out! Melodramatic words, no doubt, yet our many years of bewilderment, frustration and rootlessness render them valid.

My own family – the existence of two daughters whom I scarce know, and at least four grandchildren whom, alas, I don't know at all; the existence of an elderly half-sister [*Florrie*] of whom I'm quite fond but whom I don't wish to meet again for fear of her abiding zest for malicious gossip; these matters I keep well to the back of my mind – I cannot allow them to damage our lives here at Milford.

To end these several chapters of horror; you'll probably recall that my poor son was lost by drowning in 1975. We were all on holiday at the time, but not together. He was canoeing in Scotland with friends, I was at home enjoying a period of freedom from mother-in-law, and the women [*Granny and Mum*] were 'touring'. News of the calamity reached them via a BBC SOS message. They hastened to the scene, it's true – but they also STOPPED ON THE WAY TO BUY SOME CHEAP SUGAR! Am I not fortunate to have abandoned those people and married a real, decent, caring human being?

Dad's capacity for self-delusion was exceptional. His ability to make things up and then believe them to be fact was extraordinary. There are many absurd and false statements contained in the extracts from Dad's letters above; too many to highlight individually. However, the last passage I have quoted is not just untrue – it is ridiculous. I wish to make it absolutely clear: there was no "BBC SOS message". That is pure invention by Dad. The way Mum heard about her son's death was as I described earlier – she phoned the Taylors' house to have a chat with Chris, and Mrs. Taylor had to break the news to her. As for Dad's statement that Mum and Granny "stopped on the way to buy some cheap sugar". – well, I have never heard anything so utterly ludicrous.

Reading through his letters, it is hardly surprising that I felt emotionally tied in knots by him. I still do. His death did not change anything. But in writing this book I have at least been able to lay a few ghosts to rest, to expose some injustices and to feel that I have set one or two things straight. Why he behaved as he did, I shall never know. What I grieve for is the relationship that I did not have with my father – the love that I was never given.

I believe your best friends were loneliness and misery.
I believe your busiest enemies were anger and depression.
I believe joy was a game you could never play without stumbling.
I believe comfort, though you craved it, was always a stranger.
I believe music had to be melancholy or not at all.
I believe no trinket, no precious metal, shone so bright as your bitterness.
I believe you lay down at last in your coffin none the wiser and unassuaged.

A Bitterness – Mary Oliver

87
IZZY AND ME

If you can't get rid of the skeleton in your closet, you'd best teach it to dance.

Bernard Shaw

I have told the story of Chris's life, which is what I set out to do. However, there are a few loose ends concerning Izzy and myself to tie up before the final chapter. I will be brief. To remind you: Izzy and I met John Spencer at a Forest School Camp when we were seventeen-year-old Pathfinders. John and I spent the fortnight sharing a tent. However, as mentioned earlier in the book, our friend Melanie Turner always felt that John had picked the wrong twin. When Melanie married in 1983, she deliberately sat Izzy and John next to each other at the wedding breakfast. They had met occasionally over the previous years, but this time, as Melanie had predicted, they fell in love. Izzy didn't live with John, but he was a frequent visitor to our house in The Drive and Izzy stayed with him most weekends.

Izzy and I continued to staff with FSC most summers, almost always on Leslie Holden's camps. We took our children with us – they all benefitted from the unique experience of FSC and Leslie's gentle, unobtrusive leadership. My eldest son, Toby, was four months old at his first camp. Paul joined us for some of the time. Although he was never tempted to camp again, he enjoyed the majority of it. He and Leslie bonded straight away, and Leslie was thrilled to have live music for country dancing. Paul played violin and Owen Aaronovitch[1] guitar, the two musicians following the dancers as they skipped, promenaded and do-si-doed around the field. I stopped camping in 1998, but Izzy still camps every year. We were all heartbroken when Leslie died in February 2011.

Sadly, Paul and I separated. We sold 42, The Drive in 1986 – I only lived in my fairytale castle for five years. Izzy, my sons and I moved to a smaller house a couple of miles away, near enough for Toby and George to stay on at Oakdale School. Happily, Paul and I remained friends and continue to work together in the music world.

Izzy and John planned to get married. A summer wedding was proposed, but John found excuses to postpone it. Eventually, he called it off altogether and ended the relationship, declaring that he didn't feel ready to marry or have children. Two months later, he phoned Izzy to tell her that he was with someone else, she was pregnant and he was going to marry her. Izzy was shattered.

In 1987 a new partner moved in with me – Phillip Eastop. Izzy, who had always lived in peaceful harmony with Paul and me, soon realised that she could not remain under the same roof as Phillip. Within a few months she had bought her

1. Owen Aaronovitch is now an actor, famously known for portraying Jon Lindsay in *Coronation Street*.

own house and gone. We had lived together for the best part of thirty years. It was a sad moment. I had two more wonderful children – Emily, born in 1988 and Martha in 1990. My relationship with Phillip was not a happy one. We parted in 1991.

John and Izzy's story wasn't over. Izzy resisted John's many attempts to contact her, but in the end he persuaded her to meet him. What they felt for each other had not changed. Their relationship resumed, clandestinely. It was, and still is, a cruel compromise. In 1992 they had a son – Izzy's only child. She called him Rory.

Izzy always said she wanted to be an Infant School teacher, and that is what she became. She also kept up her music, playing the piano for school assemblies and children's concerts and the violin in local orchestras. For many years she was the assistant string tutor at Wortley summer school. She resigned from classroom teaching after twenty-three years and is now a peripatetic violin teacher in the London Borough of Redbridge.

I did not become an international soloist, but I did perform most of the major cello concertos with various pro-am orchestras and gave many recitals. My last concerto appearances were in 1996, when I played the Haydn C major at St. Martin-in-the-Fields with the Locrian Ensemble, and the Elgar at Ilford Town Hall in the Redbridge Youth Orchestra's thirtieth anniversary concert with Bram Tovey conducting. I still give the occasional short recital for friends, but my solo work has rarely been paid: it is as a freelance cellist that I have earned my living. The work has been diverse – from West End shows, Film, TV, jingle and album sessions, to playing in backing orchestras for rock and pop stars in live concerts. I am also what is known in the music business as a 'fixer' – I book musicians for work. Most of the fixing I have done has been for Paul, supplying him with the musicians he has needed to record the thousands of jingles (music for adverts) that he has written over the last thirty-five years. Since 2006, I have booked the band for BBCTV's *Strictly Come Dancing* for the MD and arranger, Dave Arch.

In 1994 I bought myself a concert harp and finally realised my dream of playing it. I took lessons with an inspirational harpist and teacher, Hugh Webb, practised madly for several years and even did a few paid gigs. But I could see that to get beyond the basic level I had reached would require many hours of practice a day. Frustration and laziness led to my virtually giving up – but who knows, maybe I will return to it.

I still have an uneasy relationship with food. I have never again starved myself down to the bone, nor binged and thrown up for a very long time, but the truth is, I have lost and gained the same pounds over and over again. Like many women, and some men I know, I live with a weight and eating depression: a private, interminable struggle between control and turmoil. I have learned to accept that it is something I shall probably never overcome.

I haven't had a drop of alcohol since April 2004, a month before I started writing this book. I intend to keep it that way for the rest of my life.

88
MUM

In the end
Our roles turned around
My little old child
I put in the ground.

Endings – Jean Lipkin

As Mum's Alzheimer's progressed to the point where she was no longer able to negotiate stairs safely, Izzy and I decided to make a bedroom for her on the ground floor. We went through her cupboards and drawers, deciding what needed to be taken downstairs. In every single place that we looked, there was something of Chris's – his schoolbooks, reports, certificates; his letters, his passport, his natural history notes, his drawings, his diaries. She had kept every receipt from John Ridgeon for his horn lessons. There were photographs, programmes of his concerts: the letters of sympathy. She had not disposed of so much after all. The house was full of him. At the back of a high cupboard we found his birth certificate folded up tightly in a small cracked brown leather purse. There were numerous items from our childhood and from her own – her diaries, diplomas, awards, boxes of photos, birth and death certificates relating to her mother's and father's families, the cards she received when we and Chris were born. Some of Dad's stuff was still there too – school books, reports, drawings – and four golden plaits – two from Izzy's head and two from mine when Mum cut our hair for the first time when we were seven. There were no love letters, but for some unfathomable reason Mum had kept all the notes between the two of them when Dad was holed up in Izzy's bedroom. I do not want to include them here – I find them too disturbing. Otherwise, much of the material hoarded by Mum for so long has gone into the writing of this book.

A year later, there was no option left but to move her into a care home. It was a harrowing moment, having to leave her looking lost and confused. We were afraid that she would plead with us to take her home when we visited a few days later, but that did not happen. She no longer knew where she was. We began to sort out the contents of the ground floor of Cleveland Road. The music room was a major task. Nearly every drawer was full of piano music, yet Mum, in her super-efficient way, had stored all of it systematically. Everything was in order. One drawer had programmes of her pupils' concerts from 1960 to her last in 2002, newspaper cuttings of concerts we had played in, plus a whole stack of unsold programmes of Chris's memorial concert. That was where I found the cassettes. I held my breath.

"Izzy – look. Oh my goodness, I had no idea Mum had these."

There were three tapes labelled in Mum's handwriting:

'Concerti Allegri Mar 8th 1975 Concertstück for four horns – Schumann'

'Redbridge Brass March 23rd 1975, Gregson Horn Concerto – soloist C. Giles'

– and the third was simply called 'Chris practising'.

"Have you ever seen them before?"

"I didn't even know she'd recorded those concerts," said Izzy.

"Shall we… would you feel able to listen to one?"

"Yes. Yes, put on the Gregson."

I slotted the tape into the cassette player and pressed 'play'. We heard clearing of throats, shuffling, an audience falling quiet. The tape was already set to play from the opening bar. I wondered how many times Mum had listened to this on her own, rewinding it each time to precisely the right place. I knew then that I had no idea of the vast, bleak, private grief that she had endured every day since Chris had died. Grief is so terribly lonely, I know that, but Mum, oh Mum. Her despair was palpable as I sat with Izzy on the carpet, the same carpet we had known since we were little, the four pairs of swans – two black and two white – still swimming in the pond. Then we heard Chris take a breath and he was in the room with us, living, breathing, playing. It was awesome and strange. My memory had not served me well enough – his playing was out of this world, his sound, his technical mastery, his phrasing, his breath, his heart; Mum's beautiful boy.

On August 14th 2007, Mum had a major stroke. Alzheimer's had done its worst to her; the stroke allowed her to die. Izzy and I sat at her bedside witnessing her distressing and unmercifully prolonged struggle towards death. While we waited, hoping the end would come soon, yet dreading the day when we would no longer be able to hold her hand, we planned her funeral. It was not going to be like Granny's. We were fully aware of its significance. Not only would it be for the many people who had known and loved Mum, but also for those who had never had an opportunity to bid farewell to Chris. We know that Mum would not have objected. I believe that she always meant to be less emotionally guarded, more openly demonstrative, but a complex inhibition held her back. The truth is that she loved us unconditionally, as we loved her. We decided that we would scatter her remains in Loch Lomond. It was the last thing we could do for her. She died at half past three in the hospice of Whipps Cross Hospital on the morning of September 3rd 2007.

More than a hundred people came to her funeral, including John Ridgeon (Chris's horn teacher), Margaret Sprakes, Malcolm Bidgood, Michael Crombie, Bram Tovey, my cousins David and Anne Fraser, Mum's cousin Marie and her husband Mike, my second cousin, Mark Heal, and many others mentioned in this book. The occasion began with a recording of a beautiful setting of Shakespeare's Sonnet 28 composed and sung by Bill Worrall. After the eulogy, six friends, Izzy and I played the first movement of the Mendelssohn octet, a piece that Mum had so enjoyed playing herself at Wortley. Paul Hart and our son George, together with Martin Wheatley (Nitram) and his sons closed with a performance of Fats Waller's *Honeysuckle Rose*. We invited everyone back to my house. To our pleasure most people came. Talking to Bram, he reminded me that it was on the night of September 2nd to 3rd in 1973 that he, Chris and Chris Freeman had camped by the grave of John Brinkley Easey in Dunwich. Mum had died on the same night in 2007.

Hovering near me was an elderly man I did not recognise. He began talking to me, saying I wouldn't know him, but he had known my mother for a long time and had first met Izzy and me when we were babies. He said he came to our concerts and had seen us perform at the Ilford Town Hall on many occasions. I was curious to know more, but I was called away for some reason and did not get a chance to continue the conversation. Fortunately, he started talking to Martin Wheatley, who was later able to enlighten me.

His name was Pete Perry. He had come to the funeral as a result of the notice I had placed in the *Morning Star*. It transpired that he had only spoken to Elizabeth three times in his life, but it was obvious to Martin that he had been in love with her from the moment he saw her and had been holding a candle for her ever since. The occasion was a recital that she gave at Canterbury Cathedral in 1950, where she played some Scarlatti. He was enthralled by her musicianship and by her. When he congratulated her afterwards, he joked that the name of the Italian composer, Domenico Scarlatti, could be translated as the 'Red Dean'.

Pete was a member of the Wanstead and Woodford Communist Party, so saw Elizabeth at CP events, but was too bashful to initiate conversation. The second time they briefly exchanged words, she was with Dad. Pete told Martin that they seemed such a happy couple, he realised there was no hope for him: he did not want to come between them or do anything to spoil Elizabeth's happiness, so he knew he must keep his feelings to himself. The third and last occasion was when he plucked up the courage to congratulate her on the birth of her twins.

He never spoke to her again, but he continued to look out for her; he read the *Morning Star* every day – he must have seen the notice of Chris's death, and then Granny's. When he saw our names advertised in concert promotions, he went to the events knowing that Elizabeth would be there. He must have watched her playing the cello in *Musici* concerts, observed her in the audience at our performances, but never felt able to approach her. She was the unrequited love of his life. He had come to her funeral to pay his last respects and to tell his untold story. A few days later, he placed a notice in the *Morning Star*. It read:

In Memoriam, Elizabeth Fraser (L.R.A.M., A.R.C.M., G.R.S.M.)
From distant admirer Pete Perry since she scintillated Scarlatti,
the 'Red Dean', Canterbury Cathedral, and me, circa 1950.

I was moved by many aspects of Pete's story: the fact that here was a man who had been in love with my mother for a lifetime, who had worshipped her from afar with an intensity of feeling that had never waned. She had not received the love she deserved from either of her husbands, but it was touching to know that she had had the constant love of Pete Perry.

Martin could not bring himself to tell Pete how dreadfully unhappy Elizabeth's marriage to Derek had been, or that she had been unattached for thirty years. I have no romantic thoughts about the unused possibilities of those decades. Mum would never have wanted another man in her life, of that I am certain.

When, as a child, I had asked her and Dad how they had met, I had been hoping to see their faces light up with joy as they remembered how they had fallen in love. It was strange now to hear a description of my parents looking "so happy together" before we were born, from a man I did not know, after Mum and Dad were both dead. The information made no difference, but it made sense. There was a time when they had loved each other, had known the potency of desire that brings forth not just children, but inspiration. They had also known bitter disillusionment.

In April 2008, Izzy and I flew to Glasgow with Mum's ashes, hired a car and drove northwards. We had never been to Loch Lomond, never seen the place where Chris had died. It was when we turned left into the road signposted to Balmaha and Rowardennan that I voiced what was in both our minds: "This is the final road that Chris travelled; what we are seeing for the first time are the same images he saw for the last time."

We drove onwards, neither of us inclined to talk. Just before the road comes to an end and Ben Lomond takes dominion is the Rowardennan Hotel. It is not a grand place – more akin to a B&B, and used by hikers walking the West Highland Way. I had booked the nicest room available some months previously: the one with the best views of the Loch and Ben Lomond. We parked and checked in for four nights.

After a cup of tea, we walked the short distance around the bay to Rowardennan Point – a wooded area with parking, public conveniences, picnic tables, several little beaches and a small pier jutting into the Loch. It was here where Chris had drowned. We looked out across the water – how tranquil and benign it looked: yet what tragedy that beauty hides – not just the life of Chris, but also the many lives that have been lost in Loch Lomond. We read that five people had drowned in 2007 alone, two of them experienced sailors.

The sun shone warmly, but we were glad of our coats. To our astonishment, we watched three young men strip to the waist and two of them dive from the pier into the water, screaming with the shock of the temperature as they surfaced. We laughed with them, smiling at their abandon, their desire to dare.

I imagined Gillian, Chris, Paula and Phillip arriving at that very spot on the hot summer morning of August 5th 1975 full of youthful vitality; saw them getting out of the car, the girls running to change into their swimming costumes, Mr. Taylor and the boys tugging the first canoe from the roof-rack, carrying it over boulders and stones, laying it on the narrow strip of sand and pushing it out into the Loch. They would have been joyful, excited and happy. It is that image I will keep. I did not want to envisage the horror of what happened a short time later. Mum never wanted to know the details of how or where her son had drowned, but I was immensely glad to be there, in the actual place where Chris's life had ended. My dreams had conjured numerous imaginary scenes for so long; I hadn't realised how much I had yearned for the reality.

The following day we drove into Glasgow. We crossed to the south of the River Clyde via Albert Bridge and made our way to the Linn Crematorium, so recently discovered to have been where Chris's body was cremated. A manager was coming out of the chapel as we arrived. He asked if he could help. I enquired if there were any records to tell us what had been done with Chris's ashes. He told us that they would probably have been scattered here in the garden of remembrance, but that if we wanted to know for sure, all the records were held at 20, Trongate, in Central Glasgow. As we had the date and time accurately documented, he said it shouldn't take too long to find out. Izzy and I walked around the rose garden for a little while.

Before we drove to Trongate, we decided to find 37, Albert Road, the tenement building where Davie and Annie Fraser lived their married life and where Mum and her brother, Robert, were born. We drove along the outskirts of Queen's Park, past the impressive ornamental wrought-iron gates through which Robert and Betty had frequently passed, negotiated a more recent one-way system into Albert Road and parked. How strange it was to be walking along the road that Mum's young self had known so intimately; almost breathtaking to see the numbers on the tenement walls and find ourselves standing in front of number thirty-seven. It is rather run down now. The 'closes', those open passages that led to the stairwells of the tenements, have been sealed off with rather ill-fitting doors, alongside which are panels of entry buzzers. We walked up the road to the end of the block to see if we could get a glimpse of the back of the building. Sure enough, there was the Cathcart Railway, set in a deep cutting, the top of the trains passing at the same level as the street. We leaned over the bridge as one clattered by, reminding ourselves that when Mum had lived here the locomotives would have been steam-powered, belching out smoke and soot. The 'green' that Granny and Mum talked about is just a narrow strip of land between the tenements and the sunken railway track. This is where the wash-houses would have been, and where the war wounded soldiers had begged for money and food. Now it is overgrown with weeds and littered with rubbish.

At the records office we found out that Chris's ashes had been dispersed on January 15th 1976, the day after the cremation, in the rose garden at the Linn Crematorium. Finally, we knew. We decided to place an inscription into the Book of Remembrance. It has now been entered:

Giles, Christopher
Born 24th June, 1958
Drowned in Loch Lomond, 5th Aug. 1975.
Musician, Naturalist, Artist, Comedian
Loved and admired by all who knew him.

I was reminded of a conversation I had with Bram many years ago. We happened to bump into each other and went for a drink. He said to me, "You know, Cathy, the three most extraordinary people I have known in my life are Simon Rattle, Paul Hart and your brother, Chris Giles, and you're connected to them all. What is it about you, do you think?" I laughed.

"I've been lucky… but I'm so glad you put Chris alongside Simon and Paul –"

"Alongside? To be honest, I'd say Chris was the one who shone the brightest."

Whilst planning our trip to Glasgow, I contacted Chris Stearn and Chris Freeman, who are both members of the Scottish National Opera orchestra, to ask if they would like to join us to scatter Mum's ashes.

We explained the reason for our visit to the hotel manager who kindly booked a private boat trip for us. On Thursday April 17th we did what we had come to do. Chris Stearn, Chris Freeman, Izzy and I walked to the pier to watch for the boat to arrive. As we waited, a text message came through on my mobile – which was surprising, as the signal in the area was very poor. "Thinking of you all 2day… love from Gillian". How good to hear from Gillian at that moment.

The ferry chugged towards us; a tiny vessel with a cabin at the front, and benches on each side with room for about eight people. Having tethered the boat, the ferryman, a man of maybe twenty years old, helped us aboard. He was aware of the purpose of the trip and could not have been more considerate or respectful. He stepped into the cabin and steered us out onto the Loch. The wind was cold, pulling at our hair and clothing. The sun appeared between the clouds intermittently. Spectacular beauty surrounded us. After a while, our young skipper asked if this would be a good place to stop. I agreed that it would be perfect.

As the boat slowed, I took the plastic bag containing Mum's ashes from its cardboard box and undid the fastening. Together, Izzy and I emptied Mum's remains into the water, gave the bag a final shake, and it was done. I put my arm around my sister and squeezed her. During those few moments, we both silently relinquished our mother, knowing that we had done our best by returning her to Scotland, her homeland, and ensuring that her final resting place is with her son in Loch Lomond. We stood and turned to our dear friends. They both gave us long, emotional embraces as the little boat circled back to the jetty. The young man helped us out; he refused to accept any payment.

We sat at one of the picnic tables for a while, reminding one another of some of the hilarious times we had shared in our youth. Then Chris Freeman asked why we had chosen to give Chris's body to Glasgow University. Several people have asked me this over the years. The fact that there was no funeral has been difficult for many to understand. I replied that Chris had often talked about wanting to donate his body when he died. We were sure that it would have been his wish. "That's absolutely right," Chris Stearn confirmed, "he talked to me about it several times."

"Unfortunately, his body had been in the water too long for his organs to be suitable for transplants," I explained, "which is why it was so difficult to find somewhere that would take it. Making those phone calls was one of the most surreal things I have ever had to do."

"You made the calls?" asked Chris Stearn, astounded.

"I had to – there was nobody else to do it."

"Cathy dealt with it all," said Izzy quietly, and in her voice I heard respect and acknowledgement.

"So for his body to be given to students to learn about anatomy was a marvellous tribute to Chris himself," said Chris Freeman.

"Indeed it was."

Later I visualised us all back in those years when Chris was alive. It struck me again how extraordinary it was that such a talented bunch of youngsters should have been spawned within the same small geographical area over the span of just a few years. I remembered the times, the places, the concerts, the parties, the feeling of it, and wished I could have it all over again. But I have to be careful with those moments; I cannot allow myself too many of them: I do not want to become maudlin. The past has been experienced; the present is to be lived.

As I write these last few words, I remember little Chris settled on Granny's lap, Granny smiling lovingly at her bonny boy and singing:

> Ye'll take the high road, and I'll take the low road,
> And I'll be in Scotland afore ye;
> But me and my true love will never meet again
> On the bonnie, bonnie banks of Loch Lomond.

Delving into the past has been painful and sorrowful at times. It has dredged up long-submerged experiences and revived the ache of loss. I was prepared to face those inevitable moments and cannot deny that parts of this have been written from the seabed of grief. What I hadn't envisaged was how stimulating, engaging, uplifting and fun most of the research and remembering would be. Ultimately, producing this book has not only been enriching and cathartic, it has changed my life.

I like to imagine we are each born with our own individual bottled sunshine. There are no instructions as to how to use that stored energy, but it is there. Chris gave the world every drop of his bright and beautiful sunshine – a rare vintage of exquisite flavour that sadly was not made for laying down. I only hope that the silent-footed butler who serves at my table will be sufficiently benevolent to open my bottle quietly before it is corked. For that I will be truly grateful.

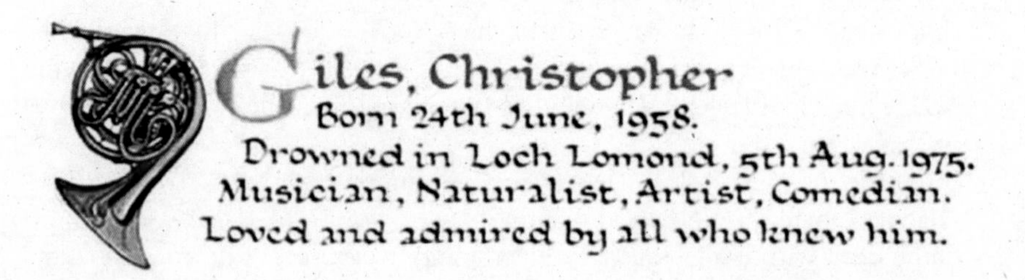

To develop to the utmost our genius and love – that is the only true religion.
To do that which needs to be written, to write that which deserves to be read, to tend the sick, to comfort the sorrowful, to animate the weary, to keep the temple of the body pure, to cherish the divinity within us, to be faithful to the intellect, to elucidate those powers that have been entrusted to our charge and to employ them in the service of humanity – that is all we can do.

Glorious Apollo is the parent of us all. Animal heat is solar heat; a blush is a stray sunbeam: Life is bottled sunshine and Death the silent-footed butler who draws out the cork.

The Martyrdom of Man – Winwood Reade

Looking across Loch Lomond from the small beach at Rowardennan Point where Chris launched the canoe. I took these pictures in April 2008. In August 1975, with sunshine and blue skies, these were some of the last images that Chris saw.

ABOVE: The pier beside the small beach.

BELOW: Looking back to Rowardennan Point from the water. The pier is on the right. The building near the centre is where Gillian and Paula changed into their swimming costumes.

ABOVE:
Dad, the last time I saw him, when I took my daughters to visit him in Derbyshire in 1997.

He died in November 1999

LEFT:
Mum in 2004, by which time she was in the mid-stages of Alzheimer's disease.

She died in September 2007.

ABOVE:
Rory Allam, our fairy-god-clarinettist, with his namesake, Rory Giles, Izzy's son. I took this photograph in 1992 when Rory, wheelchair-bound, was living in sheltered accommodation in north London. Soon after this, he moved back to Scotland, where his parents cared for him until his untimely death from multiple sclerosis in April 1995.

TOP RIGHT:
Granny in May 1988 holding the third of her great grandchildren, my daughter Emily. Granny lived to see four of her six great grandchildren.

She died in July 1991.

RIGHT:
The same day in 1988 when Emily was one day old. Mum brought Granny to the hospital so that they could both see the new baby. I have included this photograph to show Mum as we would like her to be remembered, when she was her own lovely self.

Bram Tovey, Chris Freeman, Chris Stearn and Russell Jordan in Aldeburgh, c1976

Photo by Roderick Elms

At the RYO Jubilee Hall concerts in Aldeburgh, Bram used to be pushed on stage in a wheelchair with a rug over his knees. With Paul Hart at the piano and sometimes Chris adding bits on the horn, Bram sang the Flanders and Swann song to the tune of the *Rondo* from Mozart's fourth horn concerto in E flat (K495). Bram tells me he has performed it on numerous occasions since then and it is still his party piece.

ILL WIND

I once had a whim and I had to obey it,
To buy a French horn in a second hand shop.
I polished it up and I started to play it
In spite of the neighbours who begged me to stop.

To sound my horn, I had to develop my embouchure.
I found my horn was a bit of a devil to play.
So artfully wound, to give you a sound, a beautiful sound so rich and round.
Oh, the hours I had to spend before I mastered it in the end.

But that was yesterday and just today I looked in the usual place.
There was the case, but the horn itself was missing.
Oh where can it have gone?
Haven't you, hasn't anyone seen my horn?
Oh where can it have gone?
What a blow. Now I know I'm unable to play my allegro.

Who swiped that horn?
I'll bet you a quid, somebody did,
Knowing I'd found a concerto and wanted to play it,
Afraid of my talent at playing the horn.
For early today to my utter dismay it had vanished away like the dew in the morn.

I've lost that horn, I know I was using it yesterday.
I've lost that horn, lost that horn, found that horn, gone.
There's not much hope of getting it back, though I'd willingly pay a reward.

I know some hearty folk, whose party joke's pretending to hunt with the Quorn,
'Gone away, gone away', was it one of them took it away?
Will you kindly return that horn.
Oh where is the devil who pinched my horn?
I shall tell the police, I want that French horn back.

Cadenza: I miss its music more and more and more,
without that horn I'm feeling sad and so forlorn.

I'd found a concerto and wanted to play it,
Displaying my talent at playing the horn.
But early today to my utter dismay it had totally vanished away.
I practised the horn and I wanted to play it, but somebody took it away.
I practised the horn and was longing to play it, but somebody took it away.
My neighbour's asleep in his bed,
I'll soon make him wish he were dead.
I'll take up the Tuba instead. Wah, Wah.

At which point, Bram threw the rug from his lap, which had been concealing his tuba, leapt up and played the last section of the Rondo.

MEMORIAL CONCERT

BUCKHURST HILL COUNTY HIGH SCHOOL FOR BOYS

October 23rd 1975

Conducted by John Rippin*

Violins
Susan Sheppard*
Reginald Adler
Alan Baldwin
Pavlo Beznosiuk
Linda Brewin
Ian Brown*
Nicholas Buckley*
Alistair Clapp*
Patricia Harwood
Roberta Prade
David White

Violas
Clifford Oliver*
Ian Theodoreson*
Norman Thurston

Celli
Pat Arrowsmith*
David Beckett*
Drummond Clapp*
Cathy Giles
Abigail Hall
Melanie Turner
Cleo Wood

Bass
Mary Ibbotson*

Piano
Paul Hart

Flute
Jeremy Dibble*

Oboes
Gillian Taylor
Martin Wheatley*

Clarinets
Adrian Iles*
Susan Theodoreson

Bassoon
Michael Maxwell*

Horns
Phillip Eastop
Alison Jenkins
Gareth Mollison

Trumpets
David Applegate
Antony Chittock*
Neill Cotton*
Graeme Cunningham
Brian Harper*
Phillip James*

Euphoniums
Paul Davey*
Andrew Williams*

Trombones
Martin Koch*
Simon Mansfield*
Christopher Stearn

Tuba
André de Haan

Madrigal group: Timothy Bentham, Neill Cotton, Jeremy Hayes, Nicholas Patience, Jeremy Tredinnick, Simon Hicks, Graham Wiskin, David Beard, Simon Bone, Jeremy Dibble, Geoffrey Willis, Ian Mack, Neil Selby, Adrian Sutton

* Buckhurst Hill County High School pupils and staff

A CONCERT IN MEMORY OF CHRISTOPHER GILES

ILFORD TOWN HALL

Sunday January 11th 1976

BRUCKNER: Symphony No. 4 (Romantic)

Conducted by Simon Rattle

Violins
Louise Williams
Ruth Crouch
Charles Pollard
Isabel Giles
Alison Kelly
Mary Hart
Paul Mayes
Marshall Marcus
Jane Doody
Hywel Davies
Tom Jones
Robert Heard
Sally Phillips
Leslie Phillips
Edward Garner
Miranda Fulleylove
Fiona Love
Nigel Gilmore
Ben Holland
Judy Mayhew
Sarah Streatfeild
Keith Gurry
Josi Herivel
Dave White
Patricia Harwood
Nick Warner

Stage Manager
Ian Crosswell

Violas
Trevor Snoad
Aileen Morrison
Paula Midgley
Len Davis
Bridget Crouch
Andy Sippings
Norman Thurston
Cathy Marwood
Nigel Bielby
Rona Wilson
Stewart Eaton
Judy Baum

Celli
Rod McGrath
Cathy Giles
Lowri Blake
Melanie Turner
Corinne-Ann Frost
James Potter
David Lockington
Anne Baker
John Hormbrey

Bassi
Randal Shannon
Ian Anderson
Chris Freeman
Clare Long
Sara Dobson
Caroline Maguire

Flutes
Andy Findon
Joanne Boddington

Oboes
Stella Dickinson
Gillian Taylor

Clarinets
Pete Dunkley
Rory Allam

Bassoons
Sue Eversden
Robin Kennard

Horns
Phillip Eastop
Gareth Mollison
Alison Jenkins
Jim Handy
Danny Crowley

Trumpets
Clive Miller
Bill Ramsey
Chris Larnder

Trombones
Graham Chambers
Martin Koch
Chris Stearn

Tuba
Bram Tovey

Timpani
Ben Hoffnung

ACKNOWLEDGEMENTS

To my mother, Elizabeth Fraser: for her unconditional love, her strength, loyalty and integrity. I shall always miss her.

To my sister, Isabel Giles, without whom this book could not have been written.

To my son, Toby Hart: for his help and expertise with the initial scanning of images, layout and set-up, and for showing me how to use Adobe Creative Suite software.

To my son, George Hart, and my daughters, Emily Rose Eastop and Martha Giles: for reading drafts of this book and encouraging me to finish it. I cannot thank my children enough for their love, affection and support; and for their sustained interest in this book during the many years it has taken to get it written and published.

To my friend, Justin Pearson: for his all-embracing love towards my children and me, his generosity, humour, perception and kindness.

To my friend, Maggie Baron: for her psychological insight, wisdom and empathy.

For invaluable help and advice with editing, corrections and proof-reading, I thank:

Natalie Baron
Emily Rose Eastop
Judy Gahagan
Justin Pearson
Marie Smith
Mike Smith

I am particularly indebted to my cousin, David Fraser, for his meticulous fact checking, corrections to typing and spelling, tactful suggestions and thoroughness, which he applied to several drafts. Any remaining errors are mine.

For help with my mother's side of family research, I thank:

Brenda Glass Alexander
David Fraser
Anne Frick
Ann Goddard
Sheila Jelley
Ailsa Land
Audrey Paine (1924-2008)
Marie and Mike Smith

For help with my father's side of family research, I thank:

Sallie Anstruther (1931-2009)
Mark Elliot Anstruther Heal
Amanda Heath
Melissa Heath

For assistance with other research, I thank:

Graham Frankel, editor of the *Old Buckwellians News* magazine
Neil MacInnes, Service Development co-ordinator of the Mitchell Library, Glasgow
John Saunders, manager of the Dunwich Museum
Henry Sullivan, Archivist of the Mitchell Library, Glasgow

I am most grateful to the authors and poets who graciously gave me their consent to quote their words:

Nicholas Comfort	Jean Lipkin*
Ivor Matanle	Mel Rolfe
Carole Satyamurti	Gregory Warren Wilson

*I would like to pay tribute to Jean Lipkin, whose poetry has added so much to this book. Sadly, Jean died in 2006.

To others who kindly read drafts at various stages:

Brigitte Beraha	Steve Cladingboel
Cindy Foster	Dorothy Hart
Tim Isted	Pat Lancaster
Jane Miller née Doody	Kate Musker
Martin Wheatley	Paul Willey

I would like to express my gratitude to the following people for their help, interest and support, and to those who contributed letters, photographs and memories:

Clare Adani née Ziman, Bill Ashton, Guy Barker, Edward Barnes, Lowri Blake, Vyvian Bronk née Howat, Graham Chambers, Helen Chapman, Steve Cladingboel, Robert Cooper, Melanie Cortese née Turner, Roderick Elms, Sue Eversden, Andy Findon, Bruce Fox-Lefriche, Chris Freeman, Laurence Gold, Ian Grainger, Paul Hart, Russell Jordan, Martin Koch, David Long, Simon Mansfield, Paul Mayes, Dr. Paula Midgley, Clive Miller, Gareth Mollison, Aileen Morrison, Chi-chi Nwanoku MBE, Cliff Oliver, Charles Pollard, Sir Simon Rattle, John Ridgeon, Linda Ridgeon, François Rive, John Rogers, Dr. Sonu Shamdasani, John Spencer, Chris Stearn, Gillian Taylor, Dr. Nicholas Terry, Ruth Thackeray, Alan Torrance, Bramwell Tovey, Pat Turner, Desmond Turner (d.2010), Richard Tyler, Richard Watkins, Martin Wheatley, Bill Worrall, Sigrid Zahner née Turnlund.

I owe enormous thanks to Leighton Brown, designer and Managing Director of Darwin Press, for his patience, advice and willingness to work with me to turn this book into a reality. Many thanks also to Ashley Brown in production and designer Antonio Pujante.

I would also like to thank Gerard Luskin (www.luskinet.com) for designing the T-GEM website.

In addition, I must salute the greatest research tool that has been constantly at my fingertips – the phenomenal world of the Internet. I have used a number of genealogical sites, in particular scotlandspeople.gov.uk, as well as 1837online.com, now known as findmypast.com, freeBMD.org.uk, nationalarchives.gov.uk and ancestry.com. Friendsreunited.com and genesreunited.com have been useful, as have many other interesting, informative sites too numerous to mention.

Finally, I thank you, the reader, for accompanying me on this journey and listening to my story. If you wish to contact me, please email me at cathy@t-gembooks.com. I would be pleased to receive your comments. You can also visit www.t-gembooks.com. Copies of *The Silent-footed Butler* can be purchased via the website.

BIBLIOGRAPHY

I have quoted from or referred to the following:

BOOKS

Animal Travellers – Igor Akimushkin (1929-1993) (MIR Publishers, Moscow, 1970)

There Is No Coda – The story of NYJO – Bill Ashton (NYJO Magazine, Spring 1992)

The Innsbruck Story (British Youth Festival Committee, 1951)

Table Talk – Bede Bailey, O.P., from *Opening the Scrolls*, a collection of Essays in Catholic History (Downside Abbey, Bath)

Lord Minto, a Memoir (1924) – John Buchan (1875-1940)

The Lost City of Dunwich – Nicholas Comfort (Terence Dalton Ltd., Suffolk, 1994)

The Teacher's Handbook of the Tonic Sol-Fa System – Alexander T. Cringan (Canada Publishing Co. Ltd., 1889)

David Copperfield, Great Expectations – Charles Dickens (1812-1870)

Life and Death – Andrea Dworkin (The Free Press, New York, 1997)

The Mill on the Floss – George Eliot (1819-1880) (Penguin Classics, London, 1985)

The Prophet – Kahlil Gibran (1883-1931) (Oneworld Publications, Oxford, 1998)

Memories of a Childhood in Brixton – Derek Giles (1920-1999) (unpublished)

Letters of John Keats (1795-1821) – edited by Robert Gittings (Oxford University Press, 1970)

Tales and Traditions of Ayrshire and Galloway – Andrew Glass (1820-1895) (Dunn & Wright, Glasgow, 1873)

Scottish Legends and Stories – Andrew Glass (Hamilton, Adams & Co., London 1889 and also Thomas D. Morrison, Glasgow, 1889)

A Norfolk Notebook – Lilias Rider Haggard (1892-1968) (Faber and Faber Ltd., 1946)

Dunwich Story – Allan Jobson (1889-1980) (Flood & Son, Ltd., Lowestoft, 1969)

Reminiscences – Ailsa Land (unpublished)

Letter to Florrie and Memoirs – Barry Lupino (1884-1962) (unpublished)

World War II – Ivor Matanle (Century Hutchinson Ltd., 1989)

The Martyrdom of Man – Winwood Reade (1838-1875) (Watts & Co., London, 1924)

Brass for Beginners – John Ridgeon (Boosey and Hawkes, London 1976)

When Marnie Was There – Joan G. Robinson (Collins, London, 1967)

Norfolk Fowler – Alan Savory (Boydell Press, Ipswich, 1953)

As You Like It, *The Rape of Lucrece*, *Macbeth*, *A Midsummer Night's Dream*, *Romeo and Juliet*, *The Tempest*, Sonnets 30 and 60 – William Shakespeare (1564-1616)

Frankenstein – Mary Shelley (1797-1851) (Oxford University Press, 1969)

Lady Windermere's Fan, *The Importance of Being Earnest* – Oscar Wilde (1854-1900)

A Room of One's Own – Virginia Woolf (1882-1941)

POEMS and COLLECTIONS of POETRY

The Maidens Came from Book of English Verse (Harper Collins, Glasgow, 2001)

Touched by an Angel – Maya Angelou

Auguries of Innocence, *The Marriage of Heaven and Hell*, from *The Complete Poems* – William Blake (1757-1827) (Penguin Classics, 1977)

The Pied Piper of Hamelin – Robert Browning (1812-1889) from *A Book of a Thousand Poems* (Evans Brothers Ltd., London, 1957)

Dainty Davie, *Man was Made to Mourn* from *The Complete Poems, Songs and Ballads* – Robert Burns (1759-1796) (Reed International Books, 1990)

Lines Inscribed Upon a Cup Formed from a Skull – George Gordon Byron (1788-1824)

Poems 1945-1950 – Jenefer Carlyon (1927-1962) (unpublished)

"Hope" is the Thing with Feathers –, *They Say That "Time Assuages" –*, *This World is not Conclusion* – Emily Dickinson (1830-1886)

Hyperion – John Keats (1795-1821) (J. M. Dent & Sons Ltd. 1974)

I Ask You, Pandora from the collection *Among Stones* – Jean Lipkin (1926-2006) (David Philip, Cape Town, 1975)

Recycling the Dream, *Yet Further Fragments*, *Young Girl* from the collection *Winter Walk* – Jean Lipkin (Batseye, London)

Condole, *Family Tree – Endings*, *Fragments i, iii, iv*, *The Necessary Period of Mourning*, *Walking from Dunwich* from the collection *With Fences Down* – Jean Lipkin (GPI Ltd., 1986)

A Bitterness from the collection *Wild Geese* – Mary Oliver (Bloodaxe Books Ltd., 2004)

Firesong from *Collected Poems* – Sylvia Plath (1932-1963) (Faber and Faber, London, 1983)

A Community of the Spirit, *Acts of Helplessness*, *Green Ears*, from *Selected Poems* – Mowlana Jalaluddin Rumi (1207-1273) translated by Coleman Banks (Penguin Classics, London, 1995)

Brave Face from *The Other Woman*; *Leasehold*, *Mouthfuls*, *Partners*, from *Stitching the Dark*, a collection of new and selected poems – Carole Satyamurti (Bloodaxe Books Ltd., 2005)

I Loved from *Thirty-one Poems* – Umberto Saba (1883-1957) translated by Felix Stefanile (Elizabeth Press, New York)

A Child's Thought and *Happy Thought* – Robert Louis Stevenson (1850-1894) from *A Book of a Thousand Poems* (Evans Brothers Ltd., London, 1957)

Number III of *A Correspondence Course in Singing* from the collection *Preserving Lemons* – Gregory Warren Wilson (Staple New Writing, 1996)

The Ungiven from the collection *Jeopardy* – Gregory Warren Wilson (Enitharmon Press, London, 2003)

In Time of Famine, number II of *Six Misapprehensions* from the collection *The Mercury Fountain* – Gregory Warren Wilson (Enitharmon Press, London, 2008)

Song of Myself – Walt Whitman (1819-1892)

A Woman Young and Old, *The Circus Animals' Desertion* from *The Poems* – William Butler Yeats (1865-1939) (J. M. Dent & Sons Ltd., London, 1990)

LYRICS

Do You Know the Way to San Jose? – Burt Bacharach/Hal David

Wild Eyed Boy from Freecloud from the album *Space Oddity* – David Bowie

A Prelude to a Kiss – Irving Gordon/Irving Mills lyrics to Duke Ellington song

Look for the Silver Lining – Buddy DeSylva lyrics to Jerome Kern song

Circle Game – Joni Mitchell

Somewhere from *West Side Story* – Stephen Sondheim lyrics to Leonard Bernstein song

Ill Wind – words of song by Donald Flanders/Michael Swann from the album *At the Drop of Another Hat* 1964 on EMI 7243 8 29399 2 4

Buckhurst Hill County High School Song – R. Steele/S. Campbell (1940)

LIST OF ABBREVIATIONS:

4tet, 5tet and similar: Quartet, quintet etc.
AAC Army Air Corps
ARCM Associate of the Royal College of Music
ATS Auxiliary Territorial Service – a branch of the Army to which women enlisted
BBCSO British Broadcasting Corporation Symphony Orchestra
BHCHS Buckhurst Hill County High School
BM British Museum
BSO Bournemouth Symphony Orchestra
CND Campaign for Nuclear Disarmament
ECG Electrocardiogram
ECO English Chamber Orchestra
FSC Forest School Camps
GRSM Graduate of the Royal Schools of Music
GYO Goldsmiths Youth Orchestra
IFYO International Festival Youth Orchestra
ITC International Typeface Corporation
LPO London Philharmonic Orchestra
LRAM Licentiate of the Royal Academy of Music
LSE London School of Economics
LSO London Symphony Orchestra
MAYC Methodist Association of Youth Clubs
MD Musical Director
NASA National Aeronautics and Space Administration
NYJO National Youth Jazz Orchestra
NYO National Youth Orchestra
OP *Ordo Praedicatorum*, Order of Preachers, the official name of the Dominican Order
QEH Queen Elizabeth Hall
RAM Royal Academy of Music
RCA Radio Corporation of America
RFH Royal Festival Hall
RI Religious Instruction
RK Religious Knowledge
RPO Royal Philharmonic Orchestra
RSPB Royal Society for the Protection of Birds
RYO Redbridge Youth Orchestra
TNT Trinitrotoluene – a chemical compound with the formula $C_6H_2(NO_2)_3CH_3$
TUC Trades Union Congress
USSR Union of Soviet Socialist Republics
VD Venereal disease, nowadays known as STD, sexually transmitted disease
WAAF Women's Auxiliary Air Force
WMA Workers Music Association

MAP of GREAT BRITAIN, IRELAND and NORTHERN FRANCE

a geographical guide to most of the places named in this book

A: County Antrim
B: Isle of Arran
C: Norfolk
D: County Sligo
E: Normandy

1. Aldeburgh, Suffolk
2. Ayr
3. Belfast
4. Bournemouth
5. Bristol
6. Cardiff
7. Carlisle
8. Carlyon Bay, Cornwall
9. Cork
10. Croydon
11. Dundee
12. Dunrossness
13. Dunwich, Suffolk
14. Edinburgh
15. Girvan, South Ayrshire
16. Glasgow
17. Great Ryburgh, Norfolk
18. Guernsey, Channel Islands
19. Holbrook, Suffolk
20. Leeds
21. Liverpool
22. Loch Lomond
23. London, Central
24. Melksham, Wiltshire
25. Merionethshire camp site, Harlech
26. Montgomeryshire camp site near Llanbrynmair
27. Newbury, Berkshire
28. Oban, Argyll
29. Pegasus Bridge
30. Plymouth
31. Ramsgate
32. Randalstown
33. Redbridge
34. Salisbury Plain
35. Sheringham
36. Southport
37. Stirling
38. Swindon, Wiltshire
39. Torquay
40. Wakefield
41. West Bromwich
42. Wortley, Nr. Sheffield

Shetland
Islands
12

Orkney
Islands
Outer
Hebrides
SCOTLAND
NORTH
ATLANTIC
OCEAN
NORTH
SEA
11
28
22
37
16
14
B
2
15
A
32
7
NORTHERN
IRELAND
3
D
Irish Sea
REPUBLIC
OF
IRELAND
20
40
36
21
42
35
17
C
ENGLAND
25
26
41
13
1
19
WALES
9
33
38
23
31
6
5
24
27
10
34
4
30
39
8
English Channel
N
50 km
50 miles
18
Channel
Islands
29
E
FRANCE
www.artefactestudio.com

THE BENNETT/ANSTRUTHER

MYSTERY MAN or MEN

Birth and baptismal records of Mary Henry's eldest child, Edgar, have a father named **FREDERICK CROCKFORD**. The father named on Mary's youngest six children's birth and/or baptismal registrations is **ROBERT GEORGE BENNETT**. No records of birth, marriage or death have yet been found for either man. The children were brought up to beleive that their father was **Colonel ROBERT ANSTRUTHER** and thought their last name was Anstruther. It was around 1883 that the man they knew as their father disppeared from their lives.

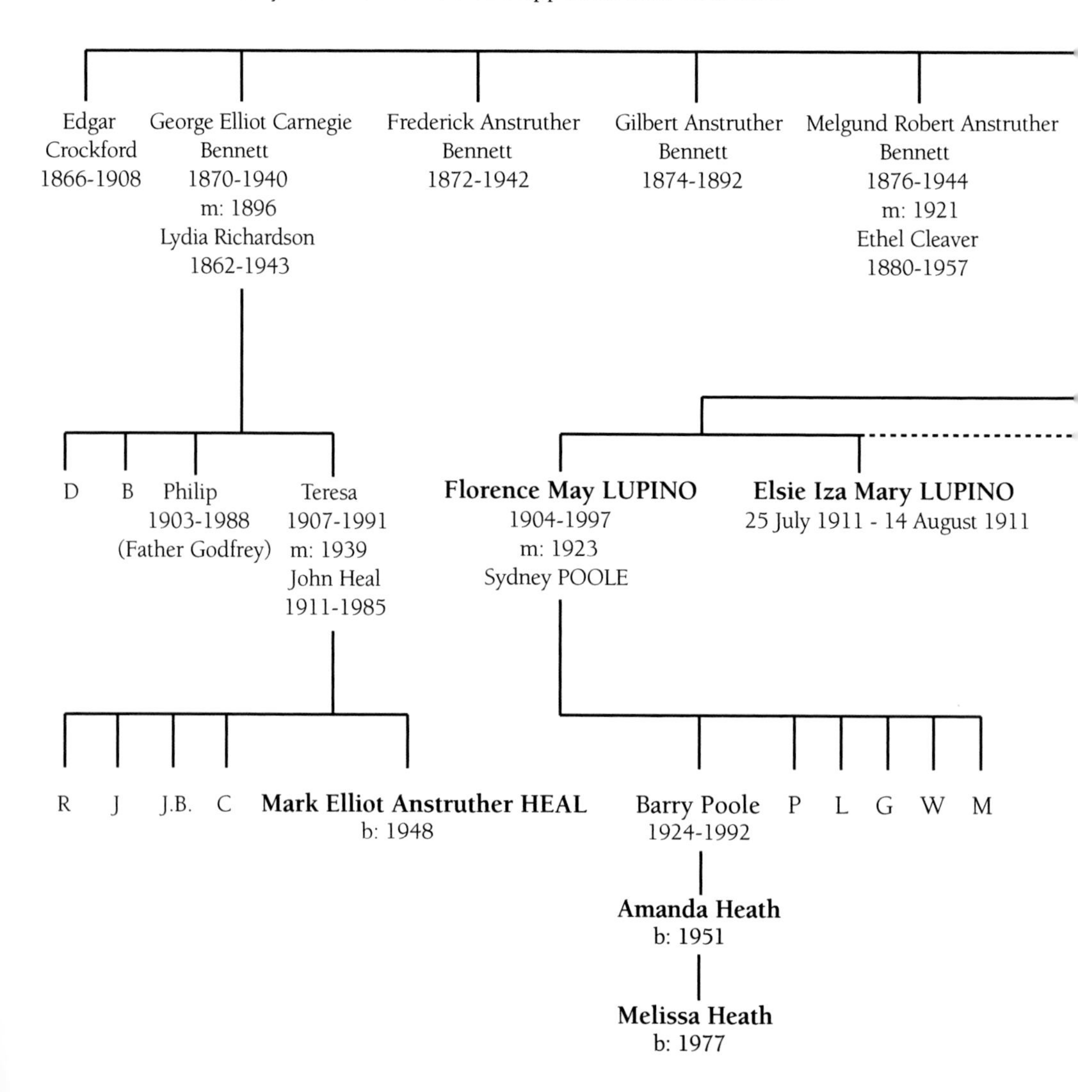

AND LUPINO/GILES FAMILY TREE

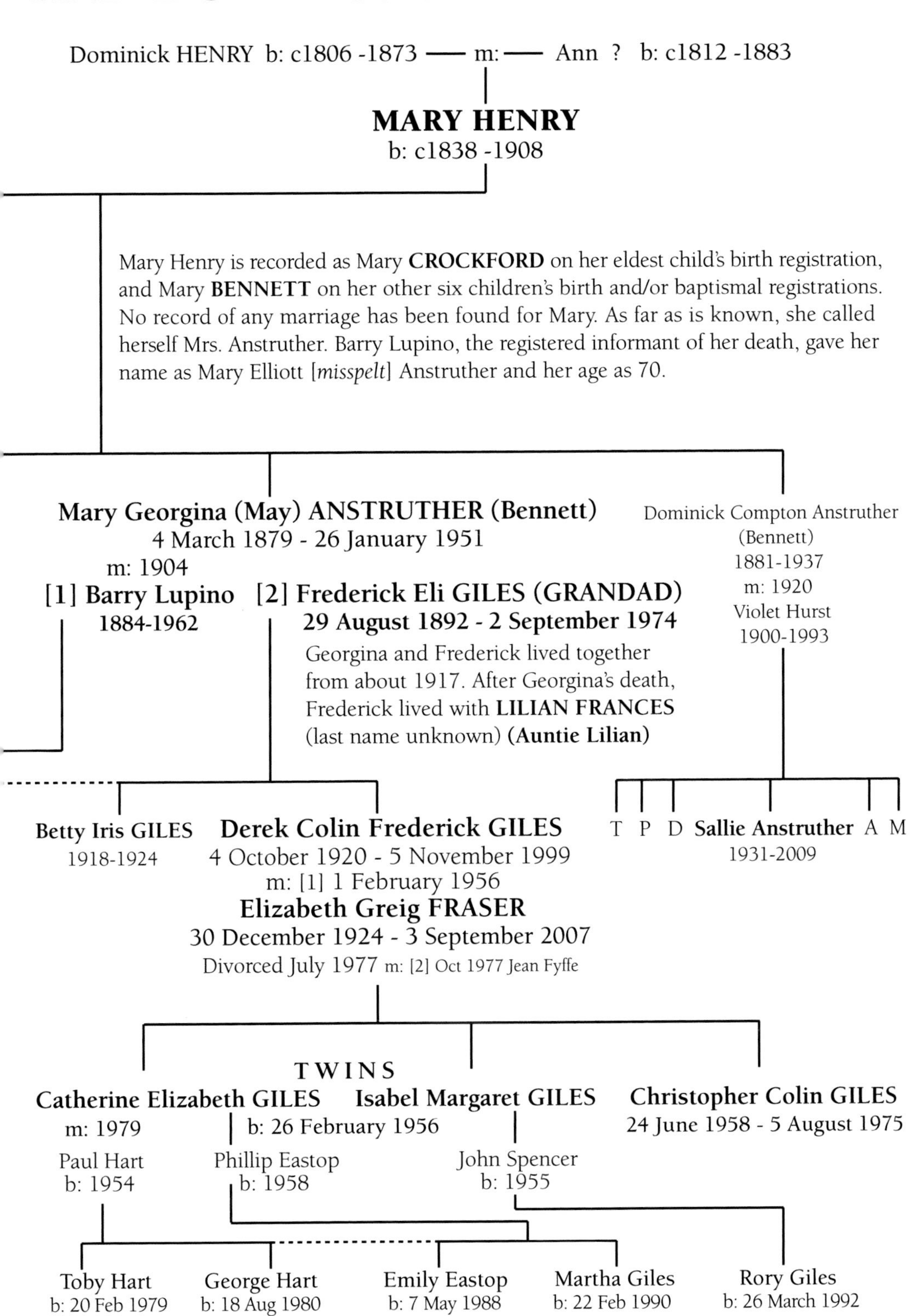

THE GREIG, GLASS

THE GREIGS (ORIGINALLY GREGG) FROM NORTHERN IRELAND

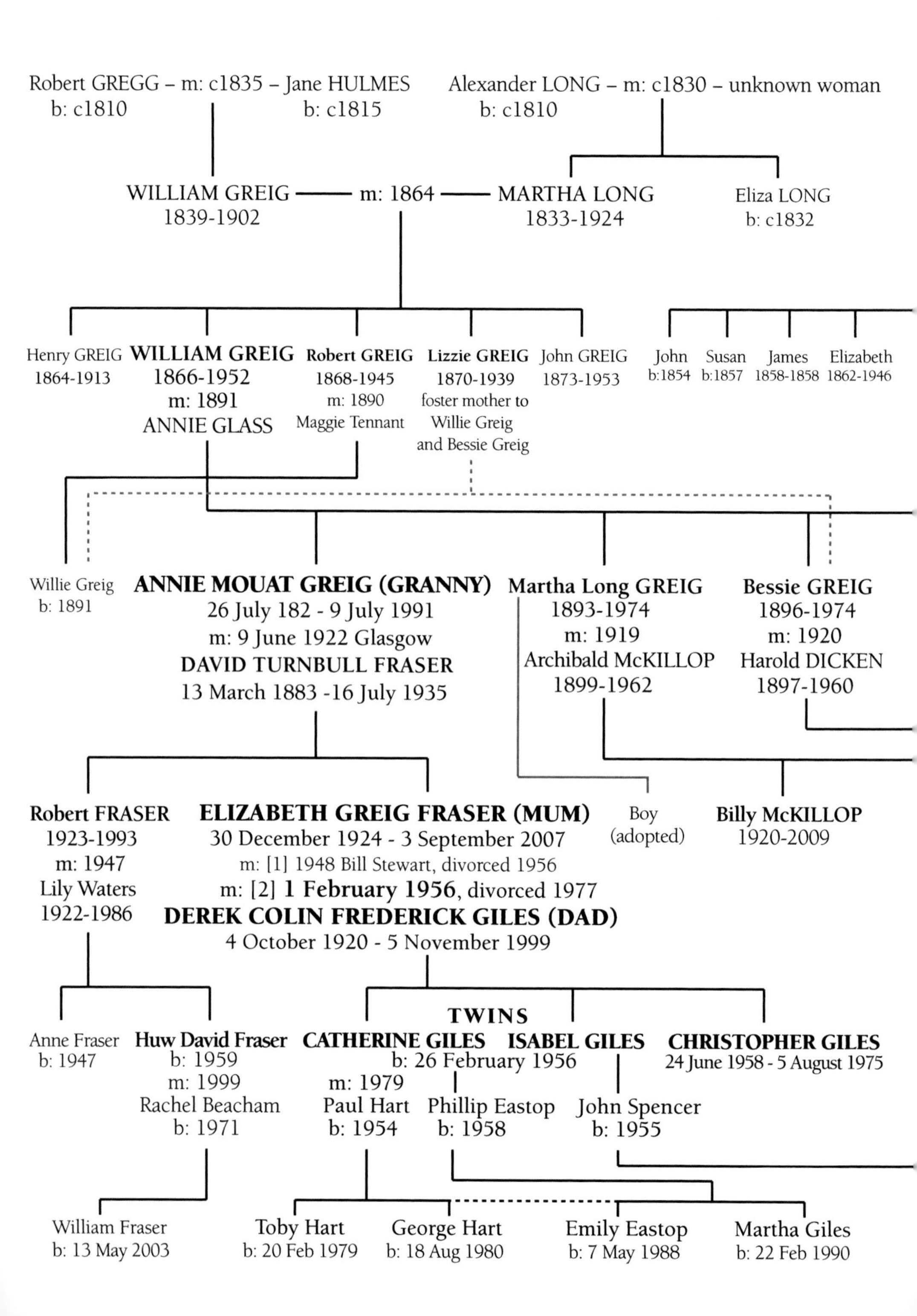

One of the displays of butterflies and moths from Chris's extensive Natural History Collection.
Most of the above hatched in jars in Chris's bedroom from pupae that he either found or bought.

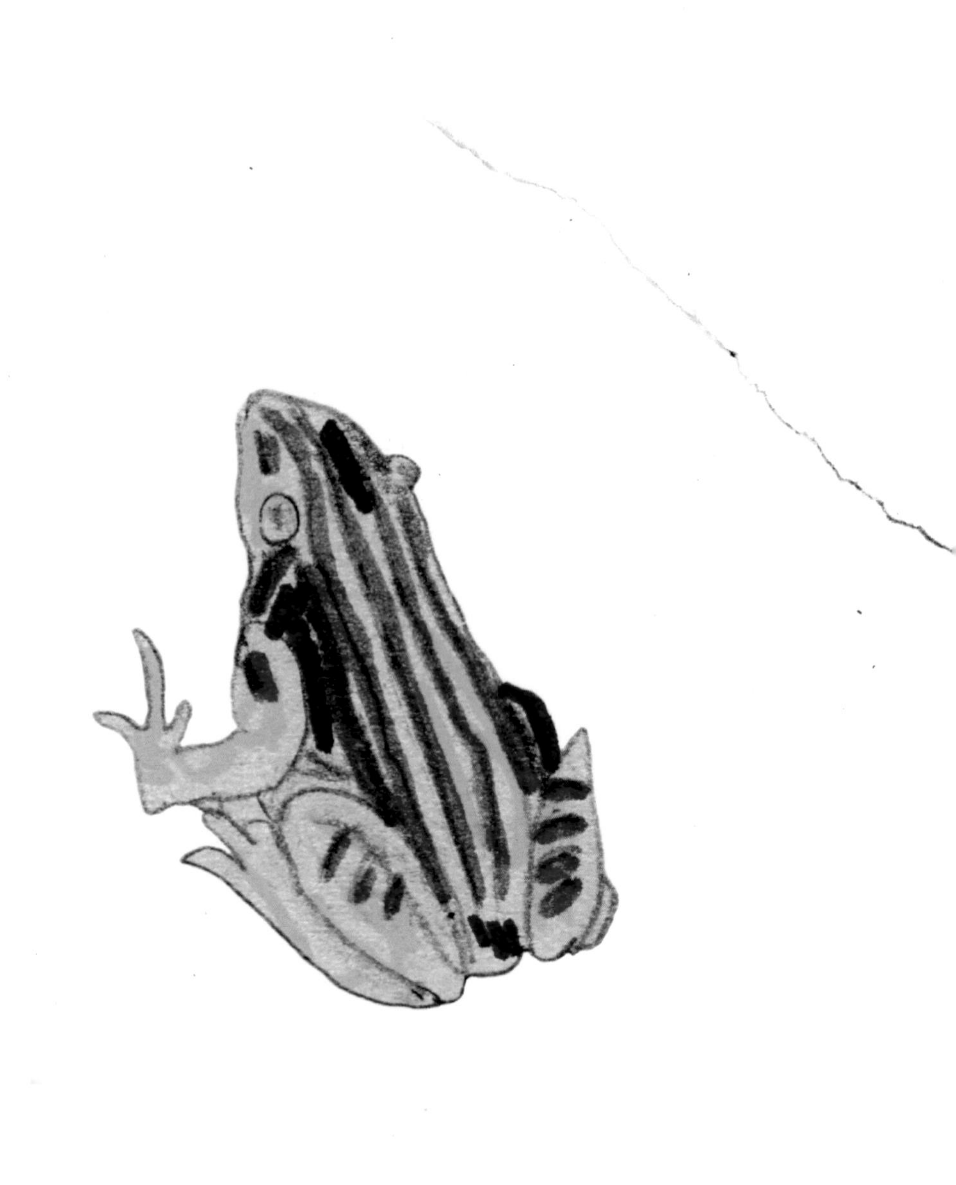